THE BEST PLAYS OF 1981–1982

THE
BURNS MANTLE
YEARBOOK

THE
BEST PLAYS
OF 1981–1982

EDITED BY OTIS L. GUERNSEY JR.

*Illustrated with photographs and
with drawings by* HIRSCHFELD

DODD, MEAD & COMPANY

NEW YORK • TORONTO

inquiries should be addressed to: Jeannine Edmunds, J. Michael Bloom, Ltd., 400 Madison Avenue, New York, N.Y. 10017.

Al Hirschfeld is represented exclusively by The Margo Feiden Galleries, New York.

EDITOR'S NOTE

ACKNOWLEDGING ALL individual contributions to *The Best Plays of 1981–82* would require a line-by-line review of each of its 500-plus pages of information about the living American theater from the sun-washed shores of San Diego to soot-stained SoHo, from crisp Seattle to gentle Sarasota. This *Best Plays* volume, like the previous 62 published by Dodd, Mead & Company, is superabundantly endowed with the concern and the fact-digging labors of a hundred theatrical press offices on, off and off off Broadway and from coast to busy coast. Their contributions of hard information, illustrations and above all the shared commitment of getting it all and getting it straight are invaluable to this and future generations of readers. We're grateful to every one of them, named (after the notation "press" in the New York program listings) or unnamed, for their indispensable help in assembling this latest in the oldest continuing series of annual American publications.

Likewise, the publisher's commitment to this series has been total, personified by Jonathan Dodd supervising and lending a hand at every stage of development. The editor's wife, painstakingly reviewing the listings, can take credit for much of the accuracy and is responsible for none of the very, very few (we hope) inaccuracies herein. Among the many not connected directly with this enterprise but to whom we owe our thanks for their personal interest and important help are Sally Dixon Wiener, Jeffrey Sweet, Hobe Morrison of *Variety*, Ralph Newman of the Drama Book Shop, Henry Hewes, Alan Hewitt and Thomas T. Foose.

The personality of this and other *Best Plays* volumes is immeasurably enhanced by Al Hirschfeld's drawings of the major theater events of the season, and by the illustrations of outstanding designs, generously contributed for use in these pages by their creators: Theoni V. Aldredge and William Ivey Long. And the extroverted vitality of 1981–82 stage presentations everywhere is vividly expressed in the photographs of Martha Swope, Peter Cunningham and Dean Abramson, Bert Andrews, Linda Blase, Robert Burroughs, Susan Cook, Jack Donohue, Anita Feldman-Shevett, Bruce Goldstein, Gerry Goodstein, Brownie Harris, Ken Howard, Lanny Nagler, Carol Rosegg, Stephanie Saia, Antony Stein, Donna Svennevik, Joseph Tenga, George Whitear and Katherine Wisniewski.

We take particular pleasure and admiration in speaking our thanks to the men and women who annually provide departmental coverage which speaks for itself in its comprehensive record of the stage year. We point with pride to our listings of regional theater as provided by Ella A. Malin (and our American Theater Critics Association survey of outstanding theater across the country, nominated by ATCA members and selected by an ATCA committee chaired by Ann Holmes of the Houston *Chronicle*); off off Broadway by Camille Croce; necrology and publications by Rue Canvin; replacements by Stanley Green; and Tony Awards details by William Schelble. Also, in this year's volume we offer a review of the off-off-Broadway season's highlights by Mel Gussow of the New York *Times*, undeniably one of the most perceptive and ubiquitous observers of the whole New York theater scene. In every direction our reach extends as far as our theater chooses to go, wherever its unfailing energy exerts new forces of creativity in the 1980s.

The heart of the matter, as always, is the collection of new playscripts, those acts of literary faith and aspiration which provide a solid foundation for the theater of the present and the grand design of the theater of the past in those that stand the test of time. Ten on and off-Broadway productions are Best Plays; but many more than ten (we are delighted to say) are strong enough to have a continuing life of their own in stages around the world; and an unknowable number of them now listed among tributary programs will rise to the top of national attention in the months ahead. Then there are the dramatists who, this time out, were unable to get a firm grasp on an effective form—but wait till next year or the year after that. As long as these authors, successful and (temporarily) unsuccessful, activate their commitment to the American theater by annually providing it with new scripts by the hundreds, there will continue to be no end to its possibilities, no limit to its excitement—nor to these *Best Plays* volumes celebrating its achievements.

OTIS L. GUERNSEY Jr.

July 1, 1982

CONTENTS

Drawings by HIRSCHFELD

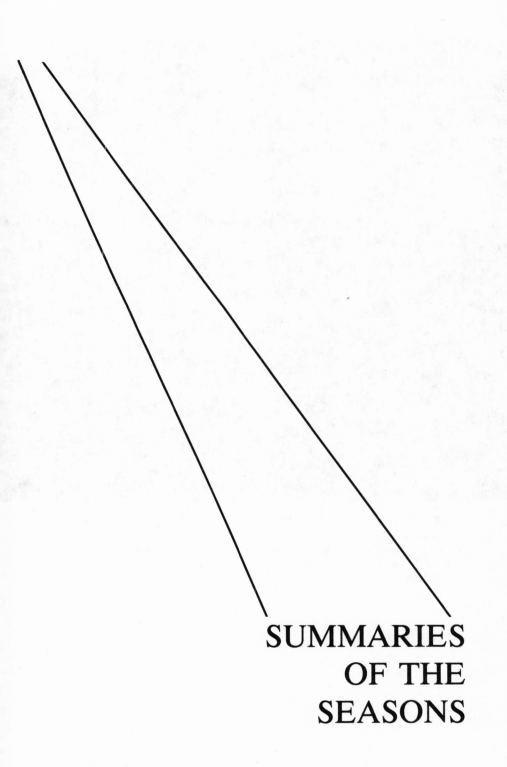

SUMMARIES
OF THE
SEASONS

THE LIFE & ADVENTURES OF NICHOLAS NICKLEBY—Roger Rees as Nicholas Nickleby *(center)* waves goodbye in a cloud of dust as he leaves for London to seek his fortune. His "stagecoach" is formed from wicker hampers and a table, and men are its wheels, in this imaginatively staged Royal Shakespeare Company production.

THE SEASON IN NEW YORK

By Otis L. Guernsey Jr.

THIS WAS THE SEASON that the Royal Shakespeare Company's production of *The Life & Adventures of Nicholas Nickleby* came to Broadway for a 49-performance visit in which it changed some of our ideas about modern theater, reaffirmed others and was so far outstandingly 1981–82's best play that some of its rivals grumbled about its eligibility for consideration in the Tony Award nominations—which it swept.

The adaptor of the Charles Dickens novel, David Edgar, described some of his and the company's intentions to a group of New York theater people: from the outset, they determined to dramatize *all* of *Nicholas Nickleby*. No subplot was to be cut, though incidents here and there could be dropped (and sometimes the status of "subplot" vs. "incident" was hotly debated during production). Much of the Dickens dialogue was used verbatim onstage, but in places Dickens's purposes were better served by invented dialogue—for example, when characters have an important presence in the novel but little to say. Requiring an eight-and-one-half-hour running time to tell its whole tale, *Nicholas Nickleby* changed, first, our estimate of how long an audience will tolerate a single sitting (broken three times for intermissions, plus an hour-long interval between Parts I and II) and end up shouting for more. Because of its extraordinary length, its adaptor tried to make material cuts in his initial working script but found that the threatened passages suddenly developed more importance than expected, taking on so much weight of continuity that most turned out to be unexcisable.

Nicholas Nickleby also changed, and probably not for the better in the long run, our notion of how much the audience might be induced to pay for a ticket to a unique experience of live theater. The impetus didn't come from the reviews, some of which were lukewarm. *Nicholas Nickleby* started slowly, but word of mouth worked its magic until theatergoers were eager to pay $100 (or $50 at the performances which offered only one part at a time) for any seat anywhere in the house during this limited engagement. "It would have been a bargain at $1,000 a ticket," declared one noted Dickens authority—hinting at unimaginable economic terrors lying in wait for the theater of the future.

What made this *Nicholas Nickleby* a bargain at $100 and up, captivating for all of its eight and one-half hours, was its reaffirmation of basic stage values: insightful faith in its source and purpose; clear-cut conflicts of good and evil, love and hate; superbly imaginative design, direction and performing. For example, we could swear that we saw a stagecoach loaded, hitched and setting out on its journey with passengers, including Nicholas, perched on its roof—but on second thought it must have been merely an illusion created with a few common objects and a group of uncommon actors under the direction of Trevor Nunn and John Caird. The design by John Napier and Dermot Hayes reached out with both arms to embrace the stage on several levels and parts of the auditorium for its travels, carnivals, duels, etc.—big enough to contain *Nicholas Nickleby* in its multifarious entirety, at the same time permitting the most intimate exchange. Here were infamous Dotheboys Hall and the preposterous Crummles troup of Shakespearean players; rakes at their insidious seduction of innocent maidens, climbers flattering a rich relative with attentions; fashion houses and counting houses whose financiers occupied no middle ground but were either so charitable as to be almost saintly (the Cheerybles) or so ruthless as to be almost demonic (Ralph Nickleby). The saga of young Nicholas trying to support his widowed mother and sister in the largely uncaring 19th century world was not what kept the audience on the edge of their seats hour after hour—after all, the general direction and final outcome of a Dickens plot could hold little mystery even for the majority who had never read this novel. The suspense was not in what was to happen, but in how it happened in episode after episode whose every detail was worth watching carefully.

Forty-two Royal Shakespeare Company performers appeared in 138 speaking roles in an ensemble display that brought to mind for comparison the same group's great *Marat/Sade* in 1965—and not to the disadvantage of *Nicholas Nickleby*. The quality of the acting varied only in length and prominence of role, the standouts being Roger Rees (the Tony winner) as Nicholas, Edward Petherbridge as humane and tipsy Newman Noggs and David Threlfall as the unfortunate Smike (Tony nominees); and, on another level, Emily Richard as Nicholas's sister Kate, John Woodvine as his sinister uncle Ralph, Alun Armstrong as the abusive schoolmaster Squeers, Patrick Godfrey as Mr. Kenwigs the paterfamilias, Christopher Benjamin and Lila Kaye as the performing Crummles's, Bob Peck as vicious Sir Mulberry Hawk, David Lloyd Meredith and Hubert Rees as the Cheerybles—and many, many others who took part in this triumph. Certainly *Nicholas Nickleby* was not merely the best play of New York's 1981–82 season, winning both the Tony and the New York Drama Critics Circle Awards, it was a stage achievement to be remembered for many years to come.

The 1981–82 theater season in New York was additionally and vividly memorable for a banner off-Broadway year. Four off-Broadway productions are Best Plays: Charles Fuller's Pulitzer Prize and Critics Award-winning drama of hatred and murder in a World War II barracks of black soldiers, *A Soldier's Play;* David Henry Hwang's enchanting two-character tribute to 19th century Chinese immigrant laborers, *The Dance and the Railroad;* Harvey Fierstein's touchingly sympathetic presentation of the life and times of a drag queen, *Torch Song Trilogy;* and A.R. Gurney Jr.'s emotionally and comically needling variations on a theme of WASP family life and times, *The Dining Room.* Furthermore, these off-Broadway bests were backed in depth by other scripts of considerable note: Jonathan Reynolds's *Geniuses,* David Pownall's *Livingstone and Sechele,* Christopher Durang's *Sister Mary Ignatius Explains It All for You* and Amlin Gray's *How I Got That Story,* to name the standouts.

Following *Nicholas Nickleby,* two foreign and two American scripts and one international inspiration reached Broadway and were designated Best Plays of this season. From England there was Ronald Harwood's sensitive dramatization of the relationship between an aging star and his devoted attendant, *The Dresser*. South African Athol Fugard premiered his *"MASTER HAROLD"* ... *and the boys* in this country, first in regional theater and then on Broadway, with the excrement of racism odoriferously present onstage. The leading American scripts were both concerned with forms of religious faith: Bill C. Davis's sometimes charming, sometimes acerbic headon collision of an elderly priest and an idealistic seminarian, *Mass Appeal*, brought across town from off-Broadway production two seasons ago; and John Pielmeier's more pungently rendered *Agnes of God*, analyzing the psychological and spiritual motivations of a nun who has apparently conceived, borne and murdered an infant. And, better late than never, the innovative musical *Nine* came in under the 1981–82 wire to redeem the Broadway musical season. Behind these Best Plays flared other conspicuously interesting events like Harold Pinter's *The Hothouse*, Ernest Thompson's *The West Side Waltz*, Percy Granger's *Eminent Domain* and Jules Feiffer's *Grown Ups*, brightening the Broadway year.

So the Best Plays list in 1981–82 consists of one Broadway musical (*Nine*) and nine plays, of which five were Broadway productions (*Nicholas Nickleby, The Dresser, Mass Appeal, Agnes of God* and *Master Harold*) and four off-Broadway (*A Soldier's Play, Torch Song Trilogy, The Dance and the Railroad, The Dining Room*). Three of these Best Plays were foreign scripts, six American and one international (*Nine*, a basically American concept which nevertheless owes its beginnings to a translation from the Italian). *Nine* was also the only one of this year's Best Plays produced directly for Broadway. *Nicholas Nickleby* and *The Dresser* came to New York from London, *Master Harold* and *Agnes of God* from regional theater. *Mass Appeal, The Dance and the Railroad, A Soldier's Play, Torch Song Trilogy* and *The Dining Room* were produced in New York off Broadway, in some cases after OOB workshops.

Taking a few paces backward to view the Broadway season as an economic whole, the box office gross continued to expand like a gas under steadily reducing pressure. During the early part of the season this one rising-gross statistic tended to conceal the truth about prosperity, which was attenuating along Broadway as it was in almost every other area of American life. The first sign of trouble was noticed in attendance figures, which began to sink below comparable 1980–81 levels and had shrunk 500,000 admissions by mid-season. "B'way Season Looms as Worst in Years," decried *Variety* in midwinter, in a story that deplored the shortage of original musicals and of the "capacity smash" amid "a substantially lower total of new productions." About a month later, *Business Week* echoed the gloomy conclusion that "the lights are dimmer on Broadway," with falling admissions and rising ticket prices and production costs, in a crisis in which "virtually every Broadway play and musical . . . . . is trying to lure patrons with half-price tickets." Twofers were lying about on counters all over town, and the TKTS booth in Times Square, purveyors of cut-rate theater tickets to last-minute show-shoppers, was doing a business amounting to more than 10 per cent of Broadway's total gross.

Looking back at the 12 months as the dust settled on June 1, *Variety* finally concluded that 1981–82 was a "nervous" Broadway theater season which grossed

TRAGEDY AND COMEDY—*Left,* Judith Anderson and Zoe Caldwell *(seated)* in *Medea; above,* Katharine Hepburn *(left)* and Dorothy Loudon in Ernest Thompson's *The West Side Waltz*

a record $221,234,791 in New York (over $200 million for the first time, compared with $194, $143, $128 and $103 million in the past four years) and a "staggering" $249,531,109 on the road. An important proportion, if not all, of this 13.7 per cent increase over 1980–81 was caused by inflation, with the Broadway top (not counting *Nicholas Nickleby*) rising to $40, with $35 becoming commonplace, and with the *average* Broadway ticket price at $23.08 by June 1 as compared with $19.72 a year before.

Further evidence that this phenomenal gross was mere inflation is provided by the general falling-off of activity elsewhere in *Variety's* final 1981–82 count. Attendance was down to just over 10 million as compared with 10.8 million in 1980–81 (but handsomely above the 9.4, 9.1 and 8.6 million attendance of the three previous years). And playing weeks (if ten shows play ten weeks, that's 100 playing weeks) took a dive to 1,461, reversing the upward movement of the recent past: 1,360, 1,472, 1,541 to the record 1,545 in 1980–81. As the season ended, there were only 26 shows playing on Broadway, compared to 30 at the same time the previous year—but again, handsomely above the 23 a decade and 21 two decades ago.

By our own count, there has been a continuing decline in the volume of Broadway production during recent seasons, becoming sharply steeper in this one. Not counting specialties, 1981–82 provided only 45 new Broadway productions, compared with 51 last year and 58 at a 1979–80 peak. This year's 45 included 12 revivals, so that the total number of new plays and musicals amounted to 33 (four fewer than last season) including three transfers and a revision. The hits were running longer (14 of the shows playing June 1, 1981 were still playing a year later), and it was taking considerably longer for a show to pay off its cost and thereby achieve hit status, and no wonder: the capitalization tab for the musical *Nine* was an estimated $2,750,000, and straight plays were lucky to get on at $500,000. As of the end of the year, only three Broadway productions other than *Nicholas Nickleby* were deemed by *Variety* to have reached the black: the off-Broadway transfer *Crimes of the Heart,* the revival of *Othello* and Katharine Hepburn's vehicle *The West Side Waltz.*

Under these conditions, a failed musical, *The First,* cost its backers $3 million (according to a *Wall Street Journal* estimate). *Colette* dropped $1,500,000 in tryout without ever reaching Broadway. *Barnum* recouped its $1.2 million Broadway cost but dropped $2 million in a Paris production and folded on the road. The popular *Woman of the Year* was still in the red, and the celebrated *Piaf* was estimated to have lost $670,000 of its $725,000 cost as of the end of its run.

Nevertheless, it was still possible to make a bundle with the right Broadway show, though accurate prediction of which show would be "right" still eluded the vast majority of investors. With 30 productions running in Broadway theaters and playing to 89.8 per cent of capacity the last week in December, the total week's gross rose over $6 million for the first time to a record $6,477,866 according to *Variety* estimate. Among the holdovers in 1981–82, *Deathtrap* had paid its backers $1,460,000 (365 per cent) on their $200,000 investment and *Children of a Lesser God* $2,500,000 (237 per cent) on $400,000. Off Broadway, *Cloud 9* had paid off its $175,000 cost and was earning $5,000 weekly. *Ain't Misbehavin'* had brought in $3,028,500 (403 per cent) for its $375,000 cost, and one of the all-time box office champs, *Fiddler on the Roof,* had reached $10,889,500 profit (1,452 per cent) on its original $375,000—and still counting.

Under present conditions, getting a Broadway show on could require a consortium of producers. There were, for example six producers' names above the title of the musical *Nine* and four more associates listed down with the design assistants and hair stylists. The corollary also obtained: the more prominent producers could be found taking part in a good many shows, the most active by our reckoning being Warner Theater Productions, led by Claire Nichtern, with eight (*Mass Appeal, Crimes of the Heart, Einstein and the Polar Bear, The Dresser, Duet for One, Little Me, Pump Boys and Dinettes* and *Beyond Therapy*). James M. Nederlander participated in six (*Fiddler on the Roof, The Supporting Cast, Nicholas Nickleby, The Dresser, Little Johnny Jones* and *Nine*), Emanuel Azenberg in five (*Einstein and the Polar Bear, Grown Ups, Duet for One, Little Me* and *Master Harold*) and The Shubert Organization in four (*Nicholas Nickleby, Grown Ups, Dreamgirls* and *Master Harold,* a perfect record if you count both hits and *successes d'estime*). The 1981–82 record of Elizabeth I.

DREAMGIRLS—The increasingly sophisticated taste of show business aspirants climbing the ladder to stardom is artfully visualized in these costumes designed by Theoni V. Aldredge for the musical. *Left to right above,* the photos of original Aldredge sketches picture the progression of some of the costumes worn by the "Dreamgirls," as follows: *(this page)* Jennifer Holliday in Act I, Scene 1; Holliday in Act I, Scene 6; Sheryl Lee Ralph in Act II, Scene 3; *(opposite page)* Deborah Burrell in Act II, Scene 3; Loretta Devine in Act II, Scene 6; Devine, Ralph and Burrell in Act II, Scene 8.

Below, Ralph, Devine and Burrell *(left)* with Cleavant Derricks, and Obba Babatunde *(right),* observe Ben Harney and Jennifer Holliday *(foreground)* in the "And I Am Telling You I'm Not Going" scene from *Dreamgirls*

McCann and Nelle Nugent was slightly smaller but even shinier: *Nicholas Nickleby, The Dresser* and *Mass Appeal,* all three of them Best Plays. The actor Wayne Rogers took a firm hold on the bottom rung of the Broadway stage production ladder with three flops (*Einstein and the Polar Bear, Duet for One* and *Little Me*), just below Kennedy Center with the very short-lived musicals *Oh, Brother!* and *Little Johnny Jones* (plus *Medea*) and Zev Bufman with *Oh, Brother!* and *The First* (plus *Joseph and the Amazing Technicolor Dreamcoat*).

Among the directors, the triumph of Trevor Nunn and John Caird in putting on *Nicholas Nickleby* dominated the field, in which other distinguished accomplishments included Michael Elliott's direction of *The Dresser,* John Lone's poetically eloquent choreography and staging of the little gem *The Dance and the Railroad,* Tommy Tune's endlessly inventive *Nine,* Athol Fugard's sure-handed staging of his own *Master Harold,* Adrian Hall's careful timing of Harold Pinter's *The Hothouse* in its regional theater production imported to Broadway, and John Madden's handling of two difficult but rewarding scripts, Jules Feiffer's *Grown Ups* and Christopher Durang's *Beyond Therapy.* Michael Bennett's rocking *Dreamgirls* (including its choreography in association with Michael Peters) and Michael Lindsay-Hogg's *Agnes of God* shook their theaters with the volume of their passion, while Douglas Turner Ward's staging of *A Soldier's Play* and David Trainer's of *The Dining Room* scored by more subtle means. Andrei Serban, Louis Malle, Robert Altman and Karel Reisz commanded with their various productions more critical attention than audience enthusiasm. Actors who dipped into direction this season, for the most part successfully, included Michael Cristofer (*Candida*), Colleen Dewhurst (*Ned and Jack*), Geraldine Fitzgerald (*Mass Appeal*), Nicol Williamson (*Macbeth*) and of course Melvin Van Peebles, a one-man band of authorship, direction and performance with his latest Broadway offering, *Waltz of the Stork.*

Actors who confined themselves to acting didn't always find themselves on the safe side of their profession. Unquestionably superior performers who this season bogged down in shows which could not make the grade were Rita Moreno, James Coco (twice), Sally Struthers, Hope Lange, Betty Garrett, Sandy Dennis (twice), Jack Gilford (twice), Claudette Colbert, Jean-Pierre Aumont, Peter Strauss, Roy Dotrice, Anne Bancroft, Max von Sydow, Suzanne Pleshette—and Cher. Even Rex Harrison repeating one of the memorable performances of all time as Professor Henry Higgins in *My Fair Lady* could not re-magnetize the 1981–82 theatergoers.

Indelible memories of characterization linger, however, when one thinks of the *Nicholas Nickleby* ensemble and those of *The Dining Room* (led by Remak Ramsay and Pippa Pearthree), *Agnes of God* (Amanda Plummer, Geraldine Page and Elizabeth Ashley) and *Master Harold* (Danny Glover, Zakes Mokae and Lonny Price) . . . the threesome of Katharine Hepburn, Dorothy Loudon and Regina Baff in *The West Side Waltz* . . . the twosomes in opposition or duet: Tom Courtenay and Paul Rogers in *The Dresser,* Jennifer Holliday and Ben Harney in *Dreamgirls,* James Earl Jones and Christopher Plummer in *Othello,* Charles Brown and Adolph Caesar in *A Soldier's Play,* Zoe Caldwell and Judith Anderson in *Medea,* Bernadette Peters and Christine Baranski in *Sally and Marsha,* Irene Worth and Constance Cummings in *The Chalk Garden* . . . and the blazing individual contributions of Raul Julia in the forefront of an extraordinary feminine ensemble in *Nine* . . . Richard Kavanaugh as the unflappable Gibbs in *The Hothouse* . . . Afemo in his striking impersonation of an African chieftain in *Livingstone and Sechele* . . . Joanne Camp as sex subject and predicate in *Geniuses* . . . plus Bob Gunton in *How I Got That Story,* Milo O'Shea in *Mass Appeal,* Bob Dishy in *Grown Ups,* Philip Bosco in *Eminent Domain,* John Lone in *The Dance and the Railroad,* Harvey Fierstein in *Torch Song Trilogy* and Elizabeth Franz in *Sister Mary Ignatius Explains It All for You.*

As in other creative and interpretive categories, John Napier's costumes and sets (with Dermot Hayes) for *Nicholas Nickleby* were in a class by themselves. Other eminently striking designs were the sets by William Ritman for *The Supporting Cast,* Laurie Dennett for *The Dresser,* David Chapman for *Othello* and the short-lived *The First,* David Gropman for *Family Devotions,* Eugene Lee for *The Hothouse* and Patricia Woodbridge for *How I Got That Story;* and the costumes by Stephen Doncaster for *The Dresser,* Robert Fletcher for *Othello* and Carol Oditz for *How I Got That Story.* The standout musical design was *Nine,* a black and white masterpiece of scenery (by Lawrence Miller) and costumes (by William Ivey Long), with Robin Wagner's sets and Theoni V. Aldredge's costumes for *Dreamgirls* also a marked success.

The ultimate insignia of New York professional theater achievement (we insist) are the Best Play citations in these volumes, designations which are 16 years older than the Critics Awards and only three years younger than the Pulitzer Prizes. Each Best Play selection is now made with the script itself as the first consideration, for the reason (as we've stated in previous volumes) that the script is the spirit of the theater's physical manifestation. It is not only the quintessence of the present, it is most of what endures into the future. So the Best Plays are the best scripts, with as little weight as humanly possible given to comparative production values. The choice is made without any regard whatever to a play's type—musical, comedy or drama—or origin on or off Broadway, or popularity at the box office, or lack of same.

We don't take the scripts of other eras into consideration for Best Play citation in this one, whatever their technical status as American or New York "premieres" which didn't happen to have a previous production of record. We draw the line between adaptations and revivals, the former eligible for Best Play selection but the latter not, on a case-by-case basis. We likewise consider the eligibility of borderline examples of limited-engagement and showcase production one at a time, ascertaining that they are probably "frozen" in final script version and no longer changeable works-in-progress, before they are considered for Best Play citation (and in the case of a late-season arrival the final decision may not be made until the following year, as with *Mass Appeal*).

If a script influences the very character of a season, or by some function of consensus wins the Critics, Pulitzer or Tony Awards, we take into account its future historical as well as present esthetic importance. This is the only special consideration we give, and we don't always tilt in its direction, as the record shows.

The ten Best Plays of 1981–82 are listed here for visual convenience in the order in which they opened in New York (a plus sign + with the performance number signifies that the play was still running after May 31, 1982).

The Dance and the Railroad
  (Off Broadway; 181 perfs.)

Nicholas Nickleby
  (Broadway; 49 perfs.)

The Dresser
  (Broadway; 200 perfs.)

Mass Appeal
  (Broadway; 214 perfs.)

A Soldier's Play
  (Off Broadway; 221+ perfs.)

Torch Song Trilogy
  (Off Broadway; 117 perfs.)

The Dining Room
  (Off Broadway; 131+ perfs.)

Agnes of God
  (Broadway; 64+ perfs.)

"MASTER HAROLD" . . . *and the boys*
  (Broadway; 32+ perfs.)

Nine
  (Broadway; 25+ perfs.)

George Martin and Richard Kavanaugh in Harold Pinter's *The Hothouse*

Broadway

Nicholas Nickleby arrived early in the season to light up the midtown sky and left early, as the year turned, at the end of its limited engagement, with its Royal Shakespeare troupe physically exhausted and its producers breathing sighs of relief that this supremely distinguished undertaking managed to break even on the balance sheets. Ronald Harwood's *The Dresser* remained, however, to demonstrate all season long the power of British theater at its best. This script concerned itself with the last day in the life of a provincial Shakespeare touring-company star (Paul Rogers), and more particularly with this star's close relationship with the admiring dresser (Tom Courtenay) who fusses over him, catering to his every need and seeing that he is ready to go on at curtain time. Courtenay's finicky performance of this mannered, single-minded creature stood at the center of a bustling play, busy with the backstage activity before, during and after a provincial performance of *King Lear.* The dresser's bewildered grief at the death of his master, his *raison d'etre,* even more acute than that of the star's wife (Rachel Gurney), climaxed this extremely skillfully acted, directed (by Michael Elliott) and designed (by Laurie Dennett and Stephen Doncaster) piece of introverted theater.

For the second year in succession, Athol Fugard provided a hard-hitting script for the Best Plays list. Like last season's *A Lesson From Aloes,* Fugard's *"MASTER HAROLD"* . . . *and the boys* was a harsh reflection of racial attitudes in his apartheid-plagued native land of South Africa, viewed in this case through the friendship, almost to the point of father-and-son kinship, between a white youth (Lonny Price) and the older black man (Zakes Mokae) who has served his family for many years. A third character, a black man (Danny Glover) menially employed in the white family's tea room, acts and reacts as a kind of Greek chorus accenting the values of the play. Under its author's direction, and with this superbly coordinated acting trio, *Master Harold* subjects the white youth to gradually increasing emotional stress until, like a skunk at bay, the boy releases his inbred racism on his longsuffering friend. The play, performed without intermission, is essentially a one-acter stretched to carry more weight that it can comfortably bear in the opening stages, but it finally arrives at a shattering collision. Whereas Fugard's *A Lesson From Aloes* was indigenously South African in its characters and situation, *"MASTER HAROLD"* . . . *and the boys* is a universal, potent variation on the theme of racism in general, anywhere, any time, and may well prove as durable as anything ever written for the stage on this subject.

Two days after *Master Harold* arrived on Broadway in its regional (Yale Repertory Theater) production, still another notable foreign script, Harold Pinter's *The Hothouse,* came to Broadway in its American premiere production by the Trinity Square Repertory Company in Providence, R.I. *The Hothouse* (written in 1958 between Pinter's *The Birthday Party* and *The Caretaker* but put away in his drawer until now) was a classic example of absurdist comedy trimmed with black at the edges. It was set in a madhouse ruled by the Establishment (a penetrable metaphor), and it ridiculed the excesses and shortcomings of bureaucracy and other conceits cherished by everyone from the director down to his lowliest eager-beaver employee (the inmates never put in an appearance). As usual in vintage Pinter, least menacing is most dangerous (remember the glass of water in *The Homecoming?*), with Richard Kavanaugh perfectly portraying the director's impeccable assistant—correct, straightforward and therefore the square backdrop against which all the ragged-edged absurdity is silhouetted, as well as the detonating device which increasingly threatens to touch everything off. The "Pinter pauses"—those beats of silence punctuating the dialogue—were carefully observed in the direction by Adrian Hall. *The Hothouse* made only a brief appearance on Broadway, but it left long memories. Not so another import from London, Tom Kempinski's *Duet for One,* about a psychiatrist treating a musician whose career is ended prematurely by a crippling disease, despite the formidable acting services of Max von Sydow in the former and Anne Bancroft in the latter roles.

Economic and social conditions being what they are in the 1980s, no longer can the state of American playwriting be appraised by its Broadway experience. Of this year's 18 new American scripts on Broadway, fewer than a handful possessed the right stuff—whatever it is—to survive even modestly in an artistically forbidding environment beset by enormous costs, discouraging ticket prices and audience tastes that are narrowing as the audience shrinks. The American script most comfortable under these conditions was Bill C. Davis's Best Play *Mass Appeal*, well polished under Geraldine Fitzgerald's direction in this and a previous production at Manhattan Theater Club and having the very great advantage of a memorable performance by Milo O'Shea of a good-natured, easygoing, middle-aged Catholic priest brought face-to-face with his own compromises by the penetrating comments of a young seminarian. For this once, Broadway audiences settled for charm and intelligence and kept *Mass Appeal* going all season long.

The theme of *Mass Appeal*—an examination of aspects of Roman Catholic style and dogma—recurred on and off Broadway in such scripts as *Sister Mary Ignatius Explains It All for You, Catholic School Girls* and even in a short-lived musical set in a Parochial School and antically entitled *Do Black Patent Leather Shoes Really Reflect Up?* On Broadway, *Agnes of God* by John Pielmeier was an emotionally violent study of a young nun who has been convicted of killing her own infant immediately after its birth. Under pressure from a court-appointed psychiatrist (Elizabeth Ashley) and under the wing of a Mother Superior (Geraldine Page), the nun gradually reveals an ascetic, child-of-God nature that transcends the most dreadful reality with sublime spiritual, even miraculous interpretations. This duality—sublime cause and brutal effect—was beautifully handled in Amanda Plummer's acting of the nun, who may be possessed by the Holy Ghost, or the devil, or merely a pathetically wracked slip of humanity, or a combination of all three. Miss Plummer's interpretation was the season's female acting peak, and Mr. Pielmeier's potent Best Play, first produced in regional theater and cited by the American Theater Critics Association in last year's *Best Plays* volume, was certainly one of the highlights of the season.

Another accomplished American script with a forceful theme—stated to more effect in individual scenes than as a structural unit—was Jules Feiffer's *Grown Ups,* in which Bob Dishy played a family man fighting simultaneous battles against his demanding parents, his self-centered child and his abrasive wife, with diminishing hope of victory. Percy Granger's *Eminent Domain,* about a college professor at a critical stage of his career and his family relationships, was given a solidly satisfying production by Circle in the Square under the direction of Paul Austin, with Philip Bosco as the professor and Betty Miller as his ex-alcoholic wife. Beth Henley's *Crimes of the Heart* transferred to Broadway this season, and Mary Beth Hurt and company repeated their celebrated off-Broadway performance of family members in crisis over a wife's attempted murder of her husband. The writing-acting team of the 1966 Best Play *Hogan's Goat* was reunited with Faye Dunaway playing a Brooklyn Irish woman looking back over the tribulations of her life and pronouncing it a triumph in William Alfred's *The Curse of an Aching Heart.* The year's further stage contemplations of rather serious matters included Elan Garonzik's *Scenes and Revelations* (19th century family strife in Lancaster, Pa.), Edward Sheehan's *Kingdoms* (ideological confrontation between Napoleon and Pope Pius VII), Tom Dulack's *Solomon's Child* (deprogramming a youngster who has been brainwashed by a religious cult) and Sheldon's Rosen's *Ned and Jack* (Edward Sheldon and John Barrymore on the brink of hitting the skids)—which last, with Bernard Slade's *Special Occasions* (the ongoing love affair between a divorced husband and wife) and an updated revival

The 1981–82 Season on Broadway

PLAYS (18)

Wally's Cafe
Scenes and Revelations
The Supporting Cast
A Talent for Murder
Einstein and the Polar Bear
Crimes of the Heart
  (transfer)
Ned and Jack
MASS APPEAL
  (transfer)
The West Side Waltz
Grown Ups
Kingdoms
The Curse of an Aching
  Heart
Special Occasions
Come Back to the 5 &
  Dime Jimmy Dean,
  Jimmy Dean
Eminent Domain
AGNES OF GOD
Solomon's Child
Beyond Therapy
  (revised version)

MUSICALS (10)

Marlowe
Oh, Brother!
Merrily We Roll Along
The First
Dreamgirls
Waltz of the Stork
Pump Boys and Dinettes
  (transfer)
Is There Life After High
  School?
NINE
Do Black Patent Leather
  Shoes Really Reflect Up?

FOREIGN PLAYS IN ENGLISH (5)

THE LIFE & ADVENTURES OF NICHOLAS NICKLEBY
THE DRESSER
Duet for One
"MASTER HAROLD" . . . AND THE BOYS
The Hothouse

REVIVALS (12)

A Taste of Honey
  (transfer)
Fiddler on the Roof
My Fair Lady
Circle in the Square:
  Candida
  Macbeth
Camelot
Little Me
  (revised version)
Joseph and the Amazing Technicolor Dreamcoat
  (transfer)
Othello
The World of Sholom
  Aleichem
Little Johnny Jones
Medea

SPECIALTIES (3)

This Was Burlesque
  (return engagement)
An Evening With Dave
  Allen
Encore

HOLDOVERS WHICH PROBABLY BECAME HITS in 1981–82

42nd Street
Sophisticated Ladies
The Little Foxes
Lena Horne

Categorized above are all the new productions listed in the Plays Produced on Broadway section of this volume.
Plays listed in CAPITAL LETTERS have been designated Best Plays of 1981–82.
Plays listed in *italics* were still running after May 31, 1982.
Plays listed in **bold face type** were classified as hits in *Variety*'s annual estimate published June 2, 1982.

of George M. Cohan's *Little Johnny Jones* starring Donny Osmond shared the harsh experience of closing after their opening performance.

On the lighter side, Ernest Thompson's vehicle for Katharine Hepburn, *The West Side Waltz*, costarred with *Mass Appeal* in this year's Broadway parade. Thompson's is a play of spirit in the ascendancy, with Miss Hepburn as a pianist who manages to keep her fingers on the keys and her good-humored wits about her even as the aging process lays upon her one infirmity after another. We have seen this gifted actress play women of indomitable courage before, and now we have seen her do it again, in full Hepburn style and with the help of Dorothy Loudon as a friend who provides the pianist with disbelieving encouragement as well as competent violin accompaniment. George Furth's *The Supporting Cast* benefited from its casting of an accomplished ensemble (Hope Lange, Betty Garrett, Sandy Dennis, Jack Gilford and Joyce Van Patten) playing the subjects of an author's embarrassingly tattle-tale memoirs, under Gene Saks's direction in an attractive Malibu beach house set designed by William Ritman.

The latest Broadway effort of Sam Bobrick and Ron Clark, *Wally's Cafe*, with Rita Moreno, James Coco and Sally Struthers hanging out in a Las Vegas roadside cafe, was a nonentity on Broadway, like most of their other work—and like it may also go on to wide international popularity. Audiences around the world dig Bobrick & Clark, Broadway to the contrary notwithstanding. Still another pair of renowned comedy writers, Jerome Chodorov and Norman Panama, missed their step with a comic murder intrigue, *A Talent for Murder*, about a mystery writer (Claudette Colbert) confined to a wheelchair in the midst of a multi-million-dollar art collection and a bunch of acquisitive relatives. *Einstein and the Polar Bear* (eager beaver young female reporter thrusts herself upon a reclusive novelist played by Peter Strauss) greatly disappointed its regional theater partisans, as did *Come Back to the 5 & Dime Jimmy Dean, Jimmy Dean* (the fan club 20 years after Dean's *Giant*, with Cher on parade among a sizeable cast). Christopher Durang scored a resounding hit off Broadway with his one-acter *Sister Mary Ignatius Explains It All for You*, but his effort to whip his *Beyond Therapy* (which played 30 performances at the Phoenix last season) into Broadway shape in a revised version, a farcical treatment of sexuality, psychiatry and an assortment of other foibles, divided his audience into pros and cons.

Chagrin at the faltering step of the 1981–82 Broadway musicals (including three major efforts, *Say Hello to Harvey, The Little Prince and the Aviator* and *Colette*, which closed out of town or in previews) was relieved at the last possible moment, on the day before the Tony nominations closed in May, by the arrival of the exciting *Nine*, staged by Tommy Tune in determination to try anything once—and imagining an abundant number of new things to try in a musical theater context. The Arthur Kopit book was based on a Mario Fratti translation of his own Italian version, apparently taking off (though unbilled in the program) from Federico Fellini's celebrated movie *8½* about an internationally renowned director gone dry of ideas but struggling to make one more "film." Raul Julia played the director in *Nine*, the only other male characters being children (the movie director at age 9 and several of his Parochial School classmates). A harem of females is grouped around the introspective hero, however, each doing her own thing, mostly with sexual overtones. The patient forbearance of a wife

Here is a sampling of William Ivey Long's sketches for the costume designs of the musical *Nine*. The first three *(left to right)* are for leading female characters. The fourth is for the romantic movie scene-within-the-play.

(Karen Akers), the hilariously overblown seductions of a mistress (Anita Morris), the sleek and savage attentions of a movie producer (Liliane Montevecchi) are a few of the enticements found here, where every musical number in Maury Yeston's compelling score stopped the show. The design (scenery by Lawrence Miller, costumes by William Ivey Long) was literally out of this world, relentlessly confined to black and white except for one sequence depicting the filming of a movie scene, when the colors spilled out into pastel in a romantic insert bringing to mind the Valentine sequence in the otherwise stark *Follies*. The black-clad silhouettes of the performers were sharply defined within the shiny, sanitary white surroundings of this Venetian spa setting, with Venice itself a mirage glimpsed in the far distance. This whole show, a Best Play, was a triumph of imagination in every department. No wonder *Nine* collected so many of the Tony Awards for which it arrived just barely in time to contend.

Dreamgirls, too, had its moments; it was a burst of color and energy with Michael Bennett staging, designs by Robin Wagner (sets) and Theoni V. Aldredge (costumes) and most conspicuously with the performance of Jennifer Holliday as the lead singer of a female rock trio. Miss Holliday's violent protest when she is both professionally and emotionally jilted at the end of Act I in the number "And I Am Telling You I'm Not Going" was a powerful outburst on a scale seldom realized outside grand opera—a performing moment to remember. The musical itself explored narrow passageways of the personal-appearance and recording entertainment world, with Ben Harney in major support as a selfish impresario. It was reverberantly loud in every sense, and, except for Miss Holliday and Mr. Harney, mostly forgettable.

A young, bright and cheerful exception to this year's rule of faltering musicals was *Pump Boys and Dinettes,* not a Broadway native but a transfer from off Broadway. Conceived and written by Jim Wann and other members of the cast, it packaged a group of country music numbers in a modern highway setting, the girls being waitresses in the diner on one side of the road and the boys gas jockeys on the other side. Also among the strivers was *Waltz of the Stork,* a "comedy with music" that sprang full-grown from the brain of Melvin Van Peebles and then walked around in his shoes. He wrote, directed, produced and starred in this series of autobiographical monologues joined by musical elaborations.

A disappointment to remember was *Merrily We Roll Along*—first, because it occupied a season of one of our theater's most valued musical artists, Stephen Sondheim; and second, because after all was said and done it didn't seem to be worth even the time required to play or watch it in the theater. It goes without saying that Harold Prince's staging of the piece was in precise control, or that there were numbers in the Sondheim score that sent his fans running out to acquire the original cast album. The Kaufman-Hart play from which the musical was adapted by George Furth travels backwards in time to show how its idealistic young hero ruined his life. This version moves back from 1980 to 1955, as a young stage hopeful on the threshold of success decides to abandon a difficult wife, an irritatingly dogmatic collaborator and the hellish strictures of the theater itself to follow the evil gleam of the recording industry. He winds up master of all he surveys, damned by affluence and the love of the woman of his choice. Well, this material was supposed to run backwards, and it certainly did, in more ways than one.

Also on the disappointing side was the economically massive failure of a large-scale musical about Jackie Robinson's entry into professional baseball, *The First,* with David Alan Grier impersonating the famous Brooklyn Dodger first baseman. *Marlowe* (a rock musical imposition on the Elizabethan dramatist), *Oh, Brother!* (a modernized spinoff from *The Comedy of Errors*), *Is There Life After High School?* (growing up can be half the fun) and *Do Black Patent Leather Shoes Really Reflect Up?* (antics at the Parochial School) fell even farther short of inspiration.

This year's specialty shows included a new production at Radio City Music Hall, *Encore,* celebrating that theater's golden jubilee with re-enactments by the Rockettes and others of noble Music Hall stage-show numbers of the past 50 years. Ann Corio's *This Was Burlesque* paid Broadway a return-engagement visit. The only straight specialty was *An Evening With Dave Allen,* with the BBC-TV star presenting his comedy monologues at the Booth Theater.

Here's where we list the *Best Plays* choices for the top individual achievements of the season. In the acting categories, clear distinction among "starring," "featured" or "supporting" players can't be made on the basis of official billing, which is more a matter of contracts than of esthetics. Here in these volumes we divide acting into "primary" and "secondary" roles, a primary role being one which might some day cause a star to inspire a revival in order to appear in that character. All others, be they vivid as Mercutio, are classed as secondary.

Furthermore, our list of individual bests makes room for more than a single choice when necessary. We believe that no useful purpose is served by forcing

Cheryl Giannini, Jennifer Dundas and Bob Dishy as a family in Jules Feiffer's *Grown Ups*

ourselves into an arbitrary selection of a single best when we come upon multiple examples of comparable quality. In that case we include them all in our list.

Here, then, are the *Best Plays* bests of 1981–82:

PLAYS

BEST PLAY: *The Life & Adventures of Nicholas Nickleby* adapted by David Edgar from the novel by Charles Dickens

BEST AMERICAN PLAY: *A Soldier's Play* by Charles Fuller

BEST REVIVAL: *Othello* by William Shakespeare, directed by Peter Coe

BEST ACTOR IN A PRIMARY ROLE: Tom Courtenay as Norman in *The Dresser;* Milo O'Shea as Father Tim Farley in *Mass Appeal;* Roger Rees as Nicholas Nickleby in *Nicholas Nickleby*

BEST ACTRESS IN A PRIMARY ROLE: Amanda Plummer as Agnes in *Agnes of God*

BEST ACTOR IN A SECONDARY ROLE: Edward Petherbridge as Newman Noggs and David Threlfall as Smike in *Nicholas Nickleby*

BEST ACTRESS IN A SECONDARY ROLE: Dorothy Loudon as Cara Varnum in *The West Side Waltz;* Geraldine Page as Mother Miriam Ruth in *Agnes of God*

BEST DIRECTOR: Trevor Nunn and John Caird for *Nicholas Nickleby*

BEST SCENERY: John Napier and Dermot Hayes for *Nicholas Nickleby*

BEST COSTUMES: John Napier for *Nicholas Nickleby*

MUSICALS

BEST MUSICAL: *Nine*

BEST BOOK: *Nine* by Arthur Kopit, adapted from the Italian by Mario Fratti

BEST MUSIC: Maury Yeston for *Nine*

BEST LYRICS: Stephen Sondheim for *Merrily We Roll Along*

BEST REVIVAL: *Joseph and the Amazing Technicolor Dreamcoat,* music by Andrew Lloyd Webber, lyrics by Tim Rice, directed by Tony Tanner

BEST ACTOR IN A PRIMARY ROLE: Raul Julia as Guido Contini in *Nine*

BEST ACTRESS IN A PRIMARY ROLE: Jennifer Holliday as Effie Melody White in *Dreamgirls*

BEST ACTOR IN A SECONDARY ROLE: Ben Harney as Curtis Taylor Jr. in *Dreamgirls*

BEST ACTRESS IN A SECONDARY ROLE: Karen Akers as Luisa, Liliane Montevecchi as Liliane La Fleur and Anita Morris as Carla in *Nine*

BEST DIRECTOR-CHOREOGRAPHER: Tommy Tune for *Nine*

BEST SCENERY: Lawrence Miller for *Nine*

BEST COSTUMES: William Ivey Long for *Nine*

Don Scardino and Bob Gunton in *How I Got That Story* by Amlin Gray

Off Broadway

In the smaller New York playhouses in 1981–82, there was a perception that the status of what we call "off Broadway" was evolving—not exactly changing, not exactly increasing in stature, but in the process of evolving from a tributary theater into what could become the main event of the New York stage in this decade.

The narrowing circumstances of Broadway acceptance (the smash musical, the popular comedy, the shock-treatment drama) are causing the creative baton to be passed elsewhere. It could be argued, for example, that a finely-drawn script like Charles Fuller's Pulitzer Prize and Critics Award-winning Best Play *A Soldier's Play* wouldn't find an economically sustaining audience in a Broadway production, any more than Samm-Art Williams's *Home* was able to do so a season ago. What to do, then? A theater that cannot support *Home* or *A Soldier's Play* doesn't deserve the name of a national art form; and the New York theater is certainly that, even if Broadway isn't any more. At this point, an alternative seems to lie in evolving off Broadway into the principal bearer of creative theater, raising the price of the top ticket to more than $20 and pushing the production cost well up into six figures, hoping it will become economically feasible to maintain such a theater in the dozens of smaller auditoriums scattered throughout the city. If this sounds like past Broadway mistakes—raise prices and costs and hope for the best—it should serve as a warning to off Broadway against playing follow-the-leader over the same cliff. Right now, good plays and willing audiences exist in abundance off Broadway, even at $14 to $20 a seat. Whether this will enable off Broadway to establish an economically stable outlet for its creative energies is still very much an ongoing question.

We must take pains to explain what we mean by "off Broadway." Its border lines are smudging at both the Broadway and off-off-Broadway ends, as most other publications including *Variety* and the New York *Times* apply the term loosely, in some cases to productions that are straight OOB (weekend or Wednesday-to-Saturday performances only, $6 admission, special Equity concessions) and frequently to "mini-contract" OOB productions (Equity concessions and closed-end engagements). We cannot draw indelible lines, but we must distinguish between professional and experimental categories; between what is probably a work-in-progress which may itself evolve as it rises to a higher level, and what is probably a "frozen" script facing the world for better or for worse as a completed work in production or publication. Only the latter is regularly considered for Best Play designation, for obvious reasons. Full off-Broadway plays and musicals are thus eligible for Best Play designation on the same terms as those listed under the Broadway heading, whereas works-in-progress are not.

By the lights of these *Best Plays* volumes, an off-Broadway production is one a) with an Equity cast b) giving 8 performances a week c) in an off-Broadway theater d) after inviting public comment by reviewers on opening nights. And according to Paul Libin, president of the League of Off-Broadway Theaters, an off-Broadway theater is a house seating 499 or fewer and situated in Manhattan *outside* the area bounded by Fifth and Ninth Avenues between 34th and 56th Streets, and by Fifth Avenue and the Hudson River between 56th and 72d Streets.

Obviously, we make exceptions to each of these rules; no dimension of "off" or "off off" Broadway can be applied exactly. In each *Best Plays* volume we stretch them somewhat in the direction of inclusion—never of exclusion. The point is, off Broadway isn't an exact location either geographically or esthetically, it's a state of the art, a level of expertise and professional commitment. In these *Best Plays* volumes we'll continue to categorize it, however, as accurately as we can, as long as it seems useful for the record, while reminding those who read these lines that distinctions are no longer as clear as they once were—and elsewhere in this volume we publish the most comprehensive list of 1981–82 off-off-Broadway productions anywhere, plus a review of the season OOB by the incomparably well qualified Mel Gussow of the New York *Times*.

This said, let us note that 1981–82 production of new scripts off Broadway was on the rise after a three-year falloff. There were 60 productions including 45 American straight plays (of which two were return engagements), 9 musicals and 7 foreign plays in English. This compares favorably with the totals of the past two seasons, 55 (33-14-8) in 1981 and 58 (39-7-12) in 1980, and is gaining on the 64 (38-15-11) of 1979; and the large number of American straight play productions last season indicates where the action was. In addition to the above, there were 4 revues and 40 revival productions off Broadway in 1981–82, a number which is not significantly out of line with other recent seasons.

Last year at this time we wrote, "Foreign playwrights stole the show off Broadway," but this year the American dramatists overwhelmed the list with

The 1981–82 Season Off Broadway

PLAYS (45)

The Fuehrer Bunker
Isn't It Romantic
The Butler Did It
A Tale Told
The Diviners
(return engagement)
How It All Began
Zooman and the Sign
(return engagement)
Key Exchange
Public Theater:
THE DANCE AND THE RAILROAD
Family Devotions
Twelve Dreams
Red and Blue
Goose and Tomtom
Sea Marks
Particular Friendships
Grace
2 by South
Manhattan Theater Club:
Crossing Niagara
Sally and Marsha
Gardenia
Playwrights Horizons:
Sister Mary Ignatius & The Actor's Nightmare
THE DINING ROOM
Geniuses

Fighting Bob
Circle Repertory:
Threads
Confluence
Snow Orchid
The Great Grandson of Jedediah Kohler
Young Playwrights Festival (three programs)
Negro Ensemble:
A SOLDIER'S PLAY
Colored People's Time
The Good Parts
TORCH SONG TRILOGY
Clownmaker
Chucky's Hunch
How I Got That Story
Lydie Breeze
Weekends Like Other People
Poor Little Lambs
Scenes Dedicated to My Brother, etc.
Catholic School Girls
The Six O'Clock Boys
The Freak

MUSICALS (9)

El Bravo!
The Heebie Jeebies
Pump Boys and Dinettes
Double Feature
Head Over Heels
Francis
Oh, Johnny
Lullabye and Goodnight
T.N.T.

FOREIGN PLAYS IN ENGLISH (7)

Hunting Scenes From Lower Bavaria
Maggie & Pierre
After the Prize
No End of Blame
Zastrozzi
Three Acts of Recognition
Livingstone and Sechele

REVUES (4)

The Laundry Hour
Pigiazz, II
Tomfoolery
Maybe I'm Doing It Wrong

SPECIALTIES (12)

"No"
Shay Duffin as Brendan Behan
Oscar Remembered
Everybody's Gettin' Into the Act
The Ballad of Dexter Creed
Behind the Broken Words
My Own Stranger
Cotton Patch Gospel
Whistler
Kaufman at Large
Cast of Characters
The Regard of Flight

REVIVALS (40)

American Buffalo
Entertaining Mr. Sloane
Misalliance
Delacorte:
The Tempest
Henry IV, Part 1
What the Butler Saw
Chekhov on the Lawn
Roundabout:
Miss Julie & Playing With Fire
The Caretaker

Roundabout (cont'd):
The Browning Version
The Chalk Garden
The Broken Pitcher
LOOM:
The Red Mill
H.M.S. Pinafore
A Night in Venice
(13 operettas in running repertory)
Taken in Marriage
Classic Stage:
Peer Gynt I
Peer Gynt II
The Cherry Orchard
King Lear
Ghost Sonata
Joseph and the Amazing Technicolor Dreamcoat
The Unseen Hand & Killer's Head
Birdbath & Crossing the Crab Nebula
Acting Company:
Twelfth Night
The Country Wife
Antigone

Categorized above are all the new productions listed in the Plays Produced Off Broadway section of this volume.
Plays listed in CAPITAL LETTERS have been designated Best Plays of 1981–82.
Plays listed in *italics* were still running off Broadway after May 31, 1982.

outstanding scripts. The aforementioned prizewinning Best Play *A Soldier's Play* made a distinguished name for itself as the opening production of The Negro Ensemble Company's tenth anniversary season, becoming virtually the whole NEC season in itself, held over all year in the group's Theater Four just west of the Broadway area. NEC wisely decided not to move this Charles Fuller hit to Broadway, where it couldn't possibly have grown any bigger than it already was, in any important way. In form it was a whodunit, with the murder of a spit-and-polish black sergeant (Adolph Caesar) in a World War II training camp for black recruits. The murder is investigated by a black captain (Charles Brown) assigned by the adjutant general's office over the strong objections and prejudice of the black soldiers' white officers. The working script (but not the playbill) carries the notation that the play is based on Herman Melville's *Billy Budd,* a fact which is not self-evident in Fuller's development of theme and situation. There is indeed an exemplary young recruit, vulnerable but extremely popular except with the tough sergeant, who views the recruit's accommodating nature as a handicap to the rapid wartime advancement of the black race and promptly makes a victim out of the lad. But there are many other antagonisms to be resolved as they orbit in flashback around the murder under Douglas Turner Ward's impeccable direction, in Felix E. Cochren's serviceable set—was it a race killing (by white officers), a revenge killing (by resentful recruits) or just a brawl? And will the white officer elite permit the black lawyer to uncover the truth? *A Soldier's Play* answered these questions by means of first-rate theater in a production perfectly suited to its off-Broadway environment. NEC had to use another theater, the Cherry Lane, for its second production of the season, Leslie Lee's *Colored People's Time,* directed by Horacena J. Taylor and outlining black American history from the Civil War to the 1960s civil rights movement.

Another standout of the off-Broadway year was Harvey Fierstein's *Torch Song Trilogy,* in which homosexuality is flaunted in the form of transvestism and then profoundly and movingly empathized in a network of family relationships. This Best Play is in fact three one-acters firmly connected by the central character (played with passionate conviction by the author), introduced as a drag queen who tires of hectic promiscuity and manages to form a meaningful attachment but suffers agonies when his lover leaves him for a woman (in the first one-acter, *The International Stud*); savors some of the pleasures of a more stable existence in tandem with another lover (in the second, *Fugue in a Nursery*); and finally reaches out to help a gay teen-ager in a cruelly hostile world, acting as both mother and father (in the third and intensely affecting *Widows and Children First!*). The theme was carried forward with a good deal of gay sexual gallows humor, but physical details of the experience were few and, except for one incident, restrained. What mattered in *Torch Song Trilogy* was not sexuality but common humanity, or its absence in the treatment of some homosexuals in some circumstances—with consequent tragic emotions rising in the midst of comedy in this outstanding play. It moved to Broadway shortly after it closed off Broadway in May.

Then there was the exceptionally successful season on the mainstage of Playwrights Horizons on 42d Street's Theater Row, where artistic director Andre Bishop and managing director Paul Daniels put every other organization in the

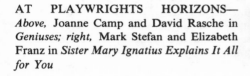

AT PLAYWRIGHTS HORIZONS—
Above, Joanne Camp and David Rasche in
Geniuses; right, Mark Stefan and Elizabeth
Franz in *Sister Mary Ignatius Explains It All
for You*

shade with a schedule made up of *Sister Mary Ignatius Explains It All for
You, The Dining Room* and *Geniuses,* all three of them still running in June when
the old New York theater season faded out and the new one faded in. The most
meticulously shaped and deeply penetrating of these three fine comedies was *The
Dining Room,* firmly positioned on the 1981–82 Best Plays list. This production
of A.R. Gurney Jr.'s play, set in that disappearing facility which in our day is
used mainly for family warfare, office space and everything else except dining, was
a triple threat of playwriting, acting and direction. The play is constructed as a
series of events with changing sets of characters of all ages flowing in and out,
but with each event a silhouetted unit of personal or family crisis, poignant or
funny, alternately and in combination. These vignettes, disconnected except by
the central theme of fading WASP glory symbolized by the fading function of the
dining room, were clearly and compellingly staged by David Trainer. The ensemble led by Remak Ramsay (appearing now as a grandfather, now as a child at
a birthday party) and Pippa Pearthree defined each of the many characters
stylishly and harmoniously. Like a well-planned feast, *The Dining Room* was
sometimes tart, sometimes sweet, always generously portioned and served with
undeniable flair.

As the record at Playwrights Horizons so eloquently demonstrates, it wasn't
only the headlining Best Plays that made this off-Broadway season such a rewarding one, it was a depth of excellent productions which might easily have made
the Best Plays list themselves in a less competitive year. Jonathan Reynolds's
Geniuses was a comedy in the boisterous tradition: literate, bawdy, hyperactive
and irreverent about both New York and Los Angeles lifestyles. With Joanne
Camp as a sexy movie star stirring libidos and egos, this three-acter played games
with some American movie makers trapped indoors by a monsoon in the Philip-

pines and beginning to give off steam. In the end, Superego (an epic movie director played by David Garrison) is a god who comes down from the sky in his machine (a helicopter) to set everybody back on proper course. Gerald Gutierrez swung his direction like a battleaxe (no needles here) in the spirit of good mean fun.

Likewise, Christopher Durang's *Sister Mary Ignatius Explains It All for You* made a strong impact on Playwrights Horizons audiences with Elizabeth Franz as a teaching nun whose devotion to her faith and dogma has crossed the border of fanaticism, so that instead of inspiring her students she rouses them to resentment and suffers their vengeance. Durang's satire was powerful acid, preceded on the program by a more frivolous one-acter, *The Actor's Nightmare,* about a player finding himself onstage in a leading role for which he has had no rehearsal.

Downtown at Joseph Papp's New York Shakespeare Public Theater there was a busy season of new plays both foreign and domestic, but it never re-attained the stature of the opening presentation, David Henry Hwang's *The Dance and the Railroad.* This was an utterly charming and subtly realized character portrait of a 19th century Chinese immigrant railroad laborer fighting the dehumanizing erosion of his daily task by practising dance steps and pantomime for a role in traditional Chinese opera. John Lone directed Hwang's piece, choreographed it, wrote the score and played the leading role, supported by Tzi Ma as a youthful laborer eager to learn opera performing too. This Best Play was a unique combination of dance movement, sound and dramatic insight, a very large entertainment in a small package. While *The Dance and the Railroad* was still running, a second play by this same author, *Family Devotions,* was produced at the Public. Its reach was broader as it compared the ways of modern Chinese Americans with those of a visiting relative from Communist China, but its grasp was far less sure.

Another leading dramatist represented on the Public Theater's schedule was James Lapine, whose *Twelve Dreams* under his own direction was a painful probing of the dreams and the sanity of a troubled 10-year-old. David Rabe too had a play at the Public this season, the gangster comedy *Goose and Tomtom,* but he can't be said to have been "represented" there, since he disavowed the production of his play before it opened. *Zastrozzi* by the Canadian George F. Walker also dealt with crime in a clash of good and evil symbols under Andrei Serban's direction, while the personal stresses of 16 characters were exposed in an art-exhibition setting in Botho Strauss's 1977 German play *Three Acts of Recognition,* staged by Richard Foreman in flamboyant style. Also mixed into the Public Theater potpourri this season were a topical revue *The Laundry Hour;* Michael Moriarty's counterattack against the critics, *The Ballad of Dexter Creed; Antigone* staged by Joseph Chaikin; a new Elizabeth Swados musical *Lullabye and Goodnight,* surveying the world of the prostitute; a pair of colored light bulbs flashing in beat with offstage conversation in *Red and Blue,* directed by JoAnne Akalaitis; plus a return engagement of Miss Swados's Old Testament-oriented *The Haggadah,* which promises to be an annual event at the Joseph Papp theater complex. Workshop and other theater-related events at the Public this season are listed in the Plays Produced Off Off Broadway section of this volume.

The off-Broadway year's best foreign play was first produced in showcase at

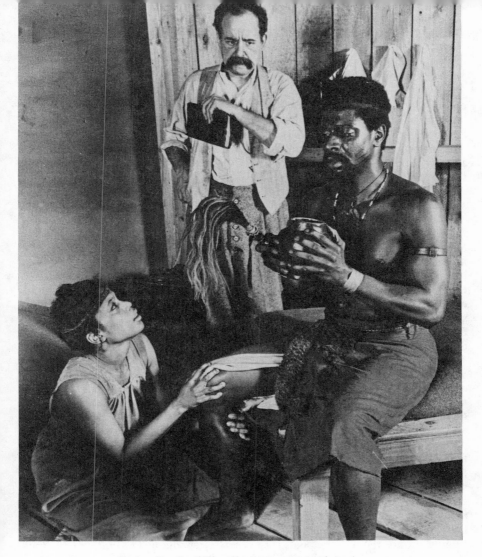

Esther Ryvlin, Mike Champagne and Afemo in
Livingstone and Sechele at the Quaigh Theater

the Quaigh Theater, then moved up to full professional status there. *Livingstone and Sechele* by David Pownall, previously produced at the Edinburgh Festival and in London, yielded very little to its contemporaries on the Best Plays list and had the advantage of a striking portrayal of a 19th century African chieftain by Afemo, an actor who, according to the Quaigh's program notes, "considers himself a child of the Yoruba culture in Nigeria." The Livingstone of the title is the one once presumed by the explorer Stanley; and the chieftain, Sechele, was the only convert achieved by the Scottish doctor's African evangelizing. The half-naked savage is more than a match, in shrewdness as well as in strength, for the Scots Presbyterian as they attempt to join their two disparate cultures by means of Christian faith and ethic. Afemo's open-eyed, indomitable Sechele was one of four strong performances, the others being by Mike Champagne as the born loser Livingstone, Prudence Wright Holmes as his wife with twice his resilience and twenty times his strength, and Esther Ryvlin as the most alluring and intractable of Sechele's wives. Directed by Will Lieberson, the Quaigh's artistic director, *Livingstone and Sechele* was one of the major contributions to this notable off-Broadway season.

Amlin Gray's *How I Got That Story* made a big splash off off Broadway a season ago and was likewise one of this year's premier events in transfer to full off-Broadway production. In the framework of an American journalist's adventures while trying to cover the Vietnam War, and in farcical style, it exposed the futilities and frustrations of that national misstep in a series of encounters with military and non-military persons on both sides. All of the latter appeared under the single character name "The Historical Event," and all were played by Bob Gunton in a virtuoso display of comedic skill. The same was said by some observers of Kevin Wade's *Key Exchange* in its WPA Theater production's season-long run at the Orpheum Theater, with three eager young people making believe that their relationships commitments were of some comic consequence— a belief we were not able to share.

Gardner McKay's *Sea Marks,* the romance of an Irish fisherman touched with the gift of poetry and the Liverpool woman who loves, encourages and exploits him—a script often produced and highly respected in regional theater— made its professional New York debut early in the season under John Stix's direction. In another part of the forest, Casey Kurtti's *Catholic School Girls* was an amusing series of incidents in a Catholic school for girls, Grades One to Eight, cleverly compressed into a small package under Burry Fredrik's direction, with four well-chosen actresses playing both the students as they grow up and the teachers who cherish or bully them. This play inaugurated a new playhouse on 42d Street's Theater Row, the Douglas Fairbanks Theater, a comfortable auditorium set back from the street behind a courtyard. Other off-Broadway plays of more than fleeting interest were Paul Rudnick's *Poor Little Lambs,* a comedy imagining that a mere woman would attempt to join the celebrated all-male Yale singing group, the Whiffenpoofs; the comedy whodunit *The Butler Did It* by Walter and Peter Marks; the Juilliard School's *How It All Began,* dramatizing the origins of West German terrorism; *Chucky's Hunch* by Rochelle Owens, with Kevin O'Connor as a disillusioned artist unburdening himself in letters to a former wife; a pair of Joel Homer one-acters at the South Street Theater; Sidney Morris's *The Six O'Clock Boys* about a middle-aged woman and the youthful visitors to her room in a Columbus Avenue welfare hotel; and *The Freak* by Granville Wyche Burgess, looking into the early life of Edgar Cayce, a faith healer.

American Place's 1981 season carried over into June with W.D. Snodgrass's own dramatization of his cycle of poems, *The Fuehrer Bunker,* with Robert Stattel as Hitler in the last days of the Third Reich. The group's 1982 season was meager in both size and scope, consisting of only one play, Jane Stanton Hitchcock's character study of the unpleasantly outspoken female operator of an Oklahoma laundromat, *Grace* (moved up from American Place workshop), plus two exceptionally attractive specialties: *Behind the Broken Words,* with Roscoe

Lee Browne and Anthony Zerbe in a collection of poetry excerpts, and *The Regard of Flight,* a comic vaudeville with Bill Irwin clowning and carrying on in pantomime routines and verbal send-ups written by himself.

The Phoenix rounded out its 1981 season with Wendy Wasserstein's *Isn't It Romantic,* about women in the big city, then went on to a pair of foreign plays: the Canadian *Maggie & Pierre* with Linda Griffiths playing both the Trudeaus and Eric Peterson as an interviewer, and the world premiere of Fay Weldon's *After the Prize,* a British script about the aftereffects of the Nobel on the emotional life of a woman laureate. The Phoenix ended 1982 with an American overview of the life of the blue collar worker, *Weekends Like Other People.*

Inevitably, there were those 1981–82 off-Broadway entries which promised much more than they were finally able to perform. For example, Lanford Wilson's attempt to round off his Talley family series (*The 5th of July, Talley's Folly*) with *A Tale Told* at Circle Repertory met with far less than the enthusiasm accorded to the two former Best Plays. The new one dealt with family frictions up in the house on the same night as the Matt Friedman-Sally Talley rendezvous down in the boathouse in *Talley's Folly.* Circle Rep continued its season's activities with two more family plays—Jonathan Bolt's *Threads* and Joe Pintauro's *Snow Orchid*—and another Lanford Wilson play, *Thymus Vulgaris,* on a program of one-acters named for its John Bishop script, *Confluence,* and including Beth Henley's *Am I Blue.* Bishop's *The Great Grandson of Jedediah Kohler,* about the descendant of a gun-totin' frontier marshal and his search for his own identity as a modern hero, was also produced by Circle in repertory with a revival of *Richard II* which closed after previews. Another 1981–82 Circle project was the production in conjunction with the Dramatists Guild Fund, Inc. of ten new plays on three programs written by children age 8 to 18, winners of the Dramatists Guild Young People's Playwriting Contest. The young people's plays were staged and performed by professionals at the Circle and were admiringly received by reviewers.

Another fully promising effort was made by John Guare with two plays in his series set in 19th century Nantucket and dealing with several generations of Americans groping for values within the rapidly-changing context of a young but maturing country. The two plays were *Lydie Breeze* (produced independently and directed by Louis Malle) taking place in the 1890s and bringing in venereal disease as a symbol of the spreading consequences of individual behavior, and *Gardenia* (produced by Manhattan Theater Club and directed by Karel Reisz) taking place after the Civil War, with the characters trying to get a running start into the new era. The plays were sensitive and eloquent, like all Guare works, but unstructured and confusing in both style and intent. Another challenging script at Manhattan Theater Club was the British *No End of Blame* by Howard Barker, subtitled "Scenes of Overcoming" chronicling the troubled career of a Middle European political cartoonist subjected to forms of censorship and suppression on both sides of the Iron Curtain. Back in June, MTC had also raised the question of the pervasiveness of Nazi evil in the 1966 German play *Hunting Scenes From Lower Bavaria.* The MTC also presented Alonso Alegria's *Crossing Niagara* about the French tightrope walker Blondin, and Sybille Peterson's *Sally and Marsha,* a sturdy vehicle for the exceptional performances of Bernadette

Josef Sommer and Ben Cross in a scene from John Guare's *Lydie Breeze*

Peters and Christine Baranski as New York and South Dakota housewives meeting across a New York City apartment hallway.

The off-Broadway straight-play season was enhanced by return engagements of *The Diviners* by Jim Leonard Jr. and last season's Best Play *Zooman and the Sign* by Charles Fuller. Israel Horovitz ventured once more briefly onto the scene with a new play about mid-life crisis *The Good Parts*. Other subjects under scrutiny in short-lived appearances off Broadway were the actress and the homosexual (*Particular Friendships*), rape (*Precious Blood* in *2 by South*), the career of Robert M. La Follette (*Fighting Bob*) and the Diaghilev-Nijinsky relationship (*Clownmaker*).

On the musical side, off Broadway came up with the cheerful and charming *Pump Boys and Dinettes,* a loose-jointed creation by its cast including Jim

Wann, with gas jockeys and diner waitresses singing to each other across the highway in an assortment of country music styles and moods. Dodger Productions offered it at the Colonnades for 112 performances and then moved it to Broadway where it brightened its corner and the whole musical season. Zev Bufman took a similar route with his hit revival of the Andrew Lloyd Webber-Tim Rice Old Testament musical *Joseph and the Amazing Technicolor Dreamcoat*, running it up to Broadway after a spell downtown. Both these off-Broadway interlopers stole a significant part of the uptown show, between them winning nine Tony nominations including Best Musical in both cases.

Among those off-Broadway musicals that did not make it to the big time were *El Bravo!* (the Robin Hood legend transposed to a New York barrio), *The Heebie Jeebies* (homage to the singing Boswell Sisters of the 1930s) and *Francis* (the life and works of St. Francis of Assisi). In the revue category, off Broadway offered a new edition of the topical, satirical *Pigjazz;* an adaptation of Tom Lehrer numbers from the 1950s and 1960s, *Tomfoolery;* and a Randy Newman pop concert entitled *Maybe I'm Doing It Wrong.*

The specialty list was crowded with historical reminiscences and nostalgia such as *Shay Duffin as Brendan Behan,* John Cullum as (James McNeill) *Whistler, Oscar* (Wilde) *Remembered,* excerpts from Anne Sexton's works (*My Own Stranger*), Bible stories set to music (*Cotton Patch Gospel*), John Lithgow in his own adaptation of (George S.) *Kaufman at Large,* a Bob Ost vaudeville revue *Everybody's Gettin' Into the Act* and Patrizia Norcia recreating Ruth Draper's character sketches in *Cast of Characters.*

Such were the individual parts of off-Broadway's contribution to the 1981–82 theater season in New York, whose whole was much greater than their sum. Off Broadway was the principal repository of American playwriting, with four very strong Best Plays—*The Dance and the Railroad, A Soldier's Play, Torch Song Trilogy* and *The Dining Room*—backed up by a dozen or more standouts. And it was the source, two seasons ago, of one of Broadway's two American plays on this year's Best Plays list, *Mass Appeal.* Its two transferred musicals supplied Broadway with half its Tony nominees for Best Musical, while the titles of its transferred holdovers were blazoned all over the Broadway marquees: *A Chorus Line, Crimes of the Heart, Oh! Calcutta!, The Pirates of Penzance, The Best Little Whorehouse in Texas.* With Broadway becoming more a display case than a production facility, off Broadway was making moves to take over. Certainly it was where most of the action and substance was in 1981–82.

OTHELLO—James Earl Jones as Othello and Christopher Plummer as Iago

Revivals on and off Broadway

New York is a year-round celebration of living theater in retrospect, from Euripides to Orton, from Shakespeare to Shepard. The former's *Medea* in the Robinson Jeffers version under Robert Whitehead's direction was one of the season's lightning bolts, with Zoe Caldwell painstakingly physical in the title role made famous in the 1940s (in a production co-produced by this same Mr. Whitehead) by Judith Anderson, who herself appeared in this production as the gauntly misgiving Nurse. In revival, Sam Shepard's *The Unseen Hand,* a manipulation of time bringing together the Old West and outer space, embellished the last half of the off-Broadway season, as did a pair of black Joe Orton comedies, *Entertaining Mr. Sloane* and *What the Butler Saw,* in the first half. As usual, Shakespeare reappeared all over the place on and off Broadway: *Othello* with Darth Vader-voiced James Earl Jones as secure in the title role as though it had been written for him, and with Christopher Plummer as a sharp-edged Iago with nerves exposed; the *Macbeth* of Nicol Williamson at Circle in the Square; *The Tempest* and *Henry IV, Part 1* (Kenneth McMillan as Falstaff) at the Delacorte in Central Park; the *King Lear* of Robert Stattel in Classic Stage Company repertory; the Acting Company's *Twelfth Night;* not to mention an aborted *Richard II* and fun-house-mirror distortions of segments of *Romeo and Juliet* and *King Lear* as plays-within-plays of *Nicholas Nickleby* and *The Dresser,* respectively.

As in other recent seasons, major undertakings to redo big Broadway musicals for the new generation that didn't see them the first time around were elegantly achieved—but they met with precious little enthusiasm this year. Herschel Bernardi as Tevye in *Fiddler on the Roof*, Rex Harrison as Professor Henry Higgins in *My Fair Lady* and Richard Harris as King Arthur in *Camelot* were all in fine fettle but failed to draw crowds. A reworked version of Neil Simon's 20-year-old musical *Little Me* made a brief reappearance with James Coco in some of the roles originally played on Broadway by Sid Caesar. As mentioned previously in this report, only *Joseph and the Amazing Technicolor Dreamcoat* among this season's musical revivals really caught on.

Chekhov? Yes, of course—the Classic Stage Company (CSC) did *The Cherry Orchard*, and the Russian dramatist also appeared as a character onstage reading and discussing his works in *Chekhov on the Lawn* by Elihu Winer, a one-man show performed by William Shust. The major achievement of CSC's season, though, was the presentation of the full text of Henrik Ibsen's *Peer Gynt* in two alternating evenings. It was translated by Rolf Fjelde, directed and designed by CSC's artistic director, Christopher Martin, and billed as the American premiere of the complete text of the play, previously presented only in abridged versions such as the Public Theater's in Central Park in 1969. Characterized by Mel Gussow as "One of our basic repositories of classics," CSC rounded off its season with Strindberg's *Ghost Sonata*.

One of the highlights of the Broadway revival year was Amanda Plummer's Tony-nominated performance in a Roundabout Theater Company revival of Shelagh Delaney's *A Taste of Honey* moved up from its off-Broadway origins. If Miss Plummer's double Tony nomination in this and the featured-actress category, which she won for her Agnes in *Agnes of God,* is not a first, surely the added fact that her father Christopher's Iago was also nominated makes it a unique family triple. Joanne Woodward played Shaw's *Candida* for Circle in the Square uptown, and Jack Gilford and Joe Silver appeared in a revived series of Arnold Perl sketches based on stories by various authors and entitled *The World of Sholom Aleichem,* who was one of them.

In addition to *A Taste of Honey,* Gene Feist's and Michael Fried's Roundabout had a fruitful and stimulating twelve months, ending their 1981 season in late June with Shaw's *Misalliance,* beginning again in September with Strindberg's *Miss Julie* and *Playing With Fire* and ending their 1982 season in full stride with Irene Worth and Constance Cummings sweeping through the leading roles of Enid Bagnold's *The Chalk Garden.* In between, this active and steadily achieving organization kept its two playhouses attractively filled with Harold Pinter's *The Caretaker* (not seen here in a major production since the Roundabout did it nine years ago) and Terence Rattigan's *The Browning Version,* with Lee Richardson as the aging misfit schoolteacher, in its first major New York revival, with J.M. Barrie's *The Twelve-Pound Look* as a curtain raiser. Revival may be the name of the Roundabout's game, but it is not now and never has been a follower.

Uptown at the Light Opera of Manhattan (LOOM), melody was in fashion as usual, heavily accented with Gilbert & Sullivan but frequently branching into Romberg, Friml, Herbert and Lehar. Three new productions were inserted in the

Elizabeth Burgess-Harr and Raymond Allen in LOOM's production of the comic opera *A Night in Venice* by Johann Strauss

group's broad operetta repertory this season. LOOM did over its versions of
H.M.S. Pinafore and *The Red Mill,* then in May mounted a production of Johann
Strauss's 1883 comic opera *A Night in Venice,* the romance of a street singer and
a senator's daughter. Remembered like so many operettas more fondly for its
score than for its book, *A Night in Venice* was freely adapted in this version by
LOOM's producer-director, William Mount-Burke, in collaboration with Alice
Hammerstein Mathias, who also supplied new lyrics.

Wycherley? Certainly, with the Acting Company's *The Country Wife.* Scat-
tered elsewhere among off Broadway's 1981–82 revival offerings were Leonard
Melfi's *Birdbath;* Heinrich von Kleist's 1808 German comedy *The Broken
Pitcher* (originally *Jug*) in a Jon Swan translation produced by Goethe
House; the Public Theater's new translation of Sophocles's *Antigone* (which,
theater historian Thomas T. Foose reminded us, has been produced in New York
in three major adaptions—by Jean Cocteau, Bertolt Brecht and Jean
Anouilh, which was actually named a Best Play in the 1946 volume—and at least
12 minor ones); and Thomas Babe's *Taken in Marriage* revived by The Woman's
Ensemble.

And finally, among the first of the 1981–82 revivals in importance as well as
in point of time was the June 3 reappearance of David Mamet's Best Play
American Buffalo in a production directed by Arvin Brown at the Long Wharf
Theater in New Haven, Conn. and brought into town by Elliot Martin. Al
Pacino vividly recreated the leading role of Teach done on Broadway by Robert
Duvall. The show suspended performances in midwinter but returned and was
still a prominent feature of New York City's multi-theater revival program as the
season ended. From Mamet to Sophocles off Broadway, from Delaney to
Euripides on, our revival year was eclectic as usual and sparkled across an
impressive proportion of its broad surface.

Offstage

All year the battle over the block on the west side of Broadway between 45th and 46th Streets was joined in court and committee, and then the inevitable happened. A final rejection in Federal and New York State courts of the organized efforts of theater folk to save the Morosco, Helen Hayes and Bijou Theaters was handed down. At the end of March, with tearful actresses and angry playwrights sounding their last-minute objections, and in a society which has come to value a sweet real estate deal more than a cultural treasure, the bulldozers had their way. Steel bent and buckled; brick and plaster fell; and soon, where noble theaters once stood, there was only a level plain of rubble to be occupied in the fulness of time-and-a-half-for-overtime by a huge new hotel tower.

Granted that the Morosco and the Hayes were run down and economically inconvenient in design (with second balconies, unsellable to today's audiences); granted that a new theater will be built like a sentient Jonah in the digestive system of the juggernaut; granted that even though other recently-built theaters like the Uris and the Minskoff have proven uncomfortable for most legitimate stage productions, we ought not to prejudge the potential of this one. Such reasoning convinced committees, mayors and judges that these theaters should fall that a hotel might rise; but it is not reason that prevails when a theater lover stares at the ropes hanging from the bared flies like the entrails of a cadaver. The emotional shock of coming upon the empty place where a legitimate theater was destroyed is a function of the body's warning system against danger—real danger. Whatever the economics, it is viscerally appalling to lose theaters to a glass-faced monster that will certainly distort the scale of the whole district, let alone exacerbate all the logistic problems of the area. We must remember, not *why* it happened, but how it *felt,* and be instinctively, politically, emotionally on guard against it ever happening again.

Now for the good news: in May, the New York City Board of Estimate beefed up the zoning regulations to place a prohibition against the demolishing of Broadway theaters for a period of one year, during which the Planning Commission is to draw up new regulations concerning them. And in line with the apparently expanding popularity of the Broadway stage in the early 1980s, there is movement afoot to bring some or all of nine former legitimate theaters, now grind houses, on 42d Street in the Broadway-to-Eighth-Avenue block, back into the fold. The Shuberts, the Nederlanders and the Brandts are looking closely at the possibilities there, with the 1,500-seat New Amsterdam Theater, former home of some of the New York stage's most effulgent glories, seemingly the most desirable. The Brandts have already refurbished their Apollo and Rialto for Broadway and own the Selwyn, Victory, Times Square, Lyric (in process of refurbishing), Empire and Liberty Theaters in that area. The Nederlanders are set to begin conversion of the New Amsterdam and Harris Theaters, and no doubt there will soon be further developments (excuse the expression) of this nature.

There were other complications, as well as some traffic, in legitimate stage houses over the course of the season. One morning, just as *The Dresser* was all set to open at the Brooks Atkinson, the house took fire from an electrical short circuit. The sprinkler and alarm systems worked perfectly, but there was some $300,000 damage to scenery and the interior before the fire was extinguished, with a consequent delay in the play's opening. Jujamcyn Theater Corporation (James and Virginia Binger), which owns the St. James and the Martin Beck, acquired the ANTA (which is now renamed the Virginia after its co-owner), the Eugene O'Neill (formerly owned by Neil Simon) and the 958-seat Ritz, now being redone to the tune of $1.5 million for a return to the legitimate stage.

Playwrights found themselves in almost continuous conflict with other branches of the profession. The disagreement of the Dramatists Guild (their craft organization) with Actors' Equity over terms and enforcement of a showcase code (so that in certain instances actors who perform in workshop projects must be offered the same roles or salary compensation in certain future productions of same script) was outlined in detail in the Offstage section of this report in *The Best Plays of 1980–81*. The focus of the controversy was a suit brought against Equity by Michael Weller and other authors, but its effects continued widespread, inhibiting some dramatists from offering their scripts for showcases, since any lien on a script's future might reduce its chances of being produced elsewhere. In a settlement of this suit out of court in November, Equity agreed to free the authors of showcases from all obligation for future payments to actors in future productions. This was hailed by some as a settlement of the entire controversy; others pointed out that Equity has subsidiary rights agreements with groups other than dramatists, such as the League of Resident Theaters, who might still be required to hire or compensate showcase actors; so that a lien of sorts might remain against the script, even though the author is free of it. Whether the Equity showcase code continues to inhibit experimental production, as it did in New York City over the previous season, remains to be seen.

Just as the author-actor dispute began to cool, the Dramatists Guild found its negotiations with the League of New York Theaters and Producers over revision of the terms of the Minimum Basic Contract heating up. Virtually unchanged since the 1920s, this contract lays out the uniform terms for producers' leasing of dramatists' scripts and scores (in the theater, authors do not *sell* their works or become employees of producers, they retain ownership of their works and *rent* them to producers for a fixed percentage of the box office gross). It had been hoped to revise the contract to bring it into line with changed economic circumstances in the modern theater, with authors waiving royalty payments while a show was earning back its cost, and with producers in exchange guaranteeing authors a down payment of "front money" based on a percentage of the show's capitalization. These advances might amount to about $50,000 in the case of Broadway musical authors, $20,000-plus for playwrights (at present the down payment is only a token as little as $500). *Variety* reported that the author-producer talks broke down over definition of terms like "net gross" and "gross gross." At season's end the situation didn't seem to be resolving itself, and a new point of author-producer friction arose after the Guild's two Tony winners (Tom Eyen for best book of a musical, Maury Yeston for best score) were given their awards off-camera at the League-organized TV ceremonies, while hordes of producers tripped over each other at the winners' podium; and even the televised announcement of the authors' having won was accidentally garbled. Dramatists

Guild members were not amused, and their Council soon made public a statement that authors will take no further part in the Tonys until they are assured on-camera representation equal to that of other winners. The official relationship between dramatist and producer deteriorated further in midsummer with the filing of a producers' anti-trust suit against the Dramatists Guild—a development which occurred too late to be evaluated here before we went to press.

In negotiations with the musicians (Local 802 of the American Federation of Musicians) the League granted a $50-a-week increase for each musician working in a Broadway show each year for three years, which will raise the pay scale from the present $470 a week to $620 a week by 1985. Fringe benefits include an additional $10 a week for instrument maintenance ($40 for harpists) and a premium of $50 for first-chair trumpeters. Musicians appearing onstage get $30 extra and $20 more if in costume. Requirements for employment minimums attached to theaters remained in effect and caused a controversy over the continuing run of *The Best Little Whorehouse in Texas.* According to *Variety,* this show uses nine musicians but was required to pay 16 additional "walkers" (who are not contractually required to attend a performance) at the 46th Street Theater, because that theater calls for the employment of 25 musicians. The management of the show stated its intention of moving to the Music Box, a nine-musician house; the union insisted on continued enforcement of a 25-musician run-of-the-play agreement, with its $6,000-a-week extra cost. *Whorehouse* suspended New York performances in March, moved to Boston, then moved back to Broadway May 31, still obligated to pay 16 "walkers" in yet another nine-musician house, and with both union and producer still adamant. The two sides finally reached a private (as opposed to formal arbitration) agreement unique in its terms: the "walkers" would be required to check in at the show, remain for the performance and check out afterwards, or suffer a one-eighth reduction in weekly pay. By what amount these provisions reduced, in practise, the show's expenses hadn't been determined at this writing.

Among organizations, the Off Off Broadway Alliance (OOBA) of 94 tributary-theater producing organizations moved into a new headquarters on Spring Street under the new executive directorship of Jane S. Moss and adopted a new name: Alliance of Resident Theaters/New York, abbreviated as ART/NY. Volume 1, Number 1 of a new ART/NY bimonthly, *Theater Times,* stated two principal aims: "First, expanded management and marketing services must be developed and new strategies for their implementation explored. Second, state-of-the-art issues must be addressed." Across the forest at the leading edge of the trees, The Shubert Organization was partially freed from the restrictions of the Federal consent decree which has limited its operations for the past 25 years. A Federal judge ruled that the Shubert group can begin acquiring additional theaters outside New York immediately and will be free of the decree's other restrictions as of Jan. 1, 1985. *Variety* concluded that the Shuberts will be the eventual managers of the new theater in the Portman Hotel complex and will be bidding for 42d Street theaters to be returned to legit operation. And the executive directorship of the League of New York Theaters and Producers changed hands, as Harvey Sabinson took over this post and its distinguished longtime incumbent, Irving W. Cheskin, became the group's director of pension and welfare affairs.

In the largest voting turnout in its history, Actors' Equity Association elected its first woman president: Ellen Burstyn, the choice of the nominating committee, who defeated her independently-nominated rival by a three-to-one margin. Merle Debuskey also swept away all opposition and was re-elected to yet another two-year term as president of the Association of Theatrical Press Agents and Managers. At the end of Circle Repertory Company's season, the group's artistic director, Marshall W. Mason announced that he will take an indefinite leave of absence. Brendan Gill, drama critic of *the New Yorker,* moved up from vice president to president of the New York Drama Critics Circle, as Edmund Wilson of the Wall Street Journal was elected vice president and Richard Hummler of *Variety* was elected to membership. And the larger circle of American critics was greatly diminished by the retirement of Elliot Norton June 1 as drama critic of the Boston *Herald-American.* Unquestionably one of the most influential and distinguished critics of our time, the 79-year-old Mr. Norton will no doubt continue to serve the theater in ways other than that with which he has favored his readers so articulately and tastefully for 48 years of daily reviewing.

Turbulence is the first word that comes to mind as we glance back for a last look at the twelve months of the 1981–82 New York theater season on and off Broadway; economic turbulence tossing the biggest pretenses in an unaccustomed chaos of inflation; social turbulence forcing the experimental fringe to rechannel its efforts and reconsider its context; esthetic turbulence seemingly draining creative energy from both the top and bottom of the scale and concentrating it in the center, in the theatrical halfway house we call off Broadway. And there is new turbulence on the way in the sure-to-be-irresistable influence of cable TV and its possibilities for the afterlife of stage productions. The cloud no larger than a man's hand has already passed overhead in Home Box Office's purchase of the cable rights to *Camelot* for $1.2 million and the first taping of a live play on Broadway, *It Had To Be You.* The theater has weathered other storms as well and even better than could reasonably have been expected, and it is getting ready for another one surely on the way. While it prepares for the worst, it hopes for the best: that the turbulence to come will prove to be a storm of technical advantages, new opportunities and stimulating challenges.

OFF OFF BROADWAY

By Mel Gussow

OFF OFF BROADWAY (OOB) is theater at large. By definition, it is eclectic, anarchic and undefinable. There are no rules, except those imposed under the showcase code by Actors' Equity in regard to length of run and and actors' salaries (usually minimal, and scarcely enough for cab fare). OOB is decidedly not for profit, except of the artistic variety. Geographically, it is the subway system of New York theater, running all over Manhattan, from the Lower East Side to Harlem, from Greenwich Village to within a half block from Broadway —and also extending to the outer boroughs. It takes place in storefronts, churches, lofts, theaters and even in the streets. As it expands, OOB continues to specialize in the experimental, but there is also room for the popular (and the prices certainly are popular). While some of the most provocative theater occurs OOB, quality is variable, and some companies could be categorized as community theater. In at least one case, the Manhattan Punch Line, it is a cameo version of Broadway in the 1930s and 1940s, presenting crowd-pleasing comedies. Essentially, OOB is where one can afford to be adventurous—a statement that is as true for theatergoers as it is for producers, playwrights, directors and actors.

A survey of the season OOB must begin with Ellen Stewart. As founder and guiding director of La Mama, she is the mother of the movement and an institution unto herself, nurturing new talent and spreading La Mamas all over the world. This season she celebrated the 20th anniversary of her theater, and more than any other event it made one realize the continuing value and vitality of OOB. On her three stages, Miss Stewart sponsored a season-long festival of revivals of plays from her past, some with members of the original casts. As usual, she also welcomed distinguished foreign companies. Several of the revivals moved into full-fledged off-Broadway engagements, including *The Unseen Hand,* a vintage fantasy by Sam Shepard about the reawakening of the American pioneer spirit, with Beeson Carroll recreating his role as a crusty desperado. Leonard Melfi's *Birdbath* also returned with its stars, Kevin O'Connor and Barbara Eda-Young, playing a would-be poet and a waitress in a wistful tale of urban isolation.

La Mama played host to a number of visiting experimental companies, and each visit became a gala international occasion. The Tokyo Kid Brothers, a youth-oriented musical theater, returned with a new show, *Shiro,* a visually opulent folk play. Late in the season, the innovative Japanese director, Tadashi Suzuki, presented his version of *The Bacchae,* a bilingual, ritualized performance piece starring Kayoko Shiraishi in the twinned roles of Agave and Dionysus. Though she spoke in Japanese, it was clear that Miss Shiraishi is an actress with elemental force and a density of emotions. The most notable event at La Mama—and the apex of the OOB season—was the presence of the Polish director-playwright, Tadeusz Kantor with an arresting new play, *Wielopole Wielopole,* about his life and the life of his country during World War II. This was another instance of a work communicating through a language barrier.

Experimental American directors also had a place of honor at La Mama. Ping Chong, as playwright, director, designer and visual artist, presented *A.M./A.M. —The Articulated Man,* an entrancing, abstract multi-media event. Joseph Chaikin's Winter Project offered *Trespassing,* a haunting tableau about dying, with a cast headed by Gloria Foster, one of several instances of experienced classical actors joining experimental companies. Paul Zimet's Talking Band was in residence with a pair of folk tales, *Tristan and Isolt* and *Gioconda and Si-Ya-U* (the latter first presented at the Dance Theater Workshop's Economy Tires Theater).

Under the leadership of Robert Applegarth, that latter group has become a primary showcase for fresh performing talent, often of a vaudeville variety, offering a first New York stage to Bill Irwin, a brilliant San Francisco clown, dancer and mime. Mr. Irwin performed the antic *Not Quite/New York* as a late-night entertainment and then followed it up later in the season with *The Regard of Flight* at the American Place Theater. Returning to Economy Tires was puppeteer Bruce D. Schwartz with *The Rat of Huge Proportions,* in which Mr. Schwartz performed while wearing a puppet stage around his body as if it were a large cloak. On another bill was *Is 60 Minutes Enough?,* an hour of clowning, juggling and tomfoolery.

Along with off Broadway and regional theater, OOB has become a generator of new work for the commercial theater. In two cases this season, shows eventually moved to Broadway: Harvey Fierstein's *Torch Song Trilogy* (one of the three short plays in the trilogy was originally done at La Mama, and all three were seen in tandem at the Richard Allen Center) and *Pump Boys and Dinettes,* a country western hoedown. This was a prolific year for Asian-American dramatists and actors. Tisa Chang's Pan-Asian Repertory produced a number of works including a three-play cycle about the internment of Japanese Americans during World War II. *The Dance and the Railroad* by David Henry Hwang, the season's most promising young playwright, was first staged as part of the ethnic heritage series last year at Henry Street Settlement's New Federal Theater, moved to the Public Theater for a long run this year, and was later presented on cable television. One of the other outstanding plays of the season was Genny Lim's *Paper Angels,* also in the Henry Street ethnic heritage series. Miss Lim dealt poetically with the dreams and fantasies of Asian immigrants to America. Both *The Dance and the Railroad* and *Paper Angels* were imaginatively staged by John Lone. Among Asian-American actors, Henry Yuk was the busiest and one of the most talented. Woodie King Jr.'s Henry Street theater also offered two musicals with potential: Rob Penny's *Who Loves the Dancer* (starring Giancarlo Esposito) and Damien Leake's *Child of the Sun,* as well as the less than auspicious return of Amiri Baraka with *Boy and Tarzan Appear in a Clearing.*

Curt Dempster's Ensemble Studio Theater, a creative company of actors, playwrights and directors, specializes in new American plays, and each year it sponsors a festival of one-acts. The E.S.T. *Marathon 82* was highlighted by Romulus Linney's *Goodbye Howard,* Mary Gallagher's *Buddies* and Willie Reale's *Many Happy Returns.* In its tenth anniversary season, the E.S.T. was honored with a Creative Arts Award citation from Brandeis University.

The Performing Garage was a busy arena for experimentation. Chris Hard-

John Schimmel, Mark Hardwick, Debra Monk, Cass Morgan, Jim Wann and John Foley in *Pump Boys and Dinettes,* which originated OOB before passing through off Broadway on its way to Broadway and a Tony nomination

man, a San Francisco playwright-director-designer, came to New York with *Vacuum,* a zestful satiric investigation of the intertwined lives of salesmen and housewives. This art-performance event combined mime, dance, puppetry—and wizardry—into a comedy of consumerism. The Wooster Group, the Garage's resident company, presented the controversial *Route 1 & 9 (The Last Act),* directed by Elizabeth LeCompte; *Hula,* a lip-synching, hip-swinging rendition of

Hawaiian music and dancing; and Spalding Gray's *47 Beds,* a freewheeling monologue about Mr. Gray's eccentric intercontinental adventures.

Charles Ludlam, founder and major domo of the Ridiculous Theatrical Company, spoofed everything from infidelity to exercise in his *Secret Lives of the Sexists,* and the San Francisco Mime Troupe returned with *Factwino Meets the Moral Majority,* a superhero cartoon that attacked book-burners and right-to-lifers, among others. *Forbidden Broadway,* a cabaret revue, saved its cynicism for the sacred cows of Broadway.

The Theater for the New City is another firmly established center of OOB activity, under the artistic direction of George Bartenieff and Crystal Field. Among the events there this season were the Bread and Puppet Theater's fable, *The Story of One Who Set Out to Study Fear;* Eric Bass's adult puppet show, *Autumn Portraits;* and the Otrabanda Company's odd *Salt Speaks,* a play about a salt shaker, a household match for Mr. Hardman's vacuum cleaner.

In the past few years, the WPA has sent a number of new plays and musicals into the commercial theater. One of this year's successes was *Little Shop of Horrors,* a musical creature feature about a man-eating plant, based on a Roger Corman movie. In a series of shows at the WPA, the sets by Edward T. Gianfrancesco have been exceptional. In other musical news, Al Carmines, former resident minister and composer at the Judson Memorial Church—and a founding father of OOB—returned after a brief absence with a jubilant new musical, *The Evangelist,* about Bible Belt soulsavers. Sam Henry Kass's *Side Street Scenes* was a congenial comedy with music about a young composer on the rise. Sam Shepard and Patti Smith's slashing *Cowboy Mouth* was given a hard-rock concert revival. *A Metamorphosis in Miniature,* was a chamber play with music, drawn from Kafka's story, with an acting transformation by David Rounds. This was a production of the Music-Theater Group/Lenox Arts Center, which also presented a South African musical, *The Long Journey of Poppie Nongena,* based on the novel by Elsa Joubert. A stirring tale of apartheid, it was elevated by the voice of Sophie Mgcina.

New York's Hispanic theaters—INTAR, the Puerto Rican Traveling Theater, and others—had active seasons, producing plays in English and in Spanish. *The Extravagant Triumph of Jesus Christ, Karl Marx and William Shakespeare* was an extravagant polemical comedy by Fernando Arrabal, starring Ron Faber as a chameleon-like island dictator. A somewhat similar role was undertaken by Rip Torn in José Ruibal's *The Man and the Fly,* directed by Jack Gelber.

Among interesting British plays receiving a first New York production off off Broadway were Snoo Wilson's fantastical *The Soul of the White Ant* (about South Africa); David Mercer's *The Arcata Promise* (adapted from a television play and starring Brian Murray as a self-destructive actor); one-acts by James Saunders collected under the title, *Savoury Meringue;* and Ted (E.A.) Whitehead's *The Sea Anchor* (about young Liverpudlians partying in Ireland).

Ibsen's last play, *When We Dead Awaken,* appeared at the Open Space in a production starring Anne Twomey and Kim Hunter. Gorky's *Philistines* had a brief run at Theater at St. Clement's. Strindberg's *The Stronger* and O'Neill's *Hughie* were given respectful treatment at the South Street Theater—one of a number of lively theaters on Theater Row on far West 42d Street. The Lion Company had a season of repertory, featuring a youthful *Caucasian Chalk Circle*. At the Jean Cocteau on the Bowery, there was a rousing version of Cyril Tourneur's *The Revenger's Tragedy,* staged by Toby Robertson of the Old Vic. On the other hand, Mrozek's *Vatzlav* and von Kleist's *The Broken Pitcher* suffered in their productions. Among other active theaters were the AMAS company, the No Smoking Playhouse, the Labor Theater, the Irish Rebel Theater and the Apple Corps.

Choosing from the hundreds of shows that are produced OOB, a theatergoer has to be prepared for anything. One surprise was *Garbage,* the New York debut of a rowdy, nerveless and very funny clown named Jango Edwards. On the opposite end of the spectrum, there was a festival of modern Italian theater, and a pretentious play called *Sacco* or *Sack,* which was just that—about a man who was trapped inside a sack, hung on a hook and poked and prodded by a sadistic accomplice. Perhaps that was intended as a visual metaphor for audiences taking part in environmental theater. As usual, the view from off off Broadway was unpredictable.

○
○
○

THE SEASON
AROUND THE UNITED STATES

with

A DIRECTORY OF PROFESSIONAL
REGIONAL THEATER

Including casts and credits of new plays

and

OUTSTANDING NEW PLAYS
CITED BY
AMERICAN THEATER CRITICS
ASSOCIATION
○
○
○

THE American Theater Critics Association (ATCA) is the organization of more than 250 leading drama critics of all media in all sections of the United States. One of this group's stated purposes is "To increase public awareness of the theater as a *national* resource" (italics ours). To this end, ATCA has cited a number of outstanding new plays produced this season across the country, to be listed and briefly described in this volume; and has designated one of them for us to offer as an introduction to our coverage of "The Season Around the United States" in the form of a synopsis with excerpts, in much the same manner as Best Plays of the New York season.

The critics made their citations, including their principal one of *Talking With* by Jane Martin, in the following manner: member critics everywhere were asked to call the attention of an ATCA committee to outstanding new work in their areas. The 1981–82 committee was chaired by Ann Holmes of the Houston *Chronicle* and comprised Elliot Norton of the Boston *Herald-American*, William Gale of the Providence *Journal*, Julius Novick of the *Village Voice*, Damien Jacques of the Milwaukee *Journal*, Sylvie Drake of the Los Angeles *Times* and Bernard Weiner of the San Francisco *Chronicle*. These committee members studied scripts of the nominated plays and made their choices on the basis of script rather than production, thus placing very much the same emphasis as the editor of this volume gives to the script in making his New York Best Plays selections. There were no eligibility requirements (such as Equity cast or formal resident-theater status) except that a nominee be the first full professional production of a new work outside New York City within this volume's time frame of June 1, 1981 to May 31, 1982.

The list of other 1981–82 plays nominated by members of ATCA as outstanding presentations in their areas, with descriptions written by the critics who saw and nominated them, follows the synopsis of *Talking With*. The synopsis itself was prepared by the Best Plays editor.

Cited by American Theater Critics as an Outstanding New Play of 1981–82

TALKING WITH

A Program of 11 Monologues in Two Acts

BY JANE MARTIN

JANE MARTIN was born like Athena full-grown from the brain of the creator of these monologues in Talking With. *In other words, it is a pen name for an author or authors who want to keep his/her/their identity a secret for one reason or another, possibly to protect privacy. We presume that Jon Jory, producing director of Actors Theater of Louisville, and probably some other members of the group's staff know who Jane Martin is, but they're not telling. Here's what the Actors Theater program note had to say about the author of* Talking With *on the occasion of its production at the resident theater group's 6th annual Festival of New American Plays Feb. 23–April 4, 1982:*

"Jane Martin is a Louisvillian. Her play Twirler *was produced in last spring's Festival of New American Plays and then went on to critically-acclaimed productions at the Toronto and Dublin international festivals.* 15 Minutes *and* Rodeo *received their world premieres at the Dublin Theater Festival this past fall. Ms. Martin's play* The Boy Who Ate the Moon, *her only two-character play, was originally produced as part of the Apprentice Showcase entitled* Stages. *Also seen again during '81 Shorts were her monologues* 15 Minutes, Twirler, Rodeo, Marks, Handler, Lamps, Clear Glass Marbles *and* Cul de Sac."

Because of the nature of the material in Talking With, *we are presenting three of the 11 monologues—*Handler, Lamps *and* Rodeo—*almost in their entirety, with brief outlines of the other eight. There is one fact about "Jane Martin's" identity that openly betrays itself in the work: he/she/they is/are an extraordinary writing talent.*

ACT I

1. Fifteen Minutes

An actress in her dressing room 15 minutes before curtain time is getting ready to go on. While doing so, she pours out her thoughts and feelings about the meaning of her life and career, her gnawing misgivings: "You know, the self-doubt and everything . . . the feeling that you're not lovable . . . that you're a mutt, too much of a mutt to be loved . . . and that you have . . . I don't know . . . a crisis of confidence . . . is that a good description? That it's hard to *act* . . . hard to be entertainment for people you don't know. . . ."

2. Handler

On the floor before a young woman in a simple country print dress is a handmade wooden box about two feet long and 18 inches high with a sliding wire screen top.

YOUNG WOMAN: My Dada was gonna do this tonight but the Lord froze his face, so he sent me. I learned this from my Dada and he learned it up from Great Gran who took it on from the Reverend Soloman Bracewood who had him a mule ministry round these parts way back when. Dada taught Miss Ellie, my ma, and my brother Jamie he was in it too, fore he went for Detroit.

See, what I got in here is snakes. Lotta people don't like snakes. Gives it it's nature, I guess. This here is prairie rattlers. Jamie, he said they got the dirtiest, nastiest bite of all . . . plus they's big. Lotta venom. You milk you a rattler, you can half fill up a juice glass. Dada said Jamie should do rattlers, but he never. Did "heads," copperheads. Now, they're slower and safer, but it ain't such a good show. You know those dang snakes smell like cucumbers? Well, they do. Miss Ellie, she favored moccasins. Dada too, well Dada he did all kinds, all ways. Your moccasin now, he's your good ol' boy snake. Flat out mean an lots of get-up-and-go. Heck, they'll chase ya. They will. Once when I was just belt size I was headin' down to the dry goods an Walsh Booker he runs outta the corn on one side and inta the corn on the other, and right behind him, hell for leather, comes this moccasin. Walsh always says he lost him at the Bowling Green turnoff. Dada he didn't like Miss Ellie doin' em. "You lay off them mocs fore they lay you down." Made Miss Ellie laugh. Me, I think they're slimy. Couldn't get me to touch one. Rattlers got him a nice dry feel. Little bit sandpapery. Rattler can find ya in the pitch dark though. They git on to yer body heat. Snake handlin'. *All* my blood does it. Only Dada and me now, though. Snake handlin', with the Holiness Church. Down where I come from we take God pretty serious. If you got the spirit, snake don't bite. If he bites you, you know you ain't got the spirit. Makes the difference real clear, don't it? It's right there in the scripture . . . Mark, Chapter 16, verses 17 and 18, "And these signs shall follow them that believe. In my name they shall cast out devils; they shall speak in new tongues; they shall take up serpents; and if they shall drink any deadly thing, it shall not hurt them; they shall lay hands on the sick and they shall recover." Don't figure it could be much clearer than that. There's some churches don't use snakes, use strychnine, powdered poison, same idea though. They mix it with cherry Kool-Aid, sing 'em a hymn, drink it off, and then just stand around waitin' to see if they fall over. Ain't much of a show. Not like snakes. Dada does fire, but I can't do it. Pours some kerosine in a Coke bottle, sticks a rag in the top and lights it up. Holds that fire under his chin, passes it down the arm, puts his hand in it, you know, that kind of stuff. He says there's people do blow torches down to Tennessee. I don't know. Jamie gave it a try fore he went to Detroit. Just about burned his ass off. Sorry.

When I handle, I keem 'em in this box. Dada gimme this and some Heidi doll on my ninth birthday. Sometimes I'll just open up the lid and put my foot in or, uh, maybe stick it open side to my chest. There's some lay it to their face. I don't. Scares my eyes. Durin' service we take 'em right out, pass 'em around. At's more dangerous than a single handler. Snake gets to comparin' who got the spirit a whole lot and who jes got it some. Somebody's just about bound to come in second. See what I mean? Don't get me wrong now. Y'don't die everytime yer bit. Dada been bit thirty-two times an never saw him a doctor. Used to let me kiss him on the marks. Last one got him here. *(Points to eye.)* Froze him right up. Dada says he'll thaw, but I don't know. I only been bit seven times. Four times by the same serpent. Dada says he got the sweet tooth for me. I went to the doctor on the sly.

Day after Jamie took off, Miss Ellie did moccasins standin' in the back of the pickup over to Hard Scrabble. Shouldn't ought to, 'cause her mind weren't there. Coal truck backfired, and she got bit. Snake bit her three more times fore she hit the ground. Dada laid hands on her, but she died anyway. There was ten of us handled right there at the funeral.

Snake handlin'. Back a few years there was a lot of people lookin' to see if they had the spirit. When I was real little there was one time four thousand people came together over to Evarts. There was two hundred handlers worked that day. There was so much God on that mountain you could stick a serpent inside your shirt, play seven innings of softball and not get bit.

Ain't so much God now, though. Big day if you see five or six handlers. There's a colored church up in Louisville wants us to bring over a busload of handlers, but Dada says they just ain't there to be got. Not a busload in the whole state.

Snake knows what you feel. You can fool a person, but you can't fool a snake. You got the spirit, God locks their jaws. Keeps you safe. Tell you what, though . . . I don't believe in a God. Left me. Gone with Miss Ellie. I was handlin' when I knew it sure. Snake was jes' comin' on down the line. Martita she yells out, "The Lord! Lord's in me and with me. In me and with me." Noah he was ululatin', talkin' in tongues. Couple of folks was rollin' and singin'. Dada was doin' switch grips. Had Miss Ellie's weddin' ring on his little finger. And it came on me, heck, there ain't no God in here. There's just a bunch of shouters gettin' tranced. There ain't no God in here at all. Bout that time they layed that serpent to me. Felt fussy. Nasty. Just lookin' for an excuse, y'know? An I was an empty vessel, worse nor a Pharisee, grist for the mill. My blood went so cold I coulda crapped ice cubes. Snake knew. Started to get leverage. So I said, "Snake. You Satan' handmaiden. You're right, there ain't no God in me. I'm just a woman, but I'm the only woman in my Dada's house, and he needs me home. Outa his faith and his need, you lock your jaws!" I let that snake feel a child's pure love, and it sponged it up offa my hands, and then ol' wiggly went limp. I tranced it. It was a real good service. Didn't nobody handlin' get bit. *(Takes snake out of the box.)* Yes, you got to

Anne Pitoniak in the *Lamps* portion of *Talking With*

believe. Holiness Church is dead right about that. Makes me wonder, you know? I git to lookin' at people and wonderin' if they got anything in 'em could lock a serpent's jaws. Any power or spirit or love or whatever. I look at 'em and I wonder, could they handle? Tell you what though, you can see it in a face. You can read it. You look me full in the face, it don't take me thirty seconds. It's like I was the snake, some ol' pit viper, an I can read yer heart. Maybe you could handle and maybe you can't, but there's one thing sure in this world . . . Yer empty, yer gonna get bit.

3. Cul de Sac

The intended victim of a mugger-rapist pulls a .38 from her purse and turns the tables on him: "Freeze! Sorry, sucker. You figured you had a real Kleenex here, didn't you? A real three-minute special? . . . . . Big petrified eyes. Funny little terrified smiles. . . . ." She is also carrying a razor in her purse, and at gun point she orders her attacker to mutilate himself with it: "I know it is very hard for you to take a woman seriously because of cultural stereotyping and your internationalized male models, but I am one of many women who mean exactly what they say. I'm going to give you fifteen seconds, and then you'll be a dead mugger." On pain of death, the mugger obeys.

4. Scraps

A woman in a Patchwork Girl of Oz costume tells of her obsession with the fantasy world of the Oz books. Since turning 35, she's spent more and more time within her fantasy: "I live in Oz. I see it all. I've gotten so I can smell it. 'Two or three hours walk along this trail brought Ojo and Scraps to a clear level country where there were a few farms and some scattered octagonal houses, all bright Quadling red and smelling of peppermint.' I can live in that sentence for the full three hours." She realizes she's becoming alienated from husband and friends, but she prefers her fantasy world to the dreary world of demographics and electronic games.

5. Twirler

The mystique of baton-twirling is conveyed by a young woman who won her first state title at the age of six and who scored high in national competition before her hand was crushed in an accident that "clipped my wings." She overcame the handicap but never rose to championship status again. "People think you're a twit if you twirl," she says, but she believes it is "the physical parallel of revelation. . . . . Twirling is the throwing of yourself up to God. It's a pure gift, hidden from Satan because it is wrapped and disguised in the midst of football. It is God throwing, spirit fire, and very few come to it." She decides to leave her silver baton here for someone to take up and use: "It can be yours, it can be your burden. It is the eye of the needle. I leave it for you."

ACT II

6. Lamps

A woman of about 65 stands in the midst of a dozen or more lamps, some on tables, some standing, but all of them turned on. *"There is no other theatrical illumination."*

WOMAN: The older I become, the more I'm drawn to light. To radiance of all kinds. Both the light and the shadows, they fascinate me. Perhaps it's a sort of primitive fire syndrome or, I suppose, simply fear of the dark. I've rented this loft and filled it with lamps. I spend most evenings here. It is both eccentric and childlike, isn't it? I would prefer to think of it as a kind of playing. The hours fly. I draw enormous energy from it. And there's the actual heat, of course.
She begins to move through the room.
I hope I'm not embarrassing you. May I show you? It's delightful to move at random, extending a hand, weaving in and through these pools of warmth. Each

lamp gives its heat differently. Uniquely. And then in between, and there are many in betweens, you can receive, feel, several sources at once. Any movement, and the balance is changed. And then, when you've exhausted these relationships, why you can change them, don't you see? Is this quite mad? I'm a little, a little frightened this will bore you . . . sharing this . . . it's so difficult to share our enthusiasms, don't you think? Does light interest you? Do you respond to it? Night flying? Like costume jewelry on velvet. Wet neon. Trees covered with ice under street lamps. I suppose these are sentimental images of my generation. Might I show you something? It won't take a moment.

She snaps several of the lamps off.

There. Now, moving through.

She walks a pattern through the lamps.

Now this.

She moves again, holding a handled mirror in each hand.

Now see.

She turns two or three off and another on.

I can *feel* that difference. Acutely. Pleasurably. Is this senility on the hoof? Look.

She hunkers down on the floor and looks up.

Seeing the lights above makes me laugh. Why, do you suppose?

She stands up.

You probably suspect that it's a history as well. Of course. Some of these are from the Catsafall Farm. Catsafall, that's Iowa. Several of these are from family and friends. And my son.

She touches a lamp.

My husband. Oh fiddle, they're all personal. No, I won't bore you. Memories, I believe, are patterns of a sort. And these, you see, make patterns and are memories.

She sits in a rocker off to one side.

I endlessly wondered what older age, later years would *be*, feel like. As have you. A diminishment? A narrowing? There are so many things one obviously cannot do. Many of the people once central to one's life are gone or dispersed. One is less often . . . useful. My grandfather when he was very rich in years used to call himself "deneeded and unpacked." There are necessarily fewer people. Thinking about it, it seemed sensible then to invest more feeling in objects, enrich my relationship to them so that I . . . so that I wasn't without intimacy.

She rises and during the next speech turns out all the lamps except the one by the chair.

I have one sister, Amelia, and she resides in a sort of Leisure World, a planned community in Albuquerque . . . New Mexico. Her husband was a thoracic surgeon, and she is very well off. She moved there from Catsafall and tells me that she is ever so busy with . . . activities. She has many, many friends there, she says. Imagine. Amelia has not a single solitary acquaintance who knew her before she was sixty. There she is, a sort of amnesiac with many friends and no memories, baking herself in the sun like a pop-tart. Quite beyond me. Several years ago she visited me here. She sat there, just where you are and shared this odd mixture of patterns, heat and memory. I showed her, for instance, how extraordinarily hands take light. Lovely. Well, after a very long silence, a very nice silence really, she rose and said, "Lila, you are mad as a March hare." She flew home to a card tournament.

She stands up behind the one remaining lamp.

It has been my experience that light is the more pleasurable as you diminish it, and that when a single glow remains there is an agony of pleasure and anticipation while you wait for the moment it will be extinguished. It is ever so lovely, ever, ever so. It bewilders and thrills me, this light, radiance, that has become my friend to succor and sustain me. The warmth! the fascination of the waiting. And then, finally, of course . . .

She stands above the lamp, illuminated for several seconds, and then snaps it off.

The dark . . .

7. Dragons

A young woman, nine months pregnant, is in labor, lying on a hospital trolley. With the contractions one minute apart, she knows that she is giving birth to a deformed child—a "dragon"—and she prays that others will tolerate this abnormality: "Gives me a certain ironic pleasure to give birth to a dragon in a Catholic hospital. . . . . I'm going to have a baby that isn't right. You deliver and I'll cope. Just get off my back, O.K.?" She prays for the life of her child and happiness with her husband, who is very understanding of her attitude.

8. Audition

An actress in her late 20s, desperate for a job, comes to an audition leading a cat on a leash, which she nails to the floor. She explains to her listeners that she plans, as her classical audition piece, to strip naked to display the classical form of her body and, as her contemporary piece, to kill the cat with a blow of her hammer if they don't give her the part. She agrees that her listeners might be thinking, "We could give her the part *now,* and then when she splits, she and the furry hostage, we could take it away from her on the basis that she needs . . . shhh, psychiatric attention." She warns them in such a case she might decide to take revenge by killing both the cat *and* herself. She begins taking off her clothes.

9. Clear Glass Marbles

A young woman holds up a crystal bowl filled with clear glass marbles, explaining that when the doctor gave her mother three months to live her mother bought 90 of the marbles, $700 worth of new nightgowns and took to her bed to study French. "And all day, every day, she would hold one of those marbles in her hand. Why? She said it made the day longer." At bedtime, daughter and father would hear her roll the marble across the floor, "learning to let go of them." There came a time when "She told Dad and me that she would like to spend more time alone. 'I'm afraid,' she said, 'that I'm going to have to do this more or less by myself.' She said that she was glad, and she hoped we would be, that this was arranged so you got less attached to the people you loved at the end." Toward dawn one day there was the sound of all the marbles rolling on the floor. They found the bedside table overturned and the mother dead, still holding one marble. Her daughter kept this marble and now holds it in *her* hand to make each day seem longer.

10. Rodeo

A young woman in her late 20s, dressed in jeans, boots and work shirt is working on a piece of tack and listening to a country western song with a can of Lone Star beer nearby. As the song ends, the woman speaks.

YOUNG WOMAN: Shoot—rodeo's just goin' to hell in a handbasket. Rodeo used to be somethin'. I loved it. I did. Once, Daddy an a bunch of 'em was foolin' around with some old bronc over to our place and this ol' red nose named Cinch got bucked off and my Daddy, he hooted and said he had him a nine-year-old girl, namely me, wouldn't have no damn trouble with that horse. Well, he put me on up there, stuck that ridin' rein in my hand, gimme a kiss and said, "Now, there's only one thing t'remember Honey Love, if ya fall off just don't come home." Well, I stayed up. You gotta stay on a bronc eight seconds, otherwise the ride don't count. And from that day on my daddy called me Big Eight. Heck, that's all the name I got anymore . . . Big Eight.

Used to be fer cowboys, the rodeo did. Do it in some open field, folks would pull their cars and pick-ups round it, sit on the hoods, some ranch hand'd bull dog him some rank steer and everybody's wave their hats and call him by name. Ride us some buckin' stock, rope a few calves, git throwed off a bull and then we'd jest git us to a bar and tell each other lies about how good we were.

Used to be a family thing. Wooly Billy Tilson and Tammy Lee had them five kids on the circuit. Three boys, two girls and Wooly and Tammy. Wasn't no two-beer rodeo on Oklahoma didn't have a Tilson entered. Used to call the oldest girl Tits. "Tits Tilson." Never seen a girl that topheavy could ride so well. Said she only fell off when the gravity got her. Cowboys used to say if she landed face down you could plant two young trees in the holes she'd leave. Ha! Tits Tilson.

Used to be people came to a rodeo had a horse of their own back home. Farm people, ranch people—lord, they *knew* what they were lookin' at. Knew a good ride from a bad ride, knew hard from easy. You broke some bones er spent the day eatin' dirt, at least ya got appreciated.

Now they *bought* the rodeo. . . . . Damn, it gets me! . . . . . There's some guy in a banker's suit runs the rodeo now. Got him a pinky ring and a digital watch, honey. Told us we oughta have a watchamacallit, choriographus or somethin', some ole ballbuster used to be with the Ice damn Capades. Wants us to ride around dressed up like Mickey Mouse, Pluto, crap like that. Told me I had to haul my butt thru the barrel race done up like Minnie damn Mouse in a tutu. Huh uh, honey! Them people is so screwed up they probably eat what they run over in the road.

Listen, they got the clowns wearin' astronaut suits! I ain't lyin'. You know what a rodeo clown does. You go down, fall off, whatever—the clown runs him in front of the bull so's ya don't git stomped. Pin stripes, he got 'em in space suits tellin' jokes on a microphone. First horse see 'em done up like the Star Wars went crazy. Best buckin' horse on the circuit, name of Piss 'n' Vinegar, took one look at them

Margo Martindale in the *Rodeo* portion of *Talking With*

clowns, had him a heart attack and died. Cowboy was ridin' him got hisself squashed. Twelve hundred pounds of coronary arrest jes' fell right thru 'em. Blam! *Vaya con dios.* Crowd thought that was funnier than the astronauts. I swear it won't be long before they're strappin' ice skates on the ponies. Big crowds now. Ain't hardly no ranch people, no farm people, nobody I know, buncha disco babies and di-vorce lawyers—designer jeans and day-glo Stetsons. Hell, the whole bunch of 'em wears French perfume. Oh, it smells like money now! Got it on the cable T and V—hey, you know what, when ya rodeo you kick yourself up some dust—well now, seems like that fogs up the ol' TV camera, so they told us a while back that from now on we was gonna ride on some new stuff called Astro-dirt. Dust free. Artificial damn dirt, honey. Lord have mercy.

Banker Suit called me in the other day and said, "Lurlene . . ." "Hold it," I said, "who's this Lurlene? Round here they call me Big Eight." "Well Big Eight," he said, "my name's Wallace." "Well that's a real surprise t'me," I said, "'cause aroun' here everybody jes calls you dumbags." My, he laughed real big, slapped his big ol' desk and then said I wasn't suitable for the rodeo no more. Said they was lookin' for another type, somethin' a little more in the showgirl line, like the Dallas Cowgirls maybe. New image, he said. Said the ridin' and ropin' wasn't the thing no more. Talked on about floats, costumes, dancin', chor-eog-aphy; if I was a man I woulda pissed on his shoe. Said he'd give me a lifetime pass, though. Said I could come see his rodeo any time I wanted.

Rodeo used to be people ridin' horses for the pleasure of people who rode horses—made you feel good about what you could do. Rodeo wasn't worth no money to nobody. Money didn't have nothin' to do with it. Used to be seven Tilsons riding in the rodeo. Wouldn't none of 'em dress up like Donald damn Duck, so they quit. That *there's* the law of gravity.

There's a bunch of assholes in this country sneak around until they see ya havin' fun, and then they buy the fun and start in sellin' it. See, they figure if ya love it, they can sell it. Well you look out, honey. They want to make them a dollar out of what you love. Dress *you* up like Minnie Mouse. Sell your rodeo. Turn *yer* pleasure into Ice damn Capades. You hear what I'm sayin'? You're jus' merchandise to them, sweetie. You're jus' merchandise to them.

11. Marks

On every visible part of a woman sitting on a bar stool and wearing a black cocktail dress are blue and red tattoos of all descriptions—except for the left side of her face, which *"bears a single scar about three inches long below the cheek."* The woman recalls her obedient childhood, bland schooling, conventional marriage, home and children: "And then on our 15th anniversary Arthur left me, saying I had nothing further to give. I was, he said, unmarked by life." She tried the singles bars and was slashed in a parking lot by a lover—but the resulting scar gave her a kind of confidence, and she decided to display on her skin the symbols of her life: "This bird in flight, horror struck, would be my mother. . . . . This day lily, which blooms, decays and is remembered is Marian, who instructed me with her death." It is important to be marked, she advised, because to be marked is to remember. "Sometimes the unmarked are attracted to me. . . . . and in the parking lots, I cut them. Make a small mark. *(She touches her cheek.)* Like this. And it is then their lives begin. With a little pain." She lifts her glass in a toast to the unmarked.

Other Outstanding New Plays Cited
By American Theater Critics Association Members

Breaking Out (Return of the Tyler Street Kid) by Michael Lynch (San Francisco: One Act Theater Company)—"Nothin' is yours! Everything you got, boy, is because of me! Me! I give you life in your body, I give you clothes to put on your back, I give you beans to put in your belly, me!"

Tyler Street Kid talking there. That impassioned speech comes in Michael Lynch's *Breaking Out,* the second of three one-act plays called *The San Joaquin Blues. Breaking Out* is a work filled not only with crisp writing but with the pulse of daily life. It knows that life comes from moment after moment and is only punctuated by major incidents.

Lynch has created a rich field from the very dailiness of his character's actions. The Skaggs family and their friends are from the "poorer" side of the tiny town of Coalinga, California.

Mackil Skaggs and his son Charlie are the focal point. Charlie is off to college in the fall—at least until Mackil loses his oil field job and calls in the family money put aside for Charlie's college expenses. "You don't tell me what's yours, son. I figger you owe me. What do you figger?"

In the end, the dilemmas of *Breaking Out* are solved by an all-too-obvious stroke of good luck designed to send you out of the theater with a warm glow. But before that, at least, Lynch has rendered some splendid characters. His play touches you with emotions we have all felt: The yearning to (and impossibility of) staying forever young; the inevitable conflicts between father and son and the precarious balance of life itself.

Breaking Out concerns everyday lives and universalizes them. In its modest way, it contains the germ of the first essence of living. Near the end, Mackil's longsuffering, always loving wife puts it this way: "We . . . survive . . . we go on . . . that's all anybody can do. That's all anybody can hope for."

WILLIAM GALE
Providence *Journal-Bulletin*

Chapter and Verse by Ken Jenkins (Louisville: Actors' Theater)—*Chapter and Verse* consists of two monologues and moves from birth to death.

The first monologue, *Rupert's Birthday,* is spoken by a farm woman seated in a rocking chair. Her name is Louisa May. She tells us that she never celebrates the usual public holidays: "Rupert's birthday is my holiday." On Louisa May's 13th birthday, while her mother was in the hospital giving birth to her brother Orville, Louisa May had her first period and felt herself to be a woman. Then she discovered that a cow was in labor, and she, Louisa May, was the only one there to help with the difficult birth of a bull calf, which she named Rupert. Exactly a year later, "Daddy and I loaded Rupert into the truck and carried him into town to be slaughtered for meat. I didn't cry." Having seen the light in Rupert's eye flash on when he was born, she "saw it go out when he was killed." And Rupert's birthday, that day of many births and one death, is still the most important day on her calendar.

Cemetery Hill, the second monologue, begins with a shotgun blast. Then the lights come up on an old man holding a shotgun. He is the gravedigger—or was; he is to be replaced by "that diesel machine, that *backhoe,* they left setting over there." So he is shooting at the machine. "If I hit the fuel tank I might blow up the whole durn thing!" He refuses to quit: "They need me out here. More than they know." He has plenty of stories to tell about people who ended up on

Cemetery Hill, and a fair amount of wisdom to dispense. At the end, to quote the stage directions, "He fires! The fuel tank on the backhoe explodes! BLACK-OUT."

JULIUS NOVICK
Village Voice

Close Ties by Elizabeth Diggs (Los Angeles: Public Theater)—On the surface, *Close Ties* is a simple story about one family and how it comes to grips with the approaching senility of its matriarch. But on a larger scale, *Close Ties* touches each of us. It forces us to examine our attitudes about our aging loved ones, our feelings of guilt and responsibility towards them, the unpleasant alternatives which we must face when someone we love becomes too old to care for himself or herself, and the "ties" that bind those who love.

It is the middle of summer, and the Frye family has come together to relax in their summer home in the Berkshires. Years ago, the house was given to Bess and Watson Frye, but Josephine Whitaker, Bess's 84 year old mother, is still trying to run it. She transplants flowers, dictates the dinner menu to her daughter and constantly berates Watson for not being as interesting a lawyer as her deceased husband. All of which would create an uncomfortable situation under the best of circumstances. Lately, however, Josephine has become very "forgetful". She forgets where she is, who she's talking to and what she's doing. She confuses the present with the past and can't seem to remember what she did the previous evening. "You tell me when I'm over the line," she tells her high-strung divorced granddaughter Evelyn. But even though Evelyn promises to do so, her own problems keep her from recognizing the moment.

And as Josephine marches grandly out the door to face her last days in a nursing home, it becomes painfully clear to every member of the family that this feisty old woman needs more care than they are able to give her.

DEBBI WASSERMAN
Westchester

Little Joe Monaghan by Barbara Lebow (Atlanta: T.H.E. Theater, Ltd., Callanwolde Theater) *Little Joe Monaghan* is a poignant, humorous, fanciful projection of what might have been the thoughts and emotions of Josephine Monaghan—a real-life 19th century Buffalo debutante who chose to pass her life as a bronco-busting cowboy in the Wild West in order to support her illegitimate son, whom she left in her sister's care. She died without anyone in her new life knowing her sexual identity.

The play opens in the early 1900s as a stooped, gray-haired old man is rummaging through an old suitcase that contains a pink satin dress. Joe holds the ball gown in front of "him" and awkwardly begins to dance and sing fragments of a waltz. Gradually he straightens and whirls, and his voice becomes a girlish soprano. Thus old cowboy Joe becomes young Josephine, spinning back into her past.

As the play progresses, going back and forth in time and slipping in and out of fantasies, we discover Joe's story: her sacrifice, her pain, her dreams and her bravery in a man's world.

Lebow's style is lyrically vernacular, with humanity, warmth and a piquant sense of humor exhibited in the snappy dialogue. The title role is a tour de force for a versatile actress. There are four other characters in the play, which can be played by three actors: Joe's sister, Helen; her deceitful lover and her grown son (one actor); and her pal, Fred. Fred and Joe are the only characters who exist in the present and the past. The others are seen in flashback and dream sequences. *Little Joe* is an intriguing and compassionate play.

HELEN C. SMITH
Atlanta *Constitution*

Oldtimers Game by Lee Blessing (Louisville: Actors' Theater)—*Oldtimers Game,* a tightly focused play confined to the limited world of male professional sports and performed entirely in the locker room of a minor-league baseball team, dramatizes a collection of types—almost cliches—in both characters and situations; but the characters are all so individually realized that they illustrate the validity of types. The nine men are current players for the Northshore Otters, some on their way up and others on their way down; a major-league superstar alumnus; a couple of retired old men; and such non-players as the aggressive new owner, the brash manager, and the conciliating public relations man. The writing is so good that the play's appeal does not depend on a knowledge or a love of baseball, and technical terms are clear without condescension.

WILLIAM T. LISTON
Muncie *Star*

Rundown by Robert Auletta (Cambridge, Mass.: American Repertory Theater)—*Rundown* is not just another painful epic about yet another battered Vietnam vet returned from the wars. It is a probing theatrical invention that pits emotional and intellectual recall against the spectrum of forces without and within us that channel and forge our lives—ultimately destroying, or, as playwright Robert Auletta suggests in the case of his anti-hero, Pay, bolstering our ability to go on even when we think we can't.

Auletta guides Pay, a "very disturbed vet," through a dreamlike recapitulation of his life mostly before and after a shattering tour of duty in Vietnam. By means of recollection and fantasy, Pay relives distant and more recent experiences that involve two school friends and the girl all three of them loved or lusted after. Unlike Pay, the friends—Spear and Trace—turned their backs on the war and suffered consequences of another, but not less critical, order. So did the woman, Laure, though her suffering stemmed from an absence of commitment to anything, rather than the pursuit of a cause or noncause.

The strong subtext here is that outside circumstances play a significant role in shaping our lives and that the action of our days makes little difference in the end. What ranks this piece above the commonplace is its impressionistic style, arresting metaphors and vivid imagery. The vigorous writing speaks in human terms. The poetic drama remembers to create characters of flesh and blood while discussing ideas.

SYLVIE DRAKE
Los Angeles *Times*

Vacuum by Chris Hardman (San Francisco: Antenna Theater)—Antenna, a division of the award-winning, internationally celebrated Snake Theater, has as its aim to "receive, transform and transmit." For this complex play centered around a most simple subject, the vacuum cleaner, Hardman solicited comments from and initiated interviews with ordinary salesmen, housewives, bartenders et al., and then used their responses and taped comments in constructing the verbal text that accompanied the extraordinary visuals and music score.

Though abstract in presentation, there is a through-line story. Walter, a novice salesman, insecure and self-negating, faces constant rejection as he goes door-to-door trying to sell his vacuum cleaners. Finally he arrives at the home of Mary, a bored, lonely housewife who is able to connect to people only when they are selling her something. (This is a very American story.) Eventually, the two have an affair, and a child is conceived; however, Mary utilizes another kind of vacuum-related machine, a vacuum-extractor, as an aborting device. Mary returns to her previous life; Walter goes through agony and confusion. And reaches some disturbing conclusions.

In sum, this is a powerfully allegorical tale—using masked performers, performance-art techniques, evocative lighting, choreographed movement, electronic sound score—about vacuums in our life and how we fill them, as well as a commentary upon the kind of buying/selling relationships that underly much of American society. The funny/serious play was first performed in a micro-chip warehouse in Sausalito, then in a church in Berkeley, then in several San Francisco locations—including a 900-seat house—before going to Europe and New York, where it earned rave reviews and captivated audiences.

BERNARD WEINER
San Francisco *Chronicle*

A DIRECTORY OF PROFESSIONAL
REGIONAL THEATER

Compiled by Ella A. Malin

Professional 1981–82 programs and repertory productions by leading resident companies around the United States, plus major Shakespeare festivals, are grouped in alphabetical order of their locations and listed in date order from May, 1981 to June, 1982. This list does not include Broadway, off-Broadway or touring New York shows (unless the local company took some special part), summer theaters, single productions by commercial producers or college or other non-professional productions. The Directory was compiled by Ella A. Malin for *The Best Plays of 1981–82* from information provided by the resident producing organizations at Miss Malin's request. First productions of new plays—American or world premieres—in regional theaters are listed with full cast and credits, as available. Figures in parentheses following title give number of performances and date given is opening date, included whenever a record of these facts was obtainable from the producing managements.

Summary

This Directory lists 479 productions of 324 plays (including one-acters, workshops, staged readings, plays-in-progress productions) presented by 49 groups in 60 theaters in 45 cities during the 1981–82 season. Of these, 184 were American plays in regular and workshop productions, 65 were world premieres, 15 were American premieres, 1 was a U. S. premiere, 1 was a professional premiere. In addition, 34 groups presented 14 productions for children and youth, and 21 groups presented 21 productions of *A Christmas Carol* by various adaptors. Some groups presented selected plays from their regular repertory for special matinees for high school and college students. Guest productions listed in the Directory were not included in this summary, unless the host theater was directly involved in the production or was the first point of origin. Producing organizations continued community outreach programs for special audiences and many theaters have installed special facilites, and sometimes performances, for the physically handicapped.

Frequency of productions of individual scripts was as follows.

> 1 play received 21 productions *(A Christmas Carol)*.
> 2 plays received 8 productions *(Talley's Folly, Tintypes)*.

  1 play received 7 productions *(A Lesson From Aloes)*.

10 plays received 4 productions *(As You Like It, Billy Bishop Goes to War, Betrayal, Da, The Gin Game, A Midsummer Night's Dream, Much Ado About Nothing, Of Mice and Men, True West, Tartuffe)*.

11 plays received 3 productions *(Another Part of the Forest, Artichoke, Deathtrap, King Lear, Loose Ends, Othello, Pantomime, Romeo And Juliet, Whose Life Is It Anyway?, Johnny Bull, The Workroom)*.

 86 plays received 2 productions

213 plays received 1 production

Listed below are the playwrights who received the greatest number of productions. The first figure is the number of productions, the second figure (in parentheses) is the number of plays produced, including one-acts.

Shakespeare	31	(19)	Mamet	4	(3)
Shaw	12	(8)	Tennessee Williams	4	(3)
Fugard	12	(6)	Hellman	4	(2)
Wilson	11	(4)	Ayckbourn	3	(3)
Molière	7	(4)	Henley	3	(3)
Pinter	6	(3)	O'Neill	3	(3)
Kaufman	5	(5)	Feydeau	3	(2)
Ibsen	5	(4)	Barrie	2	(2)
Arthur Miller	5	(4)	Christopher Hampton	2	(2)
Walcott	5	(3)	Hamilton	2	(2)
Shepard	5	(2)	Nolte	2	(2)
Coward	4	(4)	Shenkkan	2	(2)
Chekhov	4	(3)	Stoppard	2	(2)
Christie	4	(3)	Tally	2	(2)
Simon Gray	4	(3)	Ernest Thompson	2	(2)

ABINGDON, VA.

Barter Theater: Mainstage

(Producing director, Rex Partington)

DULCY (23). By George S. Kaufman and Marc Connelly. June 3, 1981. Director, George Touliatos. With Mary Benson, Byron Grant, James Hilbrandt, Carolyn Clark.

ON GOLDEN POND (23). By Ernest Thompson. June 24, 1981. Director, Fred Chappell. With Harry Ellerbe, Patricia Place, Marion Hunter.

ARMS AND THE MAN (23). By George Bernard Shaw. July 15, 1981. Director, Ada Brown Mather. With Carolyn Olga Kruse, Del Green, George Hosmer, Gerald Walling.

DEATHTRAP (23). By Ira Levin. August 5, 1981. Director, John Olon. With Ross Bickell, Cleo Holladay, Edward Gero, Eunice Anderson, Mike Champagne.

TALLEY'S FOLLY (23). By Lanford Wilson. August 26, 1981. Director, Lawrence Kornfeld. With Eugene Troobnick, Katie Grant.

OH, COWARD! (23). Words and music by Noel Coward, devised by Roderick Cook. September 16, 1981. Director/choreographer, Pamela Hunt; musical director, Marvin Jones. With Suzanne Dawson, Larry Hansen, Richard Kevlin-Bell.

LOVE'S LABOUR'S LOST (22). By William Shakespeare. April 30, 1982. Director, Ada Brown Mather. With Edward Gero, Victor Slezak, Zeke Zaccaro, Lee Alexander, Paula Mann, Anderson Matthews.

Barter Theater: Playhouse

GALLOWS HUMOR (31). By Jack Richardson. July 1, 1981. Director, Mark Sumner. With Ray Hill, Carol Schultz, Craig Kuehl.

TWO BY FIVE (31). Conceived by Seth Glassman, music by John Kander, lyrics by Fred

Ebb. July 29, 1981. Director/choreographer, Pamela Hunt; musical director/arranger, Marvin Jones. With Susan Edwards, Larry Hansen, Karl Heist, Marion Hunter, Marvin Jones.

Designers: scenery, Rex Partington, Lynn Pecktal, John C. Larrance, David W. Weiss, Bob Phillips, Daniel H. Ettinger, C. L. Hundley. Lighting, Christopher H. Shaw; costumes, Mary Jane McCarty, C. L. Hundley, Rachel Kurland, Nancy Atkinson, Sigrid Insull, Judianna Makovsky.

Note: From November 1981 to March 1982, Barter Theater presented *The Corn Is Green* by Emlyn Williams, *Deathtrap* by Ira Levin, *On Golden Pond* by Ernest Thompson, *Talley's Folly* by Lanford Wilson and *The Heiress* by Ruth and Augustus Goetz at George Mason University. The 1980 production of *The Heiress* toured Virginia during March and April 1982.

ANCHORAGE, ALASKA

Alaska Repertory Theater: Sydney Laurence Auditorium

(Artistic director, Robert J. Farley; producing director, Paul Brown)

THE MAN WHO CAME TO DINNER (16). By George S. Kaufman and Moss Hart. November 12, 1981. Director, John Going. With John Wylie, Monica Merryman, Brian Keeler, Moultrie Patten, Maeve McGuire.

A CHRISTMAS CAROL (32). By Charles Dickens; adapted by Martin L. Platt, as conceived and directed by Robert J. Farley. December

ber 10, 1981. With A. D. Cover, Charles Berendt, Charles Antalosky, Sharon Harrison, Lisa Brailoff, Benjamin Ryken.

AN ENEMY OF THE PEOPLE (16). By Henrik Ibsen, adapted by Arthur Miller. January 14, 1982. Director, Irene Lewis. With James Hurdle, Ron Frazier, Cynthia Judge, Cara Duff-MacCormick.

THE HOT L BALTIMORE (16). By Lanford Wilson. February 11, 1982. Director, Robert J. Farley. With Richard Riehle, Deirdre Owens, Linda Atkinson, Arthur Hammer, Donn Ruddy.

FOOLS (16). By Neil Simon. April 8, 1982. Director, Walton Jones. With James Maxwell, Harry Frazier, Virginia Hammer, Douglas Fisher, Richard Riehle.

Designers: scenery, William Schroder, Jamie Greenleaf, Hugh Landwehr, Kevin Rupnik; lighting, James Berton Harris, James D. Sale, Pat Collins, Judy Rasmuson, Lauren MacKenzie Miller; costumes, Spencer Mosse, Nanrose Buchman, Linda Fisher, Dunya Ramicova.

Note: Following performances in Anchorage, *Fools* toured 15 Southcentral and Southeastern communities for a month, including a week of performances in Juneau May 14–22, 1982.

ASHLAND, ORE.

Oregon Shakespearean Festival: Elizabethan Stage

(Founder, Angus L. Bowmer; producing director, Jerry Turner; general manager, William W. Patton)

TWELFTH NIGHT (32). By William Shakespeare. June 12, 1981. Director, Pat Patton. With Richard Elmore, Joan Stuart-Morris, Linda Alper, Wayne Ballantyne, Lawrence Paulsen, Larry Friedlander.

HENRY IV, Part 1 (31). By William Shakespeare. June 20, 1981. Director, James Edmondson. With Dennis Smith, Cal Winn, Barry

Kraft, Kathleen Brady, Jeanne Paulsen, Philip Davidson.

THE TWO GENTLEMEN OF VERONA (40). By William Shakespeare. June 21, 1981 Director, David Ostwald. With Joe Vincent, Barry Kraft, Michael Newell, Jeanne Paulsen, Joyce Harris.

Oregon Shakespearean Festival: Angus Bowmer Theater

DEATH OF A SALESMAN (34). By Arthur Miller. June 5, 1981. Director, Robert Loper. With James Edmondson, Anne Krill, Richard Elmore, Bruce T. Gooch, Wayne Ballantyne.

'TIS PITY SHE'S A WHORE (44). By John Ford. June 6, 1981. Director, Jerry Turner. With Philip Davidson, Joan Stuart-Morris, Kathleen Brady, Stuart Duckworth, Wayne Ballantyne.

WILD OATS (38). By John O'Keeffe. June 6, 1981. Director, Jerry Turner. With Richard Riehle, Annette Helde, Stuart Duckworth, Denis Arndt, Shirley Patton.

OTHELLO (46 and 20). By William Shakespeare. August 2, 1981 and February 27, 1982. Director, Sanford Robbins. With James Avery, Denis Arndt, Joyce Harris, Annette Helde/Gayle Bellows, James Carpenter.

JULIUS CAESAR (27). By William Shakespeare. February 26, 1982. Director, Jerry

Turner. With Cal Winn, Barry Kraft, Philip Davidson, Joan Stuart-Morris, Shirley Patton, Joyce Harris.

INHERIT THE WIND (19). By Jerome Lawrence and Robert E. Lee. February 27, 1982. Director, Dennis Bigelow. With Luther Hanson, Wayne Ballantyne, Philip Davidson, Stuart Duckworth.

BLITHE SPIRIT (24). By Noel Coward. February 28, 1982. Director, Pat Patton. With Joan Stuart-Morris, Priscilla Hake Lauris, Richard Elmore, JoAnn Johnson Patton, Tina Marie Goff.

SPOKESONG (9). By Stewart Parker with Jimmy Kennedy. May 1, 1982. Director, Denis Arndt. With James Finnegan, Richard Poe, Gayle Bellows, Richard Elmore, Jeanne Paulsen, Stuart Duckworth.

Oregon Shakespearean Festival: Black Swan Theater

ARTICHOKE (14). By Joanna M. Glass. June 5, 1981. Director, Joy Carlin. With Richard

Riehle, Jeanne Paulsen, Patricia Slover, Joe Vincent.

THE BIRTHDAY PARTY (46). By Harold Pinter. June 6, 1981. Director, Andrew J. Traister. With Jeffry Woolf, Phyllis Courtney, Bill Geisslinger, Joan Stuart-Morris, Cal Winn, James Carpenter.

THE ISLAND (60). By Athol Fugard. July 11, 1981. Director, Luther James. With J. Wesley Huston, James Avery.

WINGS (35). By Arthur Kopit. February 28, 1982. Director, James Moll. With Jeanne Paulsen, Karen Norris, Daniel Mayes, Wayne Ballantyne, Helen Machin-Smith.

HOLD ME! (15). By Jules Feiffer. March 27, 1982. Director, Paul Barnes. With JoAnn Johnson Patton, Sam Pond, Cal Winn, Joan Stuart-Morris, Tina Marie Goff.

Designers: scenery, Richard L. Hay, William Bloodgood, Jesse Hollis, James Sale, Bryan Saint Germain, Karen Gjelsteen; lighting, Richard Riddell, Robert Peterson, Peter W. Allen; costumes, Deborah M. Dryden, Barbara Affonso, Jeannie Davidson, Michael Olich, Martha Burke, Bryan Saint Germain, Carole Wheeldon, Candice Cain.

ATLANTA

Alliance Theater Company: Mainstage

(Managing director, Bernard Havard; artistic director, Fred Chappell; associate director, Charles Abbott)

WHOSE LIFE IS IT ANYWAY? (27). By Brian Clark. October 21, 1981. Director, Fred Chappell. With Linda Stephens, Terry Beaver, Jim Peck, Tom Campbell.

BRIGADOON (32). Book and lyrics by Alan Jay Lerner; music by Frederick Loewe. November 25, 1981. Director, Charles Abbott; choreographer, Susi McCarter; musical director, Michael Fauss. With Mark Jacoby, Lynn Fitzpatrick, Adrian Elder.

PRIVATE LIVES (27). By Noel Coward. January 6, 1982. Director, Fred Chappell. With Judith Robinson, Brooks Baldwin, Rob Roper, Lynn Fitzpatrick.

LOOSE ENDS (27). By Michael Weller. February 10, 1982. Director, Kent Stephens. With

James Sheridan, Sherry Steiner, Marianne Hammock, David Head.

CABARET (27). Book by Joe Masteroff, music by John Kander, lyrics by Fred Ebb; based on John van Druten's play and Christopher Isherwood's stories. March 17, 1982. Director, Fred Chappell; musical director, Michael Fauss; musical stager/choreographer, Bick Goss. With Charles Abbott, Lorna Erickson, Kurt Johnson, Woody Romoff, Libby Whittemore.

A MIDSUMMER NIGHT'S DREAM (27). By William Shakespeare. April 21, 1982. Director, Charles Abbott. With Terry Beaver, Diane D'Aquila, Marianne Hammock, David Head, David McCann, Chondra Wolle, Scott Isert.

Designers: scenery, Mark Morton, Michael Stauffer; lighting, Michael Orris Watson; costumes, Thom Coates, Stanley Simmons, Fannie Schubert.

Alliance Theater Company: Studio Theater

BILLY BISHOP GOES TO WAR (16). By John Gray with Eric Peterson. February 3, 1982. Director, Charles Abbott. With Robert Browning, Joe Collins.

SONS AND FATHERS OF SONS (11). By Ray Aranha. March 10, 1982. Director, Ray Aranha. With Ernest L. Dixon, Jihad Babatunde, Rob Cleveland.

A COUPLA WHITE CHICKS SITTING AROUND TALKING (11). By John Ford Noonan. April 14, 1982. Director, Billings LaPierre. With Jan Maris, Nancy Jane Clay.

THE DIVINERS (11). By James Leonard Jr. May 26, 1982. Director, Fred Chappell. With Al Hamacher, Don Spalding, Rudolph A. Goldschmidt, Bea Swanson, Charlie Hensley.

Alliance Theater Company: Atlanta Children's Theater

DUNGEONS AND GRYPHONS (16). By Linden Petersen. September 28, 1981 (world premiere). Director, Charles Abbott. With Magician Abb Dickson and the Children's Theater Company.

SNEAKERS (32). By Judith Weinstein and Ar-

nold Somers; music by Elissa Schreiner; lyrics by Sunnie Miller. January 18, 1982 (world premiere). Director/choreographer, Charles Abbott; music director/arranger, Michael Fauss. With members of the Children's Theater Company.

Designers: scenery, R. C, Torri, Tony Loadholt, Deborah Jasien, lighting, Paul Ackerman, Kevin Myrick, Mark Lecato, Peter H. Shinn; costumes, Susan E. Mickey, Jean Mills, Joyce Andulot, Susan Hirschfeld.

Note: *Harlem to Broadway: The Black Musical,* November 20, 1981, played three weeks at the Studio Theater. *On Golden Pond* by Ernest Thompson was presented for 5 performances at the Peachtree Playhouse, March 10–14, 1982, as part of the Alliance Theater Company's seven-state, Southeastern tour.

BALTIMORE

Center Stage: Mainstage

(Artistic director, Stan Wojewodski Jr; managing director, Peter W. Culman)

A LESSON FROM ALOES (37). By Athol Fugard. September 22, 1981. Director, Jackson Phippin. With Beth Dixon, James Hurdle, Charles Henry Patterson.

MUCH ADO ABOUT NOTHING (37). By William Shakespeare. November 3, 1981. Director, Stan Wojewodski Jr. With Tana Hicken, Terrance O'Quinn, John Wojda, Wendel Meldrum, Emery Battis, Peter Vogt, Lance Davis.

THE AMEN CORNER (37). By James Baldwin. December 15, 1981. Director, Walter Dallas. With Frances Foster, Leila Danette, Verna Lee Day, Deloris Gaskins, Jeffrey V. Thompson, Peter Wise.

L'ATELIER (THE WORKROOM) (37). By Jean-Claude Grumberg, adapted by Daniel A. Stein and Sara O'Connor. February 2, 1982. Director, Stan Wojewodski Jr. With Nancy Donohue, Rosemary Knower, Pamela Pascoe, Susan Sharkey, Larry Block, Barbara Spiegel.

TERRA NOVA (37). By Ted Tally. March 23, 1982. Director, Stan Wojewodski Jr. With Brian Murray, Peter Burnell, J. Kenneth Campbell, Beth Dixon.

SAVAGES (37). By Christopher Hampton. May 11, 1982. Director, Jackson Phippin. With George Morfogen, Joaquim De Almeida, Stanja Lowe, Malcolm Stewart, Nesbitt Blaisdell. Original music by Teiji Ito.

Designers: scenery, Tony Straiges, Wally Coberg, Richard R. Goodwin, Hugh Landwehr; lighting John Tissot, Bonnie Ann Brown, Donald Edmund Thomas; costumes, Lesley Skannal, Robert Wojewodski; puppets and masks for *Savages,* Julie Taymor.

Center Stage: First Stage

(Play Reading Series of workshop premieres, conceived and developed by Stan Wojewodski Jr., each play presented twice, with members of the company)

THE OCTETTE BRIDGE CLUB by P. J. Barry, January 21, 1982, director, Jackson Phippin. LAST LOOKS by Grace McKeaney, January 22, 1982, director, Jackson Phippin. TOWN CRIER by Mark Eisman, January 23, 1982, director, Michael Engler. THE HEADHUNTERS by Henry Denker, March 11, 1982, director, Walter Dallas. ANDY DUNDEE IS

ANTIWAR by Theodore Faro Gross, March 12, 1982, director, Lisa Bailey. THE HOUSE ACROSS THE STREET by Darrah Cloud, March 13, 1982, director, Robert Allan Ackerman. New versions of LAST LOOKS, THE HOUSE ACROSS THE STREET and ANDY DUNDEE IS ANTIWAR were presented April 29, April 30, May 1, 1982.

Note: Center Stage's Young People's Theater toured Maryland schools in 23 counties and Baltimore City, 1981–82, with *Griffin! Griffin!* by Russell Davis, based on Frank Stockton's story; music by Lance Mulcahy; director, Lenore Blank.

BERKELEY, CALIF.

Berkeley Repertory Theater: Mark Taper Mainstage

(Producing director, Michael W. Leibert; general manager, Mitzi Sales)

THE CHERRY ORCHARD (32). By Anton Chekhov. September 29, 1981. Director, James Moll. With Joy Carlin, Kimberly King, Judith Marx, Irving Israel, Hope Alexander-Willis, Brian Thompson.

THE BELLE OF AMHERST (32). By William Luce. November 1, 1981. Director, Michael W. Leibert. With Joy Carlin.

SAVAGES (32). By Christopher Hampton. January 19, 1982. Director, Tony Amendola. With Brian Thompson, Roberta Callahan, Charles Dean, Stephen J. Godwin.

AFTER THE FALL (32). By Arthur Miller. February 23, 1982. Director, Peter Layton. With Brian Thompson, Charles Dean, Emily Hubner, Joy Carlin, Judith Marx.

Berkeley Repertory Theater: Addison Street Playhouse

AS YOU LIKE IT (32). By William Shakespeare. December 8, 1981. Director, Gregory Boyd. With Hope Alexander-Willis, Judith Marx, Joe Miksak, Dennis Parlato.

HEARTBREAK HOUSE (32). By George Bernard Shaw. March 30, 1982. Director, Albert Takazaukos. With Joseph Miksak, Barbara Oliver, Kimberly King, Tony Amendola, Hope

Alexander-Willis, Kim Gayton, Brian Thompson.

THE DIARY OF ANNE FRANK (32). By Albert Hackett and Frances Goodrich. May 4, 1982. Director, Joy Carlin. With Kimberly King, Michael Leibert, Barbara Oliver, Vincent Barnett, Bob Babish, Kim Gayton.

Designers: scenery, Jesse Hollis, Gene Angell, Ron Pratt, Warren Travis, Victoria Smith; lighting, Greg Sullivan, Larry French, Robert Peterson, Tom Ruzika, Derek Duarte; costumes, Robert Blackburn, Robert Morgan, Lorraine S. Forman, Toni Lovaglia, Deborah Brothers-Lowry, Deborah Dryden, Walter Watson.

Note: *Woza Albert* by Percy Mtwa and Mbongeni Ngema, played June 1–5, 1982 at the Berkeley Repertory Theater. Noel Coward's three plays comprising *Tonight At 8:30,* director, Alex Kinney; played in repertory June 15–August 22, 1982.

BUFFALO

Studio Arena Theater

(Artistic director, David Frank; managing director, Barry Hoffman)

WHOSE LIFE IS IT ANYWAY? (32). By Brian Clark. September 25, 1981. Director, David Frank. With Munson Hicks, Dale Helward, Patricia Kilgarriff, Moultrie Patten.

THE MISS FIRECRACKER CONTEST (32). By Beth Henley. October 30, 1981. Director, Davey Marlin-Jones. With K. T. Barnum, Robert Darnell, Donna Davis, Kathryn Grody, Cam Kornman, Stephen Tobolowsky.

DEATHTRAP (32). By Ira Levin. December 4, 1981. Director, David Frank. With Robert

Darnell, Andrew Davis, Steven Gilborn, Margery Shaw, Mickey Hartnett.

TARTUFFE (32). By Molière. January 8, 1982. Director, David Frank. With William Kiehl, Holly Baron, Donald Gantry, Lisa Goodman, Charles Shaw Robinson.

DERELICT (32). By Robert Schenkkan. February 12, 1982 (world premiere). Director, A. J. Antoon; scenery and lighting, Quentin Thomas; costumes, Robert Morgan.
Capt. Craig .... William Cain

Brand .... Robert Darnell
Simms.................... Everett Ensley
Tom .... Evan Handler
Countess................. Sharon Laughlin
Crew........... Dan Oreskes, Tod Wheeler
Time: 1878. Place: Off the Coast of Nova Scotia and on the San Cristobal, an abandonned vessel.

OF MICE AND MEN (32). By John Steinbeck. March 19, 1982. Director, Geoffrey Sherman. With Don Perkins, Michael Starr, Pamela Lewis, William Preston.

RHINO FAT: From Red Dog Notes (32). Conceived and directed by Davey Marlin-Jones; written by Patrick Desmond, the Studio Arena Company, Davey Marlin-Jones. April 23, 1982 (world premiere). Researchers, Kathryn Long, Barbara Fran. Musical director, Tony Zito; music and lyrics by Tony Zito and Studio Arena Company; conductor, John Hassalback; scenery, John Arnone, David Woolard; lighting, Robby Monk; costumes, Andrew Blackwood Marlay; sound, Rick Menke. With members of the Studio Arena Company.

Sesquicentennial musical revue, a collage of Buffalo history, performed in two acts. One intermission.

Designers: scenery, Wally Coberg, Grady Larkin, Paul Wonsek; lighting, Robby Monk, Paul Wonsek; costumes, Lewis D. Rampino, Bill Walker, Janice Lines, Robert Morgan.

CAMBRIDGE, MASS.

American Repertory Theater: Loeb Drama Center

(Artistic director, Robert Brustein; managing director, Robert J. Orchard)

SGANARELLE (39) An Evening of Molière Farces translated by Albert Bermel, December 1, 1981. Director, Andrei Serban. With John Bottoms, Francois de la Giroday, Thomas Derrah, Jeremy Geidt, Richard Grusin, Cherry Jones, Karen MacDonald, Jonathan Marks.

ORLANDO (38). By George Friederic Handel. December 16, 1981 (American stage premiere). Director, Peter Sellars; music director-conductor, Craig Smith; scenery, Elaine Spatz-Rabinowitz; lighting, James F. Ingalls; costumes, Rita Ryack.
Zoroastro .... Robert Honeysucker/
                              James Maddalena
Orlando .... Jeffrey Gall/Sanford Sylvan
Dorinda .... Susan Larson/Sharon Baker
Angelica .... Jane Bryden/Jane Brown
Medoro....... Mary Kendrick/Pamela Gore.
Act I, Scene 1: Cape Canaveral, Kennedy Space Center. Scene 2: Florida Everglades. Act II. Florida Everglades. Act III. Mars.

THE JOURNEY OF THE FIFTH HORSE (35). By Ronald Ribman. January 27, 1982. Director, Adrian Hall. With Marianne Owen, Tony Shalhoub, Paul Benedict, Jeremy Geidt, Shirley Wilber, John Bottoms, Richard Grusin.

GHOSTS (35). By Henrik Ibsen, adapted by Robert Brustein. May 19, 1982. Director, Robert Brustein. With Kathleen Widdoes, John Belucci, Alvin Epstein, Cherry Jones, Jeremy Geidt.

ORCHIDS IN THE MOONLIGHT (35). By Carlos Fuentes. June 9, 1982. (world premiere). Director, Joann Green; scenery, Elaine Spatz-Rabinowitz; lighting, James F. Ingalls; costumes, Nan Cibula.
Dolores..................... Ellen Holly
Maria .... Rosalind Cash
The Fan .... Frank Licato.
Place: Venice. One intermission.

American Repertory Theater: Hasty Pudding Theater

TRUE WEST (20). By Sam Shepard. April 7, 1982. Director, David Wheeler. With John Bottoms, Francois de la Giroday, Richard Grusin, Shirley Wilber.

RUNDOWN (16). By Robert Auletta. April 15, 1982 (world premiere). Director, William Foeller; scenery, Kate Edmunds; lighting, James F. Ingalls; costumes, Nancy Thun.

Frank Payovski .... Stephen Rowe
William Spear .... Tony Shalhoub
Laura Harvey .... Karen MacDonald/
                              Marianne Owen
Allen Trace .... Thomas Derrah.
Time: Spring, 1975. Place, New York City. One intermission (see synopsis in introduction to this section).

GOODMAN THEATER, CHICAGO—Frank Hamilton and Peg Murray in *A House Not Meant to Stand,* new Tennessee Williams play

Designers: scenery, Michael H. Yeargan, Elaine Spatz-Rabinowitz, Kevin Rupnik, Kate Edmunds, Tony Straiges; lighting, James F. Ingalls; costumes, Dunya Ramicova, Rita Ryack, Nancy Thun, Nan Cibula.

Note: A.R.T. also sponsors special events and staged readings of new plays. In 1981–82, these included: *They All Want to Play Hamlet* by Jon Lipsky and Vincent Murphy, a Theater/Works of Boston production; *Mummenschanz;* Tennyson's *Enoch Arden* with Luise Rainer; Claire Bloom in *These Are Women,* a portrait of Shakespeare's heroines. A.R.T. toured New England and New York

State in the fall, playing 30 cities. The company embarked on a ten-week, 12-cities, six-countries tour of Europe and the Middle East in the summer of 1982.

CHICAGO

Goodman Theater: Mainstage

(Artistic director, Gregory Mosher; managing director, Roche Schulfer).

THE FRONT PAGE (34). By Ben Hecht and Charles MacArthur. October 8, 1981. Director, Michael Maggio. With W. H. Macy, Colin Stinton, Robert Thompson, William Munchow, Bonnie Sue Arp, Mayo Bank.

A CHRISTMAS CAROL (41). By Charles Dickens; adapted by Barbara Field. November 24, 1981. Director, Tony Mockus. With William J. Norris, Robert Thompson, Aaron Kramer, Del Close, Robert Scogin.

PANTOMIME (34). By Derek Walcott. January 21, 1982. Director, Gregory Mosher. With Roscoe Lee Browne, Brian Murray.

LAKEBOAT (34). By David Mamet. March 4, 1982. Director, Gregory Mosher. With Mike Nussbaum, Jack Wallace, Nathan Davis.

A HOUSE NOT MEANT TO STAND (34). By Tennessee Williams. April 16, 1982 (world premiere of revision). Director, Andre Ernotte; scenery, Karen Schulz; lighting, Rachel Budin; costumes, Christa Scholtz.

Cornelius .... Frank Hamilton
Bella .... Peg Murray
Jessie....................... Scotty Bloch
Charlie .... Scott Jaeck
Emerson.................... Les Podewell
Stacey..................... Cynthia Baker
Officer Bruce Lee Jackson ... Brooks Gardner
Dr. Crane.................. Nathan Davis
    Three Spectral Children: Jeremy Sisto, Meadow Sisto, Jamie Wild.
    One intermission.

THE WOOLGATHERER (34). By William Mastrosimone. April 14, 1982. Director, Sandra Grand. With Emilie Borg, Jack Wallace. (At the Studio Theater.)

Designers: scenery, Joseph Nieminsi, David Gropman, Michael Merritt, Philip Eickhoff; lighting, Jennifer Tipton, Robert Christen, Kevin Rigdon; costumes, William Ivey Long, James Edmund Brady, David Gropman, Christa Scholtz, Philip Eickhoff.

Note: A series of one-woman shows appeared at the Goodman during the 1981–82 season: Estelle Parsons in *Miss Margarida's Way* by Roberto Athayde; Pat Carroll in *Gertrude Stein, Gertrude Stein, Gertrude Stein* by Marty Martin; Uta Hagen in *Charlotte* by Peter Hicks.

CINCINNATI

Cincinnati Playhouse in the Park: Robert S. Marx Theater

(Producing director, Michael Murray; managing director, Robert W. Tolan)

BORN YESTERDAY (32). By Garson Kanin. October 6, 1981. Director, Ron Lagomarsino. With Linda Lee Johnson, Lou Criscuolo, Samuel Maupin.

PETER PAN (32). By J. M. Barrie; music by Mark Charlap and Jule Styne; lyrics by Carolyn Leigh, Betty Comden and Adolph Green. November 24, 1981. Director/choreographer, George Bunt; musical director, Boyd Staplin. With Jan Neuberger, George Cavey, Susan Glaze.

BETRAYAL (32). By Harold Pinter. January 19, 1982. Director, Michael Hankins, Laura Copland, Eberle Thomas.

MACBETH (32). By William Shakespeare. March 9, 1982. Director, Michael Murray. With Donald MacKechnie, John Milligan.

TEN LITTLE INDIANS (32). By Agatha Christie. April 27, 1982. Director, Donald MacKechnie. With Ellen Fiske, Julian Barnes, Jonathan Moore.

TALLEY'S FOLLY (32). By Lanford Wilson. June 1, 1982. Director, Michael Murray. With Steven Gilborn, Lynn Ritchie.

Cincinnati Playhouse in the Park: Thompson Shelterhouse Theater

I LOVE MY WIFE (44). Book and lyrics by Michael Stewart; music by Cy Coleman; based on a play by Luis Rego. June 25, 1981. Director, Worth Gardner. With Jill Hoel, Nancy Hoffman, Scott Bakula, Stephen Joseph.

HOME (22). By Samm-Art Williams. November 5, 1981. Director, Woodie King Jr. With Carl Crudup, Elizabeth Van Dyke, Nadyne C. Spratt.

A LIFE IN THE THEATER (22). By David Mamet. December 31, 1981. Director, James

Milton. With John Wylie, Josh Clark.

A COUPLA WHITE CHICKS SITTING AROUND TALKING (22). By John Ford Noonan. February 18, 1982. Director, Josephine Abady. With Cynthia Crumlish, Peggy Cosgrave.

A LESSON FROM ALOES (22). By Athol Fugard. April 8, 1982. Director, Thomas Bullard. With Eugene Troobnick, Tanny McDonald, Leonard Jackson.

Designers: scenery, Lowell Detweiler, David Ariosa, Robert Soule, Paul Shortt, Alan Kimmel, John Jensen; lighting, William Mintzer, Victor En Yu Tan, Neil Peter Jampolis, Spencer Mosse, Amy Merrell, Jay Depenbrock; costumes, Caley Summers, Rebecca Senske, Elizabeth Covey, Ann Firestone.

CLEVELAND

The Cleveland Play House: Drury Theater

(Director, Richard Oberlin; general manager, Janet Wade)

TINTYPES (39). Conceived by Mary Kyte with Mel Marvin and Gary Pearle. October 9, 1981. With Cliff Bemis, Theresa Peteo, Yvetta, Sharon Bicknell, Wayne S. Turney.

SHERLOCK HOLMES AND THE CURSE OF THE SIGN OF THE FOUR (43). adapted by Dennis Rosa from Arthur Conan Doyle. December 4, 1981. Director, Paul Lee. With Joe D. Lauck, Mary Adams-Smith, James P. Kisicki, Richard Halverson.

BETRAYAL (32). By Harold Pinter. January 29, 1982. Director, Dennis Sacek. With Kenneth Albers, Carolyn Reed, Joe D. Lauck.

TALLEY'S FOLLY (32). By Lanford Wilson. March 5, 1982. Director, Evie McElroy. With Ralph Gunderman, Catherine Albers.

CHEKHOV IN YALTA (32). By John Driver and Jeffrey Haddow. April 9, 1982. Director, Kenneth Albers. With William Rhys, Allan Leatherman, Mary Adams-Smith, Richard Halverson, James Richards, Carolyn Reed.

The Cleveland Play House: Euclid-77th Street Theater

TRANSLATIONS (32). By Brian Friel. October 23, 1981. Director, Kenneth Albers. With Joe D. Lauck, Cassandra Wolfe, Paul Lee, Maggie Thatcher, Gary Smith, Mary Adams-Smith, Richard Halverson, James Richards, Morgan Lund, Allan Leatherman.

A CHRISTMAS CAROL (43). By Charles Dickens; adapted by Doris Baizley. November 25, 1981. Director, William Rhys. With Wayne S. Turney, Morgan Lund, Carolyn Reed, Gary Smith, Paul A. Floriano, William Rhys.

ROMEO AND JULIET (32). By William Shakespeare. January 22, 1982. Director, William Rhys. With Morgan Lund, Sharon Bicknell, James Richards, Evie McElroy, James P. Kisicki.

COLE (53). Devised by Benny Green and Alan Strachan; songs by Cole Porter. March 19, 1982. Director, Judith Haskell; musical director, David Gooding. With members of the Cleveland Play House Company

The Cleveland Play House: Brooks Theater

DAUGHTERS (26). By John Morgan Evans. October 30, 1981. Director, Edward Stern. With

Evie McElroy, Carolyn Reed, Catherine Albers, Judy Nevits, Alden Redgrave.

PANTOMIME (26). By Derek Walcott. February 5, 1982. Director, David Connell. With Wayne S. Turney, Kenneth W. Daughty.

TRESPASSERS WILL BE PROSECUTED (25). By Peter Kenna. April 16, 1982 (American premiere). Director, Harper Jane McAdoo.

The man...................... Paul Lee
The boy .... Allan Byrne
  Place: A pit underneath the tracks of a railway freight line. Act I, Scene 1: Saturday morning. Scene 2: Saturday afternoon. Act II. Sunday afternoon.

Designers: scenery, Richard Gould, James Irwin, Charles Berliner, Gary Eckhart, Wayne Merritt; lighting, Richard Gould, James Irwin, Wayne Merritt; costumes, Estelle Painter, Mary H. Carey, Larry Bauman, Charles Berliner, Richard Gould, Elizabeth A. Streeter, Colleen Muscha.

Great Lakes Shakespeare Festival

(Producing director, Vincent Dowling; managing director, Mary Bill)

THE MATCHMAKER (25). By Thornton Wilder. July 1, 1981. Director, Dorothy Silver. With Bernard Kates, Tom Blair, Michael John McGann, Beatrice O'Donnell.

STREETSONGS (8). Conceived by Geraldine Fitzgerald and Richard Maltby Jr. July 6, 1981. With Geraldine Fitzgerald.

KING LEAR (14). By William Shakespeare. July 16, 1981. Director, Vincent Dowling. With Larry Gates, Bernard Kates, Robert Elliott, Holmes Osborne, Sarah Nall, Anne Atkins, Madylon Branstetter.

A DOLL'S HOUSE (12). By Henrik Ibsen. August 13, 1981. Director, Edward Stern. With members of the Company.

MUCH ADO ABOUT NOTHING (14). By William Shakespeare. August 27, 1981. Director, Vincent Dowling. With Holmes Osborne, Dan Westbrook, Robert Elliott, Bairbre Dowling, Madylon Branstetter.

MY LADY LUCK (1). By James A. Brown. August 5, 1981. Director, Dorothy Silver. With Vincent Dowling.

Designers: scenery, John Ezell; lighting, Susan A. White, Joseph Appelt, Kirk Bookman; costumes, Estelle Painter, Kurt Wilhelm, Lewis D. Rampino, Mary-Anne Aston.

COCONUT GROVE, FLA.

Players State Theater

(Artistic and producing director, David Robert Kanter; managing director, G. David Black)

DA (28). By Hugh Leonard. October 9, 1981. Director, David Robert Kanter. With Bill Hindman, Bruce MacVittie, Virginia Mattis, Paul Vincent, Kelly Pino, William Pitts.

OEDIPUS REX (28). By Sophocles; adapter/director, Charles Nolte. November 6, 1981. With Richard Allen, E. Wright, Barbara Montgomery, Mel Johnson Jr., Robert Colston.

A CHRISTMAS CAROL (28). By Charles Dickens, adapter/director, David Robert Kanter. December 4, 1981. With Donald Ewer, Harold Bergman, Anne Gilliam, Thom Haneline, Glenn Swan.

THE SUMMER PEOPLE (28). Written and directed by Charles Nolte. January 8, 1982. With Ellen Adamson, Booth Colman, Norma Davids, Greg Gilbert, Joseph Jamrog, Jane Lowry, Virginia Mattis, Paul Vincent.

A MOON FOR THE MISBEGOTTEN (28). By Eugene O'Neill. February 5, 1982. Director, Lou Salerni. With Peter Galman, Lisa McMillan, Fred Thompson, Robert Donley, Robert Gaston.

TALLEY'S FOLLY by Lanford Wilson (28). March 5, 1982. Director, James Riley. With Jeff David, Linda Stephens.

BLACK COFFEE (28). By Agatha Christie. April 2, 1982. Director, David Robert Kanter. With Ron Johnston, Philip Le Strange, Max Howard, Mary Benson, Harold Bergman.

Designers: scenery, Marsha Hardy, Ron Fondaw, Kenneth N. Kurtz, David Trimble; lighting, Michael Newton-Brown, Kenneth N. Kurtz, David Martin Jacques, Pat Simmons; costumes, Claire Gatrell, Barbara A. Bell, Maria Marrero, Barbara Forbes, Jill Young Zuckerman.

Note: The Players State Theater Cultural Caravan toured an original trilingual rock musical for children statewide during the winter of 1981–82: *Fugue for Four Frogs,* book by Rafael V. Blanco; music and lyrics by Fernando Fonseca, who also directed.

COSTA MESA, CALIF.

South Coast Repertory: Mainstage

(Artistic directors, David Emmes, Martin Benson)

AH, WILDERNESS! (40). By Eugene O'-Neill. September 15, 1981. Director, Martin Benson. With Mark Herrier, Anne Gerety, K. Callan, Robert Cornthwaite, James Gallery, Joe McNeely, Irene Arranga.

LOOSE ENDS (40). By Michael Weller. October 29, 1981. Director, David Emmes. With Paul Rudd, Marnie Mosiman, Anni Long, Michael MacRae, Lois Foraker.

A CHRISTMAS CAROL (22). By Charles Dickens; adapted by Jerry Patch. December 9, 1981. Director, John-David Keller. With Hal Landon Jr., John Ellington, Noreen Hennessy, Charlie Cummins, Don Tuche.

THE PLAY'S THE THING (40). By Ferenc Molnar; adapted by P.G. Wodehouse. January 12, 1982. Director, Lee Shallat. With Jonathan

Farwell, Nicholas Walker, Linda Thorson, Robert Machray.

HENRY IV, Part 1 (40). By William Shakespeare. March 2, 1982. Director, John Allison. With David Chemel, David Darlow, Anni Long, Thomas Hill, Ron Boussom, Martha McFarland.

DA (40). By Hugh Leonard. April 13, 1982. Director, David Emmes. With Dean Santoro, Thomas Toner, Katherine MacGregor, John Greenleaf, William Glover.

TINTYPES (46). Conceived by Mary Kyte with Mel Marvin and Gary Pearle. May 25, 1982. Director, John-David Keller; musical director, John Ellington. With Andrea Frierson, Stanley Grover, Ken Jennings, Angelina Réaux, Susan Watson.

South Coast Repertory: Second Stage

TRUE WEST (21). By Sam Shepard. November 4, 1981. Director, Lee Shallat. With E. D. Harris, John Ashton, Richard Doyle, Iris Korn.

BODIES (21). By James Saunders. January 20, 1982. Director, Richard Gershman. With Christina Pickles, Tandy Cronyn, Matthew Faison, Lawrence Pressman.

THE BLOOD KNOT (21). By Athol Fugard. March 10, 1982. Director, Martin Benson. With Tom Bower, Sydney Hibbert.

COMING ATTRACTIONS (21). By Ted

Tally; music by Jack Feldman; lyrics by Bruce Sussman and Jack Feldman. April 21, 1982. Director, Paul Rudd; musical director, John Ellington; choreographer, Diane dePriest. With Diane dePriest, Richard Doyle, John Ellington, Art Koustik, Anni Long, Howard Shangraw, Don Tuche.

THE MAN WHO COULD SEE THROUGH TIME (21). By Terri Wagener. June 2, 1982. Director, Martin Benson. With Charles Lanyer, Linda Purl.

Designers: scenery, Michael Devine, Mark Donnelly, Cliff Faulkner, Ralph Funicello, Lisette Thomas, Steve Lavino, Keith Hein; lighting, Susan Tuohy, Tom Ruzika, Donna Ruzika, Cameron Harvey, Paulie Jenkins; costumes, Merrily Ann Murray, Nanrose Buchman, Dwight Richard Odle, Charles D. Tomlinson, Tom Rasmussen, Barbara Cox, Skipper Skeoch.

DALLAS THEATER CENTER—Russell Henderson,
John Henson and Lynne Moon in *Pigeons on the Walk*

DALLAS

Dallas Theater Center: Kalita Humphreys Theater

(Artistic directors, Paul Baker, Mary Sue Jones; general manager, Albert Milano)

DEATHTRAP (38). By Ira Levin. July 7, 1981. Director, Christopher Pennywitt. With William Hootkins, Royal Brantley, Mary Sue Jones, Judith David, Ryland Merkey.

WAR AND PEACE (40). By Leo Tolstoy; adapted by Alfred Neumann, Erwin Piscator, Guntram Prufer; English adaptation, Robert David MacDonald. October 13, 1981. Director, Joan Vail Thorne. With Roger DeKoven, Richard Dow, John Figlmiller, Norma Moore, Randy Moore, Mary Rohde.

TINTYPES (47). Conceived by Mary Kyte with Mel Marvin, Gary Pearle. December 8, 1981. Director, David Pursley; musical director, Raymond Allen. With David Pursley, Marcee Smith, Randolph Tallman, Lou Williford, Mary Yarbrough.

OF MICE AND MEN (40). By John Steinbeck. February 9, 1982. Director, Anton Rodgers. With Cliff Osmond, Warren Hammack, Ryland Merkey, Deborah A. Kinghorn.

TARTUFFE (39). By Molière; translation by Barnett Shaw. March 30, 1982. Director Paul Baker. With Russell Henderson, Barnett Shaw. With Candy Buckley, Ronni Lopez, Randy Moore, Jo Livingston, Mary Sue Jones.

BLACK COFFEE (41). By Agatha Christie. May 18, 1982. Director, Walter Learning. With Eric House, Tim Green, Russell Henderson, Susan McDaniel Hill, Jeffrey Kinghorn, Owen Page, Mary Rohde.

Dallas Theater Center: Down Center Stage

UNDER DISTANT SKIES (25). By Jeffrey Kinghorn. November 3, 1981 (world premiere). Director, Randy Bonifay.

Barry .... Paul Munger
Sam.......................... Bob Hess
Francine.................. Shelley McClure
Place: The ninth floor of a run-down hotel in New York City. One intermission.

PIGEONS ON THE WALK (16). By Andrew Johns. January 12, 1982 (world premiere). Director, Candy Buckley.

Walter...................... Paul Munger
Frank .... William Kirk
Richie.................. Russell Henderson
Albert...................... Lynn Mathis
Victor...................... John Henson
Kid...................... Lee Lowrimore
Girl.................... Susan Engbrecht
Louis.................. Malcolm Wittman
Adolf .... Stella McCord
Irene...................... Lynne Moon
Susan.................. Nancy Lewis
Steve................... Andrew Gaupp
Cowboy .... Bill Jenkins
O.T.B. Announcer.......... Spencer Prokop
Time: Sunday. Place: An off-track betting parlor in New York. Act I. The daily double. Act II, Scene 1: The fifth race. Scene 2: The ninth race.

THE WISTERIA BUSH (15). By Jo Vander Voort. March 2, 1982 (professional premiere). Director, Michael Scudday.

Ruthie Ann Castro .... Judith Davis
Mama Wallace............. Lynn Trammell
Acia Darling .... Elly Lindsay
Miss Elly .... Synthia Rogers
Sybil Parker................ Cheryl Denson
Time: April, 1973. Place: Living room of Mama Wallace in Coleridge, Alabama. Act I. Late afternoon. Act II, Scene 1: The next morning. Scene 2: The same night.

BEOWULF—NOCTURNAL SOLSTICE (15). By Jim Marvin. April 20, 1982 (world premiere). Director, Robyn Flatt.

Old Beowulf............... Ryland Merkey
Young Beowulf .... Paul Munger
Old Unferth, King of the Brongs;
Young Unferth .... Dennis Vincent
Scop .... Bob Hess
Hrothgar, King of the Danes; Onela,
King of the Swedes .... Lee Lowrimore
Grendel.................... Peter Lynch
Grendel's Dam .... Nance Williamson
Hildebuh; Freawaru .... Carol Miles
Danish Soldier; Wiglaf;
Geatish Soldier........... Gary Whitehead
Advisor; Wealhtheow .... Susan Neely
Danish soldier; Haethcyn, King of the Frisians;
Geatish soldier; Aeschere ...... Barry Nash
Danish soldier; Wulfgar;
Geatish soldier .... Daniel Stephens
Ingeld, King of the Heathobards; Elder;
Danish Soldier .... Jim McClellan
One intermission.

Dallas Theater Center: Stemmons Auditorium

A CHRISTMAS CAROL (11). By Charles Dickens; adapted by John Figlmiller and Sally Netzel. December 18, 1981. Director, Judith Davis. With Randy Moore, Arthur Olaisen, Jeffrey Kinghorn, Ronni Lopez, Brendan Kelly.

Dallas Theater Center: Magic Turtle Children's Theater

THE LEGEND OF SLEEPY HOLLOW (8). Adapted by Frederick Gaines from Washington Irving's story. October 24, 1981. Director, Peter Lynch.

HANSEL AND GRETEL (6). By Glenn Allen Smith. January 9, 1982. Director, Carol Miles.

MERLIN AND ARTHUR (6). By Eleanor Lindsay; composer/musical director, Merlaine Angwall. February 20, 1982.

THE MIRACLE WORKER (6). By William Gibson. April 10, 1982. Director, Robyn Flatt.

Dallas Theater Center: Eugene McKinney New Play Readings

HIGH COCKALORUM by Joan Vail Thorne; October 19, 1981; Director, Mary Lou Hoyle. RAGGLE (2) by Mary Rohde; November 9, 1981; director, Michael Scudday; DUB, A

PLAY ABOUT WHALES by Ronald Wilcox; January 18, 1982; directors Paul Baker, Bryant J. Reynolds, Ronald Wilcox. TOPEKA SCUFFLE by Paul Munger; February 22, 1982; director, Mary Lou Hoyle; DUTCHMAN'S BREEZE by Allen Hibbard; March 15, 1982; director, John Logan; LAST STAGE EAST by David Hall; April 12, 1982; director, Randy Bonifay. Plays read by Dallas Theater Center Company.

Designers: scenery, Robert Duffy, Virgil Beavers, David Pursley, Mary Sue Jones, Peter Wolf, Cheryl Denson, Zak Herring, Sally Askins, Yoichi Aoki, Norman D. Schultz; lighting, Donald Edmund Thomas, Robyn Flatt, Allen Hibbard, Randy Moore, Robert Duffy, Zak Herring, Raynard Harper, Barbara Sanderson, Ken Hudson, Scott L. Hammar; costumes, Peter Lynch, John Henson, Virgil Beavers, David Pursley, Mary Lou Doyle, Sally Askins, Deborah A. Kinghorn, Ann Stephens, Lynne Moon, Stella McCord, Ken Hill, Kathy Byrne.

EVANSTON, ILL.

North Light Repertory: Mainstage

(Artistic director, Eric Steiner; managing director, Jeffrey Bentley)

PLYMOUTH ROCK ISN'T PINK (38). By William Hamilton. September 12, 1981. Director, Eric Steiner. With Ellen Crawford, Ann McDonough, Susan Dafoe, Jack McLaughlin-Gray, Mike Genovese, Greg Vinkler.

THE GLASS MENAGERIE (38). By Tennessee Williams. November 14, 1981. Director, Eric Steiner. With Glenne Headly, Tom Irwin, Terry Kinney, Peg Murray.

THE REAR COLUMN (38). By Simon Gray. January 23, 1982. Director, John Malkovich. With Roger Mueller, Joe Van Slyke, Rick Snyder, James Sudik, Peter Syversten, Michael Tezla, Billie Neil.

LES BELLES SOEURS (38). By Michel Tremblay; translated by John Van Burek and Bill Glassco. March 31, 1982 (American professional premiere). Director, Eric Steiner; scenery, Nels Anderson; costumes, Kate Bergh; lighting, Dawn Hollingsworth.
Germaine Lauzon . . . . Sheila Keenan

Linda Lauzon . . . . Joyce O'Brien
Rose Ouimet . . . . Megan McTavish
Gabrielle Jodoin . . . . Caitlin Hart
Lisette de Courval . . . . Jane MacIver
Marie-Ange Brouillette . . . . Allison Giglio
Yvette Longpré . . . . Joann Cameron
Des-Neiges Verrette . . . . Mary Ellen Falk
Thérèse Dubuc . . . . Anne Edwards
Olivine Dubuc . . . . Gail Silver
Angeline Sauve . . . . Fern Persons
Rhéauna Bibeau . . . . Marji Bank
Lise Paquette . . . . Lora Staley
Ginette Menard . . . . Elizabeth Perkins
Pierette Guerin . . . . Ann Goldman
Time: Spring 1965. Place: Germaine Lauzon's kitchen in Montreal's East End. Act I: One evening. Act II: The same.

THE PROMISE (38). By Aleksei Arbuzov, translated by Ariadne Nicolaeff. May 22, 1982. Director, Gus Kaikkonen. With Jonathan Fuller, Barbara E. Robertson, James W. Sudik.

Designers: scenery, Gary Baugh, Jeremy Conway, Michael Merritt, Bob Barnett, Nan Zabriskie; lighting, Dawn Hollingsworth, Rita Pietraszek, Michael Merritt, Stuart Duke; costumes, Kate Bergh, Jessica Hahn, Michael Merritt, Julie A. Nagel.

North Light Repertory: Satellite Season

SHIRLEY BASIN (7). By Jack Gilhooley. January 6, 1982 (world premiere) Director, John Malkovich. Trailer camps in the forlorn wilderness of Wyoming, the small mining town of Shirley Basin. The struggle is in the minds of its women trying to survive the monotony and desolation of their lives.

DOUBLE FEATURE: MATINEE IDYLL and PLAY IT AGAIN, MR. GOODBAR (7). By Dean Corrin. March 10, 1982 (world premiere). Director, Mary F. Monroe. Two plays about the films and their affect on a boy and a girl.

HIGH ROLLING (7). By Robert Litz. May 12, 1982 (world premiere). Director, Sharon Ott. Time: The present. Place: A Casino, the Madison home, an apartment house, a university residence, a Congressional hearing room.

With Dawn Atenman, Mary Becker, Anne Edwards, Aaron Freeman, Caitlin Hart, Sheila Keenan, Kathleen Melvin, Mark Millikin, Joyce O'Brien, Robert Scogin, Beth Shields, Aiden Quinn.

HARTFORD

Hartford Stage: John W. Huntington Theater

(Artistic director, Mark Lamos; managing director, William Stewart)

ANTONY AND CLEOPATRA (44). By William Shakespeare. September 25, 1981. Director, Mark Lamos. With Keith Baxter, Patricia Conolly, Michael Tolaydo, Kim Staunton.

KEAN (44). By Alexandre Dumas; adapted by Jean-Paul Sartre; translated by Frank Hauser. November 13, 1981. Director, Mark Lamos. With Keith Baxter, Mary Layne, Patricia Conolly, Timothy Meyers, David Schramm, Jean Smart.

THE WAKE OF JAMEY FOSTER (44). By Beth Henley. January 1, 1982 (world premiere). Director, Ulu Grosbard.

Marshael Foster	Susan Kingsley
Leon Darnell	Stephen Tobolowsky
Katty Foster	Belita Moreno
Wayne Foster	Adam LeFevre
Collard Darnell	Pat Richardson
Pixrose Wilson	Amanda Michael Plummer
Brocker Slade	Brad Sullivan

Place: Marshael Foster's house and yard in Canton, Miss. Act I, Scene 1: Morning. Scene 2: Supper time. Act II, Scene 1: Late that night. Scene 2: Throughout the night. Scene 3: The following morning.

THE GREEKS: *The War, The Murders, The Gods* (39). Trilogy including nine plays; adapted by Kenneth Cavander and John Barton. February 19, 1982. Directors, Mark Lamos and Mary B. Robinson. With Alan Mixon, Jennifer Harmon, Jean Smart, Margaret Phillips, Mary Layne, Richard Mathews, Kevin Conroy, Jay O. Sanders.

THE ISLE IS FULL OF NOISES (44). By Derek Walcott. April 16, 1982 (world premiere). Director, Douglas Turner Ward.

Sir Lionel Robinson	Graham Brown
James as a boy	Ventura Edgerson
Achille	Antonio Fargas
Papa	Douglas Turner Ward
Lady Isadora	Jean Smart
Sir Geoffrey Thwaite	Gwyllum Evans
James	Robert Jason
Babsie Hercules	Sullivan Walker
Punkin	Jeffrey St. L. Anderson-Gunter
Archbishop	George Bowe
Patience	Kim Staunton
Volumna	Ethel Ayler
Vox Populi	Leon Morenzie
MacGregor	Antonio Fargas
Oates	Peter DeMaio
Photographer; Reporter	Jeffrey Matthews

Mapipire Secret Police Squad: Steve Carter, Terry Woodberry, Maurice Young. Three Unities: Dana Manno, Betty K. Bynum, Olivia Virgil Harper. Party Guest; Party Attendants: Carla Dean, Maree Rogers, Steve Carter, Frances Sharp.

Time: A single Day. Prologue. Act I, Scene 1: A tropical beach in the Caribbean. Scene 2: A beach house. Act II, Scene 1: The beach house. Scene 2: A cave. Scene 3: The beach house. Scene 4: The cave. Act II. The beach.

GREATER TUNA (44). By Jaston Williams, Joe Sears, Ed Howard. June 4, 1982. Director, Ed Howard. With Joe Sears, Jaston Williams.

Hartford Stage: Lunchtime Theater—The Old Place

TWINKLE, TWINKLE (7). By Ernest Thompson. October 5, 1981 (world premiere). Director, Mary B. Robinson.

Andrea Jackson	Dana Ivey
Bo Jackson	Adam LeFevre
Ted Talbot	Paul Geier

Time: the present. Place: Brookville, Ohio.

FORBIDDEN COPY (7). By Percy Granger. October 12, 1981 (world premiere). Director, Mary B. Robinson.

Christine Wasserbecker........ Gina Barnett

HARTFORD STAGE—Joe Sears and Jaston Williams in *Greater Tuna*

Marge Logan .... Janet Zarish
Glen Larson .... Joseph Adams
Alice .... Sylvia Gassell
Renata Goetz .... Dana Ivey
Bill Krogel .... Adam LeFevre
Fritz Phipps .... Paul Geier
    Time: The present. Place: Goshen, Indiana

AM I BLUE (7). By Beth Henley. October 19, 1981 (world premiere). Director, R. Stuart White.
John Polk .... Jeff McCracken
Ashbe Williams .... June Stein

Hilda .... Dana Ivey
    Street People: Ross McKenzie, Diane Mac-
Donald, Pan Riley
    Time: 1968. Place: New Orleans French Quarter.

MOJO (7). By Alice Childress. October 26, 1981 (world premiere). Director, Clay Stevenson.
Teddy .... Howard Rollins
Irene .... Carolyn Lawson
    Time: Fall, 1969. Place: Teddy's apartment.

Hartford Stage: Children's Theater—The Old Place

THE ENORMOUS EGG (11). By Oliver Butterworth; adapted and directed by Mary B. Robinson. November 21, 1981. With David London, Adam LeFevre, Emily Bly, David O. Peterson, Pirie MacDonald.

Hartford Stage: The Old Place—Special

THE GENTLE ART OF MAKING ENEMIES (32). Adapted by Lawrence and Maggie Williams, from Mr. Williams's novel, *I, James McNeill Whistler*. May 22, 1982. Director, Jerome Kilty. With John Cullum.

Designers: scenery, Kevin Rupnik, John Conklin, David Gropman, Ruth A. Wells; lighting, Judy Rasmuson, Pat Collins, William Armstrong, Michael A. Rice; costumes, Linda Fisher, John Conklin, Anne Thaxter Watson.

Note: Amanda Plummer was billed with her middle name, Michael, in *The Wake of Jamey Foster* (see cast above) but omitted it from the billing of her two New York performances this season.

INDIANAPOLIS

Indiana Repertory Theater: Mainstage

(Artistic Director, Tom Haas; producing director, Benjamin Mordecai)

HAMLET (26). By William Shakespeare. October 16, 1981. Director, Tom Haas. With James Sutorius, Edmund Lyndeck, Bella Jarrett, Bernard Kates, Priscilla Lindsay, Scott Wentworth.

A LESSON FROM ALOES (42). By Athol Fugard. November 13, 1981. Director, Edward Cornell. With Bernard Kates, Nancy Franklin, Thomas Martell Brimm.

A CHRISTMAS CAROL (33). By Charles Dickens; adapted and directed by Tom Haas. November 25, 1981. With Scott Wentworth, Frank Raiter, Donn Ruddy, Demian Hostetter.

COMING ATTRACTIONS (27). By Ted Tally. January 8, 1982. Director, Tom Haas; musical director, James Kowal. Music and lyrics by Jack Feldman and Bruce Sussman. With Craig Fuller, Gordan Hedahl, Henry J. Jordan, Priscilla Lindsay, Karen Nelson, Frank Raiter, Rae Randall, James Tasse, Scott Wentworth.

SHE STOOPS TO CONQUER (27). By Oliver Goldsmith. February 12, 1982. Director, William Peters. With Bernard Kates, Bella Jarrett, Priscilla Lindsay, Karen Nelson, Scott

Wentworth, Henry J. Jordan, Christopher Chisholm.

RAIN (30). By W. Somerset Maugham; adapted by John Colton and Clemence Randolph. March 6, 1982. Director, Tom Haas. With Ronee Blakley, David Little, Bernard Kates, Darrie Lawrence.

OPERETTA, MY DEAR WATSON (30). By Tom Haas; music and lyrics by W. S. Gilbert and Arthur Sullivan. April 20, 1982 (world premiere). Director, Tom Haas; musical director-adaptor, Hank Levy; scenery, Tom Lynch; lighting, Robert Jared; costumes, Susan Hilferty.

Mrs. Hudson	Sue Robinson
Dr. John H. Watson	Henry J. Jordan
Sherlock Holmes	Scott Wentworth
Wiggins	Don Wagner
The Prince	Walter Charles
Irene Adler	Sophie Schwab
Nanki Poo	Cris Groenendaal
Lord Chancellor	Frank Raiter
Governess	Bella Jarrett
Lady Rose	Alison Brown
Lady Ida	Bernadette Galanti
Empress of Bohemia	Bernard Kates
Captain of the Pinafore	Donn Ruddy

Time: The late Victorian world. One intermission.

Indiana Repertory Theater: Upper Stage

THE SIEGE OF FRANK SINATRA (12). By Denis Whitburn. January 22, 1982 (American premiere). Director, Ted Weiant; scenery, Bob Barnett; lighting, Stuart Duke, Augie Mericola.

Leo Coote	George Taylor
Ken Ackman	Robert Thaler
June Shaw	Angela Stotler

Time: July 11, 1974. Place: An executive suite on the 22nd floor of the Boulevard Hotel, Sydney, Australia. Act I: 9:30 a.m. Act II: 8:30 p.m.

BILLY BISHOP GOES TO WAR (11). By John Gray with Eric Peterson. February 26, 1982. Director, Ben Cameron. With Robert Burke, Michael Deep.

HOME (22). By Samm-Art Williams. April 8, 1982. Director, Israel Hicks. With Thomas Martell Brimm, Carolyn Lawson, Janet Louise Hubert.

Designers: scenery, Steve Rubin, Bob Barnett, Karen Schulz, Kate Edmunds; lighting, Rachel Budin, Stuart Duke, Frances Aronson, Craig Miller; costumes, Steven Rubin, Michel Yeuell, Susan Hilferty, Leon I. Brauner, William Walker.

KANSAS CITY, MO.

Missouri Repertory Theater: Helen F. Spencer Theater Center

(Producing director, Patricia McIlrath)

THREE SISTERS (16). By Anton Chekhov; translated by Elizaveta Fen. July 9, 1981. Director, Cedric Messina. With Juliet Randall, Cynthia Dozier, Deborah Bremer, Jim Birdsall, Rosemary John, Robert Lewis Karlin, James Robert Daniels.

PICNIC (16). By William Inge. July 30, 1981. Director, Patricia McIlrath. With Elizabeth Ross, James Robert Daniels, Jacquelyn Riggs, Barbara Houston.

THE GOOD PERSON OF SZECHWAN (16). By Bertolt Brecht; translated by Ralph Manheim; acting version by John Reich. August 6, 1981. Director, John Reich. With Richard Halverson, Jim Birdsall, Juliet Randall, Edith Owen.

A CHRISTMAS CAROL (30). By Charles Dickens; adapted by Barbara Field. December 3, 1981. Director, James Assad. With Robert Elliott, Peter Umbras, John Q. Bruce, Jim Birdsall, Piper Carter.

THE ROYAL FAMILY (17). By George S. Kaufman and Edna Ferber. January 28, 1982. Director, Albert Pertalion. With Kevin Paul Hofeditz, Becca Ross, Roberta Wallman, R. L. Smith, Alice White, Richard Gustin.

LOOSE ENDS (15). By Michael Weller. February 4, 1982. Director, Francis J. Cullinan. With Mark Robbins, Becca Ross, Susan Warren, Jim Birdsall, Kay Christ.

CROWN OF THORN (16). By Wendy MacLaughlin. February 16, 1982 (professional premiere). Director, James Assad.

Teilhard de Chardin	Mark Robbins
Father Maurice Vendel	Peter Aylward
Lillian	Glenna Forde
Guigite (Marguerite)	Becca Ross
Charles Banois	R. L. Smith
Father-General	Robert Lewis Karlin
Teilhard as a child	John O'Byrne
Guigite as a child	Laura Schaeffer
Jacques	Bruce Roach
Henri	Steven Passer
Tea Server	Brian Peebles
Nurse	Bickie S. Little

Jesuit Review Board, Questioners: Craig Handel, George Kuhn, Mark A. Klemersrud.

Times and Places: the United States today, and, in recall, the life of Teilhard de Chardin from 1881 to 1955 in France, China, India, Africa, Italy and the U. S. One intermission.

MACBETH (17). By William Shakespeare. February 25, 1982. Director, Norris Houghton. With David Schramm, Alice White, Jim Birdsall, George Kuhn, Kay Christ.

Designers; scenery, Harry Feiner, John Ezell, Carolyn L. Ross, Howard Jones; lighting Susan White, Ruth E. Ludwick, Joseph Appelt, Keri Muir; costumes, Michelle Bechtold, Mariann Verhayen, Vincent Scassellati, Douglas E. Enderle, John Carver Sullivan, Baker S. Smith.

LOS ANGELES

Center Theater Group: Ahmanson Theater

(Artistic director, Robert Fryer)

THE LITTLE FOXES (77). By Lillian Hellman. September 25, 1981. Director, Austin Pendleton. With Elizabeth Taylor, Maureen Stapleton, Robert Lansing, J. D. Cannon, Nicholas Coster.

MORNING'S AT SEVEN (51). By Paul Osborn. December 11, 1981. Director, Vivian Matalon. With Maureen O'Sullivan, Kate Reid, Elizabeth Wilson, Teresa Wright, Russell Nype.

ANOTHER PART OF THE FOREST (51). By Lillian Hellman. February 12, 1982. Director, George Schaefer. With Dorothy McGuire, Richard Dysart, David Dukes, Tovah Feldshuh, Laurence Guittard.

MARK TAPER FORUM, LOS ANGELES—Gerald Hiken as
Brecht and Paul Sorvino as von Horvath in *Tales From Hollywood*

THE HASTY HEART (51). By John Patrick. April 16, 1982. Director, Martin Speer. With Gregory Harrison, Lisa Eichorn, Kurt Russell, Michael Evans.

Designers: scenery, Andrew Jackness, William Ritman, Douglas W. Schmidt, A. Clark Duncan; lighting, Paul Gallo, Richard Nelson, Martin Aronstein; costumes, Florence Klotz, Linda Fisher, Noel Taylor, Madeline Ann Graneto.

Center Theater Group: Mark Taper Forum—Mainstage

(Artistic director, Gordon Davidson)

A LESSON FROM ALOES (54). By Athol Fugard. August 20, 1981. Director, Daniel Petrie. With Peter Donat, Roberta Maxwell, Louis Gossett Jr.

A TALE TOLD (54). By Lanford Wilson. October 22, 1981. Director, Marshall W. Mason. With Trish Hawkins, Helen Stenborg, Fritz Weaver, Timothy Shelton, Richard Holden.

NUMBER OUR DAYS (54). By Suzanne Grossman; based on the book by Barbara Myerhoff; conceived and directed by John Hirsch. January 21, 1982 (world premiere). Musical director/composer, Michael Isaacson.
Faegl Dresner . . . . Frances Bay

1st Skater................. Gordon Haight
2d Skater .... Jason Fitz-Gerald
3d Skater .... Dominic Hoffman
Basha Rubin .... Eda Reiss Merin
Elijah Kravitz .... John Randolph
Bernie Schwartz............... Jack Bernardi
Jacob Benowitz .... Michael Fox
Rachel Mishkin.............. Estefle Omens
Ezra Posner................ Milton Selzer
Esther Reitman .... Sonia Zomina
Bette Milner............... Marti Maraden
Harry Perlman.............. Zachary Berger
Pinje Sosinski.......... Manny Kleinmuntz
D'Vorah Posner................ Erica Yohn
Rabbi Mintz.................. Hale Porter
    Members of the Community: Lillian
Adams, Sam Nudell, Stephen Roberts, Constance Sawyer, Susan Tanner, Oscar Mekler
    Place: Venice, Calif. One intermission.

TALES FROM HOLLYWOOD (54). By Christopher Hampton. March 25, 1982 (world premiere). Director, Gordon Davidson; film segments compiled by Michael Webb.
Odon von Horvath .... Paul Sorvino
Young man;
    Johnny Weissmuller.......... Scott Feraco
Thomas Mann .... David Hooks

Charles Money;
    Leon Feuchtwanger .... Bruce Kirby
Heinrich Mann .... Joseph Maher
Helen Schwartz............ Kathleen Lloyd
Salka Viertel .... Nancy Jeris
Katja Mann............... Gwen Van Dam
Marta Feuchtwanger..... Dinah Anne Rogers
Toni Spuhier .... Donna Fuller
Waiter; Chico Marx;
    Jacob Lomakhin.......... Tony Papenfuss
Nelly Mann .... Linda Carlson
Bertolt Brecht .... Gerald Hiken
Helene Weigel .... Gina Collens
Angel; Greta Garbo .... Jocelyn Jones
Hal; Harpo Marx .... Michael McNeilly
Art Nicely .... Tom Henschel
    Time: 1938–1960. One intermission.

In repertory:
A FLEA IN HER EAR (41). By Georges Feydeau; adapted by Suzanne Grossman and Paxton Whitehead. May 27, 1982. Director, Tom Moore. With James R. Winker, William Schallert, Katherine McGrath, Elizabeth Huddle, Keene Curtis, Rene Auberjonois.
THE MISANTHROPE (30). By Molière; verse translation by Richard Wilbur. June 12, 1982. Director, Diana Maddox. With Rene Auberjonois, Keene Curtis, Madolyn Smith.

Center Theater Group: Mark Taper Forum—New Theater for Now, Aquarius Theater

AMERICAN MOSAIC (19). Adapted by William Storm from the book by Joan Morrison and Charlotte Fox Zabusky. March 23, 1982 (world premiere). Director, Gordon Hunt.
    Cast: Tacwyn Morgan, Rennie Stennett, Michael Blumenthal—Nathan Cook; Bridget Fitzgerald, Pauline Newman—Tandy Cronyn; Maria Nikitin, Vo Thi Tam—Silvana Gallardo; Nguyen Cao Ky, Taro Murat—Soon-Teck Oh; Walter Lindstrom, Cesar Le Clair—Jeffrey Tambor; Riccardo Massoni, Miquel Torres—Michael Tucci; Lydia Orloff, Denise Levertov—Stephanie Zimbalist.
    One intermission.

A SONG FOR A NISEI FISHERMAN (21). By Philip Kan Gotanda. April 14, 1982. Directors, Mako and Shizuko Hoshi. With Mako, Dian Kobayashi, Leigh Kim, Nelson Mashita.

WOZA ALBERT! (24). Conceived by Percy Mtwa, Mbongeni Ngema, Barney Simon. May 4, 1982 (American premiere). Director, Barney Simon. With Percy Mtwa, Mbongeni Ngema.

STILL LIFE (20). Written and directed by Emily Mann. May 27, 1982. With John Spencer, Mary McDonnell, Timothy Near.

Center Theater Group: Mark Taper Forum Lab

(Play developmental program)

JOHNNY BULL (13). By Kathleen Betsko; director, Dana Elcar; November 6, 1981.

A SONG FOR A NISEI FISHERMAN (13). By Philip Kan Gotanda; directors, Mako and Shizuko Hoshi; December 2, 1981.

THREE FOR A FULL MOON and BOCAS (13). By Ntozake Shangé; director, Oz Simmons; choreographer, Michelle Simmons; April 28, 1982.

Center Theater Group: Mark Taper Forum—Christmas Programs

A CHRISTMAS CAROL (20). By Charles Dickens; adapted by Doris Baizley. December 12, 1981. Director, Frank Condon.

HOLIDAY PUDDING (10). Conceived and supervised by Philip Himberg; Composer/arranger, Susan Seamans Harvey; choreographer, Andrea Sherman. December 17, 1981. Stories, songs and dances.

Designers: scenery, Edward Burbridge, John Lee Beatty, Ralph Funicello, Fred Chuang, Tom Lynch, Peter Wexler, Michael Devine, Charles Berliner; lighting, Arden Fingerhut, Dennis Parichy, Martin Aronstein, Fred Chuang, Brian Gale, John Gleason, Tharon Musser, Greg Sullivan, Anna Belle Kaufman; costumes, Laura Crow, Carrie F. Robbins, Sam Kirkpatrick, Terence Tam Soon, Tom Lynch, Csilla Marki, Julie Weiss, Carol Brolaski, Alan Armstrong, Charles Berliner.

LOUISVILLE

Actors' Theater of Louisville: Pamela Brown Auditorium

(Producing director, Jon Jory)

THE THREE MUSKETEERS (32). Adapted by Peter Raby; from the novel by Alexandre Dumas. October 1, 1981. Director, Jon Jory. With Bruce Kuhn, Peggity Price, Dierk Toporzysek, Randle Mell, Patrick Tovatt.

A CHRISTMAS CAROL (27). By Charles Dickens; adapted by Barbara Field. December 3, 1981. Director, Frazier Marsh. With William McNulty, Anthony De Fonte, Brian Tibbs, Randle Mell, Michael Kevin.

THE SPIDER'S WEB (34). By Agatha Christie. December 31, 1981. Director, Adale O'-Brien. With Andy Backer, Ray Fry, Laura Hicks, Adale O'Brien.

TINTYPES (27). Conceived by Mary Kyte with Mel Marvin and Gary Pearle. February 4, 1982. Director, Larry Deckel; musical director, Dan Glosser. With Fred Sanders, Eleanor Reissa, Gail Grate, Tanny McDonald, Erick Devine.

THE INFORMER (8). By Thomas Murphy; based on Liam O'Flahery's book. March 5, 1982.

Director, Jon Jory. With Christopher Cooper, Patrick Tovatt, Sally Fay Reit, Laura Hicks, Michael Kevin.

THE GRAPES OF WRATH (19). By John Steinbeck; adapted and directed by Terrence Shank. March 7, 1982. With Ray Fry, Kathryn Fuller, Daniel Jenkins, Adale O'Brien.

OLDTIMERS GAME (5). By Lee Blessing. March 18, 1982. Director, Patrick Tovatt. With Anthony DeFonte, Ray Fry, Mel Johnson, Ken Latimer (see synopsis in introduction to this section).

BILLY BISHOP GOES TO WAR (27). By John Gray with Eric Peterson. April 8, 1982. Director, Amy Saltz. With Clayton Corzatte, David Colacci.

THE OLDEST LIVING GRADUATE (28). By Preston Jones. May 5, 1982. Director, Ken Jenkins. With Ray Fry, Adale O'Brien, Jeanne Cullen, Andy Backer, Ken Latimer.

Actors' Theater of Louisville: Victor Jory Theater

THE GIFT OF THE MAGI (27). By O. Henry; adaptation, music and lyrics by Peter Ekstrom. December 1, 1981 (world premiere). Director, Larry Deckel; musical director, Peter Ekstrom.

Della . . . . Beverly Lambert
Jim . . . . Peter Boynton
    Time: Christmas Eve 1905. Place: New York City.

Actors' Theater of Louisville: Children's Theater—Pamela Brown Auditorium

SNOW WHITE (10). January 23, 1982. Adapted and directed by Robert Spera. With Apprentice Company.

A MIDSUMMER NIGHT'S DREAM (13). By William Shakespeare. October 10, 1981. Director, Larry Deckel. With Apprentice Company.

Actors' Theater of Louisville: New Plays Program

(Monologues, short shorts and one-act plays presented in both theaters, November 5–29, 1981 and February 24–April 4, 1982)

Monologues by Jane Martin, Larry Atlas, Jim Beaver, Dare Clubb, Isabell Monk, Ken Jenkins, Trish Johnson, Robert Schenkkan. SAINT OF THE DAY by Judy Romberger; THE NEW GIRL by Vaughn McBride; DAMN EVERYTHING BUT THE CIRCUS by Terri Wagener; CLARA'S PLAY by John Olive; director, Patrick Tovatt. GUN FOR THE ROSES, book by Patrick Tovatt, music and lyrics by Jim Wann, director, Ken Jenkins; PRIVATE SHOWING by Jeffrey Sweet, director Bekki Jo Schneider; IN BETWEEN TIME by Ara Watson, director, Adale O'Brien; MERRY-GO-ROUND by Wendy Kesselman, director, Adale O'Brien; EYE OF THE BEHOLDER by Kent Broadhurst, director, Larry Deckel; A PALE LION by Michael Neville, director, Ray Fry; WASH, RINSE, SPIN DRY by Richard Whelan, director, Larry Deckel; INTERMISSION by Robert Schenkkan, director, Frazier Marsh; A DIFFERENT MOON by Ara Watson, director, Sam Blackwell; FULL HOOKUP by Conrad Bishop and Elizabeth Fuller, director, Jon Jory. Also TALKING WITH, 11 monologues by Jane Martin (see synopsis in the introduction to this section).

Designers: scenery, Paul Owen, Joseph A. Varga, Richard Wilcox, Grady Larkins; lighting, Jeff Hill, Karl Haas, Phillipa Gordon, Diana S. Cain; costumes, Kurt Wilhelm, Jess Goldstein, Phillipa A. Gordon.

MADISON, N.J.

New Jersey Shakespeare Festival: Drew University

(Artistic director, Paul Barry; producing director, Ellen Barry)

ROMEO AND JULIET (29). By William Shakespeare. June 23, 1981. Director, Paul Barry. With Denise Bessette, Scott Walters, Patrick Beatey, Victoria Boothby, Ronald Martell, Stephen McNaughton.

CYMBELINE (24). By William Shakespeare. July 7, 1981. Director, Paul Barry. With Richard M. Davidson, Chris Weatherhead, Peter Burnell, Bob Ari, Geddeth Smith, Eric Tavaris.

TARTUFFE (24). By Molière. August 4, 1981. Director, Paul Barry. With Clarence Felder, Eric Tavaris, Geddeth Smith, Chris Weatherhead.

THE ENTERTAINER (24). By John Osborne. September 22, 1981. Director, Ronald Martell. With Paul Barry, Faith Catlin, David S. Howard, Mary Hara, Curtis Armstrong.

DA (24). By Hugh Leonard. October 20, 1981. Director, Paul Barry. With David S. Howard, Kenneth Gray, Mary Hara, Casey Childs, Curtis Armstrong, Geddeth Smith.

VANITIES (24). By Jack Heifner. November 17, 1981. Director, Alex Dmitriev. With Ellen Barry, Laura Mirsky, Susanne Marley.

Designers: scenery, Peter Harrison; lighting, Richard Dorfman; costumes, Erica Hollmann, Alice S. Hughes.

MILWAUKEE

Milwaukee Repertory Theater: Todd Wehr Theater—Mainstage

(Artistic director, John Dillon; managing director, Sara O'Connor)

FRIDAYS (46). By Andrew Johns. September 11, 1981 (world premiere). Director, John Dillon.
Holly Crawford .... Victor Raider-Wexler
George Herrick .... Larry Shue
Chuck Hart .... William Leach
Douglas Herrick .... Eric Hill
Gail Herrick .... Ellen Lauren
Miss Strong .... Jane Gabbert-Wilson
Place: The basement of George's house. Act I: A Friday night. Act II, Scene 1: A Friday night the following week. Scene 2: A Friday night two weeks later.

HAVE YOU ANYTHING TO DECLARE? (46). By M. A. Hennequin and P. Veber. October 23, 1981 (American premiere). Director, Braham Murray.

Lise Dupont . . . . Rhonda Aldrich
Gontran de Barbettes . . . . Eric Hill
Ernestine . . . . Rose Pickering
La Baule . . . . James Pickering
Adelaid Dupont . . . . Dilys Hamlett
Benjamin Dupont . . . . Kurt Knudson
Phillipe Couzan . . . . Henry Strozier
Frontignac . . . . Victor Raider-Wexler
Oaykette de Trivelin . . . . Ellen Lauren
Vicomte Robert de Trivelin . . . . . Larry Shue
Zeze . . . . Sheila Dabney
Mariette, her maid . . . . Rose Pickering
Prize Winner . . . . William Leach
Police Commissioner . . . . John Engman
Policeman . . . . Richard J. Weber

Act I: The residence Dupont, evening. Act II: Two days later, the studio, afternoon. Act III: The residence Dupont, one hour later.

BOESMAN AND LENA (46). By Athol Fugard. December 4, 1981. Director, Sharon Ott. With Delroy Lindo, L. Scott Caldwell, Sam Singleton.

KINGDOM COME (46). By Amlin Gray; based on O. E. Rolvaag's *Giants in the Earth* and other sources. January 15, 1982 (world premiere). Directors, John Dillon, Sharon Ott.

Ellefstolen Harstad . . . . James Pickering
Paal; Ship Captain . . . . Eric Hill
Parson Dagsrood . . . . Henry Strozier
Gro Endressen . . . . Rose Pickering
Ola Endressen . . . . Alan Brooks
Jens Falck . . . . Michael Patterson
Thomas Falck . . . . John Gamber
Kaja Ansen . . . . Ellen Lauren
Kai Ansen . . . . Daniel Mooney
Simen; Morton Kroll . . . . William Leach
Fredrik Selmer . . . . Jonathan Smoots

Time: The middle of the 19th century. Place: Norway and the New World. One intermission.

BORN YESTERDAY (46). By Garson Kanin. March 5, 1982. Director, Robert Goodman. With Ellen Lauren, Henry Strozier, James Pickering.

SECRET INJURY, SECRET REVENGE (46). By Calderon de La Barca; adapted by Amlin Gray; translated by Laura E. Haughton. April 16, 1982. Director, Rene Buch. With James Pickering, Rose Pickering, Eric Hill, William Leach, Alan Brooks.

Milwaukee Repertory Theater: Pabst Theater

A CHRISTMAS CAROL (25). By Charles Dickens; adapted by Nagle Jackson. December 2, 1981. Director, Nick Faust. With Henry Strozier, James Pickering, Rose Pickering, Daniel R. Poppert, Larry Shue.

Designers: scenery, Elmon Webb and Virginia Dancy, Laura Mauer, Tim Thomas, Christopher Idoine; lighting, Arden Fingerhut, Spenser Mosse, Rachel Budin; costumes, Colleen Muscha, Linda Fisher, Jay Barrett Densmore, Elizabeth Covey.

Milwaukee Repertory Theater: New Works In Progress—Court Street Theater

(Staged readings received 3 performances; full productions received 17 performances)

THE FALL GUY (17). By Linda Aronson; March 4, 1982.
COUNTERTALK and TODAY'S SPECIAL (3). By Andrew Johns; March 26, 1982.
UNTITLED (3). By Larry Shue; April 2, 1982.
AT FIFTY SHE DISCOVERED THE SEA (17). By Denise Chalem; DINAH WASHINGTON IS DEAD (17) By Kermit Frazier. April 8, 1982.
THE OEDIPUS PROJECT (3). Narration and mime by Daniel Stein. April 30, 1982.

MINNEAPOLIS

The Cricket Theater: Hennepin Center for the Arts: Mainstage

(Artistic director, Lou Salerni; managing director, Cynthia Mayeda)

THE GIN GAME (21). By D. L. Coburn. October 14, 1981. Director, Lou Salerni. With Patricia Fraser, Warren Frost.

TINTYPES (21). Conceived by Mary Kyte with Mel Marvin and Gary Pearle. November 25, 1981. Director/choreographer, Lewis Whitlock. With Richard K. Allison, Susan Long, Christopher Bloch, Molly Sue McDonald, Louise Robinson, Christopher Drobny.

BETRAYAL (21). By Harold Pinter. January 6, 1982. Director, Lou Salerni. With Camille Gifford, Allen Hamilton, James J. Lawless.

CHILDE BYRON (21). By Romulus Linney. February 17, 1982. Director, Steve Pearson. With Robert Mailand, Allison Giglio.

TRUE WEST (21). By Sam Shepard. March 31, 1982. Director, Lou Salerni. With Stephen D'Ambrose, Robert Breuler, James J. Lawless, Naomi Hatfield.

DEAR RUTH (21). By Norman Krasna. May 12, 1982. Director, Robert Moss. With Louise Goetz, Lawrence S. Wechsler, Carole Kastigar, James J. Lawless.

Designers: scenery, Vera Polovko-Mednikov, Jerry R. Williams; lighting, Michael Vennerstrom, Lisa Johnson; costumes, Vera Polovko-Mednikov, Jerry R. Williams, Colin Tugwell, James Berton Harris.

The Cricket Theater: Works-in-Progress

(Artistic Director, Sean Michael Dowse. One performance each, workshop premieres)

A LONELY HOUSE. Poetry of Robert Frost, arranged by Monroe E. Denton; January 24, 1982.
RENOVATIONS by Charles Goll; April 11, 1982.

ALEXANDER ON THE WATER by John Orlock; April 13, 1982.
MIRACLE GARDENING by Marisha Chamberlain; May 26, 1982.
All directed by Sean Michael Dowse and with members of the regular company.

The Guthrie Theater

(Artistic director, Liviu Ciulei; managing director, Donald Schoenbaum; associate artistic director, Garland Wright)

THE TEMPEST (33). By William Shakespeare. June 11, 1981. Director, Liviu Ciulei. With Ken Ruta, John Seitz, Jan Triska, Francois de la Giroday, Frances Conroy, Boyd Gaines.

DON JUAN (33). By Molière; translated by Donald Frame. June 13, 1981. Director, Richard Foreman. With Roy Brocksmith, Frances Conroy, Fred Melamed, Robert Nadir, Peter Thoemke.

OUR TOWN (53). By Thornton Wilder. July 11, 1981. Director, Alan Schneider. With Ken Ruta, Boyd Gaines, Keliher Walsh, John E. Straub, Peggy Schoditsch, William Newman, Catherine Burns.

FOXFIRE (43). By Susan Cooper and Hume Cronyn; based on the Foxfire books edited by Eliot Wigginton and his students. September 5, 1981 (U. S. premiere). Director, Marshall W. Mason; music, Jonathan Holtzman; lyrics, Susan Cooper, Hume Cronyn, Jonathan Holtzman; music director, Jeff Steitzer.
Annie Nations . . . . Jessica Tandy
Hector Nations . . . . Hume Cronyn
Prinz Carpenter . . . . William Newman
Holly Burrell . . . . Katherine Cortez

Dillard Nations . . . . Richard Cox
Doctor . . . . Oliver Cliff.
One intermission.

EVE OF RETIREMENT (15). By Thomas Bernhard; translated by Gitta Honegger. September 24, 1981 (American premiere). Director, Liviu Ciulei.
Rudolf Hoeller; Chief Justice;
Former SS officer . . . . Donald Madden
Clara . . . . Catherine Burns
Vera . . . . Betty Miller
Time: the present. Place: A town in West Germany, the house of the Hoeller family. Act I: Late afternoon on October 7, Himmler's birthday. Act II: Two hours later.

ELI (12). By Nelly Sachs; translated by Christopher Holme. September 26, 1981 (American premiere). Director, Garland Wright.
Washerwoman; Old Woman . Carol Rosenfeld
Shoemaker's wife;
Baker Woman . . . . Mim Solberg
Samuel . . . . Oliver Cliff
Bricklayer; Rabbi; Band Leader;
Shoemaker . . . . Alan Woodward
Jossele . . . . Ryan Sexton

GUTHRIE THEATER, MINNEAPOLIS—Betty Miller,
Catherine Burns and Donald Madden in *Eve of Retirement*

Ester Weinberg; Blind Girl;
    Farmer's Wife............ Kristine Nielsen
Older girl; Woman .... Keliher Walsh
Younger girl............... Elena Giannetti
Boy...................... Lance Thoemke
Michael...................... Jan Triska
Mendel; Baker............. Richard Hilder
Man; Killer .... Lawrence Overmire
Woman With Child;
    Mother................ Peggy Schoditsch
Hunchback; Postman .... Peter Thoemke
Man With Looking Glass;
    Professor .... John Patrick Martin

Dajan; Hersch .... John Lewin
Carpenter; Doctor............. Paul Laakso
Old Man................ William Newman
Farmer..................... Robert Nadir
Farmer's Child.............. Stacy Forster
    Time: After Martyrdom. Place: On both sides
of the frontier.

A CHRISTMAS CAROL (45). By Charles
Dickens; adapted by Barbara Field. November
25, 1981. Director Jon Cranney. With Richard
Hilger, Oliver Cliff, J. Patrick Martin, Peggy
Schoditsch, Peter Thoemke, Marshall Gordon,
Gregory Leifeld.

CANDIDE (32). By Voltaire; adapted by Len Jenkin. January 9, 1982. Director, Garland Wright. With Michael Butler, Kristine Nielsen, Richard Ooms, Dale Soules.

AS YOU LIKE IT (41). By William Shakespeare. February 27, 1982. Director, Liviu Ciulei. With Patti LuPone, David Warrilow, Ken Ruta, Roy Brocksmith, Jody Catlin, Val Kilmer.

Designers; scenery, Liviu Ciulei, Richard Foreman, Karl Eigsti, Jack Barkla, John Arnone, Santo Loquasto; lighting, Duane Schuler, Richard Ridell, Karlis Ozals, Craig Miller, Jennifer Tipton; costumes, Jack Edwards, Patricia Zipprodt; Marjorie Slaiman, Jack Edwards, Kurt Wilhelm, Santo Loquasto.

NEW HAVEN

Long Wharf Theater: Mainstage

(Artistic director, Arvin Brown; executive director, M. Edgar Rosenblum)

JOE EGG (41). By Peter Nichols. October 22, 1981. Director, Arvin Brown. With Stockard Channing, Richard Dreyfuss, Tenney Walsh.

A VIEW FROM THE BRIDGE (34). By Arthur Miller. December 3, 1981. Director, Arvin Brown. With Tony LoBianco, Cathryn Damon, Saundra Santiago, James Hayden, William Swetland.

THE WORKROOM (L'Atelier) (41). By Jean-Claude Grumberg; translated by Tom Kempinski. January 14, 1982. Director, Nancy Meckler. With Tanya Berezin, Jane Cronin, Christine Estabrook, Gerald Hiken, Marcia Jean Kurtz.

THE DOCTOR'S DILEMMA (41). By George Bernard Shaw. February 25, 1982. Director, Kenneth Frankel. With Emery Battis, Harris Yulin, Richard Russell Ramos, John Glover, Ellen Parker.

ETHAN FROME (31). By Edith Wharton; adapted by Owen and Donald Davis. April 8, 1982. With Jon DeVries, Frances Conroy, Valerie Mahaffey.

THE FRONT PAGE (47). By Ben Hecht and Charles MacArthur. May 20, 1982. Director, Harris Yulin. With Bruce Davison, Brian Dennehy, Lois Smith, Jake Dengel, Dick O'-Neill.

Long Wharf Theater: Stage II

THIS STORY OF YOURS (116). By John Hopkins. October 13, 1981 (American premiere). Director, John Tillinger.
Det.-Sgt. John Johnson...... John McMartin
Maureen Johnson .... Joyce Ebert
Capt. Cartwright............... John Seitz
Kenneth Baxter................ J. T. Walsh
Det.-Sgt. Jessard .... Ray Horvath
Officers ...... Paul F. Ugalde, Robert Caserta
Act I: 2:30 in the morning. Act II: Later that morning. Act III: The night before.

LAKEBOAT (36). By David Mamet. February 2, 1982. Director, John Dillon. With Donald Chianese, Walter Atamaniuk, David Marshall Grant, Larry Shue, Clarence Felder.

THE CARMONE BROTHERS ITALIAN FOOD PRODUCTS CORP'S ANNUAL PASTA PAGEANT (36). By Tom Griffin. March 30, 1982 (world premiere). Director, William Ludel.
Doober .... Robert Harper
Roxanne................. Gretchen Corbett
Slimy.................... Jeffrey De Munn
Artie...................... John Spencer
Walter.................... Sloane Shelton
Time: The present. October. Place: Artie and Roxanne's home in a medium-sized Northeastern industrial city. One intermission.

Designers: scenery, David Jenkins, Steven Rubin, Laura Maurer, Marjorie Bradley Kellogg, John Jensen, Hugh Landwehr; lighting, Judy Rasmuson, Ronald Wallace, Geoffrey T. Cunningham, Jamie Gallagher; costumes, Carol Oditz, Bill Walker, Rachel Kurland, Ann Roth, Linda Fisher.

Yale Repertory Theater

(Artistic director, Lloyd Richards; managing director, Edward A. Martenson)

UNCLE VANYA (21). By Anton Chekhov; translated by Constance Garnett. October 9, 1981. Director, Lloyd Richards. With Lee Wallace, Harris Yulin, Melissa Smith, Glenn Close, William Swetland.

MRS. WARREN'S PROFESSION (21). By George Bernard Shaw. November 6, 1981. Director, Stephen Porter. With Barbara Baxley, Frances McDorman, Thomas A. Carlin, Robert Brown, Richard Woods.

RIP VAN WINKLE (21). By Richard Nelson. December 4, 1981. Director, David Jones. With Seth Allen, Laura Esterman, Garry Bamman, Alan Rosenberg.

FLASH FLOODS (12). By Dare Clubb. January 19, 1982 (world premiere). Director, Dennis Scott.
Yvette Broken Neck Krieger . . Cecilia Rubino
Melvin Baker . . . . Vytautas Ruginis
Mike Broken Neck . . . . Ricky Grove
Harmon Stetler . . . . John Seitz
Helena Stetler . . . . Kim Beaty
    Time: Now. Place: Hamilton, Montana. Act I, 13 Scenes: Act II, 11 Scenes.

THE MAN WHO COULD SEE THROUGH TIME (12). By Terri Wagener. January 20, 1982 (world premiere). Director, David Hammond.
Professor Mordecai Bates . . . . . Theodore Sorel
Ellan Brock . . . . Jane Kaczmarek
    Time: The future. Place: A lecture hall; an attic studio. Act I: Three scenes. Act II: Four scenes.

GOING OVER (10). By Stuart Browne. January 21, 1982 (world premiere). Director, Jim Peskin.
Albert Prosser . . . . James Green
Allun Prosser . . . . Gary Basaraba
Gwen Prosser . . . . Paddy Croft
Gareth Evans . . . . Jon Krupp
Archie Lumm . . . . John Lloyd
Sarge . . . . William Mesnik
    The play takes place in two interwoven time periods. The first is in 1916 during the days preceding the first attack of the battle of the Somme, July 1. The second is in 1966, a village in South Wales, on the day before and the day of the 50-year celebration of the return of the valley war hero.

BEEF, NO CHICKEN (11). By Derek Walcott. January 22, 1982 (world premiere). Director, Walton Jones.
Suminatra . . . . Elly Koslo
Otto Hogan . . . . Norman Matlock
Euphony . . . . Barbara Montgomery
The Limer . . . . Sullivan Walker
Eldridge Franco . . . . Leon Morenzie
Drusilla Douglas . . . . Angela Bassett
Cedric Hart . . . . Herb Downer
Bandits . . . . . . D. A. Green, Michael C. Night
Hernando Cadiz . . . . Clark Morgan
Mitzi Almandoz . . . . Mary Louise
Mr. Mongroo . . . . Charles S. Dutton
Mr. La-Fook . . . . William Kux
Alwyn Davies . . . . Gilbert Lewis
The Deacon . . . . Keith Grant
    Time: The present. Place: Couva, a small town in central Trinidad. One intermission.

'MASTER HAROLD' . . . and the boys (21). By Athol Fugard. March 12, 1982 (world premiere). Director, Athol Fugard.
Sam . . . . Zakes Mokae
William . . . . Danny Glover
Hally . . . . Zeljko Ivanek
    Time: 1950. Place: St. Georges Park Tea Room on a wet and windy afternoon in Port Elizabeth, South Africa.

JOHNNY BULL (21). By Kathleen Betsko. April 9, 1982 (world premiere). Director, Lloyd Richards.
Iris Malenko . . . . Anna Levine
Marie Malenko . . . . Suzanne Shepherd
Katrine Malenko . . . . Rikke Borge
Stephan Malenko . . . . Jamie Schmitt
Joe Malenko . . . . Kevin Geer
    Time: Early Autumn, 1959, a period of severe economic recession in this region of the United States. Place: Willard Patch, a tiny coal mining hamlet in the Monongahela Valley in Pennsylvania. One intermission.

LOVE'S LABOUR'S LOST (21). By William Shakespeare. May 7, 1982. Director, Mladen Kiselov. With Keith Grant, John Lloyd, Daniel Benzall, Jane Kaczmarek, Kate Burton, Warren David Keith.

Designers: scenery, Michael H. Yeargan, Alison Ford, Douglas O. Stein, Ricardo Marin, Andrew Rubenoff, Jane Clark, Joel Fontaine, Tony Straiges; lighting, David Noling, Timothy J. Hunter, Jennifer Tipton, William B. Warfel, Stephen Strawbridge; costumes, Dunya Ramicova, Jane Clark, Gene K. Lakin, Quina Fonesca, Wing Lee, Catharine Zufer, Sheila McLamb.

PHILADELPHIA

Philadelphia Drama Guild: Zellerbach Theater—Annenberg Center

(Managing producer, Gregory Poggi)

OF MICE AND MEN (22). By John Steinbeck. October 15, 1981. Director, Kurt Reis. With Kent Broadhurst, Mike Starr, Gordon Clapp, Diane Lasko.

GEMINI (22). By Albert Innaurato. November 19, 1981. Director, Jerry Zaks. With Ron Fassler, Janice Fuller, John LaGioia.

DEAR DADDY (22). By Denis Cannan. January 14, 1982 (American professional premiere). Director, William Woodman; scenery, Eldon Elder; lighting, F. Mitchell Dana; costumes, Patricia Adshead.
Bernard.................... Joseph Maher
Mary, his second wife........ Jo Henderson
Gillian, his daughter........... Ellen Parker
Billy, his elder son .... Jack Gilpin

Frank, his solicitor .... John Leighton
Charles, his younger son ...... Robert Burns
Gwen, Charles' girl.......... Jessica Drake
Delia, Bernard's first wife... Pauline Flanagan
Time: The present. Place: The living room of Bernard's house, south of London. Act I: Late morning. Act II: Mid-afternoon.

SERVANT OF TWO MASTERS (22). By Carlo Goldoni; adapted by Tom Cone. February 25, 1982. Director, Andre Ernotte; musical staging, Theodore Pappas. With Munson Hicks, Denny Dillon, Carole Monferdini, Robert Lovitz.

THE CONTEST (22). By Shirley Lauro. April 22, 1982. Director, Jerry Zaks. With Melanie Wells, Estelle Omens, George Axler, Georgia Southcotte.

Designers: scenery, Patricia Woodbridge, Chris Nowak, John Conklin; lighting Jane Reisman, Ann Wrightson, Pat Collins; costumes, Linda Fisher, Ernest Allen Smith, Susan Tsu, Jennifer Von Mayrhauser.

PORTLAND, ME.

Portland Stage Company

(Producing director, Barbara Rosoff; general manager, Patricia Egan).

THE GLASS MENAGERIE (25). By Tennessee Williams. November 5, 1981. Director, Patricia Carmichael. With John Griesemer, Anna Minot, Faith Catlin, Derek Hoxby.

ALTERATIONS (20). By Leigh Curran. December 4, 1981 (world premiere). Director, Barbara Rosoff; scenery and costumes, Leslie Taylor; lighting, Dale Jordan.
Biesel .... Mimi Weddell
Erica........................ Jean DeBaer
Adrianna .... Joanne Camp
Phoebe .... Kate Purwin
Peter................... David Rosenbaum
Place: The Dougall apartment in Greenwich Village. Act I: Early June, late afternoon. Act II: Immediately following.

PRIVATE LIVES (27). By Noel Coward. January 1, 1982. Director, Edward Herrmann. With Leslie Dalton, Michael J. Hume, Alexander Spencer, Chris Weatherhead.

THE SEA HORSE (25). By Edward J. Moore. January 29, 1982. Director, Gordon Edelstein. With Eric Conger, Judith Drake.

THE DEATH OF A MINER (26). By Paula Cizmar. February 26, 1982 (world premiere). Director, Barbara Rosoff; scenery, Leslie Taylor; lighting, Arden Fingerhut; costumes, Heidi Hollmann.
Mary Alice.............. Mary McDonnell
Jack...................... Cotter Smith
Sallie............... Sarah Jessica Parker/
                         Margaret MacLeod
Winona.................... Kristin Jolliff
Pete...................... Dave Florek
Chester.................. John Griesemer
Bonnie Jean .... Shaw Purnell
Barney .... Ritch Brinkley
Dale .... Douglas Gower
Joseph.................... Steven Loring.
Time: The present. Place: A coal-mining town in Appalachia. One intermission.

PORTLAND STAGE COMPANY—Cotter Smith
and Mary McDonnell in *The Death of a Miner*

Designers: scenery, John Döepp, Leslie Taylor; lighting, John Döepp, Dale Jordan, Gregg Marriner, Arden Fingerhut; costumes, Rachel Kurland, Leslie Taylor, Heidi Hollmann, Ellen McCartney.

PRINCETON, N.J.

McCarter Theater Company: McCarter Theater—Mainstage

(Artistic director, Nagle Jackson)

JUST BETWEEN OURSELVES (14). By Alan Ayckbourn. September 30, 1981 (American premiere). Director, Nagle Jackson.

Dennis	Herb Foster
Vera	Peggy Cowles
Neil	Robert Lanchester
Marjorie	Joan White
Pam	Jill Tanner

Time: The present. Place: The garage and patio of Dennis's home. Act I, Scene 1: February, Saturday around noon. Scene 2: May, Saturday afternoon. Act II, Scene 1: October, Saturday evening. Scene 2: January, Saturday morning.

THE NIGHT OF THE IGUANA (14). By Tennessee Williams. October 28, 1981. Director, William Ludel. With Kevin Tighe, Kelly Bishop, Penelope Reed, Jay Doyle.

A CHRISTMAS CAROL (14). by Charles Dickens; adapted and directed by Nagle Jackson; music by Larry Delinger; musical staging by Nancy Thiel. November 28, 1981. With Herb Foster, Gerald Lancaster, Jay Doyle, Liz Fillo, Jonathan Holub.

KEYSTONE (14). Book and lyrics by John McKellar and Dion McGregor; music by Lance Mulcahy. January 13, 1982. Director, Nagle Jackson; musical director, Rick Jensen; choreographer, Douglas Norwick. With John Sloman, Randy Graff, Douglas Walker, Kim Morgan, Tommy Breslin.

IPHIGENIA AT AULIS (14). By Euripides; translated by W. S. Merwin and George E. Dimock Jr. February 24, 1982 (American premiere), Director, Spyros A. Evangelatos; scenery and costumes, Giorgos Patsas; lighting,

Frances Aronson; music, Stephanos Gazou-
leas.

Agamemnon................. Tom Klunis
Old Servant .... William Denis
Menelaos .... Neil Vipond
1st Messenger .... Robert Lanchester
1st Attendant.......... Stephen Oates Smith
2d Attendant.............. Dale M. Ducko
Clytemnestra .... Holly Barron
Orestes ... Bradford J. Morith/Michael Tesser

Iphigenia .... Monique Fowler
Achilles....................... Drew Keil
2d Messenger................. Tom Hewitt

ARMS AND THE MAN (14). By George Ber-
nard Shaw. March 24, 1982. Director, Nagle
Jackson. With Gordana Rashovich, Margaret
Hilton, Penelope Reed, Robin Chadwick, Jay
Doyle, Greg Thornton.

McCarter Theater Company: Stage Two

THE OVERLAND ROOMS (14) By Richard
Hobson. January 19, 1982 (workshop premiere).
Director, Robert Lanchester; musical arrangers
and directors, Richard Hobson, Bob Jewett.
Granada Wells.............. Anne Sheldon
Howard .... Greg Thornton

Baby...................... Susan Jordan
Sawdust Kelly .... Karl Light
Singer................... Zivia Flomenhaft
    Time: An early spring afternoon in the mid-
1960s. Place: Two rooms over a bowling alley in
a small town in the Northwest. One intermission.

Designers: scenery, Daniel Boyland, Brian Martin, Desmond Heeley, Lisa Martin Cameron; lighting Frances Aronson, Sean Murphy, F. Mitchell Dana, Lowell Achziger, Don Ehman; costumes,
Nanzi Adzima, Elizabeth Covey, Desmond Heeley, Susan Rheume.

PROVIDENCE, R.I.

Trinity Square Repertory Company

(Director, Adrian Hall)

Summer Rep:

THE ELEPHANT MAN (28). By Bernard
Pomerance. June 12, 1981. Director, Peter
Gerety. With Richard Kavanaugh, Richard
Jenkins, Ed Hall, Anne Scurria.

TALLEY'S FOLLY (28). By Lanford Wilson.
July 10, 1981. Director, Melanie Jones. With
Richard Kneeland, Amy Van Nostrand.

OF MICE AND MEN (15). By John Stein-
beck. September 8, 1981. Director, Adrian
Hall. With Richard Jenkins, Keith Jochim, Amy
Van Nostrand.

BURIED CHILD (12). By Sam Shepard. September 12, 1981. Director, Adrian Hall. With
Ford Rainey, Betty Moore, Richard Kneeland.

Trinity Square Repertory Company: Upstairs Theater

L'ATELIER (The Workroom) (36). By Jean-
Claude Grumberg; translated by Marion
Simon and Philip Minor. October 16, 1981. Di-
rector, Philip Minor. With Barbara Orson,
Cynthia Carle, Melanie Jones, Barbara Blos-
som, George Martin.

A CHRISTMAS CAROL (41). By Charles
Dickens; adapted by Adrian Hall and Richard
Cumming. December 1, 1981. Director, Melanie
Jones. With George Martin, Richard Jenkins,
Ruth Maynard, Sean Reilly/Neil Hardwicke.

A FLEA IN HER EAR (41). By Georges
Feydeau. January 22, 1982. Director, George

Martin. With Richard Jenkins, Richard Ferrone, Margot Dionne, Amy Van Nostrand, Richard Kneeland.

DEAD SOULS (35). By Nikolai Gogol; adapted
and translated by Tom Cole. March 26, 1982.
Director, Adrian Hall. With Richard Jenkins,
Richard Kneeland, Richard Ferrone, Richard
Cumming, Barbara Orson, Keith Jochim, Timo-
thy Crowe.

THE 5TH OF JULY (36). By Lanford Wilson. May 7, 1982. Director, Philip Minor. With
Timothy Daly, Timothy Crowe, Anne Scurria.

Trinity Square Repertory Company: Downstairs Theater

THE GIN GAME (44). By D. L. Coburn. December 6, 1981. Director, Philip Minor. With Margaret Phillips, Conrad McLaren.

A LESSON FROM ALOES (51). By Athol Fugard. January 2, 1982. Director, Suzanne Shepherd. With Ed Hall, Richard Kavanaugh, April Shawhan.

THE HOTHOUSE (55). By Harold Pinter. February 26, 1982 (American premiere). Director, Adrian Hall; scenery and lighting, Eugene Lee; costumes, William Lane.

Roote .... George Martin
Gibbs .... Richard Kavanaugh
Lamb .... Dan Butler

Miss Cutts .... Amy Van Nostrand
Lush .... Peter Gerety
Tubb .... Howard London
Lobb .... David C. Jones

Act I: Christmas morning. Act II: Christmas night. The action ranges back and forth from Roote's office, the sitting room, the soundproof room, hallways and stairways throughout the Institution; and finally to the Ministry in London and back.

TRUE WEST (36). By Sam Shepard. April 30, 1982. Director, David Wheeler. With Richard Jenkins, Keith Jochim, Ed Hall, Ruth Maynard.

Designers: Scenery, Eugene Lee, Robert D. Soule; lighting, Eugene Lee, John F. Custer; costumes, William Lane. Composer-in-residence and musical director, Richard Cumming.

Note: Trinity Square Repertory Company presented *The Flying Karamazov Brothers* (30), during the Summer Rep, August 7, 1981. *Of Mice and Men* and *Buried Child* toured India and Syria for five weeks during 1981. High school students continued to be present at special 10:30 A.M. performances of the regular season's productions as part of the school's curriculum.

RICHMOND, VA.

Virginia Museum Theater: Mainstage

(Artistic director, Tom Markus; managing director, Ira Schlosser)

COUNT DRACULA (27). By Ted Tiller; based on Bram Stoker's novel. September 25, 1981. Director, Tom Markus. With Peter D. Umbras, Margery Murray, Jean Sincere, Robert Walsh.

TINTYPES (27). Conceived by Mary Kyte with Mel Marvin and Gary Pearle. November 6, 1981. Director, Darwin Knight; musical director, Robert J. Bruyn. With Wendy-Jo Belcher, Catherine Gaines, Olivia Virgil Harper, James LeVaggi.

A CHRISTMAS CAROL (27). By Charles Dickens; adapted by Tom Markus. December 4,

1981. With Donald Christopher, Walter Williamson, John Winn III.

TALLEY'S FOLLY (27). By Lanford Wilson. January 22, 1982. Director, Terry Burgler.

THE FATHER (27). By August Strindberg; adapted by Tom Markus. February 19, 1982. With Walter Rhodes, Jane Moore.

CANDIDE (27). Book by Hugh Wheeler; music by Leonard Bernstein. April 2, 1982. Director, Darwin Knight. With Richard Kintner, Todd Taylor, Valerie Toth.

Virginia Museum Theater: Studio Theater

MOVE (10). By Margaret Mitchell Dukore. October 23, 1981 (world premiere). Director, Tom Markus. With Donald Gantry, Marilyn McIntyre, Elizabeth Perry.

Time: Now. Place: California. One intermission.

JUST ACROSS THE BORDER (12). By Robert Potter. March 19, 1982 world premiere). Director, Tom Markus.

Kris .... Sherry Skinner

Ashby .... Geddeth Smith
Hector .... Francisco Prado
Mrs. Piltz.................. Anne Sheldon

Time: Now. Place: Playa de la Frontera, Baja California, Norte, Mexico.

NEVER THE TWAIN (10). By Bertolt Brecht and Rudyard Kipling; compiled by John Willett; music by Weill, Eisler, Dessau, Cobb, Dalby, Druce and others; additional music by Raphael Crystal. January 8, 1982 (American pre-

MEADOW BROOK THEATER, ROCHESTER, MICH.—Wil Love, Jody Broad, Barbara Berge, Randall Forte and Carl Schurr in *End of Ramadan*

miere) Director, Wal Cherry; musical director, Raphael Crystal. With Gary Brubach, Ted Pejovich, Ian Stuart, Henrietta Valor. One intermission.

ROCHESTER, MICH.

Oakland University Professional Theater Program: Meadow Brook Theater

(Artistic director, Terence Kilburn; production manager, John Walker)

OTHELLO (28). By William Shakespeare. October 8, 1981. Director, Arif Hasnain. With Richard Jamieson, Clayton Corbin, Yolanda Lloyd, Nancy Linehan.

ON GOLDEN POND (28). By Ernest Thompson. November 5, 1981. Director, Terence Kilburn. With Harry Ellerbe, Anne Shropshire, Nancy Linehan, Spencer Cox.

HAY FEVER (28). By Noel Coward. December 3, 1981. Director, Terence Kilburn. With Jeanne Arnold, George Gitto, Fredi Olster, Beth Taylor, Lee Toombs.

A VIEW FROM THE BRIDGE (28). By Arthur Miller. December 31, 1981. Director, John Ulmer. With Stephen Daley, Gretchen Lord, Victor Slezak, Colleen Smith-Wallnau.

END OF RAMADAN (28). By Charles Nolte. January 28, 1982 (world premiere). Director, Terence Kilburn.

Max Murray	Carl Schurr
Acrim	Randall Forte
Finley	Wil Love
Pamela	Jody Broad
Phyllis Murray	Barbara Berge
Youra Geyer	Jillian Lindig
Margaret Larson	Mary Pat Gleason

Ruth Spicer	Mary Benson
Mrs. Shadbolt	Anne Shropshire

Time: Ramadan, the Muslim month of fasting. Place: Villa Adonis, a small hotel near the ancient Roman ruins of Baalbek, the final days of the holiday. Act I, Scene 1: A morning in autumn, 1939. Scene 2: Afternoon, a week later. Act II, Scene 1: That evening. Scene 2: The following day.

A MAN FOR ALL SEASONS (28). By Robert Bolt. February 25, 1982. Director, Charles Nolte. With Booth Colman, Donald Ewer, Jillian Lindig, Sara Morrison, David Regal.

WAIT UNTIL DARK (28). By Frederick Knott. March 25, 1982. Director, Terence Kilburn. With Wil Love, Phillip Locker, John LaGioia, Bethany Carpenter, Andrew Barnicle.

CHAPTER TWO (28). By Neil Simon. April 22, 1982. Director, Charles Nolte. With Fran Brill, Jane Lowry, David Regal, Paul Vincent.

Designers: scenery, Peter Hicks, Barry Griffith; lighting, Barry Griffith, Reid G. Johnson, Larry A. Reed, Deatra Smith; costumes, Mary Lynn Bonnell, Maria Marrero, Mary Lynn Crum.

ROCHESTER, N.Y.

GeVa on Stage: GeVa Theater

(Producing director, Gideon Y. Schein)

THE PASSION OF DRACULA (26). By Bob Hall and David Richmond. October 30, 1981. Director, Gideon Y. Schein. With Peter Murphy, Arn Weiner, Alice White, Fritz Sperberg, Francisco Prado.

PANTOMIME (26). By Derek Walcott. November 21, 1981. Director, Ben Levit. With John Swindells, Basil Wallace.

SHE STOOPS TO CONQUER (26). By Oliver Goldsmith. January 1, 1982. Director, Beth Dixon. With Mark Arnott, John Scanlan, Nick Stannard, Matthew Kimbrough, Patricia Kilgarriff, J. Smith-Cameron, Rhada Delamarter.

HOW I GOT THAT STORY (26). By Amlin Gray. January 29, 1982. Director, Stephen Katz. With Joe Morton, Richard Zobel.

ARTICHOKE (26). By Joanna M. Glass. February 26, 1982. Director, Sharon Ott. With Gisela Caldwell, Edward Cannan, Joan Shangold, Tom Blair.

CONSTANCE AND THE MUSICIAN (26). Book and lyrics by Caroline Kava; music by Mel Marvin. March 26, 1982. Director, Gideon Y. Schein; musical stager, Theodore Pappas; musical director, Guy Strobel. With Marilyn Caskey, Guy Strobel, Mary Jay, Margaret Lamee, Peter Boynton, Charles Michael Wright, Ray Gill.

Designers: scenery, Richard M. Isackes, Jeremy Conway, Susan Hilferty, Richard Hoover, Gary Baugh, John Jensen; lighting, Sid Bennett, Ann Wrightson, John Gisondi, Rachel Budin; costumes, Pamela Scofield, Karen Matthews, Ellen Kozak.

ST. LOUIS

The Repertory Theater of St. Louis: Mainstage

(Artistic Director, Wallace Chappell)

THE THREEPENNY OPERA (33). Book and lyrics by Bertolt Brecht; music by Kurt Weill; adaptation by Marc Blitzstein. September 11, 1981. Director, Wallace Chappell; music director, Byron Grant. With Swen Swenson, Joel Colodner, Mary D'Arcy, Judith Roberts, Joneal Joplin, Lynnie Greene.

BURIED CHILD (32). By Sam Shepard. October 16, 1981. Director, Timothy Near. With Jack Hollander, B. Constance Barry, Raymond Barry, Holly Hunter.

A CHRISTMAS CAROL (35). By Charles Dickens, adapted by Addie Walsh. November 29, 1981. Director, Wallace Chappell. With Philip Kerr, Joneal Joplin, Skip Foster, Sarah-Jane Gwillum, Ryan Bollman.

ONE FOR THE ROAD (33). By Max Morath. January 1, 1982 (world premiere). Director/choreographer, Neal Kenyon; arranger/conductor, Manny Mendelson.
Piano Player.................. Max Morath
Bartender .... Peter Walker
Woman..................... Carol Morley
Younger Woman............. Molly Scates
Man .... Gerald J. Quimby

Younger Man............... Davis Gaines
Time: 1855–1982. Place: A bar in America.
Musical numbers (drinking songs), Act I: "In the Sweet Dry and Dry," "At the Prohibition Ball," "The Prohibition Blues," "Just a Little Drink," "Whiskey Blues," "Don't Marry a Man if He Drinks," "Champagne Charlie," "Comrades, Fill No Glass for Me," "Something Cool," "Make It Another Old-Fashioned, Please," "John Barleycorn."
Act II: "Vodka," "Hello Montreal," "You Cannot Make Your Shimmy Shake," "Show Me the Way to Go Home," "Never No More," "Just a Little Drink," "B-A-R Rag," "On the B-A-R," "One Little Drink," "Saloon," "Everybody Wants a Key to My Cellar," "Ten Little Bottles," "Rollin'," "Fermentation."

ROMEO AND JULIET (35). By William Shakespeare. February 5, 1982. Director, Philip Kerr. With David Gwillim, Kitty Winn.

CHARLEY'S AUNT (35). By Brandon Thomas. April 9, 1982. Director, Ian Trigger. With Ian Trigger, Michael Rothhaar, Mark Capri, Susie Wall, Susan Leigh, Paddy Croft.

The Repertory Theater of St. Louis: Studio Theater

BRECHT ON BRECHT (27). Compiled and translated by George Tabori. October 31, 1981. Arranger/director, Jan Eliasberg; music director, Byron Grant; choreographer, Swen Swenson. With Skip Foster, Chris Limber, Byron Grant, Lynnie Greene, Judith Roberts, Swen Swenson.

A LESSON FROM ALOES (27). By Athol Fugard. February 7, 1982. Director, Jan Eliasberg. With Jack Davidson, Caroline Kava, Zakes Mokae.

Designers: scenery, Carolyn L. Ross, John Roslevich Jr., Karen Connolly, Tom H. John, Tim Jozwick; lighting, Peter E. Sargent, Gilbert V. Hemsley Jr., Glenn Dunn, Max DeVolder; costumes, Dorothy L. Marshall, John Carver Sullivan, Jane Alois Stein.

ST. PAUL

Actors Theater of St. Paul: Foley Theater

(Artistic Director, Michael Andrew Miner; general director, Jan Miner).

HEDDA GABLER (25). By Henrik Ibsen. October 30, 1981. Director, Michael Andrew Miner. With Barbara Kingsley, David M. Kwist, James Cada.

ABSURD PERSON SINGULAR (25). By Alan Ayckbourn. December 4, 1981. Director, Robert Mailand. With Louise Goetz, Spencer Beckwith, Dianne Benjamin Hill, James Cada.

WAITING FOR THE PARADE (26). By John Murrell. January 8, 1982. With Louise Goetz, Barbara Kingsley, Mari Rovang, Jane MacIver, Sally Wingert.

THE SUBJECT WAS ROSES (25). By Frank Gilroy. February 5, 1982. Director, Jeff Steitzer. With Spencer Beckwith, Jane MacIver, Ted Chase.

THE INCREASED DIFFICULTY OF CONCENTRATION (25). By Vaclav Havel. March 5, 1982. Director, James Cada. With Paul Eiding, Vada Russell, Sally Wingert, Michael Dalby.

TARTUFFE (25). By Molière. April 2, 1982. Director, Jeff Steitzer. With James Cada, David M. Kwist, Barbara Kingsley, Louise Goetz, Spencer Beckwith, Michael Andrew Miner.

Actors Theater of St. Paul: Mixed Blood Theater

HOW I GOT THAT STORY (20). By Amlin Gray. January 7, 1982. Director, Jon Cran-ney. With James Cada, David M. Kwist.

Designers; scenery, James Guenther, Dick Leerhoff, Larry Kaushansky, Chris Johnson, Don Yunker; lighting, Chris Johnson, Michael Vennerstrom, Don Yunker; costumes, Michael L. Hansen, Jill Hamilton, Arthur Ridley, Don Yunker.

SAN DIEGO

Old Globe Theater: Simon Edison Center for the Performing Arts—Festival Stage

(Executive producer, Craig Noel; artistic director, Jack O'Brien; managing director, Tom Hall)

KING LEAR (23. By William Shakespeare. June 9, 1981. Director, Jack O'Brien. With David Ogden Stiers, G. Wood, John Glover, Katherine McGrath, Lisa Banes, Leslie Geraci.

MUCH ADO ABOUT NOTHING (25). By William Shakespeare. June 10, 1981. Director, Edward Berkeley. With John Glover, Lisa Banes, Kevin Conroy, Leslie Geraci, G. Wood, G. W. Bailey.

MEASURE FOR MEASURE (24). By William Shakespeare. July 11, 1981. Director, Gerald Freedman. With Tovah Feldshuh, John Glover, Kristoffer Tabori, Ron Randell.

THE COUNTRY WIFE (28). By William Wycherley. August 11, 1981. Director, Jack O'Brien. With Tovah Feldshuh, Kristoffer Tabori, G. Wood, John Glover, Katherine McGrath.

Old Globe Theater: Edison Center—Cassius Carter Center Stage

DEAR LIAR (92). By Jerome Kilty. June 23, 1981. Director, Craig Noel. With Katherine McGrath/Tandy Cronyn, Jonathan McMurtry/Norman Welsh.

SORROWS OF STEPHEN (44). By Peter Parnell. January 19, 1982. Director, Andrew J. Traister. With Bruce Davison, Barbara Dirickson, Bill Geisslinger.

OH COWARD! (44). Devised by Roderick Cook, with selected songs, dialogue, poems and quotes by Noel Coward. March 9, 1982. Director, G. Wood. With G. Wood, Ann Mitchell, Joe Vincent.

MOBY DICK REHEARSED (44). By Orson Welles, adapted from Herman Melville's novel. April 27, 1982. Director, David McClendon. With Jonathan McMurtry, Francisco Laqueruela, Bill Geisslinger, Larry Drake.

Old Globe Theater: Edison Center

AS YOU LIKE IT (50). By William Shakespeare. January 14, 1982. Director, Craig Noel. With Deborah May, George Deloy, James R. Winker, Ellis Rabb.

YANKEE WIVES (5). By David Rimmer. March 4, 1982 (world premiere). Director, Jack O'Brien; scenery, Steven Rubin; lighting, Craig Miller; costumes, Ann Roth.

OLD GLOBE THEATER, SAN DIEGO—Joan Pringle, Ronnie Claire Edwards, Annette O'Toole and Barbara Anderson in *Yankee Wives*

Sally Hite . . . . Ronnie Claire Edwards
Pam Monday . . . . Barbara Anderson
Connie Antonelli . . . . Deborah Taylor
Ronnie Roberts . . . . Alice Playten
Marceline Davis. . . . . Joan Pringle
Wyla Lee . . . . Annette O'Toole
Bob Dolan . . . . Jonathan McMurtry

Scamper Frizem. . . . . Bill Geisslinger
One intermission.

MISALLIANCE (50). By George Bernard Shaw. April 22, 1982. Director, Paxton Whitehead. With G. Wood, Tandy Cronyn, Kristin Griffith, Jonathan Miller.

Designers: scenery, Sam Kirkpatrick, Steven Rubin, Richard Seger, Kent Dorsey, Mark Donnelly, Richard Hay; lighting, Gilbert V. Hemsley Jr., Donald Darnutzer, Richard Seger, Bob Peterson, Kent Dorsey, John B. Forbes, John McLain, Craig Miller; costumes, Robert Morgan, Sam Kirkpatrick, Steven Rubin, Mary Gibson, Ann Roth, Sally Cleveland, Deborah Dryden.

Note: Old Globe's Play Discovery Project (1 performance each of staged readings, under the aegis of Andrew J. Trasister) presented: *America Was* by Jack Heifner, February 8, 1982, director Giles Colahan; *The Prisoner of Quai Dong* by Harold Willis, March 15, 1982, director James Bush; *Gym Rats* by Farrell J. Foreman, April 5, 1982, director Andrew J. Traister; *Banjo* by James L. Dickson, May 10, 1982, director David Hay. Once again, Old Globe presented an Educational Tour during the fall of 1981 and the spring of 1982.

SAN FRANCISCO

American Conservatory Theater: Geary Theater

(General director, William Ball)

KING RICHARD II (31). By William Shakespeare. September 30, 1981. Director, Elizabeth Huddle. With John Noah Hertzler, William Paterson, Sydney Walker, Stacy Ray.

I REMEMBER MAMA (39). By John van Druten. October 13, 1981. Director, Allen Fletcher. With Anne Lawder, Julia Fletcher, Richard Kuss, Dakin Matthews.

THREE SISTERS (13). By Anton Chekhov. October 27, 1981. Director, Tom Moore. With DeAnn Mears, Elizabeth Huddle, Stacy Ray, Peter Donat/Lawrence Hecht, Ray Reinhardt, Sally Smythe.

THE ADMIRABLE CRICHTON (29). By James M. Barrie. November 18, 1981. Director, Michael Winters. With John Noah Hertzler, Mimi Carr, Richard Kuss, Frank Savino.

A CHRISTMAS CAROL (22). By Charles Dickens; adapted by Laird Williamson and Dennis Powers. December 3, 1981. Directed by Laird Williamson. With Sydney Walker/Raye Birk, John Hutton, Delores Y. Mitchell, Steven Rubens.

HAPPY LANDINGS (27). By William Hamilton. January 6, 1982 (world premiere). Director, Edward Hastings.
Constance Treadwell Madison . . . Sally Smythe
Nicholas Madison . . . . Tom Parker
Carl Von Eltz . . . Nicholas Stanton Freedman
Dede Von Eltz . . . . Jill Hill
Topping Treadwell . . . . William Paterson
Klaus Von Eltz . . . . John Noah Hertzler
Red . . . . Lawrence Hecht
Bartender . . . . Frank Savino

Other Drinker . . . . Thomas Oglesby
Aunt Hopey . . . . Marrian Walters
Place: San Francisco, an apartment in Pacific Heights and a bar in the Tenderloin. One intermission.

BLACK COMEDY by Peter Shaffer and THE BROWNING VERSION by Terence Rattigan (21). January 27, 1982. Director, James Edmondson. With Janice Garcia-Hutchins, Sydney Walker, Bruce Williams, Greg Patterson, Mark Murphey, DeAnn Mears, Raye Birk.

MOURNING BECOMES ELECTRA (27). By Eugene O'Neill. February 24, 1982. Director, Allen Fletcher. With Dakin Matthews, Anne Lawder, Julia Fletcher, Thomas Oglesby, John Hutton.

CAT AMONG THE PIGEONS (27). By Georges Feydeau. March 23, 1982. Director, Nagle Jackson. With Raye Birk, Sally Smythe, William McKereghan, Ray Reinhardt, Mimi Carr.

ANOTHER PART OF THE FOREST (12). By Lillian Hellman. April 20, 1982. With Ray Reinhardt, Barbara Dirickson, Bruce Williams, Mark Murphey, Anne Lawder.

Designers: scenery, Richard Seger, Ralph Funicello, Richard L. Hay, Robert Blackman; lighting, Dirk Epperson, Mark Bosch, Duane Schuler, F. Mitchell Dana, Joseph Appelt, James Sale; costumes, Robert Morgan, Michael Casey, Michael Olich, Martha Burke.

American Conservatory Theater: Plays-in-Progress—The Playroom

TEN MINUTES FOR TWENTY-FIVE CENTS (8). By Janet Thomas. February 24, 1982. Director, Eugene Barcone.
AN AMERICAN FAIRYTALE (8). By Howard Burman, based on a novel by James Drought. March 17, 1982. Director, James Haire.

LIZZIE BORDEN IN THE LATE AFTERNOON (8). By Cather MacCallum, based on a short story by Robert Herson. April 30, 1982. Director, Janice Garcia-Hutchins.
MAMMON AND FIST (8). By Ethan Coen and William Robertson. May 7, 1982. Director, John Noah Hertzler.

SARASOTA

Asolo State Theater Company: Ringling Museums' Court Playhouse

(Artistic director, Robert Strane/Stuart Vaughan; managing director, David S. Levenson; executive director/founder, Richard G. Fallon.

THE THREE MUSKETEERS (36). Adapted by Eberle Thomas from Alexandre Dumas's novel. June 25, 1981. Director, Eberle Thomas. With James Hunt, Wesley Stevens, Barbara Redmond, Robert Murch, Jeffrey Bryan King.

PICNIC (34). By William Inge. July 3, 1981. Director, Bernerd Engel. With Isa Thomas,

Carolyn Ann Miloy, Alan Brooks, Barbara Redmond, Elizabeth Harrell.

ONCE IN A LIFETIME (33). By Moss Hart and George S. Kaufman. July 10, 1981. Director, Jim Hoskins. With Jeffrey Bryan King, Kathleen Klein, Isa Thomas, Philip Lestrange.

A MIDSUMMER NIGHT'S DREAM (48). By William Shakespeare. February 18, 1982. Director, Gregory Abels. With Robert Murch, Viveca Parker, Douglas Jones, Denise Bessette, Mary Elizabeth Horowitz, Wesley Stevens, Rob Ferguson.

MRS. WARREN'S PROFESSION (38). By George Bernard Shaw. February 27, 1982. Director, Donald Madden. With Isa Thomas, Viveca Parker, Robert Murch, Karl Redcoff.

THE SHOW-OFF (36). By George Kelly. March 5, 1982. Director, Thomas Gruenewald. With Bette Oliver, Douglas Jones, Denise Bessette, David S. Howard.

ALL NIGHT STRUT (35). Conceived by Fran Charnas; musical celebration of the big band era. May 21, 1982. Director/choreographer, Jim Hoskins; musical director, John Franceschina. With Paul M. Elkin, Ellia English, P. J. Hoffman, Lance Roberts.

Designers: scenery, William Barclay, John Ezell, Holmes Easley, Thomas Michael Cariello, Peter Dean Beck, Sam Bagarella; lighting, Martin Petlock, Dean Markosian; costumes, Paige Southard, Sally Kos Harrison, Catherine King, Ellis Tillman.

Note: The Asolo Touring Theater toured Florida and the Southeast for seven months during the 1981–82 season with *Pinocchio, Comedies of Courtship* and *The Ice Wolf* by Joanna Kraus, directed and performed by the ATT Company.

SEATTLE

A Contemporary Theater

(Founder/director, Gregory A. Falls)

GETTING OUT (24). By Marsha Norman. June 4, 1981. Director, Gregory A. Falls. With Elaine Bromka, Cynthia Darlow, Nesbitt Blaisdell, Jeffrey Covell, Sheila Crofut.

BILLY BISHOP GOES TO WAR (24). By John Gray with Eric Peterson. July 2, 1981. Director Robert Loper. With Thomas Hill, David Collaci.

NIGHT AND DAY (24). By Tom Stoppard. July 30, 1981. Director, Robert Egan. With Katherine Ferrand, John Aylward, William Cain, Neil Fitzpatrick.

LOOSE ENDS (24). By Michael Weller. August 27, 1981. Director, Richard Edwards. With Neil

Bestwick, David Colacci, Heidi Helen Davis, R. A. Farrell, Maureen Kilmurry.

WHOSE LIFE IS IT ANYWAY? (24). By Brian Clark. September 24, 1981. Director, Clayton Corzatte. J. Kenneth Campbell, Jeffrey Prather, Robert Loper.

A CHRISTMAS CAROL (52). By Charles Dickens, adapted by Gregory A. Falls. December 1, 1981. Director, Eileen MacRae Murphy. With John Gilbert/Michael Santo, R. A. Farrell, Richard Riehle.

DA (24). By Hugh Leonard. May 6, 1982. Director, Richard Edwards. With James Hilbrandt, R. A. Farrell, Kathryn Mesney, Ursula Meyer, Allen Nause.

Designers: scenery, Scott Weldin, Bill Raoul, Shelley Henze Schermer, William Forrester, Karen Gelsteen; lighting, Jody Briggs, Donna Grout, Randall G. Chiarelli, Phil Schermer; costumes, Nanrose Buchman, Susan Min, Julie James.

Note: A Contemporary Theater's Young ACT Company presented *Ali Baba and the Forty Thieves* (69), written and directed by Gregory A. Falls, during the 1982 winter-spring season, to schools in all parts of the state, including Seattle, Yakima, Sunnyside, Pasco, Moses Lake.

Seattle Repertory Theater: Seattle Center Playhouse—Mainstage

(Resident director, Daniel Sullivan; producing director, Peter Donnelly; associate director, Robert Egan)

ANOTHER PART OF THE FOREST (31). By Lillian Hellman. October 28, 1981. Director, Ed-

ward Hastings. With John Kellogg, Keith Carradine, Kim Hunter, Kate Mulgrew.

THE TWO GENTLEMEN OF VERONA (33). By William Shakespeare. December 2, 1981. Director, Daniel Sullivan. With Clayton Corzatte, Byron Jennings, John Christopher Jones, Nora McLellan, Katherine Ferrand, Eve Roberts.

AWAKE AND SING (31). By Clifford Odets. January 6, 1982. Director, Robert Loper. With William Myers, Eve Roberts, Charles Mayer, Eva Charney, Michael Albert Mantel, Mark Jenkins.

BEDROOM FARCE (31). By Alan Ayckbourn. February 10, 1982. Director, Daniel Sullivan. With Clayton Corzatte, Susan Ludlow, Ted D'Arms, Megan Cole.

SAVAGES (31). By Christopher Hampton. March 17, 1982. Director, Robert Egan. With Derek Ralston, Mark Jenkins, Megan Cole, Joseph Siravo.

MAJOR BARBARA (33). By George Bernard Shaw. April 21, 1982. Director, Daniel Sullivan. With Nathan Haas, Eve Roberts, Kate Mulgrew, Ray Dooley, Bernard Behrens, Laurence Ballard, John Procaccino.

Designers: scenery, Robert Dahlstrom, Robert Blackman, John Kasarda, Ralph Funicello; lighting, Richard Nelson, Spencer Mosse, James F. Ingalls, Richard Dahlstrom; costumes, Robert Blackman, Kurt Wilhelm, Laura Crow, Robert Wojewodski.

Seattle Repertory Theater: New Plays in Process Project

(Artistic director, Robert Egan. Workshop premieres)

THE DUEL by David Gild; adapted from a Chekhov story. January 11, 1982. Director, Robert Egan.
THE GRASS WIDOW by Snoo Wilson. January 25, 1982. Director, Robert Egan.
AN OUNCE OF PREVENTION by Hal Cor-

ley. February 8, 1982. Director, Roberta Levitow.
WHAT I DID LAST SUMMER by A. R. Gurney Jr. February 22, 1982. Director, Daniel Sullivan.

STAMFORD, CONN.

The Hartman Theater

(Artistic director, Edwin Sherin; executive director, Harris Goldman)

HEDDA GABLER (23). By Henrik Ibsen; translated by Eva Le Gallienne. September 30, 1981. Director, Edwin Sherin. With Jane Alexander, Lee Curran, Edward Herrmann, Pamela Payton-Wright, Lee Richardson, David Selby.

CATHOLICS (23). By Brian Moore. November 11, 1981. Director, Tom Kerr. With Michael Higgins, Alan Scarfe, Maurice Good.

THE MILLIONAIRESS (23). By George Bernard Shaw; including a prologue adapted by Jerome Kilty from On the Rocks and other Shaw writings. December 16, 1981. Director, Jerome Kilty. With Tammy Grimes, Richard Council, Ken Ruta, Paul Sparer.

NIGHT MUST FALL (23). By Emlyn Williams. January 20, 1982. Director, Edwin Sherin. With Jan Miner, Bill Sadler, Richard Merrell, Jeanne Ruskin, Samuel Maupin.

THE MAGISTRATE (23). By Arthur Wing Pinero. March 3, 1982. Director, Edward Hastings. With John Cullum, Jerome Kilty, Katherine McGrath, Fredi Olster, George Ede.

MAHALIA (23). Book and lyrics by Don Evans; music by John Lewis; based on the book by Laurraine Goreau. April 1, 1982. Director, Gerald Freedman; musical supervisor, Joyce Brown; choreographer, Talley Beatty. With Esther Marrow, Fran Bennett, Michelle Weeks, Danny Miller Beard, Keith David.

Designers: scenery, Dan Beaman, Marjorie Bradley Kellogg, Robin Wagner, Robert Fletcher, James Leonard Joy, Richard M. Isackes; lighting, Marcia Madeira, Bill Williams, John McLain, Sid Bennett, Roger L. Meeker; costumes, Nancy Potts, Robert Fletcher, Jane Greenwood, Anne Wallace, David Murin, Judy Dearling.

SYRACUSE STAGE—Michael Tolaydo and Jay Patterson in *K2,* which had simultaneous premieres at the Arena Stage in Washington, D.C. and in Portsmouth, N.H. Theater by the Sea

STRATFORD, CONN.

American Shakespeare Festival

(Artistic director, Peter Coe)

HENRY V (32). By William Shakespeare. July 7, 1981. Director, Peter Coe. With Christopher Plummer, Roy Dotrice, Isabelle Rosier.

OTHELLO (39). By William Shakespeare. August 4, 1981. Director, Peter Coe. With James Earl Jones, Christopher Plummer, Shannon John.

Designers: Scenery and costumes, Robert Fletcher; lighting, Marc B. Weiss.

SYRACUSE, N. Y.

Syracuse Stage

(Producing director, Arthur Storch; managing director, James A. Clark)

BETRAYAL (32). By Harold Pinter. November 30, 1981. With Lynn Milgrim, Richard Greene, Edmond Genest.

A CHRISTMAS CAROL (32). By Charles Dickens. December 11, 1981. Director, Stephen Willems. With Syracuse Stage Company.

THE MERCHANT OF VENICE (32). By William Shakespeare. January 15, 1982. Director, Ken Jenkins. With Gary Armagnac, Yusef Bulos, Erika Peterson, Yolanda Lloyd.

TWICE AROUND THE PARK (32). By Murray Schisgal. Feberuary 19, 1982 (world premiere). Director, Arthur Storch.

Edie Frazier; Margaret Heinz .. Anne Jackson
Gus Frazier; Leon Rose . . . . Eli Wallach

TALLEY'S FOLLY (32). By Lanford Wilson. March 26, 1982. Director, John Ulmer. With

David Rosenbaum, Ellen Barry.

K2 (32). By Patrick Meyers. April 30, 1982. Director, Terry Schreiber. With Michael Tolaydo, Jay Patterson.

Designers; scenery, Charles Cosler, Hal Tiné, Quentin Thomas, James Tilton, John Döepp; lighting, Charles Cosler, Judy Rasmuson, Robert F. Strohmeier, Paul Mathiesen, Michael Newton-Brown; costumes, David Toser, Nanzi Adzima, James Berton Harris, Anne Shanto.

TUCSON

Arizona Theater Company: Tucson Community Center Theater

(Artistic director, Gary Gisselman; managing director, David Hawkanson)

THE RAINMAKER (24). By N. Richard Nash. November 5, 1981. Director, Michael Maggio. With Jane Murray, Logan Pope, Paul C. Thomas.

A CHRISTMAS CAROL (26). By Charles Dickens; adapted by Frederick Gaines. December 1, 1981. Director, Gary Gisselman; musical director, Maida Libkin. With Henry Kendrick, Penny Metropulos, John Cannon Nichols, Hilary Quick, Benjamin Stewart.

WAITING FOR GODOT (22). By Samuel Beckett. January 14, 1982. Director, Gary Gisselman. With Paul Ballantyne, Robert Ellenstein, Benjamin Stewart, Clifford Rakerd, Michael E. Goodsite.

MISALLIANCE (24). By George Bernard Shaw. February 11, 1982. Director, Michael

Maggio. With Jane Murray, Patricia Fraser, Tim Halligan, Clifford Rakerd, Benjamin Stewart, Tony DeBruno.

AS YOU LIKE IT (25). By William Shakespeare. March 11, 1982. Director, Gary Gisselman. With Lynnie Green, Tim Halligan, Roy Henderson, Penny Metropulos, Jane Murray, Clifford Rakerd, Benjamin Stewart.

THE GIN GAME (29). By D. L. Coburn. April 8, 1982. Director, Jon Cranney. With Robert Ellenstein, Patricia Fraser.

TINTYPES (30). Conceived by Mary Kyte, with Mel Marvin and Gary Pearle. May 13, 1982. Directors, Gary Gisselman, Lewis Whitlock; choreographer, Lewis Whitlock. With Ross Lehman, Benjamin Stewart, Nedra Dixon, Kitty Carroll, Penny Metropulos.

Designers: scenery, Kent Dorsey, Jack Barkla, Peter A. Davis, Gene D. Buck; lighting, John B. Forbes, Don Darnutzer, Kent Dorsey, Steven B. Peterson; costumes, Christopher Beesley, Gene D. Buck, Bob Bish, Bobbi Culbert.

Note: Arizona Theater Company presented part of its season at the Phoenix Little Theater, including: *The Gin Game* (20); *As You Like It* (14); *Tintypes* (20), March to May, 1982.

WASHINGTON, D. C.

Arena Stage: Arena Theater

(Producing director, Zelda Fichandler; executive director, Thomas C. Fichandler)

MAJOR BARBARA (39). By George Bernard Shaw. October 16, 1981. Director, Martin Fried. With Biff McGuire, Christine Estabrook, Mikel Lambert, Kevin Donovan, Robert W. Westenberg.

A MIDSUMMER NIGHT'S DREAM (39). By William Shakespeare. December 4, 1981. Director, David Chambers. With Avery Brooks, Kath-

leen Turner, Charles Janasz, Christina Moore, Mary McDonnell, Thomas A. Hewitt, Robert W. Westenberg.

A DELICATE BALANCE (39). By Edward Albee. January 22, 1982. Director, Zelda Fichandler. With Robert Prosky, Myra Carter, Halo Wines, Leslie Kass.

UNDISCOVERED COUNTRY (39). By Arthur Schnitzler; adapted by Tom Stoppard. March 12, 1982. Director, Garland Wright. With Richard Bauer, Barbara Andres, Richard W. Westenberg, Stanley Anderson, Mark Hammer.

ANIMAL CRACKERS (39). Book by George S. Kaufman and Morrie Ryskind; music and lyrics by Bert Kalmar and Harry Ruby; additional music by Eric Stern. May 7, 1982. Director, Douglas C. Wager; musical director, Robert Fisher; arranger/orchestrator, Russell Warner; choreographer, Baayork Lee. With Stephen Mellor, Charles Janasz, Donald Corren, J. Fred Shiffman, Peggy Hewett.

Arena Stage: Kreeger Theater

A LESSON FROM ALOES (39). By Athol Fugard. November 12, 1981. Director, Douglas C. Wager. With Stanley Anderson, Halo Wines, Zakes Mokae.

TOMFOOLERY (39). By Tom Lehrer. January 1, 1982. Director, Douglas C. Wager; musical director, Robert Fisher; stager/choreographer, Geoffrey Ferris. With Terrence Currier, Timothy Jerome, Ellen March, Eric Weitz.

K2 (39). By Patrick Meyers. April 23, 1982. Director, Jacques Levy. With Stanley Anderson, Stephen McHattie.

Designers: scenery, Ming Cho Lee, Tony Straiges, Heidi Landesman, Karl Eigsti, Adrianne Lobel, Zack Brown, Tom Lynch; lighting, Hugh Lester, Arden Fingerhut, William Mintzer, Allen Lee Hughes; costumes, Marjorie Slaiman, Marie Anne Chiment, Mary Ann Powell, Noel Borden.

Folger Theater Group

(Artistic producer, John Neville-Andrews)

JULIUS CAESAR (64). By William Shakespeare. October 5, 1981. Director, Louis W. Scheeder. With Ralph Cosham, Earl Edgerton, Fran Dorn, Peter Webster, Sherry Skinner.

THE ROVER (54). By Aphra Behn. December 21, 1981. Director, Michael Diamond. With Jack Wetherall, Lucinda Jenney, Celeste Morrow, John Thomas Waite, Jerry Whiddon.

THE TEMPEST (37). By William Shakespeare. March 8, 1982. Director, Roger Hendricks Simon. With Joseph Wiseman, Paul Anderson, Liane Langland, Herb Davis, Charles Turner, Michael Nostrand.

THE COMEDY OF ERRORS (61). By William Shakespeare. May 10, 1982. Director, John Neville-Andrews. With David Cromwell, Gregory Roberts, Diana Van Fossen, Cecelia Riddett, Tim Rice, Lance Davis, Stephen Mottram.

Designers: scenery, Lewis Folden, Russell Methany, Hugh Lester; lighting, Richard Winkler, Robby Monk, Hugh Lester; costumes, Bary Allen Odom, Kay Haskell.

WATERFORD, CONN.

Eugene O'Neill Theater Center: National Playwright's Conference

(President, George C. White; artistic director, Lloyd Richards. New Works in Progress; 2 performances each, in one of three theaters, July 16, 1981—August 8, 1981

HAGE—THE SEXUAL HISTORY by Robert Auletta; director, Walt Jones.

C-SECTION by William di Canzio; director, Bill Ludel.

THE END OF THE TEFLON-COATED LIFE by June Calender; director, Dennis Scott.

STILL LIFE WITH COW by John Gehm; director, Walt Jones.

JOHNNY BULL by Kathleen Betsko; director, Bill Ludel.

LAST LOOKS by Grace McKeaney, director, Tony Giordano.

FLASH FLOODS by Dare Clubb; director,

Dennis Scott.

SONS AND FATHERS OF SONS by Ray Aranha; director, Walt Jones.

FIRE AT LUNA PARK by Theodore Faro Gross; director, Robert Graham Small.

GOING OVER by Stuart Browne; director, Bill

Partlan.

STARTERS by Jack Gelber; director, Dennis Scott.

HOME REMEDIES by Paul Minx; director, Barnet Kellman.

Designers: Fred Voelpel, Frances Aronson, Ian Calderon, Hugh Landwehr.

Dramaturgs: Martin Esslin, Michael Feingold, Corinne Jacker, Lee Kalcheim, Edith Oliver, Max Wilk.

WEST SPRINGFIELD, MASS.

Stage West

(Producing director, Stephen E. Hays; managing director, Robert A. Rosenbaum)

TERRA NOVA (28). By Ted Tally. October 22, 1981. Director, Harold Scott. With Curt Dawson, Adrian Sparks, Tania Myren.

TALLEY'S FOLLY (28). By Lanford Wilson. November 19, 1981. Director, Stephen E. Hays. With Eugene Troobnick, Erika Petersen.

TINTYPES (28). Conceived by Mary Kyte with Mel Marvin and Gary Pearle. December 17, 1981. Director, Wayne Bryan; musical director, Barry Koron. With Sal Biagini, Richert Easley, Ursuline Kairson, Carol Lugenbeal, Robin Taylor.

HELLO AND GOODBYE (28). By Athol Fugard. January 14, 1982. Director, Donald Hicken. With Richard Pilcher, Tana Hicken.

DEAD WRONG (28). By Nick Hall. February

11, 1982 (world premiere). Director, Richard Gershman.

Craig Blaisdell	Curt Dawson
Peggy Blaisdell	Judith McConnell
Allen Gautier	Glenn Schere
Walter Scott	Richard Zavaglia

Time: The present. Place: The living room of the Blaisdell home in Mt. Kisco, New York. One intermission.

ARTICHOKE (28). By Joanna M. Glass. March 11, 1982. Director, Timothy Near. With Lewis Arlt, Gary Armagnac, Lisabeth Shean, Holly Hunter.

YOU NEVER CAN TELL (28). By George Bernard Shaw. April 8, 1982. Director, Stephen E. Hays. With, Mary Fogarty, Nancy Boykin, Bernard Frawley, Henry Thomas.

Designers: scenery, Frank J. Boros, Joseph Long, Jeffrey Struckman, Wally Coberg, Jeffrey Fiala, Thomas Michael Cariello; lighting, Barry Arnold, Paul J. Horton, Bonnie Ann Brown, Margaret Lee; costumes, Elizabeth Covey, Leslie Miller, Deborah Shaw, Jan Morrison, Jeffrey Struckman, Anne Thaxter Watson.

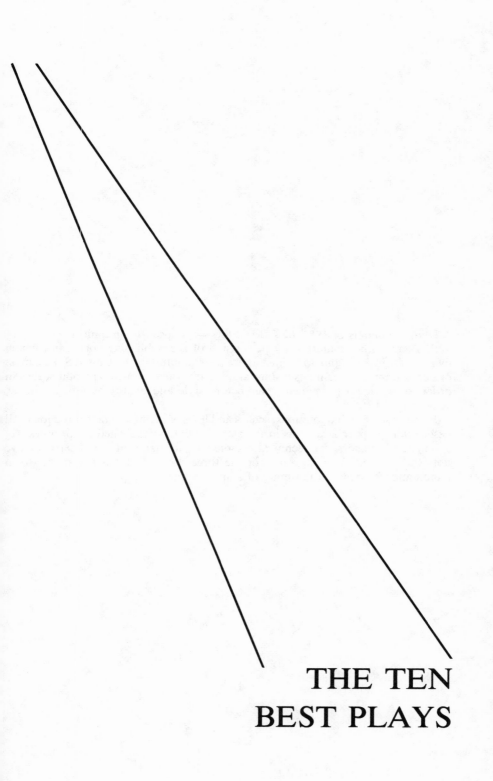

THE TEN
BEST PLAYS

Here are details of 1981–82's Best Plays—synopses, biographical sketches of authors and other material. By permission of the publishing companies which own the exclusive rights to publish these scripts in full in the United States, most of our continuities include substantial quotations from crucial/pivotal scenes in order to provide a permanent reference to style and quality as well as theme, structure and story line.

In the case of such quotations, scenes and lines of dialogue, stage directions and descriptions appear *exactly* as in the stage version or published script unless (in a very few instances, for technical reasons) an abridgement is indicated by five dots (. . . . .). The appearance of the three dots (. . .) is the script's own punctuation to denote the timing of a spoken line.

THE DANCE
AND THE RAILROAD

A Play in One Act

BY DAVID HENRY HWANG

Cast and credits appear on page 355

DAVID HENRY HWANG is the son of first-generation Americans who immigrated from China and settled in California. He was born in 1957 in Los Angeles and graduated from Stanford University, where he was already trying his hand at playwriting and developing his play entitled FOB. *Further work on and staging of this script took place at the O'Neill Playwrights Conference in Waterford, Conn. in the summer of 1979. It was soon presented by New York Shakespeare Festival Public Theater in an off-off-Broadway production May 27, 1980, then moved up to a full off-Broadway production by the same group June 8, 1980.* FOB *won the Obie Award for Best Play of the 1980–81 season.*

Following this triumphant playwriting debut, Hwang gave New York audiences their first look at The Dance and the Railroad *in an off-off-Broadway production at the New Federal Theater March 21, 1981. It subsequently was produced at New York Shakespeare Festival July 16, 1981 for 181 off-Broadway performances and its author's first Best Play citation. Still another Hwang playscript,* Family Devotions *(about a Chinese American family's problems in blending the values of both its heritages), was produced this season by New York Shakespeare Festival October 18 for 76 performances. Hwang is unmarried and lives in New York City.*

John Lone and Tzi Ma in *The Dance and the Railroad*

Time: June 1867

Place: A mountain top near the transcontinental railroad

Scene 1: Afternoon

SYNOPSIS: Lone *("20 years old, Chinaman railroad worker")* is practising the balletic movements of a Chinese opera, standing on a stump and swinging his long hair. As he leaps from the stump to the ground, Ma *("18 years old, Chinaman railroad worker")* comes to watch Lone from a hidden vantage point (the names "Lone" and "Ma" were the names of the performers in the New York production).

Lone spots Ma and whips his hair into Ma's face to express his displeasure at having his performance spied on and enjoyed for free. Ma has come to warn Lone about his attitude toward "the guys" down at the camp. Their co-workers call Lone "Prince of the Mountain" because he thinks he's too good to spend time and share songs and stories with them. Ma warns Lone that they may take reprisals, throw him into the latrine or remove his tongue because he never speaks to them.

LONE: There's no one here worth talking to.

MA: Cut it out, Lone. Look, I'm trying to help you, all right? I got a solution.

LONE: So young yet so clever.

MA: The stuff you're doing—it's beautiful. Why don't you do it for the guys down at camp? Help us celebrate.

LONE: What will "this stuff" help celebrate?

MA: C'mon. The strike, of course. . . . .

There was a time when the workers feared that "the white devils" might set upon them with soldiers, but now the Chinese workers are beginning to feel their collective strength. Their bosses may even be a little afraid of them. In any case, Lone isn't interested in Ma's "solution"—he wishes only that Ma would go back to camp and leave him alone. Ma warns Lone again of possible reprisals for his detached attitude, but Lone merely resumes his practising.

Scene 2: Afternoon, a day later

Ma again interrupts Lone's practising with the presumptuous announcement that he "forgives" Lone for brushing him off the day before. Ma finally gets around to asking Lone to teach him dance steps for the opera so that he can show off and perform when he returns to China. Lone informs Ma that a mother who learns that her child has become an actor "beats her head against the ground until the ground, out of pity, opens up and swallows her." Ma replies, "Well, I don't wanna become an 'actor.' That sounds terrible. I just wanna perform." He will return to China rich, talented, in triumph, holding his audience spellbound with stories about America.

MA: I'll say, "We laid tracks like soldiers. Mountains? We hung from cliffs in baskets and the winds blew us like birds. Snow? We lived underground like moles for days at a time. Deserts? We—"

LONE: Wait, wait, wait, wait, wait! How do you know these things after only four weeks?

MA: They told me—the other Chinamen on the gang. We've been telling stories ever since the strike began.

LONE: They make it sound like it's very enjoyable.

MA: They said it is.

LONE: Oh? And you believe them?

MA: They're my friends. Living underground in winter—sounds exciting, huh?

LONE: Did they say anything about the cold?

MA: Oh, I already know about that. They told me about the mild winters and the warm snow.

LONE: Warm snow?

MA: When I go home, I'll bring some back to show my brothers.

Lone has been here two years, so Ma expects he knows all about the warm snow on this Gold Mountain (Lone takes him to task for being so gullible as to believe such stories). Once again, Ma asks Lone to teach him to perform. He shows Lone that he's been practising the walk, only to be told that he looks like "a duck in heat."

Instead, Lone proposes to play "Die Siu," a game with two dice which Lone produces. The two commence to roll. Ma has been playing with "the guys," has lost some money, but "Here in America—losing is no problem. You know—End of the Year Bonus?" Lone knows—and hints that it is a myth. Ma suggests that Lone ought to play with his fellow-workers sometimes. Ma understands that Lone prefers to practise performing, but "You don't have to overdo it, either. You don't have to treat 'em like dirt. I mean, who are you trying to impress?" Lone throws the dice into the bushes. When Ma retrieves them, Lone tells him to keep them. Ma promptly offers to pay Lone for lessons by giving him the dice which are now his.

Lone orders Ma to feel the sweat on his brow, challenging him: "Are you willing to come up here after you've spent the whole day chipping half an inch off a rock, and punish your body some more?" Ma declares that he is, yes, even after a day's work—but even so, Lone doesn't have to act as though he thought himself superior to his fellow-workers.

LONE: . . . . . You haven't even begun to understand. To practise every day, you must have a fear to force you up here.

MA: A fear? No—it's cause what you're doing is beautiful.

LONE: No.

MA: I've seen it.

LONE: It's ugly to practise when the mountain has turned your muscles to ice. When my body hurts too much to come up here, I look at the other Chinamen and think, "They are dead. Their muscles work only because the white man forces them. I live because I can still force my muscles to work for me. Say it. "They are dead."

MA: No. They're my friends.

LONE: Well, then, take your dice down to your friends.

MA: But I want to learn—

LONE: This is your first lesson.

MA: Look, it shouldn't matter—

LONE: It does.

MA: It shouldn't matter what I think.

LONE: Attitude is everything.

MA: But as long as I come up, do the exercises—

LONE: I'm not going to waste time on a quitter.

MA: I'm not!

LONE: Then say it—"They are dead men."
MA: I can't.
LONE: Then you will never have the dedication.
MA: That doesn't prove anything.
LONE: I will not teach a dead man.

Ma finally says, "All right. I'm one of them," but he returns to his plea: he will come up the mountain to practise every night after work—but he won't say that "the guys" are dead, not when they have the gumption to strike against the imposition of a ten-hour day. They are demanding an eight-hour day, like the white man's, and a $14 raise. Lone agrees with Ma that this is a sign of life among his compatriots, and he will instruct Ma so long as the strike lasts.

Scene 3: Late afternoon, four days later

As the two men go through their exercises, Ma wonders how long before he'll be able to play the role of Kwan Kung (about as long as it takes a dog to learn the violin, Lone observes). Ma wants to start by learning a few steps, but Lone informs him that if he works very, very hard, he may be able to play the Second Clown by the time they are ready to return to China. It will certainly be years before Ma can think of playing Kwan Kung, "the god of Adventurers, the God of Fighters" in Chinese opera.

MA: You mean, I'm going to have to practise here every night—and in return, all I can play is the Second Clown?
LONE: If you work hard.
MA: Am I that bad? Maybe I shouldn't even try to do this. Maybe I should just go down.
LONE: It's not you. Everyone must earn the right to play Kwan Kung. I entered Opera School when I was ten years old. My parents decided to sell me for ten years to this opera company. I lived with eighty other boys, and we slept in bunks four beds high and hid our rice cakes and candy from each other. After eight years, I was studying to play Kwan Kung.
MA: Eight years?
LONE: I was one of the best in my class. One day, I was summoned by my master, who told me I was to go home for two days, because my mother had fallen very ill and was dying. When I arrived home, mother was standing at the door waiting, not sick at all. Her first words to me, the son away for eight years, were, "You've been playing while your village has starved. You must go to the Gold Mountain and work."
MA: And you never returned to school?
LONE: I went from a room with eighty boys to a ship with three hundred men. so you see, it does not come easily to play Kwan Kung.

Ma thinks maybe Lone has "the best of both worlds" this way, making his fortune before settling into an ill-paid career as an actor. Lone crouches, waddles and quacks, imitating a duck, and orders Ma to do the same. Ma obeys and is ordered to continue impersonating a duck after Lone stops. Lone puts Ma through many duck's paces and finally frightens Ma by imitating a tiger pouncing on the duck. Lone continues to harry Ma, imitating a voracious locust, then making Ma do the same. Ma protests that he wasn't born to be either duck or locust, and Lone tells him, "Exactly. Well, I wasn't born to work on a railroad, either. 'Best of both worlds.' How can you be such an insect?" Lone has never told his story to anyone before, and he considers Ma's comment fatuous. It proves, Lone declares, that Ma doesn't have the dedication, the extreme and unvarying dedication, needed to become an opera performer. Ma pleads that he does. Lone gives him a chance to prove it: stay here and hold this muscle-cracking pose of a locust until morning.

Scene 4: Late that evening

Much later, Ma is holding his pose and talking to himself about locusts, remembering how swarms wiped out crops back in China. An uncle of his lost his eldest son and his wife in a famine that followed a locust invasion. This uncle became deranged, living in a cave and expressing his emotions by torturing grasshoppers.

Scene 5: Just before dawn the following day

Ma is still holding his pose, as Lone enters singing. He releases Ma from his contorted position, but Ma can only lie there on the ground waiting for strength to return and pain to subside from his tortured legs.

Lone has lain awake all night thinking, and now he has much to tell Ma. First, he says, Ma will play Kwan Kung. Ma can think of nothing other than his aching legs, but Lone has brought him rice, duck and a little whiskey to revive his flesh and spirits. It seems that the blockade of the workers' food supplies has ended, along with the strike. "Yes, the Chinamen have won," admits Lone, "They can do more than just talk."

Ma exults: "In nine days we civilized the white devils. I knew it. I knew we'd hold out till their ears started twitching."

Lone is ready to celebrate the victory with Ma (though the workers themselves are not holding a celebration). First, Ma must wash his body to ready it for the role of Kwan Kung.

Ma explains to Lone that he suffered the ordeal of last night, not out of ambition to star in opera, but out of loyalty and honor to Lone for his having told Ma his story. Instead of a traditional opera with Kwan Kung as hero, Ma would like to act out an opera about himself: "I just won a great victory. . . . . I'll immortalize my story." Lone refuses, but Ma challenges him: "Don't think I'm worth an opera? No, I guess not. I forgot—you think I'm just one of those dead men."

> *Silence. Lone pulls out a gong. Ma gets into position. Lone hits the gong. They do the following in mock Chinese opera style.*

MA: I am Ma. Yesterday I was kicked out of my house by my three elder brothers calling me the lazy dreamer of the family. I am sitting here in front of the temple trying to decide how I will avenge this indignity. Here comes the poorest beggar in the village.

He cues Lone.

LONE: Wait, wait, wait, wait, wait!

MA: He is called Fleaman because his body is the most popular meeting place for fleas from around the province.

LONE *(sings):*
Fleas in love
Find your happiness
In the gray scraps of my suit.

MA: Hello, flea—

LONE *(continuing, sings):*
Fleas in need
Shield your families
In the gray hairs of my beard.

MA: Hello, flea—

Lone cuts Ma off, continues an extended improvised aria.

Hello, Fleaman.

LONE: Oh, hello, Ma. Are you interested in providing a home for these fleas?

MA: No!

LONE: This couple here—seeking to start a new home. Housing today is so hard to find. How about your left arm?

MA: I may have plenty of my own fleas in time. See, I have been kicked out of my house by my three elder brothers.

LONE: Are you seeking revenge? A flea epidemic on your house? *(To a flea.)* Get back there. You should be asleep. Your mother will worry.

MA: Nothing would make my brothers angrier than seeing me rich.

LONE: Rich, ha! After the bad crops of the last three years, even the fleas are thinking of moving north.

MA: I heard a white devil talk yesterday.

LONE: Oh—with hair the color of a sick chicken and eyes as round as eggs? The fleas and I call him Chicken-Laying-an-Egg.

MA: He said we can make our fortunes on the Gold Mountain, where work is like play and the sun scares off snow.

LONE: Don't listen to chicken-brains.

MA: Why not? He said gold grows like weeds.

LONE: I have heard that it is slavery.

MA: Slavery? What do you know, Fleaman? Who told you? The fleas? Yes, I will go to the Gold Mountain.

They pick up fighting sticks and do a water-crossing dance. Dance ends. They stoop next to each other and rock.

I have been in the bottom of this boat for thirty-six days now. Tang, how many have died?

LONE: Not me. I'll live through this ride.

MA: I didn't ask how you are.

LONE: But why's the Gold Mountain so far?

MA: We left with three hundred and three.

LONE: My family's depending on me.
MA: So tell me how many have died?
LONE: I'll be the last one alive.
MA: That's not what I wanted to know
LONE: I'll find some fresh air in this hole.
MA: I asked, how many have died?
LONE: Is that a crack in the side?
MA: Are you listening to me?
LONE: If I had some air—
MA: I asked, don't you see—?
LONE: The crack—over there—
MA: Will you answer me, please?
LONE: I need to get out.
MA: The rest here agree—
LONE: I can't stand the smell.
MA: That a hundred and eighty—
LONE: I can't see the air.
MA: —of us will not see.
LONE: And I can't die.
MA: Our Gold Mountain dream.

The two continue their improvised opera: Tang (Lone) dies, and Ma throws his body overboard. Ma pretends that one of the fighting sticks is a pickaxe and does a dance of labor to the accompaniment of a song by Lone. Ma battles the mountain with pickaxe and dynamite, as they both work the battle sticks. Lone breaks away and declares, "I am a white devil! Listen to my stupid language: "Wha Dee Doo Doo Bee Bee Blah Blah.' Look at my wide eyes—like I have drunk seventy-two pots of tea. Look at my funny hair, turning, twisting, like a snake telling lies."

They do not understand the white man's language, but they know when they are being exploited by his efforts to make them work ten-hour shifts when he works only eight. They strike, and they win: "We forced the white devil to act civilized." They are both amazed and elated by their success.

As they work the battle sticks, Ma tires of performing and decides to bring the opera to an end simply by dropping his stick. In doing so, he is accidentally struck by Lone who, after seeing that Ma is all right, informs him that they can't end the opera with a celebration—they have to go back to work tomorrow. And they did not win all that they struck for: they had asked for a $14 dollar raise but were forced to compromise on $8. Ma would prefer to continue the strike until total victory—and besides, he is tired of the work itself: "I get so frustrated sometimes. At the rock. The rock doesn't give in. It's not human. I wanna claw it with my fingers, but that would just rip them up. I wanna throw myself head first onto it, but it'd just knock my skull open. The rock would knock my skull open, then just sit there smiling, still, like nothing had happened, like a faceless Buddha."

Lone knows what Ma is beginning to suspect: that they'll never get out of here until the railroad is finished or they get rich—neither of which is likely to happen.

MA: Lone, has anyone ever gone home rich from here?

LONE: Yes. Some.

MA: But most?

LONE: Most . . . do go home.

> (Beat.)

MA: Do you still have the fear?

LONE: The fear?

MA: That you'll become like them—dead men?

LONE: Maybe I was wrong about them.

MA: Well, I do. You wanted me to say it before. I can say it now: "They are dead men." Their greatest accomplishment was to win a strike that's gotten us nothing.

LONE: They're sending money home.

MA: No.

LONE: It's not much, I know, but it's something.

MA: Lone, I'm not even doing that. . . . .

Ma is too soft and gullible (he believed "warm snow") to get rich, Lone tells him, and Ma agrees—he'll have to toughen himself up. He has now caught the fear from Lone. He has decided he doesn't have time to turn himself into a Second Clown, though Lone is ready to admit Ma might become "a fair actor." Ma must now get himself ready to go to work—with his sore legs, it's going to be an especially tough day. Lone will remain on the mountain to practise.

MA: Practise? But you said you lost your fear. And you said that's what brings you up here.

LONE: I guess I was wrong about that, too. Today I am dancing for no reason at all.

MA: Do whatever you want. See you down at camp.

LONE: Could you do me a favor, please?

MA: A favor?

LONE: Could you take some of this down so I don't have to take it all?

MA: Well, O.K. *(Pause.)* But this is the last time. *(Exits.)*

LONE: Of course, Ma. See you soon. The last time. I suppose so.

> *Lone resumes practising. He ends up on top of the tree stump swinging his hair, as in the opening. Curtain.*

THE LIFE & ADVENTURES OF NICHOLAS NICKLEBY

A Play in Two Parts With Five Acts

BY DAVID EDGAR

ADAPTED FROM THE NOVEL BY CHARLES DICKENS

Cast and credits appear on pages 313–315

DAVID EDGAR is a British dramatist much produced on stage and screen in his own country and abroad. Born Feb. 26, 1948 and educated at Oundle School and Manchester University, he wrote his first play Two Kinds of Angel *in 1970 while still working as a journalist. It was soon staged at a university, beginning the long march of his British theater productions:* Still Life, Man in Bed *(1971);* Excuses Excuses, Rent or Caught in the Act, England's Ireland *(1972);* A Fart for Europe, Baby-Love *(1973);* The Dunkirk Spirit, Dick Deterred *(1974);* Fired, O Fair Jerusalem *(1975);* Events Following the Closing of a Motorcycle Factory, Blood Sports, Saigon Rose, Destiny *(1976);* Wreckers *(1977);* Our Own People, The Jail Diary of Albie Sachs, Mary Barnes *(1978);* Teendreams *(1979);* The Life & Adventures of Nicholas Nickleby *(1980). His television plays include* The Eagle Has Landed *and* I Know What I Meant; *his* Destiny *and* Baby-Love *have also been shown on TV, and he is the author of the radio play* Ecclesiastes.

Edgar's American stage productions began with Death Story *OOB at Manhattan Theater Club in 1975 and have included* The Jail Diary of Albie Sachs *off*

Broadway at the same group in 1979, Mary Barnes *at the Long Wharf Theater in New Haven in 1980 and now* Nicholas Nickleby, *his first Broadway play and first Best Play, adapted from the Dickens novel on commission from the Royal Shakespeare Company and brought to New York after its successful London engagement.*

Edgar has also been active as a teacher of writing at Leeds Polytechnic and the University of Birmingham, at whose repertory theater he served for two years as resident playwright. He was a UK/US Bicentennial Arts Fellow resident in the United States in 1978–79 and is a founder-member of the Theater Writers' Union. He is married, and his home base is London.

Speaking to a group of theater journalists in New York, David Edgar asserted that it was his and the Royal Shakespeare Company's intention from the outset to dramatize ALL of Charles Dickens's The Life & Adventures of Nicholas Nickleby. *None of the subplots was to be dropped, though incidents within them could be cut (and sometimes the status of "subplot" vs. "incident" was hotly debated). The full synopsis of this magnificent chronicle is, therefore, available from the many sources which carry a synopsis of the novel, let alone in the pages of the novel itself.*

To offer a full synopsis of the stage version here would be redundant. Our method of hailing Nicholas Nickleby *in these pages differs from that of the other Best Plays: instead of synopsizing, we present two complete scenes selected by Mr. Edgar to represent his script. His stage adaptation was presented in two parts, Part I of four hours in two acts and Part II of four and one-half hours in three acts. The portion chosen consists of Part I, Act I, Scenes 9 and 10, preceded by a summary of events leading up to these scenes, prepared by Mr. Edgar.*

Time: Mid-Nineteenth Century

Place: London and Yorkshire

Nicholas Nickleby, his sister and his mother come to London following the death of their father, to throw themselves on the mercy of their only living relative, the businessman Ralph Nickleby. Keen to dispose of the burden of their upkeep as quickly as possible, Ralph makes Nicholas accept employment at Dotheboys Hall, a boarding school in Yorkshire.

Nicholas meets the school's headmaster, the sinister Wackford Squeers, in London (which Squeers has visited to collect boys for his school from their parents). But Nicholas suppresses his alarm at the character and demeanor of Squeers, for the sake of his mother and sister, and agrees to depart on the coach for Yorkshire the next morning, in the company of Squeers and three small boys: the Snawley brothers and young Belling. Just before leaving, however, Nicholas is handed a note by Newman Noggs, Ralph Nickleby's sad and sallow clerk, who immediately disappears into the crowd.

Roger Rees as Nicholas Nickleby and David Threlfall
as his friend Smike in a scene from *Nicholas Nickleby*

Arriving at the school, Nicholas begins to realize, with growing horror, the true nature of the "educational establishment" he is now serving.

Scene 9: Outside and inside Dotheboys Hall

> *A bare stage. Snow falls. Wind blows. Squeers, Nicholas, Belling and the two Snawleys walk downstage with the luggage. They stop.*

NICHOLAS: Dotheboys Hall.

SQUEERS: Oh, sir, you needn't call it a hall up here.

NICHOLAS: Why not?

SQUEERS: Cos the fact is, it ain't a hall.

> *Squeers leads the party round to the side of the stage,*

NICHOLAS *(speaks to the audience):* A host of unpleasant misgivings, which had been crowding upon Nicholas during the whole journey, thronged into his mind. And as he considered the dreary house and dark windows, and the wild country round covered with snow, he felt a depression of heart and spirit which he had never experienced before.

SQUEERS: No, we call it a hall up in London, because it sounds better, but they don't know it by that name here.

> *He bangs on an imaginary door. Someone makes the sound.*

A man may call his house an island if he likes; there's no Act of Parliament against that, I believe?

NICHOLAS: No, I think not, sir.

SQUEERS (banging): Well, then. Hey! Door!

>From the darkness, Smike appears, He is about 19, but bent over with lameness, and dressed in ragged garments which he has long since outgrown. He pulls open the huge door, and the wind howls as Squeers strides into the house.

Smike. Where the devil have you been?

SMIKE: Please, sir, I fell asleep.

SQUEERS: You fell what?

SMIKE: Please, sir, I fell asleep over the fire.

SQUEERS: Fire? What fire? Where's there a fire?

During the following, Squeers, Smike, Nicholas and the boys with their luggage move round the stage—as if passing along corridors—as the Squeerses' servant Phib brings on a big chair and then a table to center stage. This is the Squeerses' parlor, and Phib goes out again to bring on a tray of brandy, glasses and water, placing it on the table.

SMIKE: Please, sir, Missus said as I was sitting u—, I might be by the fire for a warm . . .

SQUEERS: Your missus is a fool. You'd have been a deuced deal more wakeful in the cold.

From off, we hear the voice of Mrs. Squeers.

MRS. SQUEERS (off): Squeers!

SQUEERS (calls): My love!

MRS. SQUEERS (off): Squeers!

By now, Squeers is in the parlor area, the boys are standing in the corridor with their luggage and Nicholas is between them, as if in the doorway, not knowing quite what to do.

SQUEERS (to Smike): There's boys. The boys, to bed.

Smike takes the boys out, leaving their luggage, as Mrs. Squeers enters.

MRS. SQUEERS: Oh, Squeers. How is my Squeery, dearie.

The Squeerses embrace.

SQUEERS: Well, well, my love. How are the cows?

MRS. SQUEERS: All right, every one of 'em.

SQUEERS: And the pigs?

MRS. SQUEERS: As well as they were when you went.

SQUEERS: Well, that's a great blessing.

These sweet nothings over, Squeers leaves Mrs. Squeers and takes letters and documents from his pocket.

(As an afterthought.) The boys all as they were, I suppose?

MRS. SQUEERS (taking the letters from Squeers and placing them on the table, glancing at one or two): Oh, yes, they're well enough. But young Sprouter's had a fever.

SQUEERS (taking off his greatcoat): No! Damn the boy, he's always at something of that sort.

Phib takes Squeers's huge coat and stands there, holding it. Squeers

*goes to the table, sits. Mrs. Squeers pours him a brandy and tops it up
with water.*

MRS. SQUEERS: Never was such a boy, I do believe. Whatever he has is always
catching, too. I say it's obstinacy, and nothing shall ever convince me that it isn't.
I'd beat it out of him, and I told you that six months ago.

SQUEERS: So you did, my love. We'll try what can be done.

> *Slight pause. Mrs. Squeers nods in the direction of Nicholas, who is still
> standing near the door, not knowing what to do.*

Ah, Nickleby. Come, sir, come in.

> *Nicholas comes a little further into the room.*

This is our new young man, my dear.

MRS. SQUEERS *(suspiciously):* Oh. Is it?

SQUEERS: He can shake down here tonight, can't he?

MRS. SQUEERS *(looking round):* Well, if he's not particular . . .

NICHOLAS *(politely):* Oh, no, indeed.

MRS. SQUEERS: That's lucky.

> *She looks at Squeers and laughs. Squeers laughs back. They laugh at
> each other. Meanwhile, Smike reappears. Mrs. Squeers looks at Phib
> and snaps her head towards the door. Phib goes out with the big coat.
> Slight pause.*

(With a wink to Squeers, as if to ask if Nicholas should be given a drink.) Another
brandy, Squeers?

SQUEERS *(nodding back):* Certainly. A glassful.

> *Mrs. Squeers pours a large brandy-and-water for Squeers and a smaller
> one for Nicholas. She takes the drink to Nicholas. Squeers is looking
> through the letters. Nicholas takes the drink. Smike stands, staring
> fixedly at the letters on the table. Mrs. Squeers goes and picks up one
> of the boys' bags and takes it back to the table.*

Bolder's father's short.

MRS. SQUEERS: Tt tt.

SQUEERS: But Cobbey's sister's sent something.

> *Mrs. Squeers starts going through the boy's luggage, picking out the bits
> and pieces she fancies.*

MRS. SQUEERS: That's good.

SQUEERS: And Graymarsh's maternal aunt has written, with no money, but
two pairs of stockings and a tract.

MRS. SQUEERS: Maternal aunt.

SQUEERS: My love?

MRS. SQUEERS: More likely, in my view, that she's Graymarsh's maternal
mother.

> *The Squeerses look at each other. Then Squeers notices that Smike is
> very close, craning to see the letters.*

SQUEERS: Yes? What's to do, boy?

SMIKE: Is there—

SQUEERS: What?

SMIKE: Is there . . . there's nothing heard . . . ?

SQUEERS: No, not a word. And never will be.

MRS. SQUEERS *(the very idea):* Tt.

>*Pause. Squeers decides to rub it in.*

SQUEERS: And it is a pretty sort of thing, that you should have been left here all these years and no money paid after the first six—nor no notice taken, nor no clue to who you belong to? It's a pretty sort of thing, is it not, that I should have to feed a great fellow like you and never hope to get one penny for it, isn't it?

>*Squeers looking at Smike.*

NICHOLAS *(out front):* The boy put his hand to his head, as if he was making an effort to remember something, and then, looking vacantly at his questioner, gradually broke into a smile.

SQUEERS: That's right. Now, off with you, and send the girl.

>*Smike limps out. Mrs. Squeers has finished sifting the boy's bag. She looks for something on the table.*

MRS. SQUEERS: I tell you what, Squeers, I think that young chap's turning silly.

SQUEERS *(wiping his mouth):* I hope not. For he's a handy fellow out of doors and worth his meat and drink anyway. *(He stands.)* But come, I'm tired and I want to go to bed.

MRS. SQUEERS: Oh, drat the thing.

SQUEERS: What's wrong, my dear?

MRS. SQUEERS: The school spoon. I can't find it.

SQUEERS: Never mind, my love.

MRS. SQUEERS: What, never mind? It's brimstone, in the morning.

SQUEERS: Ah, I forgot. *(He helps the search.)* Yes, certainly, it is.

NICHOLAS: Uh . . . ?

SQUEERS: We purify the boys' bloods now and then, Nickleby.

MRS. SQUEERS *(crossly):* Purify fiddlesticks. Don't think, young man, that we go to the expense of flour of brimstone and molasses just to purify them; because if you think we carry on the business in that way, you'll find yourself mistaken, and so I tell you plainly.

>*Squeers is not sure this intelligence is quite discreet. Enter Phib, who tidies round the table, putting things back on the tray.*

SQUEERS: My dear . . . should you . . .

MRS. SQUEERS: Nonsense. If the young man comes to be a teacher, let him understand at once that we don't want any foolery about the boys. They have the brimstone and treacle, partly because if they hadn't something or other in the way of medicine they'd always be ailing and giving a world of trouble, and partly because it spoils their appetites and comes cheaper than breakfast and dinner. So it does them good and us good at the same time, and that's fair enough, I'm sure.

>*Squeers looking embarrassed; Mrs. Squeers shoots a glance at him.*

Now, where's the spoon.

>*Phib has picked up the tray.*

PHIB: Uh, ma'am.

MRS. SQUEERS: What is it?

PHIB: S'round your neck.

>*And indeed the spoon is round Mrs. Squeers's neck. She cuffs Phib lightly for telling her.*

MRS. SQUEERS: Why did you not say *before.*

PHIB: M'sorry, ma'am.
   Phib picks up the tray, leaving the brandy bottle, and goes out.
MRS. SQUEERS *(pleasantly):* And so, dear Mr. Nickleby, good night.
   Mrs. Squeers goes out. Pause.
SQUEERS: A most invaluable woman, Nickleby.
NICHOLAS: Indeed, sir.
SQUEERS: I do not know her equal. That woman, Nickleby, is always the same, always the same bustling, lively, active, saving creature that you see her now.
NICHOLAS: I'm sure of it.
SQUEERS *(warming further to his theme):* It is my custom, when I am in London, to say that she is like a mother to those boys. But she is more, she's ten times more. She does things for those boys, Nickleby, that I don't believe half the mothers going would do for their own sons.
NICHOLAS: I'm certain of it, sir.
SQUEERS: And so, good night, then, Nickleby.
   He tries to make a solemn exit, undetermined by spotting the brandy, which he returns to pick up.
NICHOLAS: Good night, sir.
   Squeers nods gravely and goes out. Nicholas stands a moment, then takes off his coat. He sits on the floor. He notices Newman Noggs's letter in his coat pocket. He opens it and begins to read. Noggs himself appears, with a glass of brandy. He sits on the arm of Squeers's chair, and he speaks his letter as we see Nicholas read it.
NOGGS: My dear young man. I know the world. Your father did not, or he would not have done me a kindness when there was no hope of return. You do not, or you would not be bound on such a journey. If ever you want a shelter in London, they know where I live at the sign of the Crown, in Silver Street, Golden Square. You can come at night, Once, nobody was ashamed—never mind that. It's all over. Excuse errors. I have forgotten all my old ways. My spelling may have gone with them.
NICHOLAS *(reads):* Yours obediently, Newman Noggs.
NOGGS: P.S.: If you should go near Barnard Castle, there is good ale at the King's Head. Say you know me, and I am sure they will not charge you for it. You may say *Mr.* Noggs there, for I was a gentleman then. I was indeed.
   Noggs shambles out. Nicholas crumbles to the floor. He is crying. Blackout.

Scene 10: Dotheboys Hall

   The school bell rings, the lights come up. The parlor chair and table have gone. Squeers shouts to Nicholas, who wakes.
SQUEERS: Past seven, Nickleby! It's morning come, and well-iced already. Now, Nickleby, come, tumble up, will you?
   Squeers, with his cane, strides round the stage. Nicholas jumps up and, pulling on his coat, follows. Mrs. Squeers enters, followed by Smike, who carries a bowl of brimstone and treacle. Squeers and Nicholas arrive at one side of the stage, Mrs. Squeers and Smike at the other.

Then, through the darkness at the back of the stage, we see, approaching us, the boys of Dotheboys Hall. They are dressed in the ragged remains of what were once school uniforms. They move slowly, through lameness and sullenness and fear. Then they form themselves into a kind of line, and each boy goes to Mrs. Squeers to receive a spoonful of brimstone and treacle.

SQUEERS: There. This is our shop, Nickleby.

Each boy gives his number, name, age and reason for being at the school before receiving his dose. Clearly, this is an accepted ritual.

TOMKINS: First boy. Tompkins. Nine. A cripple.

COATES: Second boy. Coates. Thirteen. A bastard.

GRAYMARSH: Third boy. Graymarsh. Twelve. Another bastard.

JENNINGS: Fourth boy. Jennings. Thirteen. Disfigured.

MOBBS: Fifth boy. *(Pause.)* Mobbs. Uh—'leven.

Pause. He doesn't know what's wrong with him. Mrs. Squeers hits him on the side of the head.

MRS. SQUEERS: Simpleton!

MOBBS: Fifth. Mobbs. Eleven. Sim-pull-ton.

BOLDER: Sixth. Bolder. Fourteen. Orphan.

PITCHER: Seventh. Pitcher. Ten.

MRS. SQUEERS: Yes!

Pause.

PITCHER: I'm very. Very. Slow.

MRS. SQUEERS: Move on. Move *on.*

JACKSON: Eighth. Johnny.

MRS. SQUEERS: Johnny?

JACKSON: Jackson. Thirteen. Illegitimate.

COBBEY: Ninth. Cobbey. Fifteen. Cripple.

PETERS: Tenth Uh—Peters. Seven. Blind.

SPROUTER: Eleventh. Sprouter. Seven. My father killed my mother.

MRS. SQUEERS: Yes?

SPROUTER: Sent away.

ROBERTS: Twelfth. Roberts. Ten. There's something wrong—my brain.

Squeers's young son Wackford, well-dressed and stout, pushes forward the two Snawley boys and Belling.

SNAWLEY SENIOR: Robert Arthur Snawley.

MRS. SQUEERS: Number!

SNAWLEY SR.: I'm eleven.

MRS. SQUEERS *(twisting Snawley Senior's ear):* Number, is thirteen.

SNAWLEY SR.: Thirteen.

SNAWLEY JUNIOR: Uh—fourteen-th. Snawley, H. Uh—seven.

BELLING: Fifteen. Anthony Belling. Seven years of age. A classical and modern —moral, education.

Mrs. Squeers wipes her hands on Smike.

SQUEERS *(to Wackford):* Thank you, young Wackford. Thank you, son. And what do you say? And what d'you say, to this?

Pause.

BOYS: For what we have received, may the Lord make us truly thankful.
SQUEERS: Amen.
BOYS: Amen.
SQUEERS: That's better. Now, boys, I've been to London, and have returned to my family and you, as strong and well as ever.
> *Pause. Mrs. Squeers gestures to a boy.*
COATES *(feebly):* Hip hip . . .
BOYS *(equally feebly):* Hooray.
COATES: Hip hip . . .
BOYS: Hooray.
COATES: Hip hip . . .
BOYS: Hooray.
> *Squeers takes various letters from his pockets and wanders around among the boys as he speaks.*
SQUEERS: I have seen the parents of some boys, and they're so glad to hear how their sons are doing that there's no prospect at all of their going home, which of course is a very pleasant thing to reflect upon for all parties. *(He continues to perambulate.)* But I have had disappointments to contend with. Bolder's father, for an instance, was two pounds ten short. Where is Bolder?
> *The boys around Bolder kick him, and he puts up his hand. Squeers goes to Bolder.*
Ah. Bolder. Bolder, if your father thinks that because—
> *Squeers suddenly notices warts on Bolder's hand. He grabs the boy's arm.*
What do you call this, sir?
BOLDER: Warts, sir.
SQUEERS: What, sir?
BOLDER: Warts, sir.
SQUEERS: Warts?
BOLDER: I can't help it, sir. They will come . . . It's working in the garden does it, sir, at least I don't know what it is, sir, but it's not my fault . . .
SQUEERS: Bolder. You are an incorrigible young scoundrel, and as the last thrashing did you no good, we must see what another will do towards beating it out of you.
> *Bolder looks terrified.*
La-ter.
> *He lets Bolder go and walks on.*
(Reading.) Now, let's see . . . A letter for Cobbey. Cobbey?
> *Cobbey puts his hand up. Squeers hardly acknowledges, but walks on.*
Oh, Cobbey's grandmother is dead, and his Uncle John has took to drinking, which is all the news his sister sends, except eighteenpence, which will just pay for that broken square of glass. Mobbs!
> *Mobbs, not sure whether this will be good or bad news, nervously puts up his hand. It is clear it is not good news when Squeers walks to him and stands near.*
Now, Mobbs's stepmother took to her bed on hearing that he would not eat fat, and has been very ill ever since. She wishes to know by an early post where he

expects to go to, if he quarrels with his vittles; and with what feelings he could turn up his nose at the cow's liver broth, after his good master had asked a blessing on it. She is disconsolate to find he is discontented, which is sinful and horrid, and hopes Mr. Squeers will flog him into a happier state of mind. *(Into Mobbs's ear.)* Which—he—will. *(Long pause to let this sink in to everyone.)* Right, boys. I'd like you all to meet my new assistant, Mr. Nickleby. Good morning, Mr. Nickleby.

BOYS: Good morning, Mr. Nickleby.

NICHOLAS: Good morning.

SQUEERS: Now, this is the first class in English spelling and philosophy, Nickleby. We'll soon get up a Latin one and hand that over to you.

Nicholas joins Squeers.

Now, then, where's Smallpiece?

BOYS: Please, sir . . .

SQUEERS: Let any boy speak out of turn, and I'll have the skin off his back!

JENNINGS: Please, sir, he's cleaning the back parlor window.

SQUEERS: So he is, to be sure. We go on the practical mode of teaching, Nickleby; c-l-e-a-n, clean—

BOYS: Clean.

SQUEERS: Verb active, to make bright, to scour. W-i-n, win—

BOYS: Win—

SQUEERS: D-e-r, der—

BOYS: Der, winder—

SQUEERS: Winder, a casement. When a boy knows this out of a book, he goes and does it. It's just the same principle as the use of the globes. Where's Grinder?

Coates puts his hand up. Squeers points to Coates.

COATES: Please, sir, he's weeding the garden.

SQUEERS: To be sure. So he is. B-o-t, bot—

BOYS: Bot—

SQUEERS: T-i-n, tin—

BOYS: Tin—

SQUEERS: Bottin—

BOYS: Bottin—

SQUEERS: N-e-y, ney—

BOYS: Ney—

SQUEERS: Bottiney—

BOYS: Bottiney—

SQUEERS: Noun substantive, a knowledge of plants. When he has learned that bottiney means a knowledge of plants, he goes and knows 'em. That's our system, Nickleby. What do you think of it?

NICHOLAS: It's a very useful one, at any rate.

SQUEERS: I believe you. Graymarsh, what's a horse?

GRAYMARSH: A beast, sir.

SQUEERS: So it is. A horse is a quadroped, and quadroped's Latin for beast, as anybody that's gone through the grammar knows, or else where's the use in having grammars at all?

NICHOLAS: Where indeed.

SQUEERS *(to Graymarsh):* And as you're so perfect in that, go to *my* horse and rub him down well, or I'll rub *you* down. The rest go and draw water up till somebody tells you to leave off, for it's washing day tomorrow, and they'll want the coppers filled.

> *The boys hurry out, Mobbs and Bolder hurrying more than the others.*

Except—for Mobbs and Bolder.

> *Everyone stops. Some of the boys push Mobbs and Bolder forward, towards Squeers. Then the others go out, as Mrs. Squeers and Wackford go too. Smike tried to go as well.*

Stay there, Smike. They'll need taking to their beds. *(He turns to Nicholas.)* This is the way we do it, Nickleby.

> *Squeers lifts his cane. Blackout. Some of the older men of the company appear in a little light. As they speak this narration, we see Nicholas sit morosely down at the side of the stage. Squeers, Smike, Mobbs and Bolder have gone.*

NARRATORS: And Nicholas sat down, so depressed and self-degraded that if death could have come upon him then he would have been happy to meet it. The cruelty of which he had been an unwilling witness, the coarse and ruffianly behavior of Squeers, the filthy place, the sights and sounds about him, all contributed to this feeling. And when he recollected that, being there as an assistant, he was the aider and abetter of a system which filled him with disgust and indignation, he loathed himself.

> *Blackout.*

THE DRESSER

A Play in Two Acts

BY RONALD HARWOOD

Cast and credits appear on page 319

RONALD HARWOOD was born in Cape Town, South Africa, Nov. 9, 1934. He attended Sea Point Boys High School in his native city before moving to England in 1951 to study at the Royal Academy of Dramatic Art. In 1953 he joined Donald Wolfit's Shakespeare company at the King's Theater, Hammersmith and for the next seven years concentrated on acting, often touring with Wolfit and his troupe, where his experiences (including a stint as the star's dresser) were the source material for his Best Play The Dresser.

Harwood turned to playwriting in 1960. His works for the stage have included Country Matters *(1969), the libretto for* The Good Companions *(1974), an adaptation of Evelyn Waugh's* The Ordeal of Gilbert Pinfold *(1977),* A Family *(1978) and now* The Dresser *(1980) produced at the Royal Exchange Theater, Manchester and the Queen's Theater, London, winning the New Standard and Drama Critics Awards before its importation to Broadway Nov. 9, 1981 for a 200-performance run.*

Harwood's many other credits include, for the screen, One Day in the Life of Ivan Denisovitch; *for TV,* The Guests, A Sense of Loss *(documentary about Evelyn Waugh),* The Barber of Stamford Hill, Private Potter *and* Evita Peron; *a biography of Donald Wolfit and numerous novels, among them* The Girl in Melanie Klein, Articles of Faith, The Genoa Ferry, Caesar and Augusta *and* One. Interior. Day.

Harwood is currently at work on a 13-part history of the theater entitled All the World's a Stage *to be presented on BBC2 in 1983. He is a fellow of the Royal Society of Literature and has served as a member of the literature panel of the Arts*

Tom Courtenay as Norman and Paul Rogers as Sir (in costume for the title role of *King Lear*) in *The Dresser*

Council and as chairman of his country's Writers Guild. He is married, with three children, and lives in Hampshire, England.

The following synopsis of The Dresser *was prepared by Jeffrey Sweet.*

Time: January 1942

Place: A theater in the English provinces

ACT I: BEFORE CURTAIN UP

SYNOPSIS: Norman is alone in Sir's dressing room wearing "a lost, almost forlorn expression." On the floor are a Homburg and an overcoat in a much-abused condition. Norman hears footsteps and rises as Her Ladyship enters and reports that Sir, whom Norman took to a hospital earlier, appears to be in a state of collapse. She asks Norman for an explanation. He suggests she sit, then recounts how he happened upon Sir in the street after a bomb raid. With voice and gestures familiar from Sir's portrayal of King Lear, the old actor dramatically removed his coat and hat and trampled them, raging, "How much further do you want me to go?" as a crowd gathered.

HER LADYSHIP: You shouldn't have let the public see him like that.

NORMAN: It's easy to be wise after the event, if you don't mind my saying so, your ladyship, but I tried to spirit him away, not easy with a man of his proportions, only just then, a woman approached, quite old, wearing bombazine under a tweed coat but perfectly respectable. She'd picked up his clothes and wanted to help him dress. I just stood there, amazed, utterly amazed. He said to the woman, "Thank you my dear, but Norman usually looks after me. I'd be lost without Norman," so I thought to myself this is your cue, ducky, and said, "I'm Norman, I'm his dresser." The woman—she had her hair in curlers—took his hand and kissed it, saying, "You were lovely in *The Corsican Brothers.*" He looked at her a long while, smiled sweetly, you know the way he does when he's wanting to charm, and said, "Thank you, my dear, but you must excuse me. I have to make an exit," and ran off.

HER LADYSHIP: He said, I have to make an exit?

NORMAN: Well, of course, I went after him, fearing the worst. I didn't know he could run so fast. I just followed a trail of discarded clothing, jacket, waistcoat, and thought we can't have Sir doing a striptease round the town. But then I found him. Leaning up against a lamp-post. Weeping.

HER LADYSHIP: Where?

NORMAN: Outside the Kardomah. Without a word, hardly knowing what I was doing, I led him to the hospital. The Sister didn't recognize him, although later she said she'd seen him as Othello last night. A doctor was summoned, short, bald, bespectacled, and I was excluded by the drawing of screens.

HER LADYSHIP: And then you telephoned me.

NORMAN: No. I waited. I lurked, as Edmund says, and heard the doctor whisper, "This man is exhausted. This man is in a state of collapse." Then the Sister came out and said I must fetch you at once. That's when I telephoned. And that's how it happened.

When Her Ladyship left, Sir was weeping in his hospital bed, saying nothing. She awaits the stage manager, Madge, to seek her advice as to what to do about the performance of *King Lear* scheduled to start in an hour. Sir's collapse is not a total surprise to Norman and Her Ladyship. They describe to each other Sir's curious and unsettling behavior and comments of late. If the doctors had had an inkling of this pattern, they might have tried to lock him up for good. Norman now regrets having taken him to the hospital, but Her Ladyship insists he did right. Norman insists no doctor would understand the pressure Sir has been under as an actor-manager trying to maintain a company made up of those not fit for service—not to mention the problem with Mr. Davenport-Scott, who was both a member of the company (playing the Fool to Sir's Lear) and business manager. Mr. Davenport-Scott has fallen into the hands of the police, and so they have no business manager and will have to scramble for a Fool.

Her Ladyship is all for cancelling, but the idea strikes Norman as too drastic. Sir has never cancelled. Norman is near tears at the thought. He recalls meeting

Sir 16 years before. He had lent a hand one night in dressing Sir for a Lear and had even pounded the timpani for the storm scene. That night, Sir had proclaimed Norman to be an artist and hired him to be his dresser.

Madge, the stage manager, enters to discuss the logistics of cancelling the performance. Norman tries to get Her Ladyship to refrain from a decision.

NORMAN: Forgive me, your ladyship, it's not *a* decision you have to make, it's the *right* decision. I had a friend, before one's face was lined, as the saying goes, in a very low state he was, ever so fragile, a pain to be with. You weren't safe from him on top of a bus. If he happened to sit beside you, he'd tell you the ABC of unhappiness between request stops. Someone close to him, his mother, I believe, though it was never proved, understandably upset, made a decision. A little rest, she said, among those similarly off-center, in Colwyn Bay, never a good date, not in February, wrapped in a grey rug, gazing at a grey sea. Talk about bleak. Mother-dear made a decision, but it was the wrong decision. My friend never acted again.

MADGE *(to Her Ladyship):* We have to face the facts.

NORMAN: I've never done that in my life, your ladyship, and I don't see why I should start now. I just like things to be lovely. No pain, that's my motto.

MADGE: But things aren't lovely, Norman.

NORMAN: They aren't if you face facts. Face the facts, it's facing the company I worry about. Poor lambs. What'll happen to them? And the customers? There was a queue at the box office this afternoon, if four elderly spinsters constitute a queue. Pity to give them their money back, they've likely had enough disappointment in life as it is. It's no good Sir talking about responsibility and service and struggle and survival and then you go and cancel the performance.

MADGE *(to Her Ladyship):* It's a disease.

HER LADYSHIP: What is?

MADGE: Hopefulness. I think we should discuss this in private. I'll be in my room.

She goes. Her Ladyship is about to follow.

NORMAN: Yes, well, perhaps it is a disease, but I've caught something much worse from Sir.

HER LADYSHIP: What?

NORMAN: A bad dose of Holy Grail.

He laughs, but the laughter turns to tears. . . . .

Her Ladyship, in an attempt to make Norman recognize that reality necessarily affects the stage, recounts the story of an accident her father sustained playing Macbeth that left his face so badly cut the only part left to him was Caliban. "It's not the same thing," says Norman.

Her Ladyship is about to announce the cancellation of both the performance and the engagement, when a dishevelled Sir enters and greets them both, informing them he decided to check himself out of the hospital. Then he breaks into tears. Norman goes to tell Madge that Sir has arrived, leaving Her Ladyship alone with Sir. She tries to persuade him not to go on, but he is determined.

HER LADYSHIP: Where have you been all day? Don't tell me you found a brothel in this town.

SIR: I can't remember all I've done. I know towards evening I was being pursued but I couldn't see who the villains were. Then the warning went. I refused to take shelter. I'm accustomed to the blasted heath. Acrid smell. Eyes watering. Wherever I went I seemed to hear a woman crying. Suddenly, I had a clear image of my father on the beach near Lowestoft, plans in his hands, inspecting the boats his men had built. "An actor?" he said, "Never. You will be a boat builder like me." But I defied him and lost his love. Father preferred people to cower. But I had to chart my own course. I decide when I'm ready for the scrap-yard. Not you. I and no one else. I.

He sits and stares.

HER LADYSHIP: The woman you heard crying was me.

Sir calls for Norman and tells him to stick by him. Madge appears too. She tries to persuade Sir not to go on, but he insists that in the 20 years she's been with him he's never missed a performance, and he's not about to let this be a first time. Norman sends Madge and Her Ladyship to prepare for the show. Bracing himself with a nip of brandy, Norman tries to jolly Sir into getting started on his makeup, talking to him as if he were a child. *"Sir. . . . . suddenly grabs hold of Norman, buries his face in his neck and sobs."* Norman tries to comfort Sir by telling him of a friend of his (in reality Norman) who was once similarly emotionally distressed when he received an offer of work. The offer prompted him to recover. "Meant someone had thought of him and that's ever such a comfort." Sir releases Norman.

Norman tells him there will be a full house tonight. The news prompts Sir to ask what he's to play. Lear. He doesn't want to play it. He talks of not going on, but Norman continues to pressure him. Sir has apparently forgotten many of the events of the day. He has a vague memory of working on his memoirs. Norman looks for the pages, but there is nothing to be found. Sir bemoans the prospect of playing another Lear, as Norman pressures him to begin making up. At first Sir seems to be willing, but he stops suddenly.

SIR: Where's my hat? I'm getting out of here. I'm not staying in this place a moment longer. I'm surrounded by vipers, betrayal on every side. I am being crushed, the life blood is draining out of me. The load is too great. Norman, Norman, if you have any regard for me, don't listen to him—

NORMAN: Who? Who?

SIR: More, more, more, I can't give any more, I have nothing more to give. I want a tranquil senility. I'm a grown man. I don't want to go on painting my face night after night, wearing clothes that are not my own, I'm not a child dressing up for charades, this is my work, my life's work, I'm an actor, and who cares if I go out there tonight or any other night and shorten my life?

He sits, buries his face in his hands.

NORMAN: I had a friend once said, "Norman, I don't care if there are only three people out front, or if the audience laugh when they shouldn't, or don't when they should, one person, just one person is certain to know and understand. And I act for him." That's what my friend said.

SIR: I can't move that which can't be moved.

NORMAN: What are we on about now?

SIR: I'm filled inside with stone. Stone upon stone. I can't lift myself. The weight is too much. I know futility when I see it. I dream at night of unseen hands driving wooden stakes into my feet. I can't move, and when I look at the wounds I see a jellied, leprous pus. And the dream is long and graceless. I wake up, sweat-drenched, poisoned. And the whole day long there is a burning heat inside me, driving all else from my mind. What did I do today?

NORMAN: You walked. You thought you wrote. You were in Market Square. A woman kissed your hand and said you were lovely in *The Corsican Brothers.*

SIR: How do you know all this? Has someone been talking?

   Pause.

NORMAN: I don't wish to hurry you, Sir, no, I lie, I do.

SIR: I hate the swines.

NORMAN: Who?

SIR: He's a hard task-master, he drives me too hard. I have too much to carry.

Madge appears. Norman, keeping her from entering, tells her he is working on getting Sir prepared and shoos her away. He tells Sir that Madge says everything is working like clockwork. He tells Sir that he is where he belongs, safe in a nice theater, about to play in front of a full house. Sir is still not moved to action. He is brooding over the fact that the theater in which he made his debut was bombed by the Germans.

Norman tries to pull Sir back to the present by bringing up problems at hand with the company. "*Sir is suddenly alert.*" Mr. Davenport-Scott is being detained by police, casting has to be shifted. Sir is disgruntled at the changes: "Thornton toothless as Fool. Browne lisping as Oswald. Oxenby limping as Edmund. What have I come to? I've never had a company like this one. I'm reduced to old men, cripples and nancy-boys. Herr Hitler has made it very difficult for Shakespearean companies." The shifting means they will be under strength for the sound effects for the storm. Oxenby could lend a hand, but is likely to resist the idea. Sir asks to talk to Oxenby to urge him to help. He also wants to talk to Thornton.

Sir is now acting more or less normally. Encouraged, Norman goes to tell Oxenby and Thornton of their summonses and Sir begins to make up—except it's makeup for the wrong play. Norman returns to see Sir under a face full of black for Othello. Norman helps him remove the black as Sir tells him a long-familiar anecdote.

Irene, a young actress in the company, enters to pick up the triple crown to polish it, evidently a nightly ritual. As Sir entrusts the crown to her care, "*he pats her bottom.*" This evidently is also part of the ritual. Irene exits.

Norman guides Sir through the beginning of making up for Lear, Sir snapping at Norman in response to an offhand remark and brooding on the terrible weight of being an actor-manager. As he applies Lear's age lines, he muses that once they had to be painted on. "Now I merely deepen what is already there."

Madge comes to the door. Norman assures her that the performance will go on as scheduled and she should have the house let in. "*He closes the door on her.*"

SIR: What is going on, who was that?

NORMAN: Just a minion, minioning.

SIR: Too many interruptions—my concentration—Norman!

NORMAN: Sir?

SIR: How does the play begin?

NORMAN: Which play, Sir?

SIR: Tonight's, tonight's, I can't remember my first line.

NORMAN: "Attend the Lords of France and Burgundy, Gloucester."

SIR: Yes, yes. What performance is this?

Norman consults a small notebook.

NORMAN: Tonight will be your two hundred and twenty-seventh performance of the part, Sir.

SIR: Two hundred and twenty-seven Lears and I can't remember the first line.

NORMAN: We've forgotten something, if you don't mind my saying so.

Sir looks at him blankly.

We have to sink our cheeks.

Sir applies the appropriate make-up.

SIR: I shall look like this in my coffin.

As Norman takes another nip of brandy, Sir applies spirit gum in preparation for the beard. Then it's on with the beard. Sir has forgotten his first line again. He complains that Norman's conversation has disrupted his concentration.

SIR: You've put it from my head. You must keep silent when I'm dressing. I have work to do, work, hard bloody labor, I have to carry the world tonight, the whole bloody universe—

NORMAN: Sir, Sir—

SIR: I can't remember the first line. A hundred thousand performances behind me and I have to ask you for the first line—

NORMAN: I'll take you through it—

SIR: Take me through it? Nobody takes you through it, you're *put* through it, night after night, and I haven't the strength.

NORMAN: Well, you're a fine one, I must say, you of all people, you disappoint me, if you don't mind my saying so. You, who always say self-pity is the most unattractive quality on stage or off. Who have you been working for all these years? The Ministry of Information? Struggle and survival, you say, that's all that matters, you say, struggle and survival. Well, we all bloody struggle, don't we? I struggle, I struggle, you think it's easy for me, well, I'll tell you something for nothing it isn't easy, not one little bit, neither the struggle nor the bloody survival. The whole world's struggling for bloody survival, so why can't you?

Silence.

SIR: My dear Norman, I seem to have upset you. I apologize. I understand. We cannot always be strong. There are dangers in covering the cracks.

Sir asks help making up his hands as they are shaking. So are Norman's, but Norman does help him.

SIR: I can face the division of my kingdom. I can cope with Fool. I can bear the reduction of my retinue. I can stomach the curses I have to utter. I can even face being whipped by the storm. But I dread the final entrance. To carry on Cordelia dead, to cry like the wind, howl, howl, howl. To lay her gently on the ground. To die. Have I the strength?

NORMAN: If you haven't the strength, no one has.

SIR: You're a good friend, Norman.

NORMAN: Thank you, Sir.

SIR: What would I do without you?

NORMAN: Manage on your own, I expect.

SIR: You'll be rewarded.

NORMAN: Pardon me while I get my violin.

SIR: Don't mock me. I may not have long.

NORMAN: My father used to say that. Lived to be ninety-three. May still be alive for all I know. There! Albert Dürer couldn't have done better.

> *He rises. He powders Sir's hands. Her Ladyship enters, wigged and costumed as Cordelia but wearing a dressing-gown.*

HER LADYSHIP: Bonzo, how do you feel?

SIR: A little more myself, Pussy.

NORMAN: You see? Once he's assumed the disguise, he's a different man. Egad, Madam, thou hast a porcupine wit.

HER LADYSHIP: And you're sure you're able to go on?

SIR: On and on and on.

NORMAN: Don't start that again, please.

SIR: Pussy, I thought it was the Black One tonight.

HER LADYSHIP: My dear.

SIR: Pussy, did I wake in the night? Did I thank you for watching over me? Was there talk of violence?

> *Pause.*

HER LADYSHIP: No, Bonzo, you dreamt it.

SIR: I still have the feeling.

Her Ladyship informs him that Thornton and Oxenby are ready to see him, but Sir changes his mind about seeing Oxenby. Oxenby frightens him, though Sir allows he's a fine actor.

Her Ladyship gives Norman a precious piece of chocolate to thank him for his work. She leaves, and Sir grumbles that Her Ladyship's chocolate habits aren't making it easier for him to lift her when Lear carries on the dead Cordelia.

Geoffrey Thornton enters. An old man, he looks lost in the Fool's costume. Sir gives him words of encouragement and warning. "Feel it, my boy, feel it, that's the only way. Whatever takes you," says Sir, "But do not let too much take you. Remain within the bounds. And at all costs remain still when I speak." With a final injunction that he keep his teeth in, the feeble Thornton is dismissed.

Oxenby now must be seen. He limps in, dressed as Edmund. He is a dour man. Norman speaks for Sir to him. Has he heard the news of Mr. Davenport-Scott's arrest? Oxenby allows that when you share a dressing room with homosexuals, you hear that kind of news. "It upsets the pansy fraternity when one of their number is caught."

Norman explains that with the necessary shifting of personnel, they'll be one man short on the wind machine for the storm scene. Oxenby refuses to help out. He asks if Sir has read the play he wrote. Receiving no response, he exits, limping and glowering. Sir ascribes Oxenby's bad temper to his Bolshevik sympathies. He's sure Oxenby hates him and all he stands for. "I wouldn't read his play, not if he were Commissar of Culture." "I've read it," Norman replies. "Is there a part for me?" asks Sir. Norman replies yes, but the language wouldn't get by the censors.

Norman goes off to find Irene and the triple crown. She slips into the dressing room as soon as he is gone. Sir and Irene have interests apart from the crown. Sir has her face between his hands and is saying something about, "Next week. In Eastbourne—" when Norman reenters and shoos Irene away.

Madge comes by to let them know that the curtain is in fifteen minutes. Sir begins to ramble again about cancelling the performance. Madge thinks cancelling is a good idea, but Norman insists Sir will get through it fine and hustles her out. Sir asks Norman to help him remember the lines, wandering through passages from a variety of Shakespeare's plays. He inadvertently quotes *Macbeth,* an unlucky play according to theatrical superstition. As Sir goes through the ritual to remove the curse of *Macbeth,* Her Ladyship returns *"carrying a cloak and dressed as Cordelia. Sir looks at her and takes her face in his hands."*

SIR: "And my poor fool is hang'd. No, no, no life!
    Why should a dog, a horse, a rat have life
    And thou no breath at all?
    Thou'lt come no more.
    Never, never, never, never, never!"
    Silence.
NORMAN: Welcome back, Sir, you'll be all right.
    Sir puts on the triple crown. Her Ladyship puts the cloak around Sir's shoulders. A ritual.
HER LADYSHIP *(kissing his hand):* Struggle, Bonzo.
SIR *(kissing her hand):* Survival, Pussy.
    Knock on door.
IRENE *(off):* Five minutes, please, Sir.
NORMAN: Thank you.
SIR: Let us descend and survey the scene of battle.
    They are about to go when the air-raid sirens sound. They freeze.
The night I played my first Lear there was a real thunderstorm. Now they send bombs. How much more have I to endure? We are to speak Will Shakespeare tonight and they will go to any lengths to prevent me.
NORMAN: I shouldn't take it so personally, Sir—
SIR *(looking heavenward):* Bomb, bomb, bomb us into oblivion if you dare, but each word I speak will be a shield against your savagery, each line I utter protection from your terror.
NORMAN: I don't think they can hear you, Sir.
SIR: Swines! Barbarians!

Sir begins to shiver uncontrollably, and to whimper.

NORMAN: Oh Sir, just as we were winning.

HER LADYSHIP: Perhaps it's timely. He can't go on. Look at him.

She comforts him.

(To Norman): Fetch Madge.

SIR: Norman!

NORMAN: Sir.

SIR: Get me down to the stage. By Christ, no squadron of Fascist-Bolsheviks will stop me now.

> *He continues to shiver. Her Ladyship and Norman look at each other uncertainly.*

Do as I say!

> *Norman and Her Ladyship help him.*

HER LADYSHIP: Who'll make the announcement?

SIR: Davenport-Scott, of course.

> *Silence.*

NORMAN: Oh dear. Mr. Davenport-Scott isn't here tonight. Everyone else is in costume.

SIR: You then Norman.

NORMAN: Me Sir? No, Sir. I can't appear!

SIR: You, Norman.

NORMAN: But, Sir, I shall never remember what to say—

SIR: Do not argue, I have given my orders, I have enough to contend with—

NORMAN: But, Sir, Sir, I'm not equipped.

SIR: Do it.

Her Ladyship helps him. As they go—

Why can't I stop shaking?

> *Sirens continue loudly. Bombs begin to fall. Norman swigs deeply from the brandy bottle and finishes it. Sirens. Bomb. Blackout. Sirens and bombs continue. A bright spotlight on Norman.*

NORMAN *(softly):* Ladies and gentlemen . . . *(louder)* Ladies and gentlemen, the—the warning has just gone. An air-raid is in progress. We shall proceed with the performance. Will those—will those who wish to live—will those who wish to leave do so as quietly as possible? Thank you.

> *He stands rooted to the spot. Bombs. Blackout.*

ACT II: AFTER CURTAIN UP

From the wings of the theater we hear a repeat of Norman's announcement. Madge calls cues to begin the performance. From offstage comes the sound of the performance in progress. Backstage, Norman seeks reassurance that he did a satisfactory job on the announcement.

The cue for Sir's entrance approaches, but Sir doesn't rise from his seat. Norman and Madge try to get him to his feet, but he doesn't move. Norman pleads, "Please, Sir, it's your entrance. Mr. Oxenby's having to extemporize." And, indeed, we hear some Shakespeareanish language on the whereabouts of the

Tom Courtenay, Douglas Seale, Paul Rogers, Marge Redmond and Lisabeth Bartlett in a scene from *The Dresser*.

King. Oxenby strides backstage to demand if Sir intends to join them. Norman says he will, and Oxenby returns to the stage saying, "I am assured, my Lord, the King *is* coming."

Meanwhile, in the wake of a nearby explosion, Norman has managed to get Sir to his feet and now aims him at the stage saying, "Struggle and survival, Sir, it's a full house," reminding him of his opening line. Sir snaps to, steps out onstage to an ovation, then begins his performance. Norman starts on a new bottle of brandy as the lights black out.

Lights come up again later in the play. The storm scene is about to begin. Just then the "all-clear" signal sounds. The air raid is over. This is too bad in Sir's book. At least the Germans could have kept bombing through the storm scene and augmented the sound effects. Sir and Geoffrey go on as Norman and Irene make as much racket as they can muster. Her Ladyship tells them they need to be louder still. Oxenby, who has been standing aside in a surly mood, suddenly decides to help. The result is a wonderful din. Blackout.

A little later, Sir rages into the wings, furious that the storm wasn't loud enough. Grumbling, he returns to his dressing room with Norman in attendance.

Sir insists that if only the storm had had more of the real stuff he could have been spurred to glory. Norman is full of praise for the performance so far. He tells Sir that Her Ladyship thought his acting tonight "mighty." As he readies Sir for his interval nap, he tells of Oxenby's jumping in to help.

NORMAN: . . . . . Afterwards, just before the interval, I thanked him. "Get stuffed," he said which wasn't nice, and added scornfully, "I don't know why I helped." And I said, "Because we're a band of brothers, and you're one of us in spite of yourself." I did, that's what I said, quite unabashed. He hobbled away, head down, and if he was given to muttering, he'd have muttered. Darkly. *(Pause.)* More tea? Are you asleep, Sir?

SIR: To be driven thus. I hate the swines.

NORMAN: Who? Who is it you hate? The critics?

SIR: The critics? Hate the critics? I have nothing but compassion for them. How can one hate the crippled, the mentally deficient and the dead? Bastards.

NORMAN: Who then?

SIR: Who then what?

NORMAN: Who then what is it you hate?

SIR: Let me rest, Norman, you must stop questioning me, let me rest. But don't leave me till I'm asleep. Don't leave me alone. *(Pause.)* I am a spent force. *(Pause.)* My days are numbered.

Norman leaves the dressing room, encountering Her Ladyship going in. "Norman tells me you thought I was mighty tonight," Sir says. She denies having said any such thing and resumes what is apparently an ongoing campaign to get him to retire before it's too late. Sir insists he performs now only because he has a duty to fulfill. This talk of duty doesn't impress Her Ladyship. "You do nothing without self-interest," she says. And we discover that they are not married. He was afraid to ask his wife for a divorce because he didn't want to jinx his chance for a knighthood (which he never got).

Sir keeps talking of the sacrifices and the necessary ruthlessness that accompany a great tragedian's career. Her Ladyship refuses to subscribe to his romantic view. She talks of acting almost as if it were a profession to be embarrassed by. If she doesn't believe in the nobility of the work, at least Norman does, says Sir. Norman understands Sir's gift and his burden. There is a long pause.

SIR: . . . . . I thought tonight I caught sight of him. Or saw myself as he sees me. Speaking "Reason not the need," I was suddenly detached from myself. My thoughts flew. And I was observing from a great height. Go on, you bastard, I seemed to be saying or hearing. Go on, you've more to give, don't hold back more, more, more. And I was watching Lear. Each word he spoke was fresh invented. I had no knowledge of what came next, what fate awaited him. The agony was in the moment of acting created. I saw an old man and the old man was me. And I knew there was more to come. But what? Bliss, partial recovery, more pain and death. All this I knew I had yet to see. Outside myself, do you understand? Outside myself.

He holds out his hand. She does not take it.

Don't leave me. I'll rest easy if you stay. Don't ask of me the impossible. Otherwise, I know, without you, in darkness, I'll see a locked door, a sign turned in the window, closed, gone away, and a drawn blind.

HER LADYSHIP: I'll stay till Norman returns.

SIR: Longer. I meant longer. Please. Please, Pussy. Reassure me. I'm sick—

Her Ladyship replies that she, too, is sick. Sick of the transient and uncomfortable life they lead. Sick of reading notices that tear her down in comparison to him. She wishes she had taken an offer she once received in America to go into movies. But Sir had not also received an offer, so she let the opportunity go by.

Irene calls out that the second act is about to begin. Sir still has time to rest before he goes on. Norman returns with stories of the extravagant praise for Sir's performance he has overheard in the lobby. Her Ladyship leaves for her room. Norman encourages Sir to rest and leaves.

Sir suddenly rises, goes to the door, where he finds Irene standing with the triple crown. He sends her to fetch Madge and makes attempts to write in his exercise book until Madge arrives. Alone with Madge now, Sir tells her how very frightened he is. She appears not to be interested, wrenching her hand from his grip. She has a show to run. What did he want?

SIR: I look on you as my one true friend—

MADGE: I have to go back to the corner.

SIR: Twenty years, did you say twenty years?

MADGE: Yes.

SIR: Have you been happy? Has it been worth it?

    Pause.

MADGE: No, I've not been happy. Yes. It's been worth it.

    Pause.

SIR: Madge-dear, in my will I've left you all my press-cutting books—

MADGE: I don't want to hear what you've left me in your will—

SIR: Cuttings that span a lifetime, an entire career. I've kept them religiously. Good and bad notices alike. Not all that many bad. Talk of me sometimes. Speak well of me. Actors live on only in the memory of others. Speak well of me.

MADGE: This is a ridiculous conversation. You are in the middle of a performance of *Lear,* playing rather less mechanically than you have of late, and you talk as if you're organizing your own memorial service.

SIR: The most wonderful thing in life is to be remembered. Speak well of me. You'll be believed.

MADGE: You'll be remembered.

    Pause.

SIR: Madge-dear, I have something for you.

    He opens a box on his dressing table and finds a ring.

I want you to have this ring. If possessions can be dear then this ring is the dearest thing I own. This ring was worn by Edmund Kean in a play whose title is an apt inscription for what I feel: *A New Way to Pay Old Debts.* When you talk of it, say Edmund Kean and I wore it.

    He puts the ring into her hand. She tries not to show her feelings.

I once had it in mind to give it to you years ago, but you were younger then, and I thought you would misunderstand.

MADGE: Yes. A ring from a man to a woman is easily misunderstood.

SIR: I know I'm thought insensitive, but I'm not blind.

MADGE: No. I've always known you were aware of what the spinster in the corner felt. *(Pause.)* You were right not to give me a ring years ago. I lived in hope then. *(Pause.)* At least I've seen you every day, made myself useful to you. I settled for what I could get. I was always aware of my limitations.

SIR: You are the only one who really, truly, loves me.

> *She gives him back the ring and goes quickly from the room. He puts the ring on. . . . .*

Irene now appears to return the triple crown. She tells him it has been an honor to be on the same stage with him tonight. He tells her to lock the door and quizzes her about her desire to act. He examines her, feeling her all over. At one point, he seems on the verge of kissing her; then, suddenly, he lifts her up into his arms. "That's more like it!" he roars. He puts her down. "Too late, too late," he says, waving her away.

She unlocks the door and leaves his dressing room to be confronted by Norman, who heard much of this through the keyhole. He demands to know what happened in there, threatening to strike her. She in turn threatens to tell Sir on him. Norman is not very impressed by this and again demands to know what went on; particularly what Sir meant when he cried out "That's more like it!" Irene tells Norman of being lifted in his arms and her understanding of the situation —namely that Sir was transported by her youth. "And with my eyes closed," she continues, "I imagined what it would be like to be carried on by him, Cordelia, dead in his arms, young."

Norman snaps that Sir is not concerned with age so much as weight. Irene would make a lighter Cordelia than Her Ladyship. That's the extent of Sir's interest in her, Norman insists. He warns her not to attempt distracting Sir any more if she values her job. Her Ladyship enters and leaves with Irene in tow for an errand.

Norman, fortified by another nip from the brandy bottle, returns to Sir's dressing room, wakes him and helps him change costumes for the final scenes.

NORMAN: I talked to the girl. She's not as light as she looks. We're none of us strong enough for a change of cast.

> *Pause. Sir, suddenly and fiercely, embraces Norman.*

SIR: You cannot be properly paid. *In pectora,* I name you friend. The debt is all mine. And I shall find a way to repay you. I must, must settle all my debts.

NORMAN: Don't, you're making me tearful—

SIR *(letting go of him):* God, your breath smells of stale tights. How much have you had?

NORMAN: Not enough.

SIR: Iago, Iago—

NORMAN: Wrong play.

SIR: I have to wake in bliss, I have to carry on Her Ladyship, I need you sober.

NORMAN: I am. Sober. Diction perfect. Deportment steady. Temper serene.
Norman smiles.
SIR: It is no laughing matter! *(Pause.)* The final push. I hope you're up to it.
NORMAN *(under his breath):* And you, dear.
SIR: What?
NORMAN: And you, Lear.
They begin to go. Lights fade to blackout.

In the wings, Sir spits on his hands before lifting Her Ladyship into his arms
for Lear's entrance with the dead Cordelia. Soon the play is over and the performers take their calls, Sir getting an ovation.

Prompted by Norman, Sir addresses the audience, talking of the importance,
in these days of world war, of keeping alive Shakespeare's plays. He will continue
his part in the crusade by playing Richard III and Shylock in the next few days,
followed by another Lear. Next week, their company will travel to Eastbourne,
and Sir urges the audience to encourage friends in that area to see their productions.

Back in Sir's dressing room, Sir is drinking as Norman tends to the costume
and beard. Sir asks Norman what he would do if Sir were unable to continue.
Norman says there's no chance of Sir not being able to continue and cuts the topic
off. Geoffrey enters in street clothes. Sir congratulates him on his playing the
Fool. Geoffrey feels gratified at having been able to prove his ability, even at this
late age. Geoffrey talks a bit about the satisfaction he's had touring as a small part
player. It's been a good life. Getting to the point, he tells Sir that he would very
much like to be considered for better parts, should the occasion arise: "I shouldn't
want an increase in salary." Sir promises to keep him in mind, and Geoffrey
stumbles out.

As Norman begins to help Sir finish up for the evening, Her Ladyship stops
by to say she'll go back to the hotel ahead of Sir. Sir promises he'll be along soon.
Turning to Norman, Her Ladyship says she isn't certain whether she should
thank him or not. "Not," says Norman. "I can't bear being thanked." She leaves.

Oxenby turns up. Sir doesn't wish to see him, so Norman deals with him at
the door. Oxenby wants his manuscript back. As Norman returns it, Oxenby
makes comments meant to be overheard along the lines of "Death to all tyrants."
With a final insult "Your nose is browner than usual tonight, Norman," Oxenby
limps off into the night. Irene also stops by to say goodnight. Norman speeds her
on her way.

His face covered with cold cream, Sir suddenly moans. He cannot move.
Norman helps him to the couch and starts cleaning Sir's face. Sir begins to cry.
"There's nothing left," he says. Norman talks of his "friend" again, saying that
his friend never despaired as long as he was working in a theater.

This seems to have an effect on Sir. He talks of the beginning he has made on
his memoirs. At Sir's request, Norman fetches the exercise book and begins by
reading the dedication.

NORMAN *(reads):* My Life. Dedication. This book is dedicated to My Beloved
Pussy who has been my splendid spur. To the spirit of all actors because of their

faith and endurance which never fails them. To Those who do the work of the theater yet have but small share in its glory: Carpenters, Electricians, Scene-shifters, Property-men. To the Audiences, who have laughed with us, have wept with us and whose hearts have united with ours in sympathy and understanding. And finally—ah Sir—to the memory of William Shakespeare in whose glorious service we all labour.

      Silence.

SIR: *My Life* will have to do.

      Silence.

Norman realizes with a start that there is no mention of him in this dedication. He turns to Sir, but Sir doesn't answer. "We're not dead are we?" Norman asks Sir is, indeed.

Terrified, and with the full effect of all he's drunk finally hitting him, Norman calls out for help. Madge comes running. The death is a bad shock to her, but she covers her feelings. She begins to take charge of things, leaving to make necessary phone calls.

Alone with Sir in the dressing room, Norman looks again at the dedication.

NORMAN: "Carpenters, electricians, property men?" Cruel bastard. You might have remembered.

      Silence. Norman looks about to make sure he is unobserved. He finds a pencil and writes in the exercise book. Then, like an angry child, he turns on Sir's body and thumbs his nose at it violently. But he begins to whimper again. He drinks brandy from Sir's drinks tray. Madge returns.

MADGE: Her Ladyship's coming at once. She took it very calmly. She asked for him to be covered in his Lear cloak. Where is it?

NORMAN: Covered in his Lear cloak? Fetch the photographer, ducky. Covered in his Lear cloak? This isn't the death of Nelson, you know.

MADGE: Where is it?

      He points. She gets the cloak. Norman looks away. She is about to cover Sir but first surreptitiously slips the ring off his finger and pockets it. Then she covers him. Norman suddenly laughs.

NORMAN: There's no mention of stage managers, either.

MADGE: Come out of here.

NORMAN: Are we going to get paid? I mean, is there money in the till after deductions for income tax? We've got to be paid the full week, you know. Just because the man dies on a Thursday doesn't mean we should get paid *pro rata.*

MADGE: Wait outside.

NORMAN: You're nothing now, ducky. He took away your stripes. And mine. How could he be so bloody careless?

MADGE: Come away.

NORMAN: And then where will I go? Where? I'm nowhere out of my element. I don't want to end up running a boarding house in Westcliffe-on-Sea. Or Colwyn Bay. What am I going to do?

MADGE: You can speak well of him.

NORMAN: Speak well of that old sod? I wouldn't give him a good character, not in a court of law. Ungrateful bastard. Silence, ducky. My lips are sealed.

MADGE: Get out. I don't want you in here.

NORMAN: Holy, holy, holy, is it? Are we in a shrine? No pissing on the altar—

MADGE: Stop it.

NORMAN: He never once took me out for a meal. Never once. Always a back seat, me. Can't even remember him buying me a drink. And just walks out, leaves me, no thought for anyone but himself. What have I been doing here all these years? Why? Yes, well, reason not the need, rotten bugger. Beg your pardon, leave the room, turn round three times and come back—come back—

He breaks off and turns away from her.

Speak well of him? I know what you'd say, ducky. I know all about you. I've got eyes in my head. We all have our little sorrows.

Madge goes but Norman does not notice.

I know what you'd say, stiff upper, faithful, loyal. Loving. Well, I have only one thing to say about him and I wouldn't say it in front of you—or Her Ladyship, or anyone. Lips tight shut. I wouldn't give you the pleasure. Or him. Specially not him. If I said what I have to say he'd find a way to take it out on me. No one will ever know. We all have our little sorrows, ducky, you're not the only one. The littler you are, the larger the sorrow. You think *you* loved him? What about me?

Long silence.

This is not a place for death. I had a friend—

He turns suddenly as if aware of someone behind him, but realizes he is alone.

Sir? Sir?

Silence. He hugs the exercise book. He sings:

"He that has and a little tiny wit,
With hey, ho, the wind and the rain."

He falls silent. He stares into space. Lights fade. Curtain.

MASS APPEAL

A Play in Two Acts

BY BILL C. DAVIS

Cast and credits appear on page 320

BILL C. DAVIS was born in 1951 in Ellenville, N.Y., where his father ran a clothing store in nearby Poughkeepsie. Davis was educated in Poughkeepsie schools and received his B.A. degree from Maris College in Poughkeepsie in 1974 after transferring from Emerson College in Boston. He began writing plays in high school ("I just started to do it, I don't know why") and is the author of seven full-length plays and 15 one-acts performed in upstate New York and in city showcases. His Gentle Catapults *won an award at the state festival in 1976, and his* The Wrestlers *was acclaimed at the Westchester Theater Festival in 1978.*

Mass Appeal was its author's first New York production of record, as a Circle Repertory Project in Progress in October 1979. In April 1980 the leading role of Mass Appeal *and Milo O'Shea found each other in the off-Broadway production at Manhattan Theater Club. The match was so felicitous that the Broadway transfer of the play was delayed until the actor's commitments would permit him to resume the role.*

Davis now serves as Manhattan Theater Club's resident playwright and is at work on a new script commissioned by them. He is single and lives in Connecticut.

The following synopsis of Mass Appeal *was prepared by Sally Dixon Wiener.*

Time: Autumn

*Place: The Church of St. Francis and Father Tim Farley's
       adjacent office*

ACT I

Scene 1: Sunday morning, 10:15 mass

SYNOPSIS: The central portion of the stage is taken up with Father Tim Farley's old-fashioned parish priest's office, conventionally furnished with prie-dieu, desk and chairs. Downstage right is the pulpit of St. Francis Church, from which the audience, as congregation, is addressed.

As the lights come up on the opening scene, the church organ is playing. Father Tim Farley, a middle-aged priest, *"is discovered in the pulpit wearing a green chasuble over the white alb. It is Sunday morning, the 10:15 mass. The music stops."* Tim tells the congregation that today's sermon concludes the 3-C series on "Current Crises in Catholicism" and that a new series, "the most important and inspiring I've ever given," although he does not yet know what it is, will begin the next Sunday. He discusses the most recent crisis of the church, "Should women be priests?", and proposes a dialogue sermon on the question. He entertains two questions from members of the congregation before we hear Mark Dolson's voice from the rear of the church questioning him as to what he himself thinks about women priests. Tim avoids the issue by saying that he doesn't like to "sway people's viewpoints," but Mark comes down the aisle insisting that this is a dialogue sermon.

Mark, now revealed in the light as a young man in gray sweat pants and a red sweat jacket, is questioned by Tim and admits that this is his first visit to this church. Tim welcomes him and attempts to turn the dialogue elsewhere but is interrupted by Mark who says he hasn't given his "unswayed viewpoint" yet and that he thinks women should be priests. It seems Mark attends St. Francis seminary. Tim tells him to give his rector, Monsignor Burke, his regards and again tries to turn to another parishioner—only to be pressed further by Mark, who asks Tim if he doesn't want to know *why* he thinks women should be priests. Tim gives up and allows Mark to continue. Mark comes close to the pulpit.

MARK: Well—you said that priests should be in the image of Christ.
TIM: No, I did not say that. The Pope did.
MARK: Whoever. But when Christ was crucified, only three people stayed with him to the very end, and two of the three were women. At the foot of his cross was his youngest apostle . . .
TIM: St. John . . .
MARK: . . . his mother . . .
TIM (*concurring*): Right . . . his mother . . .
MARK: . . . and an ex-hooker.

Pause—Tim is taken aback.

All of the men either denied him or were hiding out. On the way to being crucified —it was a woman who pushed through a hostile crowd and wiped all the blood and "male" spit off his face. The first person he appeared to after his resurrection was Mary Magdalene. I really feel that the courage and loyalty these women showed the actual person Jesus *is* in his image, and I think it's foolish to continue depriving ourselves of the beautiful qualities a woman could bring to the priesthood.

Tim advises Mark to invest in a portable pulpit and again attempts to continue the dialogue with the rest of the congregation; but his efforts come to nothing, and the scene ends after Tim makes a few parish announcements about the Tuesday bingo game and a car that is blocking the exit. The organ music comes up as the lights go to black.

Scene 2: Wednesday afternoon

The lights come up immediately on the office, where Mark has arrived in his running clothes. The organ music fades out as Tim enters in his shirtsleeves reading a racing paper. He comments on Mark's sweat suit and says he hopes he hasn't tracked mud across the clean floors. Mark explains that he tries to run eight miles a day and that this is when he usually runs, and that when Tim called him he'd agreed without thinking to come at this time. He admits to not thinking very clearly on the phone. Tim tells him he thinks very clearly at mass and Mark says he feels "at home" in church.

Tim asks Mark if he knows that Tim's an advisor at the seminary. Mark says Father DeNicola plays tapes of Tim's sermons in his homily class and that the faculty talk about him a lot and seem proud that he's on their "team." Tim, pouring wine into one of two glasses, says he's asked the faculty about Mark, who has quite a reputation. Mark "certainly lived up to that reputation last Sunday," and Tim wanted to tell him how much he admired the things Mark said during mass, and "don't ever do anything like that again."

Mark refuses a glass of wine. Tim says Mark challenged him in front of his congregation, that he did not take a stand, he took a "grandstand," and that as a seminarian, if he wants to become a deacon, he should go to mass at the seminary. Mark explains that Monsignor Burke sent him to Tim's mass because "he said that you were the most tactful priest in the diocese, and that tact was something I needed to learn." Tim laughs and tells him that the monsignor is aware of his dialogue sermons as well as Mark's reputation and that this was his subtle way of getting back at him for cancelling a dinner engagement (with Monsignor Burke and his sister to see pictures of a trip to Yugoslavia). Mark's reaction is that if he was used as a pawn, it's the players' problem, but Tim says it's his problem if he wants to be a priest in the same church as the players.

Tim, under questioning, admits to using a "harmless lie" to get out of the dinner. Mark states that he didn't know there was such a thing and asks if he can leave. Tim offers him a ride back to the seminary, as he has a meeting there with the monsignor about two seminarians, Frank Kearney and Alfred Virasi

Mark knows them and thinks well of their work with emotionally disturbed children. Tim says they seem to be together a lot, and Mark says they are best friends.

TIM: How do you know?

MARK: I usually see them together during the day, so I assume . . .

TIM: I probably shouldn't be discussing this with you, but this meeting was prompted by rumors which have been reaching Monsignor Burke that not only are they together all day, but all night as well. Do you know if that's true?

MARK: No—I don't.

He takes a step toward Tim.

But so what if they are?

TIM: Don't play innocent, Mark. When I was at the seminary we could only travel in threes. Things have loosened up a little since then. But there are still strong tabus. Frank and Alfred are fooling around with the ultimate tabu.

MARK: They haven't taken any vows yet.

TIM: There's serious question they'll be allowed to—ever.

MARK: That's ridiculous—one meeting can't decide that.

TIM: You're right. These meetings never decide anything. They only help Monsignor Burke decide.

MARK: How are you going to advise him?

TIM: The only purpose of the rector's advisor is to find out exactly what the rector really wants to do and then advise him to do that.

MARK: That must make you feel awfully insignificant.

TIM: Yes—well—I'd love to discuss this with you further, but if I don't leave now, I'll be late. And the one thing he loves more than chastity is punctuality.

Mark starts to leave.

Are you sure I can't give you a lift?

Mark stops and turns.

MARK: Is that your Mercedes out there?

TIM: Yes.

MARK: I'd rather run.

A pause.

Listen—I don't know if your and Monsignor Burke's game rules apply to seminarians, but I hope you won't use your position at the seminary over me. I only spoke up at your mass because it was important to me. Becoming a priest is important to me.

He comes closer to Tim.

Please don't play games with it.

The lights black out as Mark starts to exit. Tim is still.

Scene 3: Friday, one week later

We hear Tim's taped sermon in the darkness before the lights go up on Tim in the office. The sermon, the beginning of the "On the Road to the Priesthood" series, is about being a deacon—"primarily and most importantly a big pain in the ass." He changes the word to "neck" and goes on taping, reminiscing about the summer when, in a hat and a too-large deacon's suit, he had to give sermons from a soap box on a street corner, beginning each one by assuring everybody that he was not a Marxist or Trotskyite. "All kinds of people. And we . . . talked." He continues, then replays the last few phrases. "Old men in faded plaid shirts . . . just about everyone wore some kind of sandal, and I know I haven't been as close to Christ . . . since."

He answers the buzzing house phone and is told that Mark is here. Mark enters. Tim tells him that Monsignor Burke has suggested that Mark take a year off to decide whether or not he really wants to be a priest (Latin for "Get lost"). Mark admits that he called the monsignor a "homophobic autocrat" when he went to play knight-errant on behalf of his fellow-seminarians Kearney and Virasi, but Tim has spoken up for Mark (which Mark appreciates) and he will be made a deacon, on the condition that Tim works with him.

The work will consist of three lessons, Tim tells Mark, as he pours out a glass of sparkling burgundy (a gift from the congregation). Lesson One is sermons. Tim positions Mark at the prie-dieu as a rehearsal pulpit to give his most recent student sermon. Mark begins with "Jesus is not impressed with your mink hats and your cashmere coats and your blue hair . . ."

Tim stops him and tells him it's "we" and "our." Mark starts again. When he gets to "our blue hair," Tim tells him to cut that. Then he criticizes Mark's correct grammar as not being necessarily helpful—"sermons should be understood," and he's only telling him "what works."

"Do you like my sermons?" he asks Mark. Mark replies that he's never liked "song and dance theology," and he complains about an Ascension Thursday when he was a teenager and the hip hymn committee sang "Leavin' on a Jet Plane." Mark believes people feel more secure with someone who states his position clearly, but Tim warns him that if it's not their position, they will turn on him. Mark asks Tim if the only reason he gives sermons is to be liked, and Tim tells him he likes being liked—that and wine are the only warmth he gets, and he's not going to give up either one. Mark says he'll be liked more for being "real and sober." Tim says Mark doesn't have to respect him, but that Mark is not giving this "kick-ass" sermon to his congregation.

Mark asks Tim why he drinks so much. Tim defends himself by saying that he's never missed a mass, a class or an appointment and by telling him about the problems "this drunken minstrel" has dealt with during the last week. Mark bets he was too easy on all of them. "That's how you are from the pulpit." Tim tells Mark his sermon "sucks"—the rest of it could be the Sermon on the Mount, but after "two minutes of this they'd just turn you off". He tells Mark not to kick ass, and Mark says that's better than to kiss it.

Tim tears up Mark's sermon. Mark starts to leave, but Tim stops him by saying he's doing it for his own good. Tim tells Mark the only thing that can influence Monsignor Burke more than Tim can is the congregation. He wants him to give a friendly sermon and assigns him a theme—"Why go to mass?"—and tells him to be charming, to be personal, that the congregation needs to see him in "a nice Norman Rockwell setting."

When Mark happens to mention that he and his family used to go to the bakery after mass for jelly doughnuts, Tim latches onto this and tells him to go back to the seminary and start work on a jelly doughnut sermon. But he cautions Mark that he must have an alternate sermon in case the one he's giving isn't working. "Coughs," he explains. "If you hear a lot of coughs, it means they're bored." Mark wonders how the spirit can move him if he's listening for coughs, but Tim is giving him the "facts" of this campaign. If Mark finds approval in his parish, the monsignor will know of it, and if the parishioners think he is a "Bangladesh Granola Head" he could end up in a Trappist monastery working in a bakery. Mark asks what they bake there. The lights black out, and we hear organ music.

Scene 4: Sunday, 10:15 mass, one week later

The lights come up on the pulpit as *"Tim enters upstage in his white alb and goes down to the pulpit. He enters the pulpit and waits for the music to stop. He tries to speak, but the organ continues. He holds up his hand toward the choir loft in the rear of the church in an attempt to stop the organist. Finally he entreats her by calling her name: 'Philomena . . .' "*

When the music stops, Tim reports that one of the sisters with the Maryknoll Marionettes has injured her hand and that they will not be performing today, but that he does have a treat in store. In keeping with his "On the Road to the Priesthood" series, the congregation will hear a first sermon by a newly-installed deacon, whom he says some may remember from the last dialogue sermon. He asks the members of the congregation to welcome Deacon Dolson.

> *Tim leaves the pulpit. Mark enters upstage wearing his white alb. He goes into the pulpit and turns to Tim.*

MARK: Thank you, Father Farley.

> *Tim exits. Mark faces the congregation.*

It's funny—I never stopped to think that on my way to becoming a priest I'd have to live with the name "Deacon Dolson." It sounds pretty silly, don't you think? "Deacon Dolson."

> *A single cough—he freezes.*

Can I ask all of us a question? Why did we come to mass today? What brought us to church this morning? As a teenager I had a friend who answered this question by saying, "I go to mass because my parents go." But one day I heard his father talking to my father: "Betty and I go to mass for the kids."

> *Several coughs are heard.*

I know when I was young, I liked going to church because right after mass my father would take us to the bakery. And all four of us—my two sisters and my brother and myself—would pick out what we'd like. I'd almost always get jelly doughnuts, and I'd never wait to get home before having one . . .

> *A loud wheeze from the congregation.*

But jelly doughnuts aren't a very good reason for going to mass are they?

> *Many coughs.*

What are your reasons . . .

> *Two loud coughs. Mark erupts.*

I wonder if the coughing lot of you know, or *try* to know why you pull yourselves out of bed every Sunday morning and come here?

Silence.

Do you need to come to mass? Do you need the church? Ideally, the purpose of the church is to become obsolete. But until it is, we need the habit of coming together and collectively recognizing that there is another world. There is a world that coexists and gives order to this world. Individually, we come to mass with our own personal chaos, and together we look to be ordered. We must come with our hearts open for that.

Many coughs.

But you come with your mink hats and your cashmere coats and your blue hair ... Those things are your shackles—they are accessories you have *made* essential. *You* are essential.

The scene ends with a cross-fade to the office.

Scene 5: That afternoon

Tim is talking on the telephone to a woman parishioner who has called about Mark's sermon. He says Mark is "very young and high-spirited—like a thoroughbred at the starting gate". The house phone buzzes and interrupts their conversation. He thanks her for the "bubbly" and for calling.

Tim is pouring a glass of wine as Mark enters, in a black clerical suit. Tim tells him "the parish poll is in". The feeling is that Mark and the spirit "should move each other" to that Trappist monastery, but possibly he can persuade them to expand the bakery and have jelly doughnuts every day. Mark wants to know why Tim invited the faculty to his sermon. Tim denies doing so. They were there to see the Maryknoll Marionettes, but they were surprised to hear that "the purpose of the church was to become obsolete." Mark points out that the congregation did stop coughing. "They also stopped breathing," Tim replies.

The phone buzzes again. Mr. Hartigan, another parishioner, is on the line. Tim repeatedly kow-tows to him. Mark asks Tim at the end of the conversation, "Why do you let them do that to you?" Tim describes his long struggle to achieve a level of "beloved" in the parish, a level he enjoys, and for which he's never had to fight for as hard as he's had to this afternoon.

Tim asks Mark what happened in the pulpit. Mark says he gave his alternate sermon. He admits he lost control but says he's glad, and that he felt like a priest for the first time. Tim doesn't want to hear about the spirit moving him. Mark can't explain it any other way, that it was a mystery to him. Tim says his congregation is not a "primitive tribe who'll watch in awe as their priest becomes possessed by some preternatural force". He also reports the collection went down 30 percent: "It's like the Nielson rating." Mark says that if he's making things difficult here for Tim he'll speak to Monsignor Burke, ask him to let Tim off the hook and go back to the seminary.

There is a brief silence between them, during which the town hall clock strikes the quarter hour, and then Tim suggests that they get on with Lesson Two: Consolations. Tim is aware of Mark's special projects (prison work, meals on wheels, playing piano for senior citizens' dances), but the faculty reports Mark

Michael O'Keefe as Mark Dolson and Milo O'Shea as Father Tim Farley in *Mass Appeal*

has difficulty communicating empathy to an average person going through a life crisis. Mark believes everything he thinks of to say sounds "stupid." Tim says "consolations *should* sound stupid so that the person in grief will realize how inconsolable their grief is." He explains that inconsolable grief gives people a feeling of exaltation that helps them through most tragedies. He asks Mark to think of a tragedy. Mark comes up with "My mother passed away last night, Father," and Tim suggests saying, "Well, she had a good life;" or, if she had been ill, "It was a merciful release." Mark comes up with another: "My baby died in his crib last night." Tim is horrified, but says he could say, providing the mother was young, that she could have another. "Like an hors d'oeuvre," Mark comments. Does he have to say something . . . couldn't he just listen?

TIM: No. Now I'll give you one. My father beats me.
MARK: Now I'm supposed to say something inane?
TIM: Right.
MARK: Okay—let me think . . . Your father beats you . . .
TIM: Right.
MARK: *(facing him):* You don't have any scars; you'd never know it.
TIM: I go to school with black eyes.
MARK: Catholic school?
TIM: What difference would that make?
MARK: Well—they're always fighting in Catholic schools, so they all have black eyes. You must fit right in.
TIM: My father left us. We don't know whether he's dead or alive.
MARK: Well—that's okay. Who needs a sadist like that for a father anyway? How am I doing?
TIM: My mother remarried. I hate her new husband.
MARK: Why?
TIM: The church says she can't remarry until it's certain her first husband is dead.
MARK: That's no reason to hate him.
TIM: I cry myself to sleep because I'm sure she's going to hell.
MARK: Do you believe there can be such a thing as hell?
TIM: After a while—I just wouldn't talk to her.
MARK: You talk to her now—don't you?
TIM: She died. We hadn't exchanged a word in two years.
      Silence.
MARK: Go on. I'm listening.
TIM: I went into the preparatory seminary when I was thirteen. I believed everything I was taught. Followed all the rules—to the letter. I wanted everyone to be perfect. Especially my mother. When I thought she wasn't, I cut her off. She'd write—she'd call—I never answered. Once she called, and I came so close —I had the phone in my hand. But I hung up. Three weeks later, she was dead. You ask me if I believe there's such a thing as hell. There are hints of it, here, on this earth.
      Mark touches Tim. Tim backs away.
. . . That's enough on consolations. Let's move on to Lesson Three: Converts.

The phone buzzes again. Tim answers and then asks Mark to go into the kitchen, as the call is private. Monsignor Burke is calling. Tim makes a new dinner date with him and says he's already spoken to Mark about what was wrong with his sermon. But what the monsignor is calling about is that he wants to see Mark himself, and the implication is that he is suspicious about him and his defense of the two seminarians. Tim backs Mark up but agrees to send him over. He calls Mark in to tell him the monsignor wants to see him, not about the sermon, but because of the vehemence of his defense of Kearney and Virasi. He wants to talk to him about a possible connection. Mark wants to know if he has to put up with this and asks if he can't see the bishop. Tim tells him the bishop is paranoid on the subject and will let Burke do as he wishes.

To prepare Mark for the interview, Tim suggests they act it out, with Tim playing Monsignor Burke. He tells him to relax. "You don't have to be afraid of anything, do you?" Mark doesn't want to play a "psycho game," but Tim tells him he can't afford a repeat of his last encounter with the monsignor. The "game" begins. The subject of Mark's family and his departure from home at age 16 comes up. Tim, arms folded across his chest as Burke, wants to know where Mark went. Mark avoids that question and returns to the question of the two seminarians. Tim, as Burke, asks him if he thinks priests should be allowed to sleep together. Mark says they weren't priests, not even deacons, and that the celibacy vow was "far off for them." Tim, as Burke, continues to probe, asking Mark if he thinks such practises are easily dispensed with.

MARK: Is your question something along the lines of "How you gonna keep 'em down on the farm after they've seen Paree?"

TIM *(as Burke):* Stop your verbal acrobatics and give a response to whatever you interpret my question to be.

MARK: Yes—I think Frank and Alfred would have stayed down on the farm after they had seen Paree.

TIM: *(as Burke):* How do you know?

MARK: I said "I think". I did not say I know.

TIM *(as Burke):* Let me ask my next question in your native tongue. Have *you* ever seen Paree?

    Silence.

And if you have seen Paree . . . *(Takes a few steps right.)* were they Parisiettes or . . . *(Turns and faces Mark.)* Parisians?

    Long pause.

MARK: Both.

TIM *(unfolds arms; as himself):* Really?

    Mark goes to edge of platform up left, as if to leave.

MARK: That's it—no more. You were shocked.

TIM: I was playing Monsignor Burke. Both?

MARK *(comes back):* Yes—women and men—two sexes. Monsignor—before I came to the seminary, I enrolled myself in a three-year orgy that laid waste to every fibre of my character. Does that sound apologetic enough? How about this? Monsignor Burke—please understand—I explored the world by indulging my sexual ambivalence. I searched with my own body, and I discovered that I could never reconcile my inner emotional world that way. Others have—but my unique, personal and human condition called for another way. So I invite celibacy. I will be happy to stay down on the farm, because it's there I will be calm enough to help others. And helping other people is the only real joy in this world. I feel determined and perfectly prepared to become a priest. What would he say to that?

TIM *(folds his arms; as Burke):* Both?

MARK: Will you stop?

Tim apologizes and says he's never seen him "in this light" before, but tells him that if Monsignor Burke asks him, Mark should say he made love with "Parisiettes." Mark says that's a half-truth, that he won't become a priest on a lie. Tim says that's better than not becoming one. Mark can't believe him, and he won't listen to him. Tim says once Mark becomes a priest he can fight the monsignor. "You'll probably end up hearing confessions in the cornfields of Iowa," he tells him, "but at least give yourself a chance." He tells him what Christ told his apostles: "Be as innocent as doves and as cunning as serpents."

MARK: Does cunning mean lying?

TIM: If you can afford not to be a priest—tell the truth. If you want to be a priest—lie.

   Silence.

Mark—I want you to become a priest. I asked for you.

MARK: You asked for me? You said . . .

TIM: I know. I told you Monsignor Burke made me do this, that he forced this special assignment on me. He didn't. I asked him to let me help you.

MARK: Why?

TIM: Because you're a lunatic. And the church needs lunatics—you're one of those priceless lunatics that come along every so often and make the church alive. The only problem with lunatics is they don't know how to survive. I do.

   Pause. He holds out his keys.

Here—take my car.

   Mark hesitates, then takes the keys as the lights black out. Curtain.

ACT II

Scene 1: Immediately after the 5:20 mass

The organ is playing as the lights come up on Tim, in the office. The phone buzzes, announcing the arrival of Mark, who enters and places the car keys on Tim's desk. Tim wants to know what happened and, after a pause, Mark gives a jump into the air and says it was great. He is jubilant and tells Tim how confident he felt at the interview. Tim comments that "nothing is more antagonistic than confidence" but Mark is convinced that everything's okay. Tim assumes Monsignor Burke didn't ask *the* question, but Mark says he did and that he told the truth. Mark feels Tim was wrong about the monsignor. Tim asks what he said when Mark said "both." Mark tells him the monsignor said "Thank you for being so honest—good day." Tim repeats the phrase twice, and Mark tells him he can interpret it his way, and he (Mark) will interpret it his own way. Mark then repeats the phrase himself and realizes that he's in trouble. He asks Tim's help. Tim says he can't help him, because he told the truth, and if he defended Mark to the monsignor the same thing would happen to him.

Mark complains that "Burke gets away with this crap" because only one or two people will speak up. He feels the entire parish should go after him. He reminds Tim that he said the people in his parish can be an influence on the monsignor, and that Tim has an influence on the people in his parish. Mark asks Tim if he can't talk to them about it, but Tim says that, after Mark's sermon, if he were to tell the people in his parish that the monsignor was going to dump Mark, they would send the monsignor "thank you" cards. Mark questions why it should matter what they think of him, that there's an issue here. Tim tells him *he* is the issue.

What he would be willing to do, Tim tells Mark, is let him give a redemption sermon. The monsignor hasn't yet told Tim that Mark can't give more sermons. He advises Mark to forget about Norman Rockwell and to delve deeper into what made him decide to be a priest, to think of specifics—a teacher, a best friend, a saint, a confirmation name, a pet, for instance. Mark tells him he had a tank of tropical fish, but Tim thinks they won't relate to guppies. Mark wonders what they can relate to—bingo, a car sweepstake, the lottery? Tim thinks maybe it's more of a problem of getting Mark to like people than getting people to like Mark. Tim asks him what he feels for people and digs it out of Mark that he loves them and doesn't mean to offend them, that they're his family. He tells Tim they get to him, and asks Tim to show him how to reach them.

As the clock chimes the three-quarter hour, Tim tells Mark how St. Francis undressed in the town square and gave his clothes back to his father and then was ready to begin. He advises Mark to do the same thing, and talk to them as if they were just one person; as if they were me, he says.

Mark begins to speak about his tank of tropical fish again and *"the lights on the pulpit get brighter as the lights in the office start to dim."* "Someone turned up the tank heater and they all boiled," Mark says as he moves toward the pulpit.

Scene 2: Sunday, next week, 5:20 mass

MARK *(in the pulpit):* I woke up on a Friday morning and I went to feed them —and there they were—all of my beautiful fish floating on the top. Most of them split in two. Others with their eyes hanging out. It looked like violence, but it was such a quiet night. And I remember wishing that I had the kind of ears that could hear fish screams because they looked as if they had suffered, and I wanted so badly to save them. *(He leans on top of pulpit toward congregation.)* That Sunday in church, I heard that Christ told his apostles to be fishers of men. From then on, I looked at all the people in the church as fish. I was young, so I saw them as beautiful tropical fish, and so I knew they were all quiet screamers. Church was so quiet. And I thought everyone was boiling. And I wanted the kind of ears that could hear what they were screaming about, because I wanted to save them. *(He stands up straight during a pause.)* A few years later, the people in the church lost the stained-glass look of tropical fish, and they were become catfish to me

—over-dressed scavengers. So I drowned out whatever I might be able to hear. I made my world—my tank—so hot that I almost split. So now I'm back—listening—listening for the screams of angels.

The lights dim to black, as Mark leaves the pulpit. The organ music is heard. Mark exists up center.

Scene 3: Monday morning

The lights come up on the office. Tim, who has been drinking, is singing along with the organ music. He opens the drapes as the organ music ends and *"crosses to the wall cabinet, opens it and takes a bottle in his right hand, a glass in his left."*

Mark comes in and watches Tim, who uncorks the bottle and pours, but the bottle is empty. Tim sees Mark and tells him there are a lot of reactions to his sermon. Mark asks Tim if it isn't a little early to be drinking. Tim points out that it's just wine and gets another bottle from a cupboard under the window seat. He tells Mark that making wine was Christ's first miracle and that He knew what He was doing.

Mark asks Tim if he's had breakfast, but Tim *("after emptying this wine bottle, he has less than half a glass of wine")* says never mind about that . . . Tim wants Mark to hear the reactions. "They're not bad," he tells him, taking another bottle out of the top of the prie-dieu. He thinks they might have a chance and wants to read Mark some of the reactions, but Mark says, "Only if you put down the wine."

Tim starts with the worst, from Mr. Jennings, a convert, who wrote, "We have no choice but to be catfish with garbage like that being thrown at us." Mark doesn't want to hear any more, but Tim continues, saying they get better: "He shows unusual sensitivity . . . Can he give sermons every Sunday?" Tim says there's hope, they're starting to like Mark. Mark asks what they do next, and Tim says he's going to call up Mr. Jennings and tell him he's a jerk. Mark won't let him phone.

The house phone buzzes—it's the monsignor. Mark fights Tim for the phone and tells the monsignor he's taking Father Farley's calls. Monsignor Burke informs Mark that he wants Mark out, in two weeks.

After hanging up the phone, Mark asks Tim to let him make his own appeal in his own way at Tim's mass on the one Sunday Mark has left. Tim comments, "That's like nominating yourself for President" and tells Mark he'll handle it. Tim is going to phone Monsignor Burke. Mark puts his hand on the telephone: "No—you're drunk." Tim insists that he's at his best when he's drunk, so that this is the best possible time for him to call the monsignor—which he proceeds to do.

TIM *(to Monsignor Burke, on the phone):* Oh, hello, Tom—Mark told me you called . . . Now just slow down, Tom—I can do whatever I want in my parish. Don't presume more authority than you . . .

Tim reaches for swivel chair. Mark pushes it to him. Tim sits.

It was a good sermon. Mark has made incredible strides . . . Yes, he told me, and I totally disagree with your decision. This whole sexual question is ridiculous.

Celibacy is celibacy even if your thing is goats . . . goats. He will keep his vows
. . . What? . . . Yes—I'm keeping mine. What are you . . . Tom—there are limits
. . . No—I will not be threatened. Tom . . . Tom . . . If I decide Mark gives another
sermon, then that's what he'll do. If I decide to give a sermon about Mark, than
that's what I'll do. You are not going to intimidate me with your Gestapo tactics.
And another thing—I had a terrible time in Yugoslavia. Goodbye, Monsignor.
    He hangs up the phone.
I'll do it.
    MARK: What?
    TIM: I'll make an appeal for you.
    MARK: You don't mean it. It's the wine . . .
    TIM: I do mean it. It's not the wine. I'm going to cash in my popularity stock
for power.

Tim says his people will flood the monsignor with letters and calls. Mark
wonders what will happen to Tim if it doesn't work. Tim says that if his appeal
doesn't work, the monsignor will go to the bishop and make sure he's in Iowa
by Tuesday. But he's sure his people won't let him go, that they won't let anything
happen to him, and he's not afraid of the monsignor. He's prayed not to be afraid,
and he's not. The lights black out and organ music is heard.

Scene 4: 10:15 mass, that Sunday

    Tim approaches the pulpit as the music ends.
    TIM: There are all forms of persecution. I'm sure if we watch the six o'clock
news for a week, we'd be bound to see almost every kind. But what about the ones
that occur right here in this parish? The ones we can do something about. For
example: Mark Dolson. He is being persecuted, and we should respond.
    Pause.
Now I'm not trying to impose a sense of guilt in all of us. We're trying to get
away from that sort of thing in the church today. All the same, Mark is being
persecuted.
    Pause.
Well—perhaps persecuted is too strong a word. Mark has run into some trouble
at St. Francis Seminary, and he needs our help.
    Pause.
Now some of you might say that Mark can take care of himself. And that's true.
Others of you might say that Mark asks for trouble. And that is also true. We've
all seen how vehement he can be. So you might say Mark *doesn't* need our help.
And you're probably right. But it's good to know that if he did need our help—
we would be there. Let us pray.
    The lights quickly fade to blackness.

Scene 5: That afternoon

    The lights come up on the office as the town clock is striking five. Mark is there,
wearing jeans, striped shirt and navy sweater, carrying a red sweat jacket, as Tim

comes in *"with the white chasuble on a wooden hanger. The green stole is folded over the left side of the hanger."* Mark is there because Tim wants to see him. He's been at the seminary, packing. He's not sure what he will do. Tim says that maybe there's some other diocese he could go to, that he'll make inquiries, but he supposes that whoever he calls will want references from the monsignor.

Tim is sorry if he got Mark's hopes up. His people *would* let him go: he saw it in their faces. He tells Mark he'll have to understand that "whatever I said I'd do was above and beyond the call of duty". He asks Mark if he knows what a town in Iowa is like, that it might have a Main Street, that if there's a movie theater it only shows "chain saw" films, and that the people wouldn't understand his humor and wouldn't talk to him—and he has to talk to people. Mark asks him why he doesn't, then, and Tim says he does.

Tim says to let him know if he can help Mark find a job; but Mark must leave now because Tim has an appointment. *"Mark starts to leave"*, then *"stops, turns to face Tim"* and tells him he doesn't have an appointment. Mark tells Tim he doesn't know why he lies, but he can tell when he does: "But it's all right. They're all harmless lies. You only do it to spare other people's feelings. Right?" Tim says Mark must go.

TIM: I know you think you have a right to be angry with me . . .

MARK: I'm not angry with you.

TIM: You are . . . you think I betrayed you.

MARK: What you did or didn't do for me doesn't make any difference now. I believed you, because I needed to believe you. I set myself up—that's not your fault. But the people who come to you for help deserve more.

TIM: Never mind about the people that come here for my help. They're taken care of.

MARK: You handle them—I've seen it—the way you handled me. You say what everyone wants to hear. Doesn't matter if it's true or if you can back up what you say, so long as you pacify whoever is on the other side of the desk. You'll say anything to get a person in need off your back.

TIM: Mark, get out.

MARK: No. I think I should wait here until your "appointment" comes.

TIM: Would you please leave?

MARK: I should warn whoever it is.

Mark puts his hand on Tim's shoulder.

People should be warned about you.

TIM: Don't push me.

MARK: They all come here thinking they're being helped—But really, all they're doing is pouring their guts out to a drunk who catalogs their anguish.

Tim tells Mark once more to get out, and when *"Mark goes toward him . . . . . Tim punches Mark in the stomach."* There is a pause before Tim says that he thinks he's broken his wrist, it bent back. Mark helps him into a chair and tells him to twirl his arm around, demonstrating. Tim wants to know what that's supposed to do. Mark confesses he doesn't know and he laughs. *"Tim joins the laughter. Tim's laughter turns to tears."*

TIM: I tried, Mark—I wanted to help you—but I need them.

MARK: I understand.

TIM *(turns upstage, facing Mark):* Do you?

MARK: I do. During those three years—whenever someone I loved, loved me, I did all I could to keep it constant. Bit by bit—through trial and error—I learned all the rules—what to say—what to give—what to withhold—so I could keep the love constant. But to go through all that—to worry about who's got the upper hand—who's going to change first—it made the love worthless. I found out that the constant is up to me. Promises are broken; friends will be fickle; love goes its own course, and all of it has to ultimately not matter. And what you believe has to be more important than what your congregation thinks of you.

TIM: Mark . . . I'm not sure what I believe anymore.

"The clock chimes the quarter hour." It is time for the 5:20 mass, and Tim hurriedly goes to get his vestments. (". . . the most attended mass of the day . . . standing room only.") But Tim has nothing prepared and says he can't face them. Mark says he can, and he helps Tim into his vestments to make sure he is ready. Mark says "I'll be fine"; he'll go, for now, back to the seminary and finish packing. When the men shake hands, Tim winces "Ow," and says he now thinks he knows why Christ sent his apostles out into the world in twos. Organ music is heard as the scene ends with Tim going toward the pulpit.

Scene 6: 5:20 mass

The organ music is fading out as Tim enters the pulpit.

TIM: This evening we were supposed to conclude our "On the Road to the Priesthood" series. But I have nothing prepared. And that's not like me. I'm always prepared. So much so, that I haven't really talked to you since I've been here. Because—you see—I've lost Christ. I missed him. I just tap danced right past him. But when I was on the street corner . . . There you were just people on your way to somewhere, but you stopped, to listen, to me. And there—I knew what I wanted to say to you, but I didn't know how. Now—I know how . . .

> *He takes off the sash from around his neck and puts it on the top of the pulpit.*

But from here—I haven't really been a very good priest to you.

> *He takes off the chasuble and places it on the pulpit.*

From here—I never really cared enough to run the risk of losing you.

> *He starts taking off his alb and puts it on the pulpit.*

From here—I can't really see your faces. I need to get back to the street corner.

> *Tim leaves the pulpit and goes to the "street corner".*

Monsignor Burke has expelled Mark Dolson from St. Francis Seminary, and consequently he is barred from the priesthood. Monsignor Burke will tell you that he has expelled Mark because of his past . . . because prior to his decision to become a priest, Mark made love with women and men. But I don't believe that's the real reason. I believe Mark's past is irrelevant. I believe Monsignor Burke has looked for and found a way to get rid of Mark, because Mark threatens Monsignor Burke's picture of what the church should be. But this is not only Monsignor Burke's church. I believe it is our church. Fight for it. Tell him you will not accept his decision. We have to show him what Mark has shown me—that you and I and Mark must be allowed help shape the thing that has shaped us.

Pause.

This is the first time I haven't tried to win your love. Only now is love possible.

Pause.

Oh—by the way—if you don't see me up here next week, I'll probably be in Iowa. But for now, for as long as I'm here . . . Let us . . . begin.

The lights fade to black as the organ music swells. Curtain.

A SOLDIER'S PLAY

A Play in Two Acts

BY CHARLES FULLER

Cast and credits appear on pages 380–381

CHARLES FULLER was born in Philadelphia March 5, 1939, the son of a printer. He has first-hand experience of the U.S. Army, having served in it from 1959 to 1962, after which he was educated at Villanova and LaSalle College. Between the Army and college he ran the Afro-American Art Theater in Philadelphia. As a playwright, his first New York production was The Perfect Party *off Broadway for 21 performances in 1969. He followed this with* In the Deepest Part of Sleep *at The Negro Ensemble Company for 32 performances in 1974;* Candidate *at New Federal Theater and the musical* Sparrow in Flight *at Amas Repertory Theater, both in 1974;* The Brownsville Raid, *first offered in a staged reading at the O'Neill Playwrights Conference in 1975 and then produced off Broadway by NEC in 1976 for 112 performances; and last season's* Zooman and the Sign, *Fuller's third production at NEC and first Best Play, which played 33 performances and won its author a 1981 Obie Award in playwriting.*

Now for the second season in a row Fuller receives a Best Play citation for still another drama produced off Broadway by NEC: A Soldier's Play, *which opened November 20, and has won many awards and citations (see the Awards section of this volume), including the 1982 Pulitzer Prize and New York Drama Critics Circle Award as best American play. Fuller is the author of film and TV scripts including an adaptation of Ernest J. Graves's* The Sky Is Gray *in the American Short Story series. He has been a recipient of Guggenheim, Rockefeller Foundation, National Endowment and CAPS fellowships in playwriting. He is married, with two sons, and lives in Philadelphia.*

Larry Riley as C.J. and Adolph Caesar as Sgt. Waters in *A Soldier's Play*

Time: 1944

Place: Ft. Neal, La.

ACT I

SYNOPSIS: A few pieces of furniture at stage right suggest an office area, with a picture of President Franklin D. Roosevelt; at stage left a barracks area, with a picture of Joe Louis in uniform. Upstage center a bare platform, the highest of several levels in this horshoe-shaped arrangement, serves as a kind of limbo representing any of several areas of action.

Tech Sergeant Vernon C. Waters appears in this upstage limbo, while the song "Don't Sit Under the Apple Tree" is heard being sung by the Andrews Sisters. Waters is *"a well-built light brown-skinned man in a World War II winter Army uniform."* He is down on all fours, obviously drunk, trying to stand up and mumbling.

> WATERS: They'll still hate you! They still hate you . . . They still hate you!
> *Waters is laughing as suddenly someone steps into the light (we never see this person). He is holding a .45 caliber pistol. He lifts it swiftly and ominously toward Waters's head and fires. Waters is knocked over backward. He is dead. The music has stopped and there is a strong silence.*
> VOICE: Les' go!
> *The man with the gun takes a step, then stops. He points the gun at Waters again and fires a second time.*

The limbo area upstage goes to black, while lights come up at stage left on the barracks area of Company B, 221 Chemical Smoke Generating Company. Standing at parade rest are five black men: Corporal Bernard Cobb *("a man in his mid to late 20s, dressed in a T-shirt, dog tags, fatigues and slippers");* Private James Wilkie *("in his early 40s, a career soldier, dressed in fatigues from which his stripes have been removed, a baseball cap, smoking a cigar");* Private Louis Henson *("thin, in his late 20s or early 30s, wearing a baseball T-shirt that reads 'Ft. Neal' on the front and '#4' on the back, fatigues and boots");* Private First Class Melvin Peterson *("in his late 20s, wears glasses, looks angelic. . . . . his stripe is the most visible, his boots the most highly polished");* and Private Tony Smalls *("late 30s, a career man, as small as his name feels").* These five are being searched by Corporal Ellis, black, a "spit and polish" soldier, while Captain Charles Taylor, a white man in his 30s, looks on and seems a bit disturbed.

Capt. Taylor explains to the men that the search is a necessary precaution against the possibility of revenge for the murder of Sgt. Waters, which may or may not have been a sort of lynching: "We don't want anybody from Fort Neal going into Tynin looking for rednecks." Their war is with the Japanese and

Germans, not U.S. civilians, the Captain reminds them, though he himself is shocked and upset by Waters's death. Men found with unauthorized weapons will be court martialed (but no such weapon is found in this barracks).

PETERSON: Who do they think did it, sir?
TAYLOR: At this time there are no suspects.
HENSON: You know the Klan did it, sir.
TAYLOR: Were you an eyewitness, soldier?
HENSON: Who else goes around killin' Negroes in the South? They lynched Jefferson the week I got here, sir! And that Signal Corps guy, Daniels, two months later!
TAYLOR: Henson, unless you saw it, keep your opinions to yourself! Is that clear?
      Henson nods.
And that's an order! It also applies to everybody else!
ALL *(almost simultaneously):* Yes, sir!

The Captain gives out assignments (including cleaning out the Colonel's stables), tells them the town of Tynin is now off limits and the Friday night dance has been cancelled. After he departs with Ellis, the men see through the window that the whole place is surrounded by armed Military Police. They complain among themselves of menial duties, diseases caught from the women they're able to find. Wilkie especially feels a need to toe the line in order to get his stripes back and support his wife and children. Smalls is upset by the others' apparently casual acceptance of Waters's murder, but Henson reminds him that there is nothing they can do about it here in the South, so "don't start acting like we guilty of somethin' . . . . . Besides, whoever did it didn't kill much anyway."

The lights go down in the barracks. Captain Richard Davenport enters carrying a briefcase. He is a self-assured black officer *"dressed sharply in an MP uniform, his hat cocked to the side and 'strapped' down the way the airmen wear theirs . . . . . very confident and self-assured."* He sets down the briefcase and cleans his glasses, smiling, as he addresses the audience, introducing himself with "I'm a lawyer the segregated Armed Services couldn't find a place for. My job in this war? Policing colored troops." He reviews the facts of the Waters case: a black tech sergeant stationed here with his company prior to shipping out to Europe was brutally shot to death a couple of hundred yards from the NCO club. After rumors began to spread that the Klan arranged the killing, Colonel Barton Nivens took steps to see that his 90 per cent black troops didn't attempt to retaliate. He succeeded—there were no racial incidents.

"The NAACP got me involved in this," Davenport declares, "Rumor has it, Thurgood Marshall ordered an immediate investigation of the killing, and the Army, pressured by Secretary of War Stimson, rather randomly ordered Col. Nivens to initiate a preliminary inquiry into the Sergeant's death." The Colonel passed the case along to the Provost Marshal with a low priority, and it has now landed in Davenport's hands.

Davenport's first step is to introduce himself to Capt. Taylor, who comments,

"Forgive me for occasionally staring, Davenport, you're the first colored officer I've ever met." He is curious about where Davenport attended law school (Howard University) and whether his family was rich (they weren't). Taylor himself attended West Point, where there were no Negroes ("I never saw a Negro until I was twelve or thirteen.") Taylor had no idea they'd assign a black officer to this case. He warns Capt. Davenport that the local people will be extremely hostile to his investigation, and it will be impossible to fix the guilt on a white man.

DAVENPORT (calmly): Captain, like it or not, I'm all you've got. I've been ordered to look into Sergeant Waters's death, and I intend to do exactly that.
    There is a long pause.
TAYLOR: Can I tell you a little story? (Davenport nods.) Before you were assigned here, Nivens got us together after dinner one night, and all we did was discuss Negroes in the officer ranks. We all commanded Negro troops, but nobody had ever come face to face with colored officers—there were a lot of questions that night—for example, your quarters—had to be equal to ours, but we had none—no mess hall for you. (Slight pause.) Anyway, Jed Harris was the only officer who defended it—my own feelings were mixed. The only Negroes I've ever known were subordinates—My father hired the first Negro I ever saw—man named Colfax, to help him fix the shed one summer—nice man—worked hard —did a good job, too. (Remembering; smiles thoughtfully.) But I never met a Negro with any education until I graduated the Point—hardly an officer of equal rank. So I frankly wasn't sure how I'd feel—until right now—and—(Struggles.) I don't want to offend you, but I just can not get used to it—the bars, the uniform —being in charge just doesn't look right on Negroes!
DAVENPORT: Captain, are you through?
TAYLOR: You could ask Hines for another assignment—this case is not for you! By the time you overcome the obstacles to your race this case would be dead!
DAVENPORT (sharply): I got it. And I am in charge! All your orders instruct you to do is cooperate!
    There is a moment of silence.
TAYLOR: I won't be made a fool of, Davenport. (Straightens.) Ellis! (To Davenport.) You're right, there's no need to discuss this any further.
ELLIS (appears on the edge of the office): Yes, sir!
TAYLOR: Captain Davenport will need assistance with the men—I can't prevent that, Davenport, but I intend to do all I can to have this so-called "investigation" stopped.
DAVENPORT: Do what you like. If there's nothing else, you'll excuse me, won't you, Captain?
TAYLOR (sardonically): Glad I met you, Captain.

The men exchange salutes, and Davenport leaves Taylor's office accompanied by Ellis. Questioned by Davenport, Ellis says that the murder is rumored to have been a Klan job, or possibly the work of two officers. Davenport sets up with a table and chair in the barracks section and orders Ellis to send the men in one by one for questioning. Ellis obeys with the comment, "It sure is good to see one of us wearin' them captain's bars, sir," and calls in Pvt. Wilkie, who is dressed in fatigues, boots and cap. Wilkie takes a seat as Ellis exits.

Wilkie tells Davenport he'd known Sgt. Waters about a year. His company was assembled from the best baseball players available, some of them veterans of the Negro League. They were assigned to a good deal of dirty work during the week, but Saturdays they spent on the baseball diamond. Sgt. Waters was a sort of team manager, and all spit and polish as a military man.

> *At that moment in limbo a spotlight hits Sgt. Waters. He is dressed in a well-creased uniform, wearing a helmet-liner and standing at parade rest facing the audience. The light around him, however, is strange— it is blue-gray like the past. The light around Davenport and Wilkie abates somewhat. Dialogue is continuous.*

DAVENPORT: Tell me about him.

WILKIE: He took my stripes! *(Smiles.)* But I was in the wrong, sir!

> *Waters stands at ease. His voice is crisp and sharp, his movements minimal. He is the typical hard-nosed NCO—strict, soldierly.*

WATERS: Sergeant Wilkie! You are a non-commissioned officer in the army of a country at war—the penalty for being drunk on duty is severe in peacetime, so don't bring me no po'-colored-folks-can't-do-nothin'-unless-they-drunk-shit as an excuse! You are supposed to be an example to your men—so, I'm gonna send you to jail for ten days *and* take them goddamn stripes. Teach you a lesson—you in the Army! *(Derisively.)* Colored folks always runnin' off at the mouth 'bout what y'all gonna do, if the white man gives you a chance—and you get it, and what do you do with it? You wind up drunk on guard duty—I don't blame the white man—why the hell should he put colored and white together in this war? You can't even be trusted to guard your own quarters—no wonder they treat us like dogs—Get outta my sight, *Private!*

The light fades on Waters as Wilkie remembers that Waters, from the North, was hard on Southern soldiers—all except C.J. Memphis, their best baseball player. Wilkie tells Davenport, "He didn' mess with C.J., you know what I mean? Not like he did with everybody else." At this moment, *"in limbo the spotlight illuminates C.J. Memphis, a young, handsome black man. He is in a soldier's uniform, cap on the side. He is strumming a guitar . . . . . C.J. begins to sing, his voice deep, melodious and bluesy."*

Sgt. Waters was a fan of blues singing and admired C.J.'s talent. Wilkie agrees that C.J. was "a good man" (as the lights fade on C.J. and Wilkie joins the memory figure of Waters who sits and puffs on his pipe). Wilkie remembers how Waters was always showing off snapshots of his family.

WATERS: I hope this kid never has to be a soldier.

WILKIE: It was good enough for you.

WATERS: I couldn't do any better—and this Army was the closest I figured the white man would let me get to any kind of authority. No, the Army ain't for this boy. When this war's over, things are going to change, Wilkie—and I want him to be ready for it—my daughter too! I'm sendin' both of 'em to some big white college—let 'em rub elbows with the whites, learn the white man's language—how he does things. Otherwise we'll be left behind—you can see it in the Army. White men runnin' rings around us.

WILKIE: A lot of us didn't get the chance or the schoolin' the white folks got.

WATERS: That ain't no excuse, Wilkie. Most niggahs just don't care—tomorrow don't mean nothin' to 'em. My daddy shoveled coal from the back of a wagon all his life. He couldn't read or write, but he saw to it we did! Not havin' ain't no excuse for not gettin'.

WILKIE: Can't get pee from a rock, Sarge.

WATERS (rises abruptly): You just like the rest of 'em, Wilkie—I thought bustin' you would teach you something—we got to challenge this man in his arena —use his weapons, don't you know that? We need lawyers, doctors—generals—Senators! Stop thinkin' like a niggah!

WILKIE: All I said—

WATERS: Is the equipment ready for tomorrow's game?

WILKIE: Yeah.

WATERS: Good. You can go now, Wilkie.

Wilkie is stunned.

That's an order!

Wilkie turns back to Davenport explaining that Waters could be two people, "warm one minute—ice the next." All things considered, he was an all right guy, Wilkie concludes, though he had been drinking heavily at the NCO club the night of his death. Wilkie points out to Davenport that Waters was wearing all his military insignia when his body was found; the Klan resents such insignia on black soldiers and would have stripped it off if this had been a Klan killing.

Wilkie exits (as the humming of C.J. is heard in the background) and is replaced in this interrogation by Pfc. Melvin Peterson, "the model soldier," who salutes Davenport and stands at attention. Davenport returns the salute and waves the private to a chair. Peterson disliked Waters, called him "Stone-ass," felt that he ran the baseball team like a chain gang.

As Peterson tells his story, it is acted out in retrospect by C.J. Memphis, Henson, Cobb and Smalls, who enter the barracks dressed in their baseball uniforms and carrying equipment. They are shouting about the events of the game they just played and won by a score of 9 to 1. While C.J. (who hit a home run) strums his guitar, Peterson observes, "Every time we beat them at baseball, they get back at us every way they can—seems like it makes it that much harder for us."

Sgt. Waters enters with Wilkie and calls for their attention, cutting off C.J.'s "guitar playin'-sittin'-round-the-shack music." Waters orders the men to form a work detail to paint the lobby of the Officers Club.

Collective groans.

SMALLS: The officers can't paint their own club?

COBB: Hell no, Smalls! Let the great-colored-clean-up-company do it! Our motto is: Anything you don't want to do, the colored troops will do for you!

HENSON (*like a cheer*): Anything you don't want to do, the colored troops will do for you!

He starts to lead the others.

OTHERS: Anything you don't . . . . .

WATERS: That's enough!

The men are instantly silent.

HENSON: When do we get a rest? We just played nine innings of baseball, Sarge.

SMALLS: We can't go in the place, why the hell should we paint it?

COBB: Amen, brother!

There is a moment of quiet before Waters speaks.

WATERS: Let me tell you fancy-assed ball-playin' Negroes somethin'! The *reasons* for any orders given by a superior officer is none of y'all's business! You obey them! This country is at war, and you niggahs are soldiers—nothin' else! So baseball teams—win or lose—get no special privileges! They need to work some of you niggahs till your legs fall off! (*Intense.*) And something else—from now on when I tell you to do something, I want it done—is that clear?

The men are quiet.

Now, Wilkie's gonna take all them funky shirts you got on over to the laundry. I could smell you suckers before I hit the field!

PETERSON: What kinda colored man are you?

WATERS: I'm a soldier, Peterson! First, last and always! I'm the kinda colored man that don't like lazy, shiftless Negroes!

PETERSON: You ain't got to come in here and call us names!

WATERS: The Nazis call you schvatza! You gonna tell them they hurt your little feelings?

C.J. Don't look to me like we could do too much to them Nazis wit' paint brushes, Sarge.

The men laugh. The moment is gone, and though Waters is angry, his tone becomes overly solicitous, smiling.

WATERS: You tryin' to mock me, C.J.?

C.J.: No sah, Sarge.

WATERS: Good, because whatever an ignorant, low-class geechy like you has to say isn't worth paying attention to, is it?

Pause.

Is it?

C.J.: I reckon not, Sarge.

PETERSON: You a creep, Waters!

WATERS: Boy, you are something—ain't been in the company a month, and already everybody's champion!

C.J. (*interjecting*): Sarge was just jokin', Pete—he don't mean no harm!

PETERSON: He does! We take enough from the white boys!

WATERS: Yes you do—and if it wasn' for you Southern niggahs, yessahin', bowin' and scrapin', scratchin' your heads, white folks wouldn' think we were all fools!

The two men nearly come to blows, but their quarrel is interrupted by the arrival of Capt. Taylor, who has come to congratulate them on their baseball victory (if they keep on winning they'll earn the right to play the Yankees in an exhibition game) and give them the rest of the day off. Waters wants the men to go through with the paint detail, but Taylor overrules him.

When the Captain leaves, Waters turns back to Peterson and challenges him to a fist fight behind the barracks, to be witnessed by all the other NCOs. Smalls warns Peterson that Waters will fight dirty, and C.J. offers some magic dust to make Peterson extra strong. But Peterson is annoyed by C.J.'s attitude toward Waters: "Let that bastard treat you like a dog . . . . . the man despises you!" C.J. feels the Sergeant has done him no harm, has even been good to him. C.J. begins his singing again, and the lights fade.

In the present, Peterson tells Davenport, "He beat me pretty bad that day, sir. The man was crazy!" Peterson never reported the incident (and they were beaten by another team and never got to play the Yankees).

After Peterson leaves, Davenport is summoned to Capt. Taylor's office. Taylor wants to report that he's asked Col. Nivens to call off the investigation, for reasons that have nothing to do with anything personal.

DAVENPORT: Only the color of my skin, Captain.

TAYLOR *(sharply):* I want the people responsible for killing one of my men found and jailed, Davenport!

DAVENPORT: So do I!

TAYLOR: Then give this up! Whites down here won't see their duty—or justice. They'll see *you!* And once they do, the law—due process—it all goes! And what is the point of continuing an investigation that can't possibly get at the truth?

DAVENPORT: Captain, my orders are very specific, so unless you want charges brought against you for interfering in a criminal investigation, stay the hell out of my way and leave me and my investigation alone!

TAYLOR *(almost sneering):* Don't take yourself too seriously, Davenport. You couldn't find an officer within five hundred miles who would convey charges to a Court Martial board against me for something like that, and you know it.

DAVENPORT: Maybe not, but I'd—I'd see to it that your name, rank and duty station got into the Negro press! Yeah, let a few colored newspapers call you a Negro-hater! Make you an embarrassment to the United States Army, Captain —like Major Albright at Fort Jefferson—and you'd never command troops again —or wear more than those captain's bars on that uniform, Mr. West Point!

TAYLOR: I'll never be more than a captain, Davenport, because I won't let them get away with dismissing things like Waters's death. I've been the commanding officer of three outfits. I raised hell in all of them, so threatening me won't change my request. Let the Negro press print that I don't like being made a fool of with phony investigations!

Davenport has found that there are two white officers somehow involved. Taylor knew about this and would like to see the two men charged but can't prove anything against them; besides, he was ordered not to report this involvement. Waters was killed by two bullets from an Army .45, but if there had been any suggestion that they might have been fired by white officers, there might have been an explosion among the black troops.

Davenport demands to know the names of the two white officers in question. "Byrd and Wilcox," Taylor replies. "Byrd's in Ordnance—Wilcox's with the 12th Hospital Group. I was captain of the guard the night Waters was killed. About 2100 hours, Cobb came into my office and told me he'd just seen Waters and two white officers fighting outside the colored NCO club." But when Taylor went over to break it up, everyone had disappeared, and Waters's body wasn't found until the next morning. Taylor received the Colonel's permission to question Byrd and Wilcox, but "since the situation at the Fort was potentially dangerous," Taylor could make no report; but he has put in a request daily for a follow-up investigation.

TAYLOR: . . . . . When I saw you, I exploded—it was like he was laughing at me.

DAVENPORT: Then you never believed the Klan was involved?

TAYLOR: No. Now can you see why this thing needs—someone else?

DAVENPORT: What did they tell you, Captain? Byrd and Wilcox?

TAYLOR: They're not going to let you charge those two men!

DAVENPORT *(snaps):* Tell me what they told you!

> *Taylor is quiet for a moment. At this time at center stage in limbo, Sgt. Waters is staggering. He is dressed as we first saw him. Behind him a blinking light reads "221st NCO Club." As he staggers toward the stairs leading to center stage, two white officers, Lieutenant Byrd (a spit-and-polish soldier in his 20s) and Captain Wilcox (a medical officer) walk onstage. Both are in full combat gear—rifles, pistol belts, packs—and both are tired. Taylor looks out as if he can see them.*

TAYLOR: They were coming off bivouac.

> *The two men see Waters. In the background is the faint hum of C.J.'s music.*

They saw him outside the club.

> *He rises, as Waters sees Byrd and Wilcox and smiles.*

WATERS: Well, if it ain't the white boys!

> *Waters straightens and begins to march in a mock circle and then down in their direction. He is mumbling, barely audibly: "One, two, three, four! Hup, hup, three four! Hup, hup, three four!"*

BYRD: And it wasn't like we were looking for trouble, Captain—were we, Wilcox?

> *Wilcox shakes his head "no," but he is astonished at Waters's behavior and stares at him, disbelieving.*

WATERS: White boys! All starched and stiff! Wanted everybody to learn all that symphony shit! That's what you were saying in France—and you know, I listened to you? Am I all right now? Am I?

BYRD: Boy, you'd better straighten up and salute when you see an officer, or you'll find yourself without those stripes! *(To Wilcox, as Waters nears them smiling the "coon" smile and doing a "Juba.")* Will you look at this niggah? *(Loud.)* Come to attention, Sergeant! That's an order!

WATERS: No, sah! I ain't straightenin' up for y'all no more! I ain't doin' nothin' white folks say do, no more! *(Sudden change of mood, smiles, sings.)* No-more, no-more/No-more, no-more, noooo! No-more, no-more/No-more, no-more, noooooo!

Both officers thought Waters must be out of his mind, or at the very least extremely drunk. They told Taylor they tried to shake some sense into Waters, who began to weep, declaring "I've killed for you . . . . . and nothin' changed!"

Frustrated, Byrd threw Waters to the ground and began to beat and kick him. Wilcox pulled Byrd off Waters, and the Sergeant was groveling on his knees as the officers left. Their stories stood up under interrogation, but Davenport believes they were lying to protect each other and that Taylor himself should be placed under arrest.

TAYLOR: What charges?

DAVENPORT: It was *your* duty to go over Nivens's head if you had to!

TAYLOR: Will you arrest Colonel Nivens too, Davenport? Because he's part of their alibi—he was there when they came in—played poker—from 2100 to 0330 hours the following morning, the Colonel—your Major Hines, "Shack" Callahan —Major Callahan, and Jed Harris—and Jed wouldn't lie for either of them!

DAVENPORT: They're all lying!

TAYLOR: Prove it, hotshot—I told you all I know, now you go out and prove it!

DAVENPORT: I will, Captain! You can bet your sweet ass on that! I will!
Davenport starts out as the lights begin to fade and Taylor looks after him and shakes his In the background, the sound of "Don't Sit Under the Apple Tree" comes up again and continues to play as the lights fade to black. Curtain.

ACT II

In the same setting, introduced again by a few bars from "Don't Sit Under the Apple Tree," Capt. Davenport is telling the audience how it was in May, 1944: black soldiers would soon be in combat alongside white soldiers, and Davenport was ever more determined to see this case through. "I had two prime suspects —a motive and an opportunity!" and he received permission from Col. Nivens to question Byrd and Wilcox. But he also decided "to spend some time finding out more about Waters and Memphis. Somehow the real drama seemed to be there, and my curiosity wouldn't allow me to ignore it."

In the barracks area, Davenport questions Ptv. Henson about the relationship between C.J. Memphis and Sgt. Waters. Henson doesn't like "tattle-talin' ", let alone talking to officers of any color, but he admits that Waters was always especially hard on C.J.

HENSON: C.J. wasn' movin' fast enough for *him*. Said C.J. didn' have enough *fire-under-his-behind* out on the field.

DAVENPORT: You were on the team?

HENSON: Pitcher.

Charles Brown *(left)* as Capt. Davenport confronts the officers (Peter Friedman, Sam McMurray, Stephen Zettler) in *A Soldier's Play*

> *Pause. Davenport urges with a look.*

He jus' *stayed* on C.J. all the time—every little thing, it seemed like to me—and the shootin' went down, and C.J. caught all the hell.

DAVENPORT: What shooting?

HENSON: The shooting at Williams Golden Palace, sir—here, las' year! Happened last year—way before you got here. Toward the end of the baseball season.

> *Davenport nods his recognition.*

The night it happened, a whole lotta gunshots went off near the barracks. I had gotten drunk over at the Enlisted Men's Club, so when I got to the barracks I just sat down in a stupor!

> *Suddenly shots are heard in the distance and grow ever closer as the eerie blue-grey light rises in the barracks over the sleeping figures of men in their bunks. Henson is seated, staring at the ground. He looks up once as the gunshots go off. As he does, someone—we cannot be sure who—sneaks into the barracks as the men begin to shift and awaken.*

This person puts something under C.J.'s bed and rushes out. Henson watches—surprised at first, rising, then disbelieving. He shakes his head, then sits back down as several men wake up.

Henson is sure he saw someone, but he doesn't know who. Henson remembers that Waters then entered the barracks (acted out as Henson talks to Davenport), waking the men up and telling them that the shooting started when a black man bucked the line at a pay phone, and now there are three dead, two black soldiers and a white MP. Waters tells the men, "Now the man who bucked the line, he killed the MP, and the white boys started shootin' everybody—that's how our two got shot. And this lowdown niggah we lookin' for, got chased down here—and was almost caught, 'til somebody in these barracks started shootin' at the men chasin' him."

Waters orders anyone involved in this incident to step forward (no one does) and sets Wilkie to searching the barracks. Waters questions the men about their whereabouts earlier tonight as the search continues—and of course Wilkie finds a .45 automatic under C.J.'s bunk. Waters confronts C.J., who denies vehemently that the weapon is his and points out that anyone could have put it where it was found.

WATERS: Liar!

C.J.: No, Sarge—I hate guns! Makes me feel bad jes' to see a gun!

WATERS: You're under arrest—Wilkie, escort this man to the stockade!

PETERSON *(steps forward):* C.J. couldn't hurt a fly, Waters, you know that!

WATERS: I found a gun, soldier—now get out of the way!

PETERSON: Goddamit, Waters, you know it ain't him!

WATERS: How do I know?

HENSON: Right before you came in, I thought I saw somebody sneak in.

WATERS: You were drunk when you left the club—I saw you myself!

WILKIE: Besides, how you know it wasn't C.J.?

COBB: I was here all night. C.J. didn't go out.

WATERS *(looks at them, intense):* We got the right man. *(Points at C.J., empassioned.)* You think he's innocent, don't you? C.J. Memphis playin' cotton-picker, singin' the blues, bowin' and scrapin'—smilin' in everybody's face—this man undermined us! You and me! The description of the man who did the shooting fits C.J.! *(To Henson.)* You saw C.J. sneak in here! *(Points.)* Don't be fooled— that yassah boss is hidin' something—niggahs ain't like that today! This is 1943 —he shot that white boy!

> *C.J. is stunned, then suddenly the enormity of his predicament hits him and he breaks free of Wilkie and hits Waters in the chest. The blow knocks Waters down, and C.J. is immediately grabbed by the other men in the barracks. Cobb goes to Waters and helps him up slowly. The blow hurt Waters, but he forces a smile at C.J., who has suddenly gone immobile, surprised by what he has done.*

What did you go and do now, boy? Hit a non-commissioned officer.

COBB: Sarge, he didn't mean it!

WATERS: Shut up! *(Straightens.)* Take him out, Wilkie.

Wilkie grabs C.J. by the arm and leads him out. C.J. goes calmly, almost passively. Waters looks at all the men quietly for a moment, then walks out without saying a word. There is a momentary silence in the barracks.

SMALLS: Niggah like that can't have a mother.

HENSON: I know I saw something!

PETERSON: C.J. was sleepin' when I came in! It's Waters—can't y'all see that? I've seen him before—we had 'em in Alabama. White man gives them a little ass job as a servant—close to the big house—and when the "boss" ain't lookin' old copy-cat niggahs act like they the new owner! They take to soundin' like the boss —shoutin', orderin' people aroun'—and when it comes to you and me, they sell us to continue favor. They think the "high-jailers" like that. Arrestin' C.J.— that'll get Waters another stripe! Next it'll be you—or you—he can't look good unless he's standin' on you! Cobb tol' him C.J. was in all evening—Waters didn' even listen! Turning somebody in. *(Mimics.)* "Look what I done, Captain-Boss!" They let him in the Army 'cause they know he'll do anything they tell him to —I've seen his kind of fool before. Someone's going to kill him.

It's been done before in similar circumstances on other bases, the men note. They decide to go over to the stockade and tell the MPs what they know and believe about C.J.'s innocence.

Henson repeats to Davenport that he saw a man run in and out (and as far as he knows, Wilkie was the only man out of his bunk that night; he came in later with Waters). Henson departs, as Cobb enters and becomes the next man to be interrogated, as Davenport sends Ellis to find and bring both Wilkie and Peterson to him for questioning.

Cobb—who like C.J. is from Mississippi and played baseball in the Negro League—is still convinced that C.J. was innocent of any complicity in the telephone shootings. Confinement in a cell was particularly hard on C.J., a farm boy: "He looked pale and ashy, sir—like something dead." In limbo, in the blue-grey lighting of the past (as Cobb remembers it) Waters visited C.J. in his cell.

WATERS *(calmly):* You should learn never to hit sergeants, boy—man can get in a lot of trouble doin' that kinda thing durin' wartime—they talkin' 'bout givin' you five years—they call what you did mutiny in the Navy. Mutiny, boy.

C.J.: That gun ain't mine!

WATERS: Oh, we know that, C.J.!

C.J. is surprised.

That gun belonged to the niggah did the shootin' over at Williams place—me and Wilkie caught him hidin' in the Motor Pool, and he confessed his head off. You're in here for striking a superior officer, boy. And I got a whole barracks full of your friends to prove it! *(Smiles broadly, as C.J. shakes his head.)*

DAVENPORT *(to Cobb, at once):* Memphis wasn't charged with the shooting?

COBB: No, sir—

WATERS: Don't feel too bad, boy. It's not your fault entirely—it has to be this way. The First War, it didn't change much for us, boy—but this one—it's gonna change a lot of things. Them Nazis ain't all crazy—a whole lot of people just can't fit into where things seem to be goin'—like you, C.J. The black race can't afford you no more. There useta be a time when we'd see somebody like you singin', clownin'—yas-sah-bossin'—and we wouldn't do anything. *(Smiles.)* Folks liked that—you were good—homey kinda niggah—they needed somebody to mistreat —call a name, they paraded you, reminded them of the old days—cornbread bakin', greens and ham cookin'—Daddy out pickin' cotton, Grandmammy sit on the front porch smokin' a pipe. *(Slight pause.)* Not no more. The day of the geechy is gone, boy—the only thing that can move the race is power. It's all the white respects—and people like you just make us seem like fools. And we can't let nobody go on believin' we all like you! You bring us down—make people think the whole race is unfit! *(Quietly pleased.)* I waited a long time for you, boy, but I gotcha! And I try to get rid of you wherever I go. I put two geechies in jail at Fort Campbell, Kentucky—three at Fort Huachuca. Now I got you—one less fool for the race to be ashamed of! *(Points.)* And Ima git that ole boy Cobb next!

The lights fade out on Waters. Cobb remembers a visit to C.J. in the stockade, and how C.J. despaired of ever getting out, because of Waters's ferocious hostility. Cobb tried to reassure his friend, but C.J. simply became more and more depressed and desperate, and the next day he committed suicide by hanging himself from the bars of his cell. In memory of C.J., the team threw its next game. Angered at the loss, the commanding officer broke up the team and reassigned the men to their present duty. About that time, Waters "started actin' funny . . . . . stayed drunk—talked to hisself all the time." Cobb never wholly believed that he was next on Waters's enemies list, as C.J. had reported. Anyway, Waters never waged any vendetta against Cobb. And Cobb has an alibi for the night the Sergeant was killed. He was listening to the radio with Henson and playing checkers with Wilkie. Cobb remembers that Smalls and Peterson were the last to come back to the barracks that night.

As Cobb departs, Capt. Taylor enters with the information that the Colonel has granted Davenport permission to question the two white officers. The Colonel has ordered Taylor to assist Davenport, because neither Byrd nor Wilcox would submit to questioning without a white officer present.

TAYLOR: But there's something else, Davenport. The Colonel began talking about the affidavits he and the others signed—and the discrepancies in their statements that night. *(Mimics.)* He wants me with you because he doesn't want Byrd and Wilcox giving you the "wrong impression"—he never elaborated on what he meant by the "wrong impression." I want to be there!

DAVENPORT: So you're not on *that* side any more—you're on *my* side now, right?

TAYLOR *(bristles):* I want whoever killed my Sergeant, Davenport!

DAVENPORT: Bullshit! Yesterday you were daring me to try! And today we're allies? Besides, you don't give that much of a damn about your men! I've been around you a full day and you haven't uttered a word that would tell me you had any more than a minor acquaintance with Waters! He managed your baseball team—was an NCO in your company—and you haven't offered *any* opinion of the man as a soldier—sergeant—platoon leader! Who the hell was he?

TAYLOR: He was one of my men! On my roster—a man these bars make me responsible for! And no, I don't know a helluva lot about him—or a lot of their names, or where they come from, but I'm still their commanding officer, and in a little while I may have to trust them with my life! And I want them to know they can trust me with theirs—here and now!

Questioned about C.J., Capt. Taylor repeats much of what others have said. C.J. was "more a boy than a man" and killed himself before Taylor could get very far into the facts of the charge against him. Davenport thinks Waters probably tricked C.J. into striking him. Taylor disagrees, angering Davenport by observing that "colored soldiers aren't devious like that."

Meanwhile, Byrd and Wilcox, in dress uniform, are ready for questioning in the office area.

TAYLOR (as he moves to his desk): This is *Captain* Davenport—you've both been briefed by Colonel Nivens to give the Captain your full cooperation.
    Davenport puts on his glasses. Taylor notices and almost smiles.
BYRD (to Davenport): They tell me you a lawyer, huh?
DAVENPORT: I'm not here to answer your questions, Lieutenant. And I am Captain Davenport, is that clear?
BYRD (to Taylor): Captain, is he crazy?
TAYLOR: You got your orders.
BYRD: Sir, I vigorously protest as an officer—
TAYLOR (cuts him off): You answer him the way he wants you to, Byrd, or I'll have your ass in a sling so tight you won't be able to pee, soldier!
    Byrd backs off slightly.
DAVENPORT: When did you last see Sergeant Waters?
BYRD: The night he was killed, but I didn' kill him—I should have blown his head off, the way he spoke to me and Captain Wilcox here.
DAVENPORT: How did he speak to you, Captain?
WILCOX: Well, he was very drunk—and he said a lot of things he shouldn't have. I told the Lieutenant here not to make the situation worse, and he agreed, and we left the Sergeant on his knees wallowing in self-pity. (Shrugs.)
DAVENPORT: What exactly did he say?
WILCOX: Some pretty stupid things about us—I mean white people, sir.
    Byrd reacts to the term "sir."
DAVENPORT: What kind of things?
BYRD (annoyed): He said he wasn't going to obey no white man's orders! And that me and Wilcox here were to blame for him being black, and not able to sleep or keep his food down! And I didn't even know the man! Never even spoke to him before that night!
DAVENPORT: Anything else?
WILCOX: Well—he said he'd killed somebody.
DAVENPORT: Did he call a name—or say who?
WILCOX: Not that I recall, sir.
    Davenport looks at Byrd.

BYRD: No—*(Sudden and sharp.)* Look—the goddam Negro was disrespectful! He wouldn't salute! Wouldn't come to attention! And where I come from colored don't talk the way he spoke to us—not to white people they don't!

DAVENPORT: Is that the reason you killed him?

BYRD: I killed nobody! I said, "Where I come from," didn't I? You'd be dead yourself, where I come from! But I didn't kill the—the *Negro!*

DAVENPORT: But you hit him, didn't you?

BYRD: I knocked him down!

DAVENPORT *(quickens pace):* And when you went to look at him he was dead, wasn't he?

BYRD: He was alive when we left!

DAVENPORT: You're a liar! You beat Waters up—you went back and you shot him!

BYRD: No! *(Rises.)* But you better get outta my face before I kill you!

DAVENPORT *(stands firm):* Like you killed Waters?

BYRD: No!

Byrd holds himself back from offering violence to Davenport, who points out that the two officers were carrying weapons that night. Wilcox tells him they turned their two .45's in to Major Hines, who had them cleared with Ballistics —they weren't the weapons which killed Waters. Colonel Nivens kept all this quiet because he didn't want the troops to know that white officers were involved in any way, however guiltless.

Taylor wants to place the two men under arrest, but Davenport lets them go without charging them. Taylor thinks everybody from the Colonel down is lying to give them an alibi, but Davenport is not sure. Taylor hints that Davenport may be letting Byrd and Wilcox go in order to avoid damaging his own chances for promotion by white superior officers. Davenport stoutly denies this.

Ellis comes in to report that Wilkie is waiting in the barracks to be questioned one more time. After another verbal clash with Taylor, Davenport leaves the office area and goes to the barracks where Wilkie is waiting. Asking Wilkie about how he lost his stripes, he gets the ex-Sergeant to admit that he resented being busted by his friend Sgt. Waters, for whom he had performed such loyal service.

DAVENPORT: Made you mad, didn't it?

WILKIE: Yeah, it made me mad—all the things I did for him!

DAVENPORT *(quickly):* That's right! You were his assistant, weren't you? Took care of the team—

Wilkie nods.

Ran all his errands, looked at his family snapshots.

Wilkie nods again.

Policed his quarters, put the gun under C.J.'s bed—

WILKIE *(looks up suddenly):* No!

DAVENPORT *(quickly):* It was you Henson saw, wasn't it Wilkie?

WILKIE: No, sir!

DAVENPORT: Liar! You lied about Waters, and you're lying now! You were the only person out of the barracks that night, and the only one who knew the layout

well enough to go straight to C.J.'s bunk! Not even Waters knew the place that
well! Henson didn't see who it was, but he saw what the person did—he was
positive about that—only you knew the barracks in the dark!

WILKIE (*pleadingly*): It was the Sarge, Captain—he ordered me to do it—he
said I'd get my stripes back—he wanted to scare that boy C.J.! Let him stew in
jail! Then C.J. hit him—and he had the boy right where he wanted him—
(*Confused.*) But it backfired—C.J. killed hisself—Sarge didn't figure on that.

Sarge despised C.J. (Wilkie testifies) because he was so popular, so innocent-
seeming, so gifted both in sports and in music. Waters hated murderously any
black who let himself be patronized by whites, as C.J. sometimes would. Waters
once told Wilkie a story about a black World War I soldier who let himself be
the butt of a joke for the amusement of the white soldiers and the French—his
black comrades slit his throat. And, Waters added, "I don't intend to have our
race cheated out of its place of honor and respect in *this* war because of fools like
C.J."

The one who clashed with Waters all the time was Peterson, but instead of
resenting him (Wilkie testifies) Waters admired him for talking back and pro-
moted him. Since C.J.'s death, Peterson has been keeping pretty much to himself
or hanging around with Pvt. Smalls.

The night Waters was killed, Wilkie got to the barracks about 9:45 and played
checkers with some of the others. Davenport is ready to put Wilkie under arrest,
when the sound of a bugle is heard and Ellis bursts in to report that their orders
have come through and they are soon to take part in the war in Europe. Henson
and Cobb enter, elated at the news that they are headed for combat at last. But
Davenport goes through with sending Wilkie out under arrest, guarded by Ellis.
Inquiring about the whereabouts of Peterson and Smalls, Davenport is informed
that Smalls has just been found and taken to the stockade by a pair of MPs.

The lights go down in the barracks and rise in limbo, where Smalls, pacing in
his cell, is visited by Davenport. Smalls tries to pretend that he went a.w.o.l. by
himself and got drunk, but Davenport insists Peterson was with him: "You left
together because Peterson knew I would find out the two of you killed Waters,
didn't you?" Smalls finally breaks into tears and protests that he only watched
while Peterson did the killing. The blue-grey light of memory builds at stage
center as Smalls tells Davenport that the night Sgt. Waters was killed he and
Peterson were coming off guard duty, so that they were fully armed. They came
upon Sgt. Waters talking to himself, so drunk he couldn't get up off his knees after
he had fallen. Over the objections of Smalls, Peterson began to taunt Waters.

> *Waters looks up; almost smiles. He reaches for Peterson, who pushes*
> *him back down.*

PETERSON: That's the kinda help I'll give ya, boy! Let me help you again—al'
right?

Kicks Waters.

Like that, Sarge? Huh? Like that, dog?

SMALLS (*shouts*): Peterson!

PETERSON: No! (*Almost pleading.*) Smalls—some people, man—If this was

German, would you kill it? If it was Hitler—or that fuckin' Tojo? Would you kill him?

> *Kicks Waters again.*

WATERS *(mumbling throughout):* There's a trick to it, Peterson—it's the only way you can win—C.J. could never make it—he was a clown!

> *Grabs at Peterson.*

A clown in blackface! A niggah!

> *Peterson steps out of reach. He is suddenly expressionless as he easily removes his pistol from his holster.*

You got to be like them! And I was! I was—but the rules are fixed. *(Whispers.)* Shhh! Listen. It's C.J. *(Laughs.)* I made him do it, but it doesn't make any difference! They still hate you! *(Looks at Peterson, who has moved closer to him.)* They still hate you! *(Laughs.)*

PETERSON *(to Smalls):* Justice, Smalls.

> *Peterson raises the pistol.*

DAVENPORT *(suddenly, harshly):* That isn't justice!

> *Smalls almost recoils.*

PETERSON *(simultaneously):* For C.J.! Everybody!

> *Peterson fires the gun at Waters's chest, and the shot stops everything. The celebration noise stops. Even Davenport in his way seems to hear it. Peterson fires again. There is a moment of quiet onstage.*

Smalls tells an angry Capt. Davenport that he was afraid of Peterson and could not prevent the killing, which so shocked him that Peterson had to help him back to the barracks. Peterson was certain the crime would be blamed on whites. "I'm sorry, sir," is Smalls's final comment as he salutes and exits.

Davenport tells the audience that Peterson was found and arrested a week later in Alabama. Col. Nivens, glad that no white officers were involved, glossed over the whole affair as "the usual, common violence any commander faces in Negro military units," adding extra insult to the injury caused by what Davenport sees as "the madness of race in America," which here caused two deaths and two imprisonments for no other material reason.

The death of Sgt. Waters (Davenport says) was reported to his New Jersey home town as a battle casualty, and he was memorialized as a hero. The whole of Company B, 221st Smoke Generating Company, officers and men, was later wiped out in the Ruhr.

> *Davenport turns toward Taylor, who enters quietly.*

DAVENPORT: Captain?

TAYLOR: Davenport—I see you got your man.

DAVENPORT: I got him—what is it, Captain?

TAYLOR: Will you accept my saying you did a splendid job?

DAVENPORT: I'll take the praise—but how did I manage it?

TAYLOR: Dammit, Davenport, I didn't come here to be made fun of—*(Slight pause.)* The men—the regiment—we all ship out for Europe tomorrow, and . . . *(Hesitates.)* . . . I was wrong, Davenport, about the bars—the uniform—about Negroes being in charge. *(Slight pause.)* I guess I'll *have* to get used to it.

DAVENPORT: Oh, you'll get used to it—you can bet your ass on that. Captain —you will get used to it.

Lights begin to fade slowly as the music of "Don't Sit Under the Apple Tree" begins to rise in the background, and the house goes to black. Curtain.

TORCH SONG TRILOGY

A Program of Three One-Act Plays: The
International Stud, Fugue in a Nursery *and*
Widows and Children First!

BY HARVEY FIERSTEIN

Cast and credits appear on page 385

*HARVEY FIERSTEIN was born June 6, 1954 in the Bensonhurst section of
Brooklyn, where he still resides and where he was educated, receiving a Fine Arts
degree from Pratt Institute. At 15 he was a drag performer (female impersonator)
at Club 82 in the East Village. In 1971 he made his professional stage acting debut
with Andy Warhol at La Mama ETC. Soon after, he took up his writing career,
and his first New York production was* In Search of the Cobra Jewels *at Playwrights' Workshop Club in 1972. Other productions followed:* Freaky Pussy *in
1974 and* Flatbush Tosca *in 1975 at New York Theater Ensemble; the first
one-acter in* Torch Song Trilogy, The International Stud, *at Theater for the New
City in 1976, at La Mama in 1978 and then off Broadway that same season, with
the author in the leading role of Arnold;* Fugue in a Nursery, *the second of the
Torch Song plays, at La Mama and then off Broadway in 1979 with Fierstein again
in the lead;* Widows and Children First!, *the final Torch Song play, at La Mama
in 1979.*

Fierstein's Torch Song Trilogy, *a program of the three plays about the "drag
queen" named Arnold, intensely portrayed onstage in the author's performance,
climbed all the way up the production ladder this season to the Best Plays list,
beginning OOB at the Richard Allen Center, moving to full off-Broadway status
January 15, 1982 for 117 performances and then to Broadway in June. The first
two one-acters technically would be classified as revivals, since they have previously*

Court Miller as Ed and Harvey Fierstein as Arnold in *Torch Song Trilogy*

appeared in full New York productions. The third and strongest has not, however, and certainly all three plays take on added strength in connection with each other. We synopsize all three in the outline which follows, with extra attention to the last.

Fierstein is the recipient of a Rockefeller grant in playwriting, a Ford Foundation grant for new American plays and a Public Broadcasting grant, among other accolades. He is accumulating others in addition to his Best Plays citation for the current work, after which he plans to suspend his acting activities for a time and devote himself to writing.

PART I: THE INTERNATIONAL STUD

Scene 1: January. Arnold backstage at nightclub

SYNOPSIS: Upstage center a singer, Lady Blues, is performing while near her on a raised platform, with chair and vanity table signifying a backstage dressing room, sits Arnold Beckoff, a female impersonater in full drag, applying a false eyelash. On either side of the stage are platforms with a chair on each, signifying apartments, and downstage center is a raised "stud" platform. As the song ends, Arnold talks to himself out loud, explaining himself and his philosophy as a homosexual on the make. He warns against certain specific kinds of affairs—for example, with one who is married, terminally ill or "discusses his wonderful relationship with his mother." He explains, "See, I'm among the last of a dying breed. Once the E.R.A. and gay civil rights bills have been passed, me and mine will find ourselves swept under the carpets like the blacks done to Amos, Andy and Aunt Jemima. But that's all right too."

Arnold has no other choice but to become a "drag queen." What he really would like, though is to meet what he calls an "International Stud," who takes whatever he wants but gives something back too. Arnold confesses that with all his multiple affairs, no one has ever said to him "Arnold, I love you." Does he care? Yes, he says, "a great deal. But not enough," as the lights to go black on Arnold and come up on Lady Blues.

Scene 2: February. Ed in the "International Stud" Bar

As Lady Blues finishes her song, barroom noises are heard and Ed *("He is tall, lean and very handsome. Although he is in his 30s his greatest charm is his boyishness")* is standing on the "stud" platform at center. In the crowded bar, Ed steps on Arnold's foot, and the two exchange names when Ed apologizes. In a monologue addressed to Arnold, Ed explains that he comes in here once in a while for quick trips to the back room—but he dates women too and has a straight roommate here in the city. Ed's real home is a farmhouse he owns about an hour from Montreal, which he and his father are restoring. Ed and Arnold leave the bar together, headed for Arnold's place.

Lady Blues sings another song over which can be heard the conversation of Ed and Arnold as they arrive at Arnold's apartment and make the first tentative, nervous connections with each other.

Scene 3: June. Ed and Arnold in their respective apartments

In his apartment, Arnold is waiting for a phone call from Ed, whom he has been seeing for the last four months. To Arnold, their relationship has become much more meaningful than merely an occasional, casual encounter.

Impatiently, Arnold phones Ed who, in his apartment, is getting ready for a date. Ed seems faintly embarrassed at Arnold's call but assures Arnold he was going to phone him soon. Arnold tries not to be too forward, but he can't resist quizzing Ed about his date and then losing his temper: "Why're you treating me like some trick you picked up last night?"

Ed is annoyed by Arnold's outburst; but Arnold can't help overplaying his hand, telling Ed he wants to be loved, whereas Ed will settle for friendship and is unwilling to make a deeper commitment—though in his way he loves Arnold. Ed lets slip that his date tonight is a woman, which adds to Arnold's distress. Ed confesses that he finds the woman very attractive, that he hasn't told her he's bisexual, and that he's taking her to meet his parents.

"What am I supposed to do?" asks Arnold in despair, and Ed replies, "I really don't want to lose you." To Arnold, their lovemaking was special, but Ed is confused about it: "I'm not like you, Arnold. I can't be happy in a ghetto of gay bars and restaurants and back rooms, scared that someone will find out that I'm gay and maybe get me fired." Arnold feels that they mean more to each other than this, but is finally angry enough to slam down the phone.

Scene 4: September. Arnold in the "International Stud" Bar

Arnold is drinking beer and talking to his friend Murray (whose presence onstage is imagined). Arnold explains to Murray that exhibitionist sex is not for him; to him, sex is a private matter. To prove to Murray he isn't scared, however, Arnold agrees to accompany him into the back room, where there is apparently a sort of sexual free-for-all. In the darkness, invisible, one of the studs has his way with Arnold, who submits without much pleasure but in good humor. Arnold tries to hold some friendly conversation with the stud, without success. Indifferent to this experience, Arnold pulls on his clothes and exits as Lady Blues sings a final song.

Scene 5: November. Ed and Arnold backstage

Ed comes to see Arnold in his dressing room, five months after having phoned Arnold and told him flatly he knew what he wanted and Arnold wasn't it. Ed wants to talk, and tells Arnold that he means a lot to him. But Arnold is wary of resuming any kind of relationship: "I have never done time in the closet and I sure as hell ain't gettin' in one for you."

Ed has no intention of trying to pick up where they left off, though he missed Arnold during a pleasant summer spent in the country with his parents and his woman friend Laurel. Ed loves Laurel, he confesses, "Like I could never love you." Still, he insists he did really love Arnold.

Ed has come to tell Arnold about a troublesome dream of committing suicide —and then waking to find the suicidal implements, a plastic bag and a turpentine-soaked rag, materially present on his pillow.

Ed tells Arnold, "This is what I've always wanted: you and me together talking. I think I love you more now than ever." Arnold reacts in frenzy, trying to punch Ed, then calms down as Ed goes to get his car to drive Arnold home.

> *Arnold watches him leave then suddenly snaps himself to work. He sits at the vanity and quickly brushes out his hair, clears the table top and begins to undress when just as suddenly he stops and stares at the audience, searching each face.*

ARNOLD *(slowly . . . innocently):* So, what now? Huh? If I take him back now, knowing all I do, maybe I could make it work. With a little understanding? Maybe even a shrink? *(Little laugh.)* I *could* just let him drive me home. Then I'd say something like . . . "The next time you feel you have to say 'I love you' to someone, say it to yourself and see if you believe it!" No, that'd go over his head. I think it went over mine. *(Another little laugh.)* Of course I could just leave him waiting out there in the cold. Just slip out the back and really cross him out of my life. That way I'd be over him in a few more months. Give or take a few more friends. I don't know. I don't know. 'Cause if we do start in again, who'd say he won't keep this shit up? Right? I don't know. Maybe that's what I want. Maybe he's treating me just the way I want him to. Maybe I use him to give me that tragic torchsinger status that I admire so in others. If that's true . . . then he's my International Stud. Wouldn't that be a kick in the rubber parts? I love him. That's for sure. *(Fighting back tears.)* But do I love him enough? What's enough? This is enough. *(Standing, chin up, confronting the audience.)* Enough.

Slow fade to black. Curtain.

PART II: FUGUE IN A NURSERY

As the house lights dim, a telephone rings. It is answered by Arnold, and as the phone conversation is heard, slides are seen on a screen showing photos of Arnold and Ed, Ed and Laurel, and Arnold and his new friend Alan. It is a year later, and the phone call is to Arnold in his apartment from Laurel, who is now living with Ed. Laurel has never met Arnold but knows he is a good friend whom Ed misses—can Arnold spent the weekend with them on the farm up north? Arnold's instinct is to refuse, but Alan (whom Ed has never met) would like to go. Laurel invites Alan too, and Arnold accepts.

A slide appears on the screen: "Nursery: a fugue."

The lights come up on the farm interior, represented only by a large raked bed which fills the stage: "*It will serve as all rooms in the house. The couples will be lit as separately as possible, using color to indicate the pairings when the more complicated conversations begin. Special care should be taken that the four characters never appear to be in bed together. The desired effect is of vulnerability, not obscenity.*"

Laurel and Ed are seen in bed, talking; Laurel calls the situation "civilized" and worries whether their guests have enough blankets. She is excited about playing hostess for the weekend, but Ed seems out of sorts, probably because he resents the presence of Alan in what he had expected would be a weekend threesome. Laurel observes, "The two of you were lovers. So little games and jealousies are bound to pop up. But I'm positive it's going to be a great weekend."

Laurel thinks Arnold and Alan make a nice couple, but Alan appears too young for Ed's tastes. The lights black out as Laurel and Ed prepare to make love.

A slide appears on the screen: "Subject."

The lights come up on the other side of the bed, where Arnold is trying to sleep but Alan is restless. They exchange one-liners describing their feelings about each other (generally affectionate), the weekend, Alan's occasional need to be held tight because he is afraid, Alan's wish to acquire a dog, and a comparison of their professions, Alan being a highly paid model. Arnold sums up the difference: "A model IS. A drag queen . . . aspires." They roll into each other's arms as the lights fade.

The lights come up on Ed and Laurel, who comments, "I don't believe I've seen you this turned on in months. If that's Arnold's effect on you then I think I'll ask him to move in." She does not mind that Ed called her "Arnold" while they were making love. Ed denies that he said any such thing and still resents Alan's presence.

The lights cross back to Arnold and Alan, who is evaluating Ed, deciding he is not attractive enough to be the love of Arnold's life and must be boring in bed. Arnold insists that he and Ed loved each other and broke up only because they wanted different things: "I wanted a husband and he wanted a wife." Alan wishes Arnold would say he loves him, but Arnold merely throws him a newspaper.

A slide appears on the screen: "Codetta."

The lights come up on Laurel and Ed, and now both couples are visible, but still separate; and both are reading a story in the newspaper about an 80-year-old woman charged with statutory rape of a 15-year old boy. Their comments on this incident range through "funny," "sexy," "disgusting," and their combined talk continues into a discussion of why, how and how much they love each other.

A slide appears on the screen: "Stretto."

Alan and Laurel are alone in their own spaces, while Ed and Arnold are at center stage together. Ed reminds Arnold that he used to call Arnold's bedroom "the Nursery. . . . . It was always so warm and comfortable and safe." Arnold admits he made something of a fuss when they broke up. Ed says he hasn't been seeing other men since he's been with Laurel: "I really do love her very much." The conversational mix continues.

ED: Are you jealous?
ARNOLD: No. Should I be?
ED: You don't love him.
ARNOLD: What's that got to do with anything?
ED: 'Cause I'm jealous of him anyway.
LAUREL (to Alan): So, tell me about yourself.
ALAN (to Arnold): I had to talk to her all afternoon. Nothing else to do with the two of you running off. Y'know she tried to make me? It's the truth. And not

even me. I mean it wasn't me she was trying to make, particularly. She's just got this thing for faggots. It's true. Ask her. She'll tell you the whole story. I think she likes to tell the story as much as she likes to make the faggots. Anyway, she's proved you wrong. You said people only went after me because of my looks, but she went after me because of my likes.

ED *(with Arnold in his arms)*: This feels wonderful.

ALAN: You know, at first I was insulted; being wanted just because I'm gay. But that's almost like being wanted for myself . . . I think I'm flattered.

ARNOLD *(to Ed)*: Hey, watch your hands. I'm a married man.

LAUREL *(to Alan; they are now lit together)*: So, tell me about yourself.

ALAN: I'm a model. Clothes, toothpaste . . . anything they can sell with an all-American puss. I'd like to be an actor, but I think I'll let that ride until I've made all I can out of being the American Dream.

Alan has a sense of humor about his relationship with Arnold, Laurel has noticed. She's glad Alan and Arnold are a unit from which Ed is now presumably excluded, because she has already lost one bisexual lover. Laurel met Ed in therapy, and she didn't know about Arnold until much later. Ed was free to choose, however, and he chose her.

Arnold instinctively drives lovers away when the affair starts going too well, he tells Ed. Otherwise, he believes he could have kept Ed—but Ed doubts this. Ed believes Arnold must be in love with someone (not Alan, however), and Arnold admits he's been meeting a stud regularly in the back room of the bar. Ed frowns on this practise, but Arnold defends it: "I'd never seen a back room until after you. . . . . That's where you would rather have taken me. If we'd met and stayed in the back room we never would have had the problems we did."

Alan and Arnold need each other, and that's why they're together whether love is present or not. Laurel and Ed haven't decided yet about having children. Arnold remembers a time when he and Ed discussed the possibility of adopting a child as homosexual parents. Just a fantasy, Ed says, but Arnold's interest in this was real, and he supposed Ed's was too.

A slide appears on the screen: "Counter Subject."

On Sunday, Laurel and Ed are off to church, where Ed plays the organ for the services. Arnold and Alan are sleeping in, or rather, speculating about Laurel: having been mixed up with bisexual more than once, perhaps she is really gay.

A slide appears on the screen: "Stretto."

After lunch, Ed and Alan go out to the barn to look at the new canning machine, leaving Laurel and Arnold to do the dishes. Laurel tells Arnold point-blank that she thinks he still loves Ed and wants him back. She knows all about their relationship (she says), Ed tells her about everything, including Arnold's frequent phone calls behind her back. It is Ed who does the phoning, Arnold corrects her, calling to tell Arnold how happy he is with Laurel. "Are you happy with Ed?" Arnold asks. "The happiest I've ever been in my life," Laurel replies.

The lights go out on Arnold and Laurel, as Alan tells Ed something of his past. Alan came to the city a blue-eyed blond of 14 and found it easy to take up hustling. He met Arnold when Arnold—in drag, imperiously—intervened in a barroom brawl and saved Alan from a knife-wielder. Alan wanted to come on this weekend to meet Ed—his competition, his predecessor, whom he has heard Arnold call "a self-centered, insensitive, boring fool who wouldn't know love if it wore wings, a diaper and shot heart-shaped arrows at your butt." Ed puts his arm around Alan, who at first pulls away but finally ceases to resist as the lights go to black on them.

In the light, Arnold is kicking himself for his tactless comments to Laurel. As Alan returns and they are packing, Arnold fears he may have hurt Laurel by quoting Ed as saying that "if all things were equal (she and I being the same sex) he never would have left me." Alan is not very sympathetic; he just wants to get out of here.

A slide appears on the screen: "Coda."

A phone rings, and Arnold answers it (though it is the same bed setting, the weekend is over and Ed is phoning Arnold in the city to make sure they got home all right). Alan is out—he has gone to take the car back to his mother. Ed asks Arnold to get in touch with Laurel, who's spending a few days in the city, and ask her out to lunch or dinner. Ed quickly reassures Arnold that this separation isn't the result of anything Arnold said or did: "We didn't have words or anything. I just felt that it would be better if we both had time to think about our relationship."

During the weekend, Arnold had mentioned a list he keeps of things he wants, with those he has achieved checked off. Ed ends the phone conversation by telling Arnold not to erase the check mark next to his name.

Ed disappears and Laurel appears in the scene.

LAUREL: So what'd you tell him?
ARNOLD: I told him I'd leave the check mark but erase the name.
LAUREL: You didn't?!?
ARNOLD: No, I didn't. But I should've. I don't know, sometimes I get the feeling he's learning, but God, it's a struggle. You going back to him?
LAUREL: I don't think so. I don't know.
ARNOLD: What'd your shrink say?
LAUREL: Not much. Nothing, as a matter of fact, nothing. He just kept asking me what I want. Over and over again, "What do you want?", "What do you want?"
ARNOLD: And what did you tell him?
LAUREL: I told him I wanted him to shut up.
ARNOLD (giggling): You didn't.
LAUREL (laughing too): No, I didn't. But I should've.

Laurel thought that what happened between Alan and Ed in the barn was the reason for Alan and Arnold leaving the weekend early—but the Alan-Ed incident is news to Arnold. It was the reason for Laurel leaving, after Ed told her about it, tearful, repentant. Just once, she says, she wishes an affair would end after the passion has worn off, not before.

LAUREL: . . . . . Just once I'd like to be standing on sure ground when the blow hits instead of crawling around on my hands and knees like a baby.

ARNOLD: You want a hell of a lot out of life. Don't'cha? I'd settle for being able to say to someone, "I love you," and whether I meant it or not, finding them still in bed the next morning.

ALAN: All you had to do was ask me.

ARNOLD: Ask you what?

ALAN: Not to fool around with anyone else, and I wouldn't have.

LAUREL: But you never asked me.

ED: Because I wanted you to feel that you could.

ALAN: You mean you wanted me to feel that *you* could. All those nights you spent out in them back rooms. How do you think I felt?

ARNOLD: That's not the same thing at all. I didn't even know those people's names.

ALAN: That makes a difference?

LAUREL: You mean you want me to see other men?

ARNOLD: No. But I want you to feel free to.

ALAN: I do. And I did. So, what are you so upset about?

ED: It's the kind of relationship you said you wanted.

LAUREL: Just because I said that's what I want doesn't mean that's what I want. I mean, that's what I want but that doesn't mean I'm necessarily ready for it.

ALAN: You're being ridiculous.

ARNOLD: You telling me that you don't see any difference between my innocent jaunts to the back room and your vile debauchery this weekend?

ALAN: Not really.

ARNOLD: Well. There you have it.

ALAN: There I have what?

The conversations continue in this way, with the dialogue interwoven, each expressing his or her emotional position and sense of injury. Arnold sums up the whole situation with the comment that maybe four wrongs make a right. The two couples are still together, still have each other. Arnold is in Alan's arms as the bed disappears offstage.

A slide appears on the screen: "Epilogue."

In a night club set upstage, Arnold rehearses a violent love song with a pianist. As he finishes, Laurel appears and is told that Arnold is buying Alan a dog as a kind of symbol and pledge of their permanent relationship, "as married as two men can legally get."

Laurel has come to tell Arnold that she and Ed, too, have decided on making it permanent and are engaged to be married. Ed is coming by tonight to tell Arnold, but Laurel decided to tell him first, to make sure that Arnold doesn't say anything disparaging when Ed tells him. The wedding is to be in Massachusetts, with only immediate family present—Arnold is obviously excluded.

Laurel departs after Arnold promises to say nothing to Ed about her visit. He then proceeds to do another torchy number, repeating the line "I can't live on love alone," climbing onto the piano as the pianist starts to play. *"The lights fade to black. Curtain."*

PART III: WIDOWS AND CHILDREN FIRST!

Scene 1: Arnold's apartment, 7 A.M. on a Thursday in June

Five years later, Ed is cooking breakfast in the kitchenette section at the right side of the combination dining-living room of Arnold's apartment near Central Park. The entrance door is at left, the door to the bathroom upstage center and the hallway to the bedrooms at right. The room is conventionally furnished, with a convertible sofa.

In the bathroom, David *("15 going on 30, a wonderfully bright and handsome boy")* is applying medicine to a black eye. Arnold enters from the hallway in his bathrobe and turns down Ed's offer of a kippered herring casserole.

DAVID *(through crack in door):* Everybody ready? Stand back from the door and hang onto your apron strings 'cause here I come. *(Enters modeling a three-piece suit.)* Well? What'cha think?

ARNOLD *(as Ed whistles approval):* What's the occasion? Mrs. Schnable isn't due till next week.

DAVID: But your mother is due today. Think she'll like me?

ARNOLD: Who'd dare not like my baby?

DAVID: And look, I put some gook on. You can't even see the black eye.

ARNOLD *(examining):* When I think of that kid hitting you, I wanna tear down to that school and beat the shit outta him.

ED *(serving the food):* Your maternal instincts are incredible.

DAVID: I can take care of myself.

Some youngster in his class called him a "douche bag"—"How Fifties," Arnold comments—so David punched him. Ed serves breakfast; he has been sleeping on the convertible couch for four nights but isn't used to it yet. David tells Ed that his wife Laurel called in the middle of the night about some papers to sign.

While Ed goes to the phone to talk to Laurel, Arnold gives David his morning instructions: he is to take his report card, which Arnold signed, to school with him; he is to stay out of trouble for the next three months of probation, when Mrs. Schnable will come to check on him every third Thursday. David looks forward to the day when the adoption papers come through, and they will have foster-care checks to help out with expenses.

On the phone, Ed promises to visit Laurel that afternoon. After he hangs up he tells the others Laurel was crying—he can't understand why.

ARNOLD: Of course it's just a wild guess, but do you suppose it's because she's confused and alone?

ED: Well, I don't see why. The separation wasn't all my idea.

ARNOLD: Look, Ed, I realize this is a trying time for you and I'll gladly supply a place to sleep, a home-thrown meal and all the amoral support I can muster, but you've got to keep the gory details to yourself.

ED *(grandly):* Ah, what price compassion!?!

ARNOLD: Fifty bucks an hour and I don't take credit cards.

ED: Fifty?

ARNOLD: Hey, talk's cheap, but listenin'll cost ya. Buck up, Bronco, things are bound to get easier.

ED: Oh, I know. I just wish she wouldn't carry on like that. You wouldn't believe the crazy accusations she was making . . .

ARNOLD: Ed, I'm serious. I really don't want to hear about it.

ED *(mock pout):* Some friend you are.

ARNOLD: I'm your ex-lover, Ed, not your friend.

DAVID: Oooooh. The heavy stuff. An it ain't even eight o'clock.

Ed's phone call reminded Arnold too much of their breakup, and Arnold wants to hear no more about it. He also instructs Ed to find some other place to stay on the days that Mrs. Schnable is expected. He doesn't want Ed's bisexuality, or homosexuality, or whatever, to become involved in the present situation.

Under Arnold's motherly but strict orders, David goes reluctantly to brush his teeth. Arnold confesses to Ed, "This parent act's all new to me. I can't quite get the hang of being mother, father, friend and confessor all rolled into one."

They speculate on what might have happened if they'd stayed together: would Arnold have met Alan, would Ed and Arnold have adopted David? Arnold admits, "When Alan died I thought a lot of crazy things. . . . . I forgave you years ago. I don't think I could have been happy with Alan if I hadn't."

Ed suggests maybe he'd better find another place to stay for the time being, to allow Arnold and his mother to spend some time alone during her forthcoming visit. But Arnold wants Ed to be present as a kind of protection. He doubts his mother will approve of his becoming an adoptive parent, and he'd like to have Ed's support. Arnold has always had a healthy relationship with his mother, however: "A delicate blend of love, concern and guilt. We never talked much, but when we did we kept things on an honest level. I mean, I told her I was gay when I was thirteen." They used to communicate freely with each other, until after Arnold's father's death, an event which for some reason she refused to talk about, almost as though she were unwilling to acknowledge it.

After Alan's death, Arnold was expected to keep a similar silence, so that "We've learned to make meaningful conversation from the weather, general health and my brother's marital status." Arnold has never even told his mother how it was that Alan was killed. His mother knows about David, as she knew about Alan, but she thinks David is merely another "friend" or roommate.

Arnold packs David off to school with his report card (which Arnold has signed as "parent") and after requiring a filial goodbye kiss and hug, which David warmly and genuinely supplies. Arnold queries Ed about his own mother and accuses Ed of hiding "in the closet" by not telling his parents about his homosexual attachments.

ARNOLD: . . . . . I figured once you got married you'd feel secure enough to tell them.

ED: Once I got married there was nothing to tell them. *(Defensive.)* And I wasn't in the closet.

ARNOLD: Ed, when the only people who know you're gay are the ones you're gaying with, that's called "in the closet."

ED: Arnold you may enjoy broadcasting your sexual preferences, but I happen to believe that who I sleep with is my business and not the world's.

ARNOLD: We'll discuss the world later, I'm asking about your mother.

ED: Why put them through that?

ARNOLD: Through what?

ED: Making them feel that in some way they failed me or did something wrong. You know the trip.

ARNOLD: But you could explain to them that they had nothing to do with it. Well, not that way, anyway.

ED: They'd still be miserable. Besides, I really don't think it's any of their business.

ARNOLD: You told them about Laurel, didn't you?

ED: We were married.

ARNOLD: You lived together for a year first. You sayin' they didn't know about her 'til after the wedding?

ED: Arnold, you told your parents, they accepted it and I'm very happy for all of you. Alright? Jesus. Your mother flies in for a visit and I get a Gay Consciousness Raising lecture.

Ed assures Arnold that his mother will be pleased with the relationship with David. Arnold has done well with the boy: "You've taken a punk kid who's spent the last three years on the streets and in juvenile court and turned him into a home-loving, fun-loving, school-going teenager in all of six months."

Ed departs but comes back almost immediately with the news that a woman who must be Arnold's mother is on her way up the stairs, arriving much earlier than expected. Before Arnold can make a move to straighten up the apartment, his mother, Mrs. Beckoff, appears in the doorway carrying a suitcase and a shopping bag. Arnold's Ma is *"sixtyish, a real Jewish mother, a fighter."* She nods at Ed, who makes his escape right after Arnold introduces him, and tells Arnold he looks better than the last time she saw him, at his friend's funeral. Ma has already noticed that if there is an Ed as well as a David, there would be three men in this two-bedroom apartment (Arnold points out the convertible sofa and declares Ed "transitory").

Ma asks Arnold whether his brother has serious intentions toward his new girl friend (Arnold doesn't know) and about Ed: "A friend-friend or a euphemism friend?" Ed used to be a euphemism, Arnold explains, but is now just a friend, separated from his wife and in need of temporary shelter.

Ma brings up the sleeping arrangements. Arnold informs her she'll have his room, David the other bedroom, and Arnold and Ed can make do on the couch. Ma wonders about the dog. Arnold had to give him away, to his friend Murray, because after Alan's death the dog would just sit by the door and whine.

Ma is worried that the Beckoff line will die out if neither Arnold nor his brother have children. Arnold refuses to concern himself with this and suggests that his mother go get settled (even though the bed is unmade) while he takes a shower. Both exit, Ma carrying her own suitcase.

> *David enters through the front door, slowly, peeking in first. Seeing a deserted room, he enters fully and looks around. He spots the shopping bag.*

DAVID: She has arrived. But where are she? *(Looks in kitchen, under table, goes to bathroom door and listens.)* We got us a live one.

> *Arnold hums a bit of something.*

Wrong one. *(He is having fun. He tiptoes to the hall and exits.)*

> *A moment of silence, then a shriek. David runs out of the hall pursued by Ma, who is swinging at him with her purse.*

Mrs. Beckoff, please. I'm not a burglar!

MA: Then what are you; some kind of weirdo who gets a kick watching middle-aged women strip beds?

DAVID: I'm not a weirdo. Believe me.

MA: Then you're a rapist. *(She screams again.)*

DAVID: What would a rapist be doing in a three-piece suit?

MA: How should I know? Maybe you got a wedding after.

ARNOLD *(entering dripping, in a robe):* What the . . . David! What are you doing out of school?

MA: This your roommate?

DAVID: Charmed, I'm sure.

MA: You know that "lonnng" talk we're gonna have? It just got lonnnnnnnger.

Arnold wonders what David is doing home from school—he got permission to come home until after lunch, to see Arnold's mother, provided Arnold phones the school to assure them it's all right. Arnold introduces David, suggests that his mother continue unpacking and then make lunch, and exits, hoping for the best. David offers to get Ma a drink, but she declines. Ma offers David a cookie she has made and asks him about college. She finds that he is only 15 years old and a freshman in high school. "That's wonderful," Ma comments, "You have your whole life ahead of you . . . while mine's flashing before my eyes" at the supposition that her son Arnold is establishing his kind of relationship with one so young.

Ma sends David off to change out of his suit and offers to phone the school on his behalf. She finds the number in the phone book, starts to dial, then calls offstage.

MA: David? What name shall I give them?

DAVID: What?

MA: Who shall I say is being excused? *(No response.)* Your last name!

DAVID *(sticking his head in):* Beckoff, of course.

MA: Really? That's quite a coincidence. Have you and Arnold ever compared notes to see if there's any family relation?

DAVID: I'm his son. What more relation could there be?

Arnold steps out of the bathroom.
MA: You're his what?
DAVID: His son.
Arnold goes right back into the bathroom.
Would you like that drink now?
Blackout.

Scene 2: Arnold's apartment, 5 P.M. that day

Ed, carrying a small paper bag and a newspaper, lets himself in with a key, only to be assailed by a flying platter, followed by a furious Arnold. Arnold berates Ed for leaving him alone to cope with his mother, who took him to task on every count from smoking to breaking up Ed's marriage. Arnold hid in the bathroom, emerging only for lunch during which no one spoke, and after which Arnold's mother walked David back to school.

The phone rings—it's Murray asking a favor, and while Arnold is talking his mother and David return home. Ma promises to teach David how to play chess and offers to help Arnold with the dinner—she'll make Latkes for them. She remembers how, during the Depression, they would eat a potato boiled with a little salt and call it soup.

David is reading a book from school, Oscar Wilde's *The Ballad of Reading Gaol.* Arnold explains to him that Wilde was imprisoned for being gay in an era when there was a law against it. When Arnold's mother tries to get them to change the subject, Ed takes David into the kitchen area where he continues explaining the poem to the boy.

ARNOLD: I wish you wouldn't interfere like that; it's very embarrassing.

MA: Excuse me, but listeining to that is very embarrassing.

ARNOLD: I'm sorry you feel that way, but I have a responsibility to his education.

MA: I'm sure the people who put him here did not have that kind of education in mind.

ARNOLD: The people who put him here had exactly that kind of education in mind. And I'll thank you not to interfere.

MA: I am only suggesting that you should consider the huge responsibility you've taken on here.

ARNOLD: You think I'm unaware of it!

MA: Then act like it. You should be setting an example for the boy.

ARNOLD: And I'm not?

MA: Not when you talk like that, you're not. You've got to consider what you say to him for the remaining time. He's at an impressionable age. After all, it's only for a few more months.

ARNOLD *(as Ed and David stop):* What's for a few more months?

MA: He's here on a nine-month program, right? And he's already been here for six months, so . . .

ARNOLD: And what do you think happens then?

MA: He leaves.

DAVID: No, you misunderstoo . . . *(Ed kicks him.)* Ow! This is getting serious.

ARNOLD: There seems to be a misinterpretation afoot. Yes, David is here on a nine-month program, but after that, if we agree and the Bureau of Child Welfare allows, I will legally adopt David. And believe me, Ma, if I have anything to say about it, he's not leaving.

> *Ma tries to say something, she is angry, confused, frustrated. She throws down whatever is in her hands and storms out. We hear the door slam.*

Ed and David (who claims he told Ma nothing of importance during their afternoon together) remain behind while Arnold goes in to his mother. Soon she comes back and sits down, followed by Arnold, as Ed takes David away to play chess.

Ma insists that Arnold didn't tell her about adopting David until now, though he's been here six months, because Arnold knew it was wrong. Arnold denies this, telling her he and Alan put in the application for adoption two years ago. After Alan died, the foster parent program decided to give Arnold a chance to take care of David by himself, on a trial basis. Arnold went through with it because he was tired of "widowing," of feeling sorry for himself after Alan died. Arnold's mother, as always since his father's death, pretends she doesn't know what Arnold means by this. But Arnold insists on coupling their two losses, making his mother indignant that he would compare his attachment to Alan with her 35-year marriage.

MA: . . . . . How could you possibly know what that felt like? It took me two months until I could sleep in our bed alone, a year to learn to say "I" instead of "We." And you're going to tell me you were "widowing." How dare you!

ARNOLD: You're right, Ma. How dare I. I couldn't possibly know how it feels to pack someone's clothes in plastic bags and watch the garbage pickers carry them away. Or what it feels like to forget and set his place at the table. How about the food that rots in the refrigerator because you forgot to shop for one? How dare I? Right, Ma? How dare I?

MA *(starting over his speech and continuing until her exit):* May God strike me dead! Whatever I did to my mother to deserve a child speaking to me this way. The disrespect! I only pray that one day you have a son and that he'll talk to you like this. The way you talk to me.

ARNOLD *(over her speech):* Listen, Ma, you had it easy. You have thirty-five years to remember. I have five. You had your children and friends to comfort you, I had me! My friends didn't want to hear about it. They said, "What're you gripin' about? At least you had a lover." 'Cause everybody knows that queers don't feel nothin'. How dare I say I loved him? You had it easy, Ma. You lost your husband in a nice clean hospital, I lost mine out there. They killed him there on the street. Twenty-three years old laying dead on the street. Killed by a bunch of kids with baseball bats.

> *Ma has fled the room. Arnold continues to rant.*

Children. Children taught by people like you. 'Cause everybody knows that queers don't matter! Queers don't love! And those that do deserve what they get!

Arnold stops, sits down to cool off, as David enters and hugs him reassuringly. Ed comes in, and he and David decide to remove themselves from the situation and go out to eat. After they've gone, Ma comes back in. She and Arnold agree to talk about David, but not about Alan. Arnold explains that David was a battered child, now in his third foster home. Ma doesn't think Arnold is capable of raising a child.

ARNOLD: This isn't Little Lord Fauntleroy we're talking about here. If this kid decided I was coming down too hard on him, he'd pack and take off and I'd never get him back again. That sweet looking little boy knows how to make more money in a night than you and I could make in a week.

MA: So you let him run wild?

ARNOLD: No. But I don't beat him up either. I teach him. I advise him, I try to set an example for him . . .

MA: Some example. Arnold, look, you live the life you want. I put my fist in my mouth, I don't say a word. This is what you want. But think about the boy. He likes you. He told me he loves you. He sees you living like this . . . don't you think it's going to affect him?

ARNOLD: Ma, David is gay.

MA: But he's only been here six months!

ARNOLD: He came that way.

MA: No one comes that way.

ARNOLD: What an opening.

MA: By you everything is a joke.

ARNOLD: Don't you understand: the whole purpose of placing him here was for him to grow up with a positive attitude about his homosexuality.

MA: That's it. I'm finished. The world has gone completely mad. . . . .

Alan was little more than a child (he was 17) when Arnold first met him, his mother points out. Arnold insists he has no intention of ever making advances to David. Ma tries to humiliate Arnold with his homosexuality, claiming it so disappointed his father that it made him sick. She's tired of hearing the word "gay" brought into every sentence, rubbing her nose in it, instead of keeping it in the bedroom: "In private. No, you're not happy unless everyone is talking about it."

Arnold doesn't mean to stress it, but it is what he *is*, he tells his mother, and he can't avoid the subject. He begs her to try to understand: "Try to imagine the world the other way around. Imagine that every movie, book, magazine, TV show, newspaper, commercial, billboard told you that you should be homosexual. But you know you're not. . . . ." It may seem like "a sickness" to his mother, but Arnold has been gay as far back as he can remember, back before it seemed "different or wrong." Unlike most of his friends, he's tried to be honest about it with his mother; and if she wants to be part of his life she'll have to accept him as he is. Arnold has learned to do everything for himself, from crocheting to fixing the plumbing; he is as self-sufficient as a person can be in his own context.

ARNOLD: . . . . . I don't have to ask anyone for anything. There is nothing I need from anyone except love and respect. And anyone who can't give me those two things has no place in my life. *(Breath.)* You are my mother, and I love you. I do. But if you can't respect me . . . then you've got no business being here.

MA: You're throwing me out?

ARNOLD: What I'm trying to . . .

MA: You're throwing me out! Isn't that nice? Listen, Mister, you get one mother in this world. Only one. Wait. Just you wait.

> *Ma exits to bedroom. Arnold is still as the next scene begins. The lights slowly crossfade.*

Scene 3: A bench in the park below, immediately following

The convertible sofa doubles for a park bench in this scene between David and Ed, whose lunch consists of a couple of hot dogs. This is the site (David tells Ed) where Alan was killed, the attacking youths coming out of hiding behind the bushes. Arnold took David out and showed him this place while the bloodstain was still visible. David thought Arnold must be crazy at first, but later he realized why Arnold had done it: to present him with an unforgettable lesson.

Ed confides to David that he saw Laurel this afternoon and hasn't made up his mind whether ever to go back to her. David, worldly-wise ("I picked up plenty of know how on my journey down the 'Leatherette Road' "), guesses Ed never will and warns him against a withdrawal like Arnold's: "Here's Arnold: attractive, sensitive, intelligent, a great conversationalist, pretty good cook, and he's living like an old Italian widow." David hints to Ed very broadly that sex might prove therapeutic for Ed as well as Arnold.

Arnold joins them in the park, bearing more hot dogs and admitting he doesn't know who won the argument between himself and his mother. He wants to talk to David alone, so Ed discreetly makes himself scarce. Arnold assures David that whatever happens between himself and his mother won't affect the Arnold-David relationship. David is not so sure—Arnold is very much like her, and what's more he reminds David of his previous three mothers.

DAVID: . . . . . What would you do if I met a girl, came home and told you I was straight?

ARNOLD: If you were happy, I'd be happy.

DAVID: Bull-China! Here you are, working your butt off showin' me all the joys of gay life, givin' me the line of dignity and self-respect . . . You tellin' me you wouldn't wonder where you went wrong?

ARNOLD: Not if you were sure that that's what you wanted.

DAVID: Yeah, I see the way you treat Ed. The guy keeps tellin' you he's bi and all you keep doin' is callin' him a closet case.

ARNOLD: See, you don't know what you're talking about. I'd be perfectly willing to believe he's bi if just once he thought about the person he was with before he considered what sex that person was.

DAVID: How could anybody do that? You ever meet someone and not know what sex they were?

ARNOLD: That's not what I mean . . .
DAVID: I know what you mean and it's just as dumb.
  Arnold tries to speak.
Shut up and let me finish. I stay with you because I want to. Dig? I really like living with you. I even like the way you try to mother me. But you can really be a shithead about things. But, you make me feel like I got a home. And a bunch of other assorted mushy stuff I don't want to get into here. But, Arnold, I'm tellin' you now: I'll walk if you try to use me as an excuse for sitting home alone, or to pick a fight with your mother or with Ed. Hey, you do what you gotta do. I ain't judgin'. Just don't blame anybody but yourself, if you get my drift.

Arnold gets David's drift and still thinks he's "swell." David heads back for the apartment, but before he goes Arnold wants to make sure David was only joking when he suggested that he might have straight tendencies.

Scene 4: The apartment, 6 A.M. the next morning

Ed is asleep on the couch, while Arnold enters from the bathroom in a robe, holding an empty glass. Ed forces himself awake and tells Arnold—who has been out all night and has just come home—that his mother's bags are packed and she is leaving as soon as she can get a plane out. As for Ed, he has seen Laurel, who pretended she was pregnant (she isn't) just to see if Ed would offer to come back to her (he didn't).

Arnold edges toward the couch-bed, sits on it and then stretches out as he talks to Ed. It seems Arnold is drunk—not insensibly, but thoroughly and deliberately drunk, trying to anesthetize himself to the point at which he'd ask his mother to stay on. It worked until he saw her again, sitting on the bed and obsessed with the mistaken idea that Arnold hates her. The fact is just the opposite: Arnold envies the life his mother has led, an idyllic marriage with two sons they were persuaded were the "smartest, handsomest, most talented, most important two people in the world. Didn't matter what we did, good or bad, it was the best. And she thinks she did something wrong."

Ed admits to Arnold that he'd like to have another chance with him (actually, he says, it was David's idea; David thinks Arnold is "pushing chastity too far"). Ed feels very much at home here with Arnold and David, and he asks Arnold to think about his suggestion. Arnold replies sharply, "Don't you know that I have? How thick can you possibly be? Can't you see that since you called that's all I've thought about? Five days ago you walked through the door and from that moment I've been playing the dutiful wife and mother to your understanding if distant father. And David? He's been having the time of his life playing baby."

This household seems much more real to Ed than the one with Laurel. He wants to take Alan's place here, but Arnold advises him to go home and look for family ties with Laurel. Ed summons up the courage to make the ultimate statement (even though Arnold's mother may overhear him) and gets as far as "Arnold Beckoff . . . I love . . ." when David comes in, interrupting. He lies down on the bed between them like a child between parents, hoping that they have come to terms with each other again, but finding from Ed (after Arnold gets up and exits into the bathroom for his morning ablutions) that they have not.

David is listening to his favorite call-in radio program, on which listeners are able to request numbers and dedicate them to friends (Alan once called in and had them play "My Funny Valentine" for Arnold). Arnold sends him to see if his mother needs anything. David reenters almost immediately with Ma, who has noticed David's black eye for the first time and is concerned about it. Ed invites David out for breakfast. Before they go, Arnold makes a point of taking Ed aside and telling him, "Y'know, six years is a long time . . . I don't know. But we can talk."

After the others have left, Ma brings her bags out and gets set to depart. Soon they are quarreling again.

ARNOLD: Do we have to start this again?

MA: Yes. Because you can't put all the blame on me. It's not fair. Some of it was my fault, but not all. You thing I didn't know about you, Arnold? Believe me, I knew. And not because you told me. I didn't need you to tell me. I knew but I said no. I hoped . . . What's the difference, I knew and I turned my back. But I wasn't the only one. There are other things you should have told me. You opened a mouth to me about your friend Alan . . . How was I supposed to know?

ARNOLD: Why? You would have understood?

MA: Maybe. Maybe not You can't know for sure. But I flew up for the funeral and you never said a word.

ARNOLD: So you could have done what? Tell me he's better off dead?

MA: Or maybe I could've comforted you. Told you what to expect. You and your "widowing."

She turns to leave, stops, takes a breath. One last try.

And about this Ed: You love him?

ARNOLD: I don't know. I think so.

MA: Like you loved Alan?

ARNOLD: No. They're very different. Alan loved all my faults; my temper, my bitchiness, my fat . . . He looked for faults to love. And Ed? Ed loves the rest. And really, who needs to be loved for their virtues? Anyway, it's easier to love someone who's dead; they make so few mistakes.

MA: You've got an unusual way of looking at things, Arnold Beckoff.

ARNOLD: Runs in the family. Ma, I miss him so much.

MA: Give yourself time, Arnold. It gets better. But, Arnold, it won't ever go away. You can work longer hours, adopt a son, fight with me . . . whatever, it'll still be there. But that's all right. It becomes part of you, like wearing a ring or a pair of glasses. You get used to it and it's good . . . because it makes sure you don't forget. You don't want to forget him, do you? *(Arnold shakes his head.)* So, it's good. *(Pause.)* I guess that's what I would have said . . .

The phone rings.

. . . if I'd known. You'd better answer that. It may be something with that . . . son of yours.

Arnold goes to the phone. As soon as he's turned his back, Ma slips out the door with her bags. Arnold doesn't notice.

ARNOLD *(answering):* Hello . . . Hi Murray . . . What? . . . The radio? It's on
. . . all right, hang on.

He puts the phone down and goes to the radio, turning up the volume.
It's Murray, something about the radio.

RADIO *(mid-sentence):* . . . no, I've just checked with my producer who took
the call and he's confirmed it. What a morning. Whatever is this world coming
to? So, here it is, a dedication from David to Arnold with all his love . . .

*Music begins to play. It is Big Maybelle singing "I Will Never Turn My
Back on You".*

ARNOLD: How do you like that? That's some kid I got there, huh? *(Turning.)*
You hear that, Ma? *(Sees she's gone.)* Ma? *(Goes to door.)* Ma?

*Runs to window and looks out as the music plays. He turns toward the
audience and listens to the song calmly. As the music ends, the lights
fade and the curtain falls.*

THE DINING ROOM

A Play in Two Acts

BY A.R. GURNEY Jr.

Cast and credits appear on page 370

A.R. GURNEY Jr. was born Nov. 1, 1930 in Buffalo, N.Y., the son of a realtor.
He was educated at St. Paul's School and Williams College where he received his
B.A. in 1952. After a stint in the Navy, he entered Yale Drama School in 1956 and
emerged with an M.F.A. degree after studying playwriting in seminars conducted
by Lemist Esler, Robert Penn Warren and John Gassner. His first production, the
musical Love in Buffalo, *took place at Yale.*

Gurney's first New York production of record was the short-lived The David
Show *off Broadway in 1968, repeated in an off-Broadway program with his* The
Golden Fleece *the following season. His* Scenes From American Life *premiered*
at Studio Arena Theater in Buffalo in 1970, then was produced by Repertory
Theater of Lincoln Center for 30 performances in 1971, winning its author Drama
Desk and Variety poll citations as a most promising playwright, and achieving
many subsequent productions at home and abroad.

Gurney next made the off-Broadway scene at Circle Repertory with Who Killed
Richard Corey? *in 1976, the same year that his* Children *premiered in Richmond,*
Va. and his The Rape of Bunny Stunte *was done OOB. The next year,* Children
appeared at Manhattan Theater Club, The Love Course *was produced OOB and*
The Middle Ages *had its premiere at the Mark Taper Forum in Los Angeles. His*
The Problem *and* The Wayside Motor Inn *were done OOB in the 1977–78 season.*
This year's The Dining Room, *produced off Broadway by Playwrights Horizons,*
is Gurney's first Best Play. Still another of his scripts, The Golden Age, *has already*
been launched in London.

Gurney is also the author of the novels The Gospel According to Joe *and*

Entertaining Strangers *and the PBS-TV adaptation of John Cheever's* O Youth
and Beauty. *He has been a recipient of Rockefeller and National Endowment
grants. He is married with four children, lives near Boston and teaches American
literature at M.I.T.*

Time: Over the course of many years

Place: A dining room—or rather, many dining rooms

ACT I

SYNOPSIS: The room's furniture consists of *"a lovely, burnished, shining dining
room table; two chairs, with arms, at either end; two more, armless, along each side;
several additional matching chairs,"* plus a sideboard and mirror upstage, where
a swinging door at left leads to the pantry and kitchen and an archway at right
leads to the rest of the house. If it were visible, French doors would line the fourth
wall. *"A sense of void surrounds the room. It might almost seem to be surrounded
by a velvet-covered, low-slung chain, on brass stanchions, as if it were on display
in some museum, many years from now."*

The many sets of characters who will use this room in the course of he ensuing
scenes should be conservatively dressed, and the table furnishings tasteful. *"The
blending and overlapping of scenes have been carefully worked out to give a sense
of both contrast and flow,"* instead of a series of blackouts. The room is empty
at curtain rise.

> *A woman real estate agent and her male client appear in the doorway.
> Both wear raincoats.*

AGENT: . . . and the dining room.

CLIENT: Oh boy.

AGENT: You see how these rooms were designed to catch the early morning
light?

CLIENT: I'll say.

AGENT: French doors, lovely garden, flowering crabs. Do you like gardening?

CLIENT: Used to.

AGENT: Imagine, imagine having a long, leisurely breakfast in here.

CLIENT: As opposed to instant coffee on Eastern Airlines.

AGENT: Exactly. You know, this is a room after my own heart. I grew up in
a dining room like this. Same sort of furniture. Everything.

CLIENT: So did I.

AGENT: Then here we are. Welcome home.

> *Pause.*

CLIENT: What are they asking again?

AGENT: Make an offer. I think they'll come down.

> *Another pause.*

John Shea, Lois de Banzie and Remak Ramsay in *The Dining Room*

CLIENT: Trouble is, we'll never use this room.

AGENT: Oh now.

CLIENT: We won't. The last two houses we lived in, my wife used the dining room table to sort the laundry.

AGENT: Oh, dear.

CLIENT: Maybe you'd better show me something more contemporary.

AGENT: That means something farther out. How long have we got to find you a home?

CLIENT: One day.

AGENT: And how long will the corporation keep you here, after you've found it?

CLIENT: Six months to a year.

AGENT: Oh, then definitely we should look farther out.
      She opens the kitchen door.
You can look at the kitchen as we leave.

CLIENT: You shouldn't have shown me this first.

AGENT: I thought it was something to go by.

ACLIENT: You've spoiled everything else.

AGENT: Oh no. We'll find you something if we've got all day. But wasn't it a lovely room?

CLIENT: Let's go, or I'll buy it!

They exit, as Arthur and Sally, a middle-aged brother and sister, enter and plan to divide the furniture, which their mother in Florida no longer wants. They discuss drawing lots for first choice—both, it seems, want the dining room furniture. (While they are debating the matter, a maid, Annie, sets the table for breakfast and Father comes in, sits and peruses his newspaper.) Arthur and Sally are bickering over who is to get the dining room furniture, as they exit.

Father chides the maid for failing to remove all the seeds from his orange juice. A little girl and little boy obtain permission to sit in the dining room and watch their father eat breakfast. The children are looking forward to the day—which has almost arrived—when they'll be old enough to have dinner in this room with their parents.

The car has come to take the girl to school, and she exits. Father hands the section containing the comics to his son and then continues reading his part of the paper.

> *Both read, the Boy trying to imitate the Father in how he does it.*
> *Finally:*

FATHER: This won't mean much to you, but the government is systematically ruining this country.

BOY: Miss Kelly told us about the government.

FATHER: Oh really. And who is Miss Kelly, pray tell?

BOY: She's my teacher.

FATHER: I don't remember any Miss Kelly.

BOY: She's new, Dad.

FATHER: I see. And what has she been telling you?

BOY: She said there's a depression going on.

FATEHR: I see.

BOY: People all over the country are standing in line for bread.

FATHER: I see.

BOY: So the government has to step in and do something.

> *Long pause. Then:*

FATHER: Annie!

ANNIE *(coming out of the kitchen):* Yes, sir.

FATHER: I'd very much like some more coffee, please.

ANNIE: Yes, sir. *(Goes out.)*

FATHER: You tell Miss Kelly she's wrong.

BOY: Why?

FATHER: I'll tell you exactly why, if the government keeps on handing out money, no one will want to work. And if no one wants to work, there won't be anyone around to support such things as private schools. And if no one is supporting private schools, then Miss Kelly will be standing on the breadlines along with everyone else. You tell Miss Kelly that, if you please.

Annie pours more coffee, then returns to the kitchen as the boy asks his father if they can leave a little early today—he is always embarrassingly late for school, and Miss Kelly has spoken to him about his tardiness. But Father refuses to alter his habits to suit his son (whose name is Charlie) or Miss Kelly.

Charlie's mother enters. Cued by Father, Charlie rises, pushes in her chair and hands her his part of the newspaper. Father comments: "Now Charlie: take a moment, if you would, just to look at your lovely mother, bathed in the morning sunlight, and reflected in the dining room table"—a memory worth a good deal more than any of school or Miss Kelly.

Father and son leave, and Mother instructs Annie to tell Irma she'll have her eggs poached this morning.

As Annie leaves, another couple (of whose presence Mother is unaware and to whom she pays no attention) enters—Ellie carrying typewriter and papers, spreading them over the table, and Howard carrying a briefcase. Ellie is going to work on a term paper here, much to Howard's irritation that she would use his family's heirloom table for such a mundane task.

Annie comes in—there has been a crisis in the kitchen, and Mother goes to see to it. Annie clears the breakfast things from the table and exits. Howard is still hovering disapprovingly while Ellie begins to type.

HOWARD: Couldn't you *please* work somewhere else?

ELLIE: I'd like to know where, please.

HOWARD: What's wrong with the kitchen table?

ELLIE: It doesn't work, Howard. Last time the kids got peanut butter all over my footnotes.

HOWARD: I'll set up the bridge table in the living room.

ELLIE: I'd just have to move whenever you and the boys wanted to watch a football game.

HOWARD: You mean, you're going to leave all that stuff *there?*

ELLIE: I thought I would. Yes.

HOWARD: All that shit? All over the dining room?

ELLIE: It's a term paper, Howard. It's crucial for my degree.

HOWARD: You mean you're going to commandeer the *din*ing room for the rest of the *term?*

ELLIE: It just sits here, Howard. It's never used.

HOWARD: What if we want to give a dinner party?

ELLIE: Since when have we given a dinner party?

HOWARD: What if we want to have a few people *over,* for Chrissake?

ELLIE: We can eat in the kitchen.

HOWARD: Oh Jesus.

ELLIE: Everybody does these days.

HOWARD: That doesn't make it right.

ELLIE: Let me get this done, Howard! Let me get a good grade, and my Master's degree, and a good job, so I can be *out* of here every day!

Howard storms out, as Ellie returns to her typing.

Grace enters the room, soon followed by her 14-year old daughter Carolyn. The daughter has a decision to make: she is to attend her first Junior Assemblies dance that evening, but her aunt has asked her to go to the theater to see *Saint Joan*—which will she choose? Carolyn opts for the theater, though Grace stresses the importance of getting acquainted with all the other young people her age at the first Junior Assemblies (as Ellie exits and as a maid, Aggie, comes in to polish the silver). Carolyn must get started with all the others or face the possibility of being left out in the future.

Grace warns Carolyn about the fate of her aunt after she ran away with her riding master: ". . . . . Your father had to track her down and drag her back. But it was too late, Carolyn! She had been . . . overstimulated. And from then on in, she refused to join the workaday world." But Grace still leaves the decision up to Carolyn, who is even more determined than before to spend the evening with her interesting aunt.

The two women exit as Michael, about 12 years old, joins the maid Aggie in the dining room. Michael has heard that Aggie is going to leave them to take another job. Michael tries to persuade her to stay, telling her in his childish fashion that money isn't everything.

AGGIE: It's not just the money, darlin'.
MICHAEL: Then *what,* Ag?
    No answer.
Don't you like us any more?
AGGIE: Oh, Michael . . .
MICHAEL: Don't you like our family?
AGGIE: Oh, Mikey . . .
MICHAEL: Are you still mad at me for peeking at you in the bathrub?
AGGIE: That's enough, now.
MICHAEL: Then what *is* it, Ag? How come you're just leaving?
    Pause.
AGGIE: Because I don't . . .
    Pause.
I don't want to do domestic service no more.
    Pause.
MICHAEL: Why?
AGGIE: Because I don't like it no more, Mike.

Michael offers to help lighten her work load and protests that his mother can't find anyone to replace Aggie, as an architect and a prospective buyer come in, measure the room and comment on the heat lost through French windows.

Michael begins to realize he may never see Aggie again, but he refuses to give her a hug and runs out of the room.

The architect suggests to the buyer—who is a psychiatrist—that he partition the dining room into an office and waiting room area. The psychiatrist wonders (as Aggie finishes polishing the silver and exits) where they will eat if they eliminate the dining room. The architect shows him the plan and replies, "Here. Right here. Look. I'm putting in an eating area. Here's the fridge, the cooking units, Cuisinart, butcher-block table, chrome chairs. See? Look at the space. The flow. Wife cooks, kids set the table, you stack the dishes. All right here. Democracy at work. In your own home."

The architect reviews the possibility of the psychiatrist's day, using the latest electronic gadgets, convenience foods, etc., but the psychiatrist has his doubts: "This room has such resonance." The architect knows all about rooms like this —he grew up in one, dining with his mother, father and sister, and "It was torture, that's all. Those endless meals, waiting to begin, waiting for the dessert, waiting to be excused so they wouldn't lean on you any more." The psychiatrist listens to the architect's family troubles as though he were a patient—but still, he has his doubts about tampering with this room.

As the men leave, Peggy comes out of the kitchen and proceeds to set the table for a children's birthday party. A mob of children pours into the room but soon is attempting to behave properly under Peggy's orders.

The father of one of the children shows up, having been sent here by his wife in the knowledge that he (Ted) is having an affair with Peggy (whose husband is off playing golf despite his daughter's birthday). Ted's wife means to nip this liaison in the bud, even if it means creating a messy situation in which she could have Ted fired from his job.

Peggy sets the children to bringing in the cake, singing "Happy Birthday," etc., while she and Ted manage segments of conversation in which they are trying to decide what to do—leave town and their spouses, seeing their children only in the summer time, or stay here and "be good little children." They decide to stay, hard as it will probably be. They exit with the children, planning the party games that are about to begin.

An 80-year-old grandfather comes in and sits to read his paper while the maid, Dora, sets a place in front of him. His grandson, Nick, 13 or 14, comes in looking for his grandfather and is invited to stay for lunch. The grandfather knows Nick must want something from him—his grandchildren always do—but Nick is not the one who wants the trip to Europe or the new automobile. What Nick wants is an education.

GRANDFATHER: Education, eh? That's a good thing. Or can be. Doesn't have to be. Can be a bad thing. Where do you want to be educated?

NICK: St. Luke's School in Litchfield, Connecticut.

GRANDFATHER: Never heard of it.

NICK: It's an excellent boarding school for boys.

GRANDFATHER: Is it Catholic?

NICK: I don't think so, Gramp.

GRANDFATHER: Sounds Catholic to me.

NICK: I think it's high Episcopalian, Gramp.

GRANDFATHER: Then it's expensive.

NICK: My parents think it's a first-rate school, Gramp.

GRANDFATHER: Ah. Your parents think . . .

NICK: They've discussed all the boarding schools, and decided that this is the best.

GRANDFATHER: They decided, eh?

NICK: Yes, sir.

GRANDFATHER: And then they decided you should get your grandfather to pay for it.

NICK: Yes, sir.

Dora has returned and set a place mat and a place for Nick.

GRANDFATHER: Another one leaving the nest, Dora.

DORA: Yes, sir. *(She waits by the sideboard.)*

GRANDFATHER: And taking a piece of the nest egg.

Nick explains to his grandfather that he wants to go away to school to broaden his horizons, meet interesting new friends—and this school offers advanced Latin and boasts an indoor hockey rink. Grandfather didn't go away to school—he points out—and wasn't even able to finish public schooling after his father died.

NICK: But you're a self-made man, Gramp.

GRANDFATHER: Oh is that what I am? And what are you? Don't you want to be self-made? Or do you want other people to make you? Hmmm? Hmmm? What've you got to say to that?

NICK (squashed): I don't know . . .

GRANDFATHER: Everyone wants to go away. Me? I went away twice. Took two vacations in my life. First vacation, took a week off from work to marry your grandmother. Went to Hot Springs, Virginia. Bought this table. Second vacation: Europe. 1928. Again with your grandmother. Hated the place. Knew I would. Miserable meals. Took a trunkload of shredded wheat along. Came back when it ran out. Back to this table.

> Pause.

They're all leaving us, Dora. Scattering like birds.

GRANDFATHER: We're small potatoes these days.

DORA: Yes, sir.

GRANDFATHER: This one wants to go to one of those fancy New England boarding schools. He wants to play ice hockey indoors with that crowd from Long Island and Philadelphia. He'll come home talking with marbles in his mouth. We won't understand a word, Dora.

DORA: Yes, sir.

GRANDFATHER: And we won't see much of him, Dora. He'll go visiting in New York and Baltimore. He'll drink liquor in the afternoon and get mixed up with women who wear lipstick and trousers and whose only thought is the next dance. And he wants me to pay for it all. Am I right?

NICK: No, Gramp! No I don't! I don't want to go! Really! I never wanted to go! I want to stay home with all of you!

> Pause.

GRANDFATHER: Finish your greens. They're good for your lower intestine.

> They eat silently. A man named Paul enters. He's in his mid-30s and wears an open shirt. He starts carefully examining the dining room chairs along the left wall, one by one, turning them upside down, testing their strength.

(Finally, with a sigh, to Nick): No. You go. You've got to go. I'll send you to Saint Whoozie's and Betsy to Miss Whatsie's and young Andy to whatever-it's-called. And Mary can go to Europe this summer, and Tony can have a car, and it's all fine and dandy.

> He gets slowly to his feet. Nick gets up too.

Go on. Enjoy yourselves, all of you. Leave town, travel, see the world. It's bound to happen. And you know who's going to be sitting here when you get back? I'll tell you who'll be sitting right in that chair. Some Irish fella, some Jewish gentleman is going to be sitting right at this table. Saying the same thing to *his*

grandson. And your grandson will be back at the *plow! (Starts out the door, stops, turns.)* And come to think of it, that won't be a bad thing, either. Will it Dora?
DORA: No sir.

Paul remains while the others exit, and Margery, a woman of about 40, appears. Paul has come to check the dining room furniture. To Margery's annoyance, he finds it in considerable disrepair, needing a lot of work. The table is beginning to come apart underneath where, as Margery checks it, she finds the name of the Wilkes-Barre maker and the date of manufacture, 1898, causing her to comment, "That's not old. It's not even an antique. It's just . . . American."

This table was well made (Paul, an ex-stockbroker turned cabinet maker, tells Margery), but not exceptionally valuable—they used to "crank them out" in those days. Paul allows as how he might be able to repair it here with glue and some screws. They depart to the kitchen for a beer to seal the bargain.

Nancy, about 30, enters carrying a stack of plates and carving implements and calling instructions to a Mrs. Driscoll who is helping in the kitchen. It is Thanksgiving, and the family is gathering around an old lady who comes in on the arm of her eldest son, Stuart. She is not quite sure where she is or what doing, though this is her own dining room and these are the members of her family.

The others try to arouse the old lady's interest with little reminders of family Thanksgiving traditions (Beth always gets the wishbone, Fred a drumstick and Ben the pope's nose). The old lady has lived here for more than 50 years, but she is troubled by the feeling that it is time for her to go "home." She is only momentarily distracted by a family rendition of "Aura Lee"; she soon heads for the hall, calling for her hat, gloves and carriage.

STUART: Look, Fred, Ben, we'll drive her down and show her everything. The new office complex where her house was. The entrance to the Thruway. The new Howard Johnson's motel. Everything! and she'll see that there's nothing there at all.
FRED: I'll bring the car around.
STUART: I'll get her coat.
BEN: I'm coming, too.
STUART: We'll just have to go through the motions.
          The brothers hurry after their mother. Nancy and Beth are left alone. Pause; then they begin to stack the dishes.
NANCY: That's scary.
BETH: I know it.
NANCY: I suddenly feel so . . . precarious.
BETH: It could happen to us all.
NANCY: No, but it's as if we didn't exist. As if we were all just . . . ghosts, or something. Even her own sons. She walked right by them.
BETH: And guess who walked right by *us.*
NANCY *(glancing off):* Yes . . .
          Pause.
Know what I'd like?
BETH: What?

Pippa Pearthree and Ann McDonough in a scene from *The Dining Room*

NANCY: A good stiff drink.
BETH: I'm with you.
NANCY: I'll bet Mrs. Driscoll could use a drink, too.
BETH: Bet she could.
NANCY *(deciding):* Let's go out and ask her!
BETH: Mrs. Driscoll?
NANCY: Let's!
　　　　Pause.
BETH: All right.
NANCY: Let's go and have a drink with Mrs. Driscoll, and then dig into this
turkey, and help her with the dishes, and then figure out how to get through the
rest of the goddamn day!
　　　　*They go off into the kitchen. The table is clear, the dining room is
　　　　empty. Curtain.*

ACT II

Sarah and her schoolmate Helen ascertain that there is nobody else home
(Sarah's mother is working at a boutique and her father is away on business) and
decide to sneak a drink of gin mixed with vodka. Helen is much impressed with
the dining room. Sarah's father insists that the whole family gather at the table
for dinner each night whenever they are all home: "We have to lug things out,

and lug things back, and nobody can begin till everything's cold, and we're supposed to carry on a decent conversation, and everyone has to finish before anyone can get up, and it sucks, if you want to know. It sucks out loud."

Helen's family eats in the kitchen (Sarah's parents did too while Sarah was away at school, but after she was kicked out they moved back to the dining room to help give Sarah "some sense of stability"). The girls are expecting some boys to join them, and Helen thinks it would be fun to have their drinks and pot in here. But Sarah is adamant: "Having *boys* in the *din*ing room? Jesus, Helen. You really are a wimp sometimes."

As they leave the room they are replaced by Kate, who has decided to make some tea. Her friend Gordon enters *"buttoning his shirt, carrying his jacket and tie slung over his shoulder."* Gordon hears a car stop outside, but Kate reassures him that her husband is in Amsterdam. Kate also becomes alarmed when they hear someone opening the front door with a key—it is Kate's son Chris, who has been let out of school two days early. Gordon makes his polite departure. Kate explains to her son that Gordon is a stockbroker helping her with investments. Chris's reply is, "Oh Mom," as he exits, followed by his protesting mother.

Tony, a young man carrying camera and photo equipment, comes in and tests the light in the room. His Aunt Harriet, 60, enters from the kitchen carrying a tray filled with china and crystal. Tony directs her to where the late afternoon light seems best, and she proceeds to set a place at the table.

HARRIET: Now I thought I'd use this Irish linen place mat with matching napkin, that my husband—who was that? Your great uncle—inherited from his sister. They have to be washed and ironed by hand every time they're used.
She places the place mat; he photographs it.
And then of course the silver, which was given to us as a wedding present by your great grandmother. You see? Three-prong forks. Pistol-handled knives. Spoon with rat-tail back. All Williamsburg pattern. This should be polished at least every two weeks.
She sets a place as he photographs each item. She becomes more and more at home with the camera.
And this is Staffordshire, as is the butter plate. All of this is Bone. The wine glasses are early Steuben, but the goblets and finger bowls are both Waterford. None of this goes in the dishwasher, of course. It's all far too delicate for detergents.
The place is all set. She surveys it proudly.
TONY: Finger bowls.
HARRIET: Oh yes. Our side of the family always used finger bowls between the salad and the dessert.
TONY: Would you show me how they worked?
HARRIET: Certainly, dear.
He continues to snap pictures of her as she talks.
You see, the maid would take away the salad plate—like this—
She puts a plate aside to her right.
And then she'd put down the finger bowls in front of us. Like this.
She does.

They would be filled approximately halfway with cool water. And there might be a little rose floating in it. Or a sliver of lemon . . . Now of course, we'd have our napkins in our laps—like this.
She sits down, shakes out her napkin, puts it discreetly in her lap.
And then we'd dip our fingers into the finger bowl . . . gently, gently . . . and then we'd wiggle them and shake them out . . . and then dab them on our napkins . . . and then dab our lips . . . then, of course, the maids would take them away . . .
She moves the finger bowl aside.
And in would come a nice sherbet or chocolate mousse!

Questioned by his aunt, Tony explains that this photography is a college project in anthropology. They are studying "the eating habits of various vanishing cultures"—two of his colleagues are studying the Kikuyus and the Crees. At his professor's suggestion, Tony is doing the WASPS of the Northeastern United States.

TONY: You can learn a lot about a culture from how it eats.
HARRIET *(with increasing coldness):* Such as what?
TONY: Well. Consider the finger bowls, for example. There you have an almost neurotic obsession with cleanliness, reflecting the guilt which comes with the last stages of capitalism. Or notice the unnecessary accumulation of glass and china, and the compulsion to display it. Or the subtle hint of aggression in those pistol-handled knives.
HARRIET: I think I'll ask you to leave, Tony.
TONY: Aunt Harriet . . .
HARRIET: I was going to invite you to stay for a cocktail, but now I won't.

Angrily, Harriet orders Tony out of the house and carries off her tray of cherished objects as Jim, about 60, enters with his daughter Meg, about 30. Jim has had a long day and would like to relax, but Meg needs to talk. Meg has always loved this room (Jim and Meg's mother still use it once a week when a woman comes in to serve them a sit-down dinner).

Meg wants to tell her father that she is leaving her husband, for good, and hopes she can move in here with her three children until she gets resettled. "Can we stay here, Dad?" she asks her father, and Jim replies, "Make us a drink, Meggie." Instead of answering her question, he tells her of one of her contemporaries, thrice married, who might have stayed with her first husband if she'd made more of an effort.

Meg comes back with the drinks (Jim's is not in the glass he wanted, the one with the pheasant on it, which apparently the children are using). Jim points out that there's not really enough room for them all to fit comfortably here. Meg emphasizes her need: her husband has been living with another woman and she with another man, the children shuttling between them.

JIM: It sounds a little . . . complicated.
MEG: It is, Dad. That's why I needed to come home.

Pause. He drinks.

JIM: Now let's review the bidding, may we? Do you plan to marry this new man?

MEG: No.

JIM: You're not in love with him?

MEG: No. He's already married, anyway.

JIM: And he's decided he loves his wife.

MEG: No.

JIM: But you've decided you don't love him.

MEG: Yes.

JIM: Or your husband.

MEG: Yes.

JIM: And your husband's fallen in love with someone else.

MEG: He lives with someone else.

JIM: And your children . . . my grandchildren . . . come and go among these various households.

MEG: Yes. Sort of. Yes.

JIM: Sounds extremely complicated.

MEG: It is, Dad. It really is.

Pause. He drinks, thinks, gets up, paces.

JIM: Well then it seems to me the first thing you do is simplify things. That's the first thing. You ask the man you're living with to leave, you sue your husband for divorce, you hold onto your house, you keep the children in their present schools, you—

MEG: There's someone else, Dad.

Pause.

JIM: Someone else?

MEG: Someone else entirely.

JIM: A third person.

MEG: Yes.

JIM: What was that movie your mother and I liked so much? *The Third Man? (He sits.)*

MEG: It's not a man, Dad.

Pause.

JIM: Not a man.

MEG: It's a woman.

JIM: A woman.

MEG: I've been involved with a woman, Dad, but it's not working, and I don't know who I am, and I've got to touch *base,* Daddy. I want to be here.

She kneels at his feet. Pause. Jim gets slowly to his feet. He points to his glass.

JIM: I think I'll get a repair. Would you like a repair? I'll take your glass. I'll get us both repairs.

He takes her glass and goes out to the kitchen, leaving the door open.

MEG *(moving around in the dining room)*: I'm all mixed up, Dad. I'm all over the ball park. I've been seeing a Crisis Counselor, and I've taken a part-time job, and I've been jogging two miles a day, and none of it's working, Dad. I want to come home. I want to take my children to the Zoo and the Park lake, and the art gallery, and do all those things you and mother used to do with all of us. I want to start again, Dad. I want to start all over again.

Jim comes out of the kitchen, now carrying three glasses.

JIM: I made one for your mother. And I found the glass with the pheasant on it. In the trash. Somebody broke it. *(He crosses for the doorway.)* So let's have a nice cocktail with your mother, and see if we can get the children to sit quietly while we do.

MEG: You don't want us here, do you, Dad?

JIM *(stopping):* Of course we do, darling. A week, ten days. You're most welcome.

MEG *(desperately):* I can't go back, Dad!

JIM *(quietly):* Neither can I, sweetheart. Neither can I. *(He shuffles on out.)*

After a moment, Meg follows her father off, as Emily, about 35, comes in with her son David, 14. Her daughter Claire, 16, joins them, and Bertha the maid appears at the kitchen door. They are all in the same quandary: the father, Standish, has been called to the phone, and they don't know whether to start the meal without him.

Standish soon appears to tell them he'll have to leave at once to go down to the club, where, it seems, one Binky Byers has insulted their Uncle Henry with a remark in the steam bath, so upsetting that Henry promptly got dressed and left the club. The whole family is curious about what actually was said. Standish tries to keep it from them but finally admits cryptically that Byers "alluded in very specific terms to his personal relationships." Emily elaborates further that Byers "must have made some unnecessary remarks about your Uncle Henry's bachelor attachments."

David infuriates his father by commenting, "You mean Uncle Henry is a fruit?" Standish exclaims, "I won't have that word in this house!", and anyway, it's beside the point. Standish's brother was insulted in his own club. An apology must be demanded—fought for, if necessary. Byers is half Standish's age, twice his size and may have been on his college boxing team—no matter, the entire family has been insulted and honor demands a reprisal. Standish bids everyone goodbye and departs, after which Emily takes over in businesslike fashion. She cancels the dinner, sends David down to the club to wait for his father and sends Claire to phone the doctor to get over to the club right away. It may be true about Uncle Henry but, as Emily tells Claire, "You don't say it to *him.* And you don't say it at the *club.* And you don't say it within a ten-mile radius of your *father.*"

The dining room empties, then the members of Standish's family are replaced by an old man, Harvey, and his middle-aged son, Dick. Upstage, the light is dim, and three women begin setting the table in elegant style. Downstage in the light, Harvey gives his son instructions for his funeral. Harvey has written out every detail including an obituary giving his lowest golf score and the weight of a sailfish caught off the Keys: "The papers will want to cut both items, but don't you let them."

Harvey wants the service to take place in the church, not squeezed into the chapel, and he has listed the music program. He hopes Dick will say a few words, neither too sentimental nor too flippant.

DICK: I won't make any cracks, Pop. I promise.
HARVEY: Thank you. *(Looks at documents, looks up again.)* Because you love us, don't you?
DICK: Yes, Pop.
HARVEY: You love us. You may live a thousand miles away, you may have run off every summer, you may be a terrible letter-writer, but you love us all, just the same. Don't you? You love me.
DICK *(touching him):* Oh yes, Pop! Oh yes! Really!
    Pause.
HARVEY: Fine.
    Puts his glasses on again; shuffles through documents.
Now at the graveside, just the family. I want to be buried beside my brothers and below my mother and father. Leave room for your mother to lie beside me. If she marries again, still leave room. She'll come back at the end.
DICK: All right, Pop.

As for the reception following the funeral, it is to take place here at the house, and the good Beefeater gin is not to be served to anyone who will mix it with tonic. Dick is to stay close to his mother and see that she is all right. And Dick is to inherit the dining room furniture.

They both have noticed a purple finch feeding its young outside the window. Harvey is glad that Dick saw it, too (he says) as he departs to put the papers in the safe.

Annie, the maid from the first scene, now grown old, enters to put the finishing touches on the table—candlesticks and a floral centerpiece. She is joined by Ruth, the hostess come to give final instructions. Ruth also gives Annie her envelope for the evening (with a little extra in it because Annie is always so helpful) and one for Velma in the kitchen. Ruth has heard that Annie isn't going to be available any more—Annie is retiring and moving to her sister's in Milwaukee. Ruth knows life will never be the same again without Annie.

The doorbell is heard, and Annie moves to answer it.

RUTH: Women's coats upstairs, men's in the hall closet.
ANNIE: Yes, Mrs. *(Starts out.)*
RUTH *(suddenly):* Annie!
    Annie stops. Ruth goes to her and hugs her. Annie responds stiffly.
Thank you, Annie. For everything.
ANNIE: You're welcome, Mrs.
    Annie goes off right to answer the door. Ruth goes to the sideboard, gets
    a book of matches. She lights the two candles on the table as she speaks
    to the audience.
RUTH: Lately I've been having this recurrent dream. We're giving this perfect party. We have our dining room back, and Grandmother's silver, before it was stolen, and Charley's mother's royal blue dinner plates, before the movers

dropped them, and even the finger bowls, if I knew where they were. And I've invited all our favorite people. Oh, I don't mean just our old friends. I mean everyone we've ever known and liked. We'd have the man who fixes our Toyota, and that intelligent young couple who bought the Payton house, and the receptionist at the doctor's office, and the new teller at the bank. And our children would be invited, too, and they'd all come back from wherever they are. And we'd have two cocktails, and hot hors d'oeuvres, and a first-rate cook in the kitchen, and two maids to serve, and everyone would get along famously!

The candles are lit by now.

My husband laughs when I tell him this dream. "Do you realize," he says, "what a party like that would cost? Do you realize what we'd have to *pay* these days for a party like that?" Well, I know. I know all that. But sometimes I think it might be worth it.

The rest of the cast now spills into the dining room, talking animatedly, having a wonderful time. There is the usual gallantry and jockeying around as people read the place cards and find their seats. The men pull out the women's chairs, and people sit down. The host goes to the sideboard, where Annie has left a bottle of wine in a silver bucket. He wraps a linen napkin around it and begins to pour people's wine. The conversation flows as well. The lights begin to dim. The host reaches his own seat at the head of the table and pours his own wine. Then he raises his glass.

HOST: To all of us.

Everyone raises his or her glass. As their glasses go down, the lights fade to black. The table is bathed in its own candlelight. Then the two downstage actors unobtrusively snuff the candles, and the play is over. Curtain.

AGNES OF GOD

A Play in Two Acts

BY JOHN PIELMEIER

Cast and credits appear on page 335

JOHN PIELMEIER was born in 1949 in Altoona, Pa. where his father ran a grocery and meat market. He was educated in Pennsylvania schools and received his B.A. summa cum laude and Phi Beta Kappa from Catholic University of America (where he started writing plays) in 1970 and his M.F.A. in playwriting from Penn State in 1978. He acted in plays at the O'Neill Conference and New York Shakespeare Festival lunchtime theater in 1977 and at the Actors' Theater of Louisville in 1979. His first major playwriting credit was Agnes of God, *produced first in a staged reading at the 1979 O'Neill Conference and in 1980 at Louisville and cited by the American Theater Critics Association as one of the year's outstanding cross-country plays in* The Best Plays of 1979–80. *It was then produced at Center Stage, Baltimore, at GeVa Theater, Rochester, N.Y., at Old Globe Theater, San Diego (staged reading), at Players State Theater, Coconut Grove, Fla. and at StageWest in West Springfield, Mass. before being mounted for its Broadway premiere March 31, 1982 and a Best Play citation.*

Other Pielmeier scripts of record include Jass *done in workshop at the Actors Studio in 1980 and* Chapter Twelve—The Frog *done at Louisville in 1981. He has received Shubert and National Endowment Fellowships and is a member of New Dramatists. Pielmeier is single (but is soon to be married) and lives in New York City.*

The following synopsis of Agnes of God *was prepared by Sally Dixon Wiener.*

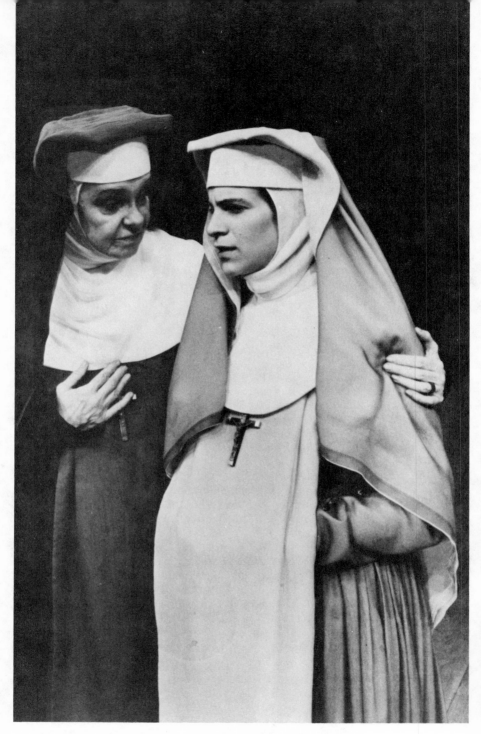

Geraldine Page as Mother Miriam Ruth and Amanda
Plummer as Agnes in a scene from *Agnes of God*

ACT I

SYNOPSIS: The raked stage that is the single playing area serves alternately as psychiatrist Dr. Martha Livingstone's office and the convent that is in Mother Miriam Ruth's charge. It is free of props, save for two ordinary but not matching wood chairs and a free-standing ash receiver. *"The scenes flow one into another, without pause."* Many lines are *"cut off or overlapped . . . Characters appear and disappear, and may even be present onstage when not in a particular scene. Because it is a play of the mind, and miracles, it is a play of light and shadows."*

The play begins in darkness. *"A beautiful soprano voice is heard, singing,"* in Latin, as *"the lights softly rise on Doctor Livingstone,"* in her 40s, professional, handsome in a beautifully-tailored suit, *"never without a cigarette, except in her monologues and one or two other moments. . . . . until a moment during the first hypnosis, after which she never smokes again."*

DOCTOR: I remember when I was a child I went to see Garbo's *Camille,* oh, at least five or six times. And each time I sincerely believed she would *not* die of consumption. . . . . . Because I believed in the existence of an alternate last reel . . . . . . I still want to believe that somewhere, somehow, there is a happy ending for *every* story. It all depends on how thoroughly you look for it. And how deeply you need it.

>   *Silence.*

The baby was discovered in a waste paper basket with the umbilical cord knotted around its neck. The mother was found unconscious by the door to her room, suffering from excessive loss of blood. She was indicted for manslaughter and brought to trial. Her case was assigned to me. . . . . as court psychiatrist, to determine whether she was legally sane. I want to help . . . this young woman, believe me.

She is interrupted by Mother Miriam Ruth, bluff, in her 50s, in the habit of the order, who tells the doctor she may call her "Sister" if she prefers. Mother Miriam Ruth has brought Agnes from the convent, where she's being allowed to stay until the trial, for her appointment with the doctor. She wants to be of help: "You must have tons of questions." The doctor wants to ask them of Agnes, but Mother Miriam Ruth says Agnes has "blocked it out, forgotten it," but that she, as the mother superior of the small contemplative order to which Agnes came four years ago, can answer the doctor's questions.

The doctor's smoking bothers Mother Miriam Ruth, once a two-pack-a-day smoker herself. The questioning reveals that no one knew of Agnes's pregnancy —the nuns dress and bathe alone, they are examined once a year, and her pregnancy fell between the doctor's visits. As to how she hid it during the day, Mother Miriam Ruth shakes her habit. "She could have hidden a machine gun in here if she wanted."

Agnes had felt unwell and retired to her room early on that night. Mother Miriam Ruth found her unconscious, sent another sister to call for an ambulance and then found the baby when she was cleaning. "There was a lot of blood." Another sister, Sister Margaret, was with her, and "it was she who called the police". There was not a clue as to the identity of the father; no men had "access to her" as far as Mother Miriam Ruth knows. She never saw the doctor; the priest, Father Marshall . . . "very shy." The doctor asks the mother superior why she didn't ask Agnes who it was, and she says that "If she doesn't even remember the birth, do you think she'd admit to the conception?" She doesn't believe the identity of the father has any importance, but the doctor says she is the one to decide what's not important and accuses the mother superior of avoiding the question. Mother Miriam Ruth says she doesn't know who the father was.

The doctor wants to see Agnes now, and Mother Miriam Ruth confesses that she disapproves of psychiatry. She warns the doctor that Agnes is a very fragile person.

DOCTOR: Sister, I'm not with the Inquisition.

MOTHER: And I'm not from the Middle Ages. I know what you are. You're a surgeon. I don't want that mind cut open.

DOCTOR: Is there something in there you don't . . . want me to see?

MOTHER: I want you to be careful, that's all.

DOCTOR: And quick?

MOTHER: Yes.

DOCTOR: Why?

MOTHER: Because Agnes is different.

DOCTOR: From other nuns? Yes, I can see that.

MOTHER: From other people. She's special.

DOCTOR: In what way?

MOTHER: She's gifted. She's blessed.

DOCTOR: What do you mean?

Agnes is heard singing.

AGNES *(off)*: *Gloria in excelsis Deo.*

MOTHER: There.

AGNES *(off)*: *Et in terra pax hominibus bonae voluntatis.*

MOTHER: She has the voice of an angel.

The doctor asks if Agnes sings when she's alone. Mother Miriam Ruth tells her that Agnes is embarrassed to sing in front of others. The doctor wonders who taught Agnes to sing. Mother Miriam Ruth doesn't know. When she first heard her singing, she "couldn't connect that voice with the simple, happy child I knew".

Mother Miriam Ruth asks if she may stay when Agnes comes in, but the doctor says no. The doctor, in another monologue, says that she wanted to maintain her objectivity, that Mother Miriam Ruth had no way of knowing that Marie, the doctor's younger sister, entered a convent at 15, where she died of "acute, and unattended appendicitis." Waiting to view the body, the doctor thought of the spotless convent room as "a metaphor for their minds" and realized that her religion, her Christ is the mind. The mother superior wouldn't understand. She reminds the doctor of her own mother.

Agnes enters, in her habit, waif-like, young, smiling, otherworldly—well, yes

—the look of an angel. The doctor tells her she has a lovely voice, but Agnes says that that wasn't her. She tells Agnes that she's pretty. Agnes denies it and suggests talking about something else. "First thing that comes to your mind," the doctor says. "God," Agnes answers.

The doctor asks Agnes if she has ever loved someone besides God. Agnes loves everyone. The doctor asks her about Father Marshall. They've been alone together, yes. "In the confessional." Agnes knows the doctor wants to talk about the baby but claims she never saw it, the police "made it up," she doesn't remember that night, she was sick—"something she ate," and it hurt "down there," and she went to sleep. The doctor asks her where the baby came from, "the baby they made up." "From their heads," Agnes tells her, but "they say it came from the waste paper basket." And before that, "from God."

The doctor wants Agnes to tell her how babies are born, but Agnes grows very impatient. The doctor suggests Agnes ask questions. Agnes asks her her name (Martha Louise Livingstone), if she's married (no), would she like to be ("Not at the moment"), does she have children (no), would she like some (she's stopped menstruating) and why does she smoke? The doctor says her smoking is an obsession, that she started when her mother died, and that her mother "was an obsession, too" and that she supposes she'll stop when she "becomes obsessed with something else." Agnes has one more question.

AGNES: Where do *you* think babies come from?
DOCTOR: From their mothers and fathers, of course. Before that, I don't know.
AGNES: Well, I think they come from when an angel lights on their mother's chest and whispers into her ear. That makes good babies start to grow. Bad babies come from when a fallen angel squeezes in down there, and they grow and grow until they come out down there. I don't know where good babies come out.
    Silence.
And you can't tell the difference except that babies cry a lot and make their fathers go away and their mothers get very ill and die sometimes. Mummy wasn't very happy when *she* died, and I think she went to hell because everytime I see her she looks like she just stepped out of a hot shower. And I'm never sure if it's her or the Lady who tells me things. They fight over me all the time. The Lady I saw when I was ten. I was lying on the grass looking at the sun and the sun became a cloud and the cloud became the Lady, and she told me she would talk to me and then her feet began to bleed and I saw there were holes in her hands and in her side and I tried to catch the blood as it fell from the sky but I couldn't see any more because my eyes hurt because there were big black spots in front of them. And she tells me things like . . . right now she's crying "Marie! Marie!" but I don't know what that means. And she uses me to sing. It's as if she's throwing a big hook through the air and it catches me under my ribs and tries to pull me up but I can't move because Mummy is holding my feet and all I can do is sing in her voice, it's the Lady's voice, God loves you!
    Silence.
God loves you.
    Silence.

DOCTOR: Do you know a Marie?
AGNES: No. Do you?
  Silence.
DOCTOR: Why should I?
AGNES: I don't know.
  Silence.
DOCTOR: Do you hear them often . . . these voices?
AGNES: I don't want to talk any more, all right? I just want to go home.

After the session, Mother Miriam Ruth is anxious to know what the doctor has decided: "Is she totally bananas or merely slightly off center? Or maybe she's perfectly sane and just a very good liar." The doctor hasn't decided. Mother Miriam Ruth believes Agnes is not crazy and not lying. The doctor wonders how she could know nothing about sex and birth under the circumstances. Mother Miriam Ruth explains that she's "an innocent", that her mother, somehow avoiding the authorities, kept her at home, that she's had very little schooling. "When her mother died, Agnes came to us. She's never been 'out there,' Doctor." Never seen television, a movie, or read a book.

The doctor wonders how anyone so innocent could murder a child, and Mother Miriam Ruth says it's manslaughter, not murder: "She did not consciously kill that baby." Because she was unconscious. The doctor asks if she's expected to believe "that she killed that baby, hid the waste paper basket, and crawled to the door, all in some sort of mystical trance?" Mother Miriam Ruth points out that the doctor is Agnes's psychiatrist, not the jury. The doctor wonders if someone else could have murdered the baby, isn't it possible? Perhaps another nun—to avoid a scandal. But Mother Miriam Ruth insists that no one, not even Agnes, knew of the pregnancy.

The doctor asks her when she first became aware of Agnes's innocence, and Mother Miriam Ruth tells her of an incident that occurred almost two years before the pregnancy. Agnes had stopped eating. Agnes did not want to explain, but finally confessed: "She said she'd been commanded by God."

"*Agnes appears. Throughout the scene*" (a memory scene) "*one of Agnes's hands is inconspicuously hidden in the folds of her habit.*" God did not speak to her directly, it was through someone else, but she won't say who it was because "she'd punish me". It was not one of the sisters, she says. Why was she told to do this? Agnes thinks it's because she's getting fat: "There's too much flesh on me . . . . . I'm a blimp." She has to be attractive to God, He hates fat people. It's a sin to be fat, she believes. The statues are all thin.

Agnes cannot be persuaded by Mother Miriam Ruth that God loves her as she is, nor will she tell who it is that tells her these things. Agnes says that "suffering is beautiful" and that she wants to be beautiful. "Christ said it in the Bible. He said, Suffer the little children, for of such is the Kingdom of Heaven.' " Mother Miriam Ruth tries to explain, but Agnes insists she *is* a little child and wants to suffer like a little child. But her body is getting bigger, and she is worried because she won't be able to "squeeze into Heaven." She won't listen when Mother Miriam Ruth tells her that Heaven is not "a place with bars or windows," and points out her own bulk. Agnes repeats that she is a blimp and is convinced that

God blew up the Hindenburg and he'll blow her up: "That's what she said."
Mother Miriam Ruth again asks "Who?", and Agnes tells her, "Mummy!" If she
stays little, then it will not happen.

MOTHER: Agnes, dear, your mother is dead.
AGNES: But she watches. She listens.
MOTHER: Nonsense. I'm your mother now, and I want you to eat.
AGNES: I'm not hungry.
MOTHER: You have to eat *something*, Agnes.
AGNES: No I don't. The host is enough.
MOTHER: My dear, I don't think a communion wafer has the Recommended
Daily Allowance of *anything*.
AGNES: Of God.
MOTHER: Oh yes, of God.
AGNES: What does that word mean? Begod?
MOTHER: Begot. You don't know?
AGNES: That God's my father?
MOTHER: Only spiritually. You don't know what that means? Begot?
AGNES: Begod. That's what *she* calls it. But I don't understand it. She says it
means when God presents us to our mothers, in bundles of eight pounds six
ounces.
MOTHER: Oh my dear.
AGNES: I have to be eight pounds again, Mother.
MOTHER: You'd even drop the six ounces. Come here.
    *Mother reaches out for an embrace. Agnes avoids the embrace, keeping
    the one hand concealed in her habit. Mother stares at the hidden hand.*
Now what's wrong?
AGNES: I'm being punished.
MOTHER: For what?
AGNES: I don't know.
MOTHER: How?
    Agnes presents a hand wrapped in a bloody handkerchief.
What happened?
    Agnes removes the handkerchief.
Oh dear Jesus. Oh dear Jesus.
AGNES: It started this morning, and I can't get it to stop. Why me, Mother?
Why me?

The doctor asks, as the memory scene ends, how long it lasted, and Mother
Miriam Ruth says that it was gone by the next morning and had not re-occurred
as far as she knew. She saw no need to take Agnes to a doctor. Agnes began eating
again.
   "I know what you're thinking," Mother Miriam Ruth tells the doctor, "She's an
hysteric, pure and simple." Not simple, the doctor opines. Mother Miriam Ruth
saw it, clean through the palm of her hand. Could hysteria do that? The doctor says
it's not unique, "She's just another victim." But God's victim, Mother Miriam
Ruth believes, and she's afraid the doctor intends to take Agnes away from God.

The doctor sees it as "opening her mind. . . . . So she can begin to heal". Mother Miriam Ruth says the doctor is to diagnose, not to heal, that's the judge's opinion. But the doctor says her duty is "to help her in whatever way I see fit." The argument continues with Mother Miriam Ruth pressing for a quick decision on Agnes's sanity. "If I say she's crazy, she goes to an institution. If If I say she's sane, she goes to prison," the doctor observes. Mother Miriam Ruth suggests temporary insanity. "A child who sees bleeding women at the age of ten, and eleven years later strangles a baby is *temporarily* insane," the doctor comments.

Does Mother Miriam Ruth think that the sooner Agnes is in prison the better off she'll be? Mother Miriam Ruth replies that she's hoping the judge will let Agnes serve her time in the convent. But the doctor wouldn't let Agnes be sent back to "the source of her problem." Mother Miriam Ruth believes that prison or an asylum would kill Agnes (the doctor doubts that), and she's fighting for her life, not her "temporal innocence." Was Mother Miriam Ruth fighting for Agnes's life when she didn't send her to a doctor when she had a hole in the palm of her hand? "That child could have died, all because of some stupid . . ." Mother Miriam Ruth defends herself. Agnes would have been public property—newspapers, psychiatrists, ridicule.

Again Agnes is singing as the doctor begins to speak (another monologue). When the doctor was 12 or 13, she told her mother that God was a moronic fairy tale. She and her mother had "terrible arguments." She hasn't thought of him in years, but she recalls the Frenchman to whom she became engaged for a brief time after her sister's death—a man whom her mother despised and whom the doctor consequently adored. "What finally happened was that I . . . well, . . . I was pregnant and I didn't exactly see myself as a . . . well, as my mother. Maurice *did*, so . . . (Silence.)"

DOCTOR: . . . . . Oh, I was never a devout Catholic—my doubts about the faith began when I was six—but when Marie died I walked away from religion as fast as my mind would take me. Mama never forgave me. And I never forgave the church. But I learned to live with my anger, forget it even . . . until *she* walked into my office, and every time I saw her after that first lovely moment, I became more and more . . . entranced.
        Silence.
Marie. Marie.

The doctor wants Agnes to tell her how she feels about babies. Agnes doesn't like them. They frighten her, and she's afraid she'll drop them. "They have a soft spot on their heads, and if you drop them so they land on their heads they become stupid. That's where I was dropped." That's why she doesn't understand things, like numbers. She wakes up and can't get hold of the world, so she talks to God. Is that's why she's a nun? Agnes supposes so—she couldn't live without Him. Couldn't the doctor talk to Him? Agnes doesn't know if He'd listen to her, because the doctor doesn't listen to Him. Has Agnes ever thought of leaving the convent? "No, just being here helps me sleep at night." She gets headaches. Her mother did, too. Her mother was very smart; she even knew things nobody else knew—the future. She knew Agnes would enter the convent. "She even knew about this. Somebody told her. . . . . An angel. When she was having one of her headaches. Before I was born."

The doctor asks Agnes if she sees angels. Agnes says no. Then the doctor asks Agnes if she believes that her mother saw them. Agnes says she doesn't, but she could never tell her because "She'd punish me," Agnes won't say how. The doctor then asks if she ever wanted to become a mother herself. Agnes could never be a mother, she doesn't think she's old enough, and besides, she doesn't want a baby. If you did, the doctor probes, how would you go about it? Agnes would adopt one from an agency. And before that, the doctor asks? From someone who didn't want one, Agnes tells her. "Like you?" Not like me, Agnes says.

The doctor keeps at her: how would the person get the baby if they didn't want it? "A mistake." How did her mother get her? Agnes repeats: "A mistake! It was a mistake!" She says the doctor is trying to make her say her mother was bad and that she hated Agnes, but That isn't so: "She did love me, and she was a good woman, a saint, and she *did* want me."

The doctor cannot imagine that Agnes knows nothing about sex, that she has no idea who the father of her child was, that she has no remembrance of her impregnation, that she doesn't believed that she carried a child. Agnes defends herself. She can't help it if she's stupid. "They made it up!" It's not her fault, it was a mistake! "What, the child?" the doctor asks. "Everything! Nuns don't have children!" Agnes knows what the doctor wants from her. "You want to take God away." She runs off.

MOTHER: You hate us, don't you?
DOCTOR: What?
MOTHER: Nuns. You hate nuns.
DOCTOR: I don't . . . understand what you're talking about.
MOTHER: Catholicism, then.
DOCTOR: I hate ignorance and stupidity.
MOTHER: And the Catholic Church.
DOCTOR: I haven't said . . . anything about the Catholic Church.
MOTHER: This is a human being you're dealing with, not an institution.
DOCTOR: I don't . . . understand.
MOTHER: Catholicism is not on trial here. I want you to treat Agnes *without* any religious prejudices or turn this case over . . . to another psychiatrist.
DOCTOR *(exploding):* How dare you march into my office and tell me how to run my affairs . . .
MOTHER: It's my affair too.
DOCTOR *(overlapping):* . . . how dare you think that I'm in a position to be badgered . . .
MOTHER: I'm only requesting that . . . you be fair.
DOCTOR *(overlapping):* . . . or bullied or whatever you're trying to do. Who the hell do you think you are? You walk in here expecting applause for the way you've treated this child.
MOTHER: She's not a child.
DOCTOR: And she has a right to *know!* That there is a world out there filled with people who don't believe in God and who are not any worse off than you!

People who go through their entire lives without bending their knees once—to *anybody!* And people who still fall in love, and make babies, and occasionally are very happy. She has a right to know that. But you, and your order, and your Church, have kept her ignorant . . .

MOTHER: We could hardly do that . . . even if we wanted to.

DOCTOR: . . . because ignorance is next to virginity, right? Poverty, chastity, and ignorance, that's what you live by.

MOTHER: I am not a virgin, Doctor. I was married for twenty-three years. Two daughters. I even have grandchildren. Surprised?

    Silence.

It might please you to know that I was a failure as a wife and mother. Possibly because I protected my children from *nothing*. Out of the womb and into the "big bad world." They won't see me any more. That's their revenge. They're both devout atheists. I think they tell their friends I've passed on. Oh, don't tell me, Doctor Freud, I'm making up for past mistakes.

DOCTOR: You can help her.

MOTHER: I am.

DOCTOR: No, you're shielding her. *Let* her face the big bad world.

MOTHER: Meaning you.

DOCTOR: Yes, if that's what you think.

MOTHER: What good would it do? No matter what you decide, it's either the prison or the nuthouse, and the differences between them are pretty thin.

DOCTOR: There's another choice.

MOTHER: What's that?

DOCTOR: Acquittal.

MOTHER: How?

DOCTOR: Innocence. Legal innocence. I'm sure the judge would be happy for *any* reason to throw this case out of court.

    Silence.

MOTHER: What do you want?

DOCTOR: Answers.

MOTHER: Ask.

The doctor wants to know if, at the time when Agnes would have conceived the child, Mother Miriam Ruth remembers anything unusual happening. Something triggers her memory. "Oh, dear God. . . . . the sheets. . . . . I should have suspected something." It was reported to her that Agnes's sheets had disappeared, and she called her in.

Agnes comes on for a memory scene, is questioned and eventually admits to burning the sheets. "They were stained." Mother Miriam Ruth is impatient at what she regards as Agnes's reaction to the "perfectly natural process" of menstruation, but Agnes tells her that it wasn't that. "It's not my time of the month." She doesn't know what happened. She woke up and there was blood on the sheets. She doesn't know what she did wrong, doesn't know why she should be punished. "For what?" Mother Miriam Ruth asks her, and she goes on repeating "I don't know! I don't know!" Mother Miriam Ruth calms her by singing with her, and the memory scene ends.

Agnes went to her room, saying it was nothing. She wouldn't see a doctor, Mother Miriam Ruth remembers, "But I should have known. . . . . that was the beginning. . . . . the night it happened." The doctor asks what else the mother superior remembers about that night. Mother Miriam Ruth says she will check in the day-book she keeps at the convent.

The doctor is alone again for another monologue. She talks about a riddle involving twins and triplets she found in an old magazine. She continues: "By this time, I was convinced that Agnes was completely innocent. I had begun to believe that someone else had murdered her child. Who that person was, and how I was to prove it, were riddles of my *own* making that I *alone* could solve. . . . . My problem was twofold: I wanted to free Agnes—legally prove her innocence—and I wanted to make her well."

The doctor and Agnes are talking again of Agnes's mother. The doctor tells Agnes that she thinks her mother was sometimes wrong. Agnes says that was because *she* was bad, not her mother—"I'm always bad," she tells the doctor. The doctor wants to know what Agnes's mother did to her and suggests that if Agnes can't talk about it she should shake her head "yes" or "no". Agnes admits that her mother made her do things she didn't want to do, that it made her uncomfortable, embarrassed her—and hurt her. Further questioning reveals that her mother made her take her clothes off and made fun of her, telling her she was ugly and stupid. "She says . . . my whole body . . . is a mistake. . . . . . if I don't watch out . . . I'll have a baby." Her mother touched her, Agnes tells the doctor, "down there," with a cigarette: "Please, Mummy. Don't touch me like that."

The doctor tells Agnes to pretend that the doctor is her mother and to say what's she's feeling. Agnes is hesitant but is finally able to answer that she's not ugly, she's pretty, not stupid and not a mistake. "How can I be a mistake if I'm really here? . . . . . You're a mistake! I wish you were dead." The doctor takes Agnes, who is crying, into her arms, and asks her permission to hypnotize her. Agnes agrees to let her.

The doctor tells Agnes she can go. Mother Miriam Ruth has entered and admits that Agnes's mother wasn't "the healthiest of women." The facts come out, bit by bit, that Mother Miriam Ruth is Agnes's aunt. When Mother Miriam Ruth's husband died and she entered the convent, her younger sister, with whom she had lost touch, began corresponding with her, telling her about Agnes and requesting that Agnes be sent to the convent. Mother Miriam Ruth had never seen Agnes until her sister died. Agnes was then 17. Her father "could have been any one of a dozen men, from what my sister told me," Mother Miriam Ruth tells the doctor, adding that her sister was afraid Agnes would follow in her footsteps.

The doctor asks Mother Miriam Ruth if she knows that Agnes's mother molested her. Mother Miriam Ruth hadn't told the doctor because she didn't think it was important, and she had only learned that the girl was kept from school and that her mother was an alcoholic after the fact.

Mother Miriam Ruth has the day-book with her. Agnes was sick the Sunday before she told her about the sheets. They probably became stained on Saturday night, but that night one of the older nuns had died and Mother Miriam Ruth was in the sick room. The doctor points out that Father Marshall must have been at the convent if extreme unction was given that night. Again Sister Miriam Ruth states he couldn't have been responsible for the child. The doctor says she'll find out: she has Agnes's permission to hypnotize her.

Mother Miriam Ruth is not happy about this. She takes a new tack and asks the doctor, "What have we done to hurt you?" She tells her she can spot an ex-Catholic a mile away. She admits that the church burned a few heretics and sold some indulgences, but that that was when the Church was in power. "We let government do those things today," she shrugs. The doctor tells her about a friend of hers in the first grade who was killed in an accident on her way to school. A nun said she died because she hadn't said her morning prayers.

Agnes is heard singing.

DOCTOR: Why is that so important to you, her singing?

MOTHER: When I was a child I used to speak with my guardian angel. Oh, I don't ask you to believe that I heard loud, miraculous voices, but just as some children have invisible playmates, I had angelic conversations. Like Agnes's mother, you might say, but I was a lot younger then, and I am not Agnes's mother. Anyway, when I was six I stopped listening, and my angel stopped speaking. But . . . . . I remembered that voice. . . . . and shortly after I was chosen Mother Superior, I looked at myself one day and saw nothing but a survivor of an unhappy marriage, a mother of two angry daughters and a nun who was certain of nothing. Not even of Heaven. . . . . Not even of God. And then one evening while walking in a field beside the convent wall, I heard a voice, and looking up I saw one of our new postulants standing in her window, singing. It was Agnes. . . . . and all of my doubts about God and myself vanished in that one moment. I recognized the voice.

Silence.

Don't take it away from me again, Doctor Livingstone. Those years after six were very bleak.

DOCTOR: My sister died in a convent. And it's *her* voice *I* hear.

The doctor asks Mother Miriam Ruth if her smoking still bothers her, and if she thinks the saints would have smoked. Mother Miriam Ruth is sure they would have, except for the ascetics. "Saint Joan would chew Mail Pouch."

DOCTOR *(taking a toke):* And what, do you suppose, are today's saints smoking?

MOTHER: There are no saints today. Good people, yes. But extraordinarily good people? I'm afraid those we are sorely lacking.

DOCTOR: Do you believe they ever existed, these extraordinarily good people?

MOTHER: Yes, I do.

DOCTOR: Would you like to become one?

MOTHER: To become? One is born a saint. Only no one is born a saint today. We've evolved too far. We're too complicated.

DOCTOR: But you can try, can't you? To be good?

MOTHER: Oh, yes, but goodness has very little to do with it. Not all the saints are good. In fact, most of them were a little crazy. But their hearts were with God, left in His hands at birth. "Trailing clouds of glory." No more. We're born, we live, we die. Occasionally one might appear among us, still attached to God. But we cut that cord very quickly. No freaks here. We're all solid, sensible men and women, feet on the ground, money in the bank, innocence trampled underfoot. Our minds dissected, our bodies cut open, "No soul here, must have been a delusion." We look at the sky, "No God up there, no heaven, no hell." Well, we're better off. Less disease, for one thing. No *room* for miracles. But, oh my dear, how I miss the miracles.

DOCTOR: Do you really believe miracles happened?

MOTHER: Of course I do. I believe in the miracle of the loaves and fishes two thousand years ago as strongly as I would doubt it today. What we've gained in logic we've lost in faith. We no longer have any sort of . . . primitive wonder The closest we come to a miracle today is in bed. And we give up everything for it. Including those bits of light that might still, by the smallest chance, be clinging to our souls, reaching back to God.

The doctor asks her if she believes Agnes is still attached to God, and Mother Miriam Ruth says only, "Listen to her singing." It is time to begin the hypnotism. The doctor will allow Mother Miriam Ruth to be present. *Curtain.*

ACT II

Agnes is again heard singing—this time, in French, as the doctor begins to speak, downstage.

DOCTOR: The hypnosis took weeks, not minutes. An hour a day, spaced in between a kleptomaniac and an exhibitionist. . . . . Between sleepless nights. Endless weekends. But *my* memories, oh, *they* come *too* easily. . . . . I know, if only I could finish the thought, they would . . . go away.

The doctor is ready to hypnotize Agnes. She tells her not to be frightened, that she can't make her say or do anything she doesn't wish to say or do. She tells her to imagine that she is listening to an angel chorus. "Their music is so beautiful and so real that you can touch it. It surrounds you like a very warm and comfortable pool of water. . . . . Close your eyes, Agnes. . . . . When I count to three, you will wake up."

The doctor begins to ask questions, and Agnes says she is there because she is in trouble and frightened. She had a baby, she knew it was going to "come out," and didn't want it to, as she felt unworthy to become a mother. Agnes admits that she knew from the beginning she was going to have a baby. She drank milk so it would be healthy but wouldn't go to a doctor for fear no one would believe her—she won't say about what, certainly not about the baby. Another Sister guessed about the baby but made Agnes promise not to tell.

The doctor tells Agnes she will ask her to open her eyes soon and see her room in the convent on the night about four months ago when she was sick. Agnes had had supper and gone to vespers, but left early, she was "just tired," and she thinks

Elizabeth Ashley as Doctor Martha Livingstone in *Agnes of God*

it was Sister Margaret who gave her some milk. The doctor asks her if it was Sister Margaret who knew about the baby but Agnes won't answer. The doctor tells her to open her eyes. Agnes is seeing her room, the usual—a bed, a chair, a crucifix —and the unusual—a waste paper basket. She thinks it is there for her "to get sick in." She feels as if she's eaten glass and begins to have contractions. The doctor asks why nobody comes. Everyone is at vespers on the other side of the building. Agnes has more contractions. She answers the doctor that she's on the bed, and she says, "Get away from me . . . . . I don't want you here!"

> DOCTOR: Is someone in the room with you? Agnes?
> AGNES: Don't touch me! Don't touch me! Please! Don't touch me!
>   *Contraction.*
> No, I don't want to have the baby now. I don't want it! Why are you making me do this?
>   *Contraction. She begins to scream.*
> DOCTOR: It's all right, Agnes. No one's going to hurt you.
> AGNES: You want to hurt my baby! You want to take my baby!
>   *Contraction.*
> MOTHER: Stop her, she'll hurt herself.
> DOCTOR: No, let her go . . . for a moment.
> MOTHER *(rushing to Agnes):* I'm not going on with this . . . any more.

DOCTOR: No!

>As Mother touches her, Agnes screams, striking Mother and pushing
>her away.

AGNES: You're trying to take my baby! You're trying to take my baby!
>Scream and contraction.

Stay in! Please stay in!

>Several violent and final contractions.

MOTHER: Stop her! Help her!

AGNES: BITCH! It's not my fault, Mummy. WHORE! It's a mistake, Mummy.
LIAR!

DOCTOR: Agnes, it's all right. One, two, three. It's all right.

Agnes relaxes. The doctor thanks her. "*After this point in the evening, the doctor
doesn't smoke another cigarette.*" Agnes leaves the office and is heard singing
again, in Latin.

Mother Miriam Ruth believes the doctor has formed her opinion about Agnes,
but the doctor doesn't feel "that's all there is to it." Her job is done, Mother
Miriam Ruth tells her, but the doctor says only as far as the court is concerned,
not personally. Mother Miriam Ruth declares that the doctor wasn't expected to
become personally involved and orders her out. If they want a psychiatrist for
Agnes, they'll get their own: "One who'll approach this matter with some objectivity and respect! . . . . . She's a remarkable person."

The doctor asks if the fact that Agnes sings is unique. Is she supposed to be
convinced that Agnes "shouldn't be touched" because she hallucinates, gives up
eating and bleeds spontaneously? The doctor tells her, "Give me a miracle.
Nothing less. *Then* I'll leave her be. . . . . Something that cannot be explained."

Mother Miriam Ruth admits that everything can be explained, but "some
explanations aren't enough. They don't answer all the questions." The doctor
argues that as a scientist she must believe that the answers are there. Again
Mother Miriam argues with her. She believes that science's function is not in the
answers it finds, but in the questions it finds. It's the *unanswered* question that
makes Agnes unique. The doctor wants know what the question is. The identity
of the father, Mother Miriam Ruth replies—and she doesn't believe there was a
man at the convent that night. The doctor asks if she thinks it was "a big white
dove." Mother Miriam Ruth concedes that she doesn't think of this as the Second
Coming, but says, "People bend spoons, stop watches. . . . . If she's capable of
putting a hole in her hand without benefit of a nail, why couldn't she split a tiny
cell in her womb?" Hysterical parthenogenesis, the doctor suggests: "If frogs can
do it, why not Agnes?" About as much an explanation as Father Marshall,
Mother Miriam Ruth replies. She believes the answer is Agnes and that Agnes
is also the question, and that is miracle enough for anyone.

The doctor accuses Mother Miriam Ruth of not wanting to face up to Agnes's
having been raped, seduced or having done the seducing; that everything Agnes
has done can be explained by modern psychiatry; that she's not an enigma; that,
yes, she is the sum of her psychological parts. Then why is the doctor so obsessed
with her? Mother Miriam Ruth asks. "This is murder we're talking about" the
doctor says. She believes in Agnes's innocence, too, and if there is proof, she'll

find it. She wants to know who that other person in the room was and asks Mother Miriam Ruth if it was her. Mother Miriam Ruth says if she believes it was murder she should consult the district attorney, not her, nor Agnes. She has decided to have the doctor taken off the case. Mother Miriam Ruth adds that, as for the miracle the doctor wanted, that has happened, a small one, but she'll notice it eventually (the doctor, who chain-smoked obsessively, has stopped smoking). Mother Miriam Ruth leaves as Agnes enters.

DOCTOR (*quickly and secretly*): Agnes, listen. You must help me. Has Mother Miriam ever threatened you in any way?
AGNES: No.
DOCTOR: Or frightened you?
AGNES: Why are you asking that?
DOCTOR: Because I believe she . . . may have something to do with . . .
MOTHER (*offstage*): Sister Agnes!
AGNES: Coming, Mother!
DOCTOR: Agnes, who . . . was in the room with you?
AGNES: I won't see you again, will I?
DOCTOR: Yes, you will. I promise. Agnes, who was in the room with you?
    Silence.
Do you know?
AGNES: Yes.
DOCTOR: Who was it? For the love of God, tell me.
AGNES: It was my mother.

The doctor, alone again, tells of the dream she had that night: In some hospital far away, she is about to perform a Caesarean, but as she cuts into the woman's belly and reaches in, a tiny hand grabs her finger and begins to draw her in. When she awakened, she discovered her sheets were blood-stained—her menstrual cycle, which had ceased three years before, had begun again. "What would I have done with a child?" she wonders.

The next day the doctor got a court order to have Agnes put back in her care. "I was so sure I was right," she says, but she wonders if, as a doctor, she should have known better. "But as a person. . . . . I am made of flesh and blood . . . and heart . . . and soul . . ."

Mother Miriam Ruth enters, not pleased that the doctor is back on the case. The doctor plans to hypnotize Agnes again, but also wants answers to some questions from Mother Miriam Ruth, and she wants the truth, not evasions. The mother superior admits that Agnes did say something to her about not feeling well while she was pregnant, but that she hadn't sent her to a doctor because Agnes wouldn't go—she was afraid. The doctor asks of what? Mother Miriam Ruth suggests the doctor is persecuting her, that she hates nuns. The doctor wants to know if she knew Agnes was pregnant. "*Mother desperately tries to fight back and hide her tears.*" She admits that she did, but she didn't guess it until it was too late to stop the scandal. She got Agnes to promise not to tell so she would have time to think. But she didn't get that time, the doctor says. And then the time ran out.

The doctor accuses Mother Miriam Ruth of wanting the child out of the way, and of hiding the waste paper basket in the room, and of tying the cord around the baby's neck. But Mother Miriam Ruth says the waste basket was for the blood and dirty sheets. She wanted Agnes to have the baby when no one was around. She would have taken it to a hospital and left it with them. "But there was so much blood, I panicked." She went for help.

Mother Miriam Ruth exits to get Agnes. *"Alone, the doctor begins to cross herself, but stops."* The two nuns return, and Agnes allows the doctor to hypnotize her again. The doctor wants her to remember a Saturday night about a year ago—"The night when Sister Paul died." She tells Agnes to imagine that she is in her room. Agnes says she woke up while it was still dark, that she didn't see anything at first. "But. . . . . Someone is in the room." She is frightened.

DOCTOR: What do you do?
> *Silence.*
Agnes?
AGNES: Who is it?
> *Silence.*
Who's there?
> *Silence.*
Is it you?
> *Silence.*
But I *am* afraid.
> *Silence.*
Yes.
> *Silence.*
Yes I do.
> *Silence.*
Why me?
> *Silence.*
Wait. I want to see you!
> *She gasps and opens her eyes.*
DOCTOR: What do you see?
AGNES: A flower. Waxy and white. A drop of water, sinking into the petal, flowing through the veins. A tiny halo. Millions of halos, dividing and dividing, feathers are stars, falling into the iris of God's eye. Oh my God, he sees me. Oh, it's so lovely, so blue, yellow, green leaves brown blood, no, red, His Blood, my God, my God, I'm bleeding, I'M BLEEDING!
> *She is bleeding from the palms of her hands.*
MOTHER: Oh my God.
AGNES: I have to wash this off, it's on my hands, my legs, my God, it's on the sheets, help me clean the sheets, help me, help me, it won't come out, the blood won't come out!

As Mother Miriam Ruth grabs her, Agnes (still under hypnosis) says, "Let go of me! . . . . . You prayed for this to happen, didn't you? . . . . . I don't want you anymore! . . . . . I wish you all were dead!" The doctor informs her they didn't have anything to do with the man in her room, that he did "a very bad thing" to her, that it isn't her fault. Agnes calls out "Mummy's fault!", and, to Mother Miriam Ruth, "It's all your fault!" The doctor again asks Agnes who did this. Agnes says it was God and that she'll "burn in hell because she hates Him."

Over Mother Miriam Ruth's protests that Agnes has had enough, the doctor continues. She wants to know what happened to the baby—"It was alive, wasn't it?" Mother Miriam Ruth protests again, but Agnes finally admits that it was, and that Mother Miriam Ruth was with her. "She took the baby in her arms," says the doctor, and Agnes says "Yes." The doctor asks Agnes what Mother Miriam Ruth did then.

AGNES *(simply and quietly):* She left me alone with that little . . . thing. I looked at it and thought, this is a mistake. But it's my mistake, not Mummy's. God's mistake. I thought, I can save her. I can give her back to God.
Silence.
DOCTOR: What did you do?
AGNES: I put her to sleep.
DOCTOR: How?
AGNES: I tied the cord around her neck, wrapped her in the bloody sheets and stuffed her in the trash can.
MOTHER: No.
Mother turns away, Silence.
DOCTOR: One. Two. Three.
Agnes slowly rises and walks away, humming "Charlie's Neat" softly to herself.

Mother Miriam Ruth admits to the doctor that Agnes did remember. "Thank you, Doctor Livingstone. We need people like you to destroy all those lies that ignorant folk like myself pretend to believe. . . . . But I'll never forgive you for what you've taken away."

AGNES *(speaking to an unseen friend):* Why are you crying?
The doctor and the mother superior turn to her. Silence.
But *I* believe. I *do.*
Silence.
Please, don't you leave me too. Oh no. Oh my God, O sweet Lady, don't leave me. Please, please don't leave me. I'll be good. I won't be your bad baby any more.
She sees someone else.
No, Mummy. I don't want to go with you. Stop pulling me. Your hands are hot. Don't touch me like that! Oh my God, Mummy, don't burn me! DON'T BURN ME!
Silence. She turns to the mother superior and the doctor and stretches out her hands, like a statue of the Lady, showing her bleeding palms. She smiles and speaks simply and sanely.
I stood in the window of my room every night for a week. And one night I heard the most beautiful voice imaginable. It came from the middle of the wheat field beyond my room, and when I looked I saw the moon shining down on Him. For

six nights He sang to me. Songs I'd never heard. And on the seventh night He came to my room and opened His wings and lay on top of me. And all the while He sang. *(Smiling and crying, she sings:)*
    "Charlie's neat and Charlie's sweet,
    And Charlie he's a dandy,
    Every time he goes to town,
    He gets his girl some candy. . . . ."

Agnes continues singing as Mother Miriam Ruth leads her offstage.

DOCTOR: . . . . . I never saw them again. The following day I removed myself from the case. Mother Miriam Ruth threw Agnes on the mercy of the court, and she was sent to a hospital . . . where she stopped singing . . . and eating . . . and where she died. Why? Why was a child molested, and a baby killed, and a mind destroyed? What kind of God can permit such a wonder one as her to come trampling through . . . *(Striking her chest.)* . . . this well-ordered existence? I want a reason! An explanation, a miracle, *anything* to help me to understand! All she's given me are packs of unopened cigarets . . . and the knowledge that I . . . miss her . . . and the hope that she has left something, some little part of herself with me. I guess that would be reason, answer, and miracle enough.
    Silence.
Wouldn't it?
    Curtain.

"MASTER HAROLD" . . . AND THE BOYS

A Play in One Act

BY ATHOL FUGARD

Cast and credits appear on pages 336–337

ATHOL FUGARD was born June 11, 1932 in Middelburg in the semi-desert Karoo country of South Africa. His mother was an Afrikaner, his father of Irish and Hugenot descent. He studied motor mechanics at Port Elizabeth Technical College and philosophy at the University of Cape Town and spent three years in the Merchant Marine, mostly in the Far East. He married an actress, Sheila Meiring, and for a time they ran an experimental theater in Cape Town. His first play, No-Good Friday, *was produced in 1959 with an all-black cast. His next was* Nongogo *(1961) which had its American premiere in 1978 for 20 performances at Manhattan Theater Club.*

In 1963 The Blood Knot *won Fugard an international reputation and reached these shores in an off-Broadway production starring James Earl Jones March 1, 1964 for 240 performances (it is about two black half-brothers, one light-skinned and one dark). His next play,* People Are Living There, *was done in Glasgow in 1968 and then in London during the 1971–72 season. His* Hello and Goodbye *appeared off Broadway with Martin Sheen and Colleen Dewhurst Sept. 18, 1969 for 45 performances and was produced in London in the season of 1972–73. Fugard's* Boesman and Lena *was done off Broadway with James Earl Jones, Ruby Dee and Zakes Mokae June 22, 1970 for 205 performances—and was named a Best Play of its season—a year before its subsequent London premiere. Another Fugard work of that period,* Mille Miglia, *was aired on BBC television, as was* The Blood Knot.

Fugard's second Best Play, The Island, *had strong mimetic as well as literary*

Athol Fugard *(left)*, author of *"MASTER HAROLD"*. . .*and the boys,* with the actors who portrayed his characters onstage: Danny Glover (Willie), Lonny Price (Hally) and Zakes Mokae (Sam)

elements and is credited as a collaboration "devised" by the author and the actors who appeared in it, John Kani and Winston Ntshona. It reversed the direction of the previous Fugard Best Play by stopping in London before coming to New York, appearing under the auspices of the Royal Court Theater on a two-play program with the effective Sizwe Banzi Is Dead *by the same authors. The two plays then had their American premieres in tandem, first at the Long Wharf Theater in New Haven, Conn. in October 1974 and then in alternating repertory (Sizwe Banzi for 159 performances,* The Island *for 52) in November 1974 in mini-Broadway productions at the Edison Theater.*

Fugard's third Best Play, A Lesson From Aloes, *first appeared on this side of the Atlantic in a production at the Centaur Theater in Montreal on Jan. 1, 1980; then was produced at the Yale Repertory Theater in New Haven March 26 and finally on Broadway Nov. 17 for 96 performances (winning the 1981 New York Drama Critics Circle award as the best play of the season), in all three cases under its author's direction. Fugard also directed his fourth Best Play, this year's "MASTER HAROLD" . . . and the boys, which opened on Broadway May 4, 1982 in a production which had originated at Yale Rep.*

Other recorded instances of production of Fugard's work in this country have included the short play Statements After an Arrest Under the Immorality Act *for 35 performances at Manhattan Theater Club in November 1978 and* The

Drummer *at Actors' Theater of Louisville in the 1979–80 season. His works are revived perennially on off-off-Broadway and regional theater programs.*

Some of Fugard's training for what has turned out to be his triple profession of actor-director-writer was acquired at Rehearsal Room in Johannesburg's Dorkay House (the headquarters of South Africa's Union Artists, the organization that cares for the cultural interests of non-Europeans in the Transvaal). Later, as resident director of Dorkay House, he staged the work of many modern playwrights including Steinbeck and Pinter. Since the mid-1960s he has been closely associated with Serpent Players of New Brighton, Port Elizabeth, a theater workshop for black Africans experimenting in collaborative "play-making" of works dealing with the contemporary South African scene. Rehearsals and performances of Serpent Players are customarily carried on after hours, with black participants sometimes classified technically as "household employees" of their white colleague Athol Fugard, because "artist" is not an accepted employment category for South African blacks.

Fugard now lives near Port Elizabeth with his wife, and they have a daughter, Lisa-Maria. He has often been a focal point of controversy in his politically controversial land and was once denied a passport by his government when he wanted to come to New York for rehearsals of Boesman and Lena *in the spring of 1970.*

Time: 1950

Place: The St. Georges Park Tea Room on a wet and windy afternoon in Port Elizabeth, South Africa

SYNOPSIS: The entrance to the tea room is at right, the counter and door to the kitchen are at left, with a wall of windows upstage looking onto the park. A small table with single chair is set for a meal for one (and holds a pile of comic books in addition to the place setting); otherwise the chairs and tables are stacked. The other furnishings include a blackboard listing prices, a telephone, soft drink and cigarette dispensers, jukebox, etc.

Sam, a black man in his late 30s wearing a waiter's white coat, is looking over the comic books. Willie, also black and about Sam's age, is on his knees cleaning the floor with rag and bucket. He is singing as he works, and then he gets up and whirls around in a dance, showing Sam how he has mastered the steps. Sam counsels Willie not to try too hard but to glide and make it look easy, so that the ballroom dancing contest judges two weeks from now will look at Willie and his partner Hilda and "see a man and a woman who are dancing their way to a happy ending."

Willie has been practising quickstep; he'd also like to try out his slow foxtrot, but he needs music for that, and neither of the men can afford to put a coin in the jukebox—they have no more than homegoing bus fare on them. Willie complains that Hilda has failed to show up for recent practise sessions and is always after him for money to support a baby he isn't sure is his. Sam advises Willie to be gentler with his partner—he beats her for missing steps. Sam's comments anger

Willie, but Sam calms him down and then demonstrates proper ballroom dancing technique: "Don't start worrying about making mistakes or the judges or the other competitors. It's just you, Hilda and the music, and you're going to have a good time."

As Sam is showing Willie quickstep, Hally enters, *"a 17 year old white boy, wet raincoat and school case."* Hally applauds with Willie when Sam finishes his steps, then Willie salutes Hally as the latter takes off his raincoat. He is dressed in school blazer, grey flannels, khaki shirt and tie, black shoes. His mother, proprietor of this place, has gone to the hospital to see his father (Sam tells Hally) after receiving a phone call. Sam thinks she may be going to bring Hally's father home, a thought which seems to upset Hally. He has come here to have his lunch but wants only soup. He notices the pile of comic books.

HALLY: And these?
SAM: For your Dad. Mr. Kempston brought them.
HALLY: You haven't been reading them, have you?
SAM: Just looking.
HALLY: God what rubbish! Mental pollution. Take them away.
  Sam exits waltzing into the kitchen. Hally turns to Willie.
Did you hear my Mom talking on the telephone, Willie?
WILLIE: No, Master Hally. I was at the back.
HALLY: And she didn't say anything to you before she left?
WILLIE: She said I must clean the floors.
HALLY: I mean about my Dad.
WILLIE: She didn't say anything to me about him, Master Hally.
HALLY *(with conviction):* No! It can't be. They said he needed at least another three weeks of treatment. Sam's definitely made a mistake.

Hally takes a book out of his bag and settles down to read it, but soon he is discussing the dance competition with Willie and Sam, who comes back with a bowl of soup. Sam keeps needling Willie about his dancing, until Willie, becoming angry, throws the slop rag at him. It misses Sam and hits Hally, who is suddenly angry, throwing the rag back and demanding, "Cut out the nonsense now and get on with your work. And you too, Sam. Stop fooling around."

But Hally again questions Sam about the phone call, after which Hally's mother specifically stated, "When Hally comes in, tell him I've gone to the hospital and I'll phone him." There was no mention of bringing Hally's father home, so Hally assumes his mother must be seeing his father through a bad turn.

Among Hally's things Sam notices a drawing, a supposed likeness of one of his teachers. Hally was punished for this impudence, six strokes of the cane. They don't pull down the culprit's pants for school punishment, but they do, Sam declares, when in court the judge dishes out a sentence of "strokes with a light cane."

SAM: They make you lie down on a bench. One policeman pulls down your trousers and holds your ankles, another one pulls your shirt over your head and holds your arms . . .

HALLY: Thank you! that's enough.

SAM: . . . and the one that gives you the strokes talks to you gently and for a long time between each one. *(He laughs.)*

HALLY: I've heard enough, Sam! Jeasus! It's a bloody awful world when you come to think of it. People can be real bastards.

SAM: That's the way it is, Hally.

HALLY: It doesn't *have* to be that way. There is something called progress, you know. We don't exactly burn people at the stake any more.

SAM: Like Joan of Arc.

HALLY: Correct. If she was captured today she'd be given a fair trial.

SAM: And then the death sentence.

HALLY *(a world-weary sigh):* I know, I know! I oscillate between hope and despair for the world as well, Sam. But things will change, you wait and see. One day somebody is going to get up and give history a kick in the backside and get it going again.

Hally's school history books are full of social reformers, and surely there will be one to set things right in this day and age. Sam reads an obscure reference to "magnitude of the quantities" in Hally's math textbook (Hally doesn't understand it either; English is his best subject). Sam then reads a passage about Napoleon from Hally's history book, and they discuss the qualifications of a man of "magnitude." Hally's candidate for magnitude is Darwin; Sam picks Abraham Lincoln, causing Hally to comment, "Don't get sentimental, Sam. You've never been a slave, you know. And anyway we freed your ancestors here in South Arica long before the Americans."

Sam tries again with William Shakespeare, but Hally reminds him that he has read only one play, *Julius Caesar,* as has Hally. Hally counters with Tolstoy, who worked with his peasants, freed his serfs and wrote *War and Peace* despite being not very good at his school studies, like Hally himself.

Sam's next candidate for magnitude is Jesus Christ, but he takes him back when Hally rules out religious figures. Sam finally comes up with Sir Alexander Flemming, discoverer of penicillin, and for once Hally agrees wholeheartedly: "If it wasn't for him we might have lost the second World War." Hally congratulates himself on Sam's discernment, because it is from Hally, in discussions of his school lessons, that Sam has acquired his erudition. Sam agrees.

SAM: . . . . . And my first lesson was geography.

HALLY *(intrigued):* Really? I don't remember.

SAM: My room there at the back of the old Jubilee Boardinghouse. I had just started working for your Mom. Little boy in short trousers walks in one afternoon and asks me seriously, "Sam, do you want to see South Africa?"

HALLY: Was that me?

SAM: Hey man! Sure I wanted to see South Africa! . . . So the next thing I'm looking at a map you had just done for homework. It was your first one and you were very proud of yourself.

HALLY: Go on.

SAM: Then came my first lesson. "Repeat after me, Sam: gold in the Transvaal, mealies in the Free State, sugar in Natal and grapes in the Cape." I still know it!

HALLY: Well I'll be buggered. So that's how it all started.

SAM: And your next map was one with all the rivers and the mountains they came from. The Orange, the Vaal, the Limpopo, the Zambesi . . .

HALLY: You've got a phenomenal memory.

SAM: You should be grateful. That is why you started passing your exams. You tried to be better than me. *(They laugh together.)*

Willie joins them and recalls how Hallie would spend his time with them at the boarding house, even though his mother objected to his "hanging around the servant's quarters." To a ten-year-old boy, the company of Sam and Willie was a blessed relief from the disturbances of his own home. Hally would come to see Sam every chance he got, entering Sam and Willie's room without knocking and once surprising Sam with a woman. The room, Hally remembers, was very modestly furnished, with pin-ups on the wall and a picture of Joe Louis, plus Sam's first ballroom dancing prize, a silver cup for third place. They would play checkers or chess (at which Willie never won because, he is convinced, the others cheated).

Then there was that special afternoon, Hally remembers; Sam was sitting on the floor: "You had two thin pieces of wood and you were smoothing them down with a knife. It didn't look particularly interesting, but when I asked you what you were doing you just said, 'Wait and see, Hally. Wait . . . and see' in that secret sort of way of yours, so I knew there was a surprise coming. . . . . It was only when you tied them together in a cross and put that down on the brown paper that I realized what you were doing. Sam is making a kite? And you said: 'Yes . . .!' *(Shaking his head with disbelief.)* The sheer audacity of it took my breath away. I mean seriously, what the hell does a black man know about flying a kite?"

When they took it up the hill, Hally was afraid they were going to be laughed at. Sam set things up, and then . . . he wants to hear in Hally's own words what happened next. Hally thinks for a minute and then says, "You went a little distance from me down the hill, you held it up ready to let it go . . . this is it, I thought. Like everything else in my life here comes another fiasco. Then you shouted 'Go, Hally!' and I started to run. *(Pause.)* I don't know how to describe it, Sam. Ja! The miracle happened! I was running, waiting for it to crash to the ground, but instead suddenly there was something alive behind me at the end of the string, tugging at it as if it wanted to be free."

Hally let it out to the end of the string, as both he and Sam were laughing for joy at this splendid sight. Sam made it dive close to the ground and then swoop back into the air. Sam left Hally with the kite tied to a bench ("I had work to do, Hally"). By the time he finally had to bring the kite down, Hally had a stiff neck from gazing up at it. Sam does not remember quite why he made the kite. Hally feels that it's now time for another one, though for some reason he would feel out of place as a kite flyer in any situation he can imagine—white boy with older black man or white boy with crippled father. But Hally remembers the old

Jubilee Boardhouse days fondly, because life then was somehow in the proper scale: "It's got so bloody complicated since then."

The phone rings: it's Hally's mother calling from the hospital—instead of taking a bad turn, Hally's father has somehow improved, and now he wants to come home. This piece of news Hally views with obvious alarm: "You know what it's going to be like if he comes home . . . Well then, don't blame me when I fail my exams at the end of the year . . ."

Hally asks his mother to keep his father in the hospital on any pretext. He promises to lock up the tea room, and the men are staring at him as the phone conversation comes to an end.

HALLY: My Mom says that when you're finished with the floors you must do the windows. Don't misunderstand me, Sam. All I want is for him to get better. And if he was I'd be the first person to say: bring him home. But he's not, and we can't give him the medical care and attention he needs at home. That's what hospitals are there for. *(Brusquely.)* So don't just stand there! Get on with it!
    Sam clears Hally's table.
You heard right. My Dad wants to go home.

SAM: Is he better?

HALLY *(sharply):* No! How the hell can he be better when last night he was groaning with pain. This is not an age of miracles!

SAM: Then he should stay in the hospital.

HALLY *(seething with irritation and frustration):* Tell me something I don't know, Sam. What the hell do you think I was saying to my Mom? All I can say is fuck-it-all.

SAM: I'm sure he'll listen to your Mom.

HALLY: You don't know what she's up against. He's already packed his shaving kit and pyjamas and is sitting on his bed with his crutches, dressed and ready to go. I know him when he gets in that mood. If she tries to reason with him we've had it. She's no match for him when it comes to a battle of words. He'll tie her up in knots. *(Trying to hide his true feelings.)*

SAM: I suppose it gets lonely for him in there.

HALLY: With all the patients and nurses around? Regular visits from the Salvation Army? Balls! It's ten times worse for him at home. I'm at school and my mother is here in the business all day.

SAM: He's at least got you at night.

HALLY *(before he can stop himself):* And we've got him! *(Another cover.)* Please! I don't want to talk about it any more.
    Unpacks his school case, slamming down books on the table.
Life is just a plain bloody mess, that's all. And people are fools.

SAM: Come on, Hally.

HALLY: Yes they are! They bloody-well deserve what they get.

SAM: They don't complain.

HALLY: Don't try to be clever, Sam. It doesn't suit you. Anybody who thinks there's nothing wrong with this world needs to have his head examined. Just when things are going along all right, without fail someone or something will come along and spoil everything. Somebody should write that down as a fundamental

Lonny Price, Zakes Mokae and Danny Glover in a
scene from "*MASTER HAROLD*". . .*and the boys*

law of the universe. The principle of perpetual disappointment. If there is a God
who created this world, he should scrap it and try again.

SAM: All right, Hally, all right. . . . .

Sam changes the subject to Hally's homework, an assignment to write 500
words describing an annual event of importance. Hally bends over his books, and
the men return to their task. While doing so, they resume discussing the forthcoming dance competition. Willie beat Hilda so hard the last time, she may not
want to be his partner any more. Sam keeps on kidding Willie about his dancing
(though Sam was the one who encouraged Willie to take it up in the first place)
until Willie is angry again. Their horseplay distracts Hally, who orders them back
to their work, lecturing them on their behavior: "I allow you chaps a little
freedom in here when business is bad, and what do you do with it? The foxtrot!"

Sam defends the harmless pleasure of dancing, while Hally derides it and sneers
at Sam for taking it seriously as an art. Hally dismisses it as mere "entertainment," but Sam challenges him to come and see for himself. It's going to be a
big event, beautifully decorated, with big band music, contestants elegantly
dressed in evening attire and the 1950 Eastern Province Championships at stake.
Hally goes so far as to admit it is an "occasion," and then it occurs to him that
it might become the subject of his assigned essay, as a cultural event: "Old Doc

Bromely—he's my English teacher—is going to argue with me, of course. He doesn't like natives. But I'll point out to him that in strict anthropolitical terms the culture of a primitive black society includes its dancing and singing. To put my thesis in a nutshell: the war-dance has been replaced by the waltz."

Hally takes notes on the physical setup of the contest: the six finalists, the band, the spectators, the long table with the three judges. Sam acts out the climactic procedure, pretending to be the master of ceremonies and naming Willie among the finalists (Willie, excited, begs for jukebox music, but Hally doesn't dare borrow a shilling from the cash register). Sam explains the scoring, Hally asks about penalty points in case one of the couples bumps into another one.

SAM: Hally, Hally . . .!

HALLY *(perplexed):* Why? What did I say?

SAM: There's no collisions out there, Hally. Nobody trips or stumbles or bumps into anybody else. That's what that moment is all about. To be one of those finalists on that dance floor is like . . . like being in a dream about a world in which accidents don't happen.

HALLY *(genuinely moved by Sam's image):* Jeasus, Sam! That's beautiful!

WILLIE *(can endure waiting no longer):* I'm starting!

Willie dances while Sam talks.

SAM: Of course it is. That's what I've been trying to say to you all afternoon. And it's beautiful because that is what we want life to be like. But instead, like you said, Hally, we're bumping into each other all the time. Look at the three of us this afternoon: I've bumped into Willie, the two of us have bumped into you, you've bumped into your mother, she's bumping into your dad . . . None of us knows the steps, and there's no music playing. And it doesn't stop with us. The whole world is doing it all the time. Open a newspaper, and what do you read? America has bumped into Russia, England is bumping into India, rich man bumps into poor man. Those are big collisions, Hally. They make for a lot of bruises. People get hurt in all that bumping, and we're sick and tired of it now. It's been going on for too long. Are we never going to get it right? . . . learn to dance life like champions instead of always being just a bunch of beginners at it?

HALLY *(deep and sincere admiration for the man):* You've got a vision, Sam!

SAM: Not just me. What I'm saying to you is that everybody's got it. That's why there's only standing room left for the Centenary Hall in two weeks' time. For as long as the music lasts we are going to see six couples get it right the way we want life to be.

Sam extends his vision to naming the teachers trying to help all humanity get the steps right: Mahatma Gandhi, the Pope, General Smuts, the United Nations. But the ringing of the telephone brings them all back to earth. It's Hally's mother informing him that she has brought Hally's father home. Hally, upset, calls this development "the end of the peace and quiet we've been having" and continues unburdening himself to his mother on the phone.

HALLY *(to the telephone):* . . . . . I know only too well he's my father! . . . I'm not being disrespectful, but I'm sick and tired of emptying stinking chamber pots full of phlegm and piss. . . . . For your information, I still haven't got that science textbook I need. And you know why? He borrowed the money you gave me for it . . . Because I didn't want to start another fight between you two . . . He says that every time . . . Alright, Mom! *(Viciously.)* Then just remember to start hiding your bag away again, because he'll be at your purse before long for money for booze. And when he's well enough to come down here, you better keep an eye on the till as well, because that is also going to develop a leak . . . Then don't complain to me when he starts his old tricks . . . Yes, you do. I get it from you on one side and from him on the other, and it makes life hell for me. I'm not going to be the peace maker any more. I'm warning you now; when the two of you start fighting again, I'm leaving home . . . Mom, if you start crying I'm going to put down the receiver . . . Okay . . . *(Lowering his voice to a vicious whisper.)* Okay, Mom. I heard you. *(Desperate.)* No. Because I don't want to. I'll see him when I get home! Mom! . . .

> Pause. When he speaks again, his tone changes completely. It is not simply pretense. We sense a genuine emotional conflict.

Welcome home, chum! . . . What's that? . . . Don't be silly, Dad. You being home is just about the best news in the world. . . . .

Hally sympathizes with his father; he'll bring home a stack of comic books and they'll have a talk (he tells his father) and no, he won't forget to bring a bottle of brandy (he tells his mother, after his father gets off the phone).

The phone conversation ends, and so at the same time does the bright, temporary vision of a world without collisions. All their afternoon's talk has been "just so much bullshit." Sam has forgotten to include the cripples in his vision—Hally tells him—the cripples who stagger around the dance floor and bump into everybody else. The grand prize (Hally insists with an ugly laugh) is a brimming chamber pot, "and guess who I think is going to be this year's winner?"

SAM *(almost shouting):* Stop now!
HALLY *(suddenly appalled by how far he has gone):* Why?
SAM: Hally? It's your father you're talking about.
HALLY: So?
SAM: Do you know what you've been saying?

> Hally can't answer. He is rigid with shame. Sam speaks to him sternly.

No, Hally, you mustn't do it. Take back those words and ask for forgiveness! It's a terrible sin for a son to mock his father with jokes like that. You'll be punished if you carry on. Your father is your father even if he is a . . . cripple man.
WILLIE: Yes, Master Hally. Is true what Sam say.
SAM: I understand how you are feeling, Hally, but even so . . .
HALLY: No you don't!
SAM: I think I do.
HALLY: And I'm telling you you don't. Nobody does.

> Speaking carefully as his shame turns to rage at Sam.

It's your turn to be careful, Sam. Very careful! You're treading on dangerous ground. Leave me and my father alone.
SAM: I'm not the one who's been saying things about him.

HALLY: What goes on between me and my Dad is none of your business!

SAM: Then don't tell me about it. If that's all you've got to say about him, I don't want to hear.

For a moment Hally is at a loss for a response.

HALLY: Just get on with your bloody work and shut up.

SAM: Swearing at me won't help you.

HALLY: Yes it does! Mind your own fucking business and shut up!

SAM: Okay. If that's the way you want it, I'll stop trying.

He turns away. This infuriates Hally even more.

HALLY: Good. Because what you've been trying to do is meddle in something you know nothing about. All that concerns you in here, Sam, is to try and do what you get paid for—keep the place clean and serve the customers. In plain words, just get on with your job. My mother is right. She's always warning me about allowing you to get too familiar. Well, this time you've gone too far. It's going to stop right now.

No response from Sam.

You're only a servant in here, and don't forget it.

Still no response. Hally is trying hard to get one.

And as far as my father is concerned, all you need to remember is that he is your boss.

SAM *(needled at last):* No he isn't. I get paid by your mother.

HALLY: Don't argue with me, Sam!

SAM: Then don't say he's my boss.

HALLY: He's a white man and that's good enough for you.

SAM: I'll try to forget you said that.

HALLY: Don't! Because you won't be doing me a favor if you do. I'm telling you to remember it.

A pause—Sam pulls himself together and makes one last effort.

SAM: Hally, Hally . . .! Come on, now. Let's stop before it's too late. You're right. We *are* on dangerous ground. If we're not careful somebody is going to get hurt.

But Hally persists, grabbing Sam and turning him around when Sam turns his back. Hally demands that Sam call him "Master Harold" from now on, or risk losing his job. Sam warns Hally, "If you make me say it once, I'll never call you anything else again," but Hally insists, calling it "a little lesson in respect that's long overdue." To demean Sam further, Hally repeats a crude joke of his father's about a "kaffir's arse." Sam resents the joke's discourtesy to Willie even more than to himself, because Willie has always shown Hally the respect he now demands. As a gesture of self-respect and defiance, Sam drops his trousers and presents his naked backside for Hally's inspection, telling him, "Now you can make your Dad even happier when you go home tonight. Tell him I showed you my arse. . . . . and if it will give him an even better laugh next time, I'll also let him have a look."

Sam laughs and turns away with Willie to tidy up the tea room. Hally is motionless, but when Sam passes him, Hally spits in Sam's face. Sam wipes his face, then tells Hally, "You've hurt yourself, Master Harold. I saw it coming. I warned you, but you wouldn't listen. You've just hurt yourself *bad*. And you're

a coward, Master Harold. The face you should be spitting in is your father's
. . . but you used mine, because you think you're safe inside your fair skin
. . . . ."

Willie agrees with Sam that being spat at like a dog would make anyone want
to strike back, and for a moment there is a threat of violence in the air . . . but
it subsides, leaving Sam with a feeling of having been dirtied, and of having failed
in one of his life's objectives. Years ago, Sam felt sorry for the little white boy
whose drunken father had to be carried home, hoped he could prevent the boy
from feeling ashamed, but obviously he failed. He made the kite to induce the
little boy to look up for a change, instead of down at the ground, ashamed of the
drunken father whom he loved. It worked, too. The little boy with the kite tied
to the bench was at last proud of himself—but there was "a twist in our ending.
I couldn't sit down there and stay with you. It was a 'whites only' bench. You
were too young, too excited to notice then. But not any more. If you're not careful
. . . Master Harold . . . you're going to be sitting up there by yourself for a long
time to come, and there won't be a kite in the sky."

Sam exits into the kitchen, taking off his coat. Hally, stricken, gathers his
belongings, empties the cash register and starts to leave, when Sam comes back
and stops him by calling him "Hally."

SAM: I've got no right to tell you what being a man means if I don't behave
like one myself, and I'm not doing so well at that this afternoon. Should we try
again, Hally?

HALLY: Try what?

SAM: Fly another kite, I suppose. It worked once, and this time I need it as
much as you do.

HALLY: It's still raining, Sam. You can't fly kites on rainy days, remember.

SAM: So what do we do? Hope for better weather tomorrow?

HALLY (helpless gesture): I don't know. I don't know anything any more.

SAM: You sure of that, Hally? Because it would be pretty hopeless if that was
true. It would mean nothing has been learnt in here this afternoon, and there was
a hell of a lot of teaching going on . . . one way or the other. But anyway, I don't
believe you. I reckon there's one thing you know. You don't *have* to sit up there
by yourself. You know what that bench means now, and you can leave it any time
you choose. All you've got to do is stand up, and walk away from it.

Without a word, Hally leaves. Willie comes over to reassure Sam that everything will be O.K. tomorrow. He even promises to tell Hilda he's sorry and not
to beat her any more. He will relax as they dance, and romance her, and they'll
carry off the first prize. Impulsively, Willie puts his only coin in the juke box—
he will walk home, but at least for this moment he will have a dream. Sam and
Willie dance to the music of Lena Horne singing "little boy, you had a busy day."
Curtain.

NINE

A Musical in Two Acts

BOOK BY ARTHUR KOPIT

MUSIC AND LYRICS BY MAURY YESTON

ADAPTATION FROM THE ITALIAN BY MARIO FRATTI

Cast and credits appear on page 338

ARTHUR KOPIT (book) was born on May 10, 1937 in New York City. He was educated at Lawrence, L.I. High School and Harvard (B.A. cum laude, 1959) where he began to write plays. Nine of them were produced from 1957 to 1960 by various groups: The Questioning of Nick, Gemini, On the Runway of Life You Never Know What's Coming Off Next, Across the River and Into the Jungle, Sing to Me Through Open Windows, Aubade, To Dwell in a Place of Strangers *and* Oh Dad, Poor Dad, Mamma's Hung You in the Closet and I'm Feelin' So Sad. *The latter was first staged by Cambridge, Mass. undergraduates in January 1960, then had a short run in its professional premiere in England during the summer of 1961, prior to its production off Broadway at the Phoenix Theater under the direction of Jerome Robbins on Feb. 26, 1962 for 454 performances. It was named a Best Play of its season (at which time its author was billing himself with a middle initial, Arthur L. Kopit) and won the Vernon Rice and Outer Circle*

Awards. Oh, Dad *was revived on Broadway Aug. 27, 1963 for 47 performances.*

A double bill of Kopit one-acters, The Day the Whores Came Out to Play Tennis *and* Sing to Me Through Open Windows *appeared off Broadway March 15, 1965 for 24 performances. His second Best Play,* Indians, *was given its world premiere by the Royal Shakespeare Company in London in July 1968, its American premiere at the Arena Stage in Washington, D.C. in May 1969 and its New York premiere on Broadway Jan. 3, 1970 for 96 performances. Kopit's third Best Play,* Wings, *had its world premiere in March 1978 at the Yale School of Drama, where its author was Adjunct Professor of Playwriting. With Constance Cummings creating the central role, this full-evening one-actor moved to a limited off-Broadway engagement of 15 performances June 21, 1978 at the Public Theater. On Dec. 5 it reopened in Boston and headed for Washington and Broadway, where it played 113 performances starting Jan. 28, 1979. Now Kopit receives his fourth Best Play citation for the authorship of the book of the musical* Nine *which opened on Broadway May 9, 1982, just in time to win the Tony Award for the best musical of the season.*

Kopit's other works for the theater have included What's Happened to the Thorne's House *(1972),* Conquest of Everest *and* Fame, the Hero *(OOB in 1973),* Louisiana Territory *(1975),* Secrets of the Rich *(1977 at the O'Neill Conference),* Good Help Is Hard to Find *(OOB in 1981) and three forthcoming works: a translation of Ibsen's* Ghosts, *a new play* Repongo *and a new musical* Eureka! *with his* Nine *collaborator, Maury Yeston. He has received Guggenheim, Rockefeller, National Endowment, CBS and other grants, as well as an award in literature from the American Academy of Arts and Letters. He is a member of the Council of the Dramatists Guild, the playwrights' organization, and lives in Connecticut with his wife Leslie Gariş, who is also a writer, and their three children.*

MAURY YESTON (music and lyrics) was born Oct. 23, 1945 in Jersey City, N.J. He received his B.A. at Yale in 1967, his M.A. at Clare College at Cambridge in England in 1969 and his Ph.D. in 1976 at Yale, where at present he is Associate Professor of Music Theory and Director of Undergraduate Studies. It was as an undergraduate at Yale that he began writing music. He contributed to college shows, and in his senior year his Movement for Cellos and Orchestra *was given its premiere performance by the Norwalk Symphony Orchestra with Yo Yo Ma as guest soloist. He wrote a children's musical based on the* Alice in Wonderland *material which was produced in 1970 at the Long Wharf Theater and the incidental music for the Best Play* Cloud 9 *off Broadway in 1981; but his Broadway musical* Nine, *for which he began writing songs at the Lehman Engel BMI Musical Theater Workshop in 1973, is his first major work for the theater.*

Yeston has published two books: The Stratification of Musical Rhythm *and* Readings in Schenker Analysis. *He and his family reside in Woodbridge, Conn.*

MARIO FRATTI (adaptation) was born in Italy at L'Aquila on July 5, 1927. The son of a laborer, he pursued his education in Italy all the way to a Ph.D. in philology from Ca'Foscari University in Venice in 1951. His playwriting career began in 1957 when he won a competition with his script The Doorbell, *and in the ensuing 25 years he has had 37 plays produced—among them* The Cage, Six Passionate Women *and* The Refrigerators—*in 18 languages in more than 300 theaters around the world. He adapted* Nine *into English from his own Italian version. It was selected for workshop presentation at the O'Neill Conference in 1979 and won the Richard Rodgers Production Award in 1981. In addition to his playwriting, Mr. Fratti currently serves as the New York drama critic for nine European newspapers.*

Our method of representing Nine *in these pages differs from that of the other* Best Plays. *The musical appears here in a series of photographs recording the overall "look" of a 1982 Broadway show, with its visually expressive concept and characters. The "story" of* Nine *proceeds as a series of relationships between an internationally renowned movie director (Raul Julia, the only adult male in the cast) and the women in his life. We have tried to illustrate all these relationships here, with quotes from the script.*

These photographs of Nine *depict scenes as produced by Michel Stuart, Harvey J. Klaris, Roger S. Berlind, James M. Nederlander, Francine LeFrak and Kenneth D. Greenblatt and as directed by Tommy Tune, as of the opening May 9, 1982 at the 46th Street Theater, with scenery by Lawrence Miller and costumes by William Ivey Long.*

Our special thanks are tendered to the producers and their press representatives Judy Jacksina, Glenna Freedman, Angela Wilson, Diane Tomlinson and Susannah Blinkoff for making available these selections from Peter Cunningham's excellent photographs of the show.

NINE

ACT I

1. Guido Contini (Raul Julia, *right*), celebrated movie director, is in crisis. The women in his life run riot in his imagination, though he tries to command them as though they were an orchestra and he a conductor. He is distracted from the realities of his marriage and his next film, rumored to be in trouble.

2. Guido's marriage is in trouble too. His wife Luisa (Karen Akers, *left*) resents his inattention and declares, "If you don't change your ways I am going to leave you." Guido proposes that they get away from it all together and collect their thoughts at the Fontane di Luna, a spa near Venice. But even in this retreat, reporters recognize and badger the famous director in front of his wife about his next movie and his love life. He identifies his problem in "Guido's Song": "My body's clearing 40 as my mind is nearing 10."

3. The spa's stark white-tiled interior is relieved only by a view of Venice through huge windows. Guido continues to see himself as a conductor of women including *(above)* new acquaintances—"The Germans at the Spa"—aided by his memory figure of himself at age 9 (Cameron Johann, *right*). Suddenly intruding upon this scene and throwing Guido deeper into confusion are his domineering French movie producer Liliane La Fleur (Liliane Montevecchi, wearing hat *below, left of center*) and her sinister masked henchwoman Lina Darling (Laura Kenyon). Guido pretends he is here to shoot Liliane's movie on location and has a great script in preparation.

4. Pestered by reporters about Guido's "friendship" with such as Carla Albanese (Anita Morris, *below right*), Luisa defends his ways, in the lyrics of the song "My Husband Makes Movies":

My husband makes movies.
To make them, he lives a kind of dream

In which his actions
        aren't always what they seem.
He may be on to some
        unique romantic theme.
Some men catch fish, some men tie flies,
Some earn their living baking bread.
My husband, he goes a little crazy
Making movies instead.

5. As Guido is confessing to Luisa that he doesn't have the idea for his next film, let alone a script, the phone rings. It's Carla (visible onstage as *at left*) singing to Guido from her bedroom:

Who's not wearing any clothes?
        I'm not, my darling.
Who's afraid to kiss your toes? I'm not.
Your momma dear is blowing into your ear
So you'll get it loud and clear.
I need you to squeeze me
        here . . . and here . . . and here.

Obviously flustered, Guido assures Luisa it's only "a call from the Vatican" about his movie.

6. The crew will arrive tomorrow to start building the sets for a Western? An epic? A documentary? Which? Guido, indecisive, is desperate. Luisa suggests warmly, pointedly, that they try a gondola ride. Guido, *"clearly turned on by her,"* sings "Only With You":

> Being just me is so easy to be when I'm only with you,
> Open inside and with nothing to hide from your view.
> Seems long ago I was destined to know,
> And the moment I saw you I knew
> I could be totally happy with no one but you.

The trouble is, in certain ways Guido feels the same about Claudia Nardi, his leading lady (Shelly Burch, *above center*), and Carla, who join Luisa in Guido's imagination.

7. Guido's producer Liliane *(above center and at left)* threatens to sue if he doesn't start the film on time. She demands to see a script, reminding Guido (to his acute distress) he promised to make a *musical,* his first. Liliane expresses her love for musicals in song and dance:

Folies Bergeres—
What a showing of color,
          costumes and dancing.
Not a moment in life
          could be more entrancing
Than an evening you spend
          aux Folies Bergeres. . . . .

Think of the footlights,
          bright and gleaming,
Le strip-tease, le can-can we all adore.
Life is too short without dreaming,
And dreams are what *le cinema* is for.

8. As the pressure mounts, Guido is increasingly haunted by memories of boyhood, age 9. Meanwhile, Carla insists that Guido visit her in her room, and Luisa goads him into doing so. But even in seductive Carla's presence, where she tells him her husband has finally consented to a divorce, visions of childhood intrude and take over in Guido's imagination.

In another part of the Spa, Guido's mother tells Luisa, "I know where Guido's problems began"—when he was sent to a parochial school in hopes that he'd become a priest. Instead, with three schoolboy companions, Guido discovered sex with the buxom Saraghina (Kathi Moss, *below*) who instructs the boys suggestively, in song: "Be Italian/You rapscallion. . . . . Please be gentle/Sentimental. . . . . But be daring/And uncaring. . . . . Live today as if it may become your last!"

9. Reprimanded by a nun for visiting Saraghina, little Guido protests that he didn't know it was wrong. Big Guido remembers these nun-dominated school days at St. Sebastian, especially the sound of its church bells:

> . . . . . The music of the ringing/Was the music of our singing
> When we were singing Kyrie Eleison, Kyrie Eleison, Kyrie Eleison.
> Each day at lauds, each night at vespers
> From the tower the hour would be tolled
> For those of us at St. Sebastian/No longer young, and not yet old.

Guido's mother asks the boy why he went to visit that woman, and Guido answers emphatically, "To see what she was like!" He breaks away from the nuns to wave at Saraghina, who waves back. *Curtain. End of Act I.*

10. Claudia *(above),* star of Guido's biggest hits, has arrived in Venice. Guido hopes she'll help him to make another hit film, but Claudia doesn't want to keep on playing that same healer-of-the-spirit role in all Guido's movies.

GUIDO: . . . . . I've lost something, I don't know what. But I know you can help me find it.
CLAUDIA: Inspiration.
GUIDO: Yes!
CLAUDIA: Guido, I was never your inspiration. That's what you imagine, but it was always you. I can't play this role for you any more. I've got my own life to think about.

(continued on the next page)

(continued from the preceding page)

GUIDO: This role made you a star!

CLAUDIA: Guido, I am not a spirit. I am real. I have a life you know nothing about. And never have shown the slightest interest in. I shouldn't have come here.

GUIDO: So why did you? . . . You came because I understand you like no other person does.

CLAUDIA: You don't understand me at all!

GUIDO: That just shows how much you know about yourself.

CLAUDIA: Guido, you have invented me! No such person exists!

GUIDO: In my mind, she exists. On the screen, she exists. And now, everywhere, in people's dreams, she exists.

CLAUDIA: I came because Luisa asked me to come. . . . . She called me in Paris. She said she didn't think she could help you any more. She thought maybe I could. Well, I can't.

Guido offers to change the role and tells Claudia he loves only her—but she calls him a Casanova who needs two or three women in his life. This plunges Guido into deep thought as Claudia sings, "In a very unusual way, one time I needed you/In a very unusual way, you were my friend/Maybe it lasted a day, maybe it lasted an hour/But somehow it will never end."

11. At last Guido has found his inspiration for a film: Casanova in a romantic farce, the idol of every female on the Grand Canal *(as above)*. He can cast everyone at the Spa, including "The Germans" (in photo *at left,* Dee Etta Rowe, Linda Kerns, Lulu Downs, Alaina Warren Zachary).

Guido directs his film through several musical numbers, including those pictured here, playing Casanova: "Amor, I love them all, every beauty/Short or tall, there's a duty/To make love to each and all." But the "movie" lapses into a confused, aimless mirror image of Guido's real emotional disarray—art reflecting life. Furthermore, the scene between Casanova and his wife Beatrice (played by Claudia) is a travesty which so infuriates Luisa that she walks off the set crying, "You've made a joke of my love!" Guido and company complete the disintegration in the film's finale:

> This is the Grand Canal.
> Its resemblance to life
> Is not obscure.
> It is filled with the milk
> Of human kindness,
> In spite of the fact
> That it's really a sewer.

12. Claudia (photo *at left*) has decided what she wants, and it isn't Guido or his movie roles. It's a career of genuine acting and a home with a handsome banker she knows in Paris. "Ciao, Guido," is her exit line as she leaves him.

13. Carla still wants Guido, but not merely as a lover. She wants him as a husband and has divorce papers to prove it. But Guido absolutely refuses to leave Luisa. Disappointed, Carla *(left)* sings to him: "Simple are the ways of love. . . . . Simple as a tree. . . . . Simple are the ways we say goodbye." Then she too departs with "Ciao, Guido."

Guido cries, "Luisa!" but it's too late. Luisa also has her song of departure to sing: "Be on your own /You've always talked about your need to travel/Now go off and unravel on your own. . . . . I set you free," free to go off and live his fantasies without her. She too takes her leave of Guido.

14. In despair, Guido admits, "I can't make this movie" and wishes that someone—Luisa or his mother—would help him. Liliane's aide, Lina, obliges by leaving a pistol at his side. He decides not to use it as Young Guido appears and Guido sings "Getting Tall":

Guido, you're not crazy, you're all right.
Everyone wants everyone in sight,
But knowing you have no one
                         if you try to have them all
Is part of tying shoes, part of starting school,
Part of scraping knees if we should fall . . .
Part of getting tall.

Guido's "orchestra" of women assembles, waiting for him to conduct as usual. Only Luisa's place is empty.

15. Guido's memory of "Long Ago" flashes through his mind in the form of a song: "Guido Contini, Luisa del Forno/Actress with dreams and a life of her own/Passionate, wild and in love in Livorno/Singing together all night on the phone/Long ago." While he is singing, Luisa appears in the distance. Guido hands his baton to Young Guido and runs to embrace Luisa. *Curtain.*

A GRAPHIC GLANCE

Roger Rees and David Threlfall in *The Life & Adventures of Nicholas Nickleby*

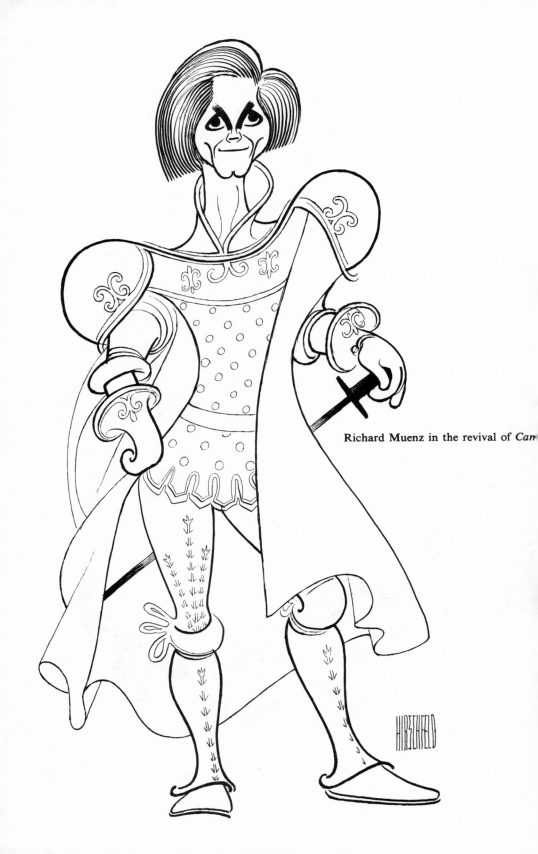

Richard Muenz in the revival of *Can*

John Lone in *The Dance and the Railroad*

Lizbeth Mackay in *Crimes of the Heart*

Elizabeth Ashley in *Agnes of God*

Raul Julia (surrounded by the 21 women in his life) in *Nine*

Victor Garber in the revival of *Little Me*

(From left) Sally Klein, Lonny Price, Jason Alexander, Jim Walton, Ann Morrison and Terry Finn in *Merrily We Roll Along*

Christopher Plummer (left) in the American Shakespeare Festival's production of *Henry V* (Stratford, Conn.) and Raul Julia in the New York Shakespeare Festival's production of *The Tempest*

James Earl Jones and Christopher Plummer in *Othello*

Tina Chen in *Family Devotions*

Lonny Price in *"MASTER HAROLD". . .and the boys*

John Wood in *Amadeus*

Katharine Hepburn and Dorothy Loudon in *The West Side Waltz*

Claudette Colbert in *A Talent for Murder*

Nancy Ringham, Rex Harrison and Milo O'Shea in the revival of *My Fair Lady*

Blanche Baker in *Poor Little Lambs*

Suzanne Pleshette and Richard Mulligan in *Special Occasions*

Betty Miller in *Eminent Domain*

Lee Richardson in *The Browning Version*

Elizabeth Franz in *Sister Mary
Ignatius Explains It All for You*

Zoe Caldwell and Judith Anderson in *Medea*

Robert Stattel in *The Cherry Orchard*

The cast of *Is There Life After High School?* (clockwise from top left): David Patrick Kelly, Alma Cuervo, James Widdoes, Maureen Silliman, Sandy Faison, Harry Groener, Cynthia Carle, Raymond Baker and Philip Hoffman

Adolph Caesar in *A Soldier's Play*

Cleavant Derricks in *Dreamgirls*

HIRSCHFELD

Estelle Getty in *Torch Song Trilogy*
and Harvey Fierstein, author and
star of the play

Barbara Bryne in *Entertaining Mr. Sloane*

Brooke Adams in *Key Exchange*

HIRSCHFELD

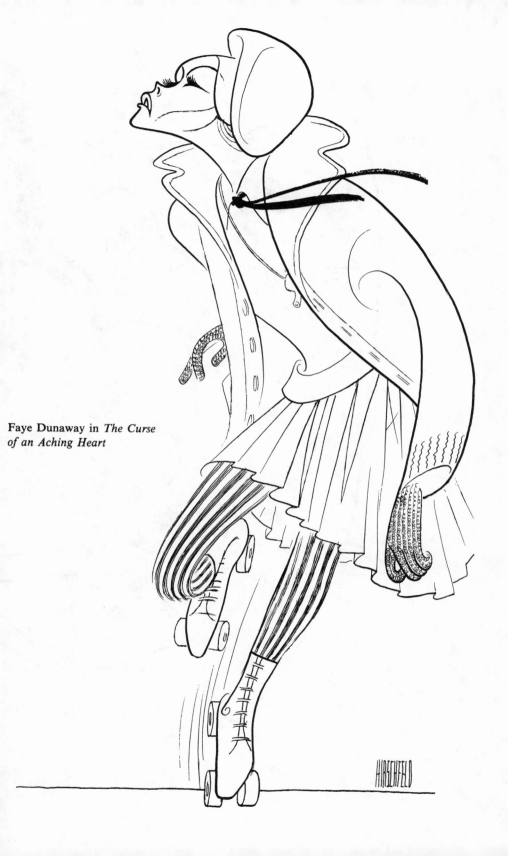

Faye Dunaway in *The Curse of an Aching Heart*

Clockwise from far right) Karen Black, Sandy Dennis, Sudie Bond, Kathy Bates, Marta
Ieflin, Cher and Mark Patton in *Come Back to the 5 & Dime Jimmy Dean, Jimmy Dean*

Bill Hutton *(left)* and Laurie Beechman
in the revival of *Joseph and the Amazing
Technicolor Dreamcoat*

Amanda Plummer *(above)* and Valerie
French in the revival of *A Taste of Honey*

Harold Gould in *Grown Ups*

Leo Burmester in *2 by South*

Deborah Burrell, Loretta Devine, Sheryl Lee
Ralph and Jennifer Holliday in *Dreamgirls*

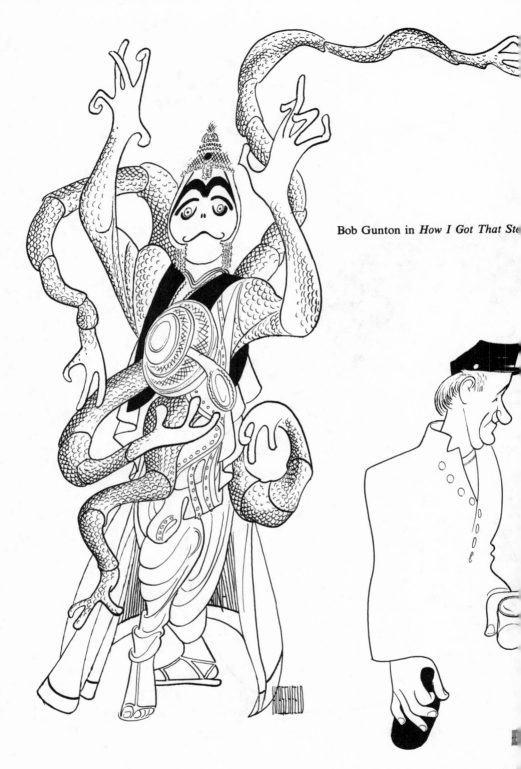

Bob Gunton in *How I Got That Ste*

Josef Sommer in *Lydie Bree*

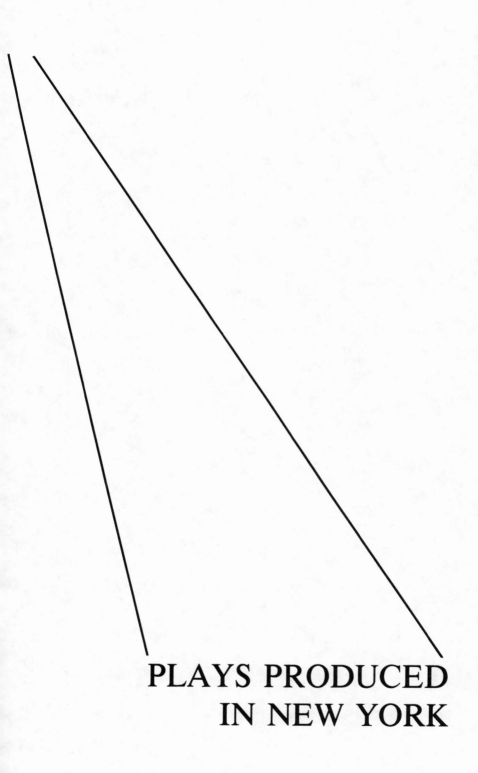

PLAYS PRODUCED
IN NEW YORK

PLAYS PRODUCED ON BROADWAY

Figures in parentheses following a play's title give number of performances. These figures are acquired directly from the production offices and do not include previews or extra non-profit performances. In the case of a transfer, the off-Broadway run is noted but not added to the figure in parentheses.

Plays marked with an asterisk (*) were still running on June 1, 1982. Their number of performances is figured through May 31, 1982.

In a listing of a show's numbers—dances, sketches, musical scenes, etc.—the titles of songs are identified wherever possible by their appearance in quotation marks (").

HOLDOVERS FROM PREVIOUS SEASONS

Plays which were running on June 1, 1981 are listed below. More detailed information about them appears in previous *Best Plays* volumes of appropriate years. Important cast changes since opening night are recorded in the Cast Replacements section of this volume.

*A Chorus Line (2,825). Musical conceived by Michael Bennett; book by James Kirkwood and Nicholas Dante; music by Marvin Hamlisch; lyrics by Edward Kleban. Opened April 15, 1975 off Broadway where it played 101 performances through July 13, 1975; transferred to Broadway July 25, 1975.

*Oh! Calcutta! (2,391). Revival of the musical devised by Kenneth Tynan; with contributions (in this version) by Jules Feiffer, Dan Greenberg, Lenore Kandel, John Lennon, Jacques Levy, Leonard Melfi, David Newman and Robert Benton, Sam Shepard, Clovis Trouille, Kenneth Tynan and Sherman Yellen; music and lyrics (in this version) by Robert Dennis, Peter Schickele and Stanley Walden; additional music by Stanley Walden and Jacques Levy. Opened September 24, 1976 in alternating performances with *Me and Bessie* through December 7, 1976, continuing alone thereafter.

*Annie (2,129). Musical based on the Harold Gray comic strip *Little Orphan Annie;* book by Thomas Meehan; music by Charles Strouse; lyrics by Martin Charnin. Opened April 21, 1977.

Gemini (1,788). By Albert Innaurato. Opened March 13, 1977 off Broadway where it played 63 performances through May 1, 1977; transferred to Broadway May 21, 1977. (Closed September 5, 1981)

*Deathtrap (1,809). By Ira Levin. Opened February 26, 1978.

*Dancin' (1,742). Musical with music and lyrics by Johann Sebastian Bach, Ralph Burns, George M. Cohan, Neil Diamond, Bob Haggart, Ray Bauduc, Gil Rodin and Bob Crosby, Jerry Leiber and Mike Stoller, Johnny Mercer and Harry Warren, Louis Prima, John Philip Sousa, Carole Bayer Sager and Melissa Manchester, Barry Mann and

Cynthia Weil, Felix Powell and George Asaf, Cat Stevens, Edgar Varèse and Jerry Jeff Walker. Opened March 27, 1978.

Ain't Misbehavin' (1,604). Musical revue with music by Fats Waller; based on an idea by Murray Horwitz and Richard Maltby Jr. Opened May 9, 1978. (Closed February 21, 1982)

***The Best Little Whorehouse in Texas** (1,577). Musical with book by Larry L. King and Peter Masterson; music and lyrics by Carol Hall. Opened April 17, 1978 off Broadway where it played 64 performances through June 11, 1978; transferred to Broadway June 19, 1978. (Closed March 27, 1982 after 1,576 performances) Reopened May 31, 1982.

They're Playing Our Song (1,082). Musical with book by Neil Simon; music by Marvin Hamlisch; lyrics by Carole Bayer Sager. Opened February 11, 1979. (Closed September 6, 1981)

The Elephant Man (916). By Bernard Pomerance. Opened January 14, 1979 off Broadway where it played 73 performances through March 18, 1979; transferred to Broadway April 19, 1979. (Closed June 28, 1981)

***Evita** (1,121). Musical with music by Andrew Lloyd Webber; lyrics by Tim Rice. Opened September 25, 1979.

***Sugar Babies** (1,105). Burlesque musical conceived by Ralph G. Allen and Harry Rigby; sketches by Ralph G. Allen based on traditional material. Opened October 8, 1979.

Children of a Lesser God (887). By Mark Medoff. Opened March 30, 1980. (Closed May 16, 1982)

Morning's at Seven (564). Revival of the play by Paul Osborn. Opened April 10, 1980. (Closed August 16, 1981)

Barnum (854). Musical with book by Mark Bramble; music by Cy Coleman; lyrics by Michael Stewart. Opened April 30, 1980. (Closed May 16, 1982)

A Day in Hollywood/A Night in the Ukraine (588). Two-part musical with book by Dick Vosburgh; music by Frank Lazarus and others. Opened May 1, 1980. (Closed September 27, 1981)

***42nd Street** (729). Musical based on the novel by Bradford Ropes; book by Michael Stewart and Mark Bramble; music and lyrics by Harry Warren and Al Dubin; other lyrics by Johnny Mercer and Mort Dixon. Opened August 25, 1980.

Fifth of July (511). Return engagement of the play by Lanford Wilson. Opened November 5, 1980. (Closed January 24, 1982)

Lunch Hour (262). By Jean Kerr. Opened November 12, 1980. (Closed June 28, 1981).

***Amadeus** (605). By Peter Shaffer. Opened December 17, 1981.

***The Pirates of Penzance** (599). Revival of the operetta with book and lyrics by W.S. Gilbert; music by Arthur Sullivan. Opened July 15, 1980 off Broadway (Delacorte Theater) where it played 42 performances; transferred to Broadway January 8, 1981.

Piaf (165). By Pam Gems. Opened February 5, 1981. (Closed June 28, 1981)

***Sophisticated Ladies** (521). Musical revue conceived by Donald McKayle; based on the music of Duke Ellington. Opened March 1, 1981.

America (264). Musical spectacle conceived by Robert F. Jani; dialogue script writer, Stan Hart; special material by Nan Mason; original music and lyrics by Don Pippin. Opened March 13, 1981. (Closed September 7, 1981)

*Woman of the Year (489). Musical based on the M-G-M film by Ring Lardner Jr. and Michael Kanin; book by Peter Stone; music by John Kander; lyrics by Fred Ebb. Opened March 29, 1981.

The Floating Light Bulb (65). By Woody Allen. Opened April 27, 1981. (Closed June 21, 1981).

The Little Foxes (126). Revival of the play by Lillian Hellman. Opened May 7, 1981. (Closed September 5, 1981)

It Had To Be You (48). By Renée Taylor and Joseph Bologna. Opened May 10, 1981. (Closed June 21, 1981)

*Lena Horne: The Lady and Her Music (308). Musical revue designed as a concert by Lena Horne. Opened May 12, 1981.

PLAYS PRODUCED JUNE 1, 1981–MAY 31, 1982

Wally's Cafe (12). By Sam Bobrick and Ron Clark. Produced by Barry M. Brown, Lita Starr, Steven Leber and David Krebs at the Brooks Atkinson Theater. Opened June 12, 1981. (Closed June 21, 1981)

Louise......................	Rita Moreno	Janet...................... Sally Struthers
Wally	James Coco	

Standby: Misses Moreno, Struthers—Joan Welles.

Directed by Fritz Holt; scenery, Stuart Wurtzel; costumes, Albert Wolsky; lighting, Ken Billington; production stage manager, James Pentecost; press, Shirley Herz, Jan Greenberg.

Place: A roadside cafe in the California desert. Act I, Scene 1: Summer 1940. Scene 2: Summer 1958. Act II: Summer—the present.

Comedy, a life in a roadside cafe near Las Vegas.

This Was Burlesque (28). Return engagement of the musical satire based on Ann Corio's recollections. Produced by MPI Productions, Ltd. and Jeff Satkin, Inc. at the Princess Theater. Opened June 23, 1981. (Closed July 17, 1981)

Lili Chanel	Charlie Naples
Ann Corio	Patrick
Phil Ford	Tami Roche
Jerry Kurland	Marilyn Simon
Dexter Maitland	Frank Vohs
Claude Mathis	

Burley Cuties: Diane Gallagher, Bonnie Wintz, Sharon Longo, Kathleen De Freest, Rusty Reigelman, Treva Hill, Christine Chulick, Erin Lareau, Tami Roche.

Supervised and directed by Ann Corio; musical conductor, Richard De Mone; choreography, Fred Albee; costumes, Rex Huntington; production manager, Peter H. Russell; press, Max Eisen, Lenny Traube.

Ann Corio's burlesque-style production originally presented off Broadway 3/6/62, transferring to Broadway 3/16/65 for 124 performances. The play was presented in two acts.

Amanda Plummer in *A Taste of Honey*

A Taste of Honey (157). Transfer from off Broadway of the revival by Shelagh Delaney. Produced by Roundabout Theater Company, Gene Feist and Martin Fried producing directors, at the Century Theater. Opened June 24, 1981. (Closed November 8, 1981)

Helen	Valerie French	Boy	Tom Wright
Jo	Amanda Plummer	Geoffrey	Keith Reddin
Peter	John Carroll		

Directed by Tony Tanner; scenery, Roger Mooney; costumes, A. Christina Giannini; lighting, Robert W. Mogel; sound, Philip Campanella; production stage manager, Howard Kolins; press, Susan Bloch & Co.

Place: Salford, Lancashire. The play was presented in two parts.

This revival of *A Taste of Honey* was produced off Broadway by the Roundabout 4/28/81 for 55 performances before transferring to Broadway.

Circle in the Square. 1980–81 schedule concluded with **Scenes and Revelations** (29). By Elan Garonzik. Produced by Circle in the Square, Theodore Mann artistic director, Paul

Libin managing director, at Circle in the Square. Opened June 25, 1981. (Closed July 19, 1981)

The Man; Samuel; Mr. Martin;		Millie	Marilyn McIntyre
Dr. Ziegler; Dennis Houser. .	Norman Snow	Uncle Jacob	Joseph Warren
Helena	Christine Lahti	Charlotte	Mary-Joan Negro
Rebecca	Valerie Mahaffey	Mr. Karonk	Nicholas Saunders

Directed by Sheldon Epps; scenery, Jane Thurn; costumes, Oleska; lighting, William Armstrong; stage manager, Rick Ralston; press, Merle Debuskey, David Roggensack.

Four sisters trying to escape from the limitations of their lives in the 1890s in Lancaster, Pa. The play was presented in two acts.

Fiddler on the Roof (53). Revival of the musical based on Sholom Aleichem's stories, by special permission of Arnold Perl; book by Joseph Stein; music by Jerry Bock; lyrics by Sheldon Harnick. Produced by James M. Nederlander and Eugene V. Wolsk at the New York State Theater. Opened July 9, 1981. (Closed August 23, 1981)

Tevye	Herschel Bernardi	Mordcha...................	Fyvush Finkel
Golde	Maria Karnilova	Rabbi	Alvin Myerovich
Tzeitel.................	Lori Ada Jaroslow	Mendel......................	Ken Leroy
Hodel	Donalyn Petrucci	Avram	Tog Richards
Chava.......................	Liz Larsen	Nachum	Ralph Vucci
Shprintze; Grandma Tzeitel. .	Susan Sheppard	Fruma-Sarah	Joyce Martin
Bielke	Eydie Alyson	Constable	Paul E. Hart
Yente	Ruth Jaroslow	Fyedka	Joel Robertson
Motel	Michelan Sisti	Shandel.....................	Bess Meisler
Perchik....................	James Werner	Fiddler	Jay Fox
Lazar Wolf.................	Paul Lipson	Yussel...................	Stephen Wright

Villagers: Bradford Dunaway, Jimmy Ferraro, Michael Fogarty, Margo F. Gruber, Michael Lane, Mark Manley, Elaine Manzel, Joyce Martin, Bess Meisler, Robert Parola, Thomas Scalise, Charles Spoerri, Marsha Tamaroff, Susan Tilson, Tim Tobin, Stephen Wright, Robert Yacko.

Standby: Mr. Bernardi—Paul Lipson. Understudies: Misses Karnilova, Ruth Jaroslow—Bess Meisler; Mr. Lipson—Fyvush Finkel; Miss Petrucci—Susan Tilson; Messrs. Robertson, Werner—Robert Yacko; Mr. Robertson (2d understudy)—Timothy Tobin; Messrs. Richards, Finkel—Tog Richards; Mr. Vucci—Vito Durante; Mr. Hart—Charles Spoerri; Miss Martin—Margo F. Gruber; Mr. Sisti—Stephen Wright; Swing Dancers—Frank Colardo, Debra Timmons.

Directed and choreographed by Jerome Robbins; associate director, Ruth Mitchell; musical direction, Richard Vitzhum; scenery, Boris Aronson; costumes, Patricia Zipprodt; lighting, Ken Billington; music supervisor, Kevin Farrell; choreography reproduced by Tom Abbott; orchestrations, Don Walker; vocal arrangements, Milton Greene; dance music arranged by Betty Walberg; associate producer, Stella Saltonstall; production stage manager, Ed Preston; stage manager, Sally Hassenfelt; press, Alpert/LeVine, Mark Goldstaub.

Fiddler on the Roof was first produced on Broadway 9/22/64 for 3,242 performances (second longest run in Broadway history) and was named a Best Play of its season and won the Critics Award for best musical. It was revived in June 1974 at Jones Beach Marine Theater and on Broadway 12/28/76 for 167 performances.

The list of musical numbers in *Fiddler on the Roof* appears on page 303 of *The Best Plays of 1964–65.*

The Supporting Cast (36). By George Furth. Produced by Terry Allen Kramer, James M. Nederlander and 20th Century-Fox at the Biltmore Theater. Opened August 6, 1981. (Closed September 5, 1981)

Ellen......................	Hope Lange	Arnold	Jack Gilford
Mae.......................	Betty Garrett	Florrie..................	Joyce Van Patten
Sally	Sandy Dennis		

Standbys: Misses Garrett, Van Patten—Chevi Colton; Misses Lange, Dennis—Claiborne Cary.
Directed by Gene Saks; scenery, William Ritman; costumes, Jane Greenwood; lighting, Richard Nelson; production stage manager, Martin Herzer; stage manager, Wayne Carson; press, Bill Evans and Associates, Sandra Manley, Howard Atlee.
Time: The present. Place: A beach house in Malibu, Calif. The play was presented in two parts.
Comedy, author embarrasses her friends by writing a revealing book about them.

My Fair Lady (119). Revival of the musical based on *Pygmalion* by George Bernard Shaw; book and lyrics by Alan Jay Lerner; music by Frederick Loewe. Produced by Don Gregory and Mike Merrick at the Uris Theater. Opened August 18, 1981. (Closed November 29, 1981)

Mrs. Eynsford-Hill . . . . Harriet Medin	Bartender; Major-Domo . . David Cale Johnson
Eliza Doolittle . . . . Nancy Ringham	Alfred P. Doolittle . . . . Milo O'Shea
Freddy Eynsford-Hill . . . . . . Nicholas Wyman	Mrs. Pearce . . . . Marian Baer
Col. Pickering . . . . Jack Gwillim	Mrs. Hopkins;
Henry Higgins . . . . Rex Harrison	Lady Boxington . . . . Mary O'Brien
Selsey Man; Harry . . . . Gary Gage	Butler . . . . Frank Bouley
Hoxton Man; Jamie;	Mrs. Higgins . . . . Cathleen Nesbitt
Ambassador . . . . Clifford Fearl	Chauffeur; Constable . . . . Alan Gilbert
Bystander . . . . Joseph Billone	Lord Boxington . . . . Richard Ammon
Bystander; 2d Cockney . . . . Ned Coulter	Flower Girl . . . . Karen Toto
1st Cockney; Footman . . . . John Caleb	Zoltan Karpathy . . . . Jack Sevier
3d Cockney; Footman;	Queen of Transylvania . . . . . . Svetlana McLee
Bartender. . . . . Ned Peterson	Grody
4th Cockney . . . . Jeffrey Calder	Mrs. Higgins's Maid . . Elizabeth Worthington

Buskers: Eric Alderfer, Alan Gilbert, Lisa Guignard. Servants: Jeralyn Glass, David Miles, Ellen McLain, Judith Thiergaard.
Singing Ensemble: Frank Bouley, Jeffrey Calder, John Caleb, Ned Coulter, Diana Lynne Drew, Julie Ann Fogt, Terri Gervais, Jeralyn Glass, David Cale Johnson, Michael McGifford, Ellen McLain, David Miles, Mary O'Brien, Ned Peterson, Cynthia Sophiea, Judith Thiergaard.
Dancing Ensemble: Eric Alderfer, Richard Ammon, Joseph Billone, Arlene Columbo, Ron Crofoot, Raul Gallyot, Alan Gilbert, Svetlana McLee Grody, Lisa Guignard, Scott Harris, Lynn Keeton, James Boyd Parker, Karen Paskow, Karen Toto, Elizabeth Worthington.
Standbys: Mr. Harrison—Michael Allinson; Miss Ringham—Valerie Lee. Understudies: Mr. Gwillim—Clifford Fearl; Mr. Wrigley—Gary Gage; Misses Nesbitt, O'Brien—Harriet Medin; Misses Baer, Medin—Mary O'Brien; Mr. Wyman—Jeffrey Calder; Mr. Gage—Jack Sevier; Messrs. Sevier, Fearl—Frank Bouley. Ensemble Alternates: Scott Harris, Lynne Savage.
Directed by Patrick Garland; original production staged by Moss Hart; musical staging and choreography, Crandall Diehl; based on the original by Hanya Holm; musical direction, Franz Allers; scenery, Oliver Smith; costumes, Cecil Beaton; co-costume designer, John David Ridge; lighting, Ken Billington; sound, John McClure; orchestra conductor, Robert Kreis; musical arrangements, Robert Russell Bennett, Phil Lang; stage managers, Jack Welles, William Weaver; press, Seymour Krawitz, Patricia McLean Krawitz, Janet Tom.
My Fair Lady was first produced 3/15/56 for 2,717 performances and was named a Best Play of its season and won the Critics Award for best musical. It has been revived previously in New York 5/20/64 for 47 performances, 6/13/68 for 22 performances and 3/25/76 for 377 performances.
The synopsis of scenes and list of musical numbers in *My Fair Lady* appear on pages 378–9 of *The Best Plays of 1955–56*.
Ben Wrigley replaced Milo O'Shea 9/22/81.

An Evening With Dave Allen (28). One-man performance by Dave Allen. Produced by Chartwell Communications, Inc. with Theater Now, Inc. at the Booth Theater. Opened September 20, 1981. (Closed October 17, 1981).

Jean-Pierre Aumont and Claudette Colbert in *A Talent for Murder*

Lighting, John Gleason; press, Lester Schecter, Barbara Schwei.
Stand-up comedy monologue by a star of BBC-TV. A foreign show previously produced in England and Australia.

A Talent for Murder (77). By Jerome Chodorov and Norman Panama. Produced by Edwin S. Lowe at the Biltmore Theater. Opened October 1, 1981. (Closed December 6, 1981)

Rashi	Shelly Desai	Lawrence McClain	Barton Heyman
Dr. Paul Marchand	Jean-Pierre Aumont	Sheila McClain	Nancy Addison Altman
Anne Royce McClain	Claudette Colbert	Mark Harrison	Stephen Burleigh
Pamela Harrison	Liane Langland		

Standby: Miss Colbert—Betty Low. Understudies: Misses Altman, Langland—Ann Convery; Messrs. Heyman, Burleigh—Leon Russom; Mr. Aumont—Maury Cooper.

Directed by Paul Aaron; scenery, Oliver Smith; costumes, David Murin; lighting, Ken Billington; Miss Colbert's costumes, Bill Blass; production stage manager, Robert Townsend; stage manager, Charles Kindl; press, Jeffrey Richards Associates, C. George Willard.

Place: The library-study of Twelve Oaks, Anne Royce McClain's estate in the foothills of the Berkshires not far from Tanglewood. Act I, Scene 1: Friday afternoon, 4 P.M. Scene 2: Same evening, after dinner. Scene 3: Saturday evening, 7:30 P.M. Scene 4: Saturday night, 9 P.M. Act II, Scene 1: Saturday midnight. Scene 2: Sunday afternoon, 5 P.M. Scene 3: Late that evening.

Comedy-mystery, woman writer of mystery stories copes with her acquisitive and designing family.

The Life & Adventures of Nicholas Nickleby (49 each of Parts I and II; 98 programs). By Charles Dickens; adapted by David Edgar. Produced by James M. Nederlander, The Shubert Organization, Elizabeth I. McCann and Nelle Nugent in The Royal Shakespeare Company production at the Plymouth Theater. Opened October 4, 1981. (Closed January 3, 1982)

The Nickleby Family:
Nicholas Nickleby .... Roger Rees
Kate Nickleby............. Emily Richard
Ralph Nickleby........... John Woodvine
Mrs. Nickleby........... Priscilla Morgan
London:
Newman Noggs ...... Edward Petherbridge
Hanna .... Hilary Townley
Miss La Creevy .... Rose Hill
Sir Matthew Pupker. . David Lloyd Meredith
Mr. Bonney............. Andrew Hawkins
Irate Gentleman .... Patrick Godfrey
Flunkey .... Timothy Knightley
Mr. Snawley .... William Maxwell
Snawley Major .... Janet Dale
Snawley Minor .... Hilary Townley
Belling .... Stephen Rashbrook
William .... John McEnery
Waitresses ..... Sharon Bower, Sally Nesbitt
Coachman .... Clyde Pollitt
Mr. Mantalini............. John McEnery
Mme. Mantalini .... Thelma Whiteley
Flunkey .... Richard Simpson
Miss Knag................... Janet Dale
Rich Ladies.... Sharon Bower, Shirley King
Milliners: Suzanne Bertish, Sharon Bower,
Lucy Gutteridge, Cathryn Harrison, Ian
East, William Maxwell, Sally Nesbitt, Stephen
Rashbrook, Hilary Townley.
Yorkshire:
Mr. Squeers............. Alun Armstrong
Mrs. Squeers................. Lila Kaye
Smike................... David Threlfall
Phib...................... Sally Nesbitt
Fanny Squeers .... Suzanne Bertish
Young Wackford Squeers ..... Ian McNeice
John Browdie .... Bob Peck
Tilda Price .... Cathryn Harrison
Boys:
Tomkins .... William Maxwell
Coates............... Andrew Hawkins
Graymarsh .... Alan Gill
Jennings .... Patrick Godfrey
Mobbs......... Christopher Ravenscroft
Bolder.................... Mark Tandy
Pitcher .... Sharon Bower
Jackson............... Nicholas Gecks
Cobbey .... John McEnery
Peters .... Teddy Kempner
Sprouter .... Lucy Gutteridge
Roberts..................... Ian East
London Again:
Mr. Kenwigs............. Patrick Godfrey
Mrs. Kenwigs............... Shirley King
Morleena Kenwigs .... Hilary Townley
Mr. Lillyvick......... Timothy Knightley
Miss Petowker .... Cathryn Harrison

Mr. Crowl.................... Ian East
George...................... Alan Gill
Mr. Cutler................. Jeffery Dench
Mrs. Cutler.................. Janet Dale
Mrs. Kenwigs's Sister .... Sharon Bower
Lady From Downstairs .... Rose Hill
Miss Green .... Priscilla Morgan
Benjamin................. Teddy Kempner
Pugstyles .... Roderick Horn
Old Lord............... Richard Simpson
Young Fiancee .... Lucy Gutteridge
Landlord .... Jeffery Dench
Portsmouth:
Mr. Vincent Crummles .... Christopher
                               Benjamin
Mrs. Crummles............... Lila Kaye
The Infant Phenomenon ... Hilary Townley
Master Percy Crummles ... Teddy Kempner
Master Crummles........... Mark Tandy
Mrs. Grudden.................. Rose Hill
Miss Snevellicci........... Suzanne Bertish
Mr. Folair.................. Clyde Pollitt
Mr. Lenville ...... Christopher Ravenscroft
Miss Ledrock .... Lucy Gutteridge
Miss Bravassa.............. Sharon Bower
Mr. Wagstaff............... Alun Armstrong
Mr. Blightey .... Jeffery Dench
Miss Belvawney .... Janet Dale
Miss Gazingi................ Sally Nesbitt
Mr. Pailey............. William Maxwell
Mr. Hetherington .... Andrew Hawkins
Mr. Bane............ Stephen Rashbrook
Mr. Fluggers........... Richard Simpson
Mrs. Lenville................ Shirley King
Mr. Curdle .... Hubert Rees
Mrs. Curdle............... Emily Richard
Mr. Snevellicci .... John McEnery
Mrs. Snevellicci.......... Thelma Whiteley
London Again:
Scaley..................... Ian McNeice
Tix .... Teddy Kempner
Sir Mulberry Hawk .... Bob Peck
Lord Frederick Verisopht .. Nicholas Gecks
Mr. Pluck .... Teddy Kempner
Mr. Pyke................... Mark Tandy
Mr. Snobb....... Christopher Ravenscroft
Col. Chowser .... Timothy Knightley
Brooker .... Clyde Pollitt
Mr. Wititterley .... Roderick Horn
Mrs. Wititterley .... Janet Dale
Alphonse............. Stephen Rashbrook
Opera Singers: Sharon Bower, Andrew
Hawkins, John Woodvine.
Charles Cheeryble.... David Lloyd Meredith
Ned Cheeryble........... Hubert Rees
Tim Linkinwater......... Richard Simpson
Man Next Door .... Patrick Godfrey

Keeper.................... Alan Gill		Westwood................... Alan Gill
Frank Cheeryble... Christopher Ravenscroft		Croupier.................. Ian McNeice
Nurse................ Thelma Whiteley		Casino Proprietor........ Patrick Godfrey
Arthur Gride............. Jeffery Dench		Surgeon............... Timothy Knightley
Madeline Bray.......... Lucy Gutteridge		Umpire................ Roderick Horn
Walter Bray....... Christopher Benjamin		Policemen.. Andrew Hawkins, Mark Tandy
Peg Sliderskew.......... Suzanne Bertish		Mrs. Snawley................ Janet Dale
Hawk's Rival....... Edward Petherbridge		Young Woman.......... Hilary Townley
Capt. Adams............ Andrew Hawkins		

Musicians: Donald Johnson conductor, piano; Mel Rodnon flute; Seymour Press clarinet; Ethan Bauch bassoon; Lowell Hershey, Robert Zittola trumpet; Christine Snyder french horn; Daniel Repole trombone; Sandra Billingslea violin; Karen Ritscher viola; Doc Solomon bass; Bruce Yuchitel banjo; Jack Jennings percussion. Wedding anthem sung by Choristers (Master of Choir, Barry Rose) from St. Paul's Cathedral.

Understudies: Catherine Brandon, Wilfred Grove, Katherine Levy.

Directed by Trevor Nunn and John Caird, assisted by Leon Rubin; music and lyrics, Stephen Oliver; scenery, John Napier, Dermot Hayes; costumes, John Napier; lighting, David Hersey; American production designed in association with Neil Peter Jampolis (scenery, costumes), Beverly Emmons (lighting), Richard Fitzgerald (sound); musical direction, Donald Johnston; production stage manager, Robert Bennett; stage managers, Sally Greenhut, Michael Townsend, David Proctor, Simon Hooper, Hilary Groves; press, Solters/Roskin/Friedman, Joshua Ellis, Louise Weiner Ment, Becky Flora, David LeShay, Cindy Valk.

The play was presented in two parts, the first with one intermission and the second with two intermissions.

Staging of virtually all the episodes of the Dickens novel in an 8½-hour production by The Royal Shakespeare Company with 42 actors in 138 speaking roles (listed above in the order of appearance). A foreign play previously produced in London.

A Best Play; see page 116.

Marlowe (48). Musical with book by Leo Rost; music by Jimmy Horowitz; lyrics by Leo Rost and Jimmy Horowitz. Produced by Tony Conforti in a John Annunziato production co-produced by Robert R. Blume in association with Billy Gaff and Howard P. Effron at the Rialto Theater. Opened October 12, 1981. (Closed November 22, 1981)

Queen Elizabeth I....... Margaret Warncke		William Shakespeare.... Lennie Del Duca Jr.
Audrey Walsingham....... Debra Greenfield		Emelia Bossana............. Lisa Merdente
Capt. Townsend................ Steve Hall		Christopher Marlowe......... Patrick Jude
Archbishop Parker......... Raymond Serra		Ingram Frizer............... Robert Rosen
Richard Burbage......... John Henry Kurtz		

Chorus: Kenneth D. Ard, Marlene Danielle, Robert Hoshour, Renee Dulaney, Timothy Tobin, Teri Gibson, Diane Pennington, Caryn Richmond.

Band: Kinny Landrum director, piano; Don Rebic assistant conductor, keyboards; John Putnam, Bill Washer guitars; Chico Rindner bass; Frank Vilardi drums, percussion.

Understudies: Mr. Jude—James Sbano; Misses Mordente, Greenfield—Diane Pennington; Mr. Del Duca—Robert Hoshour; Miss Warncke—Teri Gibson; Mr. Kurtz—Steve Hall; Mr. Hall—Timothy Tobin; Swings—Kathey Jennings, Willie Rosario.

Directed by Don Price; musical direction, Kinny Landrum; scenery, Cary Chalmers; lighting, Mitch Acker, Rick Belzer; costumes, Natalie Walker; sound, Peter Fitzgerald; orchestrations, Jimmy Horowitz; musical supervision, Larry Fallon; vocal arrangements, Jimmy Horowitz, Patrick Jude; choral direction, Billy Cunningham; fight choreography, Peter Moore; production associate, Leon Gast; associate producer, Raymond Serra; production stage manager, Alisa Adler; stage manager, Bo Metzler; press, Max Eisen, Alan Eichler, Maria Somma.

Time: 1593 A.D. Place: England. Act I, Scene 1: Queen Elizabeth's bedchamber, May 28, late morning. Scene 2: Backstage at the Globe Theater, a few hours later. Scene 3: The Mall near St. James's Palace during the Jubilee Festival; Scene 4: Sir Walter Raleigh's observatory, that evening.

Scene 5: The Privy Council Chamber at St. James's Palace, May 30, morning. Act II, Scene 1: Eleanor Bull's tavern at Deptford, May 30, early evening. Scene 2: Deptford waterfront docks, May 30, later that evening. Scene 3: The courtyard at St. James's Palace, a few days later.

Rock musical biography of Christopher Marlowe.

ACT I

Prologue .... Chroniclers
"Rocking the Boat" .... Parker, Queen, Townsend, Chorus
"Because I'm a Woman" .... Emelia, Shakespeare, Burbage
"Live for the Moment" .... Marlowe, Company
"Emelia" .... Shakespeare, Marlowe
"I'm Coming 'Round to Your Point of View" .... Marlowe, Emelia
"The Ends Justify the Means" .... Frizer, Audrey
"Higher Than High" .... Marlowe, Emelia, Burbage, Shakespeare, Chorus
"Rocking the Boat" (Reprise)... Company

ACT II

Prologue .... Chroniclers
"Christopher" .... Emelia, Chorus
"So So I" (Ode to Virginity)... Burbage, Chorus
"Two Lovers"... Emelia
"The Funeral Dirge" .... Burbage, Emelia, Shakespeare, Frizer, Townsend, Queen
"Live for the Moment" (Reprise)..................................... Marlowe, Emelia
"Emelia" (Reprise)... Marlowe, Emelia
"Can't Leave Now" .... Marlowe
"Christopher" (Reprise)........................... Emelia, Shakespeare, Company
"The Madrigal Blues" .... Marlowe, Company

Circle in the Square. Schedule of three programs. **Candida** (92). Revival of the play by George Bernard Shaw. Opened October 15, 1981. (Closed January 2, 1982) **Macbeth** (21). By William Shakespeare. Opened January 28, 1982. (Closed February 14, 1982) **Eminent Domain** (49). By Percy Granger. Opened March 28, 1982. (Closed May 23, 1982) Produced by Circle in the Square, Theodore Mann artistic director, Paul Libin managing director, at Circle in the Square.

CANDIDA

Proserpine Garnett .... Jane Curtin   Mr. Burgess .... Ronald Bishop
Rev. James Mavor Morell ...... Ron Parady   Candida .... Joanne Woodward
Maria .... Mary Jay   Eugene Marchbanks .... Tait Ruppert
Rev. Alexander Mill .... John Gilliss

Standby: Miss Woodward—Mary Jay. Understudies: Messrs. Parady, Bishop—C.B. Anderson; Misses Curtin, Jay—Allison Mackie; Messrs. Ruppert, Gilliss—Courtney Burr.

Directed by Michael Cristofer; scenery, Kenneth Foy; costumes, Richard Hornung; lighting, Paul Gallo; produced by special arrangement with Kenyon Festival Theater; stage managers, Michael F. Ritchie, Allison Mackie; press, Merle Debuskey, David Roggensack.

Time: A day in the spring of 1905. Place: The home of the Rev. James Mavor Morell. Act I: Morning. Act II: Afternoon. Act III. Evening.

The last New York revival of *Candida* took place off Broadway at Roundabout Theater 12/15/78 for 115 performances.

Ann Willis replaced Jane Curtin 12/8/81.

MACBETH

1st Witch; Gentlewoman ..... Elaine Bromka   3d Witch .... Tara Lowenstern
2d Witch .... Bette Henritze   Duncan................. Tom McDermott

Malcolm.	Ray Dooley	Macduff	J.T. Walsh
Captain.	Richard Jamieson	Lennox	Peter Phillips
Ross	Paul Falzone	Donalbain.	Mark Herrier
Macbeth	Nicol Williamson	Old Man.	Renato Cibelli
Banquo.	John Henry Cox	1st Murderer	Rik Colitti
Angus.	Gregory Mortensen	2d Murderer; Doctor	Peter McRobbie
Lady Macbeth	Andrea Weber	Lady Macduff	Joyce Fideor
Seyton.	Paul Perri	Macduff's Son	Christian Slater
Fleance.	Peter James	Messenger.	John Wojda
Porter	Rand Bridges	Cream-Faced Loon	Neal Jones

Understudies and Standbys: Messrs. Williamson, Walsh—Richard Jamieson; Miss Weber—Tara Lowenstern; Mr. Dooley—Peter Phillips; Mr. Cox—Paul Falzone; Messrs. Phillips, Falzone, McRobbie (2d Murderer)—John Wojda; Messrs. Mortenson, Herrier, James—Neal Jones; Mr. Perri—Gregory Mortensen; Mr. McDermott—Renato Cibelli; Mr. Jamieson—Peter McRobbie; Miss Fideor—Elaine Bromka; Mr. Colitti—Mark Herrier; Mr. Bridges—Rik Colitti; Mr. Cibelli—Tom McDermott; Mr. Slater—Peter James; Mr. McRobbie (Doctor)—John Henry Cox; Miss Bromka—Bette Henritze.

Directed by Nicol Williamson; scenery, Kenneth Foy; costumes, Julie Weiss; lighting, William Armstrong; music, Guy Woolfenden; production stage manager, Michael F. Ritchie; stage manager, Ted William Sowa.

The play was presented without intermission in a running time of approximately two hours. The last major New York revival of *Macbeth* took place at Lincoln Center 1/22/81 for 53 performances.

EMINENT DOMAIN

Holmes Bradford.	Philip Bosco	Stoddard Oates	Scott Burkholder
Katie Bradford	Betty Miller	John Ramsey	Paul Collins
Victor Salt	John Vickery		

Directed by Paul Austin; scenery, Michael Miller; costumes, Jennifer Von Mayrhauser; lighting, Lowell Achziger; production stage manager, Michael F. Ritchie.

Time: February, 1975. Place: A university town in the Midwest. Act I, Scene 1: Late Tuesday night. Scene 2: Wednesday morning. Scene 3: Thursday afternoon. Act II, Scene 1: Thursday night. Scene 2: Friday morning. Scene 3: Friday evening.

College professor's troubled family relationships are exposed by an interviewer seeking information about his famous son. Previously produced at the O'Neill Theater Center and at the McCarter Theater, Princeton, N.J. and Peterborough, N.H.

Einstein and the Polar Bear (4). By Tom Griffin. Produced by Max Allentuck, Wayne M. Rogers, Warner Theater Productions, Inc., Ron Dante, Tommy Valando and Emanuel Azenberg at the Cort Theater. Opened October 29, 1981. (Closed October 31, 1981)

Andrew Allenson.	John Wardwell	Bill Allenson	Peter Strauss
Charlie Milton.	Robert Nichols	Helen Bullins.	Marjorie Lovett
Diane Ashe	Maureen Anderman	Bobby Bullins	David Strathairn

Standbys: Messrs. Strauss, Strathairn—Ron Frazier; Miss Anderman—Marsha Skaggs; Messrs. Wardwell, Nichols—James Cahill; Miss Lovett—Le Clanché du Rand.

Directed by J Ranelli; scenery, Fred Voelpel; costumes, Nancy Potts; lighting, Arden Fingerhut; production stage manager, Frank Marino; stage manager, Bill McIntyre; press, Bill Evans & Associates, Leslie Anderson, Jim Baldassare.

Time: During a raging February blizzard. Place: Spider Lake, a small New England town. Act I: Friday evening, Act II: The next morning.

Young woman takes refuge from a storm in a reclusive novelist's hideaway; romance ensues. Previously produced by the Hartford, Conn. Stage Company and the O'Neill Theater Center's National Playwrights Conference.

Betty Miller, John Vickery and Philip Bosco in *Eminent Domain*

Crimes of the Heart (239). Transfer of the play by Beth Henley. Produced by Warner Theater Productions, Inc./Claire Nichtern, Mary Lea Johnson, Martin Richards and Francine LeFrak at the John Golden Theater. Opened November 4, 1981.

Lenny MaGrath	Lizbeth Mackay	Meg MaGrath	Mary Beth Hurt
Chick Boyle	Sharon Ullrick	Babe Botrelle	Mia Dillon
Doc Porter	Raymond Baker	Barnette Lloyd	Peter MacNicol

Understudies: Misses Dillon, Ullrick—Susan Greenhill; Misses Hurt, Mackay—Caryn West; Messrs. Baker, MacNicol—Harley Venton.

Directed by Melvin Bernhardt; scenery, John Lee Beatty; costumes, Patricia McGourty; lighting, Dennis Parichy; associate producer, Ethel Watt; production stage manager, James Pentecost; press, Betty Lee Hunt, Maria Cristina Pucci, James Sapp.

Time: Five years after Hurricane Camille. Place: Hazelhurst, Miss. The play was presented in three parts.

Crimes of the Heart, a comedy-drama of three sisters making difficult adjustments to life, was previously produced in regional theater at the Actors' Theater of Louisville, Ky., The California Actors' Theater, Los Gatos, the Loretto-Hilton Theater in St. Louis and Center Stage, Baltimore; and off off Broadway at Manhattan Theater Club's Upstage Theater 12/21/80 for 35 performances and was named a Best Play of its season and won the Pulitzer Prize and the Critics Award for best American play.

Tim Choate replaced Peter MacNicol 2/1/82; Tom Stechschulte replaced Raymond Baker 2/16/82; Peter MacNicol replaced Tim Choate 5/18/82.

Ned and Jack (1). By Sheldon Rosen. Produced by Ken Marsolais, Martin Markinson, All Starr Productions, Inc. and Axbell Productions, Inc. at the Little Theater. Opened and closed at the evening performance November 8, 1981.

Edward (Ned Sheldon	John Vickery	Ethel Barrymore	Barbara Sohmers
Danny	Sean Griffin	John (Jack) Barrymore	Peter Michael Goetz

Directed by Colleen Dewhurst; scenery, James Leonard Jay; costumes, David Murin; lighting, Robby Monk; production stage manager, Richard Elkow; stage manager, Buzz Cohen; press, Shirley Herz, Sam Rudy, Peter Cromarty.

Time: After midnight, Nov. 17, 1922. Place: Ned Sheldon's New York penthouse apartment. The play was presented in two parts.

Famous actor and famous playwright (Sheldon) at the party following the opening of Barrymore's *Hamlet.* Previously produced off off Broadway at Hudson Guild Theater.

The Dresser (200). By Ronald Harwood. Produced by James M. Nederlander, Elizabeth I. McCann, Nelle Nugent, Warner Theater Productions, Inc. and Michael Codron at the Brooks Atkinson Theater. Opened November 9, 1981. (Closed May 1, 1982)

Norman	Tom Courtenay	Oxenby	Don McAllen Leslie
Her Ladyship	Rachel Gurney	Electrician	Geoff Garland
Madge	Marge Redmond	Kent	Jeffrey Alan Chandler
Sir	Paul Rogers	Gloucester	Leslie Barrett
Irene	Lisabeth Bartlett	Gentleman; Knight 2	Richard Frank
Geoffrey	Douglas Seale	Knight 1; Albany	Jerome Collamore

Standbys: Mr. Courtenay—Richard Frank; Mr. Rogers—Michael Egan. Understudies: Mr. Seale —Leslie Barrett; Mr. Leslie—Jeffrey Alan Chandler; Miss Bartlett—Michele Seyler; Messrs. Chandler, Barrett, Collamore—Geoff Garland.

Directed by Michael Elliott; scenery, Laurie Dennett; costumes, Stephen Doncaster; lighting, Beverly Emmons; sound, Ian Gibson; scenery supervision, Karen Schulz; costume supervision, Jeanne Button; sound supervision, T. Richard Fitzgerald; production stage manager, Steve Beckler; stage manager, Arlene Grayson; press, Joshua Ellis, Becky Flora, Solters/Roskin/Friedman, Inc., Cindy Valk.

Time: January, 1942. Place: A theater in the British provinces. Act I: Before curtain up. Act II: After curtain up.

The faltering star of a touring British troupe is goaded by his devoted dresser into playing *King Lear* one more time. A foreign play previously produced in England at Manchester and London. A Best Play; see page 127.

Oh, Brother! (3). Musical with book and lyrics by Donald Driver; music by Michael Valenti. Produced by Zev Bufman and The Kennedy Center with The Fisher Theater Foundation, Joan Cullman and Sidney Shlenker at the ANTA Theater. Opened November 10, 1981. (Closed November 11, 1981)

Camel	Steve Sterner, Eric Scheps	Eastern Mousada	David-James Carroll
Revolutionary Leader	Larry Marshall	Balthazar	Bruce Adler
Eastern Habim	Joe Morton	Bugler	Sal Provenza

Fatatatatatima	Alyson Reed	Saroyana	Judy Kaye
Lew	Richard B. Shull	Musica	Mary Mastrantonio
Western Mousada	Harry Groener	Ayatollah	Thomas LoMonaco
Western Habim	Alan Weeks	Lillian	Geraldine Hanning

Revolutionary Men: Steve Sterner, Eric Scheps, Michael-Pierre Dean, Thomas LoMonaco, Mark Martino, Steve Bourneuf. Revolutionary Women: Kathy Mahony-Bennett, Geraldine Hanning, Suzanne Walker, Pamela Khoury, Karen Teti.

Understudies: Mr. Adler—Sal Provenza; Mr. Provenza—Steve Bourneuf; Messrs. Morton, Weeks —Michael-Pierre Dean; Messrs. Carroll, Groener, Marshall—Mark Martino; Miss Kaye—Kathy Mahony-Bennett; Miss Mastrantonio—Pamela Khoury; Miss Reed—Suzanne Walker; Miss Hanning —Karen Teti; Mr. LoMonaco—Eric Scheps; Female Swing—Nancy Meadows; Male Swing—David Michael Lang.

Directed by Donald Driver; musical direction, vocal and dance arrangements, Marvin Laird; scenery, Michael J. Hotopp, Paul De Pass; costumes, Ann Emonts; lighting, Richard Nelson; sound, Richard Fitzgerald; orchestrations, Jim Tyler; assistant choreographer, Ahmed Hussien; production stage manager, Nicholas Russiyan; stage manager, Robert O'Rourke; press, Fred Nathan and Associates, Patt Dale, Eileen McMahon.

Time: Today. Place: The Persian Gulf. The play was presented without intermission.

Plot reminiscent of *The Comedy of Errors,* with overtones of Plautus, with two sets of twins, one white and one black, stranded in a modern Middle East setting.

MUSICAL NUMBERS

"We Love an Old Story"	Revolutionary Leader, Revolutionaries
"I to the World"	Mousada and Habim Twins
"That's Him"	Musica, Revolutionaries
"How Do You Want Me?"	Saroyana
"Everybody Calls Me by My Name"	Western Mousada, Revolutionaries
"Opec Maiden"	Western Mousada, Revolutionaries
"A Man"	Eastern Mousada
"How Do You Want Me?" (Reprise)	Saroyana
"Tell Sweet Saroyana"	Eastern Mousada, Western Habim, Arabs
"What Do I Tell People This Time?"	Saroyana
"Opec Maiden" (Reprise)	Musica, Women
The Chase	Company
"I to the World" (Reprise)	Mousada, Habim Twins
"Oh, Brother"	Company

Mass Appeal (214). Transfer from off Broadway of the play by Bill C. Davis. Produced by Elizabeth I. McCann, Nelle Nugent and Ray Larsen in association with Lynne Meadow, Barry Grove and Warner Theater Productions, Inc., in the Manhattan Theater Club production at the Booth Theater. Opened November 12, 1981. (Closed May 16, 1982)

Father Tim Farley	Milo O'Shea
Mark Dolson	Michael O'Keefe

Standbys: Mr. O'Shea—Malachy McCourt; Mr. O'Keefe—Charley Lang.

Directed by Geraldine Fitzgerald; scenery, David Gropman; costumes, William Ivey Long; lighting, F. Mitchell Dana; associate producer, Peter Jedlin; production stage manager, William Dodds; stage manager, William Chance; press, Solters/Roskin/Friedman, Inc., Joshua Ellis, David LeShay, Cindy Valk.

Time: Autumn. Place: The Church of St. Francis and Father Tim Farley's adjacent office. The play was presented in two parts.

Elderly priest is persuaded to look at himself and his calling with new eyes by an idealistic young seminarian. Previously produced off Broadway by Manhattan Theater Club 4/22/80 where it played 104 performances through 7/20/80.

A Best Play; see page 144.

Camelot (48). Return engagement of the revival of the musical based on *The Once and Future King* by T.H. White; book and lyrics by Alan Jay Lerner; music by Frederick Loewe. Produced by Mike Merrick and Don Gregory at the Winter Garden. Opened November 15, 1981. (Closed January 2, 1982)

King Arthur	Richard Harris	Lady Anne	Sally Williams
Sir Sagramore	Andy McAvin	Lady Sybil	Patrice Pickering
Merlyn	James Valentine	Sir Lionel	William James
Guenevere	Meg Bussert	King Pellinore	Barrie Ingham
Sir Dinidan	William Parry	Horrid	Daisy
Nimue	Jeanne Caryl	Sir Lionel's Squire	Steve Osborn
Lancelot Du Lac	Richard Muenz	Sir Sagramore's Squire	Randy Morgan
Mordred	Richard Backus	Sir Dinadan's Squire	Richard Maxon
Dap	Robert Molnar	Tom	Thor Fields
Friar	Vincenzo Prestia		

Knights of the Investiture: Bruce Sherman, Jack Starkey, Ken Henley, Ronald Bennett Stratton. Knights, Lords and Ladies of the Court: Elaine Barnes, Marie Berry, Bjarne Buchtrup, Jeanne Caryl, Melanie Clements, John Doyle, Debra Dickinson, Kathy Flynn-McGrath, Ken Henley, William James, Norb Joerder, Kelby Kirk, Dale Kristien, Lorraine Lazarus, Lauren Lipson, Craig Mason, Richard Maxon, Andy McAvin, Robert Molnar, Randy Morgan, Ann Neville, Steve Osborn, Patrice Pickering, Joel Sager, Mariellen Sereduke, D. Paul Shannon, Bruce Sherman, Jack Starkey, Ronald Bennett Stratton, Nicki Wood. Alternates: Ellyn Arons, Gary Wales.

Understudies: Mr. Harris—William Parry; Miss Bussert—Debra Dickinson; Mr. Muenz—Bruce Sherman; Mr. Ingham—James Valentine; Mr. Backus—Andy McAvin; Mr. Valentine—Robert Molnar; Miss Caryl—Sally Williams; Mr. Parry—D. Paul Shannon, Craig Mason; Mr. James—John Doyle; Mr. McAvin—Craig Mason; Mr. Molnar—Steve Osborn; Mr. Fields—Joel Sager.

Directed by Frank Dunlop; original direction by Moss Hart; choreography, Buddy Schwab; musical direction, Franz Allers; scenery and costumes, Desmond Heeley; lighting, Thomas Skelton; conductor, Terry James; sound, John McClure; orchestrations, Robert Russell Bennett, Phil Lang; musical coordinator, Robert Kreis; artistic consultant, Stone Widney; production stage manager, Alan Hall; stage manager, Steven Adler; press, Seymour Krawitz, Patricia McLean Krawitz.

This production of *Camelot* was presented at the New York State Theater in Lincoln Center with Richard Burton as Arthur 7/8/80 for 56 performances.

The list of scenes and musical numbers in *Camelot* appears on pages 345–6 of *The Best Plays of 1980–81*.

Merrily We Roll Along (16). Musical based on the play by George S. Kaufman and Moss Hart; book by George Furth; music and lyrics by Stephen Sondheim. Produced by Lord Grade, Martin Starger, Robert Fryer and Harold Prince at the Alvin Theater. Opened November 16, 1981. (Closed November 28, 1981)

Franklin Shepard	Jim Walton	Mr. Spencer	Paul Hyams
Mary Flynn	Ann Morrison	Mrs. Spencer	Mary Johanson
Charley Kringas	Lonny Price	Meg	Daisy Prince
Gussie	Terry Finn	Ru	Forest D. Ray
Joe	Jason Alexander	Bartender	Tom Shea
Beth	Sally Klein	Evelyn	Abby Pogrebin
Franklin Shepard (age 43)	Geoffrey Horne	Valedictorian	Giancarlo Esposito
Jerome	David Cady	George; Headwaiter	James Bonkovsky
Terry	Donna Marie Elio	Girl Auditioning	Marianna Allen
Ms. Gordon	Maryrose Wood	Nightclub Waitress	Liz Callaway
Alex; Talk Show Host	Marc Moritz	Photographer	Steven Jacob
Gwen Wilson	Tonya Pinkins	Soundman	Clark Sayre
Ted	David Loud	Waiter	Gary Stevens
Les	David Shine		

Understudies: Mr. Walton—David Cady; Miss Morrison—Liz Callaway; Mr. Price—David Loud; Mr. Alexander—James Bonkovsky; Miss Klein—Daisy Prince; Miss Finn—Marianna Allen; Swing—Janie Gleason.

Directed by Harold Prince; choreography, Larry Fuller; musical director, Paul Gemignani; scenery, Eugene Lee; costumes, Judith Dolan; lighting, David Hersey; orchestrations, Jonathan Tunick; sound, Jack Mann; associate producers, Ruth Mitchell, Howard Haines; production stage manager, Beverley Randolph stage manager, Richard Evans; press, Mary Bryant, Francine L. Trevens.

Successful musical comedy author reviews his life in backward time sequence, revealing that he has lost his youthful idealism as well as some of his cherished friends, based on the 1934 Kaufman-Hart play.

ACT I

1980. Lake Forest Academy, Lake Forest, Ill.
"Merrily We Roll Along" .... Company
1979. Franklin Shepard's house, Bel Air, Calif.
"Rich and Happy" .... Frank, Guests
1979-1976
"Merrily We Roll Along" (Reprise) .... Company
1975. The Polo Lounge of the Beverly Hills, Calif., Hotel
"Like It Was" .... Mary
1973. A TV studio, New York City
"Franklin Shepard, Inc." .... Charley
1973-1969.
"Merrily We Roll Along" (Reprise) .... Company
1968. Frank's apartment, Central Park West, New York City
"Old Friends" .... Frank, Charley Mary
1968-1966
"Merrily We Roll Along" (Reprise) .... Company
1966. Outside a courthouse, Centre Street
"Not a Day Goes By" .... Frank
"Now You Know" .... Mary, Company

ACT II

1964. Outside a theater
"It's a Hit!" .... Frank, Mary, Charley, Joe
1964-1962
"Merrily We Roll Along" (Reprise) .... Company
1962. Joe and Gussie's apartment, Sutton Place
"Good Thing Going" .... Charley, Frank
1961
"Merrily We Roll Along" (Reprise) .... Company
1960. A small night club in Greenwich Village
"Bobbie and Jackie and Jack" .... Charlie, Beth, Frank, Ted
"Not a Day Goes By" (Reprise) .... Frank, Mary
1959-1957. Frank and Charley's apartment; Joe Josephson's office, Manhattan
"Opening Doors" .... Frank, Charley, Mary, Joe, Beth
1957. A rooftop on West 110th Street
"Our Time" .... Frank, Charley, Mary, Company
1955. Lake Forest Academy
"The Hills of Tomorrow" .... Company

The First (37). Musical with book by Joel Siegel with Martin Charnin; music by Bob Brush; lyrics by Martin Charnin. Produced by Zev Bufman, Neil Bogart, Michael Harvey and Peter A. Bobley at the Martin Beck Theater. Opened November 17, 1981. (Closed December 13, 1981)

Red Barber...................... Himself
Huey; Sheriff .... Jack Hallett
Noonan................... George Wallace
Eunice..................... Patricia Drylie
Sorrentino; Umpire; Trainer..... Paul Forrest
Frog; Brian Waterhouse.......... Bill Buell
Leo Durocher .... Trey Wilson
Branch Rickey........... David Huddleston
Tommy Holmes........... Sam Stoneburner
Waiter; Hatrack Harris...... D. Peter Samuel
Jackie Robinson.......... David Alan Grier
Junkyard Jones;
   Dr. Johnson .... Luther Fontaine
3d Baseman;
   Equipment Manager.......... Steven Bland
Bucky; Redcap...... Michael Edward-Stevens
Cool Minnie Edwards........ Clent Bowers
Softball................... Paul Cook Tartt
Clyde Sukeforth.................. Ray Gill
Jo-Jo.................. Rodney Saulsberry
Rachel Isum............... Lonette McKee

Swanee Rivers .... Steven Boockvor
Casey Higgins .... Court Miller
Pee Wee Reese................ Bob Morrisey
Eddie Stanky;
   Brooklyn Trainer .... Stephen Crain
Dodger Coaches ..... Jack Hallett, Bill Buell
Dodger Rookie .... Thomas Griffith
Girls at the Bar.............. Kim Criswell,
                              Margaret Lamee
Philadelphia Reporters .... Paul Forrest,
                                  Jack Hallett
Opal .... Janet Hubert
Ruby..................... Boncellia Lewis
Reds Fans .... Sam Stoneburner,
                              Stephen Crain
Dodger Wives .... Kim Criswell,
                              Margaret Lamee
Hilda Chester................ Kim Criswell
Pittsburgh Pirates .... Stephen Crain,
                              Thomas Griffith

Dodger Fans: Steven Boockvor, Stephen Crain, Kim Criswell, Tom Griffith, Margaret Lamee, Bob Morrisey. Passengers: Margaret Lamee, Sam Stoneburner, Rodney Saulsberry, Janet Hubert, Thomas Griffith, Kim Criswell, Steven Bland, Bob Morrisey, Stephen Crain, Boncellia Lewis. Fans: Boncellia Lewis, Steven Bland, Michael Edward-Stevens, Janet Hubert, Rodney Saulsberry. Ministers: Rodney Saulsberry, Michael Edward-Stevens, Paul Cook Tartt.

Understudies: Mr. Grier—Rodney Saulsberry; Miss McKee, Female Swing—Jacqueline Lowe; Mr. Huddleston—George Wallace; Mr. Bowers—Paul Cook Tartt; Mr. Fontaine—Michael Edward-Stevens; Misses Drylie, Criswell, Female Swing—Margaret Lamee; Mr. Gill—Bill Buell; Mr. Miller—Steven Boockvor; Mr. Morrisey—Stephen Crain; Mr. Wallace—Sam Stoneburner.

Directed by Martin Charnin; musical numbers choreographed by Alan Johnson; scenery, David Chapman; costumes, Carrie F. Robbins; lighting, Marc B. Weiss; sound, Louis Shapiro; conductor, Rachel Robinson; musical supervision, orchestrations and dance arrangements, Luther Henderson; musical conductor and vocal arrangements, Joyce Brown; associate producer, Roger Luby; production stage manager, Peter Lawrence; stage manager, Jim Woolley; press, Fred Nathan & Associates, Eileen McMahon, Patt Dale, Jan Greenberg.

Events in the life of the first black player admitted to major league baseball, Jackie Robinson, between August 1945 and September 1947, with a program note adding, "Some characters have been created and some chronology and situations have been altered."

ACT I

Scene 1: Noonan's Bar in Brooklyn, October 1946
   "Bums" .... Noonan, Eunice, Huey, Frog, Sorrentino, Fans
Scene 2: Gallagher's Restaurant, West 52d St., New York
   "Jack Roosevelt Robinson" .... Rickey, Durocher
Scene 3: The third base line in Comiskey Park, Chicago
Scene 4: The locker room of the Kansas City Monarchs in Chicago
   "The National Pastime"...................... Cool Minnie, Jackie, Junkyard, Monarchs
Scene 5: Union Station, Chicago
   "Will We Ever Know Each Other" .... Jackie, Rachel
Scene 6: Branch Rickey's Office, 215 Montague St., Brooklyn
   "The First" .... Jackie
Scene 7: The Havana training camp of the Brooklyn Dodgers
   "Bloat" .... Durocher, Reporters, Dodgers
Scene 8: Outside a ballpark, Jacksonville, Fla.
   "Southern Hospitality".. Jackie, Rachel, Fans

Scene 9: A roadhouse, Route 27, Richmond, Va.
"It Ain't Gonna Work"................................... Higgins, Sukeforth, Dodgers
"The Brooklyn Dodger Strike"..................................... Rickey, Durocher
Scene 10: Branch Rickey's office
"Jack Roosevelt Robinson" (Reprise)... Rickey
"The First" (Reprise).. Rachel

ACT II

Scene 1: Noonan's Bar, April 1947
"Is This Year Next Year?".................... Noonan, Eunice, Huey, Frog, Sorrentino
Scene 2: Behind first base, Crosley Field, Cincinnati
"You Do-Do-Do-It Good!".................. Cool Minnie, Jackie, Monarchs, Ruby, Opal
Scene 3: The Dodger locker room, Shibe Park, Philadelphia
"Is This Year Next Year?" (Reprise)....... Rickey, Holmes, Reporters, Sukeforth, Dodgers
Scene 4: Behind third base, the Polo Grounds, New York City
"There Are Days and There Are Days"..................................... Rachel
Scene 5: The front porch of a farmhouse, outside of St. Louis
"It's a Beginning".. Jackie, Rickey, Rachel
Scene 6: Outside Ebbets Field
"The Opera Ain't Over"................ Noonan, Regulars' Dodgers, Rickey, Hilda, Fans
Scene 7: Inside Ebbets Field

The West Side Waltz (126). By Ernest Thompson. Produced by Robert Whitehead and Roger L. Stevens in association with Center Theater Group-Ahmanson at the Ethel Barrymore Theater. Opened November 19, 1981. (Closed March 13, 1982)

Cara Varnum............. Dorothy Loudon   Robin Bird................... Regina Baff
Serge Barrescu............. David Margulies   Glen Dabrinsky............. Don Howard
Margaret Mary Elderdice. Katharine Hepburn

Standby: Miss Loudon—Ludi Claire. Understudies: Messrs. Margulies, Howard—Pat Santino. Miss Baff—Corinne Neuchateau.
Directed by Noel Willman; scenery, Ben Edwards; costumes, Jane Greenwood; lighting, Thomas Skelton; music supervised and arranged by David Krane; production stage manager, Ben Strobach ; stage manager, Valentine Mayer; press, Seymour Krawitz, Patricia Krawitz.
Time: The present. Place: the living room of a West Side New York apartment. Act I, Scene 1: Winter, afternoon ("Du und Du" by Johann Strauss). Scene 2: Spring, afternoon ("Gelaufigkeit" by Carl Czerny). Scene 3: Summer, morning ("Playing Together Is Fun" by Saul Minsch and Wolfgang Mozart). Act II, Scene 1: Winter, evening ("The Little Dog Waltz" by Frederic Chopin). Scene 2: Spring, evening ("Wein, Weib und Gesang" by Johann Strauss). Scene 3: Fall, afternoon ("One More Waltz" by Dorothy Fields and Jimmy McHugh).
Advancing age, with its infirmities, plagues but does not daunt a plucky woman pianist. Previously produced in San Diego and elsewhere on the West Coast.

Grown Ups (83). By Jules Feiffer. Produced by Mike Nichols and Emanuel Azenberg with The Shubert Organization at the Lyceum Theater. Opened December 10, 1981. (Closed February 20, 1982)

Helen .... Frances Sternhagen   Jake.......................... Bob Dishy
Jack...................... Harold Gould   Louise................... Cheryl Giannini
Marilyn........... Kate McGregor-Stewart   Edie .... Jennifer Dundas

Standbys: Mr. Dishy—Stephen D. Newman; Miss Sternhagen—Georgine Hall; Misses Giannini, McGregor-Stewart—Barbara Eda-Young; Miss Dundas—Shelly Inglis.
Directed by John Madden; scenery, Andrew Jackness; costumes, Dunya Ramicova; lighting, Paul Gallo; produced in association with Wayne M. Rogers; production stage manager, Craig Jacobs; stage manager, Wayne Carson; press, Bill Evans & Associates, Sandra Manley, Howard Atlee, Leslie Anderson.

Time: The present. Act I: Marilyn's kitchen in New Rochelle. Act II: Jake and Louise's apartment in New York, one year later. Act III: Jake and Louise's apartment, the following Sunday.

Echoes of past parental wrongs reverberate in the collapsing marital and family relationships of the son, now a middle-aged journalist. Previously produced by American Repertory Theater, Cambridge, Mass.

Kingdoms (17). By Edward Sheehan. Produced by Elliot Martin at the Cort Theater. Opened December 13, 1981. (Closed December 27, 1981)

Domestic	Joe Zaloom	Soldier; Maurice	Alex Hyde-White
Domestic; Javel	Ralph Drischell	Tailor	Arthur Burns
Cardinal Consalvi	Thomas Barbour	Radet	Michael Tolaydo
Cardinal Fesch	George Morfogen	Emperor Napoleon I	Armand Assante
Papal Chamberlain	Donald Linahan	Empress Josephine	Maria Tucci
Pope Pius VII	Roy Dotrice	Dr. Porta	Charles White
Soldier	John Martinuzzi	DuBois	Stephen Stout

Soldiers: Alex Hyde-White, John Martinuzzi, Ralph Drischell, Stephen Stout, Joe Zaloom. Monks: Stephen Stout, Arthur Burns, Joe Zaloom.

Standbys: Mr. Dotrice—George Morfogen; Mr. Assante—Michael Tolaydo, Arthur Burns; Miss Tucci—Etain O'Malley; Mr. Barbour—Donald Linahan; Mr. Morfogen—Ralph Drischell; Mr. White—Joe Zaloom; Mr. Tolaydo—Stephen Stout.

Directed by Paul Giovanni; scenery, David Hayes; costumes, Patricia Zipprodt; lighting, Paul Gallo; sound, Chuck London; associate producer, Dana Matthow; production stage manager, Tom Aberger; stage manager, Johnna Murray; press, Jeffrey Richards Associates, C. George Willard.

Time: 1804 to 1814. Place: France and Italy. The play was presented in two parts.

Napoleon and the Pope in confrontation, with the latter as the Emperor's prisoner.

Duet for One (20). By Tom Kempinski. Produced by Emanuel Azenberg, Ray Cooney, Wayne M. Rogers, Ron Dante, Tommy Valando 'and Warner Theater Productions, Inc. at the Royale Theater. Opened December 17, 1981. (Closed January 2, 1982)

Stephanie Abrahams	Anne Bancroft
Dr. Alfred Feldmann	Max von Sydow

Standbys: Miss Bancroft—Cristine Rose; Mr. von Sydow—Ron Randell.

Directed by William Friedkin; scenery, John Lee Beatty; costumes, Jane Greenwood; lighting, Dennis Parichy; production stage manager, Charles Blackwell; stage manager, Cathy B. Blaser; press, Bill Evans & Associates, Sandra Manley, Howard Atlee, Leslie Anderson.

Place: Dr. Feldmann's office on the first floor of his town house in the East 80s in Manhattan. The play was presented in six scenes and two parts.

Psychiatrist and patient, a cellist whose career has been disrupted by the onset of a crippling disease. A foreign play previously produced in London.

*Dreamgirls (186). Musical with book and lyrics by Tom Eyen; music by Henry Krieger. Produced by Michael Bennett, Bob Avian, Geffen Records and The Shubert Organization at the Imperial Theater. Opened December 20, 1981.

Charlene	Cheryl Alexander	C.C. White	Obba Babatunde
Joanne	Linda Lloyd	Effie Melody White	Jennifer Holliday
Marty	Vondie Curtis-Hall	James Thunder Early	Cleavant Derricks
Curtis Taylor Jr.	Ben Harney	Edna Burke	Sheila Ellis
Deena Jones	Sheryl Lee Ralph	Wayne	Tony Franklin
M.C.; Mr. Morgan	Larry Stewart	Frank	David Thome
Tiny Joe Dixon; Jerry	Joe Lynn	Michelle Morris	Deborah Burrell
Lorell Robinson	Loretta Devine		

The Stepp Sisters: Deborah Burrell, Vanessa Bell, Tenita Jordan, Brenda Pressley. Little Albert and the Tru-Tones: Wellington Perkins, Charles Bernard, Jamie Patterson, Charles Randolph-Wright, Weyman Thompson. The James Early Band: Charles Bernard, Jamie Patterson, Wellington Perkins, Scott Plank, Charles Randolph-Wright, Weyman Thompson. Dave and the Sweethearts: Paul Binotto, Candy Darling, Stephanie Eley. The Five Tuxedos: Charles Bernard, Jamie Patterson, Charles Randolph-Wright, Larry Stewart, Weyman Thompson. Les Style: Cheryl Alexander, Tenita Jordan, Linda Lloyd, Brenda Pressley. Film Executives: Paul Binotto, Scott Plank, Weyman Thompson.

Announcers, Fans, Reporters, Stagehands, Party Guests, Photographers: Cheryl Alexander, Phylicia Ayers-Allen, Vanessa Bell, Charles Bernard, Paul Binotto, Candy Darling, Ronald Dunham, Stephanie Eley, Sheila Ellis, Tenita Jordan, Linda Lloyd, Joe Lynn, Frank Mastrocola, Jamie Patterson, Wellington Perkins, Scott Plank, Brenda Pressley, David Thome, Charles Randolph-Wright, Larry Stewart, Weyman Thompson.

Swings: Brenda Draxton, Milton Craig Nealy.

Understudies: Miss Ralph—Phylicia Ayers-Allen; Miss Holliday—Sheila Ellis; Miss Devine—Cheryl Alexander; Miss Burrell—Linda Lloyd; Mr. Harney—Vondie Curtis-Hall; Mr. Derricks—Larry Stewart; Mr. Babatunde—Tony Franklin; Messrs. Curtis-Hall, Lynn—Milton Craig Nealy; Mr. Franklin—Weyman Thompson; Mr. Thome—Scott Plank.

Directed and choreographed by Michael Bennett; co-choreographer, Michael Peters; musical direction, Yolanda Segovia; scenery, Robin Wagner; costumes, Theoni V. Aldredge; lighting, Tharon Musser; sound, Otts Munderloh; musical supervision and orchestrations, Harold Wheeler; vocal arrangements, Cleavant Derricks; production stage manager, Jeff Hamlin; stage manager, Zane Weiner; press, Merle Debuskey, Diane Judge.

Time: Act I—the early 1960s. Act II—the early 1970s.

Romantic and career tribulations of a trio of woman singers and their associates in the high-pressure world of recordings and personal appearances.

ACT I

Scene 1: The Apollo Theater
"I'm Looking for Something" .... Stepp Sisters
"Goin' Downtown" .... Little Albert, Tru-Tones
"Takin' the Long Way Home" .... Tiny Joe Dixon
"Move (You're Steppin' on My Heart")" .... Dreamettes
"Fake Your Way to the Top" .... Jimmy Early, Jimmy Early Band, Dreamettes
"Cadillac Car" .... Curtis, Jimmy, C.C., Marty, Company
Scene 2: On the road
"Cadillac Car" (Reprise) .... Company
Scene 3: A recording studio
"Cadillac Car" (Reprise) .... Company
Scene 4: Limbo
"Cadillac Car" (Reprise) .... Dave, Sweethearts
"Steppin' to the Bad Side" .... Curtis, C.C., Jimmy, Wayne, Dreamettes, Company
Scene 5: A hotel in St. Louis
"Party, Party" .... Company
Scene 6: Miami
"I Want You Baby" .... Jimmy, Dreamettes
Scene 7: Dressing room in the Atlantic Hotel
"Family" .... C.C., Curtis, Jimmy, Deena, Lorell
Scene 8: Cleveland
"Dreamgirls" .... Dreams
"Press Conference" .... Company
"Only the Beginning" .... Curtis, Deena, Effie
Scene 9: A TV studio
"Heavy" .... Dreams
Scene 10: San Francisco
"Heavy" (Reprise) .... Dreams, Curtis

Scene 11: Las Vegas (backstage)
"It's All Over" .... Curtis, Effie, Deena, Lorell, C.C. Michele, Jimmy
"And I Am Telling You I'm Not Going" .... Effie
Scene 12: Las Vegas (on stage)
"Love Love You Baby" .... Dreams

ACT II

Scene 1: Las Vegas Hilton
Dreams Medley .... Deena Jones, Dreams, Company
Scene 2: Chicago Nightclub
"I Am Changing" .... Effie
Scene 3: Vogue Magazine photo call
"One More Picture Please" .... Company
"When I First Saw You" .... Curtis, Deena
Scene 4: National Democratic fundraiser
"Got To Be Good Times" .... Five Tuxedos
"Ain't No Party" .... Lorell, Jimmy
"I Meant You No Harm" .... Jimmy
"Quintette" .... Deena, Lorell, C.C., Michelle Jimmy
"The Rap" .... Jimmy, C.C., Marty, Curtis, Frank, Lorell, Company
Scene 5: A Chicago recording studio
"I Miss You Old Friend" .... Effie, Marty, C.C., Les Style
"One Night Only" .... Effie
Scene 6: Los Angeles
"One Night Only" (Reprise) .... Deena Jones, Dreams, Company
Scene 7: Chicago
"I'm Somebody" .... Deena Jones, Dreams
"Faith in Myself" .... Effie
Scene 8: New York
"Hard to Say Goodbye, My Love" .... Deena Jones, Dreams

Waltz of the Stork (160). By Melvin Van Peebles; music and lyrics by Melvin Van Peebles; additional music and lyrics by Ted Hayes and Mark Barkan. Produced by Melvin Van Peebles at the Century Theater. Opened January 5, 1982. (Closed May 23, 1982)

Cast: Stillman—Bob Carten; Phantoms/Memories/Backup Vocals—C.J. Critt; Phantoms/-Memories/Backup Vocals—Mario Van Peebles; Edward Aloysius Younger—Melvin Van Peebles.

Directed by Melvin Van Peebles; musical director, Bob Carten; scenery, Kert Lundell; costumes, Bernard Johnson; lighting, Shirley Prendergast; sound, Lou Gonzalez; production stage manager, Nate Barnett; stage manager, John Concannon; press, Susan L. Schulman, Bruce Lynn.

Time: Now and before. Place: Wherever and midtown Manhattan. The play was presented in two parts.

Series of autobiographical monologues by Melvin Van Peebles joined together as a self-described "comedy with music." Previously produced off off Broadway at INTAR.

MUSICAL NUMBERS, ACT I: "There," "And I Love You," "The Apple Stretching" (introduction), "Tender Understanding" (music and lyrics by Ted Hayes), "The Apple Stretching" (instrumental), "Mother's Prayer," "My Love Belongs to You", "Weddings and Funerals" (music and lyrics by Mark Barkan).

ACT II: "My Love Belongs to You" (Reprise), "One Hundred and Fifteen," "Play It as It Lays," "The Apple Stretching" (Reprise), "Shoulders to Lean On."

Little Me (36). Revised version of the musical based on the novel by Patrick Dennis; book by Neil Simon; music by Cy Coleman; lyrics by Carolyn Leigh. Produced by Ron Dante, Wayne Rogers, Steven Leber, David Krebs, McLaughlin, Piven, Inc., Warner

Theater Productions, Inc. and Emanuel Azenberg at the Eugene O'Neill Theater. Opened January 21, 1982. (Closed February 21, 1982)

Cast, Act I: Announcer, Attorney, Bandleader, Preacher, German Soldier, General—Gibby Brand; Belle (Today)—Jessica James; Charlie Drake, Greensleeves, Town Spokesman—Henry Sutton; Belle—Mary Gordon Murray; Momma—Mary Small; Ramona—Mary C. Holton; Cerine, Boom Boom Girl—Gail Pennington; Bruce—Brian Quinn; Noble Eggleston, Val du Val, Fred Poitrine—Victor Garber; Flo Eggleston, Amos Pinchley—James Coco; Ms. Kepplewhite—Maris Clement; Pinchley Junior—James Brennan; Nurse—Sean Murphy; Court Clerk, Henchman, Sergeant—Stephen Berger; Henchman—Bob Freschi; Frankie Polo—Don Correia; Boom Boom Girl—Bebe Neuwirth; Bert—Mark McGrath; Red Cross Nurse—Andrea Green.

Act II: Captain—Bob Freschi; Steward—David Cahn; Sailor I—Brian Quinn; Sailor II—Mark McGrath; Mr. Worst, Otto Schnitzler, Prince Chernet—James Coco; Assistant Director, Croupier —Henry Sutton; Pharaoh I—Kevin Winkler; Doctor—Stephen Berger; Yulnick—Gibby Brand; Baby Belle—Mary Gordon Murray; Noble Junior—Victor Garber.

Townspeople, Skylight Patrons, Nurses, Soldiers, Passengers, International Set, Peasants: Stephen Berger, Michael Blevins, David Cahn, Maris Clement, Bob Freschi, Andrea Green, Mary C. Holton, Mark McGrath, Gary Mendelson, Sean Murphy, Bebe Neuwirth, Gail Pennington, Susan Powers, Brian Quinn, Kevin Brooks Winkler. Swings—John Hillner, Meredith Murray.

Orchestra: Donald York conductor; Joel Kaye contractor, reeds; Rick Centalonza reeds; Earl Gardner, Joe Mosello trumpet; Dale Kirkland trombone; Barry Gordon piano, associate conductor; David Finck bass; Joe Passaro percussion; Luther Rix drums.

Understudies: Mr. Coco—Gibby Brand; Mr. Garber—Gibby Brand, John Hillner; Miss Murray —Susan Powers; Miss James—Mary Small; Mr. Correia—James Brennan; Mr. Sutton—Bob Freschi; Miss Small—Maris Clement; Mr. Brand—Stephen Berger; Mr. Brennan—John Hillner.

Directed by Robert Drivas; choreography, Peter Gennaro; musical director, Donald York; scenery and costumes, Tony Walton; lighting, Beverly Emmons; vocal and dance arrangements, Cy Coleman; orchestrations, Harold Wheeler; sound, Tom Morse; production manager, Martin Herzer; stage manager, Robert LoBianco; press, Bill Evans & Associates, Sandra Manley, Howard Atlee, Leslie Anderson.

The life and loves of the adventuress Belle Poitrine, previously musicalized on Broadway in the original version by the same librettist, composer and lyricist 11/17/62 for 257 performances.

ACT I

"Don't Ask a Lady" .... Belle (Today)
"The Other Side of the Tracks" .... Belle
"The Rich Kids Rag" .... Company
"I Love You" .... Noble, Belle, Company
"The Other Side of the Tracks" (Reprise)................................... Belle
"Deep Down Inside" .... Pinchley, Belle, Company
"Boom-Boom" .... Val du Val
"I've Got Your Number" .... Frankie Polo
"Real Live Girl".. Fred Poitrine
"Real Live Girl" (Reprise) .... Doughboys

ACT II

"I Love You" (Reprise).. Noble, Belle
"I Wanna Be Yours"... Belle, Worst
"Little Me".. Belle (Today), Belle, Momma
"Goodbye" .... Prince Cherney, Yulnick, Doctor, Company
"Here's to Us" .... Belle (Today), Company

The Curse of an Aching Heart (32). By William Alfred; music by Claibe Richardson. Produced by Margot Harley, John Houseman, Everett King, David Weil and Sidney Shlenker at the Little Theater. Opened January 25, 1982. (Closed February 21, 1982)

Bill Hutton and Laurie Beechman in *Joseph and the Amazing Technicolor Dreamcoat*

Prologue—1942
   Frances Walsh . . . . Faye Dunaway
Friday Night Dreams Come True—1923
   Frances Anna Duffy . . . . Faye Dunaway
   Gertrude "Lulu" Fitter . . . . . Audrie Neenan
Clothes Make the Woman—1925
   Frances Anna Duffy . . . . Faye Dunaway
   John Joseph
      "Jo Jo" Finn . . . . Bernie McInerney
The Curse of an Aching Heart—1927
   Pasquale "Packy" Malardino . . . John Polito
   Man With Newspaper . . . . Dale Helward
   Herman Crump . . . . Kurt Knudson
   Martin "Lugs" Walsh . . . Terrance O'Quinn
   Fran Duffy . . . . Faye Dunaway

Lulu Fitter . . . . Audrie Neenan
Minnie Crump . . . . Francine Beers
J. Stanislaus McGahey . . . . Colin Stinton
Aloysius "Wishy" Burke . . . . Paul McCrane
All Saints, All Souls—1935
   Frances Anna Duffy Walsh . . Faye Dunaway
   Gertrude "Lulu"
      Fitter Malardino . . . . Audrie Neenan
   Gertrude Graham Finn . . . . Beverly May
Holy Saturday—1942
   Frances Anna Duffy Walsh . . Faye Dunaway
   Martin Thomas Walsh . . . . . Raphael Sbarge
   John Joseph
      "Jo Jo" Finn . . . . Bernie McInerney

Standbys: Misses Dunaway, May—Joan MacIntosh. Understudies: Misses Neenan, Beers—Mary E. Baird; Mr. McCrane—Rich Rand; Messrs. O'Quinn, Polito, Stinton—Thomas A. Stewart; Messrs. McInerney, Knudson—Dale Helward.

Directed by Gerald Gutierrez; scenery, John Lee Beatty; costumes, Nancy Potts; lighting, Dennis Parichy; sound, David Rapkin, orchestrations, Bruce Pomahac; associate producers, David Jiranek, Frederick C. Venturelli; production stage manager, Franklin Keysar; press, Fred Nathan & Associates, Eileen McMahon, Francine L. Trevens.

Woman in her mid-30s remembers the highlights and heartbreaks of her life in Brooklyn from age 14 on. The play was presented without intermission.

*Joseph and the Amazing Technicolor Dreamcoat (219). Transfer from off Broadway of the revival of the musical based on the Old Testament story; music by Andrew Lloyd Webber; lyrics by Tim Rice. Produced by Zev Bufman, Susan R. Rose, Melvyn J. Estrin, Sidney Shlenker and Gail Berman by arrangement with The Robert Stigwood Organization, Ltd. and David Land at the Royale Theater. Opened January 27, 1982.

Narrator . . . . Laurie Beechman	Zebulon . . . . Doug Voet
Jacob . . . . Gordon Stanley	Gad; Baker . . . . Barry Tarallo
Reuben . . . . Robert Hyman	Benjamin . . . . Philip Carrubba
Simeon; Butler . . . . Kenneth Bryan	Judah . . . . Stephen Hope
Levi . . . . Steve McNaughton	Joseph . . . . Bill Hutton
Napthali . . . . Charlie Serrano	Ishmaelite; Pharaoh . . . . Tom Carder
Issachar . . . . Peter Kapetan	Ishmaelite; Potiphar . . . . David Ardao
Asher . . . . David Asher	Mrs. Potiphar . . . . Randon Lo
Dan . . . . James Rich	

Women's Chorus: Lorraine Barrett, Karen Bogan, Katharine Buffaloe, Lauren Goler, Randon Lo, Joni Masella, Kathleen Rowe McAllen, Renee Warren. Swings: Rosalyn Rahn, John Ganzer.

Understudies: Miss Beechman—Rosalyn Rahn; Mr. Stanley—David Asher; Mr. Hutton—Doug Voet; Mr. Ardao—Kenneth Bryan; Mr. Carder—James Rich.

Directed and choreographed by Tony Tanner; musical direction, David Friedman; scenery, Karl Eigsti; costumes, Judith Dolan; lighting, Barry Arnold; sound, Tom Morse; musical supervision, arrangements and orchestrations, Martin Silvestri, Jeremy Stone; associate producers, Thomas Pennini, Jean Luskin, Jerome Edson; production stage manager, Michael Martorella; stage manager, John Fennessy; press, Fred Nathan & Associates, Francine L. Trevens, Eileen McMahon.

This revival of *Joseph and the Amazing Technicolor Dreamcoat,* presented in two acts, was previously produced at Ford's Theater in Washington, D.C. and off Broadway 11/18/81–1/24/82 for 77 performances. Its list of musical numbers appears on pages 335–6 of *The Best Plays of 1976–77.* In this 1981–82 production, the number "Pharaoh's Story" has been shifted from Act II to Act I.

Othello (123). Revival of the play by William Shakespeare. Produced by Barry and Fran Weissler in association with CBS Video Enterprises by special arrangement with Don Gregory at the Winter Garden Theater. Opened February 3, 1982. (Closed May 23, 1982)

Othello . . . . James Earl Jones	Roderigo . . . . Graeme Campbell
Desdemona . . . . Dianne Wiest	Duke of Venice; Montano . . . . . . Robert Burr
Cassio . . . . Kelsey Grammer	Brabantio . . . . David Sabin
Iago . . . . Christopher Plummer	Gratiano . . . . Richard Dix
Emilia . . . . Aideen O'Kelly	Lodovico . . . . Raymond Skipp
Bianca . . . . Patricia Mauceri	Herald; Soldier . . . . Kim Bemis

Gentlemen of Cyprus, Officers: Edwin J. McDonough, Harry S. Murphy, Bern Sundstedt. Senators of Venice: Edwin J. McDonough, Harry S. Murphy. Servants to Brabantio: Randy Kovitz, Ellen Newman, Edwin J. McDonough, Bern Sundstedt. Cypriots: Ellen Newman, Randy Kovitz.

Understudies: Mr. Jones—Mel Winkler; Mr. Plummer—Robert Burr; Mr. Grammer—Bern Sundstedt, Randy Kovitz; Mr. Sabin—Harry S. Murphy; Messrs. Dix, Skipp—Kim Bemis; Mr. Burr —Edwin J. McDonough, Randy Kovitz; Misses Wiest, O'Kelly, Mauceri—Ellen Newman; Messrs. Campbell, Bemis—Bern Sundstedt.

Directed by Peter Coe; scenery, David Chapman; costumes, Robert Fletcher; lighting, Marc B. Weiss; fights, B.H. Barry; music, Stanley Silverman; production stage manager, Thomas Kelly; stage manager, Dianne Trulock; press, Seymour Krawitz, Patricia McLean Krawitz, Robert W. Larkin.

This revival of *Othello,* presented in two parts, was first produced at American Shakespeare Festival in Stratford, Conn. The last major New York revival of *Othello* was by New York Shakespeare Festival in Central Park 6/27/79 for 25 performances.

Stephen Markle replaced Graeme Campbell 3/9/82; Cecelia Hart replaced Dianne Wiest 4/12/82.

*Pump Boys and Dinettes (134). Transfer from off Broadway of the musical with music and lyrics by Jim Wann and other members of the cast. Produced by Dodger Productions (Michael David, Edward Strong, Sherman Warner), Louis Busch Hager, Marilyn Strauss, Kate Studley, Warner Theater Productions, Inc. and Max Weitzenhoffer at the Princess Theater. Opened February 4, 1982.

Jackson	John Foley	Rhetta Cupp	Cass Morgan
L.M.	Mark Hardwick	Eddie	John Schimmel
Prudie Cupp	Debra Monk	Jim	Jim Wann

Understudies: Women—Rhonda Coullet; Men—Malcolm Ruhl.

Scenery, Doug Johnson and Christopher Nowak; costumes, Patricia McGourty; lighting, Fred Buchholz; sound, Bill Dreisbach; stage manager, Mo Donley; press, Betty Lee Hunt, Maria Cristina Pucci, James Sapp.

Gas jockeys and waitresses from the diner across the highway combine in country music numbers ranging from ballads to blues. Previously produced off off Broadway at Westside Arts Theater and off Broadway 10/1/81–1/17/82 for 112 performances in a production whose musical numbers differed somewhat from those in this one.

ACT I

(Music and lyrics by Jim Wann unless otherwise noted)
"Highway 57" .... Company
"Taking It Slow" .... Pump Boys
    (by John Foley, Mark Hardwick, John Schimmel and Jim Wann)
"Serve Yourself" .... L.M.
"Menu Song" .... Dinettes
    (by Cass Morgan and Debra Monk)
"The Best Man" .... Prudie
"Fisherman's Prayer" .... Pump Boys
"Caution: Men Cooking" .... Pump Boys
    (by Debra Monk, Cass Morgan, Jim Wann and John Foley)
"Mamaw" .... Jim
"Be Good or Be Gone" .... Rhetta
"Drinkin' Shoes" .... Company
    (by Mark Hardwick, Cass Morgan and Debra Monk)

ACT II

"Pump Boys" .... Pump Boys
"Mona" .... Jackson
"T.N.D.P.W.A.M." .... L.M.
"Tips" .... Dinettes
    (by Debra Monk and Cass Morgan)
"Sister" .... Dinettes
    (by Cass Morgan)
"Vacation" .... Company
"No Holds Barred" .... Company
    (by Jim Wann and Cass Morgan)

"Farmer Tan".. L.M., Dinettes
"Highway 57" (Reprise) .... Company
"Closing Time"... Company

Special Occasions (1). By Bernard Slade. Produced by Morton Gottlieb, Ben Rosenberg and Warren Crane at the Music Box. Opened and closed at the evening performance, February 7, 1982.

Amy Ruskin .... Suzanne Pleshette
Michael Ruskin.. Richard Mulligan

Directed by Gene Saks; scenery, David Jenkins; costumes, Jennifer Von Mayrhauser; lighting, Tharon Musser; associate producers, Martin Cohen, Milly Schoenbaum; produced in association with Thornhill Productions, Inc.; stage manager, Kate Pollock; press, Solters/Roskin/Friedman, Inc., Milly Schoenbaum, Warren Knowlton, Kevin Patterson.

Time: During the past ten years. Place: Various locales in California, New York and Colorado. The play was presented in two acts.

Divorced couple finds a new piquancy in their relationship during meetings on special occasions over the next decade.

The World of Sholom Aleichem (22). Revival of dramatic sketches by Arnold Perl; adapted from stories by Sholom Aleichem, Isaac L. Peretz and others. Produced by Lee Guber and Madeline Gilford at the Rialto Theater. Opened February 11, 1982. (Closed February 28, 1982)

Mendele, The Book Seller .... Joe Silver		6th Angel .... Mark Margolis	
A Tale of Chelm		Father Abraham............. Arn Weiner	
The Melamed .... Jack Gilford		Bontche Schweig............. Jack Gilford	
Rifkele................... Renee Lippin		Presiding Angel .... Mitchell Jason	
Rabbi David .... Harris Laskawy		Defending Angel...... Olivia Virgil Harper	
The Angel Rochelle....... Robin Bartlett		Prosecuting Angel .... Harris Laskawy	
Dodi.................... Mark Margolis		*The High School*	
Goatseller .... Sally-Jane Heit		Aaron Katz................. Jack Gilford	
Dodi's Friend .... David Lang		Hannah .... Sally-Jane Heit	
The Bandit		Moishe................... Brian Zoldessy	
Bandit .... Joe Silver		1st Man at the List .... Andy Gale	
Sholom Aleichem............ Jack Gilford		Tutor.................... Mark Margolis	
Bontche Schweig		Woman at the List......... Robin Bartlett	
1st Angel................ Sally-Jane Heit		Principal .... Mitchell Jason	
2d Angel................. Robin Bartlett		Uncle Maxl.............. Harris Laskawy	
3d Angel.................... Andy Gale		Aunt Reba................. Renee Lippin	
4th Angel .... Renee Lippin		Kholyava................... David Lang	
5th Angel .... David Lang		2d Man at the List.......... Arn Weiner	

Klezmer Band: Michael Bloom violin, viola; Stan Free accordion, concertina, shofar; Brian Koonin guitar, mandolin, balalaika.

Understudies: Mark Fleischman, Sherry Lambert.

Directed by Milton Moss; stage movement, Pearl Lang; music, Stan Free; music arrangements, Earl Shandell; scenery, Karl Eigsti; costumes, Pearl Somner; lighting, Robby Monk; movement, Pearl Lang; production supervision, Larry Arrick; original production conceived by Arnold Perl and Howard DaSilva; associate producer, Joseph E. Gilford; production stage manager, Mortimer Halpern; stage manager, Sherry Lambert; press, Merle Debuskey, David Roggensack, Bruce Cohen.

The original production of *The World of Sholom Aleichem* was presented off Broadway 5/3/53. This collection of Yiddish folk tales was presented in two parts, with the intermission coming between *Bontche Schweig* (based on a story by I.L. Peretz) and *The High School* (based on a story by Sholom Aleichem).

Cher and Sandy Dennis in a scene from *Come
Back to the 5 & Dime Jimmy Dean, Jimmy Dean*

Come Back to the 5 & Dime Jimmy Dean, Jimmy Dean (52). By Ed Graczyk. Produced
by Dan Fisher, Joseph Clapsaddle, Joel Brykman and Jack Lawrence at the Martin Beck
Theater. Opened February 18, 1982. (Closed April 4, 1982)

Juanita	Sudie Bond	Edna Louise	Marta Heflin
Sissy	Cher	Martha	Ann Risley
Mona	Sandy Dennis	Alice Ann	Dianne Turley Travis
Joe	Mark Patton	Clarissa	Ruth Miller
Sue Ellen	Gena Ramsel	Joanne	Karen Black
Stella May	Kathy Bates		

Understudies: Misses Dennis, Black—Ann Risley; Misses Cher, Bates—Gena Ramsel; Miss Bond
—Ruth Miller; Miss Heflin—Dianne Turley Travis; Mr. Patton—Joey Alan Phipps.

Directed by Robert Altman; scenery, David Gropman; costumes, Scott Bushnell; lighting, Paul
Gallo; sound, Richard Fitzgerald; production stage manager, John Brigleb; stage manager, Jerry
Rice; press, Jeffrey Richards Associates, C. George Willard.

Music: Theme from *Giant* by Dimitri Tiomkin; "Sincerely" by A.H. Fried and H. Fuqua; "Seems Like Old Times" by J.J. Loeb and C. Lombardo.

Time: Alternating between Sept. 30, 1975 and 1955. The play was presented in two parts.

Members of a Jimmy Dean fan club in the locale where *Giant* was filmed are seen during their high school days, when the movie was being made, and 20 years later. Previously produced in Columbus, Ohio, Atlanta and off off Broadway.

Little Johnny Jones (1). Revival of the musical with book, music and lyrics by George M. Cohan; adapted by Alfred Uhry. Produced by James M. Nederlander, Steven Leber, David Krebs and The Kennedy Center at the Alvin Theater. Opened and closed at the evening performance March 21, 1982.

Starter; Announcer;	Sing-Song.................... Bruce Chew
Captain Squirvy .... Jack Bittner	Whitney Wilson.............. Ernie Sabella
Anthony Anstey .... Peter Van Norden	Bellboy.................... Al Micacchion
Florabelle Fly .... Jane Galloway	Johnny Jones.............. Donny Osmond
Timothy D. McGee........... Tom Rolfing	Mrs. Kenworth .... Anna McNeely
Goldie Gates .... Maureen Brennan	Newsboy................. David Fredericks

American Boys, Porters, Sailors: Richard Dodd, David Fredericks, James Homan, Gary Kirsch, Bobby Longbottom, Al Micacchion, David Monzione, Keith Savage.

American Girls: Coleen Ashton, Teri Corcoran, Susie Fenner, Linda Gradl, Debra Grimm, Lori Lynott, Annette Michelle, Mayme Paul.

Dance alternates: Tammy Silva, Jonathan Aronson, Jamie Torcellini.

Directed by Gerald Gutierrez; choreography and musical staging, Dan Siretta; musical direction, Lynn Crigler; musical consultant, Alfred Simon; scenery, Robert Randolph; costumes, David Toser; lighting, Thomas Skelton; sound, Abe Jacob; additional orchestrations, Eddie Sauter, Mack Schlefer; dance arrangements, Russell Warner; vocal arrangements and additional dance arrangements, Robert Fisher; production associate, Warren Pincus; production supervisor, Robert V. Straus; press, Fred Nathan, Eileen MacMahon.

Little Johnny Jones was originally produced on Broadway 11/7/04 for 52 performances, and this is its first New York revival of record, previously produced at the Goodspeed Opera House, Haddam, Conn. and on tour in U.S. cities.

ACT I

Overture... Orchestra
Scene 1: Exterior of the Hotel Cecil, London, 1904
    "The Cecil in London" .... Starter, Ensemble
Scene 2: Interior of the Hotel Cecil, immediately following
    "Then I'd Be Satisfied With Life" .... Anthony
    "Yankee Doodle Boy" .... Johnny, Ensemble
Scene 3: Hyde Park, immediately following
    "Oh, You Wonderful Boy" .... Goldie, Florabelle, American Girls
Scene 4: The British Derby, that afternoon
    "The Voice in My Heart" .... Mrs. Kenworth, Ensemble
    Finaletto .... Company

ACT II

Entr'acte .... Orchestra
Scene 1: Outside the pier at Southampton, a week later
    "Captain of a Ten Day Boat".................................... Captain, Ensemble
Scene 2: The pier itself, immediately following
    "Goodbye Flo" .... Florabelle, Sailors
    "Life's a Funny Proposition" .... Johnny
    "Let's You and I Just Say Goodbye".. Goldie
    "Give My Regards to Broadway"................................. Johnny, Ensemble

Scene 3: A New York street, two weeks later
"Extra! Extra!" .... Newsboys
Scene 4: Saratoga, the Fourth of July
"American Ragtime" .... Florabelle, Timothy, Johnny, Ensemble
Finale... Company

*Encore (116). Golden Jubilee Spectacular. Produced by Radio City Music Hall Productions, Robert F. Jani producer, at Radio City Music Hall Entertainment Center. Opened March 26, 1982.

Principals: Wendy Edmead, Tom Garrett, Michael Kubala, Kuniko Narai, Deborah Phelan, Justin Ross, Luis Villanueva, Karen Zjemba.

Rockettes: Lois Ann Alston, Kathy Beatty, Dottie Belle, Susan Boron, Beth Chanin, Barbara Ann Cittadino, Susan Cleland, Eileen Collins, Brie Daniels, Susanne Doris, Jackie Fancy, Deniene Fenn, Alexis Ficks, Prudy Gray, Leslie Gryzko, Jennifer Hammond, Carol Harbich, Cindy Hughes, Stephanie James, Joan Kelleher, Pam Kelleher, Dee Dee Knapp, Judy Little, Sonja Livingston, Mary McNamara, Lynn Newton, Kerri Pearsall, Cindy Peiffer, Gerri Presky, Terry Spano, Pam Stacey, Lynn Sullivan, Susan Theobold, Carol Toman, Pat Tully, Darlene Wendy, Rose Ann Woolsey, Phyllis Wujko.

New Yorkers: John Aller, David Brownlee, Rick Conant, Dale Furry, Edyie Fleming Geistman, Sonya Hensley, David Michael Johnson, Joe Joyce, Connie Kunkle, Rosemary Loar, Keith Locke, Edward Prostak, Susan Streater, Scott Willis.

Dancers: David Askler, Robert Boling, Leigh Catlett, Cisco X. Drayton, Larry Lynd, Will Mead, Jackie Patterson, David Roman, Stan Shelmire.

Directed by Robert F. Jani; staged and choreographed by Adam Grammis, Geoffrey Holder, Violet Holmes, Linda Lemac, Shozo Nakano and Frank Wagner; musical direction, Tom Bahler; scenery, Charles Lisanby; costumes, Michael Casey; lighting, Ken Billington; conductor, Joseph Klein; production stage manager, Donald Christy; stage managers, Jack Horner, Ray Chandler, Peter Aaronson; press, Gifford/Wallace, Inc., Keith Sherman.

Musical spectacle recreating numbers that were highlights of Music Hall stage shows over the 50 years of its history.

PART I: "You're at the Music Hall" (by Donald Pippin and Sammy Cahn); "Encore" (by Stan Lebowsky and Fred Tobias); Our Scrapbook of Memories—Ginny Hounsell; "The Lord's Prayer" (by Albert Hay Malotte) and "Kamenoi Ostrow" (by Anton Rubinstein); Ohka-No-Zu (Cherry Blossom), with the Doncho curtain; "Rhapsody in Blue" (by George Gershwin); "Showstoppers" (by Fred Ebb and John Kander)—Rockettes.

PART II: Entr'acte Overture—Music Hall Orchestra; "Bolero" (by Maurice Ravel); Fifty Years of American Popular Music; Dancing in Diamonds comprising "There Are No Girls Like Show Girls" (by Donald Pippin and Sammy Cahn) and "Encore" (Reprise)—Rockettes; "That's Entertainment" (by Howard Dietz and Arthur Schwartz); A Salute to the Music Hall with "You're at the Music Hall" (Reprise).

*Agnes of God (64). By John Pielmeier. Produced by Kenneth Waissman, Lou Kramer and Paramount Theater Productions at The Music Box. Opened March 30, 1982.

Agnes .... Amanda Plummer   Mother Miriam Ruth .... Geraldine Page
Dr. Martha Livingstone .... Elizabeth Ashley

Understudies: Misses Ashley, Page—Susan Riskin; Miss Plummer—Sally Klein.

Directed by Michael Lindsay-Hogg; scenery, Eugene Lee; costumes, Carrie Robbins; lighting, Roger Morgan; production stage manager, Larry Forde; stage manager, Mark Rubinsky; press, Betty Lee Hunt, Maria Cristina Pucci, James Sapp.

A postulant, rapt in her faith, is closely questioned by a psychiatrist and the Mother Superior to determine the true facts of her case: she is accused of manslaughter in the death of her newborn baby. The play was presented in two parts. Previously produced at the O'Neill Theater Center and in regional theater at Louisville, Baltimore and Seattle.

A Best Play; see page 217.

Solomon's Child (4). By Tom Dulack. Produced by FDM Productions, Inc. (Francois de Menil and Harris Maslansky) at the Little Theater. Opened April 8, 1982. (Closed April 10, 1982)

Allan	John McMartin	Balthazar	Anthony Zerbe
Joe	Ellis Williams	Naomi	Deborah Hedwall
Sam	Tom Nardini	Liz	Joanna Merlin
Shelley	Evan Handler	Trooper	Mike Houlihan

Standbys: Messrs. McMartin, Zerbe—John Seitz; Miss Hedwall—Ilvi Dulack; Messrs. Williams, Nardini, Houlihan—Munson Hicks.

Directed by John Tillinger; scenery, Marjorie Bradley Kellogg; costumes, Jennifer Von Mayrhauser; lighting, Richard Nelson; production stage manager, Franklin Keysar; press, Betty Lee Hunt, Maria Cristina Pucci, James Sapp.

Time: The present, 10:30 A.M. Place: The Solomons' summer house in the Catskills. The play was presented in two parts.

Deprogramming a youngster brainwashed by a religious cult. Previously produced at the Long Wharf Theater, New Haven, Conn.

*Medea (33). Revival of the play by Euripides; adapted by Robinson Jeffers. Produced by Barry and Fran Weissler by arrangement with Kennedy Center and Bunny and Warren Austin at the Cort Theater. Opened May 2, 1982.

Nurse	Judith Anderson	Creon	Paul Sparer
Tutor	Don McHenry	Jason	Mitchell Ryan
Children	Jason Kimmell, Christopher Garvin	Aegeus	Peter Brandon
1st Woman of Corinth	Pauline Flanagan	Jason's Slave	Lucien Douglas
2d Woman of Corinth	Harriet Nichols	Handmaidens	Emily King, Amy Lovell
3d Woman of Corinth	Giulia Pagano	Attendants to Jason	Wayne Carson,
Medea	Zoe Caldwell		Ralph Roberts

Standbys: Miss Caldwell—Giulia Pagano; Misses Anderson, Flanagan—Barbara Lester; Mr. Ryan —Peter Brandon; Messrs. Sparer, Brandon, Douglas—Wayne Carson; Mr. McHenry—Ralph Roberts; Miss Nichols—Amy Lovell; Miss Pagano—Emily King; Messrs. Kimmell, Garvin—Stephen Garvin.

Directed by Robert Whitehead; scenery, Ben Edwards; costumes, Jane Greenwood; lighting, Martin Aronstein; music and sounds, David Amram; production stage manager, Mitchell Erickson; stage manager, Stephen Nasuta; press, David Powers, Barbara Carroll, Thomas Trenkle.

Place: In front of Medea's house in Corinth. The play was presented in two parts.

This Robinson Jeffers version of *Medea* was produced on Broadway 10/20/47 for 214 performances with Judith Anderson (who plays the Nurse in this production) in the title role. It has been revived 5/2/49 for 17 performances at the City Center, 11/28/65 for 77 performances off Broadway and 10/2/74 in a free adaptation for 1 performance on Broadway.

*"MASTER HAROLD" . . . **and the boys** (32). By Athol Fugard. Produced by The Shubert Organization, Freydberg/Bloch Productions, Dasha Epstein, Emanuel Azenberg and David Geffen in the Yale Repertory Theater (Lloyd Richards artistic director) production at the Lyceum Theater. Opened May 4, 1982.

Sam	Zakes Mokae	Hally	Lonny Price
Willie	Danny Glover		

Standbys: Messrs. Mokae, Glover—Bill Cobbs; Mr. Price—Charles Michael Wright.

Directed by Athol Fugard; scenery, Jane Clark; costumes, Sheila McLamb; lighting, David Noling; stage movement, Wesley Fata; production stage manager, Neal Ann Stephens; stage manager, Sally J. Greenhut; press, Bill Evans and Associates, Sandra Manley, Leslie Anderson.

Time: 1950. Place: The St. Georges Park Tea Room on a wet and windy afternoon in Port Elizabeth, South Africa. The play was presented without intermission.

The Rockettes in the "Dancing in Diamonds"
number of *Encore* at Radio City Music Hall

Racism flares and damages the longtime affectionate relationship between a white youth and a black who works for his family. A foreign (South African) play in its American premiere in this production, previously produced at Yale Repertory Theater.

A Best Play; see page 236.

The Hothouse (29). By Harold Pinter. Produced by Arthur Cantor and Dorothy Cullman in the Trinity Square Repertory Company production at the Playhouse Theater. Opened May 6, 1982. (Closed May 30, 1982)

Roote . . . . George Martin	Lush . . . . Peter Gerety
Gibbs . . . . Richard Kavanaugh	Tubb . . . . Howard London
Lamb . . . . Dan Butler	Lobb . . . . David C. Jones
Miss Cutts . . . . Amy Van Nostrand		

Directed by Adrian Hall; scenery and lighting, Eugene Lee; costumes, William Lane; associate producer, Harvey Elliott; produced in association with Adrian Hall; production stage manager, Robert Crawley; press, Arthur Cantor Associates.

Place: Back and forth from Roote's office, the sitting room, the soundproof room, hallways and stairways throughout the Institution and finally to the Ministry in London and back. Act I: Christmas morning. Act II: Christmas night.

Comedy, the Establishment's management of a madhouse as a black metaphor of modern society. A foreign play written in 1958 but not produced until 1979 in London. This production originated this season at Trinity Square Repertory Company in Providence, R.I.

Is There Life After High School? (12). Musical suggested by the book by Ralph Keyes; book by Jeffrey Kindley; music and lyrics by Craig Carnelia. Produced by Clive Davis, Francois de Menil, Harris Maslansky and Twentieth Century-Fox Theater Productions, Inc. at the Ethel Barrymore Theater. Opened May 7, 1982. (Closed May 16, 1982)

Raymond Baker   Philip Hoffman
Cynthia Carle   David Patrick Kelly
Alma Cuervo   Maureen Silliman
Sandy Faison   James Widdoes
Harry Groener

Musicians: Edward Strauss assistant musical director, electric keyboards; James Ogden drums; Brian Koonin, Scott Kuney guitars; Lawrence Lenske, Eugene Moye cellos; Harry Max bass; Eric Cohen percussion.

Understudies: Scott Bakula, Marcus Olson, Lauren White.

Directed by Robert Nigro; scenery, John Lee Beatty; costumes, Carol Oditz; lighting, Beverly Emmons; sound, Tom Morse; musical direction and orchestrations, Bruce Coughlin; associate producer, Robert Feiden; production stage manager, Robert D. Currie; stage manager, Bernard Pollock; press, Jeffrey Richards Associates, C. George Willard.

Collection of high school memories in revue form, based on a 1976 book. Previously produced by the Hartford, Conn. Stage Company.

MUSICAL NUMBERS, ACT I: "The Kid Inside"—Company; "Things I Learned in High School"—Harry Groener; "Second Thoughts"—Raymond Baker, Sandy Faison, David Patrick Kelly, Maureen Silliman, James Widdoes; "Nothing Really Happened"—Alma Cuervo, Women; "Beer"—Baker, Groener, Kelly; "For Them"—Philip Hoffman, Company; "Diary of a Homecoming Queen"—Silliman.

ACT II: "Thousands of Trumpets"—Widdoes, Groener, Company; "Reunion"—Company; "High School All Over Again"—Kelly; "Fran and Janie"—Faison, Silliman; "I'm Glad You Didn't Know Me"—Cynthia Carle, Hoffman.

Nine (25). Musical with book by Arthur Kopit; music and lyrics by Maury Yeston; adaptation from the Italian by Mario Fratti. Produced by Michel Stuart, Harvey J. Klaris, Roger S. Berlind, James M. Nederlander, Francine LeFrak and Kenneth D. Greenblatt at the Forty-Sixth Street Theater. Opened May 9, 1982.

Guido Contini . . . . Raul Julia	Maria . . . . Jeanie Bowers
Guido at an early age . . . . . . Cameron Johann	Francesca . . . . Kim Criswell
Luisa . . . . Karen Akers	Venetian Gondolier . . . . Colleen Dodson
Carla . . . . Anita Morris	Giulietta . . . . Louise Edeiken
Claudia . . . . Shelly Burch	Annabella . . . . Nancy McCall
Guido's Mother . . . . Taina Elg	Diana . . . . Cynthia Meryl
Liliane La Fleur . . . . Liliane Montevecchi	Renata . . . . Rita Rehn
Lina Darling . . . . Laura Kenyon	The Germans:
Stephanie Necrophorus . . . Stephanie Cotsirilos	Gretchen von Krupf . . . . Lulu Downs
Our Lady of the Spa . . . . Kate Dezina	Heidi von Sturm . . . . Linda Kerns
Mama Maddelena . . . . Camille Saviola	Olga von Sturm . . . . Dee Etta Rowe
Saraghina . . . . Kathi Moss	Ilsa von Hesse . . . . Alaina Warren Zachary
The Italians:	

Young Guido's Schoolmates: Evans Allen, Jadrien Steele, Patrick Wilcox.

Standby: Mr. Julia—Clifford David. Understudies: Misses Akers, Montevecchi—Cynthia Meryl; Misses Burch, Morris—Kim Criswell; Miss Elg—Alaina Warren Zachary; Miss Dezina—Colleen Dodson; Miss Cotsirilos—Rita Rehn; Miss Moss—Camille Saviola; Miss Saviola—Lulu Downs; Master Johann—Patrick Wilcox; Germans—Julie J. Hafner; Italians—Dorothy Kiara.

Directed by Tommy Tune; musical direction, Wally Harper; scenery, Lawrence Miller; costumes, William Ivey Long; lighting, Marcia Madeira; musical supervision and orchestrations, Jonathan Tunick; choral composition and musical continuity, Maury Yeston; artistic associate, Thommie Walsh; sound, Jack Mann; associate producers, Mark Beigelman, Shulamith and Michael N. Appell, Jerry Wexler and Michel Kleinman Productions; production stage manager, Charles Blackwell; stage manager, Bruce H. Lumpkin; press, Judy Jacksina, Glenna Freedman, Angela Wilson, Diane Tomlinson, Susannah Blinkoff.

Famous Italian movie director has lost his momentum and attempts to recover it in the setting of a spa near Venice (where he is making another movie) and through the company of various women and memories of his past, in the same pattern as Federico Fellini's movie 8½. Previously produced in a reading at the O'Neill Theater Center, Waterford, Conn.

A Best Play; see page 248.

ACT I

Overture Delle Donne; Spa Music; "Not Since Chaplin" .... Company
"Guido's Song".. Guido
   Coda di Guido .... Company
"The Germans at the Spa" .... Mama, Italians, Germans
"My Husband Makes Movies" .... Luisa
"A Call From the Vatican"... Carla
"Only With You".. Guido
"Folies Bergeres" .... Liliane, Stephanie, Company
"Nine".. Guido's Mother, Company
"Ti Voglio Bene/Be Italian".............................. Saraghina, Boys, Company
"The Bells of St. Sebastian" .... Guido, Boys, Company

ACT II

"A Man Like You/Unusual Way/Duet"................................ Claudia, Guido
"The Grand Canal": Contini Submits/The Grand Canal/Tarantella/Every Girl in Venice/Marcia Di
   Ragazzi/Recitativo/Amor/Recitativo/Only You/Finale................ Guido, Company
"Simple" .... Carla
"Be on Your Own" .... Luisa
"I Can't Make This Movie" .... Guido
"Getting Tall"... Young Guido
"Nine/Long Ago/Nine" (Reprise) .... Guido

*Beyond Therapy (6). Revised version of the play by Christopher Durang. Produced by Warner Theater Productions/Claire Nichtern, FDM Productions/Francois de Menil and Harris Maslansky, at the Brooks Atkinson Theater. Opened May 26, 1982.

Bruce	John Lithgow	Charlotte	Kate McGregor-Stewart
Prudence	Dianne Wiest	Bob	Jack Gilpin
Stuart	Peter Michael Goetz	Andrew	David Pierce

Standby: Messrs Lithgow, Goetz—James Eckhouse.

Directed by John Madden; scenery, Andrew Jackness; costumes, Jennifer Von Mayrhauser; lighting, Paul Gallo; music coordinator, Jack Feldman; production stage manager, Craig Jacobs; stage manager, Trey Hunt; press, Jeffrey Richards Associates, C. George Willard.

Time: The present. Act I, Scene 1: A restaurant. Scene 2: Dr. Stuart Framingham's office. Scene 3: The office of Charlotte Wallace. Scene 4: The restaurant again. Scene 5: Dr. Framingham's office. Scene 6: Bruce's apartment. Act II, Scene 1: Mrs. Wallace's office. Scene 2: The restaurant again. Scene 3: The restaurant still.

Beyond Therapy, a sex-and-psychiatry comedy, was originally produced off Broadway by the Phoenix Theater 1/1/81 for 30 performances.

Do Black Patent Leather Shoes Really Reflect Up? (5). Musical based on a novel by John R. Powers; book by John R. Powers; music and lyrics by James Quinn and Alaric Jans. Produced by Mavin Productions, Inc., Libby Adler Mages and Daniel A. Goldman at the Alvin Theater. Opened May 27, 1982. (Closed May 30, 1982)

Eddie Ryan	Russ Thacker	Father O'Reilly	Robert Fitch
Secretary; Sister Melanie	Amy Miller	Virginia Lear	Vicki Lewis
Becky Backowski	Maureen Moore	Felix Lindor	Don Stitt
Sister Lee	Ellen Crawford	Mike Depki	Peter Heuchling

Nancy Relansky .... Karen Tamburrelli
Mary Kenny .... Christine Gradl
Louie Schlang .... Jason Graae

Sister Helen .... Elizabeth Hansen
Sister Monica Marie .... Catherine Fries

Understudies: Messrs. Thacker, Stitt, Graae—Russ Billingly; Messrs. Fitch, Heuchling—Orrin Reiley; Misses Moore, Tamburrelli, Gradl—Catherine Fries; Misses Crawford, Hansen—Amy Miller; Misses Miller, Fries, Lewis—Carol Estey.

Directed by Mike Nussbaum; musical numbers staged by Thommie Walsh; musical direction and vocal arrangements, Larry Hochman; scenery, James Maronek; costumes, Nancy Potts; lighting, Marilyn Rennagel; sound, Richard Fitzgerald; orchestrations and musical supervision, Jerome Jay Dryer; dance arrangements, Peter Larson; production supervisor, William Gardner; associate choreographer, Ronna Kaye; production stage manager, Mortimer Halpern; stage manager, Mitchell Lemsky; press, Fred Nathan, Eileen McMahon.

Parochial School shenanigans set to music, previously produced in Chicago and elsewhere.

ACT I—ELEMENTARY SCHOOL

Scene 1: St Bastion's School, the present
"Get Ready, Eddie" .... Company
Scene 2: Second Grade at St. Bastion's
"The Greatest Gift" .... Sister Helen, Kids
Scene 3: Confession at St. Bastion's Church
Scene 4: The playground—Fifth Grade
"It's the Nuns" .... Kids, Nuns
"Little Fat Girls" .... Beck, Eddie
Scene 6: Fifth Grade at St. Bastion's
"Cookie Cutters" .... Sister Lee, Becky
Scene 7: Confession at St. Bastion's Church
"Patron Saints" .... Father O'Reilly, Eddie, Kids, Nuns
Scene 8: Eighth Grade at St. Bastion's
"How Far Is Too Far" .... Nancy, Girls, Boys
Finale .... Company

ACT II—HIGH SCHOOL

Scene 1: The Freshman Mixer in the gym of St. Patrick Bremmer High School for Boys
"Doo-Waa, Doo-Wee" .... Louie, Company
"I Must Be in Love" .... Eddie
Scene 2: The front yard of Becky's house—a year later
"Friends, the Best Of" .... Becky, Eddie
Scene 3: Confession at St. Bastion's Church
Scene 4: The Parish Bazaar, senior year
"Mad Bombers and Prom Queens" .... Felix, Virginia, Kids
Scene 5: The night of the Senior Prom
"Late Bloomer" & Prom Montage .... Eddie, Kids
Scene 6: Becky's hospital room
"Friends, the Best Of" (Reprise) .... Becky, Eddie
Scene 7: The present
"Thank God" .... Company

PLAYS WHICH CLOSED
PRIOR TO BROADWAY OPENING

Productions which were organized by New York producers for Broadway presentation but which closed during their production and tryout period are listed below.

The Boys in Autumn. By Bernard Sabath. Produced by Kennedy Center and James B. McKenzie in a pre-Broadway tryout at the Marines Memorial Theater, San Francisco. Opened September 3, 1981. (Closed September 20, 1981)

Thomas Gray .... Kirk Douglas
Henry Finnigan.. Burt Lancaster

Directed by Tom Moore; scenery, Douglas W. Schmidt; costumes, Robert Blackman; lighting, Martin Aronstein; sound, Susan Harvey; associate producer, Harry Berensen.

Tom Sawyer (an ex-vaudevillian) and Huck Finn (retired hardware merchant) meet 50 years after their celebrated raft voyage on the Mississippi. The play was presented in two parts.

Say Hello to Harvey. Musical based on the play *Harvey* by Mary Chase; book, music and lyrics by Leslie Bricusse. Produced by Michael McAloney and Ed Mirvish in association with Joyce Sloane in a pre-Broadway tryout at the Royal Alexandra Theater, Toronto. Opened September 14, 1981. (Closed October 17, 1981)

Elwood P. Dowd........	Donald O'Connor	Mrs. Ethel Chauvenet........	Maxine Miller
Veta Louise Simmons	Patricia Routledge	Nurse Kelly	Patricia Arnell
Dr. William Chumley............	Joe Silver	Dr. Lyman Sanderson........	John Gardiner
Myrtle Mae Simmons......	Sheila McCarthy	Mrs. Chumley	Angela Fusco
Dr. Natalie Egremont............	Judy Sabo	Judge Gaffney	Sidney Miller

Chorus: Mary Leigh Stahl, Janet McCall, Tommy Breslin, Jack Davidson, Jim Betts, Bernard Cauchy, Keith Curran, Cynthia Dale, Mark Esposito, Rodney Freeze, William Gilinsky, Karen Giombetti, Terry Hawkes, Jacob Mark Hopkin, Sherry Lambert, Claudia Shell.

Directed by Mel Shapiro; choreography, Donald Saddler; musical direction, Milton Rosenstock; scenery and lighting, Neil Peter Jampolis; costumes, Olga Dimitrov; musical supervisor and arranger, Ian Fraser; orchestrations, Billy Byers; sound, Jack Ralph; production stage manager, Mortimer Halpern; press, Solters/Roskin/Friedman Inc., Milly Schoenbaum, Kevin Patterson.

Musicalization of the 1945 Best Play and Pulitzer Prize winner about a genial fellow and his imaginary friend, a six-foot rabbit.

MUSICAL NUMBERS: "Smalltown, U.S.A.," "The Wednesday Forum," "We Like the Very Same Things," "That Brother of Mine," "Dr. Chumley," "I'd Rather Look at You," "Do Your Own Thing," "Sue," "Bring It to the Bar," "Elwood P. Dowd," "Say Hello to Harvey," "A Lousy Life," "Be Glad," "The Perfect Person," "One Last Fling," "Human Beings."

The Little Prince and the Aviator. Musical based on *The Little Prince* by Antoine de Saint-Exupery; book by Hugh Wheeler; music by John Barry; lyrics by Don Black. Produced by A. Joseph Tandet in previews at the Alvin Theater. Opened January 1, 1982. (Closed in previews January 17, 1982)

Little Prince...............	Anthony Rapp	Cactus.....................	Joe Degunther
Toni	Michael York	Rose	Janet Eilber
Suzanne; Little Rose...........	Ellen Greene	Cap Juby Pilot #1;	
Georges; Fennec	David Purdham	Conceited Man	Robert Hoshour
Snake; Cap Juby Pilot #3.....	Chip Garnett	Cap Juby Pilot #2; King......	Alan Gilbert

Morse Code Operator;	Suzanne as a Child	Jennifer Fetten
Lamplighter. . . . . Mark Dovey	Vulture	Kenneth D. Ard
Ahmed; Georges as a Child . . . . . Lee Gordon	Drunkard	Larry G. Bailey
Nurse . . . . Brooks Almy	Businessman.	Edward Conery

Pilots: Mark Dovey, Alan Gilbert, Robert Hoshour, Larry G. Bailey, Kenneth D. Ard, Fred C. Mann III. Lotus Club Girls: Brooks Almy, Lynn Gendron, Robin Kensey, Diana Laurenson.

Directed by Jerry Adler; choreography, Billy Wilson; musical direction and vocal arrangements, David Friedman; scenery, Eugene Lee; costumes, Christa Scholtz; lighting, Roger Morgan; orchestrations, Don Walker; dance music arrangements, Grant Sturiale; environmental sound, Kirk Nurock; sound, Robert Kerzman; sound effects, Gary Harris; flying by Foy; production stage manager, Zoya Wyeth; stage manager, B.J. Allen; press, Merle Debuskey, Leo Stern, Jan Greenberg.

Time: 1911–1928. Place: The Sahara Desert, Paris and Asteroid B6–12. The play was presented in two parts.

The friendship of an airplane pilot and a small boy from another planet, stranded in the desert.

ACT I

"Par Avion" . . . . Toni, Georges, Suzanne
"Power Comes, Power Goes" . . . . Snake
"I Pity the Poor Poor Parisiennes" . . . . Toni
"Making Every Minute Count" . . . . Toni, Georges, Pilots
"Made for Each Other" . . . . Toni, Rose
"Wind, Sand & Stars" . . . . Toni, Georges, Pilots
"First Impressions" . . . . Little Prince
"A Day Will Never Be the Same" . . . . Fennec, Pilots
"I've Got You to Thank for All This" . . . . Suzanne
"I Don't Regret a Thing" . . . . Toni
"We Couldn't We Mustn't We Won't . . . . Toni, Little Suzanne, Little Georges

ACT II

"Watch Out for the Baobabs" . . . . Little Prince
"I Like My Misfortunes to Be Taken Seriously" . . . . Toni
"The Volcano Song" . . . . Little Prince
"More Than Just a Pretty Flower" . . . . Rose
"First Impressions" (Reprise) . . . . Little Prince
"Volcano Song" (Reprise) . . . . Little Prince
"Playground of the Planets" . . . . Little Prince
"It Was You" . . . . Georges
"Grain of Sand" . . . . Little Prince
"I Don't Regret a Thing" (Reprise) . . . . Toni
"Sunset Song" . . . . Little Prince
"Little Prince"/"Stars Will Be Laughing" . . . . Toni, Little Prince

The Late Christopher Bean. Revival of the play by Sidney Howard; based on *Prenez Garde a la Peinture* by Rene Fauchois. Produced by Kennedy Center, CBS Broadcast Group, Martha Scott and James M. Nederlander in a pre-Broadway tryout at the Eisenhower Theater, Washington, D.C. Opened January 25, 1982. (Closed February 27, 1982)

Dr. Haggett . . . . Pat Hingle	Warren Creamer . . . . Timothy Landfield
Susan Haggett . . . . Glynnis O'Connor	Tallant . . . . Kevin Tighe
Abby . . . . Jean Stapleton	Rosen . . . . Salem Ludwig
Mrs. Haggett . . . . Olive Dunbar	Maxwell Davenport. . . . . . . Alexander Scourby
Ada Haggett . . . . Ellen Tobie		

Directed by William Putch; scenery, William Ritman; costumes, Arnold S. Levine; lighting, Martin Aronstein; stage manager, Michael Foley; press, Solters/Roskin/Friedman Inc.

The Late Christopher Bean was first produced on Broadway 10/31/32 and was named a Best Play of its season. This is its first major New York revival.

Colette. Musical with book and lyrics by Tom Jones; music by Harvey Schmidt. Produced by Harry Rigby and The Kennedy Center with The Denver Center and James M. Nederlander in a pre-Broadway tour. Opened February 9, 1982 at the 5th Avenue Theater in Seattle. (Closed March 20, 1982 at the Auditorium Theater in Denver)

Colette	Diana Rigg	Mme. Semiramis; Pauline	Mary Stout
Sido	Marta Eggerth	Nita	Jane Lanier
Willy	John Reardon	Writer	Michael Cone
Jacques	Robert Helpmann	Ida	Nancy Callman
Maurice	Martin Vidnovic	Boudou; Collaborator	Russell Leib
Henri de Jouvenal	Ron Raines	Master of Ceremonies;	
Colette de Jouvenal	Rhoda Butler	German Officer	Ralph Braun
Missy	Marti Stevens	Danielle	Dana Moore

Ensemble: Don Bernhardt, Ralph Braun, Carol Burt, Rhoda Butler, Nancy Callman, Arlene Columbo, Michael Cone, Ron Farrar, Jane Lanier, Valerie Lemon, Dana Moore, Daryl Murphy, Harry Lee Nordyke, Peggy Parten, David Scala, Carol Schuberg, Mary Stout, Ivan Torres, Joel Whittaker, Zachary Wilde. Swing Girl: Lisa Guignard. Swing Boy: Lester Holmes.

Directed by Dennis Rosa; choreography, Carl Jablonski; musical direction and vocal arrangements, Larry Blank; scenery, John Conklin; costumes, Raoul Pène du Bois; lighting, Gilbert V. Hemsley Jr.; orchestrations, Larry Wilcox; dance music arrangements, David Krane; associate producer, Frank Montalvo; sound, John McClure; assistant choreographer, Michon Peacock; production stage manager, Robert Vandergriff; stage manager, Dan Hild; press, Henry Luhrman Associates, Bill Miller, Terry M. Lilly.

Time: Act I, 1890–1910; Act II, 1925–1954.

Musical biography covering 64 years in the life of the French writer Colette.

ACT I

Overture
Prologue: Colette's desk
  "There's Another World" .... Colette, Ensemble
Scene 1: Her mother's garden in Saint-Sauveur
  "Come to Life" .... Willy, Ensemble
  "Do Not Hold On" .... Sido
Scene 2: Willy's apartment in Paris
Scene 3: The Semiramis Bar
  "Semiramis" .... Jacques, Girls, Ensemble
  "Do It for Willy" .... Willy, Ensemble
Scene 4: Willy's apartment and the streets of Paris
  The Claudine Sequence:
    a. Claudine .... Colette
    b. Two Claudines .... Colette, Claudine Girls
    c. The Father of Claudine .... Willy, Colette, Claudine Girls, Ensemble
  "Why Can't I Walk Through That Door?" .... Colette
Scene 5: The music hall on tour
  "Music Hall" .... Jacques, Colette, Performers
Scene 6: Onstage, an Egyptian tomb
  "Dream of Egypt" .... Colette, Jacques
Scene 7: Colette's dressing room
  "I Miss You" .... Sido
Scene 8: Missy's Salon
  "La Vagabonde" .... Colette, Missy, Women
Scene 9: Onstage
  "Music Hall Scandal" .... Colette, Missy
Scene 10: Colette's dressing room
  Act I Ending .... Colette

ACT II

Entr'acte
Scene 1: Colette's villa in Saint-Tropez
    Act 2 Opening. . . . . Colette, Journalists
    "Curiosity" . . . . Sido
    "I Miss You" (Reprise) . . . . Colette
Scene 2: Club Pastiche
    "Riviera Nights". . . . . Jacques, Maurice, Colette, Ensemble
Scene 3: Colette's bedroom
    "Oo-La-La". . . . . Maurice, Colette
Scene 4: Saint-Tropez
    "Something for the Summer" . . . . Colette, Maurice, Ensemble
Scene 5: Paris
    "Something for the Winter" . . . . Colette, Maurice, Ensemble
Scene 6: A decade of honors
    "Madame Colette" . . . . Ensemble
Scene 7: Colette's apartment in the Palais-Royale
    "Be My Lady" . . . . Maurice
    "Do Not Hold On" (Reprise) . . . . Sido
Scene 8: Paris during the Occupation
    "The Room Is Filled With You" . . . . Colette
    "Victory". . . . . Colette, Maurice, Ensemble
Scene 9: Colette's apartment
    "Growing Older" . . . . Colette
Scene 10: Colette's desk
    "Joy" . . . . Colette, Ensemble

PLAYS PRODUCED
OFF BROADWAY

Some distinctions between off-Broadway and Broadway productions at one end of the scale and off-off-Broadway productions at the other were blurred in the New York theater of the 1970s and 1980s. For the purposes of this *Best Plays* listing the term "off Broadway" is used to distinguish a professional from a showcase (off-off-Broadway) production and signifies a show which opened for general audiences in a mid-Manhattan theater seating 499 or fewer and 1) employed an Equity cast, 2) planned a regular schedule of 7 or 8 performances a week and 3) offered itself to public comment by critics at a designated opening performance.

Occasional exceptions of inclusion (never of exclusion) are made to take in visiting troupes, borderline cases and a few nonqualifying productions which readers might expect to find in this list because they appear under an off-Broadway heading in other major sources of record.

Figures in parentheses following a play's title give number of performances. These figures do not include previews or extra non-profit performances.

Plays marked with an asterisk (*) were still running on June 1, 1982. Their number of performances is figured from opening night through May 31, 1982.

Certain programs of off-Broadway companies are exceptions to our rule of counting the number of performances from the date of the press coverage. When the official opening takes place late in the run of a play's regularly-priced public or subscription performances (after previews) we count the first performance of record, not the press date, as opening night—and in each such case in the listing we note the variance and give the press date.

In a listing of a show's numbers—dances, sketches, musical scenes, etc.—the titles of songs are identified wherever possible by their appearance in quotation marks (").

Most entries of off-Broadway productions which ran fewer than 20 performances or scheduled fewer than 8 performances a week are somewhat abbreviated, as are entries on running repertory programs repeated from previous years.

HOLDOVERS FROM PREVIOUS SEASONS

Plays which were running on June 1, 1981 are listed below. More detailed information about them appears in previous *Best Plays* volumes of appropriate date. Important cast changes since opening night are recorded in a section of this volume.

*The Fantasticks (9,180; longest continuous run of record in the American theater). Musical suggested by the play *Les Romantiques* by Edmond Rostand; book and lyrics by Tom Jones; music by Harvey Schmidt. Opened May 30, 1960.

Scrambled Feet (831). Musical revue by John Driver and Jeffrey Haddow. Opened June 11, 1979. (Closed June 7, 1981)

*One Mo' Time (1,084). Vaudeville show conceived by Vernel Bagneris. Opened October 22, 1979.

Really Rosie (274). Musical with book and lyrics by Maurice Sendak; music by Carole King. Opened October 14, 1980. (Closed June 13, 1981) New York Shakespeare Festival Public Theater.

The Haggadah, a Passover Cantata (72). Return engagement of the musical by Elizabeth Swados; adapted from texts by Elie Wiesel. Opened April 14, 1981. (Closed June 14, 1981)

Roundabout Theater Company. A Taste of Honey (55). Revival of the play by Shelagh Delaney. Opened April 28, 1981. (Closed June 14, 1981 and transferred to Broadway; see its entry in the Plays Produced on Broadway section of this volume) **Hedda Gabler** (51). Revival of the play by Henrik Ibsen; adapted by Christopher Hampton. Opened May 5, 1981. (Closed June 14, 1981)

The Negro Ensemble Company. Home (45). Return engagement of the play by Samm-Art Williams. Opened May 8, 1981. (Closed June 14, 1981)

I Can't Keep Running in Place (208). Musical with book, music and lyrics by Barbara Schottenfeld. Opened May 14, 1981. (Closed October 25, 1981)

*Cloud 9 (440). By Caryl Churchill. Opened May 18, 1981.

March of the Falsettos (268). Musical by William Finn. Opened May 20, 1981. (Closed September 26, 1981) Reopened October 13, 1981 (press date 11/9/81). (Closed January 31, 1982)

PLAYS PRODUCED JUNE 1, 1981–MAY 31, 1982

The American Place Theater. 1980–81 season concluded with **The Fuehrer Bunker** (21). By W.D. Snodgrass. Produced by The American Place Theater, Wynn Handman director, Julia Miles associate director, at the American Place Theater. Opened May 26, 1981; see note. (Closed June 14, 1981)

Martin Bormann	Larry Block	Hermann Goering	Jerome Dempsey
Magda Goebbels	Catherine Byers	Leader; Gottherd Heinrici	Carl Low
Heinrich Himmler	Thomas Carson	Hitler	Robert Stattel
Joseph Goebbels	Paul Collins		

Directed by Carl Weber; music and chorus supervision, Richard Peaslee; musical director and accordionist, William Schimmel; percussionist, Michael Canick; lighting supervisor, Daniel C. Abrahamsen; costumes, K.L. Fredericks; stage manager, W. Scott Allison; press, Jeffrey Richards Associates, Ted Killmer.

The last days of Hitler in the Berlin bunker, based by the playwright on his cycle of poems with the same title. The play was presented without intermission.

Note: Press date for *The Fuehrer Bunker* was 6/2/81.

The Phoenix Theater. 1980–81 season concluded with **Isn't It Romantic** (37). By Wendy Wasserstein. Produced by The Phoenix Theater, T. Edward Hambleton managing director, Steven Robman artistic director, at the Marymount Manhattan Theater. Opened May 28, 1981; see note. (Closed June 28, 1981)

Janie Blumberg	Alma Cuervo	Simon Blumberg .... Bernie Passeltiner
Harriet Cornwall	Laurie Kennedy	Lillian Cornwall .... Barbara Baxley
Salvatore; Vladimir	Fritz Kupfer	Marty Sterling .... Peter Riegert
Tasha Blumberg	Jane Hoffman	Paul Stuart.................. Bob Gunton

Directed by Steven Robman; scenery, Marjorie Bradley Kellogg; costumes, Jennifer Von Mayrhauser, Denise Romano; lighting, Spencer Mosse; sound, David Rapkin; movement consultant, Nora Peterson; press, Susan L. Schulman.

Comedy, romance and career at odds in the lives of women in the big city. The play was presented in two acts.

Note: Press date for *Isn't It Romantic* was 6/13/81.

Manhattan Theater Club. 1980–81 season concluded with **Hunting Scenes From Lower Bavaria** (40). By Martin Sperr; translated by Christopher Holme. Produced by Manhattan Theater Club, Lynne Meadow artistic director, Barry Grove managing director, at Manhattan Theater Club Downstage. Opened June 2, 1981; see note. (Closed July 5, 1981)

Barbara.................	Marge Redmond	Butcher's Widow........ Sasha Von Scherler
Boney	Dominic Chianese	George .... Tom Kopache
Mayor....................	Jack Davidson	Tonka................... Pippa Pearthree
Priest	Michael Burg	Paula....................... Ann Lange
Maria	Suzanne Costallos	Zenta .... Cristine Rose
Volker..................	Raymond Barry	Abram .... John Pankow
Rovo....................	Paul McCrane	Max .... John Beven

Standbys: Mr. Burg—John Beven; Messrs. Chianese, Beven, Kopache—William Gaynor Dovey.

Directed by Ulrich Heising; dramaturg, Jonathan Alper; scenery, Karen Schulz; costumes, William Ivey Long; lighting, Marc B. Weiss; production stage manager, Richard Elkow; stage manager, John Beven; press, Patricia Cox.

Time: Late summer, 1948. Place: In and about the small village of Reinod, lower Bavaria. The play was presented in two parts.

1966 play about the post-Nazi pervasiveness of evil in a Bavarian village. A foreign play previously produced in Germany.

Note: Press date for *Hunting Scenes From Lower Bavaria* was 6/14/81.

*American Buffalo (259). Revival of the play by David Mamet. Produced by Elliot Martin in the Long Wharf Theater production at Circle in the Square (Downtown). Opened June 3, 1981. (Suspended performances October 31, 1981) Reopened February 25, 1982.

Donny Dubrow	Clifton James	Walter Cole (Teacher) .... Al Pacino
Bobby	Thomas Waites	

Directed by Arvin Brown; scenery, Marjorie Bradley Kellogg; costumes, Bill Walker; lighting, Ronald Wallace; production stage manager, Anne Keefe; press, Jeffrey Richards Associates, Ben Morse.

American Buffalo was produced on Broadway 2/16/77 for 135 performances and was named a Best Play and won the Critics Award for Best American play. This is its first professional New York revival. The play was presented in two parts.

J.J. Johnston replaced Clifton James and James Hayden replaced Thomas Waites 8/81.

James Hayden, Al Pacino and J.J. Johnston in *American Buffalo*

The Butler Did It (70). By Walter Marks and Peter Marks. Produced by Gordon Crowe at the Players Theater. Opened June 3, 1981. (Closed August 1, 1981)

Raymond Butler	Gordon Connell	Victoria Butler	Patricia Kalember
Aldo	John Monteleone	Anthony J. Lefcourt	Alan Mixon
Angela Butler	Gerrianne Raphael	Detective Mumford	John Hallow

Understudy: Misses Raphael, Kalember—Karen McLaughlin.

Directed by Doug Rogers; scenery, Akira Yoshimura; costumes, Merrill Cleghorne; lighting, Gregg Marriner; production coordinator Barbara Carroll; stage manager, Robert Vandergriff; press, Jeffrey Richards Associates, C. George Willard.

Act I, Scene 1: Early evening. Scene 2: The following morning. Scene 3: Later that day. Act II, Scene 1: Early afternoon, the next day. Scene 2: That night. Scene 3. The next morning.

Comedy thriller taking place during rehearsals of an off-Broadway mystery play.

"No" (15). By Alexis De Veaux; adapted by Glenda Dickerson. Produced by the Henry Street Settlement's New Federal Theater, Woodie King Jr. and Steve Tennen producers, at the New Federal Theater. Opened June 5, 1981. (Closed June 24, 1981)

Directed by Glenda Dickerson; scenery, Robert Edmonds; costumes, Risë Collins, Glenda Dickerson; lighting, Marshall Williams; production stage manager, Dwight R.B. Cook; press, Warren Knowlton. With Cheryl Lynn Bruce, Risë Collins, Yvette Erwin, Gwendolen Hardwick, Judith Alexa Jackson, André Liguori, Marilyn Nicole Worrell.

Musicians: Madeleine Yayodele Nelson percussionist, Lorna Warden vocalist.

Compedium of excerpts prepared for the stage of Miss De Veaux's *Erotic Folktale #7, The Riddles of Egypt Brownstone, When the Negro Was in Vogue* and poetry. The play, presented in two parts, was first produced as an OOB offering 4/24/81 by this group.

Shay Duffin as Brendan Behan (14). Written, adapted and performed by Shay Duffin. Produced by Jonathan Reinis and Arthur Cantor at the Astor Place Theater. Opened June 9, 1981. (Closed June 21, 1981)

Directed by Denis Hayes; scenery and lighting, Joe Behan; production stage manager, Larry Bussard; press, Jeffrey Richards Associates, C. George Willard.

One-man performance of Brendan Behan (including his favorite song, "Trust in Drink," author unknown) in the following excerpts from Behan's published work: We're here because we're queer, Bells of hell *(The Hostage);* Words of introduction *(Brendan Behan's New York);* Giants of Irish literature, Down by the glenside, Pubs, whiskey, whores and porter, Parsnips and Yeats, Popes, pulpits and parish priests *(Brendan Behan's Island):* My father, English spoken in North America, Almost a smuggler, Pimp and pornographer *(Confessions of an Irish Rebel);* The sea, oh the sea, Another martyr for old Ireland, Prison cells, mass, benediction and excommunication; British justice and judges *(Borstal Boy);* Overheard in a bookshop *(Hold Your Hour and Have Another);* The old triangle, Capital punishment *(The Quare Fellow);* also Reflections written by Shay Duffin from his own collection of Behanisms.

The play was presented in two parts.

Circle Repertory Company. 1980–81 schedule continued with **A Tale Told** (30). By Lanford Wilson. Opened June 11, 1981. (Closed July 5, 1981) **The Diviners** (40). Return engagement of the play by Jim Leonard Jr. Opened August 4, 1981. (Closed September 6, 1981) Produced by Circle Repertory Company, Marshall W. Mason artistic director, at the Circle Theater.

BOTH PLAYS: Producing director, Porter Van Zandt; scenery, John Lee Beatty; lighting, Dennis Parichy; press, Richard Frankel, Jane Brandmeir.

A TALE TOLD

Viola Platt	Nancy Killmer	Emmet Young	Lindsey Ginter
Olive	Patricia Wettig	Harley Campbell	Jimmie Ray Weeks
Netta	Helen Stenborg	Mr. Talley	Fritz Weaver
Lottie	Elizabeth Sturges	Avalaine Platt	Laura Hughes
Eldon	Michael Higgins	Timmy	David Ferry
Buddy	Timothy Shelton	Sally	Trish Hawkins

Directed by Marshall W. Mason; costumes, Laura Crow; sound, Chuck London; production stage manager, Fred Reinglas.

Time: Early evening, Independence Day, 1944. Place: The front parlor of the Talley place, a farm near Lebanon, Mo. The play was presented in two parts.

Third in the author's series of plays about the Talley family: The Talley patriarch dominates his family in general and his son in particular at a gathering on the same night that his daughter Sally is meeting her lover Matt in the boathouse in the previous Talley play *Talley's Folly.*

THE DIVINERS

Basil Bennett	Jack Davidson	C.C. Showers	Timothy Shelton
Dewey Maples	Rob Gomes	Ferris Layman	Jimmie Ray Weeks
Buddy Layman	Robert MacNaughton	Norma Henshaw	Stephanie Gordon
Melvin Wilder	Gary Berner	Goldie Short	Debra Mooney
Luella Bennett	Elizabeth Sturges	Darlene Henshaw	Laura Hughes
(Jennie Mae Layman)	Patricia Wettig,	(Parentheses indicate role in which the per-	
	Rosemary Sykes	former alternated)	

Directed by B. Rodney Marriott and Porter Van Zandt; costumes, Jennifer Von Mayrhauser; stage manager, M.A. Howard.

Time: The early 1930s. Place: In the homes, fields and public gathering places of the mythical Southern Indiana town of Zion, population 40. The play was presented in two parts. This production of *The Diviners* was first offered off Broadway by Circle Repertory Company 10/16/80 for 41 performances.

Entertaining Mr. Sloane (269). Revival of the play by Joe Orton. Produced by Howard Feuer, Larry Gordon, Jeremy Ritzer and Sidney Shlenker at the Cherry Lane Theater. Opened June 12, 1981. (Closed January 31, 1982)

Kath	Barbara Bryne	Kemp	Gwyllum Evans
Sloane	Maxwell Caulfield	Ed	Joseph Maher

Standbys: Miss Bryne—Eda Seasongood. Mr. Caulfield—Richard Eddon; Messrs. Evans, Maher —Richard Lupino.

Directed by John Tillinger; scenery, Mark Haack; costumes, Bill Walker; lighting, David N. Weiss; production stage manager, Kevin Mangan; press, Fred Nathan & Associates, Eileen McMahon, Patt Dale, Anne Abrams.

Act I: Early evening. Act II: Morning, six months later. Act III: The same afternoon.

Entertaining Mr. Sloane was first produced on Broadway 10/12/65 for 13 performances. This production was previously presented off off Broadway by Penumbra Productions.

Brad Davis replaced Maxwell Caulfield and Jerome Dempsey replaced Joseph Maher 11/3/81.

El Bravo! (48). Musical based on a story by Jose Fernandez and Kenneth Waissman; book by Jose Fernandez and Thom Schiera; music and lyrics by John Clifton. Produced by Kenneth Waissman with Edward Mezvinsky and Sidney Shlenker at the Entermedia Theater. Opened June 16, 1981. (Closed July 26, 1981)

Pepe DeMarco (El Bravo)	Aurelio Padron	Aunt Rosa	Olga Merediz
Beggar	Chamaco Garcia	Willy	Ray Stephens
Alan	Dennis Daniels	The People of El Barrio:	
Juanito	Charlie Serrano	Louie Woodknot; Narrator	Duane Bodin
Honest John	Ray De Mattis	Jose Ensalada	Jesse Corti
Sgt. Noble	Keith Jochim	Betty Ensalada	S.J. Davis
Cruikshank	Michael Jeter	Julia Fairchilde	Julia Lema
Lola	Michele Mais	Duchess Hilda	
Kitty	Vanessa Bell	Pinchik	Alaina Warren Zachary
Annabelle	Starr Danias	Officer Walker	Jenifer Lewis
Father Tucker	Frank Kopyc	Officer Chase	Stephen Jay
Mrs. Krekelberg	Lenka Peterson	Officer Cruz	Quitman Fludd III
Mariana (Chiquita Bonita)	Yamil Borges		

Swings: Leilani Jones, Greg Rosatti.

Understudies: Messrs. Kopyc, De Mattis—Duane Bodin; Messrs. Jochim, Garcia—Jesse Corti; Miss Danias—S.J. Davis; Mr. Stephens—Quitman Fludd III; Messrs Daniels, Jeter—Stephen Jay; Miss Borges—Leilani Jones; Miss Mais—Julia Lema; Miss Bell—Jenifer Lewis; Misses Peterson, Merediz—Alaina Warren Zachary.

Directed and choreographed by Patricia Birch; musical direction and vocal arrangements, Herbert Kaplan; scenery, Tom Lynch; costumes, Carrie F. Robbins; lighting, Neil Peter Jampolis; sound, Tom Morse; vocal and dance arrangements and musical supervision, Louis St. Louis; orchestrations, Michael Gibson, Gary Anderson; associate producer, Barry Greene; production stage manager, Michael Martorella; stage manager, David Piel; press, Betty Lee Hunt, Maria Cristina Pucci.

Time: Once upon a time. Place: El Barrio, somewhere in New York City. The Robin Hood legend transposed to a modern metropolitan Spanish quarter.

ACT I

Prologue .... Narrator, Pepe, Beggar, Alan, Juanito, Honest John, Company
Scene 1: A street in El Barrio
    "El Bravo" .... Pepe, Alan Juanito, Company
    "Cuchifrito Restaurant"................................... Pepe, Friends
Scene 2: The Blue Bagel Luncheonette
    "Que Pasa, My Love?" .... Pepe, Mariana
Scene 3: Honest John's parlor
    "Honest John's Game" .... Honest John, Henchmen

Scene 4: The subway entrance
"Chiquita Bonita".................................... Mariana, Aunt Rosa, Company
Scene 5: The church confessional and the lobby of Honest John's hotel
"Shoes" ....Lola, Kitty, Annabelle
Scene 6: The street
"Hey Chico"... Pepe, Alan, Juanito
"Criminal".. Aunt Rosa, Mariana, Company

ACT II

Scene 1: Honest John's used formal wear shop
Scene 2: The churchyard
"He Says" .... El Bravo, Chiquita Bonita
Scene 3: The Bimbo Lounge
"The Talent Contest".... Officer Walker, Betty Ensalada, Duchess Hilda Pinchik, Annabelle
"Gotta Get out"... Willie, The Creampuffs
Scene 4: Honest John's parlor
"Honest John's Game" (Reprise) .... Honest John, Henchmen
Scene 5: The subway entrance
"Adios Barrio" .... Mariana, Aunt Rosa, Company
"Fairy Tales" .... Pepe
Scene 6: The church confessional
Scene 7: Honest John's parlor
"Torture"............................. Mariana, Aunt Rosa, Honest John, Sgt. Noble
"That Latin Lure" .... Honest John
"Congratulations"................................ El Bravo, His Band, Honest John
Scene 8: The street fiesta
"Bailar!" .... Aunt Rosa
"And Furthermore"... Beggar
Finale... Company

The Heebie Jeebies (37). Musical by Mark Hampton and Stuart Ross; original idea by Mark Hampton; script and production advisor, Vet Boswell. Produced by Spencer Tandy, Joseph Butt and Peter Alsop at Westside Arts Theater (Downstairs). Opened June 18, 1981. (Closed July 19, 1981)

Memrie Innerarity   Nancy McCall
Audrey Lavine

General Understudy: Mary-Cleere Haran.

Direction and musical staging by Stuart Ross; scenery, Michael Sharp; costumes, Carol Oditz; lighting, Richard Winkler; musical supervision, Howard A. Roberts; vocal direction, Elise Bretton; orchestrations, Christopher Bankey; associate choreographer, Terry Reiser; produced in association with Dale Ward and Doug Cole; production stage manager, Robert Bennett; stage manager, Michael Trueman; press, Jeffrey Richards Associates, Bob Ganshaw.

Self-described as "a musical tribute to the Boswell sisters," Vet, Connee and Martha, whose 1930s singing style and song numbers are recreated here. Previously produced at Berkshire Theater Festival.

MUSICAL NUMBERS, ACT I: "The Heebie Jeebies," "Spend an Evening in Caroline," "Sentimental Gentleman From Georgia," "Nights When I Am Lonely," "St. Louis Blues," "I'm Gonna Cry," "Dinah," "That's How Rhythm Was Born," "We're on the Highway to Heaven;" The California Melodies Hour: "We Gotta Put the Sun Back in the Sky," "Life Is Just a Bowl of Cherries," "Sing a Little Jingle;" "Crazy People," "Nothing Is Sweeter Than You," "When I Take My Sugar to Tea." ACT II: "The Music Goes Round and Round," "Let Yourself Go," "You Oughta Be in Pictures," "Rock 'n' Roll," "These Foolish Things," "Until the Real Thing Comes Along," "Darktown Strutters Ball," "Minnie the Moocher's Wedding Day," "Goin' Home," "Shout, Sister, Shout," "The Object of My Affection," "Everybody Loves My Baby," "The Heebie Jeebies" (Reprise).

How It All Began (32). Adaptation of the autobiography of Michael "Bommi" Baumann; written and compiled by Benjamin Donenberg, Jessica Drake, Paula Fritz, Brian Hargrove, Mary Lynn Johnson, Val Kilmer, Linda Koslowski, Liane Langland, Des MacAnuff, Gregory Mortensen, Patrick O'Connell, John Palmer, Kim Staunton, Pamela White and Richard Ziman; edited by John Palmer. Produced by Joseph Papp in the Dodger Theater Company production at the New York Shakespeare Festival Public Theater (Other Stage). Opened June 18, 1981. (Closed July 12, 1981)

CAST: Lead Singer, Antje, Farah Diba, Sohniein, Bank Teller—Kim Staunton; Michael "Bommi" Baumann—Val Kilmer; Rudi Dutschke, Tommi Weisbecker—Benjamin Donenberg; Georg von Rauch—Brian Hargrove; Peter Urbach, Policeman—Gregory Mortenson; Annekatrin, Benno, Astrid Proll—Paula Fritz; Fritz Teufel, Hans Werner—Richard Ziman; Rainer, Sgt. Kurass, Judge—Patrick O'Connell; Angela Luther—Liane Langland; Ulrike Meinhof—Jessica Drake; Gudrun Ensslin—Mary Lynn Johnson; Andress Hans Baader—Pamela M. White; Hella—Linda Kozlowski.

Directed by Des McAnuff; scenery, Heidi Landesman; costumes, Leslie Calumet; lighting, Fred Buchholz; stage manager, Mo Donley; press, Merle Debuskey, Richard Kornberg, Ed Bullins, Dennis Thread.

Documentary drama of the founding of a 1960s terrorist group in West Germany, developed at the Juilliard School and featuring Group X of its Stage Division in this Dodger Theater Company guest residency production at the Public.

The Negro Ensemble Company. 1980–81 season concluded with **Zooman and the Sign** (44). Return engagement of the play by Charles Fuller. Produced by The Negro Ensemble Company, Douglas Turner Ward artistic director, Gerald S. Krone managing director, at Theater Four. Opened June 20, 1981. (Closed July 26, 1981)

Zooman	Giancarlo Esposito	Russell Odoms	Terrance Terry Ellis
Rachel Tate	Mary Alice	Donald Jackson	Steven A. Jones
Emmett Tate	Carl Gordon	Ash Boswell	Frances Foster
Reuben Tate	Ray Aranha	Grace Georges	Carol Lynn Maillard
Victor Tate	Alvin Alexis		

Directed by Douglas Turner Ward; scenery, Rodney J. Lucas; costumes, Judy Dearing; lighting, Shirley Prendergast; production stage manager, Clinton Turner Davis; stage manager, Femi Sarah Heggie; press, Howard Atlee, Jim Baldassare.

Time: The present. Place: Philadelphia, Pa.—The home of Rachel and Reuben Tate; the street outside; various locations for Zooman. The play was presented in two parts. This production of *Zooman and the Sign* was offered off Broadway by The Negro Ensemble Company 12/7/80 for 33 performances and was named a Best Play of its season.

Oscar Remembered (23). One-man performance by and with Maxim Mazumdar. Produced by Kevin Gebhard at the Provincetown Playhouse. Opened June 23, 1981. (Closed July 12, 1981)

Production supervision, Larry Fuller; scenery, Tom H. John; lighting, Richard Winkler; production stage manager, Bill Hare; press, Jeffrey Richards Associates, Ben Morse.

Act I: 1892–1895. Act II: Some years after Oscar's death.

The actor portrays Lord Alfred Douglas recalling his ill-fated friendship with Oscar Wilde.

Roundabout Theater Company. 1980–81 season concluded with **Misalliance** (192). Revival of the play by George Bernard Shaw. Produced by Roundabout Theater Company, Gene Feist and Michael Fried producing directors, at the Roundabout Theater Stage One. Opened June 23, 1981; see note. (Closed December 6, 1981)

John Tarleton Jr.	Rand Bridges	Hypatia Tarleton	Jeanne Ruskin
Bentley Summerhays	Keith McDermott	Mrs. Tarleton	Patricia O'Connell

Mark Blum, Brooke Adams and Ben Masters in *Key Exchange*

Lord Summerhays............	Ronald Drake	Lina Szczepanowska.........	Patricia Elliott
John Tarleton	Philip Bosco	Gunner..................	Anthony Heald
Joseph Percival	Nigel Reed		

Directed by Stephen Porter; scenery, Roger Mooney; costumes, Jane Greenwood; lighting, Ronald Wallace; original score, Philip Campanella; production stage manager, M.R. Jacobs; press, Susan Bloch & Company.

Time: May 31, 1909. Place: The house of John Tarleton of Hindhead, Surrey. The play was presented in two parts.

The last professional New York revival of *Misalliance* was off Broadway by the Roundabout 3/28/72 for 46 performances.

Note: Press date for *Misalliance* was 7/15/61.

New York Shakespeare Festival Public Theater. Summer schedule of two outdoor revivals of plays by William Shakespeare. **The Tempest** (24). Opened June 26, 1981; see note. (Closed July 26, 1981) **Henry IV, Part 1** (31). Opened July 31, 1981; see note. (Closed September 6, 1981) Produced by New York Shakespeare Festival, Joseph Papp producer, at the Delacorte Theater in Central Park.

THE TEMPEST

Prospero......................	Raul Julia	Ferdinand...........	David Marshall Grant
Miranda	Jessica Nelson	Alonso	Joseph Costa
Young Miranda..............	Clove Galilee	Antonio	Steven Keats
Caliban.....................	Barry Miller	Francisco	Carl Lumbly

Gonzalo	Frederick Neumann	Trinculo	Lola Pashalinski
Sebastian	Bill Raymond	Stephano	Louis Zorich
Adrian	Stephen Rowe		

Ariel: Craig Chang, Aramis Estevez, Michael Pearlman, Lute Ramblin', Ken Seymour, Iwatora, Eric Elice, Leo Holder, Esai Morales, Terry O'Reilly, David Sotolongo. Goddesses: Maya Pailu, Hedstrom O'Reilly, Panda Weiss, Clove Galilee.

Directed by Lee Breuer with Ruth Maleczech; scenery consultant, David Mitchell; costumes, Carol Oditz; lighting, Spencer Mosse; Malaysian dance choreography, Marion D'Cruz; contact improvisation, Steven Paxton; Gamelan music, Barbara Benary; Samba music, Nana Vasconcelos; magic, Jack Adams; production stage manager, Michael Chambers; stage manager, Susan Green; press, Merle Debuskey, Richard Kornberg.

The last major New York revival of *The Tempest* was off Broadway by New York Shakespeare Festival Lincoln Center 1/26/74 for 81 performances.

HENRY IV, PART 1

Prologue; 1st Carrier; Peto	Philip Craig	Lady Percy	Margaret Whitton
Henry IV	Stephen Markle	Hotspur Servant	Val Kilmer
Lancaster	Raphael Sbarge	Francis	Richard Ziman
Westmoreland; Chamberlain	Rex Robbins	Vintner; Vernon	Robert Westenberg
Blunt	John Goodman	Mistress Quickly	Beulah Garrick
Prince Henry	John Vickery	Sheriff	Peter Rogan
Falstaff	Kenneth McMillan	Mortimer	Todd Waring
Bardolph	John Bottom	Glendower	Max Wright
Poins	Philip Casnoff	Lady Mortimer	Susan Berman
Thomas	Ralph Drischell	Archibald	Ralph Byers
Henry Percy	Clement Fowler	Scroop	George Lord
Hotspur	Mandy Patinkin	Sir Michael	Benjamin Donenberg
2d Carrier	Matthew Gottlieb	Messenger	Kevin Spacey
Gadshill	Larry Block		

Lords, Monks, Serving Women, Tavern People, Travelers, Soldiers: Susan Berman, Larry Block, Ralph Byers, Christopher Colt, Philip Craig, Brian Delate, Benjamin Donenberg, Henry Ferree, Paula Fritz, Gerald Gilmore, Matthew Gottlieb, Brian Hargrove, Mary Johnson, Val Kilmer, Linda Kozlowski, Conal O'Brien, Rick Parks, David Price, Rich Rand, Kevin Spacey, Jack Stehlin, Todd Waring, Robert Westenberg, Richard Ziman.

Directed by Des McAnuff; scenery, Stuart Wurtzel; costumes, Patricia McGourty; lighting, Richard Nelson; music, Richard Peaslee; fight sequences, B.H. Barry.

The last professional New York revival of *Henry IV, Part 1* was in Classic Stage Company repertory 10/8/78.

Note: Press date for *The Tempest* was 7/8/81, for *Henry IV, Part 1* was 8/19/81.

What the Butler Saw (12). Revival of the play by Joe Orton. Produced by '81 Theater, Inc. at the Westside Arts Theater (Cabaret Space). Opened July 3, 1981. (Closed July 12, 1981)

Dr. Prentice	Harry Reems	Nicholas Beckett	Jonathan Goldwater
Geraldine Barclay	Holly Woodlawn	Dr. Rance	George Lloyd
Mrs. Prentice	le Clanché du Rand	Sgt. Match	Brandon Brady

Understudies: Messrs. Reems, Brady, Lloyd—Edward Conery; Misses Woodlawn, du Rand—Staci Sweeden; Mr. Goldwater—John E.C. Doyle.

Directed by Jonathan Davenport. scenery, Robert Berg; costumes, Jim Stewart; lighting, Terry Alan Smith; "Sir Winnie" by Doug Johns; executive producer, Nelson Denis; production stage manager, Greta Minsky; press, Jeffrey Richards Associates, Robert Ganshaw.

What the Butler Saw was produced off Broadway 5/4/70 for 224 performances and was named a Best Play of its season. This revival was presented in two parts.

Key Exchange (352). By Kevin Wade. Produced by Frank Gero, Mark Gero, Mitchell Maxwell, Alan J. Schuster and Frederick Zollo in the WPA Theater (Kyle Renick producing director) production at the Orpheum Theater. Opened July 14, 1981. (Closed May 16, 1982)

Michael	Mark Blum	Lisa	Brooke Adams
Philip	Ben Masters		

Understudies: Messrs. Blum, Masters—Robert Schenkkan; Miss Adams—Sofia Landon.

Directed by Barnet Kellman; scenery, Terry Ariano; costumes, Robert Wojewodski; lighting, Frances Aronson; associate producer, Fred H. Krones; production stage manager, Bill McComb; press, Solters/Roskin/Friedman, Inc., Milly Schoenbaum, Warren Knowlton, Kevin Patterson.

Place: Central Park, N.Y. Scene 1: Sunday, June 20. Scene 2: Sunday, June 27. Scene 3: Sunday, July 4. Scene 4: Sunday, July 11. Scene 5: Sunday, July 18. Scene 6: Sunday, July 25. Scene 7: Saturday, July 31. Scene 8: Sunday, August 1. Scene 9: Sunday, August 8. The play was presented in two parts.

The making—or non-making—of commitments among contemporary youth. Previously produced off off Broadway at WPA Theater.

Priscilla Lopez replaced Brooke Adams 12/22/81.

*New York Shakespeare Festival Public Theater. Schedule of 11 programs. **The Dance and the Railroad** (181). By David Henry Hwang. Opened July 16, 1981. (Closed December 20, 1981) **The Laundry Hour** (8). Musical revue by Mark Linn-Baker and Lewis Black; music by Paul Schierhorn. Opened August 4, 1981. (Closed August 9, 1981) **The Ballad of Dexter Creed** (8). By Michael Moriarty. Opened October 6, 1981. (Closed October 11, 1981) **Family Devotions** (76). By David Henry Hwang. Opened October 18, 1981. (Closed December 20, 1981) **Twelve Dreams** (48). By James Lapine. Opened December 22, 1981. (Closed January 31, 1982)

Also **Zastrozzi** (49). By George F. Walker. Opened January 17, 1982. (Closed February 28, 1982) **Lullabye and Goodnight** (30). Musical writted and composed by Elizabeth Swados. Opened February 9, 1982. (Closed March 7, 1982) **Three Acts of Recognition** (48). By Botho Strauss; translated by Sophie Wilkins. Opened April 6, 1982. (Closed May 16, 1982) ***Antigone** (40). Revival of the play by Sophocles; translated by John Chioles. Opened April 27, 1982. **Red and Blue** (15). By Michael Hurson. Opened May 12, 1982. (Closed May 23, 1982). **Goose and Tomtom** (14). By David Rabe. Opened May 6, 1982. (Closed May 16, 1982). Produced by New York Shakespeare Festival Public Theater, Joseph Papp producer, at the Public Theater (see note).

ALL PLAYS: Production supervisor, Jason Steven Cohen; press, Merle Debuskey, Richard Kornberg, Ed Bullins, Dennis Thread, Anthony Sherwood.

THE DANCE AND THE RAILROAD

Lone	John Lone
Ma	Tzi Ma

Music composed by John Lone; arranged and performed by Lucia Hwong (pi-pa, percussion), Charlie Chin (bamboo flute, percussion, harp), Tzi Ma (percussion), David Henry Hwang (violin); house music from the recording "Sonic Seasonings" by Walter Carlos.

Directed and choreographed by John Lone; scenery, Karen Schulz; costumes, Judy Dearing; lighting, Victor En Yu Tan; production stage manager, Alice Jankowiak.

Time: June 1867. Place: A mountain top near the transcontinental railroad. Scene 1: Afternoon. Scene 2: Afternoon, a day later. Scene 3: Late afternoon, four days later. Scene 4: Late that evening. Scene 5: Just before dawn the following day.

Chinese railroad workers practise the exacting, ballet-like art of formal Chinese opera to counter the dehumanizing effects of their hard labor in undignified circumstances.

A Best Play; see page 107.

THE LAUNDRY HOUR

Lewis Black   Paul Schierhorn
Mark Linn-Baker

Directed by William Peters; choreography, Rick Elice; musical direction, Paul Schierhorn; lighting, Gerard P. Bourcier.

Cabaret-style show described by its authors as a spiritual adventure "from the fervent 1960s to today's loss of the liberal leading edge." The show was presented without intermission.

THE BALLAD OF DEXTER CREED

CAST: Michael Moriarty, Linda Kozlowski.

Directed by James Milton; scenery and lighting, John Gisondi; costumes, Amanda J. Klein; music composed by Michael Moriarty; arrangements, Louis Forestieri.

The drama critic criticized and satirized in a production which combines an onstage performance of an actor playing a role and a taped interview between actor and critic. The play was presented without intermission.

FAMILY DEVOTIONS

DiGou	Victor Wong	Ama	Tina Chen
Wilbur	Jim Ishida	Popo	June Kim
Joanne	Jodi Long	Robert	Michael Paul Chan
Jenny	Lauren Tom	Hannah	Helen Funai
Chester	Marc Hayashi		

Musicians: Lucia Hwong pi-pa; Charlie Chin bamboo flute, butterfly harp.

Understudies: Miss Tom—June Angela; Misses Funai, Long—Hyung-In Choi; Misses Chen, Kim —Lilah Kan; Messrs. Wong, Chan, Ishida—Fredric Mao; Mr. Hayashi—Keenan Shimizu.

Directed by Robert Allan Ackerman; scenery, David Gropman; costumes, Willa Kim; lighting, Tom Skelton; original music composed by John Lone; arrangements, Lucia Hwong, Charlie Chin; production stage manager, Michael Chambers; stage manager, Loretta Robertson.

Time: The present, late Sunday afternoon. Place: The sunroom and backyard of a home in Bel Air, Calif. The play was presented without intermission.

Affluent Chinese American family receives a visit from an uncle who lives in China, exposing false values of each.

TWELVE DREAMS

Charles Hatrick	James Olson	Sanford Putnam	Thomas Hulce
Emma Hatrick	Olivia Laurel Mates	Dorothy Trowbridge	Carole Shelley
Jenny	Marcell Rosenblatt	Miss Banton	Valerie Mahaffey
Professor	Stefan Schnabel	Rindy	Stacey Glick

Directed by James Lapine; scenery, Heidi Landesman; costumes, William Ivey Long; lighting, Frances Aronson; music, Allen Shawn; movement consultant, Wesley Fata; production stage manager, Ginny Martino; stage manager, Evan Canary.

Place: A university town in New England. Act I: Winter, 1936. Act II: Spring, 1937.

Ten-year-old-girl's strange dreams (enacted in the play) are subjected to analysis by a psychiatrist.

ZASTROZZI

Bernardo	Andreas Katsulas	Verezzi	Grzegorz Wagrowski
Zastrozzi	Jan Triska	Matilda	Judith Roberts
Victor	Robert Langdon-Lloyd	Julia	Frances Conroy

Understudies: Mr. Triska—Dan Nutu; Messrs. Langdon-Lloyd, Verezzi—Christopher McCann; Misses Conroy, Roberts—Lauren Kim; Mr. Katsulas—John Capodice.

Stefan Schnabel, Valerie Mahaffey, Thomas Hulce, Stacey
Glick and Marcell Rosenblatt in a scene from *Twelve Dreams*

Directed by Andrei Serban; scenery and costumes, Manuel Lutgenhorst; lighting, Jennifer Tipton; combat staging, Larry Carpenter; stage managers, Susan Green, Richard Jakiel.

Time: The 1890s. Place: Europe, probably Italy. The play was presented without intermission.

A fable of the battle of good and evil in the tale of a master-criminal's search for vengeance. A foreign (Canadian) play in its premiere in this production.

LULLABYE AND GOODNIGHT

Retail	Frances Asher	Trojan	Bruce Hubbard
Velvet Puppy	Gail Boggs	Snow	Larry Marshall
Deputy	Jesse Corti	Saint	Olga M. Merediz
Lullabye	Jossie de Guzman	Cody	Tim Moore
Stiletto	Ula Hedwig	Chameleon	Rudy Roberson

Understudies: Women—Vicky Blumenthal; Men—Clifford Lipson; Miss Merediz—Frances Asher; Miss Hedwig—Gail Boggs; Miss Boggs—Miss Hedwig; Miss Asher—Olga M. Merediz; Mr. Hubbard—Jesse Corti; Mr. Marshall—Bruce Hubbard; Mr. Roberson—Tim Moore; Mr. Moore—Rudy Roberson.

Directed by Elizabeth Swados; choreography, Ara Fitzgerald; scenery, David Jenkins; costumes, Hilary Rosenfeld; lighting, Marcia Madeira; production stage manager, Jeff Lee; stage manager, Sherry Cohen.

Self-labeled "a musical romance" about prostitutes and their hangers-on.

ACT I

Prologue	Company
"Gentleman of Leisure"	Snow, Women

"Port Authority" .... Company
"I Am Sick of Love"... Snow, Lullabye
"When a Pimp Meets a Whore"... Snow, Lullabye
"Love Loves the Difficult Things" .... Snow, Lullabye, Men
"In the Life"... Company
"The Moth and the Flame" .... Snow, Lullabye, Women
"Why We Do It"... Women
"Wife Beating Song" .... Lullabye
"You're My Favorite Lullabye" .... Snow, Lullabye
"When Any Woman Makes a Running Issue Out of Her Flesh"................... Company
"Now You Are One of the Family"........................... Snow, Lullabye, Company
"Turn Her Out"... Snow, Company
"You Gave Me Love" .... Lullabye

ACT II

"Let the Day Perish When I Was Born" .... Lullabye, Snow
"Keep Working" .... Snow, Company
"Deprogramming Song" .... Lullabye
"Lies, Lies, Lies" .... Lullabye, Snow
"Ladies, Look at Yourselves".................................... Lullabye, Women
"Don't You Ever Give It All Away"........................ Lullabye, Snow, Company
"Man That Is Born of Woman"................................... Snow, Men
"Sub-Babylon" .... Snow, Company
"Getting From Day to Day" .... Snow
"Sweet Words"... Snow Lullabye, Company
"The Nightmare Was Me" .... Lullabye, Company

THREE ACTS OF RECOGNITION

Vogel	Carl Don	Johanna	Kathleen Masterson
Klaus	Stephen Baccus	Franz	Sam Gray
Elfriede	Cristine Rose	Ruth	Kate Manheim
Felix	James Cromwell	Lothar	Bill Raymond
Richard	William Atherton	Answald	Frank Maraden
Suzanne	Joan MacIntosh	Peter	Christopher McCann
Moritz	Richard Jordan	Marlies	Karen Young
Vivien	Ruth Nelson	Kiepert	Wade Barnes
Martin	Leonardo Cimino		

Directed by Richard Foreman; scenery, Sally Jacobs; costumes, Franne Lee; lighting, F. Mitchell Dana; paintings, Jeanne Hedstrom; sound, Daniel M. Schreler.

1977 German play exposing the flaws and troubles of 16 people who come together at an art exhibition.

ANTIGONE

Ismene	Rosemary Quinn	Haemon	Peter Francis-James
Antigone	Lisa Banes	Tiresias	Priscilla Smith
Chorus Leader	George Lloyd	Boy	Jeffrey Bravin
Creon	F. Murray Abraham	Messenger	Raymond Barry
Guard	Roger Babb	Euridice	Shami Chaikin

Chorus: B. Constance Barry, Hunt Cole, Ann Dunnigan, Richard Frisch, Ronnie Gilbert, Clark Morgan.

Directed by Joseph Chaikin; music, Richard Peaslee; scenery and costumes, Sally Jacobs; lighting, Beverly Emmons; dramaturg, Mira Rafalowicz.

The last major New York revival of Sophocles's *Antigone* was by Classic Stage Company 10/30/80 for 57 performances.

RED AND BLUE

Blue	Randy Danson	Voice	James Hurdle
Red	Earl Hindman		

Directed by JoAnne Akalaitis; scenery and lighting, John Arnone; sound, J.B. Dallas; projections, Stephanie Rudolph; production consultant, B-St. John Schofield.

Conversation of offstage voices visualized onstage by two colored light bulbs. The play was presented without intermission.

GOOSE AND TOMTOM

Tomtom	Jerry Mayer	Lulu	Leslie Busa
Goose	Frederick Neumann	Bingo	Will Patton
Lorraine	Gale Garnett	The Man	Clarence Felder

Henchmen: Jesse Doran, Jack R. Marks, Brian Delate, Adam LeFevre, Peter Jolly.

Directed by John Pynchon Holms; scenery and costumes, Dean Tschetter; lighting, Victor En Yu Tan.

Comic jewel robbery and other criminal antics.

The New York Shakespeare Festival 1981–82 season also included the third annual engagement of *The Haggadah, a Passover Cantata,* musical adapted by Elizabeth Swados, narration adapted from Elie Wiesel's *Moses: Portrait of a Leader* and portions of the Haggadah and the Old Testament, 3/30/82–5/23/82 for 62 performances, with scenery, costumes, puppets and masks by Julie Taymor, lighting by Arden Fingerhut and a cast including Tichina Arnold, Anthony Asbury, Rebecca Bondor, Craig Chang, Victor Cook, Jesse Corti, Sheila Dabney, Nina Dova, Ron Eichaker, Tom Howe, Bruce Hubbard, Onni Johnson, Sally Kate, Esther Levy, Larry Marshall, Olga Merediz, David Schechter, Zvee Scooler, Ira Siff and Martha Wingate (see its entries in *The Best Plays of 1979–80* and *1980–81*).

In Joseph Papp's Public Theater there are many separate auditoriums. *The Dance and the Railroad* and *Three Acts of Recognition* played the Anspacher Theater, *The Laundry Hour, Zastrozzi* and *Red and Blue* played The Other Stage, *The Ballad of Dexter Creed* played LuEsther Hall, *Family Devotions, Lullabye and Goodnight* and *Goose and Tomtom* played the Estelle R. Newman Theater, *Twelve Dreams* and *Antigone* played Martinson Hall.

The Phoenix Theater, Schedule of four programs. **Maggie & Pierre** (22). By Linda Griffiths with Paul Thompson. Produced by arrangement with Garth H. Drabinsky and Norman Kean. Opened September 17, 1981; see note. (Closed October 11, 1981) **After the Prize** (22). By Fay Weldon. Opened November 19, 1981; see note. (Closed December 13, 1981) **Kaufman at Large** (22). Adapted by John Lithgow from the writings of George S. Kaufman. Opened December 25, 1981; see note. (Closed January 17, 1982) **Weekends Like Other People** (30). By David Blomquist. Opened March 4, 1982; see note. (Closed March 28, 1982) Produced by The Phoenix Theater, T. Edward Hambleton managing director, Steven Robman artistic director, at the Marymount Manhattan Theater.

MAGGIE & PIERRE

CAST: Linda Griffiths, Eric Peterson.

Directed by Paul Thompson; scenery, John Kasarda; costumes, Denise Romano; lighting, Jim Plaxton; press, Susan L. Schulman.

Canada's onetime first family, the Trudeaus, interviewed by a reporter (Eric Peterson) and with both Maggie and Pierre portrayed by Linda Griffiths. The play was presented in two parts. A foreign play previously produced in Canada.

AFTER THE PRIZE

Edwin	John Horton	Bee	Lois Markle
Wasp	Veronica Castang	Brian	David McCallum

Directed by Steven Robman; scenery, Adrianne Lobel; costumes, Linda Fisher; lighting, Arden Fingerhut; fights, B.H. Barry; sound, Tom Gould; production stage manager, J. Thomas Vivian.

Time: The present. Place: England. The play was presented in two parts.

Nobel prizewinner allows her success to jeopardize her emotional relationships. A foreign (British) play in its world premiere in this production.

KAUFMAN AT LARGE

George S. Kaufman .... John Lithgow

Directed by John Lithgow with Steven Robman; scenery, Marjorie Bradley Kellogg; costumes, Ann Roth; lighting, Ronald M. Bundt; sound, David Rapkin; assistant director, Bob Edgar.

The actor in a solo portrayal of George S. Kaufman on Aug. 21, 1936 reacting to his notoriety in the tabloids because of a love affair and tinkering with the script of *You Can't Take It With You* with Moss Hart on the long distance phone. The play was presented in two parts.

WEEKENDS LIKE OTHER PEOPLE

Laurie .... Rose Gregorio
Dan .... Kenneth McMillan

Directed by Ulu Grosbard; scenery, David Jenkins; costumes, Jennifer Von Mayrhauser; lighting, Pat Collins; sound, David Rapkin; production stage manager, J. Thomas Vivian.

Time: The present, autumn. Place: A small apartment on the Northwest side of Chicago. The play was presented in two parts.

The plight of the average, blue-collar American middle-aged couple.

Note: Press date for *Maggie & Pierre* was 9/26/81, for *After the Prize* was 11/23/81, for *Kaufman at Large* was 12/28/81, for *Weekends Like Other People* was 3/11/82.

Chekhov on the Lawn (64). Revival of the one-man show by Elihu Winer; performed by William Shust. Produced by Ruth Kalkstein at Theater East. Opened September 22, 1981. (Closed November 15, 1981)

Directed by Elihu Winer; scenery and lighting, Joe Ray; press, David Lipsky.

Time: April 17, 1900. Place: The garden of Chekhov's home in Yalta.

An impersonation of Anton Chekhov discussing his works (and reading excerpts from them) with visiting Moscow Art Theater friends, previously produced off Broadway at the Roundabout 11/22/72 for 22 performances.

*Roundabout Theater Company. Schedule of four programs. **Miss Julie** (196) and **Playing With Fire** (160). Program of two revivals by August Strindberg; translated by Michael Meyer. Opened September 22, 1981; see note. (*Playing With Fire* closed February 7, 1982; *Miss Julie* closed March 14, 1982) **The Caretaker** (69). Revival of the play by Harold Pinter. Opened January 21, 1982; see note. (Closed March 21, 1982) ***The Browning Version,** revival of the play by Terence Rattigan, and ***The Twelve-Pound Look,** revival of the play by J.M. Barrie (80). Opened March 23, 1982; see note. ***The Chalk Garden** (72). Revival of the play by Enid Bagnold. Opened March 30, 1982; see note. Produced by Roundabout Theater Company, Gene Feist and Michael Fried producing directors, at the Roundabout Theater (*The Caretaker* and *The Chalk Garden* at Stage One, *Miss Julie* and *Playing With Fire* and *The Browning Version* and *The Twelve-Pound Look* at Stage Two).

PLAYING WITH FIRE

Son	Geoffrey Pierson	Mother	Elizabeth Owens
Daughter-in-Law	Giulia Pagano	Father	Dillon Evans

Bruce Wall, Lee Richardson, Edmond Genest and Sheila
Allen in the Roundabout production of *The Browning Version*

Cousin .... Janet Zarish
Friend.................... John Michalski
   Time: A summer morning toward the end of
the last century. Place: A seaside resort in Sweden. The play was presented in one act.

MISS JULIE

Christine.................... Alma Cuervo
Jean.................. Stephen Schnetzer
Miss Julie.................. Giulia Pagano
   Country Folk: Dillon Evans, Janet Zarish,
Elizabeth Owens, John Michalski, Mickey Bes-
soir.
   Time: On a midsummer's night at the end of
the last century. Place: The Count's kitchen. The
play was presented in two parts.

Directed by Gene Feist; scenery, Roger Mooney; costumes, A. Christina Giannini; lighting, Marshall Spiller; sound, Philip Campanella; production stage manager, Michael S. Mantel; press, Susan Bloch & Company, Adrian Bryan-Brown, Ellen Zeisler.

New York professional revivals of record of *Miss Julie* took place off Broadway in the 1953–54 season; by the Phoenix Theater 2/21/56 for 33 performances; on Broadway by the Royal Dramatic Theater of Sweden 5/16/62 for 3 performances; and off Broadway 11/10/65 for 11 performances and 7/31/73 (by the Roundabout in another translation) for 16 performances. *Playing With Fire* was presented off off Broadway (last season by Shelter West).

Janet Zarish replaced Giulia Pagano and Priscilla Smith replaced Alma Cuervo in *Miss Julie* 2/7/82.

THE CARETAKER

Mick..................... Daniel Gerroll
Aston .... Anthony Heald
Davies............... F. Murray Abraham

Directed by Anthony Page; scenery, Roger Mooney; costumes, A. Christina Giannini; lighting, Ronald Wallace; sound, Philip Campanella; production stage manager, M.R. Jacobs.

Place: A house in West London. Act I, Scene 1: A night in winter. Scene 2: The next morning. Act II, Scene 1: A few seconds later. Scene 2: Later that day. Scene 3: The next morning. Act III, Scene 1: A fortnight later. Scene 2: Later that night. Scene 3: The next evening.

The last major New York revival of *The Caretaker* was by the Roundabout 6/23/73 for 36 performances.

THE BROWNING VERSION

John Taplow	Bruce Wall	Dr. Frobisher..............	James Higgins
Frank Hunter..............	Edmond Genest	Peter Gilbert	Josh Clark
Millie Crocker-Harris	Sheila Allen	Mrs. Gilbert.................	Joyce Fideor
Andrew Crocker-Harris	Lee Richardson		

THE TWELVE-POUND LOOK

Sir Harry Sims.............	Lee Richardson	Kate	Sheila Allen
Lady Sims	Joyce Fideor	Tombes...................	James Higgins

Directed by Stephen Porter; scenery, Roger Mooney; costumes, Sarah G. Conly; lighting, Walter Uhrman; sound, Philip Campanella; production stage manager, Michael S. Mantel.

The Browning Version was first produced on Broadway 10/12/49 for 69 performances. *The Twelve-Pound Look* was first produced on Broadway 2/13/11 for 32 performances.

THE CHALK GARDEN

Miss Madrigal	Irene Worth	3d Applicant	Betty Low
Maitland.................	Donal Donnelly	Mrs. St. Maugham	Constance Cummings
2d Applicant; Nurse	Eunice Anderson	Olivia	Elizabeth Owens
Laurel..................	Sallyanne Tackus	Judge	I.M. Hobson

Directed by John Stix; scenery, Roger Mooney; costumes, Judith Dolan; lighting, Martin Aronstein; sound, Philip Campanella; production stage manager, M.R. Jacobs.

The Chalk Garden was first produced on Broadway 10/26/55 for 182 performances. This is its first major New York revival. The play was presented in three parts.

Note: Press date for *Miss Julie* and *Playing With Fire* was 12/9/81, for *The Caretaker* was 2/24/82, for *The Browning Version* and *The Twelve-Pound Look* was 4/19/82, for *The Chalk Garden* was 4/29/82.

Sea Marks (62). By Gardner McKay. Produced by Dana and Deborah Matthew at the Players Theater. Opened September 24, 1981. (Closed November 15, 1981)

Colm Primrose	John Getz
Timothea Stiles	Leslie Lyles

Directed by John Stix; scenery, Leslie Taylor, Dale Jordan; costumes, Richard Hornung; lighting, Todd Elmer; production stage manager, Tom W. Picard; press, Bruce Cohen.

Liverpool lady attempts to bring out the poetic and romantic nature of an Irish fisherman. Previously produced in regional theater and in an off-off-Broadway production at Manhattan Theater Club. The play was presented in two parts.

Everybody's Gettin' Into the Act (33). Vaudeville revue by Bob Ost. Produced by Karen B. Gromis and Bunny Adir, Ltd. at Actors' Playhouse. Opened September 27, 1981. (Closed October 25, 1981)

CAST: The Loser, Outtatown Broad, Female Friend, Louise Black, Mary Smith, Evie, The Swinger —Ann Hodapp; The Piano Man—Bill McCauley; The Looker, Rich Bitch, Female Stranger, Doris Gray, Gloria Vandenberg, Lonely Lady, The Victim—Leilani Mickey; The Loner, GQ Man, Male

Friend, Herbert Gray, Egon Vandenberg, Lonely Man, The Compaliner—Tuck Milligan; The Lover, Macho Man, Male Friend Fred Black, Charles Smith, Stu, The Drag—Ross Petty.

Understudies: Misses Hodapp, Mickey—Julie Oliveri.

Directed by Darwin Knight; musical direction and arrangements, Curtis Blaine; scenery, Frank J. Boros; costumes, Dianne Finn Chapman; lighting and production stage manager, Ric Barrett; stage manager, Julie Oliveri; press, Fred Nathan & Associates, Patt Dale, Eileen McMahon, Jan Greenberg.

Vignettes of contemporary life and love. Previously produced off off Broadway.

SONGS AND SCENES—PART I

Prologue: Gettin' into the act—a bare stage
"Everybody's Gettin' Into the Act" .... Company
Act One: Singles' scene—an Eastside bar
"That First Hello" .... Piano Player
The Pickup .... The Loner, The Loser
"Perfection" .... The Lover
"Too Good" .... The Looker
Act Two: Attitudes—the hottest dance club in town
Attitude #1 .... Outtatown Broad
"So Close" .... Company
Attitude #2 .... Rich Bitch
Attitude #3/"Steppin' Back" .... GQ Man
Attitude #4 .... Macho Man
"I'm Available" .... Outtatown Broad
"Love Me Just a Little Bit" .... Company
Act Three: Performance—two bedrooms
Strange Bedfellows/"Love Duet" .... The Strangers
Nothing's Changed/"Looks Like Love" .... The Friends
Act Four: Routine—somewhere in suburbia
Life Is Perfect/"You Never Take Me Anywhere" .... Doris, Herbert
Success Stories .... Louise, Fred
Social Intercourse/First Act Finale .... Company

PART II

Entr'acte
Act Five: Appearance—a summer house in Southampton
Appearance .... Mary, Charles
"Yes, I See the Woman" .... Charles
Playing Hostess .... Mary
Party Games/"To Wit" .... Mary, Charles, Gloria, Egon
"A Party in Southampton" .... Mary
Act Six: Gettin' into the act—a theater
Sincere .... Stu, Evie
"It Always Seems to Rain" .... Lonely Lady
"Never, Never" .... Lonely Guy
"Keepin' It Together" .... Piano Man
Act Seven: In the spotlight—a stage
"Ballad of the Victim" .... The Victim
"Alive and . . . Well" .... The Complainer
"Valse Triste" .... The Drag
"And I'm There!" .... The Swinger
Epilogue: Offstage
"Don't I Know You?" .... Company
"Everybody's Gettin' Into the Act" (Reprise) .... Company

Particular Friendships (23). By Bill Elverman. Produced by David Jones and George Barimo at the Astor Place Theater. Opened September 30, 1981. (Closed October 18, 1981)

Avery Graham .... Luke Reilly
Brooke Silver.. Julie Kavner

Understudies: Miss Kavner—Betsy Tooker; Mr. Graham—Cotter Smith.
Directed by Dennis Rosa; scenery and costumes, Ben Shecter; lighting, Craig Miller; original music, William D. Brehn; production stage manager, Perry Cline; press, Jeffrey Richards Associates, Robert Ganshaw.
Time: The present. Place: Avery's New York apartment. The play was presented in two acts.
Comedy, actress meets homosexual artist. An American play which had its world premiere at the Grove Theater in London in 1980.

Pump Boys and Dinettes (112). Musical with music and lyrics by Jim Wann; additional music and lyrics by other members of the cast. Produced by Dodger Productions (Michael David, Doug Johnson, Rocco Landesman, Des McAnuff, Edward Strong, Sherman Warner), Louis Busch Hager, Marilyn Strauss, Kate Studley, Warner Theater Productions, Inc. and Max Weitzenhoffer at the Colonnades Theater. Opened October 1, 1981. (Closed January 17, 1982 and transferred to Broadway; see its entry in the Plays Produced on Broadway section of this volume)

Jackson...................... John Foley	Rhetta Cupp .... Cass Morgan
L.M...................... Mark Hardwick	Eddie .... John Schimmel
Prudie Cupp................. Debra Monk	Jim .... Jim Wann

Scenery, Doug Johnson; lighting, Fred Buchholz; press, Betty Lee Hunt Associates.
Gas jockeys and waitresses from the diner across the highway combine in country music numbers ranging from ballads to blues. Previously produced off off Broadway at Westside Arts Theater.

PART I

(Music and lyrics by Jim Wann unless otherwise noted)
"Highway 57".. Company
"Takin' My Time" .... Pump Boys
    (by Spider John Koerner, additional lyrics by John Foley)
"Who Will the Next Fool Be" .... L.M.
    (by Charlie Rich)
"Menu Song".. Dinettes
    (by Cass Morgan and Debra Monk)
"The Best Man".. Prudie
"Fisherman's Prayer".. Pump Boys
"Catfish" .... Pump Boys
    (by Jim Wann and B. Simpson)
"Mamaw"... Jim
"Be Good or Be Gone"... Rhetta
"Drinkin' Shoes" .... Company
    (by Mark Hardwick, Cass Morgan and Debra Monk)

PART II

"Pump Boys" .... Pump Boys
"Mona".. Jackson
"T.N.D.P.W.A.M." .... L.M.
"Tips" .... Dinettes
    (by Debra Monk and Cass Morgan)
"Sisters"... Dinettes
    (by Cass Morgan)
"Vacation" .... Company
"No Holds Barred" .... Company
    (by Jim Wann and Cass Morgan)

"Farmer Tan".. L.M., Dinettes
"Highway 57" (Reprise) .... Company
"Closing Time"... Company

The Broken Pitcher (23). Revival of the play by Heinrich von Kleist; translated by Jon Swan. Produced by the Kleist Company, Lily Turner and Carl Weber executive producers, and sponsored by Goethe House, at the Martinique Theater. Opened October 7, 1981. (Closed October 25, 1981)

Lisa....................... Barbara Wild	Martha Rull.................. Sylvia Short
Margaret................. Marylouise Burke	Eve .... Marta Heflin
Adam .... George Ede	Veit Puddle .... Thomas Carson
Link .... Larry Pine	Ruprecht .... Gary Kingsolver
Servant.................... Roy Cockrum	Constable .... Norman Marshall
Waiter.............. Richard M. Davidson	Bridget .... Angela Pietropinto

Directed by Carl Weber; scenery and lighting, Wolfgang Roth; costumes, Dean H. Reiter; production stage manager, John Weeks; press, Susan Bloch, Adrian Bryan-Brown.

German comedy, first produced in 1808, about honest Dutch peasants in a battle of wits with an immoral judge. Its last New York production took place on Broadway 4/1/58 for 12 performances in another translation entitled *The Broken Jug*.

Double Feature (7). Musical with book, music and lyrics by Jeffrey Moss. Produced by Allen Grossman, Karl Allison and Nan Pearlman in association with The Common at St. Peter's Church. Opened October 8, 1981. (Closed October 13, 1981)

Directed by Sheldon Larry; choreography, Adam Grammis; musical direction, Michael Lee Stockler; scenery, Stuart Wurtzel; costumes, Patricia Von Brandenstein; lighting, Marilyn Rennagel; musical arrangements and orchestrations, Michael Starobin; additional dance arrangements, Glen Rovin; production stage manager, Susan Green; press, Jeffrey Richards Associates, Bob Ganshaw. With Pamela Blair, Carole Shelley, Stephen Vinovich, Don Scardino.

The romantic problems of two contemporary couples. The play was presented in two parts. Previously produced at the Long Wharf Theater, New Haven, Conn.

*The American Place Theater. Schedule of three programs. **Grace** (24). By Jane Stanton Hitchcock. Opened October 13, 1981; see note. (Closed November 1, 1981) **Behind the Broken Words** (15). By Roscoe Lee Browne and Anthony Zerbe; devised from the works of celebrated writers. Opened December 4, 1981; see note. (Closed December 20, 1981) ***The Regard of Flight** and **The Clown Bagatelles** (16). Comedy entertainment written by Bill Irwin; original music by Doug Skinner. Opened May 23, 1982. Produced by The American Place Theater, Wynn Handman director, Julia Miles associate director, at the American Place Theater.

GRACE

Grace .... Scotty Bloch	Sissy .... Jane Fleiss
Mae...................... Catherine Byers	Dino .... Emmanuel Yesckas
Indian.................... Rino Thunder	Patterson .... James Higgins
Rose .... Karen Looze	Mrs. Meers................. Hope Cameron

Directed by Peter Thompson; scenery, William Barclay; costumes, David Griffin; lighting, Phil Monat; production stage manager, Nancy Harrington; press, Jeffrey Richards Associates, Ted Killmer, C. George Willard, Bob Ganshaw.

Dramatic portrait of an outspoken, detestable woman. Previously produced by American Place in workshop. The play was presented in two parts.

Bill Irwin airborne in *The Regard of Flight*

BEHIND THE BROKEN WORDS

CAST: Roscoe Lee Browne, Anthony Zerbe.

Production supervisor, Nancy Harrington; a Cameo Entertainment production, Howard Burman producing director.

Anthology of poetry excerpts from the works of celebrated writers. Part I: From *The Very Latest School in Art* by e.e. cummings; Junkman's Obligato by Lawrence Ferlinghetti; "Rain Comes Down" by Edna St. Vincent Millay; In My Craft or Sullen Art by Dylan Thomas; Prologue to *Amphytryon 38* by Jean Giraudoux; The Song of the Wandering Aengus by W.B. Yeats; I Knew a Woman, Lovely in Her Bones by Theodore Roethke; From *Let Us Now Praise Famous Men* by James Agee; "Mariposa" by Edna St. Vincent Millay; Musee des Beaux Arts by W.H. Auden; Between the World and Me by Richard Wright; In Spring Comes by e.e. cummings; Junkman's Obligato (continued); From *Cyrano de Bergerac* by Edmond Rostand; From *Four Questions* by James P. Vaughan; Read History: So Learn Your Place in Time by Edna St. Vincent Millay; From *Aria de Capo* by Edna St. Vincent Millay; Junkman's Obligato (concluded).

Part II: From *For the Time Being* by W.H. Auden; The Second Coming by W.B. Yeats; From *Fantasio* by Alfred de Musset; Shine, Perishing Republic by Robinson Jeffers; I Paint What I See by E.B. White; The Politicians by Roger McCough; Round by Robert Sabaroff; We Have Gone Too Far by Edna St. Vincent Millay; From *Conversation at Midnight* by Edna St. Vincent Millay; Read History, Thus Learn How Small a Space by Edna St. Vincent Millay; From *Not for a Nation* and *Conversation at Midnight* by Edna St. Vincent Millay; from *HIM* by e.e. cummings; The Love Song of J. Alfred Prufrock by T.S. Eliot; The Lake Isle of Innisfree by W.B. Yeats; If the Birds Do Not Come by Roscoe Lee Browne.

THE REGARD OF FLIGHT and THE CLOWN BAGATELLES

Bill Irwin   Doug Skinner
Michael O'Connor

Material created in collaboration with Matthew Cohen, Michael O'Connor and Doug Skinner; lighting, Joan Arhelger; production stage manager, Nancy Harrington; stage manager, Larry Woodbridge.

Mr. Irwin in a versatile comic display of mime, dance, clowning and verbal routines, loosely connected as a commentary on the styles and conventions of the modern theater. The play was presented without intermission.

Note: Press date for *Grace* was 10/19/81, for *Behind the Broken Words* was 12/8/81.

My Own Stranger (40). By Marilyn Campbell; adapted from the writings of Anne Sexton. Produced by Gintare Sileika and Linda Laundra in the Writers Theater production at the Provincetown Playhouse. Opened October 13, 1981. (Closed November 15, 1981)

Marilyn Campbell
Nancy-Elizabeth Kammer

Pat Lysinger

Understudy—Emily Nash.

Conceived and directed by Linda Laundra; scenery, Christina Weppner; costumes, Clifford Capone; lighting, Robby Monk; original music, Richard Kassel; produced in association with the Provincetown Playhouse; production stage manager, Becky Wold; press, Gifford/Wallace, Inc., Keith Sherman.

Works of the Pulitzer Prize-winning poet adapted for stage presentation. The play was presented in two parts.

Excerpts on this program were: Dancing the Jig, Angel of Beach Houses and Picnics (from *The Book of Folly*); Young, I Remember, Letters Written During a January Northeaster (from *All My Pretty Ones*); Protestant Easter, For the Year of the Insane, Flee on Your Donkey, Live (from *Live or Die*); Us (from *Love Poems*); four groups of letters and Letter to Linda (from *Anne Sexton: A Self-Portrait in Letters*); The Farmer's Wife, The Double Image (from *To Bedlam and Part Way Back*); two groups of letters and quotes from interviews; The Poet of Ignorance, Riding the Elevator Into the Sky, The Earth Falls Down, Welcome Morning, Snow (from *The Awful Rowing Toward God*); Yellow, Dr. Y (from *Words for Dr. Y*); Cigarettes and Whiskey and Wild, Wild Women (from *45 Mercy St.*)

2 by South (59). Program of two one-act plays by Frank South: *Precious Blood* and *Rattlesnake in a Cooler*. Produced by M.G.I. and Scott Bushnell in association with The Los Angeles Actors' Theater at St. Clements Theater. Opened October 14, 1981. (Closed December 5, 1981)

Precious Blood
Actor .... Guy Boyd
Actress .... Alfre Woodard

Rattlesnake in a Cooler
Actor .... Leo Burmester
Musician.................... Danny Darst

Directed by Robert Altman; scenery, John Kavelin; lighting, Barbara Ling; songs, Danny Darst; production stage manager, John Brigleb; press, Jeffrey Richards Associates, Ben Morse.

In *Precious Blood*, the two characters recall events in their past lives, which then collide in a rape. In *Rattlesnake in a Cooler*, a young doctor decides to lead a cowboy's life, which causes him to become an outlaw. Previously produced in Los Angeles.

Manhattan Theater Club. Schedule of four programs. **Crossing Niagara** (48). By Alonso Alegria. Opened October 20, 1981; see note. (Closed November 29, 1981) **No End of Blame** (48). By Howard Barker. Opened December 15, 1981; see note. (Closed January 24, 1982) **Sally and Marsha** (56). By Sybille Peterson. Opened February 9, 1982; see note. (Closed March 28, 1982) **Gardenia** (48). By John Guare. Opened April 13, 1982; see note. (Closed May 23, 1982) Produced by Manhattan Theater Club, Lynne Meadow artistic director, Barry Grove managing director, at Manhattan Theater Club Downstage.

CROSSING NIAGARA

Blondin .... Alvin Epstein
Carlo .... Paul McCrane

Standbys: Mr. Epstein—James Burge; Mr. McCrane—John Geter.
Directed by Andre Ernotte; scenery and costumes, Santo Loquasto; lighting, Jennifer Tipton; production stage manager, John Beven; stage manager, James McC-Clark; press, Patricia Cox.
Scene 1: Blondin's rooms, Niagara Falls, N.Y., a summer evening, 1859. Scene 2: The same, two days later. Scene 3: The same, during the afternoon, three weeks later. Scene 4: A promontory overlooking the falls, evening, a few days later. Scene 5: Over the falls, the next day, August 18, 1859. The play was presented in two parts with the intermission following Scene 3.
19th century tightrope walker's daredevil adventure is dramatized. Play by a Peruvian author now residing in the U.S., previously produced at the Folger Theater in Washington, D.C.

NO END OF BLAME

CAST: Peasant Woman, Tea Woman—Elizabeth Norment; Gigor Gabor—Gene O'Neill; Bela Veracek—Michael Cristofer; 1st Hungarian Soldier, Art Student, 3d Comrade, 1st Customs Officer, John Lowry, 1st Airman, 3d Male Nurse—Ralph Byers; 2d Hungarian Soldier, Art Student, 3d Airman, Mr. Mik, 2d Male Nurse—Brent Spiner; Hungarian Officer, 2d Comrade, Anthony Diver —George Ede; 1st Red Soldier, GPU Man, 2d Customs Officer, Bob Stringer, 1st Male Nurse—John C. Vennema; 2d Red Soldier, Billwitz, 1st Comrade, Frank Deeds, Hoogstraten—Michael Gross; 3d Red Soldier, Art Student, 5th Comrade, 4th Airman, Dockerill—Keith Reddin; Stella, 1st Airwoman, Dr. Glasson—Robin Bartlett; 4th Comrade, 2d Airwoman—Patricia Hodges; Ilona, Secretary— Caitlin Clarke; Soviet Gardener, 2d Airman, Sir Herbert Strubenzee, 4th Male Nurse—George Hall.
Standbys: Mr. Cristofer—John C. Vennema; Misses Norment, Bartlett—Denise Stevenson.
Directed by Walton Jones; scenery, Tony Straiges; costumes, Christa Scholtz; lighting and projections, Donald Edmund Thomas; production stage manager, Robert Kellogg; stage manager, Betsy Nicholson.
Act I, Scene 1: Somewhere in the Carpathian Mountains, 1918. Scene 2: The Institute of Fine Arts, Budapest, 1921. Scene 3: The offices of the Writers & Arts Union, Moscow, 1923. Scene 4: A garden in a suburb of Moscow, 1934. Scene 5: A street in Moscow, 1934. Scene 6: The customs shed, Dover, 1936. Scene 7: The German invasion of Russia, 1941.
Act II, Scene 1: An RAF station, Oxfordshire, 1943. Scene 2: A government office in London, 1943. Scene 3: A park in Southwark, 1960. Scene 4: An office in Fleet Street, 1973. Scene 5: The Pool of London, 1973. Scene 6: The grounds of a mental institution, London, 1973.
The life and times of a political cartoonist who finds that truth is not always respected on either side of the Iron Curtain. A foreign play previously produced in London.

SALLY AND MARSHA

Sally .... Bernadette Peters
Marsha .... Christine Baranski

Standbys: Miss Peters—Sabra Jones; Miss Baranski—Rhonda Farer.
Directed by Lynne Meadow; scenery, Stuart Wurtzel; costumes, Patricia McGourty; lighting, Marc B. Weiss; associate artistic director, Douglas Hughes; production stage manager, Tom Aberger.
Time: Over a period of seven months, in the morning. Place: A New York City West Side apartment. The play was presented in two parts.
Housewife from South Dakota meets and becomes friends with native New York housewife living across the hall. Previously produced at O'Neill Theater Center and Yale Repertory Theater.

GARDENIA

Joshua Hickman	Sam Waterston	Dan Grady	James Woods
Lydie Breeze	JoBeth Williams	Jeremiah Grady	R.J. Burke
Amos Mason	Edward Herrmann	Ambrose O'Malley	Jarlath Conroy

Bernadette Peters and Christine Baranski in *Sally and Marsha*

Directed by Karel Reisz; scenery, Santo Loquasto; costumes, Ann Roth; lighting, Craig Miller; music composed by Glen Roven; associate artistic director, Douglas Hughes.

A play in its author's series about 19th century ambitions and passions among characters in a Nantucket Island setting, its events taking place before those of Guare's previously-produced *Lydie Breeze* (see its entry elsewhere in this section of this volume). The play was presented in two parts.

Note: Press date for *Crossing Niagara* was 11/3/81, for *No End of Blame* was 12/23/81, for *Sally and Marsha* was 2/21/82, for *Gardenia* was 4/27/82.

Cotton Patch Gospel (193). Musical based on *The Cotton Patch Version of Matthew and John* by Clarence Jordan; book by Tom Key and Russell Treyz; music and lyrics by Harry Chapin. Produced by Philip M. Getter at the Lambs Theater. Opened October 21, 1981. (Closed April 11, 1982)

Matthew . . . . Tom Key

Cotton Patch String Band: Scott Ainslie fiddle, banjo, dobro, mandolin; Pete Corum Bass fiddle; Jim Lauderdale banjo, guitar; Michael Mark guitar, mandolin.

Musical understudy: Gary Oleyar.

Directed by Russell Treyz; musical direction, Tom Chapin; scenery and costumes, John Falabella; lighting, Roger Morgan; associate producer, Louis F. Burke; production stage manager, Mark Rubinsky; stage manager, Jerry Bihm; press, Susan L. Schulman, Claudia McAllister, Sandi Kimmel.

Time: Now. Place: Here.

Biblical stories, with Tom Key as Matthew and 32 other characters.

MUSICAL NUMBERS, ACT I: "Something's Brewing in Gainesville"—Band; "I Did It"—Company; "Mama Is Here"—Michael Mark; "It Isn't Easy"—Jim Lauderdale, Band; "Sho 'Nuff"

—Band; "Turn It Around"—Tom Key, Band; "When I Look Up"—Band; "There Ain't No Busy Signals/Spitball"—Band; "We're Going to Atlanta"—Band; "What Does Atlanta Mean to Me?"—Key.

ACT II: "Are We Ready"—Pete Corum, Band; "You Are Still My Boy"—Lauderdale, Mark; "We Got to Get Organized"—Company; "We're Gonna Love It"—Band; "Jubilation"—Scott Aimslie, Company; "One More Tomorrow"—Band; "I Wonder"—Company.

*Playwrights Horizons. Schedule of three programs. ***Sister Mary Ignatius Explains It All for You** and **The Actor's Nightmare** (247). Program of two one-act plays by Christopher Durang. Opened October 21, 1981. ***The Dining Room** (131). By A.R. Gurney Jr. Opened February 24, 1982; see note. ***Geniuses** (34). By Jonathan Reynolds. Opened May 13, 1982. Produced by Playwrights Horizons, Andre Bishop artistic director, Paul Daniels managing director, at Playwrights Horizons.

THE ACTOR'S NIGHTMARE

George Spelvin	Jeff Brooks	Dame Ellen Terry	Mary Catherine Wright
Meg	Polly Draper	Henry Irving	Timothy Landfield
Sarah Siddons	Elizabeth Franz	Place: A stage.	

SISTER MARY IGNATIUS EXPLAINS IT ALL FOR YOU

Sister Mary Ignatius	Elizabeth Franz	Philomena Rostovich	Mary Catherine Wright
Thomas	Mark Stefan	Aloysius Benheim	Jeff Brooks
Diane Symonds	Polly Draper	Place: A lecture hall.	
Gary Sullavan	Timothy Landfield		

Directed by Jerry Zaks; scenery, Karen Schulz; costumes, William Ivey Long; lighting, Paul Gallo; sound, Aural Fixation; production stage manager, Esther Cohen; press, Bob Ullman.

In *The Actor's Nightmare,* the performer finds himself prominently displayed onstage in material he has never rehearsed. In *Sister Mary Ignatius Explains It All for You* a teaching nun with dogmatic manner and views is attacked by former students who hate her. It was previously produced off off Broadway at Ensemble Studio Theater.

Carolyn Mignini replaced Polly Draper and Deborah Rush replaced Mary Catherine Wright 5/24/82.

THE DINING ROOM

Lois de Banzie	Pippa Pearthree
W.H. Macy	Remak Ramsay
Ann McDonough	John Shea

Directed by David Trainer; scenery, Loren Sherman; costumes, Deborah Shaw; lighting, Frances Aronson; production stage manager, M.A. Howard.

Time and place: The play takes place in a dining room—or rather many dining rooms—over the course of many years.

In a series of vignettes, the dining room is viewed as a disappearing phenomenon in WASP family life, but still useful for certain special purposes including both celebrations and crises.

Note: *The Dining Room* opened as a workshop production in Playwrights Horizons Studio 2/11/82 and transferred to the group's mainstage as an off-Broadway production 2/24/82.

Patricia Wettig replaced Pippa Pearthree 5/29/82.

A Best Play; see page 201.

GENIUSES

Jocko Pyle	Michael Gross	Eugene Winter	David Rasche
Sky Bullene	Joanne Camp	Bart Keely	Kurt Knudson
Winston Legazpi	Thomas Ikeda	Milo McGee McGarr	David Garrison

Directed by Gerald Gutierrez; scenery, Andrew Jackness; costumes, Ann Emonts; lighting, James F. Ingalls; sound, Scott Lehrer; fights, B.H. Barry; special effects, Esquire Jauchem, Gregory Meeh; production stage manager, J. Thomas Vivian.

Place: A village 200 miles north of Manila, the Philippines. Act I: Early evening in mid-May. Act II: Four days later. Act III: The following morning.

American movie makers in the Philippines, housebound by a typhoon with a sex object stirring them up comedically.

Peter Evans replaced Michael Gross 5/24/82.

Circle Repertory Company. Schedule of six programs. **Threads** (33). By Jonathan Bolt. Opened October 25, 1981. (Closed November 22, 1981) **Confluence** (36). Program of three one-act plays: *Thymus Vulgaris* by Lanford Wilson, *Confluence* by John Bishop and *Am I Blue* by Beth Henley. Opened January 10, 1982. (Closed February 11, 1982) **Snow Orchid** (39). By Joe Pintauro. Opened March 10, 1982. (Closed April 11, 1982) **The Great Grandson of Jedediah Kohler** (8). By John Bishop. Opened March 21, 1982 (Entermedia Theater). (Closed April 3, 1982; see note) **Young Playwrights Festival** (24). Three programs of ten plays. Program A opened April 27, 1982 (Closed May 16, 1982) Program B opened May 1, 1982. (Closed May 14, 1982) Program C Opened May 4, 1982 (Closed May 11, 1982) Produced by Circle Repertory Company, Marshall W. Mason artistic director, at the Circle Theater (*Young People's Festival* produced by The Dramatists Guild Fund, Inc. in association with Circle Repertory Company).

THREADS

David Owens	Ben Siegler	Jesse Sykes	Nancy Killmer
Clyde Owens	Jonathan Hogan	Nub	David Morse
Pete	Roger Chapman	Janine	Patricia Wettig
Sally Owens	Jo Henderson	Voice of a Neighbor	Alice Connorton
Abner Owens	William Andrews		

Directed by B. Rodney Marriott; scenery, David Potts; costumes, Joan E. Weiss; lighting, Craig Miller; sound, Chuck London, Stewart Werner; music, Stephen Lockwood, Patricia Lee Stotter; production stage manager, Kate Stewart; press, Richard Frankel.

Time: Summer, 1965. Place: Alamance Springs, a small mill town in the Piedmont hills of North Carolina. The play was presented in three parts.

The prodigal son returns, and the family resurrects past sorrows. Previously produced by Circle Repertory in workshop.

CONFLUENCE

Thymus Vulgaris

Ruby	Pearl Shear
Evelyn	Katherine Cortez
Cop	Jeff McCracken

Directed by June Stein.

Time: The present. Place: A trailer park in Palmdale, Calif.

Homecoming of a daughter who has worked the streets but is now trying to go straight. Previously produced at Lee Strasberg Theater Institute, Los Angeles.

Confluence

Chuck Janola	Jimmie Ray Weeks
Kathy Milan	Katherine Cortez
Earl Douchette	Edward Seamon

Directed by B. Rodney Marriott.

Time: Summer. Place: The small town of Confluence, Pa.

Two former professional athletes and an actress face change in their lives.

Am I Blue

John Polk Richards	Jeff McCracken
Ashbe Williams	June Stein
Hilda	Pearl Shear
Barker	Jimmie Ray Weeks
Bum	Edward Seamon
Hippie	Ellen Conway
Whore	Katherine Cortez

Understudy: Miss Shear—Katherine Cortez.

Directed by Stuart White.

Time: 1968. Place: New Orleans.

Boy and girl, teen agers, meet for a romantic adventure. Previously produced at Southern Methodist University.

ALL PLAYS: Scenery, Bob Phillips; costumes, Joan E. Weiss; lighting, Mal Sturchio; sound, Chuck London, Stewart Werner; acting managing director, Richard Frankel; press, Richard Frankel, Reva Cooper.

SNOW ORCHID

Blaise .... Ben Siegler	Filumena .... Olympia Dukakis
Sebbie .... Robert LuPone	Rocco .... Peter Boyle

Directed by Tony Giordano; scenery, Hugh Landwehr; costumes, David Murin; lighting, Dennis Parichy; sound, Chuck London, Stewart Werner; production stage manager, Bill Kavanagh; press, Max Eisen.

Time:· 1973. Place: The house of the Lazarra family in the Greenpoint section of Brooklyn. The play was presented in two parts.

A father returns from a sanatarium sojourn to his Brooklyn family, to find it troubled but enduring. Previously produced in a staged reading at the O'Neill Theater Center.

THE GREAT GRANDSON OF JEDEDIAH KOHLER

Death .... Jake Dengel	Ronald Hoerner .... Jonathan Bolt
Jed Kohler .... Michael Ayr	Ike McKee; Henry Jarvis...... William Hurt
Leon; Blake Kohler............. Ken Kliban	Johnny Two-Deuce.......... Lou Liberatore
Shorty Radabaugh;	Frank Graham................. Tim Morse
Doc McCullough .... Gary Berner	Brother................ Jimmie Ray Weeks
Father; Jedediah Kohler;	Jack Beck; Prescott Man;
Cop .... Edward Seamon	Coach Frankie Torski ...... Jack Davidson
Mother; Nancy .... Trish Hawkins	Joe Goldman .... Roger Chapman
Bobbi .... Katherine Cortez	Wally Silver............. Charles T. Harper
Bob Graham;	

Understudy: Mr. Dengel—Charles T. Harper.

Directed by John Bard Manulis and Marshall W. Mason; scenery, Karl Eigsti; costumes, Laura Crow; lighting, Dennis Parichy; music and songs, Jonathan Holtzman; sound, Chuck London Media, Stewart Werner; production stage manager, Fred Reinglas; stage manager, Ginny Martino.

Time: The present. Place: The city, the suburbs, Las Vegas and the Old West. The play was presented in two parts.

Comedy, the descendant of a gun-toting frontier marshal finds his own opportunity to become a hero.

Note: *The Great Grandson of Jedediah Kohler* was presented in repertory with a revival of Shakespeare's *Richard II,* which played 14 previews 3/10/82–4/4/82 without an official opening.

YOUNG PLAYWRIGHTS FESTIVAL

PROGRAM A

Bluffing by Peter Murphy, age 17

Pete..................... James Pickens Jr.	Charlie .... Ted Sod
Stew .... Jonathan Bolt	Understudy: Messrs. Pickens, Sod—David
Rick .... Timothy Busfield	Labiosa. Directed by Carole Rothman. Time:
Bill .... Burke Pearson	The present. Five men play games behind each
Tony..................... Bruce McCarty	other's backs at the poker table.

Present Tense by John McNamara, age 18

Norm Prescott........... Timothy Busfield	Margie Eaton............. Wanda de Jesus
Ann Allen .... Karen Sederholm	Directed by Marshall W. Mason. Time: The
Jerry..................... Bruce McCarty	present. Place: Norm Prescott's bedroom and in
Doug Domineri............. David Labiosa	the various reaches of his overactive imagination.
Mother's Voice .... Alba Oms	Illusions and anxieties of a teenager in love.
Blonde .... Trish Hawkins	

The Rennings Children by Kenneth Lonergan, age 18

Paul Rennings . . . . Bruce McCarty
Attendant . . . . James Pickens Jr.
Mary Jones . . . . Trish Hawkins
Parkinson . . . . Burke Pearson
Dr. Pierceson . . . . Alba Oms

Understudy: Miss Oms—Wanda de Jesus. Directed by Marshall W. Mason. Time: The present. Place: An East Coast mental institution. Sister tries to get brother out of hospital.

It's Time for a Change by Adam Berger, age 8

Mrs. Swell . . . . Alba Oms
Kirk Swell . . . . Timothy Busfield
Allan . . . . Ted Sod
Ben . . . . David Labiosa
Bruce . . . . Bruce McCarty
Jim . . . . Burke Pearson
Sally . . . . Karen Sederholm
Susan . . . . Wanda de Jesus

Amanda . . . . Trish Hawkins
Mr. Fend . . . . James Pickens Jr.
Mr. Swell . . . . Jonathan Bolt
Understudy: Miss Oms—Wanda de Jesus. Directed by Elinor Renfield. Time: The present. Place: The world of Kirk Swell, who is not good at sports but springs a surprise.

PROGRAM B

The Bronx Zoo by Lynnette Serrano, age 17

Junito . . . . David Labiosa
1st Girl . . . . Kate Anthony
2d Girl . . . . Lucy Deakins
Evie . . . . Wanda de Jesus
Bum . . . . Burke Pearson
Lucy . . . . Alba Oms
Angel . . . . Ted Sod
Clara . . . . Zaina Rivera
Elsie . . . . Trish Hawkins
Rosie . . . . Karen Sederholm

Mike . . . . Bruce McCarty
Santo . . . . James Pickens Jr.
Ramon; Doctor . . . . Jonathan Bolt
Louie . . . . Timothy Busfield
Understudies: Misses de Jesus, Hawkins—Karen Sederholm; Miss Oms—Wanda de Jesus; Miss Rivera—Linda Holmes. Directed by Gerald Chapman. Time: Today. Place: The South Bronx. A Puerto Rican family in a tough neighborhood.

Half Fare by Shoshana Marchand, age 17

Claudia . . . . Karen Sederholm
Evan . . . . David Labiosa
George . . . . Jonathan Bolt
Directed by Elinor Renfield. Time: The pre-

sent. Place: A run-down New York City apartment. Adolescent girl and hippy father in conflict.

So What Are We Gonna Do Now? by Juliet Garson, age 13

Patricia . . . . Trish Hawkins
Jennifer . . . . Lucy Deakins
Mary . . . . Alba Oms
Teresa . . . . Kate Anthony
1st Man . . . . Ted Sod
2d Man . . . . James Pickens Jr.
John . . . . Jonathan Bolt

3d Man . . . . Burke Pearson
Cop . . . . Timothy Busfield
Understudies: Mr. Bolt—David Labiosa; Miss Anthony—Linda Holmes. Directed by Arthur Laurents. Time: The present. Place: New York City. Friends plot to make parks safe to play in.

PROGRAM C

The Bronx Zoo (see Program B)
It's Time for a Change (see Program A)
Coleman, S.D. by Anne Pierson Wiese, age 18, staged reading directed by Carole Rothman
In the Way by Stephen Gutwillig, age 17, staged reading directed by Carole Rothman
Epiphany by Jennie Litt, age 17, staged reading directed by Gerald Chapman

ALL PLAYS: Scenery, John Lee Beatty; costumes, Ann Roth; lighting, Dennis Parichy; sound, Chuck London Media, Stewart Werner; original music, Louis Rosen *(It's Time for a Change)*, David Valentin *(The Bronx Zoo)*; Festival director, Gerald Chapman; Festival administrator, Peggy Hansen; production stage manager, Judy Boese; stage manager, Kate Stewart.

Ten plays by young people (ages given above at the time of submission of scripts) selected from 732 entries in the Dramatists Guild's First Annual Young Playwrights Festival for this off-Broadway production under the aegis of Circle Repertory Company.

Katherine Cortez and Pearl Shear in *Thymus Vulgaris*

The Light Opera of Manhattan (LOOM). Repertory of three new revival productions and 13 running operetta revivals. **The Red Mill** (35). Book and lyrics by Henry Blossom; music by Victor Herbert. Opened October 28, 1981. (Closed November 29, 1981) **H.M.S. Pinafore** (21). Book by W.S. Gilbert; music by Arthur Sullivan. Opened March 10, 1982. (Closed March 21, 1982) Reopened April 7, 1982 (Closed April 11, 1982). **A Night in Venice** (28). Book by William Mount-Burke and Alice Hammerstein Mathias; based freely on an idea by Zell & Genée; music by Johann Strauss; lyrics by Alice Hammerstein Mathias. Opened May 5, 1982. (Closed May 30, 1982) Produced by The Light Opera of Manhattan, William Mount-Burke producer/director, at the Eastside Playhouse. (Repertory closed May 30, 1982)

ALL PLAYS: Directed by William Mount-Burke; musical director, William Mount-Burke; associate director, Raymond Allen; choreographer, Jerry Gotham; assistant musical director and pianist, Brian Molloy; assistant conductor and organist, Stanley German; stage manager, Jerry Gotham; press, Jean Dalrymple, Peggy Friedman.

THE RED MILL

Con Kidder	James Nadeaux	Cornelius Van Hoagland	Raymond Allen
Kid Conner	Kevin Usher	Gretchen	Cheryl Savitt
Jan Van Borkem	J.J. Weber	Bertha de Hooch	Millie Petroski
Franz	Robert Barker	Tina	Joyce Bolton
Willem	Tom Olmstead	Hilda Kouker	Ann Kirschner
Capt. Doric Van Damm	Anthony Michalik		

Ensemble: John Baray, Joyce Bolton, Ed Harrison, Joanne Jamieson, Janette Jones, Ann Kirschner, Claudia O'Neill, Richard Perry, Cheryl Politzer, Suzanne Portfolio, Warren Randolph, Frank Rella, Lance Taubold, Mimi Wyche.

Scenery, Elouise Meyer; costumes, James Nadeaux; lighting, Peggy Clark; script preparation, Karen Schlotter; vocal arrangements, John Mizell; musical arrangements, Stanley German.

Time: Summer, 1906. Place: At the sign of the Red Mill, Katwky-ann-Zee, Holland.

The Red Mill was first produced on Broadway 9/24/06 for 274 performances. It was revived on Broadway 10/16/45 for 531 performances.

ACT I

Overture
"By the Side of the Mill" .... Ensemble
"Mignonette" .... Tina, Girls
"You Never Can Tell About a Woman" .... Burgomaster, Willem
"If You Love But Me" .... Gretchen, Doric
"Go While the Goin' Is Good" .... Con, Kid, Gretchen, Tina
"The Accident" .... Ensemble
"When You're Pretty and the World Is Fair" .... Bertha, Governor, Ensemble
"A Widow Has Ways" .... Bertha
"Moonbeams" .... Gretchen, Doric, Burghers
Finale .... Ensemble

ACT II

Entr'Acte
"Gossips Corner" .... Ensemble
"The Legend of the Mill" .... Burgomaster, Ensemble
"I Want You to Marry Me" .... Franz, Tina
"Every Day Is Ladies' Day With Me" .... Governor, Gentlemen
"Because You're You" .... Bertha, Governor
"In Old New York" .... Con, Kid
"The Isle of Our Dreams" .... Gretchen, Doric
"Entrance of the Wedding Guests" .... Ensemble
Finale .... Ensemble

H.M.S. PINAFORE

Sir Joseph	Raymond Allen	(Josephine) ...... Cheryl Savitt, Joyce Bolton
Captain Corcoran	Robert Barker	Hebe .... Ann J. Kirschner
Ralph Rackstraw	Anthony Michalik	(Buttercup).... Irma Rogers, Ethelmae Mason
Dick Deadeye	Vashek Pazdera	(Parentheses indicate roles in which the perform-
Boatswain	Gary Pitts	ers alternated)

Costumes, George Stinson; production supervisor, Jerry Gotham.

Sailors, Sisters, Cousins and Aunts: Christina Darnowski, Joanne Jamieson, Janette Leslie Jones, Paul Knox, Warren Randolph, Michele Scirpo, Karen Sussman, Nancy Jane Williams, Glenn Halladay, Susan Taplinger, Jerome Johnson Jr., Nicolas Glaeser, Neil Donohoe, Philip Der Margosian, Rhanda Elizabeth Spotton, Richard Liss, Bill Madden, Peter Sham, Suzanne Portfolio, Marianne Cook, Billy Hester, Jane Winslow.

Time: Act I, Noon. Act II, night. Place: The quarterdeck of H.M.S. Pinafore, off Portsmouth.

This new revival production of the operetta replaced the former LOOM production which was offered for 21 performances in August and September this season.

A NIGHT IN VENICE

Duke D'Urbino (Harlequin)...	Robert Barker	Caramello.............. Anthony Michalik
Senator Delacqua	Raymond Allen	Luisa..................... Cheryl Savitt
Nina	Sylvia Lanka	Marchesa .... Elizabeth Burgess-Harr
Siboletta	Jacqueline Kroschell	Agricola .... Ann J. Kirschner
Pappacoda	Stephen Rosario	

Contadine, Street Peddlers, Merchants, Gondoliers, etc.: Janette Leslie Jones, Ann J. Kirschner, Warren Randolph, Michele Scirpo, Karen Sussman, Nancy Jane Williams, Susan Taplinger, Nicolas Glaeser, Richard Liss, Bill Madden, Peter Sham, Marianne Cook, Billy Hester.

Caramello's Troupe: Susanna Organek, Roni Zaro, Jolene Senchur, James Siegel.

Standbys: Miss Lanka—Joyce Bolton; Miss Kroschell—Ann J. Kirschner.

Scenery, Jeremy Conway; costumes, James Brega; lighting, Peggy Clark; script preparation, Karen Schlotter; musical preparation, Dr. John Mizell, Stanley German, Brian Molloy; production supervisor, Jerry Gotham.

Time: Carnival time, circa 1750. Place: Venice.

This Strauss operetta about a senator's daughter infatuated with a street singer was first produced in Berlin in 1883.

ACT I

Introduction . . . . Caramello's Troupe
Prologue . . . . Duke (Harlequin)
Opening Chorus . . . . Ensemble
"Your Palate I Will Tickle" . . . . Pappacoda, Ensemble
"I Am Me" . . . . Nina, Ladies
"Evviva Caramello" . . . . Duke, Caramello, Ensemble
"How I Can Picture Them" . . . . Delacqua, Marchesa
"Frutti di Mare" . . . . Luisa, Ensemble
"Put on a Dream" . . . . Luisa, Siboletta, Caramello, Pappacoda
"Chop-a, Chop-a" . . . . Siboletta, Pappacoda
"Pigeons of San Marco" . . . . Ladies
Finale . . . . Ensemble

ACT II

Promenade . . . . Ensemble
"Remember" . . . . Luisa, Duke, Nina, Caramello
"Here in My Arms" . . . . Nina, Duke
"Gather Together" . . . . Agricola, Pappacoda, Caramello Delacqua, Ensemble
"Pigeons of San Marco" (Reprise) . . . . Delacqua, Caramello, Pappacoda
"Hail the Duke" . . . . Gentlemen
"Venice" . . . . Duke
"We Welcome All You Ladies" . . . . Duke, Pappacoda, Caramello, Delacqua, Ladies
"Now Is the Time to Have Fun" . . . . Principals
Ballet . . . . Troupe
    (with Susanna Organek)
"Here in My Arms" (Reprise) . . . . Nina, Duke
Finale . . . . Company

LOOM's 1981–82 repertory included 13 running productions mounted in previous seasons and presented on the following schedule (operettas have book and lyrics by W.S. Gilbert and music by Arthur Sullivan unless otherwise noted): *The Student Prince* (14), book and lyrics by Dorothy Donnelly, music by Sigmund Romberg, continued June 3 from previous season; *The Mikado* (46), opened June 17, July 15, Dec. 31 and January 27; *The Pirates of Penzance* (28), opened July 1 and January 13; *The Sorcerer* (14), opened July 22; *H.M.S. Pinafore* (21; old production), opened August 5 and September 2; *Ruddigore* (14), opened August 19; *The Vagabond King* (21), lyrics by W.H. Post and Brian Hooker, music by Rudolf Friml, opened September 9.

Also *The Desert Song* (28), Book and lyrics by Otto Harbach, Oscar Hammerstein II and Frank Mandel, music by Sigmund Romberg, opened September 30; *Babes in Toyland* (33), book by William Mount-Burke and Alice Hammerstein Mathias, lyrics by Alice Hammerstein Mathias, music by Victor Herbert, opened December 2; *Princess Ida* (14), opened February 10; *The Grand Duke* (14), libretto revised by John Wolfson, opened February 24; *The Yeomen of the Guard* (14), opened March 24; *The Merry Widow* (21), based on the book by Victor Leon and Leo Stein, music by Franz Lehar, English lyrics by Alice Hammerstein Mathias, opened April 14.

Performers in LOOM running repertory during the 1981–82 season included Raymond Allen, Jon

Brothers, Jeffrey Blane, Robert Barker, Joyce Bolton, Deborah Barnes, Richard Bitsko, John Bonk, John Baray, Mary Cohen, Cathy Cosgrove, Robert Carpenter, Dan Charnas, Steven Douglas, Neil Donohoe, Christina Darnowski, Dino Dimario, Clem Egan, Ann Ennis, Cary Frumess, Dianne Fraser, Marilyn Florez, Vince Gerardi, Neil Gregory, Bruce Gould, Nicolas Glaeser, Glenn Halladay, Lloyd Harris, Karen Hartman, Ed Harrison, Nicholas Haylett, G. Michael Harvey, Claudia Hommel.

Also Joanne Jamieson, Janette Leslie Jones, Russell Kaein, Jacqueline Kroschell, Ann J. Kirschner, Ted Kalmon, Eleanore Knapp, John Kalki, Brooks King, Paul Knox. Richard Lafica, Catherine Lankford, Anthony Michalik, Georgia McEver, Daniel Mason, Catherine Miller, Cole Mobley, Ethelmae Mason, Bruce McKillip, Marcia Mizell, James Nadeaux, Tom Olmstead, Claudia O'Neill, Susanna Organek, Richard Perry, Maria Magliaro Politano, Suzanne Portfolio, Vashek Pazdera, Cheryl Politzer, Gary Pitts, Brian Powell, David Preston.

Also Frank Rella, Mary Lee Rubens, Irma Rogers, Gary Ridley, Frank Rahls, Warren Randolph, Stephen Rosario, Craig Schulman, Richard Smithies, Cheryl Savitt, Rhanda Spotton, Michele Scirpo, Al Schmitz, Karen Sussman, Susan Taplinger, Tony Tamburello, Nancy Temple, Lance Taubold, Kevin Usher, Janet Villas, Evan Willis, Willie Wenger, J.J. Weber, Susan Winter, Nancy Jane Williams.

Taken in Marriage (25). Revival of the play by Thomas Babe. Produced by The Woman's Ensemble at the Harold Clurman Theater. Opened November 1, 1981. (Closed November 22, 1981)

Dixie Avalon . . . . Prudence Sherman	Ruth Chandler . . . . Patricia Newcastle
Annie . . . . Sammi Gavitch	Aunt Helen . . . . Barbara LeBrun
Andrea . . . . Carolyn Kennedy	

Directed by Russ Weatherford; choreography, Arthur Goldweit; lighting, Stephen and Candace Solie; assistant to the director, Ann Clay; stage manager, D. King Rodger; press, Shirley Herz Associates.

Time: The present. Place: A small town in New Hampshire. The play was presented in two parts.

The first professional New York production of *Taken in Marriage* took place off Broadway by New York Shakespeare Festival 2/22/79 for 46 performances.

Classic Stage Company (CSC). Repertory of four revivals. **Peer Gynt I** (47) and **Peer Gynt II** (46). By Henrik Ibsen; translated by Rolf Fjelde. Opened November 8, 1981. (Closed April 10, 1982) **The Cherry Orchard** (39). By Anton Chekhov; translated by Alex Szogyi. Opened January 17, 1982. (Closed April 8, 1982) **King Lear** (52). by William Shakespeare. Opened February 28, 1982. **Ghost Sonata** (22). By August Strindberg. Opened April 18, 1982. (Repertory closed May 16, 1982) Produced by Classic Stage Company, Christopher Martin artistic director, Stephen J. Holland managing director, at CSC Repertory.

ALL PLAYS: Associate costume designer, Miriam Nieves; composer, Noble Shropshire; production manager, Robert Holley; stage manager, Christine Michael; press, Dan J. Martin, Stephen J. Holland.

PEER GYNT I

1. The Briderobber

Peer Gynt . . . . Patrick Egan	Fiddler . . . . Noble Shropshire
Mother Aase . . . . Karen Sunde	Helga . . . . Susan Stern
1st Old Woman; Solveig . . . Patricia O'Donnell	Solveig's Father . . . . John Camera
2d Old Woman . . . . Carol Schultz	Wedding Guests: Richard Mover, Peter
Aslak the Smith . . . . David Snizek	Lopez, David Aston-Reese, Tom Spackman,
Mads Moen . . . . Douglas Moore	Ginger Grace, Gina Gold.
Father Moen . . . . Brian Lawson	*2. The Mountain Man*
Hegstad Farmer . . . . Tom Spiller	Peer Gynt . . . . David Aston-Reese
	Ingrid . . . . Carol Schultz

Aase .... Karen Sunde
Solveig .... Patricia O'Donnell
Solveig's Father.............. John Camera
1st Herd Girl................ Ginger Grace
2d Herd Girl .... Susan Stern
3d Herd Girl .... Gina Gold

3. *The Troll Prince*
Peer Gynt................. Tom Spackman
Green Woman............... Carol Schultz
Troll King .... Tom Spiller
Old Troll Courtier........... David Snizek
Great Boyg.................. Patrick Egan
    Troll Courtiers: Douglas Moore, Brian Law-

son, Patrick Egan, John Camera. Troll Children:
Ginger Grace, Richard Mover, Gina Gold, Peter
Lopez.

4. *The Outlaw*
Peer Gynt................ Noble Shropshire
Solveig .... Patricia O'Donnell
Helga .... Susan Stern
Boy........................ Peter Lopez
Aase .... Karen Sunde
Kari .... Ginger Grace
Green Woman............... Carol Schultz
Troll Brat................. Richard Mover

PEER GYNT II

5. *The Charleston Trader*
Peer Gynt............... Noble Shropshire
Trumpeterstraale............. David Snizek
Master Cotton .... Brian Lawson
Monsieur Ballon .... Douglas Moore
Heer Von Eberkoff .... John Camera
Moroccan Captain............ David Snizek
Old Ape..................... Tom Spiller
    Apes: Richard Mover, Brian Lawson, Douglas
Moore.

6. *The Harem Prophet*
Peer Gynt................. Tom Spackman
Thief...................... David Snizek
Fence .... John Camera
Harem Leader .... Carol Schultz
Anitra...................... Ginger Grace
    Harem Girls: Patricia O'Donnell, Gina
Gold, Susan Stern.

7. *The Emperor of Self*
Peer Gynt.............. David Aston-Reese
Solveig .... Patricia O'Donnell
Dr. Begriffenfeldt............. Brian Lawson

1st Keeper .... David Snizek
2d Keeper.................. Richard Mover
3d Keeper.................... Peter Lopez
Huhu .... Tom Spiller
King Apis .... Douglas Moore
Hussein the Scribe............ John Camera

8. *The Prodigal Onion*
Peer Gynt................... Patrick Egan
Captain; Aslak............... David Snizek
Boatswain; Pastor .... John Camera
Watch; Troll King.............. Tom Spiller
Mate; Sheriff .... Brian Lawson
Cook; Mads Moen.......... Douglas Moore
Sailors......... Richard Mover, Peter Lopez
Passenger .... David Aston-Reese
Button-Molder............ Noble Shropshire
Lean One .... Tom Spackman
Solveig .... Patricia O'Donnell
    Villagers: Richard Mover, Ginger Grace, Gina
Gold, Tom Spiller, John Camera, Peter
Lopez. Voices on the Wind: Carol Schultz, Pa-
tricia O'Donnell, Ginger Grace, Gina Gold.

Directed and designed by Christopher Martin; choreographer, Carol Flemming.

This production was billed as the American premiere of the complete text of Ibsen's play, presented
as two separate, full programs of theater in alternating performances. The last major New York
revival of an abridged version was by New York Shakespeare Festival in Central Park 7/8/69 for
19 performances.

PERFORMER	"THE CHERRY ORCHARD"	"KING LEAR"	"GHOST SONATA"
David Aston-Reese	Yasha	Burgundy; Curan	Baron; Cook
John Camera	Simeonov-Pishchik	Albany	
Kathryn Chilson	Charlotta		
Michael L.R. Devine		Messenger	
Patrick Egan		Edmund	Johansson
Ginger Grace	Dunyasha	Servant	Girl
David H. Johnson		Captain	
Brian Lawson	Firs	Gloucester	
Miles Mason		Soldier	
Douglas Moore	Yepidohov	Cornwall	Colonel
Richard Mover		Knight	

PERFORMER	"THE CHERRY ORCHARD"	"KING LEAR"	"GHOST SONATA"
Patricia O'Donnell	Anya	Cordelia	Milkmaid; Dark Lady
Carol Schultz	Varya	Regan	Concierge; Mummy
Noble Shropshire	Gayev	Fool; King of France	Old Man
David Snizek	Trofimov	Oswald	
Tom Spackman		Edgar	Student
Tom Spiller	Passerby; Stationmaster	Kent	Bengtsson
Robert Stattel	Lopahin	Lear	
Susan Stern			Fiancee
Karen Sunde	Lyubov	Goneril	

THE CHERRY ORCHARD: Directed by Rene Buch; design, Robert Weber Federico.
The last major New York revival of *The Cherry Orchard* was by New York Shakespeare Festival at Lincoln Center 6/29/77 for 48 performances. The play was presented in two parts.
KING LEAR: Director and designer, Christopher Martin; costumes, Miriam Nieves; fights, Brian Lawson.
The last major New York revival of *King Lear* was by The Acting Company repertory 4/9/78 for 9 performances. The play was presented in two parts.
GHOST SONATA: Directed by Christopher Martin and Karen Sunde; scenery, Christopher Martin; costumes, Miriam Nieves.
The only previous New York production of record of *Ghost Sonata* was by Circle Repertory Company off off Broadway in the 1971 and 1972 seasons.

Fighting Bob (8). By Tom Cole. Produced by Baraboo Productions at the Astor Place Theater. Opened November 9, 1981. (Closed November 15, 1981.

Directed by Sharon Ott; scenery, Laura Maurer; lighting, Rachel Budin; costumes, Susan Tsu; music, Mark Van Hecke; production stage manager, Marjorie Horne; press, Jeffrey Richards Associates, Bob Ganshaw. With John P. Connolly, Sonia Lanzener, Eugene J. Anthony, David E. Chadderdon, Paul Meacham.
Drama of Robert M. La Follette (1855–1925) and his try for the Presidency. Previously produced by Milwaukee Theater Company.

Pigjazz, II (30). Musical revue conceived by Michael Nee; written by Gretchen Alan Aurthur, Glenn Kramer, Michael Nee and Stephen Pell. Produced by Michael Nee and Pigjazz Productions, Ltd. in association with Gary Sales at the Actors' Playhouse. Opened November 16, 1981. (Closed December 20, 1981)

Gretchen Alan Aurthur
Glenn Kramer
Michael Nee
Stephen Pell

Directed by Michael Nee; musical director and pianist, Paul Sklar; scenery and lighting, Dorian Vernacchio; costumes, Muriel Stockdale; production coordinator, Jon Beaupré; press, Peggy Friedman.
Satirical songs and sketches based by the performers upon their own lives and experiences.

MUSICAL NUMBERS, ACT I (The Life): Overture—Paul Sklar; "When You're Not the Same" —Company; "I Have No Name"—Gretchen Alan Aurthur; "Miya Sama Dinah Shore"—Aurthur; The Hollywood Piece—Company; "Did You Notice?"—Michael Nee; The POW-MIA Benefit Show —Stephen Pell, Company; The Street Act—Company; "Phantom Affair"—Glenn Kramer; Pastiche of the first *Pigjazz:* "Don't Feed the Animals"—Kramer, Pell, Nee, "Gumby Gets a Nose"—Aurthur, "Pain(e)"—Nee, "Beetle Bailey, Won't You Please Come Home"—Company, "One-Faced Woman" —Pell, "An American Cripple Need Not Stand for the Star Spangled Banner"—Kramer, "Yankle Deedan Doodah Rag"—Paul, "Chez Adams (the Washingtons Come Too)"—Company; "The 'E' Medley"—Company.
ACT II (The Times): "Love Is a Crazy Thing"—Nee, Company; I Just Want To Be Happy—Nee;

"Yes, Yes, Yes"—Aurthur; "Bad Bar Bebop"—Company; "Job Hunting in Sodom"—Kramer; "It's the Loneliness, I Think"—Pell; "East Indian Love Call"—Nee, Company; "Too Hot to Handel"—Sklar; "The Movie Guide to Love"—Pell, Company; "Cheatin' "—Aurthur; One-Faced Woman Turns the Other Cheek, "I Only Want the Best"—Pell; "Dead Bride-To-Be"—Kramer; "The L.I. Van Gogh Blue Period Gavotte"—Pell, Aurthur; The "Real" People's Party—Company; Foster Children—Company; "Thank God" Chorus Reprise—Company.

Joseph and the Amazing Technicolor Dreamcoat (77). Revival of the musical based on the Old Testament story; music by Andrew Lloyd Webber, lyrics by Tim Rice. Produced by Zev Bufman, Susan R. Rose, Melvyn J. Estrin and Sidney Shlenker by arrangement with the Robert Stigwood Organization, Ltd. and David Land at the Entermedia Theater. Opened November 18, 1981. (Closed January 24, 1982 and transferred to Broadway; see its entry in the Plays Produced on Broadway section of this volume)

Narrator	Laurie Beechman	Zebulon	Doug Voet
Jacob	Gordon Stanley	Gad; Baker	Barry Tarallo
Reuben	Robert Hyman	Benjamin	Philip Carrubba
Simeon; Butler	Kenneth Bryan	Judah	Stephen Hope
Levi	Steve McNaughton	Joseph	Bill Hutton
Napthali	Charlie Serrano	Ishmaelite; Pharoah	Tom Carder
Issachar	Peter Kapetan	Ishmaelite; Potiphar	David Ardao
Asher	David Asher	Mrs. Potiphar	Randon Lo
Dan	James Rich	Apache Dancer	Joni Masella

Women's Chorus: Lorraine Barrett, Karen Bogan, Katharine Buffaloe, Lauren Goler, Randon Lo, Joni Masella, Kathleen Rowe McAllen, Renee Warren.

Swings: Rosalind Rahn, John Ganzer.

Directed and choreographed by Tony Tanner; musical director, David Friedman; scenery, Karl Eigsti; costumes, Judith Dolan; lighting, Barry Arnold; sound, Tom Morse; musical supervision, arrangements and orchestrations, Martin Silvestri, Jeremy Stone; associate producers, Gail Berman, Jean Luskin; production stage manager, Michael Martorella; stage manager, John Fennessy; press, Fred Nathan Associates, Patt Dale, Eileen McMahon.

Joseph and the Amazing Technicolor Dreamcoat was originally produced in England in 1968 and in America in 1970. Its professional productions have included those by the Young Vic in London in 1972, at Playhouse in the Park in Philadelphia and off Broadway by Brooklyn Academy of Music 12/30/76 for 23 performances. This 1981 revival, presented in two acts, was previously produced at Ford's Theater in Washington, D.C.

The list of musical numbers in *Joseph and the Amazing Technicolor Dreamcoat* appears on pages 335-6 of *The Best Plays of 1976-77*. In this 1981-82 production, the number "Pharaoh's Story" has been shifted from Act II to Act I.

*The Negro Ensemble Company. Schedule of two programs. ***A Soldier's Play** (221). By Charles Fuller. Opened November 20, 1981. **Colored People's Time** (32). By Leslie Lee. Opened March 30, 1982. (Closed April 25, 1982) Produced by The Negro Ensemble Company, Douglas Turner Ward artistic director, Leon B. Denmark managing director, at Theater Four (*A Soldier's Play*) and the Cherry Lane Theater (*Colored People's Time*).

A SOLDIER'S PLAY

Tech. Sgt. Vernon C. Waters	Adolph Caesar	Pvt. James Wilkie	Steven A. Jones
Capt. Charles Taylor	Peter Friedman	Pvt. Tony Smalls	Brent Jennings
Cpl. Bernard Cobb	Eugene Lee	Capt. Richard Davenport	Charles Brown
Pfc. Melvin Peterson	Denzel Washington	Pvt. C.J. Memphis	Larry Riley
Cpl. Ellis	James Pickens Jr.	Lt. Byrd	Cotter Smith
Pvt. Louis Henson	Samuel L. Jackson	Capt. Wilcox	Stephen Zettler

Understudies: Mr. Friedman—Cotter Smith; Messrs. Brown, Washington—James Pickens Jr.
Directed by Douglas Turner Ward; scenery, Felix E. Cochren; costumes, Judy Dearing; lighting, Allen Lee Hughes; sound, Regge Life; production stage managers, Clinton Turner Davis; stage manager, Femi Sarah Heggie; press, Howard Atlee.
Time: 1944. Place: Ft. Neal, La. The play was presented in two parts.
Investigation of the murder of a black Army sergeant in charge of World War II recruits in training. A Best Play; see page 161.

COLORED PEOPLE'S TIME

Prologue.............. Charles H. Patterson

ACT I

1859, Mississippi
Catherine .... L. Scott Caldwell
Sampson.................. Charles Weldon
Hannah.................. Juanita Mahone
Isaac...................... Chuck Cooper
1870, South Carolina
Jesse .... Charles H. Patterson
Aaron.................... Robert Gossett
Riverboat Captain........... Curt Williams
Early 1900s, the South
Blind John .... Chuck Cooper
1903, Richmond, Va.
Clemmie.................. Debbi Morgan
C.J..................... Charles Weldon
Roger .... Curt Williams
1919, Chicago
Addie .... L. Scott Caldwell
Abner.................... Chuck Cooper
Dewitt............... Charles H. Patterson
Berger.................... Curt Williams
1926, Harlem
Gus..................... Charles Weldon

Marcella.................. Juanita Mahone
1930s, Harlem
Alberta.................... Jackée Harry
1932, Harlem
Bud.................. Charles H. Patterson
Nadine .... L. Scott Caldwell
Riggins.................... Robert Gossett

ACT II

1938, Kansas City
Corina..................... Jackée Harry
Curtis .... Charles Weldon
Nat .... Charles H. Patterson
Alma..................... Debbi Morgan
WW II, USO Club
Belle .... Juanita Mahone
1944, Germany
Klaus .... Curt Williams
Bert....................... Chuck Cooper
Early 1950s, Detroit
Richard.................. Robert Gossett
1956, Montgomery, Ala.
Walter.................. Charles Weldon
Ida .... L. Scott Caldwell
Epilogue............. Charles H. Patterson

Directed by Horacena J. Taylor; scenery, Felix E. Cochren; costumes, Myrna Colley-Lee; lighting, Shirley Prendergast; sound, Gary Harris; production stage manager, Femi Sarah Heggie.
Series of scenes depicting highlights of black American history.

Whistler (34). Solo performance by John Cullum in a play by Lawrence and Maggie Williams; adapted from the novel *I, James McNeill Whistler* by Lawrence Williams. Produced by Frank and Mark Gero in association with Hori Productions of Tokyo at the Provincetown Playhouse. Opened December 6, 1981. (Closed January 3, 1982)

Directed by Jerome Kilty; scenery and costumes, David Gropman; scenery and costume supervisor, Keith Gonzales; lighting, William Armstrong; production supervisor, Louis Pietig; stage manager, Jonathan Gero; press, Shirley Herz, Sam Rudy, Peter Cromarty.
Comedy, with John Cullum portraying the painter Whistler in episodes from his life (1834–1903), plus 22 additional characters. The play was presented in two parts. Previously produced by the Hartford, Conn. Stage Company.

Tomfoolery (120). Musical revue with words and music by Tom Lehrer; adapted by Cameron Mackintosh and Robin Ray. Produced by Cameron Mackintosh, Hinks Shimberg and Art D'Lugoff at Top of the Gate. Opened December 14, 1981. (Closed March 28, 1982)

Charles H. Patterson, Robert Gossett and L. Scott
Caldwell in a scene from *Colored People's Time*

Donald Corren   MacIntyre Dixon
Joy Franz   Jonathan Hadary

The *Tomfoolery* Band: Ed Palermo reeds, Joel Helleny trombone, Bruce Doctor percussion, Bill Ellison bass, Eric Stern piano.

Standbys: Miss Franz—Connie Coit; Messrs. Dixon, Hadary, Corren—Michael McCormick.

Directed by Gary Pearle and Mary Kyte; musical direction, Eric Stern; scenery, Tom Lynch; costumes, Ann Emonts; lighting, Robert Jared; musical and vocal arrangements, John McKinney; original musical arrangements, Chris Walker; production stage manager, Alice Galloway; press, Solters/Roskin/Friedman, Milly Schoenbaum, Kevin Patterson.

Compilation of satirical and other numbers written by Tom Lehrer in the 1950s and 1960s. Previously produced in London.

MUSICAL NUMBERS, ACT I: "Be Prepared"—Company; "Poisoning Pigeons"—Joy Franz, Donald Corren; "I Wanna Go Back to Dixie"—MacIntyre Dixon, Company; "My Home Town"—Corren; "Pollution"—Franz, Dixon, Company; "Bright College Days"—Jonathan Hadary, Corren; "Fight Fiercely, Harvard"—Hadary, Corren, Dixon; "The Elements"—Hadary; "The Folk Song Army"—Company; "In Old Mexico"—Franz, Company; "She's My Girl"—Corren; "When You Are Old and Grey"—Company; "Wernher von Braun"—Dixon' "Who's Next"—Company; "I Got It From Agnes"—Hadary; "National Brotherhood Week"—Company.

ACT II: "So Long Mom"—Corren, Hadary; "Send the Marines"—Company; "Hunting Song"—Dixon; "Irish Ballad"—Franz, Company; "New Math"—Corren, Dixon; "Silent E"—Company; "Oedipus Rex"—Franz, Company; "I Hold Your Hand in Mine"—Corren; "Masochism Tango"—Dixon; "The Old Dope Peddler"—Hadary; "The Vatican Rag"—Company; "We Will All Go Together"—Company.

Head Over Heels (22). Musical based on the play *The Wonder Hat* by Kenneth Sawyer Goodman and Ben Hecht; book by William S. Kilborne Jr. and Albert T. Viola; music by Albert T. Viola; lyrics by William S. Kilborne Jr. Produced by Aristotle Productions at the Harold Clurman Theater. Opened December 15, 1981. (Closed January 3, 1982)

Punchinello	John Cunningham	Pierrot	Charles Michael Wright
Harlequin	Dennis Bailey	Nurse	Gwyda Donhowe
Columbine	Elizabeth Austin		

Directed by Jay Binder; musical numbers staged by Terry Rieser; musical direction and vocal arrangements, Herbert Kaplan; scenery and costumes, John Falabella; lighting, Jeff Davis; orchestrations and musical supervision, John Clifton; executive producers, Leonard Soloway, Allan Francis; associate producer, Joseph M. Sutherin; production stage manager, Laura deBuys; stage manager, John Philip; press, Shirley Herz, Sam Rudy, Peter Cromarty.

Place: Act I—A moonlit evening. Act II—A moment later.

Sweetly whimsical mixture of magic and romance.

ACT I

"New Loves for Old" .... Punchinello, Lovers
"Perfection" .... Columbine, Nurse, Punchinello
"I'm in Love" .... Harlequin
"Aqua Vitae" .... Punchinello, Nurse
"Nowhere" .... Punchinello, Harlequin
Finaletto .... Company

ACT II

"Castles in the Sand" .... Columbine, Nurse
"As If" .... Columbine
"Couldn't He Be You?" .... Punchinello, Nurse
"Lullabye to Myself" .... Pierrot
Finale.. Company

Francis (30). Musical with book by Joseph Leonardo, music by Steve Jankowski, lyrics by Kenny Morris. Produced by The Praxis Group in cooperation with The National Franciscan Communications Conference at The Common at St. Peter's Church. Opened December 22, 1981. (Closed January 24, 1982)

Francis Bernadone	John Dossett	Bernard de Quintavalle	Cris Groenendaal
Old Rufino	K.C. Wilson	Father Silvestro	Ron Lee Savin
Pietro Bernadone; Innocent III	Lloyd Battista	Juniper	Paul Browne
Lady Pica Bernadone	Tanny McDonald	Agnes	Whitney Kershaw
Clare de Favorone	Donna Murphy	Pacifica	Deborah Bendixen
Leo	Kenny Morris	Elias Bombarone	Tom Rolfing

Understudies: Misses Murphy, McDonald—Deborah Bendixen; Messrs. Browne, Morris, Saving —Chuck Newcombe; Mr. Wilson—Ron Lee Savin.

Directed by Frank Martin; musical direction and arrangements, Larry Esposito; scenery, Neil Bierbower; costumes, Martha Kelly; lighting, Thomas Bowen; production stage manager, William Hare; press, Shirley Herz, Sam Rudy, Peter Cromarty.

Time: The 12th century. Place: Umbria, a province of central Italy.

St. Francis of Assisi, on his deathbed, looks backward to evaluate the events of his life.

ACT I

"Miracle Town"	Company
Bedtime Stories	
"The Legend of Old Rufino"	Pica
"The Legend of King Arthur"	Pietro
"Serenade"	Francis, Clare
"Canticle of Pleasure"	Company
"I'm Ready Now!"	Francis
"The Fire in My Heart"	Francis
Ballet San Damiano	Women
"For the Good of Brotherhood"	Brothers
"The New Madness"	Francis, Company
"Bidding the World Farewell"	Francis, Clare

ACT II

"Oh, Brother!"	Brothers
"All the Time in the World"	Clare
"All the Time in the World" (Reprise)	Clare, Pica
"Walking All the Way to Rome"	Company
"Two Keys"	Innocent III
"The Road to Paradise"	Elias, Brothers
"Francis"	Clare, Leo
"The Legend of Old Rufino" (Reprise)	Pica
"Praises to the Sun!" (Canticle of Our Brother Sun)	Company

The Good Parts (22). By Israel Horovitz. Produced by Elena Latici, Charles Hollerith Jr., Max Weitzenhoffer and David Jones at the Astor Place Theater. Opened January 7, 1982. (Closed January 24, 1982)

Men of Greece	Robert DeFrank	Eugene Jacoby	Stephen Strimpell
Women of Greece	Nancy Mette	Maxine; Brenda	Cecelia Hart
Brian "Sonny" Levine	Tony Roberts	Eloise; Mildred	Judy Graubart

Understudy: Misses Hart, Graubart, Mette—Dorothy French.

Directed by Barnet Kellman; scenery, David Jenkins; costumes, Robert Wojewodski; lighting, Roger Morgan; sound, Michael Jay; production stage manager, Amy Pell; press, Solters/Roskin/Friedman, Milly Schoenbaum, Claudia McAllister, Kevin Patterson.

Time: The present. Place: Athens, Greece. The play was presented in two parts.

Comedy, a man in mid-life crisis flees New York family and friends for adventures in Greece.

Oh, Johnny (1). Musical with book and lyrics by Paul Streitz; music and lyrics by Gary Cherpakov. Produced by Paul Streitz in association with Stephen Harcusz at the Players Theater. Opened and closed at the evening performance January 10, 1982.

Directed and choreographed by Alan Weeks; musical direction, vocal and dance arrangements, Robert Marks; scenery, Jim Chesnutt; costumes, Gene Galvin; lighting, Tonu Goldin; press, Jeffrey Richards Associates, Bob Ganshaw. With Michael Crouch, Jo Mitchell, Nazig Edwards, Mark Frawley, Janet Wong, Jerry Coyle, Joey Ginza, Katherine Lench, Sally Yorke, Janet Donohue, David C. Wright, Clayton Davis, Robert Kellett.

World War II story of a pilot recruited for a secret mission behind the lines in China. Previously produced off off Broadway at the Off Center Theater.

Torch Song Trilogy (117). Program of three one-act plays by Harvey Fierstein: *The International Stud, Fugue in a Nursery* and *Widows and Children First!*. Produced by The Glines at the Actors Playhouse. Opened January 15, 1982. (Closed May 30, 1982 and transferred to Broadway)

Arnold Beckoff	Harvey Fierstein	Alan	Paul Joynt
Ed	Joel Crothers	David	Matthew Broderick
Lady Blues; Laurel	Diane Tarleton	Mrs. Beckoff	Estelle Getty

Directed by Peter Pope; scenery, Leon Munier; costumes, Mardi Philips; lighting, Scott Pinkney; musical direction and arrangements for *The International Stud*, Ned Levy; original music for *Fugue in a Nursery*, Ada Janik; production stage manager, Herb Vogler; press, Fred Nathan Associates, Francine L. Trevens, Eileen McMahon.

Part I: *The International Stud*—1. January, Arnold backstage at nightclub. 2. February, Ed in the "International Stud" bar. 3. June, Ed and Arnold in their respective apartments. 4. September, Arnold in the "International Stud" bar. 5. November, Ed and Arnold backstage.

Part II: *Fugue in a Nursery*—Time, one year later. Place, Arnold's apartment and various rooms of Ed's farmhouse.

Part III: *Widows and Children First!*—Time, five years later. 1. Arnold's apartment, 7 A.M. on a Thursday in June. 2. The same, 5 P.M. that day. 3. A bench in the park below, immediately following. 4. The apartment, 6 A.M. the next morning.

Three related one-acters about the life and times of a drag queen in a four-and-one-half-hour context. *The International Stud* and *Fugue in a Nursery* were previously produced off Broadway 5/22/78 for 72 performances and 1/27/80 for 53 performances, respectively, and not on the same program with each other. *Torch Song Trilogy*, including the aforementioned two plays plus *Widows and Children First!* was previously produced off off Broadway at the Richard Allen Center.

A Best Play; see page 181.

Fisher Stevens replaced Matthew Broderick 3/21/82.

The Unseen Hand (127) and **Killer's Head** (1). Revival of one-act plays by Sam Shepard. Produced by Burton Greenhouse (*The Unseen Hand* in the La Mama E.T.C. production) at the Provincetown Playhouse. Opened January 27, 1982. (Closed May 16, 1982)

Killer's Head		Willy the Space Freak	Deirdre O'Connell
Mazon	Perry Lang	Cisco Morphan	Michael Brody
The Unseen Hand		The Kid	David Watkins
Blue Morphan	Beeson Carroll	Sycamore Morphan..........	Walter Hadler

Directed by Tony Barsha; scenery, Dorian Vernacchio; costumes, Allison Connor; lighting, Anne Militello; sound, James Hardy; production stage manager, Dan Ziegler; press, Patt Dale, Jim Baldassare.

The Unseen Hand was previously produced off off Broadway at La Mama E.T.C. and off Broadway 4/1/70 for 21 performances. *Killer's Head*, a monologue, was previously produced off Broadway at American Place 4/4/75 for 34 performances. It closed after 1 performance as a curtain-raiser in this production.

Clownmaker (15). By Richard Crane. Produced by Riverside Productions with Union Square Theater at the Wonderhorse. Opened February 15, 1982. (Closed February 28, 1982).

Directed by Isaiah Sheffer; scenery, Barbara Miller, Daniel Michaelson; costumes, Daniel Michaelson; lighting, Arden Fingerhut; special consultant, Igor Youskevitch; press, Seymour Krawitz, Bob Larkin. With Stephen Lang, Jerome Dempsey, Ann Sachs, Dennis Bacigalupi, Kevin McClarnon, Alexandra O'Karma.

Play about Diaghilev, Nijinsky and his wife Romola, which won a prize at the 1975 Edinburgh festival.

The Harold Clurman Theater. Repertory of two programs. **Chucky's Hunch** (29). By Rochelle Owens. Opened February 16, 1982. **Birdbath,** revival of the play by Leonard Melfi, and **Crossing the Crab Nebula** by Lewis Black, program of two one-act plays (14). Opened March 7, 1982. (Repertory closed March 21, 1982) Produced by The Harold Clurman Theater, Jack Garfein artistic director, at the Harold Clurman Theater.

CHUCKY'S HUNCH

Chucky . . . . Kevin O'Connor	Porcupine Story . . . . Cynthia Adler
Voice, Snake &	Voice, Mother's Letter . . . . Leora Dana

Directed by Elinor Renfield; scenery, Abe Lubelski; costumes, Carla Kramer; lighting, Peter Kaczorowski; sound, Paul Garrity; associate producer, Byron Lasky; stage manager, Marc Cohen; press, Burnham-Callaghan Associates.

Monologue of a disillusioned artist, drinking and composing angry letters to a former wife, presented without intermission. Previously produced off off Broadway by Theater for the New City.

CROSSING THE CRAB NEBULA

Booney . . . . Kevin O'Connor	Mirage . . . . Barbara Eda-Young
Radio . . . . Peter Crombie	

BIRDBATH

Frankie Basta. . . . . Kevin O'Connor	City: a midtown cafeteria, the streets outside and
Velma Sparrow . . . . Barbara eda-Young	Frankie's basement apartment.
Time: A night in February. Place: New York	

Birdbath directed by Tom O'Horgan; *Crossing the Crab Nebula* directed by William Peters; scenery, Marc Cohen and Sam Gonzalez; costumes, Gabriel Perry; lighting, Laura Rambaldi; associate producer, Byron Lasky; production stage manager, David Marc; press, Burnham-Callaghan Associates, Lynda C. McKinney.

Birdbath was originally produced off Broadway 4/11/66 for 16 performances, following an off-off-Broadway production at La Mama ETC. *Crossing the Crab Nebula* is a satire on American commercialism.

How I Got That Story (111). By Amlin Gray. Produced by Harold DeFelice and Louis W. Scheeder with J.N.H. Ventures, Inc. and Margo Lion at the Westside Arts (Cheryl Crawford) Theater. Opened February 17, 1982. (Closed May 23, 1982)

The Reporter. . . . . Don Scardino
The Historical Event . . . . Bob Gunton

Directed by Carole Rothman; scenery, Patricia Woodbridge; costumes, Carol Oditz; lighting, Pat Collins; sound, Gary Harris; choreography, John Lone; creative consultant, Bob Gunton; original music and sound effects composed and performed by Bob Gunton; stage manager, Fredric H. Orner; press, Bob Ullman.

Episodes of the Vietnam War covered by a reporter, with Bob Gunton playing all the characters he meets and/or interviews on both sides. The play was presented in two parts. Previously produced at Milwaukee Repertory Theater, Folger Theater Group and last season off off Broadway.

Lydie Breeze (29). By John Guare. Produced by Roger S. Berlind and John Wulp at the American Place Theater. Opened February 25, 1982. (Closed March 21, 1982)

Jeremiah Grady................	Ben Cross	Joshua Hickman	Josef Sommer
Beaty....................	Roberta Maxwell	Jude Emerson	Robert Joy
Lydie Hickman	Cynthia Nixon	Lucian Rock	James Cahill
Gussie Hickman	Madeleine Potter		

Directed by Louis Malle; scenery, John Wulp; costumes, Willa Kim; lighting, Jennifer Tipton; music, Glen Roven; production stage manager, Jay Adler; stage manager, Scott Allen; press, Robert Ullman, Louise Ment.

Time: September, 1895. Place: Nantucket Island. The play was presented in two parts.

Emotional and physical influences from the past snowball into a multitude of crises in the present (in this case, the 1890s). Events prior to these are recounted in *Gardenia,* another in Guare's Nantucket series also produced this season (see its entry in this section of this volume).

Maybe I'm Doing It Wrong (33). Musical revue conceived by Joan Micklin Silver; music and lyrics by Randy Newman. Produced by Raphael D. Silver at the Astor Place Theater. Opened March 14, 1982. (Closed April 11, 1982)

Mark Linn-Baker	Larry Riley
Patti Perkins	Deborah Rush

Musicians: Michael S. Roth piano, Cecelia Hobbs violin, James McElwaine reeds, Don Mikkelson trombone.

Standbys: Messrs. Linn-Baker, Riley—Eric Elice; Misses Perkins, Rush—Marilyn Pasekoff.

Directed by Joan Micklin Silver; dance direction, Eric Elice; musical direction and arrangements, Michael S. Roth; scenery, Heidi Landesman; costumes, Hilary Rosenfeld; lighting, Fred Buchholz; production stage manager, Richard Elkow; press, Jeffrey Richards Associates, Bob Ganshaw, Ted Killmer.

Modern pop composer's works assembled into a show, presented without intermission. Previously produced off off Broadway by The Production Company.

MUSICAL NUMBERS: "Sigmund Freud's Impersonation of Albert Einstein in America"—Band; "My Old Kentucky Home"—Company; "Birmingham"—Mark Linn-Baker, Larry Riley; "Political Science"—Deborah Rush, Patti Perkins; "It's Money That I Love"—Company; "Jolly Coppers on Parade" (choreography, Ara Fitzgerald)—Rush, Company; "Caroline"—Company; "Simon Smith and the Amazing Dancing Bear"—Linn-Baker; "Love Story—Riley, Rush; "Tickle Me"—Perkins, Linn-Baker.

Also "Maybe I'm Doing It Wrong"—Company; "The Debutante's Ball"—Company; "Burn On" —Perkins; "Pants"—Linn-Baker; "God's Song (That's Why I Love Mankind)"—Riley; "They Just Got Married"—Company; "A Wedding in Cherokee County"—Riley, Perkins; "Yellow Man"— Company; "The Girls in My Life (Part I)"—Linn-Baker, Rush; "Rider in the Rain"—Linn-Baker, Company; "Mama Told Me Not to Come"—Rush, Company; "Old Man"—Perkins; "Lonely at the Top"—Company.

Also "Mr. President (Have Pity on the Working Man)"—Company; "Sail Away"—Riley, Company; "Theme From *Ragtime*"—Band; "Marie"—Riley; "I Think It's Going to Rain Today"— Perkins; "Let's Burn Down the Cornfield"—Riley, Linn-Baker; "Davy the Fat Boy"—Company; "You Can Leave Your Hat On"—Linn-Baker; "Rollin' "—Rush; "Short People"—Company; "I'll Be Home"—Perkins, Company; "Dayton, Ohio 1903"—Company.

Poor Little Lambs (73). By Paul Rudnick. Produced by Richmond Crinkley at the Theater of St. Peter's Church. Opened March 14, 1982. (Closed May 16, 1982)

Stu Arnstine..............	Bronson Pinchot	Ike Ennis	William Thomas Jr.
Ricky Hocheiser	Albert Macklin	Itsu Yoshiro..............	Gedde Watanabe
Davey Waldman	David Naughton	Drew Waterman Reed	Page Moseley
Frank Wozniak	Kevin Bacon	Claire Hazard	Blanche Baker
Jack Bayliss Hayes	Miles Chapin		

Understudy: Men—Scott Barnes.

Directed by Jack Hofsiss; scenery, David Jenkins; costumes, William Ivey Long; lighting, Beverly

Emmons; sound, T. Richard Fitzgerald; stage movements, Peter Anastos; musical consultant, Bob Brush; associate producer, Scott Steele; production stage manager, Janet Beroza; press, Betty Lee Hunt, Maria Cristina Pucci, James Sapp.

Time: During the current academic year. Place: Yale University, New Haven, Conn. The play was presented in two parts.

A female attempts to join the all-male college singing group known as The Whiffenpoofs.

Repertory of Songs: "Mother of Men" by Brian Hooker and Seth Bingham; "When My Sugar Walks Down the Street" by Gene Austin and Jimmy McHugh; "I Married an Angel" by Richard Rodgers and Lorenz Hart; "Bright College Years" by H.S. Durand and Carl Wilhelm; "Love for Sale" by Cole Porter; "Undertaker" (traditional); "Boola" by Allan M. Hirsch; "Bingo" by Cole Porter; "Good Night, Poor Harvard" by Douglas S. Moore.

Scenes Dedicated to My Brother and **What People Do When They're All Alone** (28). Program of two one-act plays by Joel Homer. Produced by Magpie Productions in association with David G. Watson at the South Street Theater. Opened March 15, 1982. (Closed April 11, 1982)

SCENES DEDICATED TO MY BROTHER

Father	Jack Fogarty	Woman's Voice .... Suzanne Johnson
Older Son	Stephen Hamilton	Time: Present and past. Place: Father's home.
Younger Son	Joel Fredrickson	

WHAT PEOPLE DO WHEN THEY'RE ALL ALONE

The Woman .... Patti Karr
    Time: The present. Place: A city apartment.

Directed by Maggie L. Harrer; scenery, Joshua Dachs, Maggie L. Harrer; costumes, Sara Denning; lighting, Joshua Dachs; sound, Paul Garrity; production stage manager, Renee F. Lutz; press, Jacksina & Friedman, Angela Wilson, Diane Tomlinson.

Scenes Dedicated to My Brother is about the power of control, *What People Do When They're All Alone* about self-control.

Catholic School Girls (30). By Casey Kurtti. Produced by Lucille Lortel and Mortimer Levitt in association with Burry Fredrik and Haila Stoddard at the Douglas Fairbanks Theater. Opened April 1, 1982. (Closed April 25, 1982)

CAST: Elizabeth McHugh, Sister Mary Thomasina—Lynne Born; Wanda Sluska, Sister Mary Agnes—Maggie Low; Maria Theresa Russo, Sister Mary Germaine—Shelley Rogers; Colleen Dockery, Sister Mary Lucille—Christine Von Dohln.

Understudy: Vandra Thorburn.

Directed by Burry Fredrik; scenery, Paul Leonard; costumes, Sigrid Insull; lighting, Paul Everett; associate producer, Ben Sprecher; production stage manager, Melissa Davis; stage manager, Vandra Thorburn; press, Jeffrey Richards Associates, Bob Ganshaw, Ted Killmer.

Character sketches of four pupils in a Catholic school from first to eighth grades, and of four of the nuns who are their teachers. The play was presented in two parts. Previously produced at the White Barn Theater, Westport, Conn.

The Acting Company. Tenth anniversary season schedule of two revivals. **Twelfth Night** (5). By William Shakespeare. Opened April 15, 1982. **The Country Wife** (8). By William Wycherley. Opened April 20, 1982 matinee. (Repertory closed April 24, 1982) Produced by The Acting Company, John Houseman producing artistic director, Michael Kahn and Alan Schneider artistic directors, Margot Harley executive producer, at the American Place Theater.

Lynne Born, Maggie Low, Shelley Rogers and Christine Von Dohln in a scene from *Catholic School Girls*

PERFORMER	"TWELFTH NIGHT"	"THE COUNTRY WIFE"
Casey Biggs	Sebastian	Mr. Horner
Becky Borczon		Lucy
Bonnie Bowers		Old Lady Squeamish
Tommy Bramlett	1st Sailor; 2d Officer	
Lynn Chausow	Maria	Mrs. Margery Pinchwife
Philip Goodwin	Feste	Dr. Quack
Barry Heins	Antonio	Horner's Servant
Richard S. Iglewski	Sir Toby Belch	Mr. Pinchwife
Ronna Kress	Servant	Mrs. Dainty Fidget
Pamela Nyberg	Viola	Lady Fidget
Patrick O'Connell	Orsino	Mr. Harcourt
Brian Reddy	Fabian; Sea Captain	Sir Jasper Fidget
Jeffrey Rubin	Malvolio	Bookseller
Pamela Tucker-White		Mrs. Squeamish
Ray Virta	Valentine; Friar	Servant; Tradesman
Paul Walker	Sir Andrew Aguecheek	Mr. Sparkish
Daniel Wirth	Curio; 1st Officer	Mr. Dorilant
Michele-Denise Woods	Olivia	Alithea

Understudies, *Twelfth Night:* Messrs. O'Connell, Goodwin—Casey Biggs; Mr. Biggs—Ray Virta; Messrs. Heins, Iglewski—Daniel Wirth; Messrs. Virta, Bramlett, Wirth—Randolph Foerster; Mr. Walker—Brian Reddy; Messrs. Rubin, Reddy (Sea Captain)—Barry Heins; Mr. Reddy (Fabian)—Philip Goodwin; Miss Woods—Pamela Tucker-White; Miss Nyberg—Becky Borczon; Miss Chausow—Bonnie Bowers.

Understudies, *The Country Wife:* Mr. Biggs—Patrick O'Connell; Messrs. Goodwin, Reddy—Barry Heins; Misses Borczon, Kress—Bonnie Bowers; Messrs. Wirth, O'Connell—Ray Virta; Misses Tucker-White, Chausow—Becky Borczon; Mr. Walker—Jeffrey Rubin; Mr. Iglewski—Daniel Wirth; Misses Nyberg, Woods—Pamela Tucker-White; Mr. Virta—Randolph Foerster.

BOTH PLAYS: Production stage manager, Don Judge; stage manager, Kathleen B. Boyette; press, Fred Nathan, Anne Abrams.

TWELFTH NIGHT: Directed by Michael Langham; scenery and costumes, Desmond Heeley; lighting, John Michael Deegan; music composed and directed by David Erlanger; assistant to Mr. Langham, Randolph Foerster.

Place: Illyria, an island. The play was presented in two parts. *Twelfth Night* was last revived off Broadway by Circle Repertory Company 12/12/80 for 27 performances.

THE COUNTRY WIFE: Directed by Garland Wright; scenery, Jack Barkla; costumes, Judith Dolan; lighting, Dennis Parichy; assistant to Mr. Wright, Randolph Foerster; assistant to Miss Dolan, John W. Glaser III.

Place: London. The play was presented in two parts. *The Country Wife* was last revived on Broadway by Repertory Theater of Lincoln Center 12/9/65 for 54 performances.

T.N.T. (6). Musical with book, music and lyrics by Richard Morrock. Produced by The Dynamite Limited Partnership at the Players Theater. Opened April 22, 1982. (Closed April 25, 1982)

Directed by Frank Carucci; musical numbers staged by Mary Lou Crivello; musical direction and arrangements, William Gladd; scenery and lighting, Ernest Allen Smith; costumes, Susan J. Wright; production stage manager, Irene Klein; press, Francine L. Trevens, Becky Flora, David Mayhew. With Steven F. Hall, Mary Anne Dorward, Regis Bowman, Joanne Bradley, Kenneth Boys, Mary Garripoli, Bill Boss, Gabriel Barre, Christine Campbell, Natalie Strauss.

The initials stand for "Tricephalous Neurosyllogistic Training" in a musical send-up of California cults, previously produced off off Broadway.

*Cast of Characters (31). One-woman show adapted by Patrizia Norcia, David Kaplan and William Bixby Jr.; based on *The Art of Ruth Draper* by Morton Dauwen Zabel; with Patrizia Norcia. Produced by William Bixby Jr. in association with Edwin W. Schloss and Abigail Franklin at the Cherry Lane Theater. Opened May 5, 1982.

Directed by David Kaplan; lighting, Stuart Duke; costume supervision, Dunya Ramicova; original music by Steve Lutvak; production stage manager, Nora Peck; press, Fred Nathan & Associates, Eileen McMahon, Louis Sica.

Recreations of the character sketches made famous by Ruth Draper. The program, presented in two parts, was chosen from the following Draper material: *Three Women and Mr. Clifford*, *The Italian Lesson*, *A Scottish Immigrant at Ellis Island*, *The Actress*, *A Class in Greek Poise*, *The French Dressmaker*, *A Children's Party*, *In the Court of Philip IV*, *Four Imaginary Folk Songs*, *In a Church in Italy*.

*Livingstone and Sechele (24). By David Pownall. Produced by Quaigh Theater, William H. Lieberson artistic director, at the Quaigh Theater. Opened May 11, 1982; see note.

Sechele	Afemo	Mary	Prudence Wright Holmes
Livingstone	Mike Champagne	Mokokon	Esther Ryvlin

Directed by William H. Lieberson; scenery, Geoffrey Hall; costumes, Bob Horek; lighting, Paul Bartlett; lighting assistant, Jacquelyn Clymore; production stage manager, Fred Berg; stage manager, Kathy LaCommare; press, Max Eisen, Maria Somma.

Place: The settlement of the Kwena (Crocodile) tribe on the edge of the dried-up Kolobeng River in the Kalahari Desert, southern Africa. Act I: August 1848. Act II: A few days later. Act III: January 1, 1849.

African tribal chieftain is exposed to 19th century Christian culture and religion by the explorer Dr. Livingstone. A foreign play previously produced at the 1978 Edinburgh Festival and in London.

Note: Press date for this off-Broadway production of *Livingstone and Sechele* was 5/19/82; it was previously offered as an off-off-Broadway production opening at the same theater 4/6/82.

*The Six O'Clock Boys (23). By Sidney Morris. Produced by Lester Lockwood Sr. and Lester Lockwood Jr. at the Vandam Theater. Opened May 12, 1982.

Gabie	Vera Lockwood	Tuesday Night Boy	Lee Collings
Monday Night Boy	Johnnie Collins III	Wednesday Night Boy	James Nixon

Directed by Raymond Homer; scenery and costumes, Helen Lockwood; lighting, Angus Moss; press, Howard Atlee.

Woman living in a welfare hotel entertains a series of young men. Previously produced in Los Angeles.

*The Freak (6). By Granville Wyche Burgess. Produced by Kyle Renick and Gene Persson in association with Miranda Smith in the WPA Theater production at the Douglas Fairbanks Theater. Opened May 27, 1982.

Dr. Wesley Ketchum	James Rebhorn	Edgar Cayce	Dann Florek
Squire Cayce	James Greene	Dr. Phillip Barber	Richard Patrick-Warner
Charlie Dietrich	Peter J. Saputo	Dr. Joe Quigly	Eddie Jones
Gertrude Cayce	Polly Draper	Dr. Furman Shepard	William R. Riker

Directed by Stephen Zuckerman; scenery, Christina Weppner; costumes, Susan Denison; lighting, Richard Winkler; production stage manager, Melissa Davis; press, Jeffrey Richards Associates, Ted Killmer.

The effects on his family and private life of the psychic and faith-healing activities of Edgar Cayce, an early 20th century Kentuckian. Previously produced off off Broadway at WPA Theater. The play was presented in three acts.

PLAYS PRODUCED OFF OFF BROADWAY

AND ADDITIONAL PRODUCTIONS

Here is a comprehensive sampling of off-off-Broadway and other experimental or peripheral 1981–82 productions in New York, compiled by Camille Croce. There is no definitive "off-off-Broadway" area or qualification. To try to define or regiment it would be untrue to its fluid, exploratory purpose. The listing below of hundreds of works produced by 79 OOB groups and others is as inclusive as reliable sources will allow, however, and takes in all leading Manhattan-based, new-play-producing, English-language organizations.

The more active and established producing groups are identified in **bold face type,** in alphabetical order, with artistic policies and the name of the managing director(s) given whenever these are a matter of record. Each group's 1981–82 schedule is listed with play titles in CAPITAL LETTERS. Often these are works-in-progress with changing scripts, casts and directors, sometimes without an engagement of record (but an opening or early performance date is included when available).

Many of these off-off-Broadway groups have long since outgrown a merely experimental status and are offering programs which are the equal in professionalism and quality (and in some cases the superior) of anything in the New York theater, with special contractual arrangements like the showcase code, letters of agreement (allowing for longer runs and higher admission prices than usual) and, closer to the edge of the commercial theater, a so-called "mini-contract." In the list below, all available data on opening dates, performance numbers (with a plus sign + in the case of a show still running) and major production and acting credits (almost all of them Equity members) is included in the entries of these special-arrangement offerings.

A large selection of lesser-known groups and other shows that made appearances off off Broadway during the season appears under the "Miscellaneous" heading at the end of this listing.

Amas Repertory Theater. Creative arts as a powerful instrument of peaceful change, towards healthier individuals. Rosetta LeNoire, founder and artistic director.

16 performances each
WILL THEY EVER LOVE US ON BROADWAY. Musical by Osayande Baruti. October 22, 1981. Director and choreographer, Mabel Robinson; musical director, Coleridge-Taylor Perkinson; scenery, Thomas Barnes; lighting, John Enea; costumes, Judy Dearing. With Ed Battle, Dwayne A. Grayman, Marva Hicks, James Judy, Jay Herbert Kerr Jr., L. Edmond Wesley.

American Place Theater. In addition to the regular off-Broadway subscription season, cabaret and other special projects are presented. Wynn Handman, director, Julia Miles, associate director.

AMERICAN PLACE—Trazana Beverley in *The Brothers*

The Women's Project

CONSTANCE AND THE MUSICIAN (12). Book and lyrics, Caroline Kava; music, Mel Marvin. June 10, 1981. Director, Joan Micklin Silver; choreographer, Wesley Fata; scenery, William Barclay; lighting, Judy Rasmuson; costumes, Whitney Blausen. With Jeff Brooks, Marilyn Caskey, Philip Casnoff, M'el Dowd, Caroline Kava, Mel Marvin, Stan Wilson.

THE WINDS OF CHANGE. Book, Franklin C. Tramutola; music, Joseph D'Agostino; lyrics, Gary Romero. February 4, 1982. Director, William Michael Maher; musical director, Lea Richardson; scenery, Tom Barnes; lighting, Ronald L. McIntyre; costumes, Judy Dearing. With Richard T. Alpers, Susan Berkson, Terry Kirwin, Jack Sevier, Molly Stark.

FIVE POINTS. Book, Laurence Holder; music and lyrics, John Braden. April 15, 1982. Director, William Michael Maher; choreographer, Keith Rozie; musical director, Steven Oirich; scenery, Tom Barnes; lighting, Gregg Marriner; costumes, Gabriel Berry. With Joseph Fugett, J. Herbert Kerr, Jr., Cynthia MacPherson, Nicky Paraiso, Rochelle Parker, Tonya Pinkins, Valois Mickens, Robert Lydiard.

THE DEATH OF A MINER (21). By Paula Cizmar. March 25, 1982. Director, Barbara Rosoff; scenery, Leslie Taylor; lighting, Arden Fingerhut; costumes, Heidi Hollmann. With Mary McDonnell, Cotter Smith, Margaret MacLeod, Kristin Jolliff, Dave Florek, Shaw Purnell, Ritch Brinkley, Douglas Gower, Steven Liring, John Griesmer.

THE BROTHERS (14). By Kathleen Collins. April 4, 1982. Director, Billie Allen; scenery, Christina Weppner; lighting, Annie Wrightson; costumes, K.L. Fredericks. With Trazana Beverley, Leila Danette, Duane Jones, Janet League, Seret Scott, Marie Thomas.

American Humorists Series SERIOUS BIZNESS (comedy revue) (6+). May 18, 1982. With David Babcock, Winnie Holzman, Jill Larson, Don Perman.

Circle Repertory Projects in Progress. Developmental programs for new plays. Marshall W. Mason, artistic director.

4 performances each

BING AND WALKER by James Paul Farrell. October 12, 1981. Directed by Mick Casale; with Mary Lea Floden, Conrad McLaren, Debra Mooney, Jack Davidson.

'NIGHT MOTHER by Marsha Norman. November 9, 1981. Directed by Jeremy Blahnik; with Bobo Lewis, Kathy Bates.

WHAT I DID LAST SUMMER by A.R. Gurney Jr. December 7, 1981. Directed by Porter Van Zandt; with Ben Siegler, Jeff McCracken, Debra Mooney, Mia Dillon, Mary Lea Floden, Sloane Shelton.

CAT AND MOUSE by Claris Nelson, directed by B. Rodney Marriott; HOW WOMEN BREAK BAD NEWS by John Bishop, directed by Amy Salz; PRESQUE ISLE by Joyce Carol Oates, directed by Sallie Brophy. January 18, 1982. With Ellen Conway, Jane Fleiss, Lindsey Ginter, Charles T. Harper, Trish Hawkins, Ken Kliban, Debra Mooney.

SPOOKHOUSE by Harvey Fierstein. March 15, 1982. Directed by George Ferencz; with Camille Saviola, Zane Lasky, Christine Speicher, Tom Noonan.

Encompass Theater. Dedicated to exploring the American spirit by presenting adventurous, vital productions of American opera and contemporary music theater; also provides a forum for the development of new composers and librettists. Nancy Rhodes, artistic director, Roger Cunningham, producer.

Schedule included:

FIRST STAGE FIRST (staged readings of The American Composer/Librettist Lab): MON-KEYSHINES book, music, lyrics, and directed by Michael Mooney, with Semina DeLaurentis, Steve Yudson, Georgia Spelvin; 1619 B'WAY music and lyrics by Lou Rodgers, directed by Jane Whitehill, with David Lahm, Eddie Allen, Beth Angel, Michael Ingram, Tim Strong; MÉNAGE music and lyrics by Roger Lax, directed by David Crane and Marta Kauffman; LEAPERS book, music, and lyrics by Margaret Carriel; SEVEN GABLES book and lyrics by Al Reynolds, music by George Groth; WRITINGS (songs based on letters of Emily Dickinson, Eleanor Roosevelt, Sarah Bernhardt, and Cho Wen Chun) by J. Spencer; THE CAT AND THE MOON based on William Butler Yeats's poems, by Wayne Paquette; HAWKRUN (music drama) libretto by Tom Piechowski, music and lyrics by Roger Zahab; TORQUEMADA libretto by Al Reynolds, music and lyrics by Max Kinberg; BLINDS book, music, and lyrics by Roger Lax, directed by Marta Kauffman and David Crane, with Jean Elliott, James Romick. May 1–16, 1982.

Ensemble Studio Theater. Nucleus of playwrights-in-residence dedicated to supporting individual theater artists and developing new works for the stage. 80–100 projects each season, initiated by E.S.T. members. Curt Dempster, artistic director.

THE BEST OF THE MARATHON: A SERMON written and directed by David Mamet; DUMPING GROUND by Elizabeth Diggs, directed by Pamela Berlin; THE LADY OR THE TIGER by Shel Silverstein, directed by Art Wolff; OPEN ADMISSIONS by Shirley Lauro, directed by Elinor Renfield (36). October 27, 1981. Scenery, Dale Jordan, Leslie Taylor; lighting, Richard Lund. With Bill Cwikowski, Jack Gilpin, Frank Girardeau, Judith Ivey, Russ Kupfrian, Calvin Levels, Christopher Murney, David Rasche, Marilyn Rockafellow, William Russ.

THE HOUSE ACROSS THE STREET (24). By Darrah Cloud. January 22, 1982. Director, Bruce Levitt; scenery, Brian Martin; lighting, Richard Lund; costumes, Deborah Shaw. With Lewis Arlt, Stephen Baccus, Bill Cwikowski, Cordis Heard, Jane Hoffman, Sarah Inglis.

BELLA FIGURA (24). By Brother Jonathan, O.S.F. April 2, 1982. Director, John Schwab; scenery, Brian Martin; lighting, Todd Elmer; costumes, Madeline Cohen. With Reed Birney, Dominic Chianese, James Greene, Jo Henderson, Stefano Loverso, Patricia Mauceri.

NEW VOICES (staged readings): MOTHERLESS CHILD by Rosemary McLaughlin, THE BRASS BELL SUPERETTE by Bill Bozzone, GRUNTS by Joshua Brand, DANCERS by Brendan Ward, LILY DALE by Horton Foote. March 10–21, 1982.

MARATHON 1982 (one-act play festival): FOG by Conrad Bromberg, directed by Marilyn Rockafellow; APPEARANCES by Tina Howe, directed by Douglas Johnson; THE UN-DEFEATED RHUMBA CHAMP by Charles Leipart, directed by Charles I. Karchmer; THE FOREST LAWN DIET by James G. Richardson, directed by Raymond Singer; THE FISHER WEDDING by Carol Hall, directed by Marcia Haufrecht; GOODBYE HOWARD by Romulus Linney, directed by Art Wolff; THE FORTRESS OF SOLITUDE by Jeffrey M. Jones, directed by James A. Simpson; THE SELF-BEGOTTEN by John Wellman, directed by Pamela Berlin; BUDDIES by Mary Gallagher, directed by Mary B. Robinson; ROSARIO AND THE GYPSIES (musical) book and lyrics by Eduardo Machado, music by Rick Vartorella, directed by Shirley Kaplan; ORD-WAY AMES-GAY by Susan Vick, directed by Pamela Berlin; KILO by Marc B. Berman, directed by Risa Bramon; CLASS REUNION by Kermit Frazier, directed by Madeleine Thornton-Sherwood; MANY HAPPY RETURNS by Willie Reale, directed by June Stein; ROUTED by Jeffrey Sweet, directed by Charles I. Karchmer. May 12–June 21, 1982.

Equity Library Theater. Actors' Equity sponsors a series of revivals each season as showcases for the work of its actor-members and an "informal series" of original, unproduced material. George Wojtasik, managing director.

KING OF HEARTS by Jean Kerr and Eleanor Brooke. September 24, 1981. Directed by Richard Mogavero; with Alice Elliott, Dugg Smith, Dennis Predovic.

SEESAW (musical) book by Michael Bennett, based on *Two for the Seesaw* by William Gibson, music by Cy Coleman, lyrics by Dorothy Fields. October 29, 1981. Directed by Yvonne Ghareeb; with Diana Szlosberg, Bill Tatum.

TEN LITTLE INDIANS by Agatha Christie. December 3, 1981. Directed by Philip Giberson; with Kathryn Boulé, Marcus Smythe, Fred Miller.

STREET SCENE (musical) book by Elmer Rice, music by Kurt Weill, lyrics by Langston Hughes. January 7, 1982. Directed by Robert Brink; with D. Michael Heath, Casper Roos, Sue Anne Gershenson, Jane Seaman.

LYSISTRATA by Aristophanes. February 11, 1982. Directed by Alan Fox; with Madelon Thomas, Deborah Allison, Scott Campbell.

NYMPH ERRANT (musical) book by Romney Brent, from James Laver's novel, music and lyrics by Cole Porter. March 11, 1982. With Kathleen Mahony-Bennett, Lynne Charney, Avril Gentles, Boncellia Lewis.

TEACH ME HOW TO CRY by Patricia Joudry. April 15, 1982. Directed by Don Price; with Jolene Adams, Gerry Goodman, Lynn Watson, Alan Zampese, Helen-Jean Arthur.

APPLAUSE (musical) book by Betty Comden and Adolph Green, based on the film, *All About Eve* and the original story by Mary Orr, music by Charles Strouse, lyrics by Lee Adams. May 13, 1982. Directed by Leslie Eberhard; with Renee Roy, Karen Stefko, Charles T. Harper.

Informal Series: 3 performances each

SEA DREAM (musical revue) conceived and directed by Margaret Denithorne. September 21, 1981. With Lucinda Hitchcock Cone, Lenny Foglia, Mary Gaebler, Jay Aubrey Jones, Michael Noll.

LEAVIN' CHEYENNE by Percy Granger. October 19, 1981. Directed by Constance Grappo; with Brad Sullivan, Tom McKitterick.

ACE O' DIAMONDS (musical) book by Ed Kelleher, music and lyrics by Melanie. November

23, 1981. Directed by Sparkle Finley; with Victor Caroli, Dru-Ann Chuckran, Annie Golden, Ed Hyland, Claire Jagemann, Jim Quinn.

WILLY & SAHARA written and directed by Tom Rosica. December 7, 1981. With Linda Eskenas, Todd Lewis.

HEROES by Jeffrey Arthur Beard. January 18, 1982. Directed by J. Barry Lewis; with Peter Gatto, Joel Leffert.

OUT TAKES by Donna Sorbello. February 1, 1982. Directed by Shauna Vey; with Margo Bruton, Kelly Champion, Joanna Green, Judith Reagan.

CAUGHT IN THE MIDDLE by Betta Shafran. March 15, 1982. Directed by Elowyn Castle; with Jo Deodato Clark.

STRANGER IN THE LAKE by Kate Heichler. April 26, 1982. Directed by David Butler; with Eliza Decroes, Lois Englund, Mary Lowry, William Winkler.

THE INSANITY OF MARY GIRARD by Lanie Robertson. May 10, 1982. Directed by Rene Alexander; with Stephen Gleason, Gael Hammer, Vicki Hirsch, Margaret Hunt, Judy Kelley, G. Leslie Muchmore, Elizabeth von Benken.

Gene Frankel Theater. Development of new works and revivals for the theater. Gene Frankel, artistic director.

F. SCOTT FITZGERALD TALKS ABOUT HIS CRACK-UP (15). By and with Peter Savage. August 7, 1981. Director, Noel Boode; lighting, Dan Farley.

SUNDAY PICNIC. By Abbie H. Fink and Carol Shoshanah Fink, with John Slater Reaves; director, Abbie H. Fink; with Shelia Russell, Jan Leslie Harding, Rick Weatherwax, Frank Spencer, Victor Talmadge. MARY GOLDSTEIN AND THE AUTHOR. By Oyamo; director, Patricia Benoit; with Lorey Hayes. (12). October 2, 1981. Scenery, Howard R. McBride; lighting, Daniel J. Farley; costumes, Van Broughton Ramsey, Gene Lakin.

Hudson Guild Theater. Presents plays in their New York, American, or world premieres. David Kerry Heefner, producing director, Daniel Swee, general manager.

28 performances each

SLEEP BEAUTY. By Arthur Meryash. November 18, 1981. Directors, Jordan Deitcher and Arthur Feinsod; scenery, Roger Mooney; lighting, Paul Wonsek; costumes, Edi Giguere. With Clarice Taylor, Charles Henry Patterson, Tom Everett.

BESIDE THE SEASIDE. By Stephen Temperley. January 6, 1982. Director, Vivian Matalon; scenery, William Ritman; lighting, Richard Nelson; costumes, David Loveless. With Leslie O'Hara, Charlotte Moore, Harry Groener, Jack Ryland, Kathryn C. Sparer.

WONDERLAND. By Margaret Keilstrup. February 24, 1982. Director, David Kerry Heefner; scenery and lighting, Paul Wonsek; costumes, Bob Graham. With Dennis Bailey, Thomas A. Carlin, Debra Mooney, Alice Drummond.

EMIGRÉS. By Slawomir Mrozek, translated by Maciej and Teresa Wrona with Robert Holman. April 14, 1982. Director, Thomas Gruenewald; scenery, James Leonard Joy; lighting, Jeff Davis; costumes, Mariann Verheyen. With David Leary, Sam Tsoutsouvas.

Work-in-Progress

VAMPS AND RIDEOUTS (12). Conceived by Phyllis Newman; book material, Betty Comden, Adolph Green, Arthur Laurents, Isobel Lennart, Anita Loos; music, Jule Styne; lyrics, Susan Birkenhead, Sammy Cahn, Betty Comden, Adolph Green, E.Y. Harburg, Bob Merrill, Leo Robin, Stephen Sondheim; adapted by Phyllis Newman and James Pentecost. February 4, 1982. Director, James Pentecost; scenery, Lawrence Miller; lighting, David H. Murdock. With Phyllis Newman, George Lee Andrews, Pauletta Pearson.

INTAR. Innovative culture center for the Hispanic American community of New York City, focusing on the art of theater. Max Ferra, artistic director, Dennis Ferguson, managing director.

BODYBAGS (28). By Tee Saralegui. July 30, 1981. Director, Melvin Van Peebles; scenery and costumes, Ken Holamon; lighting, Larry Crimmins. With Donna Pescow, John Snyder, Jaime Tirelli.

CRISP! (24). Book and lyrics, Dolores Prida, conceived by Max Ferra and Dolores Prida, based on Jacinto Benavente's *Los Intereses Creados;* music, Manuel Del Fuego. October 17, 1981. Director, Max Ferra; choreographer, Daniel Lewis; musical director, Tania Leon; scenery, Larry Brodsky; lighting, Tom Hennes; costumes, Debra Stein. With Manuel Martinez, Felipe Gorostiza, Cintia Cruz, C.J. Critt, Stephen Rosario, Dain Chandler, Antonia Rey, Mary Stout, Jose Antonio Maldonado, Edward Paul Allen.

THE EXTRAVAGANT TRIUMPH OF JESUS CHRIST, KARL MARX, AND WILLIAM SHAKESPEARE (24). By Fernando Arrabal, translated by Miguel Falquez-Certain. April 1, 1982. Director, Eduardo Manet; scenery and costumes, Randy Barcelo; lighting, Cheryl Thacker. With Doris Castellanos, Naseer El-Kadi, Ron Faber, Cecilia Flores, Thomas Kopache, Madeleine LeRoux, Brian Rose.

Interart Theater. A professional environment primarily for women playwrights, directors, designers, and performers to participate in theatrical activity. Margot Lewitin, artistic director.

Schedule included:

FOOD (Part I of WOMAN'S BODY AND OTHER NATURAL RESOURCES) (15). By Sondra Segal and Roberta Sklar. June 7, 1981. Lighting, Annie Wrightson. With Donna Kaz, Mary Lum, Mary Lyon, Lizzie Olesker, Linda Powell, Sondra Segal.

LaMama Experimental Theater Club (ETC). A busy workshop for experimental theater of all kinds. Ellen Stewart, founder, Wesley Jensby, artistic director.

Schedule included:

THE HOTEL PLAY. By Wallace Shawn. August 12, 1981. Director, John Ferraro; scenery, Michael Moran; lighting, Gregory C. MacPherson; costumes, Abigail Murray; music, Richard Weinstock. With Griffin Dunne, Michael Murphy, Mark Linn-Baker, Ed Bullins, Christopher Durang, Wendy Wasserstein, Frank Modell, Jim Stevenson, Ann Beattie.
YA'ACOBI AND LEIDENTAL. Written and directed by Hanoch Levine. September 8, 1981. Scenery, lighting, and costumes, Ruth Dar; music, Alex Cagan. With Zahariah Charifal, Albert Cohen, Joseph Carmon.
LA MAMA'S 20TH ANNIVERSARY CELEBRATION (revival of plays originally presented in 1960's and 1970's, including one new work by the Tokyo Kid Brothers): WHY HANNA'S SKIRT WON'T STAY DOWN written and directed by Tom Eyen, with Helen Hanft, John Patrick Hurley, William Duff-Griffin; BIRDBATH by Leonard Melfi, directed by Tom O'-Horgan, with Kevin O'Connor, Barbara Eda-Young; LITTLE MOTHER written and directed by Ross Alexander, with Jamie Donnelly, David Khouri; CLARA'S OLE MAN by Ed Bullins, directed by Robert Macbeth, with Helen Pearl Ellis, Ebony Jo-Ann, Martin Pinckney; THE NIGHT OF THE ASSASSINS by Jose Triana, directed by Endre Hules, with Christopher Deoni, Magaly Alaban, Elizabeth Pena; NIGHTCLUB by Kenneth Bernard, directed by John Vaccaro; SHIRO, book, lyrics and directed by Yutaka Higashi, music by Takashi Yoshimatsu, with Tokyo Kid Brothers; SON OF FRICKA written and directed by Bruce Kessler; HURRAH FOR THE BRIDGE by Paul Foster, directed by Tom O'Horgan; THE RIMERS OF ELDRITCH written and directed by Lanford Wilson; SOON JACK NOVEMBER by Sharon Thie, directed by John A. Coe; MOTEL from AMERICA HURRAH by Jean-Claude Van Itallie, directed by Michael Kahn; LOVE ME OR I'LL KILL YOU written and directed by Daniel Haben Clark; THE RICHEST GIRL IN THE WORLD FINDS HAPPINESS written and directed by Robert Patrick; XXXXX by William M. Hoffman, directed by John Vaccaro; GODSPELL (musical) conceived by John-Michael Tebelak, music by Stephen Schwartz; THE UNSEEN HAND by Sam Shepard, directed by Tony Barsha. October 7, 1981–January 10, 1982.

FRANKIE AND JOHNNIE by Winston Tong and Bruce Geduldig. January 5, 1982. Directed by Bruce Geduldig.

ELECTRA-CUTION, OR YOU'RE UNDER ORESTES by Erin Martin and Davidson Lloyd. January 13, 1982. Directed by James Milton.

A.M./A.M.—THE ARTICULATED MAN. Created and directed by Ping Chong. January 28, 1982. Designer-in-chief, Paul Krajniak; lighting, Blu. With Ishmael Houston-Jones, Wendelien Haveman, Jeannie Hutchins, Ciel Werts, Lois Smith, Rob List.

TRESPASSING. By The Winter Project. February 23, 1982. Director, Joseph Chaikin; music, Harry Mann, William Uttley, and Neal Kirkwood; scenery, Jun Maeda; lighting, Jane Hubbard; costumes, Mary Brecht. With Roger Babb, Cristobal Carumbo, Gloria Foster, Ronnie Gilbert, Tina Shepard, Paul Zimet.

BECOMING. By Anton Gill. March 3, 1982. Director, Mervyn Willis; scenery, Natalie Lunn; lighting, Michael Bergfeld; unicorn created by Victor Carnuccio and Kenneth Kosakoff. With Dilys Hamlett.

BON-BEAU CHER, VARIATIONS ON THE GRAIL. By KISS (Dutch theater group). March 9, 1982.

L'HOMME QUI RIT by Victor Hugo. March 24, 1982. Directed by Gerard Guillaumat; with Théâtre National Populaire.

AMERIKANONG HILAW and PET FOR COMPANY adapted by Cecile Guidote-Alvarez. March 26, 1982. Directed by Pepe Barcega; with PETAL.

PRISONERS OF THE INVISIBLE KINGDOM written and directed by Michael Kirby. April 1, 1982.

YOSSELE GOLEM. By Dan Horowitz, translated by Imri Goldstein and Michael Posnick. April 9, 1982. Director, Rina Yerushalmi; scenery, H. Peet Foster and Whitney Quesenbery; lighting, Whitney Quesenbery. With Robert Trebor, Joel Rooks, Tim Saukiavicus, Dana Zeller-Alexis.

TRISTAN & ISOLT. Adapted by Sidney Goldfarb and the Talking Band. May 8, 1982. Director, Paul Zimet; scenery, Martin Bernstein; costumes, Mary Brecht; music, Harry Mann. With Paul Zimet, Jack Wetherall, Tina Shepard. (presented in repertory with GIOCONDA AND SI-YA-U by Nazim Hikmet; with The Talking Band)

WIELOPOLE WIELOPOLE written and directed by Tadeusz Kantor. May 13, 1982. With the Cricot II company.

THE BACCHAE by Euripides. May 28, 1982. Directed by Tadashi Suzuki.

Lion Theater Company. Actors' company with an eclectic repertory. Gene Nye, artistic director, Eleanor Meglio, producing director.

VILLAGER. By Ron McLarty. July 9, 1981. Director, John Guerrasio; scenery, Linda Skipper; lighting, Norman Coates; costumes, Bud Santora. With Roy Poole, Kate Wilkinson, Winston May, Barney Martin, Janet Zarish, Bob Horen (co-production with South Street Theater).

ROMEO AND JULIET by William Shakespeare. April 21, 1982. Directed by Gene Nye.

THE CAUCASIAN CHALK CIRCLE by Bertolt Brecht, English version by Eric Bentley. April 22, 1982.

Manhattan Punch Line. Comedy theater. Steve Kaplan, Mitch McGuire, Jerry Heymann, producing directors.

BADGERS (20). By Donald Wollner. September 17, 1981. Director, Ellen Sandler; scenery, Nancy Tobias; lighting, John Hickey; costumes, Gayle Everhart. With Stephanie Murphy, Matthew Penn, Peter E. Green, Dee Ann Sexton, Gabriel Yorke, Adam Lefevre, Steve Beauchamp, Derek Hoxby.

FEROCIOUS KISSES (20). By Gil Schwartz. January 29, 1982. Director, Josh Mostel; scenery, Geoffrey Hall; lighting, Dennis Size; costumes, Amanda Aldridge. With Harry Goz, Baxter Harris, Mark Hattan, Terry Layman, John Monteith, Brian Rose.

THE ROADS TO HOME (3 related one-act plays): A NIGHTINGALE, THE DEAREST OF FRIENDS, and SPRING DANCE (41). By Horton Foote. March 25, 1982. Director, Calvin Skaggs; scenery, Oliver D'Arcy; lighting, Richard Dorfman; costumes, Edi Giguere. With Carol

MANHATTAN PUNCH LINE—John Monteith,
Brian Rose and Harry Goz in *Ferocious Kisses*

Fox, Rochelle Oliver, B. Hallie Foote, Greg Zittel, Jess Osuna, Jon Berry, James Paradise, Tony Noll, Ron Marr.

THE COARSE ACTING SHOW by Michael Green. October 29, 1981. Directed by Jerry Heymann; with Reathel Bean, Brad Bellamy, Victoria Boothby, Ellen Fiske, Joel Simon, F.L. Schmidlapp, Arthur Erickson.

AN ITALIAN STRAW HAT by Eugene Labiche and Marc-Michel, translated by Jerry Heymann. December 17, 1981. Directed by Steve Kaplan; with John Rothman, Robert Dale Martin, Eileen Albert, Getchie Argetsinger, Tom Shelton, Ron Johnston.

WHAT A LIFE! by Clifford Goldsmith. May 21, 1982. Directed by Jerry Heymann; with Rusty Jacobs, Rusti Moon, Karyn Lynn Dale, Mitch McGuire.

Manhattan Theater Club. A producing organization with three stages for fully-mounted off-Broadway productions, readings, workshop activities and cabaret. Lynne Meadow, artistic director, Barry Grove, managing director.

UpStage

HARRY RUBY'S SONGS MY MOTHER NEVER SANG (28). Musical revue of songs by Harry Ruby and Bert Kalmar, conceived by Michael S. Roth and Paul Lazarus. June 9, 1981. Director, Paul Lazarus; choreographer, Douglas Norwick; musical director, Michael S. Roth; scenery, Jane Thurn; lighting, F. Mitchell Dana; costumes, Christa Scholtz. With Indira Christopherson, Peter Frechette, I.M. Hobson.

THE RESURRECTION OF LADY LESTER (40). By Oyamo. October 20, 1981. Director, Andre Mtumi; musical director, Dwight Andrews; scenery, Kate Edmunds; lighting, William

Armstrong; costumes, Rita Ryack. With Cleavon Little, Randy Danson, Carol-Jean Lewis, Otis Young-Smith, Arthur French, Yvette Hawkins, Obaka Adedunyo, Larry Bryggman.

AND I AIN'T FINISHED YET (24+). By Eve Merriam. December 1, 1981. Director, Sheldon Epps; musical director, Patti Brown; scenery, Kate Edmunds; lighting, Robby Monk; costumes, Judy Dearing. With Lynne Thigpen, Stanley Ramsey, Robin Karfo, Bo Smith.

STRANGE SNOW (42). By Steve Metcalfe. January 19, 1982. Director, Thomas Bullard; scenery, Atkin Pace, lighting, Cheryl Thacker; costumes, Nan Cibula. With Christopher Curry, Dann Florek, Kaiulani Lee.

LIVIN' DOLLS (56). Book, music, and lyrics, Scott Wittman and Marc Shaiman. March 9, 1982. Director, Richard Maltby Jr.; musical director, Marc Shaiman; scenery, John Lee Beatty; lighting, Pat Collins; costumes, Timothy Dunleavy. With Lisa Embs, Linda Hart, Kim Milford, Zora Rasmussen, James Rich, Deborah Van Valkenburgh, Tom Wiggin.

SCENES FROM LA VIE DE BOHEME (32). By Anthony Giardina. May 4, 1982. Director, Douglas Hughes; scenery, Adrianne Lobel; costumes, Rita Ryack; lighting, Craig Miller. With John Christopher Jones, Michael Kaufman, Jed Cooper, Daniel Gerroll, Cornelia Mills, Mary Elaine Monti, Robin Karfo, John Shepard.

The New Dramatists. An organization devoted to playwrights; member writers may use the facilities for anything from private cold readings of their material to public script-in-hand readings. David Juaire, program director.

Staged readings

RED STORM FLOWER by John Patrick Shanley. June 17, 1981. Directed by Susan Gregg; with Cara Duff MacCormick, Cory Parker, Douglas Jones.

JASS by John Pielmeier. June 24, 1981. Directed by Susan Gregg; with Mia Dillon, Anne Pitoniak, James Maxwell, Milledge Mosley, Frankie R. Faison.

AMERICANA by John Patrick Shanley. September 23, 1981. Directed by Susan Gregg; with Michael Morin, Tony Shultz, Daydrie Hague, Jim Maxwell, Carol Ann Mansell.

THE BATHERS by Victor Steinbach. October 21, 1981. Directed by Gordon Edelstein; with Dominic Chianese, Martha Ferris, Robert E. Weil, Patrick Farrelly, Royce Rich, Boris Leskin.

THE SADDEST SUMMER OF VAL by Dennis McIntyre. November 4, 1981. Directed by Tom Bullard; with Morgan Freeman, Michelle Shay, John Danelle, Tony Campisi, Bill Cobbs, Roscoe Orman.

INTRODUCTION, THEME AND 'TO BE OR NOT TO BE,' SOLO RECITAL and HERMIT OF PRAGUE by Stanley Taikeff. November 18, 1981. Directed by Thomas Gruenewald; with Susan Greenhill, Anita Keal, Mark Gordon, Lynn Cohen.

MISSING PERSONS by Stephen Levi. December 2, 1981. Directed by Thomas Gruenewald; with Doug Jones, Brian Benben, Tom Bade, Tee Scatuorchio, Tim Wayne, Alan Ellington, Jay Devlin.

SKY BLUE PINK by David Hill. January 20, 1982. Directed by Scott Rubsam; with Anna Minot, Joseph Warren, Timothy Wayne, Marcella Lowry, Dolores Kenan, Leta Bonynge, Florence Leflar.

GARDENS OF EDEN by Romulus Linney. February 17, 1982. Directed by Betty Osborn; with Leon Russom, Sloane Shelton, Susan Pellegrino, Mary Jay.

THREE UNNATURAL ACTS by Dick Zigun. March 1, 1982. Directed by Matthew Maguire; with Paul Zaloom, Deirdre O'Connell, Sari Weissman.

THE GREAT GORILLA MUSICAL by John Patrick Shanley. March 31, 1982. Directed by Susan Gregg; with Allan Stevens, Robert Frink, Judith Jarosz, Willie Reale, Victoria Bradbury, Peter Phillips.

KIDS AND DOGS by Philip Bosakowski. April 14, 1982. Directed by Casey Childs; with K.C. Kelly, Sarah Jessica Parker, James Burge, Tony Blake, Marylouise Burke, Jack Honor.

DOLOROSA SANCHEZ by Stanley Taikeff, directed by Lew Shena; OUTPOST by Gus Edwards, directed by Roger Hendricks-Simon. April 28, 1982. With Socorro Santiago, Kermit Brown, Jim Doerr, William Van Hunter, Willie Carpenter, Leslie Bates.

THE RELEASE OF A LIVE PERFORMANCE by Sherry Kramer. May 12, 1982. Directed by Pat Carmichael; with Cordis Heard, Patricia Sherick, Stephen Lang, Quincy Long.
THE NAME OF THE GAME IS 'BEN' by Dennis McIntyre. May 26, 1982. Directed by Allen R. Belknap; with Michael Guido, Susan Merson, Jay Sanders.

New Federal Theater. The Henry Street Settlement's training and showcase unit for playwrights, mostly black and Puerto Rican. Woodie King Jr. and Steve Tennen, producers.

ZORA and WHEN THE CHICKENS CAME HOME TO ROOST (12) One-act plays by Laurence Holder. June 18, 1981. Directors, Elizabeth Van Dyke, Allie Woods; scenery, Robert Edmonds; lighting, Allen Lee Hughes; costumes, Judy Dearing. With Phylicia Ayers-Allen, Kirk Kirksey, Denzel Washington.

STEAL AWAY (12). By Ramona King. July 16, 1981. Director, Anderson Johnson; scenery, Llewellyn Harrison; lighting, Shirley Prendergast; costumes, Judy Dearing. With Joyce Sylvester, Minnie Gentry, Beatrice Winde, Estelle Evans, Juanita Clark, Dorothi Fox.

LOUIS (12). Book and lyrics, Don Evans; music, Michael Renzi. September 18, 1981. Director, Gilbert Moses; choreographer, Billy Wilson; musical director, Danny Holgate; scenery, Robert Edmonds; lighting, Shirley Prendergast; costumes, Judy Dearing. With Northern J. Calloway, Debbie Allen, Ernestine Jackson, Ken Page, Tiger Haynes, Marcella Lowry.

BOY AND TARZAN APPEAR IN A CLEARING (12). By Amiri Baraka. October 9, 1981. Director and scene design, George Ferencz; lighting, Marshall Williams; costumes, Sally J. Lesser. With Jack R. Marks, Willie Carpenter, Rod McLucas, Rosita Broadus, Christine Campbell.

THE BLACK PEOPLE'S PARTY (12). By Earl Anthony. October 22, 1981. Director, Norman Riley; scenery, Llewellyn C. Harrison; lighting, Marshall Williams; costumes, Judy Dearing. With Ronald Willoughby, Hunter Cain, P. Anderson Scott, Richard H. Arnold Jr., Gregory Miller, Jane Scott, John J.J. Cole, Lucy Holland, Andre Worthy.

CHILD OF THE SUN (16). Book, music, and lyrics, Damien Leake. December 1, 1981. Director, Harold Scott; choreographer, Otis Sallid; musical director, Lea Richardson; scenery, John Scheffler; lighting, Shirley Prendergast; costumes, Judy Dearing. With Nat Morris, Pauletta Pearson, Jackee Harry, Gordon Heath, Raymond Patterson, Yolanda Lee, Count Stovall, Kevin Harris.

KEYBOARD (12). By Matt Robinson. January 15, 1982. Director, Shauneille Perry; scenery, Robert Edmonds; lighting, Sandra Ross; costumes, Judy Dearing. With Cleavon Little, Zaida Coles, Giancarlo Esposito, André Robinson Jr., Lex Monson, Louise Stubbs.

WHO LOVES THE DANCER (12). By Rob Penny. February 18, 1982. Director, Shauneille Perry; scenery, Robert Edmonds; lighting, Sandra Ross; costumes, Judy Dearing. With Giancarlo Esposito, Louise Stubbs, Peter Wise, Rosanna Carter, Andre Robinson Jr., Sloan Robinson, Martin D. Pinckney.

THE WORLD OF BEN CALDWELL (12). By Ben Caldwell. April 1, 1982. Director, Richard Gant; scenery, Llewellyn Harrison; lighting, Lynne Reed; costumes, Myrna Colley-Lee. With Kirk Kirksey, Reginald Vel Johnson, Morgan Freeman, Garrett Morris, Steve Coats, B. Jerome Smith, Dianne Kirksey, Terria Joseph.

Ethnic Heritage Series

A DAY OUT OF TIME (11). By Alan Foster Friedman. November 20, 1981. Director, Harold Guskin; scenery, David Weiss; lighting, Lynne Reed; costumes, Judy Dearing. With Tim Donoghue, Tom Mardirosian, Barbara Tirrell, Jim Shankman, Jerry Matz, Robert Silver, Carol Nadell, John Capodice.

DREAMS DEFERRED (12). By Laurence Holder. January 7, 1982. Director, Allie Woods; scenery, Pete Caldwell; lighting, Marshall Williams; costumes Judy Dearing. With Erma

Campbell, Kim Sullivan, Clebert Ford, Phyllis Yvonne Stickney, Kathleen Morrison, Michael Alsen.

LA CHEFA (12). By Tato Laviera. February 11, 1982. Director, Raul Davila; scenery, Miguel Aguilar and Carmen Montalvo; lighting, Lynne Reed; costumes, Judy Dearing. With Alfonso Manosalvas, Denia Brache, Michael Yanez.

PAPER ANGELS (12). By Genny Lim. March 18, 1982. Director, John Lone; scenery, Karen Schulz; lighting, Paul Gallo; costumes, Susan Hilferty. With Kitty Mei-Mei Chen, William Hao, Lilah Kan, Toshi Toda, Victor Wong, Henry Yuk.

New York Shakespeare Festival Public Theater. Schedule of workshop productions and guest residencies, in addition to its regular productions. Joseph Papp, producer.

FRESH FRUIT IN FOREIGN PLACES (1). Based on a story by August Darnell; music and lyrics, August Darnell, additional music and lyrics, Sugar Coated Andy Hernandez. July 20, 1981. Choreography, Adriana Kaegi; lighting, Gordy Hebler; costumes, Adriana Kaegi, Leila, and Richard Kennedy. With Kid Creole and The Coconuts.

CHARLOTTE (1). By Peter Hacks, translated and adapted by Herbert and Uta Berghof. December 14, 1981. Director, Herbert Berghof; scenery, Timothy Farmer; lighting, Thomas Skelton. With Uta Hagen.

SPECIMEN DAYS (49). Conceived and directed by Meredith Monk; music, Meredith Monk. December 2, 1981. Choreography, Meredith Monk, Gail Turner; scenery and costumes, Yoshio Yabara; lighting, Beverly Emmons. With Cristobal Carambo, Shami Chaikin, Rober Een, Andrea Goodman, Paul Langland, Steve Lockwood, Meredith Monk, Nicky Paraiso, Marge Lee Sherman, Mary Shultz, Gail Turner, Mieke van Hoek, Pablo Vela. (reopened February 11 1982)

WRONG GUYS reopened September 22, 1981. (Mabou Mines production.)

No Smoking Playhouse. Emphasis on new plays and adaptation of classics, stressing the comedic. Norman Thomas Marshall, artistic director.

THOM AND JERRI. By Carol de Santa. June 13, 1981. Director, Sebastian Stuart. With Norman Thomas Marshall, Christin Cockerton.

'81 VARIETIES. Written and directed by Lou Trapani. August, 1981. With Lou Trapani, Alan Bluestone, Lori Cardille, Malcolm Gray, Sylvester Rich, Marina Posvar.

THE UNICORN (20). By Michael Kimberly. February 4, 1982. Director, Norman Thomas Marshall; scenery, Tom Schwinn; lighting, Edward R.F. Matthews; costumes, Marla R Kaye. With Hansford Rowe, Adam Redfield, Janie Kelly, Ed Van Nuys.

THE ARCATA PROMISE by David Mercer. May 27, 1982. Directed by Geoffrey Sherman; with Kermit Brown, Lisa Carling, Brian Murray.

THE WOULD-BE GENTLEMAN by Molière. November 18, 1981. Directed by Marvin Einhorn; with Greg Fellows, Malcolm Gray, Diane Heles, Cheryl Henderson, Elizabeth Horowitz, Olivia Negron, Robert Putnam, Eric Zwemer, Cathy Roskam.

A MIDSUMMER NIGHT'S DREAM by William Shakespeare. April 15, 1982. Directed by George Wolf Reily; with June Ballinger, Peter Blaxill, Mary Kay Dean, Eden-Lee Murray, Steve Pudenz, Jyll Stein, Malcolm Gray.

The Open Space Theater Experiment. Emphasis on experimental works. Lynn Michaels, Harry Baum, directors.

SIDE STREET SCENES (24). By Sam Henry. November 5, 1981. Director, Peter Kass; music and lyrics, Stuart Bloom; scenery, Bob Wallace; lighting, Greg MacPherson; costumes, Pear Somner. With Michael Lombard, Rochelle Parker, Stuart Bloom, Peter Boruchowitz, Joi Gallo, Max Mayer, Patty Stern.

WHEN WE DEAD AWAKEN by Henrik Ibsen, translated by Rolf Fjelde. January 7, 1982. Directed by Stephen Zuckerman; with Ken Costigan, Kim Hunter, Anne Twomey, Tom Klunis, Nicholas Wyman.

THE MISUNDERSTANDING by Albert Camus, translated by Stuart Gilbert. April 22, 1982. Directed by Susan Einhorn; with Paul R. Cox, Jean DeBaer, Elizabeth Lawrence, Daniel Ziske.

The Garret of the Open Space:

THE CLOUDBERRY FIELD (12). By Karen Johnson. October 14, 1981. Director, Nancy Gabor; scenery and lighting, Harry Baum. With Annette Hunt, James Johnston.

THE SEA ANCHOR (16). By Ted (E.A.) Whitehead. March 4, 1982. Director, Alex Dmitriev; scenery, Bob Phillips; lighting, Richard Dorfman; costumes, Barbara Weiss. With Caroline Lagerfelt, Peter Rogan, John Pietrowski, Amy Stoller.

THE PELICAN by August Strindberg. January 28, 1982. Directed by Rosemary Hay; with Florence Anglin, Helen-Jean Arthur, Karla Barker, Rudi Caporaso, Robin Thomas.

Pan Asian Repertory Theater. Aims to present professional productions employing Asian American theater artists, to encourage new plays exploring Asian American themes and to combine traditional elements of Far Eastern theater with Western theatrical techniques. Tisa Chang, artistic director.

YELLOW IS MY FAVORITE COLOR (16). By Edward Sakamoto. August 6, 1981. Director, Ron Nakahara; lighting, Edward R.F. Matthews; costumes, Valerie Charles. With Henry Yuk, Raul Aranas, Freda Foh Shen, Valerie Charles, Ellen Boggs, Lynette Chun, William P. Ogilvie.

BULLET HEADED BIRDS (16). By Philip Kan Gotanda. November 19, 1981. Director, Tisa Chang; musical director, Geoff Lee; scenery, Michael DeSousa; lighting, Edward R.F. Matthews; costumes, Lydia Tanji. With Gedde Watanabe, Raul Aranas, Christopher Odo, Lynette Chun, William Ogilvie, Jessica Hagedorn, Ching Valdes.

ROHWER. By Lionelle Hamanaka. March 11, 1982. Director, Ernest Abuba; scenery, Michael DeSousa; lighting, Edward R.F. Matthews; costumes, Stephanie Kerley. With Jodi Long, Ron Nakahara, Anne Miyamoto, Helen Yng Wong, Lynnette Chun, Thomas Ikeda, Tom Matsusaka.

BEHIND ENEMY LINES. By Rosanna Yamagiwa Alfaro. March 24, 1982. Director, Ron Nakahara; scenery, Ronald Kajiwara; lighting, Viveca Yrisarry; costumes, Valerie Charles. With Thomas Ikeda, Michael G. Chin, Natsuko Ohama, Carol A. Honda.

STATION J. By Richard France. April 7, 1982. Director, Tisa Chang; scenery, Atsushi Moriyashu; lighting, Victor En Yu Tan; costumes, Eiko Yamaguchi. With Alvin Lum, Elizabeth Sung, Glenn Kabota, Freda Foh Shen, Henry Yuk. (ROHWER, BEHIND ENEMY LINES, and STATION J comprise a trilogy on Japanese-American internment during World War II.)

Puerto Rican Traveling Theater. Professional company presenting bilingual productions primarily of Puerto Rican and Hispanic playwrights, emphasizing subjects of relevance today. Miriam Colon, founder and producer.

28 performances each

THE MAN AND THE FLY. By Jose Ruibal, translated by Gregory Rabassa. January 27, 1982. Director, Jack Gelber; scenery, Andrew Jackness; lighting, John Tissot; costumes, Nancy Thun. With Rip Torn, Norman Briski, Lazaro Perez, David Crommett, Felipe Gorostiza.

SHE, THAT ONE, HE AND THE OTHER. By Jacobo Morales, translated by Manuel Power Viscasillas. March 10, 1982. Director, Alba Oms; scenery, Christina Weppner; lighting, John Tissot; costumes, Maria Contessa. With Liz Torres, Shawn Elliott.

PAN ASIAN REPERTORY—Lynette Chun
and Raul Aranas in *Bullet Headed Birds*

PAPER FLOWERS. By Egon Wolff, translated by Margaret Peden. April 21, 1982. Director, Victoria Espinosa; scenery, Gary English; lighting, John Tissot; costumes, Santiago Seijo. With Gilda Miros, Ricardo Matamoros.

Quaigh Theater. Primarily a playwrights' theater, devoted to the new playwright, the established contemporary playwright and the modern (post-1920) playwright. Will Lieberson, artistic director.

DRAMATHON '81 (one-act plays in marathon). Schedule included: MOMA by Tom Coble, directed by Joe Nikola; INSIDE written and directed by Norman Biem; MONEY BACK GUARANTEED by Don Flynn, directed by Chuck Noell; THE FILLETING MACHINE by Tom Hadaway, directed by Richard Bly; THE AMBIVALENT MS. X by Michael Templon, directed by Dunsten J. McCormack; THE SEDUCTION OF PEE WEE by Judith Present, directed by Bill Fears; THE UNKNOWN SOLDIER written and directed by Linda Pallotta; MANY HAPPY RETURNS by Jeffrey Lawrence, directed by Cece Critchley; SCENES DEDICATED TO MY BROTHER by Joel Horner, directed by Maggie Harrer; CHRIS AND RONNIE by Chris Grabenstein and Ronnie Venable; PHARMACEUTICALS by Steve Currens, directed by Chuck Noell; THE BOND by Howard Brown, directed by James Paradise;

DOCTOR'S OFFICE DISCO? by Donald Kvares, directed by Ed Rubin; KEN AND CLARENCE by William Devane, directed by Tom Rosica; COURTSHIP by John Reaves, directed by Milton James Coykendall; LEAN ON THE WIND written and directed by Frank Biancamano; UNDERBELLY BLUES by Sebastian Stuart, directed by Ted Mornel; WILLY AND SAHARA written and directed by Tom Rosica; GROWING UP NAKED by Richard Barbie, directed by Pam Reed; SEX AGAINST SEX by Leslie Middlebrook and Lee Moore, directed by Barry Keating; REALOMETERS by Charles Wilbert, directed by Marc Tessler; DOG AND SUDS by Alan Ball, directed by William Sevedge Jr.; TUBA SOLO by Michael Lynch, directed by Dorothy Neuman; LIFE AFTER COMAS by Ernest McCarty, directed by Peter Forman; TWO WOMEN by Mario Fratti, directed by Cyril Simon; AH, EURYDICE by Stanley Taikeff, directed by Roger Lawson; TELEMACHUS CLAY by Lewis John Carlino, directed by George Stevenson; A WELL-RESPECTED GENTLEMAN by Dan Bothstein, directed by W.J. Lentsch; ANDY AND MAX ET AL., adapted from Arthur Schnitzler's *Anatole*, by Ron Daley and Deena Kaye. June 5–8, 1981.

YOUNG, GIFTED, & BROKE (late night revue). Conceived and directed by Daniel Herris and Edwin Gray. June 12, 1981. With Eydie Alyson, Larry Campbell, Avah Mealy, Sherry Nehmer, Luis Remesar, Marla Sterling, Edwin Gray, Daniel Herris.

FINAL HOURS (18). By Harold Steinberg. October 1, 1981. Director, Will Lieberson; scenery, Geoffrey Hall; lighting, Lisa Grossman. With Joe Jamrog, Allison Brennan, Kricker James.

VATZLAV (20). By Slawomir Mrozek, translated by Ralph Manheim. January 26, 1982. Director, Will Lieberson; scenery, Geoffrey Hall; lighting, E. St. John Villard; costumes, Jessica Fasman. With Frank Dwyer, Rebecca Wells, Ernst Muller, Tony Page, Richard Spore, Gerry Lou, Gary Klar, Dennis Lieberson, Robert Zukerman.

SOME OF MY BEST FRIENDS ARE and THEIR OWN WORST ENEMIES (10+) (one-act plays). By Laurence Blackmore. February 19, 1982. Director, Frank Biancamano; scenery and costumes, Pip Biancamano; lighting, Paul Bartlett. With Mila Burnette, Terence Cartwright, Frank Biancamano.

LIVINGSTONE AND SECHELE (20+). By David Pownall. April 5, 1982. Director, Will Lieberson; scenery, Geoffrey Hall; lighting, Paul Bartlett; costumes, Bob Horek. With Afemo, Mike Champagne, Prudence Wright Holmes, Esther Ryvlin.

Lunchtime Theater, 10 performances each

THE WIND BLOWS AND YOU CATCH A COLD by Frank Adduci, Jr. June 22, 1981. Directed by Salem Ludwig.
SCENES DEDICATED TO MY BROTHER by Joel Horner. November 2, 1981. Directed by Maggie Harrer; with Jack Fogarty, Stephen Hamilton, Joel Fredrickson, Suzanne Johnson.
FORCE OF NATURE by Paul Lambert. November 16, 1981. Directed by Ben Kapen; with James Rosin, David Higlen.
SAVOURY MERINGUE and POOR OLD SIMON (one-act plays) by James Saunders. November 30, 1981. Directed by Dennis Lieberson; with Allen Jared, Donald Pace, Jean Richards, Angelynne Bruno, Kenneth Marks, Albert Ross.
SNUFF FLICK by John Fiero. January 4, 1982. Directed by Cece Critchley; with Scott Gleason, Joel Stevens, Cindy Benson, Katherine Barefield.
DOCTOR'S OFFICE DISCO? by Donald Kvares. January 19, 1982. Directed by Ed Rubin; with Harvey Pierce, Robert McAllan, Donald Pace, Laurie Graff.
RATTLESNAKE IN A COOLER by Frank South. February 1, 1982. Directed by Ann Sackrider; with Curt Williams.
A JIVE TIME (revue) conceived and directed by Guy C. Coleman. February 15, 1982. With Darlene Curtis, Stephen Miller, Michelle Riley.
SEE NO EVIL (one-act plays) by Ann Harson. March 1, 1982. Directed by John Cameron; with Frank Nastasi, Donnah Welby, Vince Pacineo.
MOLLY BLOOM by James Joyce. March 15, 1982. Directed by Barbara Firrell; with Freda Kavanagh.
MANY HAPPY RETURNS by Jeffrey Lawrence. April 12, 1982. Directed by Cece Critchley; with Donna Lowre, Ann Clayton, Paul Kerry, Jeremiah Alexander.

THE SEDUCTION OF PEE WEE by Judith Present. April 26, 1982. Directed by Bill Fears; with Anita Keal, Stewart Schneck, Robert Levoyd-Wright.

The Ridiculous Theatrical Company. Charles Ludlam's camp-oriented group devoted to productions of his original scripts and broad adaptations of classics. Charles Ludlam, artistic director and director of all productions.

LOVE'S TANGLED WEB (16). By Charles Ludlam. June 7, 1981. Scenery, Charles Ludlam; costumes, Gabriel Berry; lighting, Lawrence Eichler; music, Peter Golub. With Charles Ludlam, Christine Deveau, Mink Stole, Everett Quinton, Bill Vehr, Black-Eyed Susan.

SECRET LIVES OF THE SEXISTS (109). By Charles Ludlam. February 9, 1982. Scenery, Jack Kelly; costumes, Gabriel Berry; lighting, Richard Currie; music, Peter Golub. With Black-Eyed Susan, Bill Vehr, Everett Quinton, Mink Stole, Georg Osterman, Charles Ludlam, Deborah Petti.

The Second Stage. Committed to producing plays of the last ten years believed to deserve another chance. Robyn Goodman, Carole Rothman, artistic directors.

PASTORALE (24). By Deborah Eisenberg. April 4, 1982. Director, Carole Rothman; scenery, Heidi Landesman; lighting, Frances Aronson; costumes, Nan Cibula. With Elizabeth Austin, Christine Estabrook, Jeffrey Fahey, Judith Ivey, Taylor Miller, Thomas Waites.

MY SISTER IN THIS HOUSE by Wendy Kesselman. November 8, 1981. Directed by Inverna Lockpez and Carole Rothman; with Lisa Banes, Brenda Currin, Beverly May, Elizabeth McGovern.

FLUX by Susan Miller. January 31, 1982. Directed by Michael Kahn; with Kevin Bacon, Jean DeBaer, Daryl Edwards, Robyn Goodman, Sam Robards, Clare Timoney, Michael Tucker.

THE WOODS written and directed by David Mamet. May 16, 1982. With Patti LuPone, Peter Weller.

Shelter West. Aims to offer an atmosphere of trust and a place for unhurried and constructive work. Judith Joseph, artistic director.

DREAMS OF FLIGHT and COUPLES (16). By Brian Richard Mori. June 10, 1981. Director, Judith Joseph; scenery, Rudy Kocevar; lighting, Shulamit Ziv; costumes, MaryAnn D. Smith. With John Robert Evans, William Lucas, Kevin Madden, Anthony DiNovi, Timothy O'Hare, Jo Tyler.

WOEMAN (20). By Paul Stephen Lim. March 11, 1982. Director, Eduardo Ivan Lopez; scenery, Gordon A. Juel; lighting, Shulamit Ziv. With Mary Charalambakis, Anthony DiNovi, Kevin Madden, Sandra Soehngen, Christy Brotherton, Judith Joseph.

THE WALK (6). By Thomas Moore. March 22, 1982. Director, Esteban Fernandez; scenery, Gordon Juel; lighting, Shulamit Ziv. With Joseph Noah, Nada Despotovitch.

RASHOMON by Fay and Michael Kanin. September 30, 1981. Directed by George Zagoren; with Joseph Noah, Richard Borg, Margot Avery, Judith Joseph, Radu Terner, Richard DeDomenico, John Marchesella.

Soho Rep. Infrequently or never-before-performed plays by the world's greatest authors, with emphasis on language and theatricality. Marlene Swartz, Jerry Engelbach, artistic directors.

DARK RIDE. Written and directed by Len Jenkin. November 12, 1981. Scenery, John Arnone; lighting, Bruce Porter; costumes, David C. Woolard. With William Sadler, John Nesci, Betty LaRoe, Melissa Hurst, Eric Loeb, Walter Hadler, Saun Ellis, JoAnne Akalaitis, Will Patton, David Brisbane.

THE GIRL WHO ATE CHICKEN BONES. Book, Stan Kaplan; music, David Hollister; lyrics, Stan Kaplan and David Hollister. April 16, 1982. Director, Marlene Swartz; choreographer, Joe

Holloway; musical director, John McMahon; scenery and costumes, Steven Birnbaum; lighting, MaryJo Dondlinger. With Terry Kirwin, Lloyd David Hart, Jody Hiatt, Marlea Evans, Steve Sterner, James Mallory, Ryn Hodes, Elizabeth Bayer, Roy Steinberg.

3 AMERICAN OPERAS: THE AUDIENCE text by Glenn W. Miller, music by Royce Dembo, directed by Scott Clugstone; MR. LION text and music by Linder Chlarson, directed by Lou Rodgers; MIYAKO text, music, and directed by Lou Rodgers. May 7, 1982. (Produced in association with Golden Fleece, Ltd.)

South Street Theater Company. Presents dramatizations of American literature and classics from the international repertory. Jean Sullivan, Michael Fischetti, co-artistic directors.

THE STRONGER by August Strindberg, translated by George Springer, directed by Gene Nye; HUGHIE by Eugene O'Neill, directed by Gino Giglio. November 4, 1981. With Margaret Warnke, Jean Sullivan, Frank Geraci, Michael Fischetti.

THE BRIXTON RECOVERY by Jack Gilhooley. January 18, 1982. Directed by Mike Houlihan; with Hazel Medina, William Russ. (co-produced with Penumbra Productions).

Theater at St. Clement's. Primarily new American plays presented in New York premieres. Michael Hadge, artistic director, Stephen Berwind, managing director.

16 performances each

BATTERY. By Daniel Therriault. June 4, 1981. Director, George Ferencz; scenery and lighting, Peter Harrison; costumes, Sally J. Lesser. With Holly Hunter, Stephen Mellor, Fritz Sperberg.

CHAINSAWS. By Margaret Ann Spiers. November 18, 1981. Director, Stephen Berwind; scenery, Michael Miller; lighting, Richard Moore; costumes, Sam Fleming. With Linda Christian-Jones, Mel Haynes, Gary Klar, Olga Druce, Jacqueline Knapp, Gregory Grove, Martin LaPlatney.

PHILISTINES. By Maxim Gorky, adapted and directed by Michael Landrum. February 17, 1982. Scenery, Lou Anne Gilleland; lighting, Victor En Yu Tan; costumes, Carla Kramer. With Susan Stevens, Stephen Mellor, Martha Greenhouse, Clarke Gordon, Seymour Penzner, Rudy Hornish, Gina Barnett, Tom Everett, Janice Lathen, Bob Morrisey, J.D. Clarke.

MAIDEN STAKES. By David Libman. April 15, 1982. Director, Anita Khanzadian; scenery and lighting, Dale F. Jordan; costumes, Margo LaZaro. With Victor Arnold, Eddie Jones, Ira Lewis, Barbara Eda-Young.

Theater for the New City. Developmental theater, incorporating live music and dance into new American experimental works. George Bartenieff, Crystal Field, artistic directors.

Schedule included:

SELMA (12). By Shami Chaikin. November 5, 1981. Director, Karen Ludwig; scenery, Sally Jacobs; lighting, Beverly Emmons; costumes, Mary Brecht. With Alice Spivak, Harvey Perr, Gordana Rashovich, Jon Huberth, Suzanne Costallos.

A VISIT (16). Created and directed by Maria Irene Fornes; music, George Quincy. December 24, 1981. Musical director, Mary L. Rodgers; scenery and lighting, Donald Eastman; costumes, Gabriel Berry. With Mary Beth Lerner, Penelope Bodry, Joseph C. Davies, Richard DeDomenico, Candace Derra, Florence Tarlow, Eduardo Machado.

ZEKS (12). By Maria A. Rasa, translated by A. Byla. December 24, 1981. Director, Jonas Jurasas; scenery and costumes, Alex Okun; lighting, Rick Butler. With Jeffrey Bingham, Robert Harper, Dane Knell, Robert Lovitz, Nicholas Saunders, Roy Steinberg, Susan Stevens, J.D. Swain, Martin Treat, Michael Thompson.

LIFE AND DEATH OF CHARLOTTE SALOMON (one-woman show), with Margo Lee Sherman; THE STORY OF ONE WHO SET OUT TO STUDY FEAR by and with Bread and Puppet Theater. January 26, 1982.

THE THUNDERSTORM OF THE YOUNGEST CHILD. By and with Bread and Puppet Theater. February 9, 1982.

THE BLONDE LEADING THE BLONDE. By Stephen Holt. February 27, 1982. Director, John Albano; scenery, Bobjack Callejo; lighting, Richard Currie. With Lola Pashalinski, Crystal Field, Helen Hanft, Alex Mustelier, Lynn Oliver.

LETTERS TO BEN. Book, music, and lyrics, Charles Choset. April 1, 1982. Director, Lisa Simon; choreographer, Sharon Kinney; musical director, Curtis Blaine; scenery and lighting, Joe Ray; costumes, Don Sheffield. With Carol Harris, Diane Irwin, Bebe Landis, John Gallogly, Michael Conant.

WHO DO YOU WANT, PEIRE VIDAL? (16). By Rochelle Owens. April 29, 1982. Director, Ernest Abuba; scenery, Mike Sullivan; lighting, Chaim Gitter. With Valerie Charles, Ron Nakahara.

THE DISPOSSESSED. By Leonard Melfi. May 6, 1982. Director, Crystal Field; scenery, Ron Kajiwara; lighting, Joanna Schielke; costumes, Edmond Felix. With Crystal Field, George Bartenieff, Vira Colorado, Anne Swift, Leonard Melfi.

Theater of the Open Eye. Total theater involving actors, dancers, musicians and designers working together, each bringing his own talents into a single project. Jean Erdman, producing artistic director.

PUNCH WITH JUDY (15). By Rosemary Foley. March 17, 1982. Director, Dana Coen; scenery, Rob Hamilton; lighting, Phil Monat; costumes, Sue Ellen Rohrer; masks and puppets, Eric Bass. With Jeff Abbott, David Combs, Kirtan Coan, Joel Bernstein, Jeanne Cullen, Julia McLaughlin, Dana Mills, Warren Sweeney.

THE SUN GETS BLUE (15). Book, lyrics, and choreography, William "Electric" Black; music, Paul Shapiro. April 14, 1982. Director, Amy Brockway; scenery and lighting, Adrienne J. Brockway; costumes, Karen Selby. With J. J. Cole, Elton Becket, Judy Thames, Matthew Idason, Carol London, Daniel Neusom, Theresa Marsh, Michele Cannon, Raymond Anthony Thomas, Randy Frazier, John Redwood.

THE SHINING HOUSE (collaborative dance opera) created and directed by Jean Erdman. June 16, 1981. With Nancy Allison, Leslie Dillingham, Maura Ellyn, William Ha'o, Susan Murakoshi, Kathy Paulo, David Rousseve, Muna Tseng.
THE COACH WITH THE SIX INSIDES written and directed by Jean Erdman, based on James Joyce's *Finnegan's Wake*. February 10, 1982.

Theater Off Park. Provides Murray Hill-Turtle Bay residents with a professional theater, showcasing the talents of new actors, playwrights, designers, and directors. Patricia Flynn Peate, executive director.

16 performances each

VONETTA SWEETWATER CARRIES ON . . . Book, music, and lyrics, Johnny Brandon. February 3, 1982. Director and choreographer, Otis Sallid; musical director, Thom Bridwell; scenery, Bob Provenza; lighting, Stephen Shereff; costumes, Ellen Lee. With Lynne Bell, Jim Cyrus, Catherine Campbell, Adele Foster, Shelton Ray.

THE WIND THAT SHOOK THE BARLEY. By Declan Burke-Kennedy. March 24, 1982. Director, Jamie Brown; scenery, Gordon A. Juel; lighting, Daniel J. Farley; costumes, Mary Hayes. With Jarlath Conroy, Kathleen Roland, Mary Tierney, Denis O'Neill.

Urban Arts Theater. Dedicated to the development of theater arts and craft skills in the black community. Vinnette Carroll, artistic director, Anita MacShane, managing director.

YOU BET YOUR SWEET— I'M A LADY by Jess Lowen. February 4, 1982. Directed by Vinnette Carroll; with Marie Thomas, Beauris Whitehead, Ray Robertson, Michael Jameson.

THEATER OF THE OPEN EYE—Randy Frazier, Michele Cannon, J.J. Cole, Elton Becket, Matthew Idason and John Redwood in *The Sun Gets Blue*

DESIRE UNDER THE ELMS by Eugene O'Neill; songs by Micki Grant. April 30, 1982. Directed by Vinnette Carroll; with Joe Davis, James Robertson, Richard Schull, Lorey Hayes.

WPA Theater. Produces neglected American classics and new American plays in the realistic idiom. Kyle Renick, producing director, Howard Ashman, artistic director, Edward T. Gianfrancesco, resident designer/technical director.

KEY EXCHANGE (20). By Kevin Wade. June 4, 1981. Director, Barnet Kellman; scenery, Terry Ariano; lighting, Frances Aronson; costumes, Robert Wojewodski. With Brooke Adams, Mark Blum, Ben Masters.

BIG APPLE MESSENGER (24). By Shannon Keith Kelley. October 15, 1981. Director, Stephen Zuckerman; scenery, Edward T. Gianfrancesco; lighting, Phil Monat; costumes, Mimi Maxmen. With Merwin Goldsmith, Joseph Warren, Michael Huddleston, Eddie Jones, Kim Sullivan, Rod Houts, Mark Soper, Gregory T. Daniel, Emil Belasco, Ken Costigan, Terrance Terry Ellis, Dave Florek, Edward Gallardo, Richard Zobel.

GHOSTS OF THE LOYAL OAKS (24). By Larry Ketron. November 27, 1981. Director, Amy Saltz; scenery, Edward T. Gianfrancesco; lighting, Craig Evans; costumes, Judy Dearing. With Linda Cook, John Goodman, Mary Elaine Monti, William Russ, Loudon Wainwright III.

THE WHALES OF AUGUST (24). By David Berry. January 29, 1982. Director, William Ludel; scenery, Edward T. Gianfrancesco; lighting, Phil Monat; costumes, David Murin. With Elizabeth Council, Bettie Endrizzi, Daniel Keyes, George Lloyd, Vivienne Smith.

WHAT WOULD JEANNE MOREAU DO? (24). By Elinor Jones. March 11, 1982. Director, Stuart White; scenery, Terry Ariano; lighting, Craig Evans; costumes, Anne Watson. With Joaquim DeAlmeida, James Hilbrandt, Lynn Milgrim, Burke Pearson.

LITTLE SHOP OF HORRORS (24). Book, lyrics, and directed by Howard Ashman, based on Roger Corman's film; music, Alan Menken. May 6, 1982. Choreographer, Edie Cowan; scenery, Edward T. Gianfrancesco; lighting, Craig Evans; puppets, Martin P. Robinson. With Sheila Kay Davis, Ellen Greene, Leilani Jones, Franc Luz, Martin P. Robinson, Ron Taylor, Michael Vale, Jennifer Leigh Warren, Lee Wilkof.

The York Players. Each season, productions of classics and contemporary plays are mounted with professional casts, providing neighborhood residents with professional theater. Janet Hayes Walker, artistic director.

THE TEAK ROOM (10). Written and performed by Margaret Beals. February 16, 1982. Director, Tony Tanner; scenery, James Morgan; lighting, Edward M. Greenberg; costumes, Sally Ann Parsons.

LOLA (20). Book and lyrics, Kenward Elmslie; music, Claibe Richardson. March 24, 1982. Director, John Going; choreographer, David Holdgreiwe; musical director, David Bishop; scenery, James Morgan; lighting, David Gotwald; costumes, William Schroeder. With Jane White, Robert Stillman, Leigh Beery, Tom Flagg, Bud Nease, John Foster, Gretchen Albrecht, Jack Dabdoub.

THE PRIVATE EAR and THE PUBLIC EYE by Peter Shaffer. November 20, 1981. Directed by William Cain; with Kristine Sutherland, Paul Murray, Guy Louthan, Timothy Hall, James Secrest, Diane Warren.
THE ENCHANTED by Jean Giraudoux, adapted by Maurice Valency. January 21, 1982. Directed by Janet Hayes Walker; with Kermit Brown, Ralph David Westfall, Susan Frazer, John Rainer, Brockman Seawell, I. Mary Carter, Arthur Hanket, Aaron Lusting.
110 IN THE SHADE (musical) book by N. Richard Nash, based on his play, *The Rainmaker*, music by Harvey Schmidt, lyrics by Tom Jones. May 19, 1982. Directed by Fran Soeder; with Jan Pessano, Mark Zimmerman, Robert Stoeckle, Jesse Cline, Belle Smith, Linda Jacobs, Nan Burling, Craig Shepherd, Jane Jensen, Scott Ellis, Ralph Gunderman, Luke Sickle.

Miscellaneous

In the additional listing of 1981–82 off-off-Broadway productions below, the names of the producing groups or theaters appear in CAPITAL LETTERS and the titles of the works in *italics*. This list consists largely of new or reconstituted works and excludes most revivals, especially of classics. It includes a few productions staged by groups which rented space from the more established organizations listed previously.

ACTORS AND DIRECTORS' THEATER. *Brontosaurus Rex* by Schuyler Bishop. October 20, 1981. Directed by Peter L. Wallace; with Frank Biancamano, Dan Ahearn. *Magic Time* by James Sherman. December, 1981. Directed by Henry Hoffman; with Ivar Brogger, Karen Ingenthron, Rick Casorla, Elizabeth Burr, Judy Tate.

ACTORS' OUTLET. *Occupations* by Trevor Griffiths. March, 1982. Directed by James Traub; with Chris Ceraso, Harris Laskawy.

AMERICAN JEWISH THEATER. *House Music* by Hans Sahl. November 14, 1981. Directed by Geoffrey Sherman; with Jean Hackett, Clement Fowler, Robert Blumenfeld, Shirin Trainer, Elaine Grollman, Eberle Thomas, Albert S. Bennett, Waltrudis Buck. *The Keymaker* by Nathan Teitel. March 6, 1982. Directed by Stanley Brechner; with Carol Teitel, Lloyd Battista. *The Raspberry Pickers* by Fritz Hochwalder. May 1, 1982. Directed by Dan Held.

AMERICAN RENAISSANCE THEATER. *Baseball Wives* by Grubb Greebner. May 6, 1982. Directed by Gloria Maddox; with Lynn Goodwin, Patti Karr, Marcella Lowery.

AMERICAN THEATER OF ACTORS. *The Last of the Knucklemen* by John Powers. March, 1982. Directed by Peter Masterson; with Gary Klar, Gene O'Neill, George Taylor, Ben George.

APPLE CORPS THEATER. *Dead Giveaway* by Mary Orr and Reginald Denham. September 24, 1981. Directed by Philip Giberson; with Roger Morden, Judith McIntyre, Judith Scarpone, Ed Van Nuys.

ARK THEATER COMPANY. *The Middle Ages* by A. R. Gurney Jr. March, 1982. Directed by Donald Marcus; with Jack Gilpin, Carolyn Mignini, Steven Gilborn, Pat Lavelle. *Unheard Songs: Solitude* and *Vivien* (one-act plays) by Percy Granger. May 16, 1982. Directed by Charles Morey; with Richard Mathews, Thomas A. Carlin, Paul Austin, Richmond Hoxie, Dana Ivey.

COLONNADES THEATER LAB. *The Man With the Flower in His Mouth, The License,* and *The Jar* by Luigi Pirandello. August 27, 1981. Directed by Michael Simone; with Danny DeVito, Val Dufour, Sam Locante, Angela Pietropinto, Ron Faber, Antonio Sordi.

ECONOMY TIRES THEATER. *Tristan and Isolt* and *Gioconda and Si-Ya-U,* with Pail Zimet's Talking Band. *Not Quite/New York,* with Bill Irwin. *The Rat of Huge Proportions,* with Bruce D. Schwartz.

ENTERMEDIA THEATER. *Garbage* concept, lyrics and performed by Jango Edwards. October 7, 1981.

THE FIRST ALL CHILDREN'S THEATER. *Nightingale* opera by Charles Strouse, based on "The Emperor and the Nightingale" by Hans Christian Andersen. April 25, 1982. Directed by Meridee Stein.

HAROLD CLURMAN THEATER (tenant). *Meegan's Game* by Elliott Caplin. March 26, 1982. Directed by Gary Bowen; with Linda Barnhurst, Aida Berlyn, Nick Ferrari Ferris, Ron Harper, Bernie Rachelle, Carlotta Sherwood, Greg Spagna.

HORACE MANN THEATER. *Welded* by Eugene O'Neill. June 13, 1981. Directed by Jose Quintero; with Philip Anglim.

JEAN COCTEAU REPERTORY. *Something Cloudy, Something Clear* by Tennessee Williams. August 25, 1981. Directed by Eve Adamson; with Craig Smith, Elton Cormier, Dominique Cieri, David Fuller, John Schmerling, Phyllis Deitschel, Meg Fisher, Harris Berlinsky. *The Two Noble Kinsmen* by William Shakespeare and John Fletcher. October 15, 1981. Directed by Eve Adamson. *The Revenger's Tragedy* by Cyril Tourneur. December 3, 1981. *The Golem* by H. Leivick, translated by Joseph C. Landis. February 11, 1982. Directed by Eve Adamson; with Harris Berlinsky, John Schmerling, Coral S. Potter. *The Count of Monte Cristo* by Alexander Dumas, adapted by Douglas McKeown and Dennis Green. March 25, 1982.

JEWISH REPERTORY THEATER. *Awake and Sing!* by Clifford Odets. October 24, 1981. Directed by Lynn Polan; with Vera Lockwood, Michael Albert Mantel, Alan Brandt. *Elephants* by David Rush. December 5, 1981. Directed by Edward M. Cohen; with Lee Wallace, Marilyn Chris, Richard Niles. *Delmore* (one-act plays): *Shenandoah* by Delmore Schwartz and *Luna Park,* adapted by Donald Margulies from Delmore Schwartz's story "In Dreams Begin Responsibilities". February 5, 1982. Directed by Florence Stanley. *Vagabond Stars* (musical) book by Nahma Sandrow, music by Raphael Crystal, lyrics by Alan Poul. May 29, 1982. Directed by Ran Avni; with Steve Sterner, Herbert Rubens, Steve Yudson, Susan Victor, Dana Zeller-Alexis.

JONES BEACH THEATER. *Damn Yankees* (musical) book by George Abbott and Douglass Wallop, music and lyrics by Richard Adler and Jerry Ross. June 30, 1981. Directed by Frank Wagner; with Joe Namath, Eddie Bracken.

LABOR THEATER. *Yours for the Revolution, Jack London* (one-man show) by and with Chuck Portz. October 30, 1981.

MEAT AND POTATOES COMPANY. *Fasnacht Day* by John Speicher. June, 1981. Directed by James E. Dwyer; with Jay Devlin, Lisa Cosman, Evan Thompson, Donald Pace.

FIRST ALL-CHILDREN'S THEATER—Death creeps up on the Emperor (John Shuck) in this scene from *Nightingale*

MODERN TIMES THEATER. *Hibakusha: Stories from Hiroshima* by Steve Friedman. February 28, 1982. Directed by Denny Partridge; with Bruce Butler, Glenn Kubota, Janet Langon, Mary Lum, Joan Rosenfels, Steve Friedman.

MUSIC-THEATER GROUP/LENOX ARTS CENTER. *A Metamorphosis in Miniature,* adapted by Martha Clarke, Linda Hunt, David Rounds, Penny Stegenga, with Jeff Wanshel, from Franz Kafka's "Metamorphosis". January 27, 1982. With David Rounds, Linda Hunt. *The Long Journey of Poppie Nongena* by Elsa Joubert, adapted by Sandra Kotze and Elsa Joubert. March, 1982. Directed by Hilary Blecher; with Nomsa Nene, Sophie Mgcina, Seth Sibanda, Tsepo Mokone, Maggie Soboll, Alan Coates.

NAT HORNE MUSICAL THEATER. *Zindel x 2* (one-act plays): *Let Me Hear You Whisper* and *The Ladies Should Be in Bed* by Paul Zindel. April 29, 1982. Directed by Ann Raychel; with Peter Baird, Saun Ellis, Yvonne Southerland, Julia Rand, Alice Spivak, Nancy Weems, Francesca DeSapio, Carol Rosenfeld, Beryl Towbin.

NEW YORK ART THEATER. *The Party* by Arnold Weinstein. February, 1982. Directed by Donald Sanders; with Guy Custis, Linda Blumberg, Clark Taylor.

NEW YORK STAGEWORKS. *The Derby* by Michael McClure. September 17, 1981. Directed by Angela Paton; with Laurence Roth, Janice Kay Young, Kevin Reilley, Maggie Schmidt, *The Bridge to Latonia* by Marc Berman, directed by Susan Gregg; *The Skirmishers* by John Bishop, directed by Ted Bank (one-act plays). January, 1982. With Joan Wooters, Robert Frederick, Tony Pasqualini, Sarah Brooke, Christopher Goutman, Diane Heles, Eddie Jones.

NEW YORK THEATER WORKSHOP. *The Potsdam Quartet* by David Pinner. February, 1982. Directed by Jacques Levy; with John Braden, Bill Moor, Roger Forbes, Gavin Reed, George Kyle.

NUOVA OPERA DEI BURATTINI. *Gentlemen, the Marionette!* by Edward Gordon Craig. October, 1981. Directed by Michele Mirabella.

OFF CENTER THEATER. *Macrune's Guevara* by John Spurling. October 21, 1981. Directed by Larry Loonin; with Harriett Kittner, Juan Wolf, Bill Olland.

OPEN EYE THEATER (tenant). *Vincent* by and with Christopher Consani. December 4, 1981. Directed by Shari Upbin; with Lou Liotta.

PALSSON'S. *Forbidden Broadway* (musical revue) lyrics by Gerard Alessandrini. January 15, 1982. Directed by Michael Chapman; with Nora Mae Lyng, Wendee Winters, Bill Carmichael, Gerard Alessandrini.

THE PERFORMING GARAGE. *Vacuum* created and directed by Chris Hardman. March, 1982. With Ernesto Sanchez, Annie Hallatt, Chris Tellis, Ray Myslewski (Antenna Theater). *Micropolis, or Five Portraits and a Landscape* created by Theodora Skipitares. April 5, 1982.

PERRY STREET THEATER. *Forty-Deuce* by Alan Bowne. October, 1981. Directed by Tony Tanner; with Orson Bean, Kevin Bacon, Tommy Citera, Mark Keyloun, John Noonan. Sixth Festival of Italian Theater, schedule included *Sack* written, directed and performed by Claudio Remondi and Riccardo Caporossi. December 14, 1981.

PRISM THEATER. *Amidst the Gladiolas* by Vito A. Gentile Jr. December, 1981. Directed by Ron Comenzo; with James Selby, Rosemary Prinz, Dorothy Holland, Sally-Jane Heit, Joe Palmieri. *Best All 'Round* by Marsha Sheiness. April, 1982. Directed by Stephen Stewart-James; with Nina Levine, Lisa Reed, Lisa Kable, Mary Caton.

RICHARD ALLEN CENTER. *Torch Song Trilogy: The International Stud, Fugue in a Nursery,* and *Widows and Children First!* by Harvey Fierstein. October 16, 1981. Directed by Peter Pope; with Harvey Fierstein, Joel Crothers, Diane Tarleton, Estelle Getty, Matthew Broderick, Paul Joynt.

SAN FRANCISCO MIME TROUPE. *Factwino Meets the Moral Majority* by Joan Holden in collaboration with the San Francisco Mime Troupe. May, 1982. Directed by Sharon Lockwood.

SOLOMON R. GUGGENHEIM MUSEUM. *The Yellow Sound* by Vasily Kandinsky. February 9, 1982. Directed by Ian Strasfogel.

SOUTH STREET THEATER (tenant). *Peep* by James Murray. August 10, 1981. Directed by Graham Leader; with Anna Maria Horsford, Linda Lee Johnson, Sioux Saloka, Jill Larson, Devon O'Brien, Jacqueline M. Sedlar, Denise Lute.

STONEWALL REPERTORY THEATER. *Thanksgiving* by Loretta Lotman. January 15, 1982. Directed by Rene Savitt; with Sylvia Stein, Demetra Karras, Elayne Wilks.

TED HOOK'S ON STAGE: *Oh, Coward!* (cabaret) words and music by Noel Coward, devised and directed by Roderick Cook. June, 1981. With Terri Klausner, Russ Thacker, Dalton Cathey, Kay Walbye. *Jerry's Girls* (cabaret revue of Jerry Herman's songs). August, 1981. Directed by Larry Alford; with Evalyn Baron, Alexandra Korey, Pauletta Pearson, Leigh Martin.

THEATER MATRIX. *Gas Station* by Shelby Buford Jr. May 14, 1982. Directed by Robert Fuhrmann.

THREE MUSES THEATER. *Bags* (musical) book and lyrics by Elizabeth Perry, music by Robert Mitchell. April 6, 1982. With Tiger Haynes, Juanita Fleming, Fiddle Viracola, Audre Johnston.

TYSON STUDIO. *A Limb of Snow* and *The Meeting* (one-act plays) by Anna Marie Barlow. September 23, 1981. Directed by Philip Gushee; with Cheryl Henderson, Richard Fancy, Elizabeth Davis, George Babiak.

WESTSIDE ARTS THEATER. *The City Suite* (musical revue) by Keith Levenson. December 3, 1981. Directed by David Jiranek; with Shari Lee Scott, Dayna Clark, Paul Harman.

WESTSIDE MAINSTAGE THEATER. *Homeboys* written and directed by John Lordan. March 25, 1982.

WONDERHORSE THEATER. *Close Enough for Jazz* (revue) book and lyrics by Joseph Keenan, music by Scott Steidl, created by Joseph Keenan and David Rothkopf. June, 1981. Directed by

David Rothkopf; with Stephen Berenson, Dietrich Snelling, Joe Joyce, Debra Jacobs, Susan J. Baum, Mary Duncan, Nina Hennessey. *The Evangelist* (musical) book, music, and lyrics by Al Carmines. March 31, 1982. Directed by William Hopkins; with Keith Baker, Donna Bullock, Paul Farin, Kate Ingram, Judith Moore.

THE WOOSTER GROUP. *Route 1 & 9 (The Last Act)* composed by the Wooster Group. October 8, 1981. Directed by Elizabeth LeCompte; with Willem Dafoe, Freya Hansell, Marisa Hansell, Simon Stimson, Kate Valk, Ron Vawter, Peyton. *47 Beds* by and with Spalding Gray. December, 1981. *Hula*. February, 1982. Directed by Elizabeth LeCompte; with Willem Dafoe, Kate Valk, Ron Vawter.

CAST REPLACEMENTS AND TOURING COMPANIES

Compiled by Stanley Green

The following is a list of the more important cast replacements in productions which opened in previous years, but were still playing in New York during a substantial part of the 1981–82 season; or were still on a first-class tour in 1981–82, or opened in New York in 1981–82 and went on tour during the season (casts of first-class touring companies of previous seasons which were no longer playing in 1981–82 appear in previous *Best Plays* volumes of appropriate years).

The name of each major role is listed in *italics* beneath the title of the play in the first column. In the second column directly opposite appears the name of the actor who created the role in the original New York production (whose opening date appears in *italics* at the top of the column). Indented immediately beneath the original actor's name are the names of subsequent New York replacements, together with the date of replacement when available.

The third column gives information about first-class touring companies, including London companies (produced under the auspices of their original New York managements). When there is more than one roadshow company, #1, #2, etc., appear before the name of the performer who created the role in each company (and the city and date of each company's first performance appears in *italics* at the top of the column). Their subsequent replacements are also listed beneath their names, with dates when available.

AMADEUS

	New York 12/17/81
Antonio Salieri	Ian McKellen
	John Wood 10/13/81
	Frank Langella 4/13/82
Wolfgang Amadeus Mozart	Tim Curry
	Peter Firth 7/7/81
	John Pankow 3/10/82
	Dennis Boutsikeris 4/13/82
Constanze Weber	Jane Seymour
	Caris Corfman 5/26/81
	Amy Irving 7/7/81
	Caris Corfman 2/16/82
	Michele Farr 3/23/82
	Suzanne Lederer 4/13/82

ANNIE

		#1 San Francisco 6/22/78
		#2 Dallas 10/3/79
	New York 4/21/77	*#3 West Point 9/11/81*
Oliver Warbucks	Reid Shelton	#1 Keene Curtis
	Keene Curtis 2/6/78	Reid Shelton 12/28/79
	Reid Shelton 2/27/78	#2 Harve Presnell
	John Schuck 12/25/79	Jack Collins 12/17/80
	Harve Presnell 12/17/80	Harve Presnell 1/7/81
	John Schuck 1/7/81	Rhodes Reason 8/31/81

415

	Rhodes Reason 6/23/81 Harve Presnell 9/1/81	#3 Ron Holgate
Annie	Andrea McArdle Shelley Bruce 3/6/78 Sarah Jessica Parker 3/6/79 Allison Smith 1/29/80	#1 Patricia Ann Patts Louanne Marisa Morell Kristi Coombs #2 Rosanne Sorrentino Bridget Walsh 3/27/81 #3 Mollie Hall
Miss Hannigan	Dorothy Loudon Alice Ghostley 8/15/78 Dolores Wilson 8/21/79 Alice Ghostley 1/29/80 Betty Hutton 9/17/80 Alice Ghostley 10/8/80 Marcia Lewis 4/29/81 Ruth Kobart 2/24/82 Marcia Lewis 3/10/82	#1 Jane Connell #2 Patricia Drylie Kathleen Freeman 3/27/81 #3 Ruth Williamson
Grace Farrell	Sandy Faison Lynn Kearney 1/22/79 Mary Bracken Phillips 8/79 Kathryn Boulé 7/29/80 Ann Kerry 4/29/81 Lauren Mitchell 1/13/82	#1 Kathryn Boulé Lisa Robinson Krista Neumann 1/7/81 Ann Peck 10/13/81 #2 Deborah Jean Templin Lauren Mitchell 3/27/81 Kathryn Boulé 1/13/82 #3 Lynne Wintersteller
Rooster Hannigan	Robert Fitch Gary Beach 1/29/80 Richard Sabellico 4/29/81	#1 Swen Swenson Tom Offt Michael Calkins 9/30/81 Gary Beach 4/30/82 #2 Michael Leeds Dennis Parlato 10/4/80 J.B. Adams 8/25/81 Jon Rider 2/22/82 #3 Guy Stroman William McClary 4/6/82
Lily	Barbara Erwin Annie McGreevey 9/78 Barbara Erwin 5/29/79 Rita Rudner 1/29/80 Dorothy Stanley 2/11/81	#1 Connie Danese Jacalyn Switzer Edie Cowan Maggie Gorrill 11/4/80 Linda Manning 11/3/81 #2 Katharine Buffaloe Wendy Kimball 10/4/80 #3 Ann Casey
FDR	Raymond Thorne	#1 Tom Hatten Alan Wikman 12/17/80 Randall Robbins 12/22/81 #2 Jack Denton David Green 3/29/82 #3 William Metzo

Note: Casts, including replacements, of the first touring company and the London company of *Annie* appear on pages 446–7 of *The Best Plays of 1980–81.* These companies ended their runs on Sept. 6, 1981, and Nov. 28, 1981, respectively.

BARNUM

	New York 4/30/80	#1 New Orleans 5/16/81 #2 London 6/11/81 #3 San Francisco 12/16/81
Phineas T. Barnum	Jim Dale Tony Orlando 5/5/81 Jim Dale 5/26/81 Mike Burstyn 10/13/81	#1 Stacy Keach #2 Michael Crawford #3 Jim Dale*
Chairy Barnum	Glenn Close Catherine Cox 3/81 Suellen Estey 1/19/82 Catherine Cox 1/26/82 Deborah Reagan 3/9/82	#1 Dee Hoty #2 Deborah Grant #3 Glenn Close
Jenny Lind	Marianne Tatum Suellen Estey 1/26/82 Marianne Tatum 2/1/82	#1 Catherine Gaines #2 Sarah Payne #3 Catherine Gaines
Tom Thumb	Leonard John Crofoot	#1 Bobby Lee #2 Christopher Beck #3 Ray Roderick
Joice Heth	Terri White Lillias White 4/14/81	#1 Terri White #2 Jennie McGustie #3 Terri White
Ringmaster	William C. Witter Terrence V. Mann 4/14/81 Kelly Walters 11/17/81	#1 Gabriel Barrie #2 William C. Witter #3 Terrence V. Mann

* For one performance a week during the second U.S. tour, the role of Barnum was played by Terrence V. Mann.

THE BEST LITTLE WHOREHOUSE IN TEXAS

	N.Y. Off Bway 4/17/78 N.Y. Bway 6/19/78 & 5/31/82
Mona Stangley	Carlin Glynn Bobbi Jo Lathan 8/6/79 Carlin Glynn 8/20/79 Fannie Flagg 5/12/80 Candace Tovar 11/24/80 Anita Morris 11/16/81 Carlin Glynn 3/10/82
Ed Earl Dowd	Henderson Forsythe Larry L. King 1/15/79 Henderson Forsythe 1/29/79 Gil Rogers 8/4/80
Jewel	Delores Hall Marilyn J. Johnson 12/21/81 Delores Hall 1/18/82
*Amber**	Pamela Blair Gena Ramsel 8/78 Tina Johnson Susann Fletcher

* Character name changed to Angel during run.

Doatsey May   Susan Mansur
                                     Carol Hall 1/1/79
                                     Susan Mansur 1/8/79
                                     Bobbi Jo Lathan
                                     Candace Tovar
                                     Becky Gelke 11/24/80

Melvin P. Thorpe   Clinton Allmon

Governor   Jay Garner
                                     Tom Avera 8/6/79
                                     Jay Garner 8/13/79
                                     Patrick Hamilton 5/80

CAMELOT

| | #1 New York 7/8/80 | #1 Dallas 9/30/80 |
| | #2 New York 11/15/81 | #2 Buffalo 2/11/82 |

Arthur   #1 Richard Burton   #1 Richard Burton
                                 #2 Richard Harris   William Parry 3/17/81
                                                                Richard Harris 4/13/81
                                                                William Parry 9/25/81
                                                            #2 Richard Harris

Guenevere   #1 Christine Ebersole   #1 Christine Ebersole
                                                                Meg Bussert 6/4/81
                                 #1 Meg Bussert   #2 Debra Dickinson

Lancelot du Lac   #1 Richard Muenz   #1 Richard Muenz
                                 #2 Richard Muenz   #2 Richard Muenz

King Pellinore   #1 Paxton Whitehead   #1 Paxton Whitehead
                                 #2 Barrie Ingham   Barrie Ingham 6/4/81
                                                            #2 Barrie Ingham

Mordred   #1 Robert Fox   #1 Robert Fox
                                 #2 Richard Backus   Albert Insinnia 6/4/81
                                                                Richard Backus 10/5/81
                                                            #2 Richard Backus

Note: This was one company that played New York on two different occasions. For the sake of clarity, the second New York engagement and the second tour are treated separately.

CHILDREN OF A LESSER GOD

| | | #1 Chicago 12/16/80 |
| | New York 3/30/80 | #2 London 8/25/81 |

James Leeds   John Rubinstein   #1 Peter Evans
                                     Robert Steinberg 11/13/80   James N. Stephens
                                                                   12/29/81
                                     John Rubinstein 12/8/80   #2 Trevor Eve
                                     David Ackroyd 12/22/80
                                     John Rubinstein 6/29/81
                                     Peter Evans 12/29/81
                                     James N. Stephens 3/82

Sarah Norman   Phyllis Frelich   #1 Linda Bove
                                                            #2 Elizabeth Quinn

A CHORUS LINE

N.Y. Off Bway 4/15/75
N.Y. Bway 7/25/75

Kristine

Renee Baughman
  Cookie Vazquez 4/26/76
  Deborah Geffner 10/76
  P.J. Mann 9/78
  Deborah Geffner 1/79
  Christine Barker 3/79
  Kerry Casserly 8/81
  Christine Barker 10/81

Sheila

Carole Bishop (name changed
to Kelly Bishop 3/76)
  Kathrynann Wright 8/76
  Bebe Neuwirth 6/80
  Susan Danielle 3/81

Val

Pamela Blair
  Barbara Monte-Britton 4/26/76
  Karen Jablons 10/76
  Mitzi Hamilton 3/1/77
  Karen Jablons 12/77
  Mitzi Hamilton 3/78
  Lois Englund 7/78
  Deborah Henry 10/79
  Mitzi Hamilton 10/80
  Joanna Zercher 6/81
  Mitzi Hamilton 7/81

Mike

Wayne Cilento
  Jim Litten 6/77
  Jeff Hyslop 1/79
  Don Correia 6/79
  Buddy Balou' 6/80
  Cary Scott Lowenstein 7/81

Larry

Clive Clerk
  Jeff Weinberg 10/76
  Clive Clerk 1/77
  Adam Grammis 2/77
  Paul Charles 12/77
  R.J.Peters 3/79
  T. Michael Reed 11/79
  Michael-Day Pitts 3/80
  Donn Simione 4/81
  J. Richard Hart 7/81

Maggie

Kay Cole
  Lauree Berger 4/26/76
  Donna Drake 2/77
  Christina Saffran 7/78
  Betty Lynd 6/5/79
  Marcia Lynn Watkins 8/79
  Pam Klinger 9/81

Richie

Ronald Dennis
  Winston DeWitt Hemsley 4/26/76
  Edward Love 6/77

A. William Perkins 12/77
(name changed to Wellington
Perkins 6/78)
Larry G. Bailey 1/79
Carleton T. Jones 3/80
Ralph Glenmore 6/80
Kevin Chinn 1/81

Judy   Patricia Garland
                          Sandahl Bergman 4/26/76
                          Murphy Cross 12/77
                          Victoria Tabaka 11/78
                          Joanna Zercher 7/79
                          Angelique Ilo 8/79
                          Jannet Horsley 9/80
                          (name changed to Jannet
                          Moranz 2/81)
                          Melissa Randel 12/81

Don   Ron Kuhlman
                          David Thomé 4/26/76
                          Dennis Edenfield 3/80
                          Michal Weir 8/81
                          Michael Danek 10/81

Bebe   Nancy Lane
                          Gillian Scalaci 4/26/76
                          Rene Ceballos 9/77
                          Karen Meister 1/78
                          Rene Ceballos 3/81
                          Pamela Ann Wilson 1/82

Connie   Baayork Lee
                          Lauren Kayahara 4/26/76
                          Janet Wong 2/77
                          Cynthia Carrillo Onrubia 11/79
                          Janet Wong 12/79
                          Lauren Tom 10/80
                          Lily-Lee Wong 10/81

Diana   Priscilla Lopez
                          Barbara Luna 4/26/76
                          Carole Schweid 5/7/76
                          Rebecca York 8/76
                          Loida Iglesias 12/76
                          Chris Bocchino 10/78
                          Diane Fratantoni 9/79
                          Chris Bocchino 12/79
                          Gay Marshall 7/80
                          Chris Bocchino 8/80
                          Dorothy Tancredi 3/82

Zach   Robert LuPone
                          Joe Bennett 4/26/76
                          Eivind Harum 10/76
                          Robert LuPone 1/31/77
                          Kurt Johnson 5/77
                          Clive Clerk 7/77
                          Kurt Johnson 8/77

Anthony Inneo 8/78
Eivind Harum 10/78
Scott Pearson 8/79
Tim Millett 3/81

Mark   Cameron Mason
Paul Charles 10/76
Timothy Scott 12/77
R.J. Peters 4/78
Timothy Wahrer 3/79
Dennis Daniels 5/80
Timothy Wahrer 6/80
Gregory Brock 8/80
Danny Herman 5/81

Cassie   Donna McKechnie
Ann Reinking 4/26/76
Donna McKechnie 9/27/76
Ann Reinking 11/29/76
Vicki Frederick 2/9/77
Pamela Sousa 11/14/77
Candace Tovar 1/78
Pamela Sousa 3/78
Cheryl Clark 12/78
Deborah Henry 10/80
Pamela Sousa 11/81

Al   Don Percassi
Bill Nabel 4/26/76
John Mineo 2/77
Ben Lokey 4/77
Don Percassi 7/77
Jim Corti 1/79
Donn Simione 9/79
James Warren 5/80
(name changed to James
Young 9/80)
Jerry Colker 5/81

Greg   Michel Stuart
Justin Ross 4/26/76
Danny Weathers 6/78

Bobby   Thomas J. Walsh
Christopher Chadman 6/77
Ron Kurowski 1/78
Tim Cassidy 11/78
Ronald Stafford 3/79
Michael Gorman 8/80
Matt West 9/80

Paul   Sammy Williams
George Pesaturo 4/26/76
René Clemente 2/78
Timothy Wahrer 9/81
René Clemente 10/81
Tommy Aguilar 5/82

Note: Original casting of the three touring companies of *A Chorus Line* appears on pages 472–3 of
The Best Plays of 1978–79. Changes have become too numerous for a continuing record.

DANCIN'

New York 3/27/78

Ciscoe Bruton

Lloyd Culbreath

Spence Ford

Dana Moore

Bebe Neuwirth

Alison Sherve

Laurie Dawn Skinner

David Thomé

Note: Because replacements do not generally succeed specific performers in *Dancin'*, listed above in alphabetical order are those new members of the company who were in it as of May 31, 1982. The casting from the opening through May 31, 1980 appears in *The Best Plays of 1979–80.*

A DAY IN HOLLYWOOD/A NIGHT IN THE UKRAINE

N.Y. B'way 5/1/80	*Toronto 12/1/81*
Kate Draper	Evalyn Baron
David Garrison	Jill Cook
Niki Harris	Mary D'Arcy
Peggy Hewett	Richard Haskin
Stephen James	Jeff Keller
Frank Lazarus	Frank Lazarus
Priscilla Lopez	Patricia Lockery
Albert Stephenson	Brad Moranz

Both casts listed above in alphabetical order.

DEATHTRAP

New York 2/26/78

Sidney Bruhl	John Wood
	Patrick Horgan 11/27/78
	John Wood 12/11/78
	Stacy Keach 1/15/79
	John Cullum 7/17/79
	Robert Reed 9/2/80
	Farley Granger 3/17/81
Myra Bruhl	Marian Seldes
Helga Ten Dorp	Marian Winters
	Elizabeth Parrish 10/78
Clifford Anderson	Victor Garber
	Daren Kelly 10/78

Steve Bassett 10/79
Ernest Townsend 7/81
Michael McBride 4/5/82
Ernest Townsend 5/3/82

Porter Milgrim   Richard Woods
William Le Massena 11/78

ENTERTAINING MR. SLOANE

New York 5/14/81

Sloane   Maxwell Caulfield
Richard Eddon 10/20/81
Brad Davis 11/3/81

Ed   Joseph Maher
Jerome Dempsey 11/3/81

EVITA

		#1 *Los Angeles 1/13/80*
		#2 *Chicago 9/30/80*
	New York 9/25/79	#3 *Detroit 2/23/82*
Eva Peron	Patti LuPone (eves.)	#1 Loni Ackerman (eves.)
	Terri Klausner (mats.)	Derin Altay (mats.)
	Nancy Opel (mats.) 10/80	Pamela Blake (mats.)
		1/10/81
	Derin Altay (eves.) 1/12/81	Derin Altay (eves.)
		4/5/82
	Loni Ackerman (eves.) 4/5/82	#2 Valerie Perri (eves.)
		Joy Lober (mats.)
		#3 Florence Lacey (eves.)
		Patricia Hemenway
		(mats.)
Juan Peron	Bob Gunton	#1 Jon Cypher
	David Cryer 10/20/80	David Brummel 3/82
		#2 Robb Alton
		#3 John Leslie Wolfe
Che	Mandy Patinkin	#1 Scott Holmes
	James Stein 10/20/80	#2 John Herrara
	Anthony Crivello 4/5/82	Anthony Crivello
		R. Michael Baker
		4/3/82
		#3 Tim Bowman

THE FANTASTICKS

New York 5/3/60

El Gallo   Jerry Orbach
Gene Rupert
Bert Convy
John Cunningham
Don Stewart 1/63
David Cryer
Keith Charles 10/63

John Boni 1/13/65
Jack Metter 9/14/65
George Ogee
Keith Charles
Tom Urich 8/30/66
John Boni 10/5/66
Jack Crowder 6/13/67
Nils Hedrick 9/19/67
Keith Charles 10/9/67
Robert Goss 11/7/67
Joe Bellomo 3/11/68
Michael Tartel 7/8/69
Donald Billett 6/70
Joe Bellomo 2/15/72
David Rexroad 6/73
David Snell 12/73
Hal Robinson 4/2/74
Chapman Roberts 7/30/74
David Brummel 2/18/75
David Rexroad 8/31/75
Roger Brown 9/30/75
David Rexroad 9/1/76
Joseph Galiano 10/14/76
Douglas Clark 5/2/78
Joseph Galiano 5/23/78
Richard Muenz 10/78
Joseph Galiano 2/20/79
George Lee Andrews 11/27/79
Sal Provenza 5/13/80
Lance Brodie 9/8/81

Luisa   Rita Gardner
Carla Huston
Liza Stuart 12/61
Eileen Fulton
Alice Cannon 9/62
Royce Lennelle
B.J. Ward 12/1/64
Leta Anderson 7/13/65
Carole Demas 11/22/66
Anne Kaye 5/28/68
Carolyn Mignini 7/29/69
Virginia Gregory 7/27/70
Leta Anderson
Marti Morris 3/7/72
Sharon Werner 12/73
Sarah Rice 6/24/74
Cheryl Horne 7/1/75
Sarah Rice 7/29/75
Betsy Joslyn 3/23/76
Kathy Vestuto 7/18/78
Betsy Joslyn 8/8/78
Kathryn Morath 11/28/78
Debbie McLeod 4/17/79
Joan Wiest 10/9/79
Marti Morris 11/6/79
Carol Ann Scott 5/20/80
Beverly Lambert 9/2/80

Judith Blazer 12/1/80
Elizabeth Bruzzese 8/15/81

Matt   Kenneth Nelson
Gino Conforti
Jack Blackton 10/63
Paul Giovanni
Ty McConnell
Richard Rothbard
Gary Krawford
Bob Spencer 9/5/64
Erik Howell 6/28/66
Gary Krawford 12/12/67
Steve Skiles 2/6/68
Craig Carnelia 1/69
Samuel D. Ratcliffe 8/5/69
Michael Glenn-Smith 5/26/70
Jimmy Dodge 9/20/70
Geoffrey Taylor 8/31/71
Erik Howell 3/14/72
Phil Kilian 7/4/72
Richard Lincoln 9/72
Bruce Cryer 7/24/73
Phil Killian 9/11/73
Michael Glenn-Smith 6/17/74
Ralph Bruneau 10/29/74
Bruce Cryer 9/30/75
Jeff Knight 7/19/77
Michael Glenn-Smith 1/9/79
Christopher Seppe 3/6/79
Howard Lawrence 12/29/81

Note: As of May 31, 1982, 29 actors had played the role of El Gallo, 26 actresses had played Luisa, and 22 actors had played Matt.

FIFTH OF JULY

New York 11/5/80

Kenneth Talley Jr.   Christopher Reeve
Phillip Clark 3/24/81
Richard Thomas 3/27/81
Michael O'Keefe 9/7/81
Richard Thomas 10/6/81
Timothy Bottoms 11/3/81
Lindsey Ginter 12/1/81
Joseph Bottoms 12/15/81

Gwen Landis   Swoosie Kurtz
Laraine Newman 10/9/81

June Talley   Joyce Roebling
Tanya Berezin
Kathy Bates 10/6/81

Sally Friedman   Mary Carver
Edith Larkin
Ruby Holbrook 10/6/81

Ted Jenkins   Jeff Daniels
John Dossett 7/81

42ND STREET

	New York 8/25/80
Julian Marsh	Jerry Orbach
Dorothy Brock	Tammy Grimes Millicent Martin 10/28/81
Peggy Sawyer	Wanda Richert Nancy Sinclair 10/15/80 Karen Prunczik 10/20/80 Wanda Richert 10/25/80
Billy Lawlor	Lee Roy Reams
Maggie Jones	Carole Cook Peggy Cass 9/81

I CAN'T KEEP RUNNING IN PLACE

	New York 4/14/81
Michelle	Marcia Rodd Jill O'Hara 8/25/81
Beth	Helen Gallagher Catherine Wolf 9/1/81

THE LITTLE FOXES

	New York 5/7/81	#1 New Orleans 9/7/81 #2 London 3/1/82
Regina Giddens	Elizabeth Taylor	#1 Elizabeth Taylor #2 Elizabeth Taylor
Birdie Hubbard	Maureen Stapleton	#1 Maureen Stapleton Sada Thompson 11/24/81 #2 Sada Thompson
Horace Giddens	Tom Aldredge J.D. Cannon 8/31/81	#1 J.D. Cannon #2 J.D. Cannon
Ben Hubbard	Anthony Zerbe Robert Lansing 8/31/81	#1 Robert Lansing #2 Robert Lansing
Oscar Hubbard	Joe Ponazecki Nicholas Coster 8/31/81	#1 Nicholas Coster #2 Nicholas Coster
Leo Hubbard	Dennis Christopher William Youmans 8/31/81	#1 William Youmans #2 William Youmans

MARCH OF THE FALSETTOS

	New York 5/20/81	Los Angeles 4/21/82
Marvin	Michael Rupert	Michael Rupert
Trina	Alison Fraser	Melanie Chertoff
Whizzer Brown	Stephen Bogardus	Stephen Bogardus
Mendel	Chip Zien	Chip Zien

MORNING'S AT SEVEN

	New York 4/10/80	*Boston 9/15/81*
Esther Crampton	Maureen O'Sullivan	Maureen O'Sullivan
Cora Swanson	Teresa Wright Carmen Mathews 7/7/81	Teresa Wright
Ida Bolton	Nancy Marchand Harriet Rogers 11/17/80 Kate Reid 12/14/80	Kate Reid Harriet Rogers 3/23/82
Aaronette Gibbs	Elizabeth Wilson Nancy Kulp 7/7/81	Rosemary Murphy Elizabeth Wilson 12/7/81
David Crampton	Gary Merrill Shepperd Strudwick 4/28/81	Russell Nype
Homer Bolton	David Rounds Robert Moberly 7/7/81	Robert Moberly
Carl Bolton	Richard Hamilton King Donovan 7/7/81	King Donovan
Myrtle Brown	Lois de Banzie Charlotte Moore 7/7/81	Elizabeth Hartman Charlotte Moore 3/23/82
Theodore Swanson	Maurice Copeland	Maurice Copeland

ONE MO' TIME

	New York 10/22/79	*#1 Philadelphia 7/2/80* *#2 London 7/14/81*
Bertha	Sylvia "Kuumba" Williams Carol Woods 7/81	#1 Sandra Reaves-Phillips #2 Sylvia "Kuumba" Williams
Ma Reed	Thais Clark Frozine Jo Thomas 7/81	#1 Jackee Harry #2 Thais Clark
Thelma	Topsy Chapman Peggy Alston 7/81	#1 Deborah Burrell #2 Topsy Chapman
Theatre Owner	John Stell James "Red" Wilcher 7/81	#1 James "Red" Wilcher #2 John Stell
Papa Du	Vernel Bagneris Bruce Strickland 7/80	#1 Vernel Bagneris #2 Vernel Bagneris

THE PIRATES OF PENZANCE

	New York 1/8/81	*#1 Los Angeles 6/3/81* *#2 London 5/26/82*
Pirate King	Kevin Kline Treat Williams 8/25/81 Walter Niehenke 1/12/82 Treat Williams 1/26/82 Gary Sandy 3/23/82	#1 Barry Bostwick Jim Belushi 9/23/81 #2 Tim Curry
Ruth	Estelle Parsons Kaye Ballard 9/15/81	#1 Jo Anne Worley Marsha Bagwell 12/1/81 #2 Annie Ross

Mabel Stanley	Linda Ronstadt	#1 Pam Dawber
	Karla DaVito 6/2/81	Caroline Peyton 9/23/81
	Maureen McGovern 9/8/81	#2 Pamela Stephenson
	Kathryn Morath 2/16/82	
	Maureen McGovern 3/2/82	
Major-General Stanley	George Rose	#1 Clive Revill
	George S. Irving 12/8/81	Leo Leyden 12/1/81
	Joseph Pichette 3/9/82	
	George Rose 3/16/82	#2 George Cole
Frederic	Rex Smith	#1 Andy Gibb
	Robby Benson 7/28/81	Patrick Cassidy 9/23/81
	Patrick Cassidy 1/5/82	Peter Noone 12/1/81
	Rex Smith 4/13/82	#2 Michael Praed
	Patrick Cassidy 4/27/82	
Sergeant	Tony Azito	#1 Paxton Whitehead
	David Garrison 12/8/81	Paul Ainsley 12/1/81
	Tony Azito 3/16/82	Wally Kurth 2/13/82
		Paul Ainsley 3/18/82
		#2 Chris Langham

SOPHISTICATED LADIES

New York 3/1/81	*Los Angeles 1/17/82*
Gregory Hines	Gregory Hines
Maurice Hines 1/5/82	
Judith Jamison	Paula Kelly
Hinton Battle	Hinton Battle
Gary Chapman 1/5/82	
Priscilla Baskerville	Leata Galloway
Phyllis Hyman	DeeDee Bridgewater
P.J. Benjamin	Mark Fotopoulos
Don Correia 3/29/82	
Terri Klausner	Terri Klausner
Donna Drake 1/5/82	
Gregg Burge	Gregg Burge
Michael Scott Gregory 1/5/82	

SUGAR BABIES

New York 10/8/79	*Knoxville 9/16/81*
Ann Miller	Jaye P. Morgan
Helen Gallagher 9/21/81	Mimi Hines
Ann Miller 10/12/81	
Mickey Rooney	Eddie Bracken
Joey Bishop 2/2/81	
Mickey Rooney 3/2/81	
Rip Taylor 6/29/81	
Mickey Rooney 7/8/81	
Rip Taylor 12/17/81	
Mickey Rooney 12/26/81	

Eddie Bracken 5/31/82
Mickey Rooney 6/13/82

Ann Jillian	Toni Kaye
Anita Morris 3/8/80	
Jane Summerhays 11/80	

| Sid Stone | Phil Ford |
| Maxie Furman | |

Michael Allen Davis*

*Mr. Davis was added to the cast 3/2/81.

SWEENEY TODD

	New York 3/1/79	*Wilmington 2/22/82*
Mrs. Lovett	Angela Lansbury	June Havoc
	Marge Redmond 9/3/79	
	Angela Lansbury 9/12/79	
	Dorothy Loudon 3/4/80	
Sweeney Todd	Len Cariou	Ross Petty
	George Hearn 3/4/80	
Anthony Hope	Victor Garber	Spain Logue
	Cris Groenendaal 8/79	
Johanna	Sarah Rice	Melanie Vaughan
	Betsy Joslyn	
Beadle Bamford	Jack Eric Williams	Calvin Remsberg
Beggar Woman	Merle Louise	Carolyn Marlow
Tobias Ragg	Ken Jennings	Steven Jacob
Judge Turpin	Edmund Lyndeck	Robert Ousley

Note: Casts, including replacements, of the London company and the first touring company of *Sweeney Todd* appear on pages 457–8 of *The Best Plays of 1980–81.* These companies ended their runs on Nov. 15, 1980, and Sept. 20, 1981, respectively.

THEY'RE PLAYING OUR SONG

		#1 Chicago 12/1/79
		#2 London 9/20/80
	New York 2/11/79	#3 Wilmington 1/19/81
Vernon Gersch	Robert Klein	#1 Victor Garber
	John Hammil 11/27/79	#2 Tom Conti
	Tony Roberts 12/17/79	Martin Shaw 7/27/81
	John Hammil	Tom Conti 3/82
	Ted Wass 4/7/81	Martin Shaw 6/82
	Victor Garber 8/4/81	#3 John Hammil
		Richard Ryder
Sonia Wolsk	Lucie Arnaz	#1 Ellen Greene
	Stockard Channing 3/6/80	Marsha Skaggs 8/80
	Rhonda Farer 6/1/80	#2 Gemma Craven
	Anita Gillette 9/23/80	Sheila Brand 12/28/81
	Diana Canova 4/7/81	#3 Lorna Luft
	Marsha Skaggs 8/4/81	June Gable
		Dawn Wells 11/29/81

THE WEST SIDE WALTZ

	New York 11/19/81	*Washington 3/17/82*
Margaret Elderdice	Katharine Hepburn	Katharine Hepburn
Cara Varnum	Dorothy Loudon	Dorothy Loudon

WOMAN OF THE YEAR

	New York 3/29/81
Tess Harding	Lauren Bacall
	Raquel Welch 12/1/81
	Lauren Bacall 12/15/81
Sam Craig	Harry Guardino
	Jamie Ross 12/1/81
	Harry Guardino 12/15/81
Jan Donovan	Marilyn Cooper
	Carol Arthur 10/13/81
	Marilyn Cooper 10/20/81

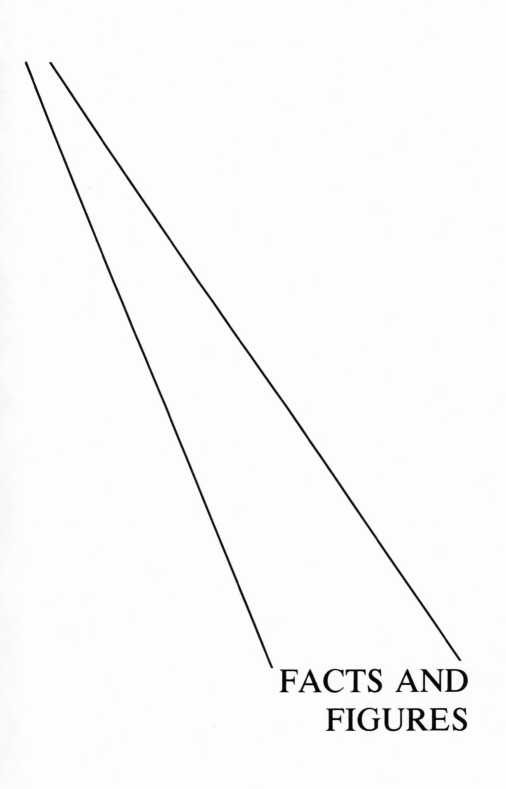

FACTS AND
FIGURES

LONG RUNS ON BROADWAY

The following shows have run 500 or more continuous performances in a single production, usually the first, not including previews or extra non-profit performances, allowing for vacation layoffs and special one-booking engagements, but not including return engagements after a show has gone on tour. In all cases the numbers were obtained directly from the shows' production offices. Where there are title similarities, the production is identified as follows: (p) straight play version, (m) musical version, (r) revival.

THROUGH MAY 31, 1982

(PLAYS MARKED WITH ASTERISK WERE STILL PLAYING JUNE, 1, 1982)

Plays	Number Performances	Plays	Number Performances
Grease.....................	3,388	How To Succeed in Business	
Fiddler on the Roof..........	3,242	Without Really Trying......	1,417
Life With Father.............	3,224	Hellzapoppin	1,404
Tobacco Road	3,182	The Music Man..............	1,375
Hello, Dolly...............	2,844	Funny Girl	1,348
*A Chorus Line.............	2,825	Mummenschanz.............	1,326
My Fair Lady	2,717	Oh! Calcutta!	1,314
*Oh! Calcutta! (r)............	2,391	Angel Street	1,295
Man of La Mancha..........	2,328	Lightnin'...................	1,291
Abie's Irish Rose............	2,327	Promises, Promises	1,281
Oklahoma!	2,212	The King and I	1,246
*Annie	2,129	Cactus Flower	1,234
Pippin.....................	1,944	Sleuth	1,222
South Pacific	1,925	1776.......................	1,217
The Magic Show	1,920	Equus	1,209
*Deathtrap.................	1,809	Guys and Dolls	1,200
Gemini	1,788	Cabaret....................	1,165
Harvey	1,775	Mister Roberts..............	1,157
Hair.......................	1,750	Annie Get Your Gun	1,147
*Dancin'...................	1,742	The Seven Year Itch	1,141
The Wiz	1,672	Butterflies Are Free..........	1,128
Born Yesterday	1,642	*Evita	1,121
Ain't Misbehavin'	1,604	Pins and Needles............	1,108
*The Best Little Whorehouse in		*Sugar Babies...............	1,105
Texas...................	1,577	Plaza Suite	1,097
Mary, Mary................	1,572	They're Playing Our Song	1,082
The Voice of the Turtle	1,557	Kiss Me, Kate	1,070
Barefoot in the Park	1,530	Don't Bother Me, I Can't Cope.	1,065
Mame (m)..................	1,508	The Pajama Game...........	1,063
Same Time, Next Year	1,453	Shenandoah	1,050
Arsenic and Old Lace........	1,444	The Teahouse of the August	
The Sound of Music	1,443	Moon...................	1,027

433

Plays	Number Performances	Plays	Number Performances
Damn Yankees	1,019	The First Year	760
Never Too Late	1,007	You Know I Can't Hear You	
Any Wednesday	982	When the Water's Running	755
A Funny Thing Happened on		Two for the Seesaw	750
the Way to the Forum	964	Death of a Salesman	742
The Odd Couple	964	For Colored Girls, etc.	742
Anna Lucasta	957	Sons o' Fun	742
Kiss and Tell	956	Candide (mr)	740
Dracula (r)	925	Gentlemen Prefer Blondes	740
Bells Are Ringing	924	The Man Who Came to Dinner	739
The Moon Is Blue	924	Call Me Mister	734
Beatlemania	920	West Side Story	732
The Elephant Man	916	*42nd Street	729
Luv	901	High Button Shoes	727
Chicago	898	Finian's Rainbow	725
Applause	896	Claudia	722
Can-Can	892	The Gold Diggers	720
Carousel	890	Jesus Christ Superstar	720
Hats Off to Ice	889	Carnival	719
Fanny	888	The Diary of Anne Frank	717
Children of a Lesser God	887	I Remember Mama	714
Follow the Girls	882	Tea and Sympathy	712
Camelot	873	Junior Miss	710
I Love My Wife	872	Last of the Red Hot Lovers	706
The Bat	867	Company	705
My Sister Eileen	864	Seventh Heaven	704
No, No, Nanette (r)	861	Gypsy (m)	702
Song of Norway	860	The Miracle Worker	700
Chapter Two	857	Da	697
A Streetcar Named Desire	855	The King and I (r)	696
Barnum	854	Cat on a Hot Tin Roof	694
Comedy in Music	849	Li'l Abner	693
Raisin	847	Peg o' My Heart	692
That Championship Season	844	The Children's Hour	691
You Can't Take It With You	837	Purlie	688
La Plume de Ma Tante	835	Dead End	687
Three Men on a Horse	835	The Lion and the Mouse	686
The Subject Was Roses	832	White Cargo	686
Inherit the Wind	806	Dear Ruth	683
No Time for Sergeants	796	East Is West	680
Fiorello!	795	Come Blow Your Horn	677
Where's Charley?	792	The Most Happy Fella	676
The Ladder	789	The Doughgirls	671
Forty Carats	780	The Impossible Years	670
The Prisoner of Second Avenue	780	Irene	670
Oliver	774	Boy Meets Girl	669
Bubbling Brown Sugar	766	Beyond the Fringe	667
State of the Union	765	Who's Afraid of Virginia Woolf?	664

Plays	Number Performances	Plays	Number Performances
Blithe Spirit	657	Show Boat	572
A Trip to Chinatown	657	The Show-Off	571
The Women	657	Sally	570
Bloomer Girl	654	Golden Boy (m)	568
The Fifth Season	654	One Touch of Venus	567
Rain	648	Happy Birthday	564
Witness for the Prosecution	645	Look Homeward, Angel	564
Call Me Madam	644	Morning's at Seven (r)	564
Janie	642	The Glass Menagerie	561
The Green Pastures	640	I Do! I Do!	560
Auntie Mame (p)	639	Wonderful Town	559
A Man for All Seasons	637	Rose Marie	557
The Fourposter	632	Strictly Dishonorable	557
Two Gentlemen of Verona (m)	627	Sweeney Todd, the Demon Barber of Fleet Street	557
The Tenth Man	623	A Majority of One	556
Is Zat So?	618	The Great White Hope	556
Anniversary Waltz	615	Toys in the Attic	556
The Happy Time (p)	614	Sunrise at Campobello	556
Separate Rooms	613	Jamaica	555
Affairs of State	610	Stop the World—I Want to Get Off	555
Star and Garter	609	Florodora	553
The Student Prince	608	Ziegfeld Follies (1943)	553
Sweet Charity	608	Dial "M" for Murder	552
Bye Bye Birdie	607	Good News	551
*Amadeus	605	Peter Pan (r)	551
Irene (r)	604	Let's Face It	547
Broadway	603	Milk and Honey	543
Adonis	603	Within the Law	541
Street Scene (p)	601	The Music Master	540
Kiki	600	Pal Joey (r)	540
Flower Drum Song	600	What Makes Sammy Run?	540
A Little Night Music	600	The Sunshine Boys	538
*The Pirates of Penzance (1980 r)	599	What a Life	538
Don't Drink the Water	598	The Unsinkable Molly Brown	532
Wish You Were Here	598	The Red Mill (r)	531
A Society Circus	596	A Raisin in the Sun	530
Absurd Person Singular	592	Godspell	527
Blossom Time	592	The Solid Gold Cadillac	526
A Day in Hollywood/A Night in the Ukraine	588	Irma La Douce	524
The Me Nobody Knows	586	The Boomerang	522
The Two Mrs. Carrolls	585	Follies	521
Kismet	583	Rosalinda	521
Detective Story	581	*Sophisticated Ladies	521
Brigadoon	581	The Best Man	520
No Strings	580	Chauve-Souris	520
Brother Rat	577	Blackbirds of 1928	518

Plays	Number Performances	Plays	Number Performances
The Gin Game	517	Shuffle Along	504
Sunny	517	Up in Central Park	504
Victoria Regina	517	Carmen Jones	503
The 5th of July	511	The Member of the Wedding	501
Half a Sixpence	511	Panama Hattie	501
The Vagabond King	511	Personal Appearance	501
The New Moon	509	Bird in Hand	500
The World of Suzie Wong	508	Room Service	500
The Rothschilds	507	Sailor, Beware!	500
Sugar	505	Tomorrow the World	500

LONG RUNS OFF BROADWAY

Plays	Number Performances	Plays	Number Performances
*The Fantasticks	9,180	The Pocket Watch	725
The Threepenny Opera	2,611	The Connection	722
Godspell	2,124	The Passion of Dracula	714
Jacques Brel	1,847	Adaptation & Next	707
Vanities	1,785	Oh! Calcutta!	704
You're a Good Man Charlie Brown	1,547	Scuba Duba	692
The Blacks	1,408	The Knack	685
Let My People Come	1,327	The Club	674
The Hot l Baltimore	1,166	The Balcony	672
I'm Getting My Act Together and Taking It on the Road	1,165	America Hurrah	634
Little Mary Sunshine	1,143	Hogan's Goat	607
El Grande de Coca-Cola	1,114	The Trojan Women (r)	600
*One Mo' Time	1,084	Krapp's Last Tape & The Zoo Story	582
One Flew Over the Cuckoo's Nest (r)	1,025	The Dumbwaiter & The Collection	578
The Boys in the Band	1,000	Dames at Sea	575
Your Own Thing	933	The Crucible (r)	571
Curley McDimple	931	The Iceman Cometh (r)	565
Leave It to Jane (r)	928	The Hostage (r)	545
The Mad Show	871	Six Characters in Search of an Author (r)	529
Scrambled Feet	831	The Dirtiest Show in Town	509
The Effect of Gamma Rays on Man-in-the-Moon Marigolds	819	Happy Ending & Day of Absence	504
A View From the Bridge (r)	780	The Boys From Syracuse (r)	500
The Boy Friend (r)	763		

John Woodvine, Roger Rees and Emily Richard in the multiple award-winning *The Life & Adventures of Nicholas Nickleby*

NEW YORK CRITICS AWARDS, 1935–36 to 1981–82

Listed below are the New York Drama Critics Circle Awards from 1935–36 through 1981–82 classified as follows: (1) Best American Play, (2) Best Foreign Play, (3) Best Musical, (4) Best, regardless of category (this category was established by new voting rules in 1962–63 and did not exist prior to that year).

1935–36—(1) Winterset
1936–37—(1) High Tor
1937–38—(1) Of Mice and Men, (2) Shadow and Substance
1938–39—(1) No award, (2) The White Steed
1939–40—(1) The Time of Your Life
1940–41—(1) Watch on the Rhine, (2) The Corn Is Green
1941–42—(1) No award, (2) Blithe Spirit
1942–43—(1) The Patriots
1943–44—(2) Jacobowsky and the Colonel
1944–45—(1) The Glass Menagerie
1945–46—(3) Carousel
1946–47—(1) All My Sons, (2) No Exit, (3) Brigadoon

1947–48—(1) A Streetcar Named Desire, (2) The Winslow Boy
1948–49—(1) Death of a Salesman, (2) The Madwoman of Chaillot, (3) South Pacific
1949–50—(1) The Member of the Wedding (2) The Cocktail Party, (3) The Consul
1950–51—(1) Darkness at Noon, (2) The Lady's Not for Burning, (3) Guys and Dolls
1951–52—(1) I Am a Camera, (2) Venus Observed, (3) Pal Joey (Special citation to Don Juan in Hell)
1952–53—(1) Picnic, (2) The Love of Four Colonels, (3) Wonderful Town
1953–54—(1) Teahouse of the August Moon, (2) Ondine, (3) The Golden Apple

1954–55—(1) Cat on a Hot Tin Roof, (2) Witness for the Prosecution, (3) The Saint of Bleecker Street
1955–56—(1) The Diary of Anne Frank, (2) Tiger at the Gates, (3) My Fair Lady
1956–57—(1) Long Day's Journey Into Night, (2) The Waltz of the Toreadors, (3) The Most Happy Fella
1957–58—(1) Look Homeward, Angel, (2) Look Back in Anger, (3) The Music Man
1958–59—(1) A Raisin in the Sun, (2) The Visit, (3) La Plume de Ma Tante
1959–60—(1) Toys in the Attic, (2) Five Finger Exercise, (3) Fiorello!
1960–61—(1) All the Way Home, (2) A Taste of Honey, (3) Carnival
1961–62—(1) The Night of the Iguana, (2) A Man for All Seasons, (3) How to Succeed in Business Without Really Trying
1962–63—(4) Who's Afraid of Virginia Woolf? (Special citation to Beyond the Fringe)
1963–64—(4) Luther, (3) Hello, Dolly! (Special citation to The Trojan Women)
1964–65—(4) The Subject Was Roses, (3) Fiddler on the Roof
1965–66—(4) The Persecution and Assassination of Marat as Performed by the Inmates of the Asylum of Charenton Under the Direction of the Marquis de Sade, (3) Man of La Mancha
1966–67—(4) The Homecoming, (3) Cabaret
1967–68—(4) Rosencrantz and Guildenstern Are Dead, (3) Your Own Thing
1968–69—(4) The Great White Hope, (3) 1776

1969–70—(4) Borstal Boy, (1) The Effect of Gamma Rays on Man-in-the-Moon Marigolds, (3) Company
1970–71—(4) Home, (1) The House of Blue Leaves, (3) Follies
1971–72—(4) That Championship Season, (2) The Screens, (3) Two Gentlemen of Verona (Special citations to Sticks and Bones and Old Times)
1972–73—(4) The Changing Room, (1) The Hot 1 Baltimore, (3) A Little Night Music
1973–74—(4) The Contractor, (1) Short Eyes, (3) Candide
1974–75—(4) Equus, (1) The Taking of Miss Janie, (3) A Chorus Line
1975–76—(4) Travesties, (1) Streamers, (3) Pacific Overtures
1976–77—(4) Otherwise Engaged, (1) American Buffalo, (3) Annie
1977–78—(4) "Da", (3) Ain't Misbehavin'
1978–79—(4) The Elephant Man, (3) Sweeney Todd, the Demon Barber of Fleet Street
1979–80—(4) Talley's Folly, (2) Betrayal, (3) Evita (Special citation to Peter Brook's Le Centre International de Créations Théâtrales for its repertory)
1980–81—(4) A Lesson From Aloes, (1) Crimes of the Heart (Special citations to Lena Horne: The Lady and Her Music and the New York Shakespeare Festival production of The Pirates of Penzance)
1981–82—(4) The Life & Adventures of Nicholas Nickleby, (1) A Soldier's Play

NEW YORK DRAMA CRITICS CIRCLE VOTING, 1981–82

The New York Drama Critics Circle voted David Edgar's adaptation of Charles Dickens's novel *The Life & Adventures of Nicholas Nickleby* the best play of the season on the first ballot, on which this Royal Shakespeare Company production from England received the necessary majority of 13 first choices among the 23 members of the Circle voting in person or by proxy. First choices on this first ballot were distributed as follows: *Nicholas Nickleby* (13)—John Beaufort, Glenne Currie, Brendan Gill, Ted Kalem, Howard Kissel, Hobe Morrison, Norman Nadel, Don Nelsen, Julius Novick, Edith Oliver, William Raidy, Allan Wallach, Edwin Wilson; *"MASTER HAROLD"* . . . *and the boys* (7)—Mel Gussow, Richard Hummler, Jack Kroll, Frank Rich, John Simon, Marilyn Stasio, Douglas Watt; *Three Acts of Recognition* (1)—Clive Barnes; *Torch Song Trilogy* (1)—Michael Feingold; *A Soldier's Play* (1)—Walter Kerr.

Having named a foreign play best-of-bests, the Circle members then proceeded to vote Charles Fuller's *A Soldier's Play* the best American play of the season on a weighted multiple-choice second ballot, after no play received a majority of first choices on the first ballot. With 3 points given for a critic's first choice, 2 for second and 1 for third, in order to win on this second ballot the Circle's voting rules require a play to receive a point total of three times the number of those voting (17 without the proxies and abstentions) divided by two, plus one, i.e. 27 points. The winning total received by *A Soldier's Play* was 29 (see the record of this ballot following this report) in competition with *Torch Song Trilogy* (25), *The Dining Room* (19), *Grown Ups* (12), *Sister Mary Ignatius Explains It All for You* (6), *The Dance and the Railroad* (3), *Geniuses* (3), *Gardenia* (2), *Eminent Domain* (1), *Lydie Breeze* (1) and *Sally and Marsha* (1).

For the second year in a row, the Circle decided not to give an award for best musical, this year by a vote of 10 to 6 among those present and voting on this question.

SECOND BALLOT FOR BEST AMERICAN PLAY

Critic	*1st Choice (3 pts.)*	*2d Choice (2 pts.)*	*3d Choice (1 pt.)*
Clive Barnes *Post*	A Soldier's Play	The Dining Room	Torch Song Trilogy
John Beaufort *Monitor*	A Soldier's Play	The Dining Room	Geniuses
Glenne Currie *U.P.I.*	The Dance and the Railroad	A Soldier's Play	Sally and Marsha
Michael Feingold *Village Voice*	Torch Song Trilogy	Grown Ups	The Dining Room
Brendan Gill *New Yorker*	A Soldier's Play	Torch Song Trilogy	Sister Mary Ignatius Explains It All For You
Mel Gussow *Times*	Torch Song Trilogy	Gardenia	Eminent Domain
Richard Hummler *Variety*	Grown Ups	Torch Song Trilogy	The Dining Room
Howard Kissel *Women's Wear*	A Soldier's Play	The Dining Room	Grown Ups
Jack Kroll *Newsweek*	Torch Song Trilogy	Sister Mary Ignatius	Lydie Breeze
Don Nelsen *Daily News*	Torch Song Trilogy	A Soldier's Play	The Dining Room
Julius Novick *Village Voice*	The Dining Room	Torch Song Trilogy	A Soldier's Play
Edith Oliver *New Yorker*	A Soldier's Play	The Dining Room	Sister Mary Ignatius
Frank Rich *Times*	Grown Ups	A Soldier's Play	Sister Mary Ignatius
John Simon *New York*	Torch Song Trilogy	Geniuses	A Soldier's Play
Marilyn Stasio *Post*	The Dining Room	Grown Ups	Torch Song Trilogy
Allan Wallach *Newsday*	A Soldier's Play	Torch Song Trilogy	Grown Ups
Edwin Wilson *Wall St. Journal*	A Soldier's Play	The Dining Room	Sister Mary Ignatius

Note: Hobe Morrison *(Variety)* and Norman Nadel (NEA) abstained; proxies of Ted Kalem *(Time),* Walter Kerr *(Times),* William Raidy (Newhouse Papers) and Douglas Watt *(Daily News)* did not specify three choices and were not counted on this ballot.

CHOICES OF SOME OTHER CRITICS

Critic	Best Play	Best Musical
Judith Crist*	Master Harold	Nine
Saturday Review, TV Guide		
John Gambling	Agnes of God	Dreamgirls
WOR Radio		
Katie Kelly	Nicholas Nickleby	Nine
WNBC-TV		
Alvin Klein	Master Harold	Abstain
WNYC Radio, *Times* L.I. Section		
Stewart Klein	Master Harold	Abstain
WNEW-TV		
Joanna Langfield*	The Dresser	Nine
WMCA		
Jeffrey Lyons	The Dresser	Nine
WCBS Radio, Independent Network		
Leida Snow*	Master Harold	Dreamgirls
WINS & ABC Radio		

*Also recommend special recognition of Nicholas Nickleby

PULITZER PRIZE WINNERS, 1916–17 to 1981–82

1916–17—No award
1917–18—Why Marry?, by Jesse Lynch Williams
1918–19—No award
1919–20—Beyond the Horizon, by Eugene O'Neill
1920–21—Miss Lulu Bett, by Zona Gale
1921–22—Anna Christie, by Eugene O'Neill
1922–23—Icebound, by Owen Davis
1923–24—Hell-Bent for Heaven, by Hatcher Hughes
1924–25—They Knew What They Wanted, by Sidney Howard
1925–26—Craig's Wife, by George Kelly
1926–27—In Abraham's Bosom, by Paul Green
1927–28—Strange Interlude, by Eugene O'Neill
1928–29—Street Scene, by Elmer Rice
1929–30—The Green Pastures, by Marc Connelly
1930–31—Alison's House, by Susan Glaspell
1931–32—Of Thee I Sing, by George S. Kaufman, Morrie Ryskind, Ira and George Gershwin
1932–33—Both Your Houses, by Maxwell Anderson

1933–34—Men in White, by Sidney Kingsley
1934–35—The Old Maid, by Zoë Akins
1935–36—Idiot's Delight, by Robert E. Sherwood
1936–37—You Can't Take It With You, by Moss Hart and George S. Kaufman
1937–38—Our Town, by Thornton Wilder
1938–39—Abe Lincoln in Illinois, by Robert E. Sherwood
1939–40—The Time of Your Life, by William Saroyan
1940–41—There Shall Be No Night, by Robert E. Sherwood
1941–42—No award
1942–43—The Skin of Our Teeth, by Thornton Wilder
1943–44—No award
1944–45—Harvey, by Mary Chase
1945–46—State of the Union, by Howard Lindsay and Russel Crouse
1946–47—No award
1947–48—A Streetcar Named Desire, by Tennessee Williams
1948–49—Death of a Salesman, by Arthur Miller

1949–50—South Pacific, by Richard Rodgers, Oscar Hammerstein II and Joshua Logan
1950–51—No Award
1951–52—The Shrike, by Joseph Kramm
1952–53—Picnic, by William Inge
1953–54—The Teahouse of the August Moon, by John Patrick
1954–55—Cat on a Hot Tin Roof, by Tennessee Williams
1955–56—The Diary of Anne Frank, by Frances Goodrich and Albert Hackett
1956–57—Long Day's Journey Into Night, by Eugene O'Neill
1957–58—Look Homeward, Angel, by Ketti Frings
1958–59—J.B., by Archibald MacLeish
1959–60—Fiorello!, by Jerome Weidman, George Abbott, Sheldon Harnick and Jerry Bock
1960–61—All the Way Home, by Tad Mosel
1961–62—How to Succeed in Business Without Really Trying, by Abe Burrows, Willie Gilbert, Jack Weinstock and Frank Loesser
1962–63—No award
1963–64—No award
1964–65—The Subject Was Roses, by Frank D. Gilroy
1965–66—No award
1966–67—A Delicate Balance, by Edward Albee
1967–68—No award
1968–69—The Great White Hope, by Howard Sackler
1969–70—No Place To Be Somebody, by Charles Gordone
1970–71—The Effect of Gamma Rays on Man-in-the-Moon Marigolds, by Paul Zindel
1971–72—No award
1972–73—That Championship Season, by Jason Miller
1973–74—No award
1974–75—Seascape, by Edward Albee
1975–76—A Chorus Line, by Michael Bennett, James Kirkwood, Nicholas Dante, Marvin Hamlisch and Edward Kleban
1976–77—The Shadow Box, by Michael Cristofer
1977–78—The Gin Game, by D.L. Coburn
1978–79—Buried Child, by Sam Shepard
1979–80—Talley's Folly, by Lanford Wilson
1980–81—Crimes of the Heart, by Beth Henley
1981–82—A Soldier's Play, by Charles Fuller

THE TONY AWARDS, 1981–82

The Antoinette Perry (Tony) Awards are voted by members of the League of New York Theaters and Producers, the governing bodies of the Dramatists Guild, Actors' Equity, the American Theater Wing, the Society of Stage Directors and Choreographers, the United Scenic Artists Union and members of the first-night and second-night press, from a list of four nominees in each category.

The four nominations in each category (Broadway shows only; off Broadway excluded) are made by a committee of critics whose personnel changes annually at the invitation of the abovementioned League, which administers the Tony Awards under an agreement with the American Theater Wing. The 1981–82 Nominating Committee was composed of Schuyler Chapin of Columbia University, Richard Coe, critic emeritus of the Washington *Post,* Miriam Colon, president and founder of the Puerto Rican Traveling Theater, Anna E. Crouse of Theater Development Fund, Brendan Gill of *The New Yorker,* William Glover, former theater critic for the Associated Press, Henry Hewes of the American Theater Critics Association, Mary C. Henderson, curator of the theater collection of the Museum of the City of New York, Norris Houghton, author, director, producer and former president of the National Theater Conference, Kevin Kelly of the Boston *Globe,* Elliot Norton of the Boston *Herald American,* Seymour Peck of the New York *Times* and Jay Sharbutt of the Associated Press.

The list of 1981–82 nominees follows, with winners in each category listed in **bold face type.**

BEST PLAY (award goes to both producer and author). *Crimes of the Heart* by Beth Henley, produced by Warner Theater Productions, Inc., Claire Nichtern, Mary Lea Johnson, Martin Richards and Francine LeFrak; *The Dresser* by Ronald Harwood, produced by James M. Nederlander, Elizabeth I. McCann, Nelle Nugent, Warner Theater Productions, Inc. and Michael Codron; *"MASTER HAROLD" . . . and the boys* by Athol Fugard, produced by The Shubert Organization, Freydberg/Bloch Productions, Dasha Epstein, Emanuel Azenberg and David Geffen; **The Life & Adventures of Nicholas Nickleby by David Edgar,** produced by **James M. Nederlander, The Shubert Organization, Elizabeth I. McCann and Nelle Nugent.**

BEST MUSICAL (award to producers). *Dreamgirls* produced by Michael Bennett, Bob Avian, Geffen Records and The Shubert Organization; *Joseph and the Amazing Technicolor Dreamcoat* produced by Zev Bufman, Susan R. Rose, Melvyn J. Estrin, Sidney Shlenker and Gail Berman; **Nine** produced by **Michel Stuart, Harvey J. Klaris, Roger S. Berlind, James M. Nederlander, Francine LeFrak and Kenneth D. Greenblatt;** *Pump Boys and Dinettes* produced by Dodger Productions, Louis Busch Hager, Marilyn Strauss, Kate Studley, Warner Theater Productions, Inc. and Max Weitzenhoffer.

BEST BOOK OF A MUSICAL. **Dreamgirls by Tom Eyen;** *Joseph and the Amazing Technicolor Dreamcoat* by Tim Rice; *Nine* by Arthur Kopit; *The First* by Joel Siegel and Martin Charnin.

BEST SCORE OF A MUSICAL. *Dreamgirls,* music by Henry Krieger, lyrics by Tom Eyen; *Joseph and the Amazing Technicolor Dreamcoat,* music by Andrew Lloyd Webber, lyrics by Tim Rice; *Merrily We Roll Along,* music and lyrics by Stephen Sondheim; **Nine,** music and lyrics by **Maury Yeston.**

OUTSTANDING ACTOR IN A PLAY. Tom Courtenay in *The Dresser,* Milo O'Shea in *Mass Appeal,* Christopher Plummer in *Othello,* **Roger Rees** in *Nicholas Nickleby.*

OUTSTANDING ACTRESS IN A PLAY. **Zoe Caldwell** in *Medea,* Katharine Hepburn in *The West Side Waltz,* Geraldine Page in *Agnes of God,* Amanda Plummer in *A Taste of Honey.*

OUTSTANDING ACTOR IN A MUSICAL. Herschel Bernardi in *Fiddler on the Roof,* Victor Garber in *Little Me,* **Ben Harney** in *Dreamgirls,* Raul Julia in *Nine.*

OUTSTANDING ACTRESS IN A MUSICAL. **Jennifer Holliday** in *Dreamgirls,* Lisa Mordente in *Marlowe,* Mary Gordon Murray in *Little Me,* Sheryl Lee Ralph in *Dreamgirls.*

OUTSTANDING FEATURED ACTOR IN A PLAY. Richard Kavanaugh in *The Hothouse,* **Zakes Mokae** in *Master Harold,* Edward Petherbridge in *Nicholas Nickleby,* David Threlfall in *Nicholas Nickleby.*

OUTSTANDING FEATURED ACTRESS IN A PLAY. Judith Anderson in *Medea,* Mia Dillon in *Crimes of the Heart,* Mary Beth Hurt in *Crimes of the Heart,* **Amanda Plummer** in *Agnes of God.*

OUTSTANDING FEATURED ACTOR IN A MUSICAL. Obba Babatunde in *Dreamgirls,* **Cleavant Derricks** in *Dreamgirls,* David Alan Grier in *The First,* Bill Hutton in *Joseph and the Amazing Technicolor Dreamcoat.*

OUTSTANDING FEATURED ACTRESS IN A MUSICAL. Karen Akers in *Nine,* Laurie Beechman in *Joseph and the Amazing Technicolor Dreamcoat,* **Liliane Montevecchi** in *Nine,* Anita Morris in *Nine.*

OUTSTANDING DIRECTION OF A PLAY. Melvin Bernhardt for *Crimes of the Heart,* Geraldine Fitzgerald for *Mass Appeal,* Athol Fugard for *Master Harold,* **Trevor Nunn and John Caird** for *Nicholas Nickleby.*

OUTSTANDING DIRECTION OF A MUSICAL. Michael Bennett for *Dreamgirls,* Martin Charnin for *The First,* Tony Tanner for *Joseph and the Amazing Technicolor Dreamcoat,* **Tommy Tune** for *Nine.*

OUTSTANDING SCENIC DESIGN. Ben Edwards for *Medea,* Lawrence Miller for *Nine,* **John Napier and Dermot Hayes** for *Nicholas Nickleby,* Robin Wagner for *Dreamgirls.*

OUTSTANDING COSTUME DESIGN. Theoni V. Aldredge for *Dreamgirls,* Jane Greenwood for *Medea,* **William Ivey Long** for *Nine,* John Napier for *Nicholas Nickleby.*

OUTSTANDING LIGHTING DESIGN. Martin Aronstein for *Medea,* David Hersey for *Nich-*

CRIMES OF THE HEART—Mia Dillon, Lizbeth Mackay and Mary Beth Hurt in *Crimes of the Heart*, a Best Play in OOB production last season, transferred to Broadway this season for a long run and multiple Tony citations for script and performances

olas Nickleby, Marcia Madeira for *Nine,* **Tharon Musser** for *Dreamgirls.*

OUTSTANDING CHOREOGRAPHY. **Michael Bennett** and **Michael Peters** for *Dreamgirls,* Peter Gennaro for *Little Me,* Tony Tanner for *Joseph and the Amazing Technicolor Dreamcoat,* Tommy Tune for *Nine.*

OUTSTANDING REPRODUCTION OF A PLAY OR MUSICAL. *A Taste of Honey* produced by Roundabout Theater Company, Inc., Gene Feist and Michael Fried; *Medea* produced by Barry and Fran Weissler, Kennedy Center, Bunny and Warren Austin; *My Fair Lady* produced by Mike Merrick and Don Gregory; *Othello* produced by **Barry and Fran Weissler** and **CBS Video Enterprises.**

SPECIAL TONY AWARDS. **The Guthrie Theater,** Minneapolis, Minnesota; **The Actors' Fund of America**; Theater Award '82 to **Warner Communications, Inc.** and **Radio City Music Hall.**

TONY AWARD WINNERS, 1947–1982

Listed below are the Antoinette Perry (Tony) Award winners in the categories of Best Play and Best Musical from the time these awards were established (1947) until the present.

1947—No play or musical award
1948—Mister Roberts; no musical award
1949—Death of a Salesman; Kiss Me, Kate
1950—The Cocktail Party; South Pacific
1951—The Rose Tattoo; Guys and Dolls
1952—The Fourposter; The King and I
1953—The Crucible; Wonderful Town
1954—The Teahouse of the August Moon; Kismet
1955—The Desperate Hours; The Pajama Game
1956—The Diary of Anne Frank; Damn Yankees
1957—Long Day's Journey Into Night; My Fair Lady
1958—Sunrise at Campobello; The Music Man
1959—J.B.; Redhead
1960—The Miracle Worker; Fiorello! and The Sound of Music (tie)
1961—Becket; Bye Bye Birdie
1962—A Man for All Seasons; How to Succeed in Business Without Really Trying
1963—Who's Afraid of Virginia Woolf?; A Funny Thing Happened on the Way to the Forum
1964—Luther; Hello, Dolly!
1965—The Subject Was Roses; Fiddler on the Roof

1966—The Persecution and Assassination of Marat as Performed by the Inmates of the Asylum of Charenton Under the Direction of the Marquis de Sade; Man of La Mancha
1967—The Homecoming; Cabaret
1968—Rosencrantz and Guildenstern Are Dead; Hallelujah, Baby!
1969—The Great White Hope; 1776
1970—Borstal Boy; Applause
1971—Sleuth; Company
1972—Sticks and Bones; Two Gentlemen of Verona
1973—That Championship Season; A Little Night Music
1974—The River Niger; Raisin
1975—Equus; The Wiz
1976—Travesties; A Chorus Line
1977—The Shadow Box; Annie
1978—Da; Ain't Misbehavin'
1979—The Elephant Man; Sweeney Todd, the Demon Barber of Fleet Street
1980—Children of a Lesser God; Evita
1981—Amadeus; 42nd Street
1982—The Life & Adventures of Nicholas Nickleby; Nine

THE OBIE AWARDS, 1981–82

The *Village Voice* Off-Broadway (Obie) Awards are given each year for excellence in various categories of off-Broadway—and frequently off-off-Broadway —shows, as close distinctions between these two areas are ignored in Obie Award-giving. The Obies are voted by a committee of *Village Voice* critics and others, which this year was made up of Eileen Blumenthal, Gus Edwards, Michael Feingold, Richard Gilman, Erika Munk, Julius Novick and Ross Wetzsteon.

BEST THEATER PIECE. **Wielopole Wielopole** by Tadeusz Kantor.

BEST NEW AMERICAN PLAY (tie). **Mr. Dead and Mrs. Free** by Squat and **A Metamorphosis in Miniature** by Martha Clarke, Linda Hunt, David Rounds, Jeff Wanshel, Noa Ain and Penny Stegenga.

SUSTAINED ACHIEVEMENT. **Maria Irene Fornes** "for the wit, imagination and social outrage she has brought to off Broadway for 20 years."

PLAYWRITING. **Caryl Churchill** for *Cloud 9*, **Robert Auletta** for *Virgins* and *Stops*.

DIRECTION: **Tommy Tune** for *Cloud 9*.

PERFORMANCE: **Kevin Bacon** in *Forty Deuce* and *Poor Little Lambs*, **James Barbosa** in *Soon Jack November*, **Ray Dooley** in *Peer Gynt*, **Christine Estabrook** in *Pastorale*, **Michael Gross** in *No End of Blame*, **E. Katherine Kerr** in *Cloud 9*, **Kenneth McMillan** in *Weekends Like Other People*, **Kevin O'Connor** in *Chucky's Hunch, Birdbath* and *Crossing the Crab Nebula*, **Carole Shelley** in *Twelve Dreams*, **Josef Sommer** in *Lydie Breeze*, **Irene Worth** in *The Chalk Garden*.

ENSEMBLE PERFORMANCE. **Adolph Caesar, Larry Riley** and **Denzel Washington** in *A*

Soldier's Play; **Lisa Banes, Brenda Currin, Beverly May** and **Elizabeth McGovern** in *My Sister in This House.*

DESIGN: **Jim Clayburgh,** sustained excellence in set design; **Arden Fingerhut,** sustained excel-lence in lighting design.

SPECIAL CITATIONS. **Harvey Fierstein** for *Torch Song Trilogy;* **Theater Communications Group; LaMama ETC 20th Anniversary Celebration.**

ADDITIONAL PRIZES AND AWARDS, 1981–82

The following is a list of major prizes and awards for achievement in the theater this season. In all cases the names of winners appear in **bold face type.**

MARGO JONES AWARD. For the producer and producing organization whose continuing policy of producing new theater works has made an outstanding contribution to the encouragement of new playwrights. 1981 Award (given in May 1982): **Lynne Meadow** and the **Manhattan Theater Club.** (1982 Award to be given in December 1982.)

1982 JOSEPH MAHARAM FOUNDATION AWARDS. For distinguished theatrical design for original New York productions (selected by a committee comprising Tish Dace, Mel Gussow, Henry Hewes and Edward F. Kook). Scenery: **David Chapman** for *The First,* **Edward T. Gianfrancesco** for *Big Apple Messenger* and *Little Shop of Horrors.* Costumes: **William Ivey Long** for *Nine.* Lighting: **Tharon Musser** for *Dreamgirls.* Special citation: **John Napier, Dermot Hayes** and **David Hersey** for their designs of *The Life & Adventures of Nicholas Nickleby,* executed in New York with Neil Peter Jampolis and Beverly Emmons.

Citations—Scenery: John Arnone and Gerald Marks for *Dark Ride,* Jim Clayburgh for *My Sister in This House,* Karl Eigsti for *Joseph and the Amazing Technicolor Dreamcoat,* David Gropman for *Family Devotions,* Chris Hardman for *Vacuum,* Andrew Jackness for *Beyond Therapy* and *Geniuses,* Ron Kajiwara for *The Dispossessed,* Eugene Lee for *The Hothouse,* Santo Loquasto for *Gardenia,* Loren Sherman for *The Dining Room,* Dean Tschetter for *Goose and Tomtom,* Robin Wagner for *Dreamgirls,* John Wulp for *Lydie Breeze.*

Citations—Costumes: Theoni V. Aldredge for *Dreamgirls,* Gabriel Berry for *Secret Lives of the Sexists,* Michael Kirby for *Prisoners of the Invisible Kingdom,* Martin P. Robinson for *Little Shop of Horrors,* Tadashi Suzuki and Suzanne Elder for *The Bacchae,* Bill Taylor for *In the Cage.*

Citations—Lighting: Frances Aronson for *The Dining Room,* Pat Collins for *How I Got That Story,* Beverly Emmons for *The Dresser,* James F. Ingalls (with Esquire Jauchem and Gregory Meek) for *Geniuses,* Marcia Madeira for *Nine,* Craig Miller for *Gardenia,* Bruce Porter for *Dark Ride,* Marc B. Weiss for *The First,* Marshall Williams for *Boy and Tarzan Appear in a Clearing* and Christopher Martin for his total design of *The Golem, Ghost Sonata* and *Peer Gynt.*

38th ANNUAL THEATER WORLD AWARDS. For outstanding new talent in Broadway and off-Broadway productions during the 1981–82 season (selected by a committee comprising Clive Barnes, Douglas Watt and John Willis). **Karen Akers** in *Nine,* **Laurie Beechman** in *Joseph and the Amazing Technicolor Dreamcoat,* **Danny Glover** in *"MASTER HAROLD" . . . and the boys,* **David Alan Grier** in *The First,* **Jennifer Holliday** in *Dreamgirls,* **Anthony Heald** in *Misalliance,* **Lizbeth Mackay** and **Peter MacNicol** in *Crimes of the Heart,* **Elizabeth McGovern** in *My Sister in This House,* **Ann Morrison** in *Merrily We Roll Along,* **Michael O'Keefe** in *Mass Appeal,* **James Widdoes** in *Is There Life After High School?* Special Theater World Award to the **Manhattan Theater Club** for its ten years of discovering and encouraging new talent.

1982 ROSAMUND GILDER AWARD. For outstanding creative achievement in the theater (selected by a committee of the New Drama Forum). **Robyn Goodman** and **Carole Rothman,** directors of The Second Stage.

CLARENCE DERWENT AWARDS. For the most promising male and female actors on the metropolitan scene during the 1981–82 season. **Joanne Camp** in *Geniuses* and **Larry Riley** in *A Soldier's Play* and *Maybe I'm Doing It Wrong.*

GEORGE JEAN NATHAN AWARD. For drama criticism. **Carolyn Clay** and **Sylviane Gold** of the Boston *Phoenix.*

2d ANNUAL JOHN F. WHARTON THEATER AWARD. For creative contributions to the producing of theater. **John Houseman.**

ELIZABETH HULL-KATE WARRINER AWARD. To the playwright whose work dealt with controversial subjects involving the fields of political, religious or social mores of the time (selected by the Dramatists Guild Council). 1980–81 season: **Shirley Lauro** for *Open Admissions.*

2d ANNUAL RICHARD L. COE AWARD. For an individual who has contributed to the development of original material for the theater. **Audrey Wood.**

5th ANNUAL JAMES N. VAUGHAN MEMORIAL AWARD. For exceptional achievement or development and growth of professional theater, presented by the Shubert Foundation. **Yale Repertory Theater-School of Drama.**

OUTER CRITICS CIRCLE AWARDS. For distinguished achievement in the New York theater season, voted by critics of foreign and out-of-town periodicals. Play: **"MASTER HAROLD"—and the boys.** Musical: **Nine.** Actors: **Zakes Mokae** in *Master Harold* and **Milo O'Shea** in *Mass Appeal.* Actress: **Amanda Plummer** for *Agnes of God* and *A Taste of Honey.* Off-Broadway Play: **A Soldier's Play.** Direction: **Athol Fugard** for *Master Harold.* Revival: **The Chalk Garden.** Debut Performances: **Matthew Broderick** in *Torch Song Trilogy* and **Lizbeth Mackay** in *Crimes of the Heart.* John Gassner Playwriting Award: **Bill C. Davis** for *Mass Appeal.* Book: **Paul Rudnick** for *Poor Little Lambs.* Off-off-Broadway Company: **The Second Stage.** Special Citation: **The Life & Adventures of Nicholas Nickleby.**

DRAMA DESK AWARDS. For outstanding achievement, voted by an association of New York drama reporters, editors and critics. Play: **"MASTER HAROLD" . . . and the boys** by Athol Fugard. Musical: **Nine.** Direction: **Tommy Tune** for *Cloud 9.* Actor in a play: **Christopher Plummer** in *Othello.* Actress in a play: **Zoe Caldwell** in *Medea.* Actress in a musical: **Jennifer Holliday** in *Dreamgirls.* Featured actor in

a play: **Adolph Caesar** in *A Soldier's Play* and **Zeljko Ivanek** in *Cloud 9* (tie). Featured actress in a play: **Amanda Plummer** in *Agnes of God.* Featured actor in a musical: **Cleavant Derricks** in *Dreamgirls.* Featured actress in a musical: **Liliane Montevecchi** and **Anita Morris** (tie) in *Nine.* Musical score: **Maury Yeston** for *Nine. Lyrics:* **Maury Yeston** for *Nine* and **Stephen Sondheim** for *Merrily We Roll Along* (tie). Scenery: **Robin Wagner** for *Dreamgirls.* Costumes: **William Ivey Long** for *Nine.* Lighting: **Marcia Madeira** for *Nine* and **Tharon Musser** for *Dreamgirls* (tie). Unique theatrical experience: **Whistler** with **John Cullum.** Revival: **Entertaining Mr. Sloane.** Special awards: **The Life & Adventures of Nicholas Nickleby; Jonathan Tunick; The Ridiculous Theatrical Company.**

48th ANNUAL DRAMA LEAGUE AWARD. Delia Austrian Medal for distinguished performing. **Milo O'Shea** in *Mass Appeal.*

9th ANNUAL JOSEPH JEFFERSON AWARDS. For outstanding work in Chicago Theater. Production of a play: **Balm in Gilead** by Steppenwolf. Production of a musical: **Follies** by Candlelight Dinner Playhouse. Director of a play: **John Malkovich** for *Balm in Gilead.* Director of a musical: **David H. Bell** for *Man of La Mancha.* Principal actor in a play: **Jack McLaughlin-Gray** in *How I Got That Story.* Principal actress in a play: **Laurie Metcalf** in *Balm in Gilead.* Principal actor in a musical: **Walter Hook** in *South Pacific.* Principal actress in a musical: **Loida Santos** in *Bye Bye Birdie.* Supporting actor in a play: **Nicholas Rudall** in *Juno and the Paycock.* Supporting actress in a play: **Glenne Headley** in *Balm in Gilead.* Supporting actor in a musical: **James Sudik** in *South Pacific.* Cameo actor: **James Deuter** in *Bent.* Cameo actress: **Debra Engle** in *Balm in Gilead.* Choreography: **David H. Bell** for *South Pacific.* Costumes: **Adrianne Lobel** for *Play Mas.* Lighting: **Kevin Rigdon** for *Balm in Gilead.* Scenery: **Michael Merritt** for *Mother Courage.* Original incidental music: **Joseph Reiser** for *Mother Courage.* Principal actor in a revue: **Bruce Jarchow** of Second City. Principal actress in a revue: **Mary Gross** of Second City. Director of a revue: **Del Close** of Second City. Ensemble: **Balm in Gilead.**

1981–1982 PUBLICATION
OF RECENTLY-PRODUCED PLAYS

Beyond Therapy. Christopher Durang. Nelson Doubleday.
Children of a Lesser God. Mark Medoff. James T. White. (Also paperback).
Class Enemy. Nigel Williams. Methuen. (paperback).
Division Street and Other Plays. Steve Tesich. Performing Arts Journal (paperback).
Dresser, The. Ronald Harwood. Grove Press (paperback).
Floating Light Bulb, The. Woody Allen. Random House.
Fools. Neil Simon. Random House.
Joseph and the Amazing Technicolor Dreamcoat. Tim Rice and Andrew Lloyd Webber. Novello
 (paperback).
Lakeboat. David Mamet. Grove Press. (Also paperback).
Lunch Hour. Jean Kerr. Doubleday.
Maggie & Pierre. Linda Griffiths with Paul Thompson. Talonbooks (paperback).
Merrily We Roll Along. Book by George Furth, music and lyrics by Stephen Sondheim, based on the
 play by George S. Kaufman and Moss Hart. Dodd, Mead.
Mister Lincoln. Herbert Mitgang. Southern Illinois University Press.
My Blue Heaven. Jane Chambers. JH Press (paperback).
No End of Blame: Scenes of Overcoming. Howard Baker. Riverrun Press/John Clader. (paperback).
No Limits to Love. David Mercer. Methuen (paperback).
Station J. Richard France. Irvington Press.
Summer. Edward Bond. Methuen (paperback).
Torch Song Trilogy. Harvey Fierstein. Gay Presses (paperback).
Translations. Brian Friel. Faber & Faber (paperback).
West Side Waltz, The. Ernest Thompson. Dodd, Mead.
Woolgatherer, The. William Mastrosimone. Nelson Doubleday.

A SELECTED LIST OF OTHER PLAYS
PUBLISHED IN 1981–1982

After the Fall: Final Stage Version. Arthur Miller, Penguin (paperback).
Anatol. Arthur Schnitzler. Methuen (paperback).
Anthology of Austrian Drama, An. Editor, Douglas A. Russell. Fairleigh Dickinson University Press.
Bacchae, The. Euripides. Mentior/New American Library (paperback).
By Popular Demand: Plays and Other Works by the San Francisco Mime Troupe. San Francisco Mime
 Troupe (paperback).
Collected Works of Maxim Gorky: Volume IV—Plays. Imported Publications.
Complete Plays of Aristophanes, The. Bantam Classics (paperback).
Complete Works of Christopher Marlowe: Second Edition, The. Cambridge University Press. Volumes
 One and Two.
Complete Works of Sophocles, The. Bantam Classics (paperback).
Coward: Plays—One. Grove Press (paperback).
Coward: Plays—Two. Grove Press (paperback).
Coward: Plays—Three. Grove Press (paperback).
Coward: Plays—Four. Grove Press (paperback).
Edward Albee: The Plays—Volume One. Coward, McCann & Geoghegan (paperback).
Edward Albee: The Plays—Volume Two. Atheneum (paperback).
Feydeau, First to Last: Eight One-Act Comedies. Cornell University Press.

Eight Plays by Henrik Ibsen. Modern Library College Editions (paperback).
Five Major Plays by Anton Chekhov. Bantam Classics (paperback).
Four Great Plays by Henrik Ibsen. Bantam Classics (paperback).
Greatest Revue Sketches, The. Editor, Donald Oliver. Avon (paperback).
King Richard III: Arden Shakespeare Edition. Editor, Antony Hammond. Methuen (Also in paperback).
Month in the Country, A. Ivan Turgenev. New translation by Isaiah Berlin. Viking Press.
Much Ado About Nothing: The Arden Shakespeare. Editor, A.R. Humphreys. Methuen (paperback).
Nine Plays of the Modern Theater. Editor, Harold Clurman. Grove Press (paperback).
Oresteia, The. Aeschylus. Bantam Classics (paperback).
Plain Dealer, The. Willian Wycherley. W.W. Norton (paperback).
Plays of David Garrick, The. Volume One: Garrick's Own Plays 1740–1766). Southern Illinois University Press.
Plays of William Wycherley, The. Cambridge University Press (Also paperback).
Rivals, The: New Mermaid Edition. Richard Brinsley Sheridan. W.W. Norton (paperback).
Seven Plays. Sam Shepard. Bantam (paperback).
Striptease/Tango/Vatzlav. J.M. Synge. Methuen (paperback).
Taming of the Shrew, The: The Arden Shakespeare. Editor, Brian Morris. Methuen (Also paperback).
Ten Plays by Euripides. Bantam Classics (paperback).
Theater of Tennessee Williams, The: Volume 6. New Directions.
Three Pieces. Ntozake Shangé. St. Martin's Press.
Three Plays. Joyce Carol Oates. Ontario Review Press (Also paperback).
Three Plays by D.H. Lawrence. Penguin (paperback).
Three Plays by Oscar Wilde. Methuen (paperback).
Three Sanskrit Plays. Translator, Michael Coulson (paperback).
Twilight Dinner, The, and Other Plays. Lennox Brown. Talonbooks (paperback)

MUSICAL AND DRAMATIC RECORDINGS OF NEW YORK SHOWS

Title and publishing company are listed below. Each record is an original cast album unless otherwise indicated. An asterisk (*) indicates recording is also available on cassettes. Two asterisks (**) indicate it is available on eight-track cartridges.

Aladdin. Stet.
Baker's Wife, The. Take Home.
Carmelina. Original.
Christy (1975). Original.
Dreamgirls. Geffen. (*).
Evening With W.S. Gilbert, An. (1980). Original.
Flowers for Algeron. Original.
Housewives' Cantata, The. OC.
In Trousers (1979). Original.
Joseph and the Amazing Technicolor Dreamcoat. Chrysallis.
Ka-Boom. CYM.
King of Hearts. CYM. (*).
Little Me. New release by RCA. (*).
March of the Falsettos. DRG. (*).
Marry Me a Little. RCA. (*).
Merrily We Roll Along. RCA. (*).
Nefertiti. Take Home.

Opening Nights: Volumes I and II. RCA. (*)
Piano Bar. Original.
Second Shepherd's Play. Broadway.
So Long, 174th Street. Original.
Tintypes. (2 records). DRG. (*).
Utter Glory of Morrissey Hall, The. Original.
Your Arms Too Short to Box With God. MCA.

NECROLOGY

MAY 1981–MAY 1982

PERFORMERS

Abbott, Betty (80)—September 11, 1981
Able, Will B. (57)—November 18, 1981
Abraham, Clara Gaiser Linder (92)—August 17, 1981
Acton, Wallace (76)—September 2, 1981
Adam, Alfred—May 7, 1982
Albertson, Jack (74)—November 24, 1981
Alson, Julia (41)—Spring 1982
Anders, Glenn (92)—October 26, 1981
Andrews, Ellen (65)—May 22, 1982
Arthur, Maxine Arnold—October 26, 1981
Asther, Nils (84)—October 13, 1981
Badel, Alan (58)—March 19, 1982
Baker, Sam (56)—May 6, 1982
Baltzell, Deborah (25)—October 24, 1981
Barnes, Charles H.—August 26, 1981
Bayer, Lenny (37)—April 12, 1982
Beaumont, Hugh (72)—May 3, 1982
Becker, Emma Sampson (85)—August 11, 1981
Bell, Brian (36)—February 10, 1982
Belushi, John (33)—March 5, 1982
Benet, Brenda (36)—April 7, 1982
Bishop, Ronald (59)—May 21, 1982
Blackwell, George C. Jr. (56)—September 13, 1981
Bledsoe, George (62)—May 12, 1982
Bond, Rudy (68)—March 29, 1982
Bordner, Cecil (70)—September 8, 1981
Brasselle, Keefe (58)—July 7, 1981
Braun, Martha (54)—May 3, 1982
Brennan, David (90)—May 17, 1982
Breslaw, Joseph (95)—March 5, 1982
Broadwell, Mary Etta (78)—September 8, 1981
Brown, Joseph (59)—April 9, 1982
Brown, Keith (30)—November 10, 1981
Bruce, Virginia (72)—February 24, 1982
Bruck, Bella (70)—April 5, 1982
Bryant, Thomas C. Jr. (51)—January 3, 1982
Buono, Victor (43)—January 1, 1982
Bussieres, Raymond (75)—April 29, 1982
Calve, Olga (82)—May 12, 1982
Carver, Tina (58)—February 18, 1982
Castner, Alan (42)—April 24, 1982
Cavanaugh, James (69)—September 30, 1981
Charles, Leon (66)—August 14, 1981

Clarke, William K. (70)—June 20, 1981
Clements, Stanley (55)—October 16, 1981
Coate, Margie (83)—May 23, 1982
Coleman, Isabel Catherine (75)—April 27, 1982
Collyer, Marian Shockley—December 14, 1981
Conliss, Edward B. (80)—August 3, 1981
Conreid, Hans (66)—January 5, 1982
Conway, Morgan (81)—November 16, 1981
Cooper, Dulcie (77)—September 3, 1981
Corbett, Harry H. (57)—March 21, 1982
Courtney, Dan (87)—April 30, 1982
Cover, Billy (65)—May 12, 1981
Crane, Jean Dale (70)—October 6, 1981
Dantine, Helmut (63)—May 2, 1982
de Bathe, Count Popo (81)—September 2, 1981
De Kova, Frank (71)—October 19, 1981
Desdevises, Madeleine (15)—April 16, 1982
Devereaux, C.R. (51)—February 13, 1982
Devi, Ragini (86)—January 23, 1982
Diamond, Daniel (52)—November 28, 1981
Dix, Constance (60)—February 1, 1982
Donahue, William Francis (86)—May 21, 1981
Donat, Sandra (47)—October 3, 1981
Doubrovska, Celia (85)—September 18, 1981
Doucet, Rober (62)—July 20, 1981
Douglas, Melvyn (80)—August 4, 1981
Doyle, Brenda (48)—November 12, 1981
Drayton, Noel (68)—December 7, 1981
Duke, Paul (86)—June 27, 1981
Durante, Marcy C. (71)—March 12, 1982
Eberly, Bob (65)—November 17, 1981
Edwards, G.H. (74)—July 19, 1981
Edwards, Joan (61)—August 27, 1981
Eldridge, Peggy Fewel—December 2, 1981
Faversham, Philip (75)—April 20, 1982
Fitzgerald, Edward (89)—March 22, 1982
Flynn, Irving (79)—January 17, 1982
Ford, Helen—January 19, 1982
Fried, Sylvia (53)—December 12, 1981
Fyodorova, Zoya (68)—December 11, 1981
Garralaga, Martin (86)—June 12, 1981
Gary, Thelma Connor (75)—October 30, 1981
George, Chief Dan (82)—September 23, 1981
Goldberg, Meyer (64)—November 30, 1981
Gorin, Igor (72)—March 24, 1982

Graham, Olive Brown (68)—May 9, 1982
Grahame, Gloria (55)—October 5, 1981
Granger, Michael (58)—October 22, 1981
Green, Cyrus (47)—March 23, 1982
Greene, Stanley N. (70)—July 4, 1981
Gresser, William (85)—May 6, 1982
Haden, Sara (82)—September 15, 1981
Hale, Richard (88)—May 18, 1981
Hall, Ella (85)—September 3, 1981
Hammond, Kay (80)—January 7, 1982
Hampton, Hope (84)—January 23, 1982
Harding, Ann (79)—September 1, 1981
Harmon, John (50s)—January 2, 1982
Harris, Robert H. (72)—November 30, 1981
Harrison, Paul (66)—January 16, 1982
Hassalevris, Constantine (68)—March 7, 1982
Hayden, Russel (70)—June 10, 1981
Hays, Lee (67)—August 26, 1981
Heming, Violet (86)—July 4, 1981
Henry, Pat (58)—February 18, 1982
Herman, Harry (68)—November 24, 1981
Hessel, Edith Bell (58)—December 16, 1981
Higgenbotham, Robert (48)—January 22, 1982
Hill, Fern Barry (71)—September 9, 1981
Hilt, Ferdinand H. (61)—September 4, 1981
Holden, William (63)—November 16, 1981
Holland, Edna (86)—May 4, 1982
Holloway, Stanley (91)—January 30, 1982
Hopkins, Sam (69)—January 30, 1982
Hough, Joe (69?)—May 26, 1982
Howard, Richard (91)—Winter 1982
Hoxie, Al (80)—April 6, 1982
Humes, Helen (68)—September 9, 1981
Hurwitz, Abraham B. (76)—September 30, 1981
Jacobson, Andrew (46)—December 18, 1981
Jackson, Larry (64)—October 10, 1981
Jamieson, Richard (38)—April 15, 1982
Johnson, Bobby (71)—April 30, 1982
Johnson, Celia (73)—April 25, 1982
Johnson, Dan (38)—April 21, 1982
Johnson, Foster (64)—October 30, 1981
Johnson, Robert (61)—January 3, 1982
Jones, Al (72)—February 17, 1982
Jory, Victor (79)—February 11, 1982
Julian, Joseph (71)—March 11, 1982
Kahalewai, M. Haunani (53)—March 2, 1982
Kaiman, Lambert H. (77)—July 7, 1981
Kalima, Willard A. (57)—May 20, 1981
Keane, Robert Emmett (96)—July 2, 1981
Keene, Patricia (34)—December 9, 1981
Keiser, Margaret (76)—March 18, 1982
Kelly, Patsy (71)—September 24, 1981
Kendall, L. Kenn (72)—May 12, 1982
Kenny, James (57)—April 17, 1982
Kertman, Betty—December 18, 1981
Kinch, Myra (77)—November 20, 1981

Kirkland, Monroe (73)—April 17, 1982
Kokic, Kazimir—February 5, 1982
Korn, Iris (about 60)—January 27, 1982
Kosta, Tessa (83)—August 23, 1981
Kovacs, Mary (80)—August 24, 1981
Lacey, Lois Lindsey (65)—April 21, 1982
Ladd, Sue Carol (72)—February 4, 1982
Landver-Davison, Rose (79)—November 28, 1981
Lane, Lola (75)—June 22, 1981
Lawrence, Reginald (64)—August 27, 1981
Lawrence, Stacy (54)—March 5, 1982
Lehman, Trent Lawson (20)—January 18, 1982
Lehmann-Haupt, Miriam (76)—August 3, 1981
Lembeck, Harvey (58)—January 5, 1982
Lenn, Robert (62)—January 15, 1982
Lenya, Lotte (83)—November 27, 1981
Lerario, Helen (61)—October 18, 1981
Lewis, Adah (83)—May 30, 1981
Lewis, Barbara Burns—September 24, 1981
Lewis, Harry—August 9, 1981
Lobato, Nelida (47)—Spring 1982
London, Jack (57)—November 13, 1981
Lopokova, Lydia (88)—June 8, 1981
Lupenui, Muriel K. (80)—June 18, 1981
Lyles, John D. (53)—September 28, 1981
Lynde, Paul (55)—January 11, 1982
Markey, Enid (91)—November 15, 1981
Markham, Dewey (77)—December 13, 1981
Marleaux, Mimi (66)—February 5, 1982
Marlowe, Hugh (71)—May 2, 1981
Martin, Ian (69)—July 25, 1981
Martin, Ross (61)—July 3, 1981
Matthews, Jessie (74)—August 20, 1981
Maule, Donovan (82)—Winter 1982
Maurice, Bobby (75)—October 17, 1981
Maxwell, Jenny (30)—June 10, 1981
May, Bobby (74)—November 7, 1981
McCullough, Philo (87)—June 5, 1981
McGraw, Sylvia (65)—September 25, 1981
McHugh, Frank (33)—September 11, 1981
McWilliams, Ralph (55)—June 23, 1981
Memminger, Robert B. (76)—September 23, 1981
Miller, Ruth (78)—June 13, 1981
Mitchell, Duke (55)—December 2, 1981
Montgomery, Robert (77)—September 27, 1981
Moran, Dolores (56)—February 5, 1982
Nazarro, Nat Jr. (78)—April 14, 1982
Negas, Christos (46)—June 21, 1981
Nelson, Dolph (68)—December 7, 1981
Nicholson, Nick (62)—February 11, 1982
Nobriga, Ted (70)—June 5, 1981
Nofer, Ferd (81)—April 14, 1982

Oates, Warren (52)—April 3, 1982
O'Brien, Adrian (73)—February 14, 1982
Oken, Jacob (52)—August 14, 1981
O'Rourke, Michael (73)—November 22, 1981
Pallay, Fran (77)—November 6, 1981
Palmer, Maria (57)—September 6, 1981
Pascal, Jean (54)—April 15, 1982
Patrick, Nigel (63)—September 21, 1981
Paxton, Frank (76)—May 1982
Peirce, Dorothy (70s)—June 18, 1981
Pell, Peter (50)—July 27, 1981
Philips, Edwin (69)—July 26, 1981
Phillips, Eddie (54)—February 28, 1982
Polk, Vernon C. (55)—August 22, 1981
Powell, Eleanor (69)—February 11, 1982
Power, L. Carleton (66)—June 29, 1981
Priore, Vincent J.—December 18, 1981
Provol, Nathan (100)—February 11, 1982
Pursell, Robert (26)—January 19, 1982
Quinn, Eunice (76)—October 30, 1981
Raymond, Dorothy—October 26, 1981
Rayner, Sydney (86)—September 14, 1981
Reader, Ralph (78)—May 13, 1982
Rhoden, Elmer C. (88)—July 14, 1981
Richards, Ann—April 1, 1982
Richards, Dan (39)—October 4, 1981
Richardson, Tony (56)—April 26, 1982
Rochelle, Claire (70s)—May 23, 1981
Romero, Enrico (54)—October 28, 1981
Rosinski, Joseph P. (53)—February 24, 1982
Ross, Glenn (27)—September 24, 1981
Rossini, Luigi (84)—February 3, 1982
Roth, Virginia Carville (87)—February 18, 1982
Rutherford, Cecil—June 10, 1981
Ryan, Harriet—May 31, 1981
Salerno, George (62)—February 24, 1982
Saroya, Blanca—July 30, 1981
Sawyer, Joe (75)—April 21, 1982
Schneider, Romy (43)—May 29, 1981
Scott, Hazel (61)—October 2, 1981
Scott, Henry (59)—April 22, 1981
Scott, Marc (44)—July 1, 1981
Shafer, Robert K.—June 19, 1981
Shaw, Leon—Summer 1981
Shaw, Reta (69)—January 8, 1982
Shaw, Wini (72)—May 2, 1982
Shdanoff, Elsa Schreiber (81)—January 9, 1982
Sheffield, Rollin (50)—January 18, 1982
Sheldon, Gene (75)—May 1, 1982
Sheriff, Ernest J. (88)—May 22, 1981
Shimoda, Yuki (59)—May 21, 1981
Sigrist, Lori (21)—December 9, 1981
Smith, Kevin H. (73)—March 14, 1982
Smith, Loring B. (91)—July 8, 1981
Smith, Ralph (57)—December 10, 1981

Sothern, Georgia (68)—October 14, 1981
Spadaro, Umberto (77)—October 11, 1981
Stalker, Bill—November 29, 1981
Stanley, Aileen (89)—March 24, 1982
Steele, Marjorie Blair (68)—October 13, 1981
Stewart, Robert (77)—August 15, 1981
Stone, Lillian (76)—July 1, 1981
Strunk, Jud (45)—October 5, 1981
Sullivan, Lee (70)—May 29, 1981
Tannen, Louis (73)—March 24, 1982
Temkin, Jeffrey (35)—Winter 1982
Thomas, Hugh (61)—June 27, 1981
Thomson, Archibald Melick (80)—September 22, 1981
Topper, Sidney (69)—June 2, 1981
Tremain, Barbara (86)—March 18, 1982
Tully, Tomy (85)—April 27, 1982
Velie, Jay (89)—April 22, 1982
Vestoff, Virginia (42)—May 2, 1982
Vera-Ellen (55)—August 30, 1981
Von Elm, Billie Breneman (79)—October 22, 1981
von Zell, Harry (75)—November 22, 1981
Voskovec, George (76)—July 1, 1981
Waddy, Henrietta (79)—August 10, 1981
Wahlstedt, John (89)—October 11, 1981
Wallis, MaLu (70)—Fall 1981
Warburton, John (78)—October 27, 1981
Ward, Marie (83)—February 18, 1982
Ward, Penelope Dudley (67)—January 21, 1982
Warner, Jack (85)—May 24, 1981
Watson, Milton (79)—January 2, 1982
West, Dave LeRoy (60)—Summer 1981
White, Louis—August 1, 1981
Wilborn, Dave (78)—April 25, 1982
Williams, Al (72)—June 30, 1981
Williams, David (61)—March 13, 1982
Wilson, Don (81)—April 25, 1982
Wilson, Helene (83)—July 29, 1981
Wilson, Louise Hunter (80)—September 13, 1981
Wood, Natalie (43)—November 29, 1981
Wright, Ned (55)—September 27, 1981
Yatir, Nisan (78)—February 17, 1982
Zacchini, Edmondo (87)—October 13, 1981
Zwerling, Yetta (93)—January 17, 1982

CONDUCTORS

Barrett, Stevenson L.—March 5, 1982
Block, Ray (79)—March 29, 1982
Boehm, Karl (87)—August 14, 1981
Camp, Byrne (41)—December 12, 1981
Carazo, Castro (86)—December 28, 1981
Fox, Roy (89)—March 22, 1982

Holmes, Herbie—December 1, 1981
King, Bernie (70)—July 4, 1981
Krueger, John H. (59)—June 13, 1981
Lucas, Clyde (80)—January 15, 1982
Neel, Boyd (76)—September 30, 1981
Osborne, Will (75)—October 22, 1981
Pelletier, Wilfrid (85)—April 9, 1982
Prince, Graham (77)—August 1, 1981
Rhul, Warney (69)—November 21, 1981
Vyner, Louis (73)—October 21, 1981

PLAYWRIGHTS

Ace, Goodman (83)—March 18, 1982
Arout, Gabriel (73)—February 12, 1982
Bell, Bobby (61)—February 28, 1982
Benchley, Nathaniel (66)—December 14, 1981
Block, Arthur J. (65)—October 17, 1981
Chase, Mary Coyle (74)—October 20, 1981
Chayesfsky, Paddy (58)—August 1, 1981
Child, Nellise (79)—June 11, 1981
Cohen, Albert (87)—October 17, 1981
Colin, Constance (84)—March 12, 1982
De Laiglesia, Alvaro (59)—August 2, 1981
de Sola Pool, Tamar (90)—June 1, 1981
Dolan, Harry (53)—September 7, 1981
Fox, Fred (78)—August 27, 1981
Gerstad, John (57)—December 1, 1981
Gielgud, Val (81)—November 30, 1981
Gostanian, Joseph Ara (41)—July 9, 1981
Greggs, Herbert Dana (49)—October 13, 1981
Gruenberg, Axel (79)—December 19, 1981
Haskell, Henry Cummings (79)—July 21, 1981
Holm, John Cecil (76)—October 24, 1981
Johnson, Pamela Hansford (69)—June 18, 1981
Jones, Elwyn (59)—May 19, 1982
Kalisky, Rene (50)—June 1981
Kharitonov, Yevgeny (40)—June 29, 1981
Levin, Meyer (75)—July 9, 1981
Loos, Anita (93)—August 18, 1981
MacLeish, Archibald (89)—April 20, 1982
Morris, Phillis (88)—February 9, 1982
O'Connor, P.J. (59)—November 26, 1981
Patterson, Tom (70)—May 3, 1982
Peman, Jose Maria (84)—July 19, 1981
Perec, Georges (45)—March 3, 1982
Romero, Ramon (74)—July 3, 1981
Ross, George (74)—February 8, 1982
Saidy, Fred M. (75)—May 14, 1982
Schaefer, Walter Erich (80)—December 28, 1981
Shabtai, Ya'akov (47)—August 5, 1981
Shevelove, Burt (66)—April 8, 1982
Taylor, Cecil P. (53)—December 10, 1981
Vos, David (41)—November 17, 1981
Weiss, Peter (65)—May 9, 1982

COMPOSERS/LYRICISTS

Aubin, Tony (73)—September 21, 1981
Barrett-Ayres, Reginald (61)—Summer 1981
Beaumont, Robert (32)—March 15, 1982
Bennett, Robert Russell (87)—August 18, 1981
Boral, Rai Chand (79)—Winter 1982
Carmichael, Hoagy (82)—December 27, 1981
Chapin, Harry (38)—July 16, 1981
Cheslock, Louis (82)—July 19, 1981
Coolidge, Peggy Stuart (67)—May 7, 1981
Coslow, Sam (79)—April 2, 1982
Crooker, Earl (82)—January 9, 1982
Diamond, Ora May—August 29, 1981
Dimey, Bernard (50)—July 1, 1981
Dostal, Nico (85)—October 27, 1981
Franklin, Malvin M. (91)—July 9, 1981
Gershwin, Arthur (81)—November 20, 1981
Gillette, Leland J. (68)—August 20, 1981
Gordon, Kelly (48)—August 1, 1981
Guion, David Wendell (88)—October 17, 1981
Harrison, Tommy (70s)—September 11, 1981
Hasquenoph, Pierre (59)—March 30, 1982
Hawk, James Leonard (77)—August 27, 1981
Hudson, Will (73)—July 27, 1981
Kay, Hershy (62)—December 2, 1981
Lasher, Leonard (40)—April 1, 1982
Leclere, Irwin (90)—September 29, 1981
Ledrut, Jean (79)—April 18, 1982
Orff, Carl (86)—March 29, 1982
Rossellini, Renzo (74)—May 14, 1982
Sauvage, Camille (71)—October 30, 1981
Searle, Humphrey (66)—May 12, 1982
Seelen, Jerry (69)—September 12, 1981
Skinner, Wilbur A. (75)—March 8, 1982
Suessdorf, Karl (70)—February 25, 1982
Warren, Harry (87)—September 22, 1981
Weiner, Lazar (84)—January 10, 1982

CRITICS

Andorn, Sidney (76)—September 25, 1981
Aston, Frank (85)—May 17, 1982
Berenson, Sam (77)—September 2, 1981
Brady, John R.P. (77)—February 4, 1982
Crisler, Benjamin (77)—May 16, 1982
Frankenstein, Alfred (74)—June 22, 1981
Gosling, Nigel (73)—May 21, 1982
Hale, Wanda (80)—May 24, 1982
Holliday, Kate (64)—June 3, 1981
Humphries, Clem (82)—Winter 1982
Jenom, William (68)—Spring 1982
Joseph, John (83?)—June 16, 1981
Keen, Eleanor (75)—September 26, 1981
Lawrence, Robert (69)—August 9, 1981

Nichols, Lewis (78)—April 29, 1982
Petrucci, Antonio (74)—September 1, 1981
Probst, Leonard (60)—March 19, 1982
Rhodes, Barbara (58)—October 22, 1981
Seaman, Julian (86)—April 1, 1982
Swerdlin, Nathan (75)—June 9, 1981
Wachner, Audrey Kearns (75)—May 25, 1981
Wilson, Arthur (101)—April 24, 1982

DESIGNERS

Battersby, Martin (68)—April 3, 1982
Delano, Irene—February 4, 1982
Enoch, Vernon (59)—November 4, 1981
Harrison, Wallace K. (86)—December 2, 1981
Head, Edith (82)—October 24, 1981
Lissum, Simon (81)—May 10, 1981
Sassi, Marusia Toumanoff—March 13, 1982

MUSICIANS

Aitken, Webster (72)—May 11, 1981
Allsop, Brian (23)—September 25, 1981
Amidon, Harry C. (85)—February 10, 1982
Baum, Carlton U. (73)—Febrary 22, 1982
Broste, Terry Dale (37)—November 23, 1981
Buffington, James (59)—July 20, 1981
Burke, James F. (58)—June 26, 1981
Butts, Ashton (68)—September 24, 1981
Chertok, Pearl (63)—July 31, 1981
Church, Charles F. Jr. (77)—August 24, 1981
Coleman, Bill (77)—August 24, 1981
Coyle, Marion J. (84)—May 23, 1981
Cron, William E. (70)—April 14, 1982
Davidson, Jim (77)—April 9, 1982
Davis, Leroy Buddy (51)—September 4, 1981
Del Regno, Ugo (84)—June 14, 1981
Debra, James J. Jr. (46)—July 11, 1981
Dougherty, William (81)—March 20, 1982
Erwin, Pee Wee (68)—June 20, 1981
Floyd, Chick (76)—October 31, 1981
Foley, Madeline (59)—February 2, 1982
Fortune, Betty (81)—Fall 1981
Gainsborg, Lolita Cabrera (85)—May 23, 1981
George, Catty (54)—May 1982
Glass, Henry (101)—June 25, 1981
Glow, Bernie (56)—May 8, 1982
Gold, Leona Wolson (71)—March 28, 1982
Greer, William Alexander (78)—March 23, 1982
Horton, Walter (64)—December 8, 1981
Johnson, Floyd H. (59)—June 28, 1981
Kaplan, Rosalind—April 13, 1982
Kell, Reginald (75)—August 5, 1981

Kellem, Ted (69)—March 25, 1982
Lanoix, August (79)—November 17, 1981
Leiendecker, William (73)—April 17, 1982
Lewis, Herb (73)—January 13, 1982
Lewis, Walter (88)—September 14, 1981
Lippus, Ervin F. (71)—September 20, 1981
Maeric, Eduardo (28)—March 12, 1982
Major, Lester B. (100)—October 18, 1981
Marlowe, Sylvia (73)—December 10, 1981
Mayo, Walter L. (83)—April 10, 1982
McEachern, Murray (67)—April 28, 1982
Metcalf, Louis (76)—October 27, 1981
Minor, Brian Morris (42)—September 1, 1981
Monk, Thelonious (64)—February 17, 1982
Montgomery, William (60)—May 20, 1982
Moore, Oscar (64)—October 8, 1981
Morey, John Rushton (32)—July 1, 1981
Mosley, Lawrence Leo (71)—July 21, 1981
Murphy, Harry (51)—July 5, 1981
Musso, Vido (68)—January 9, 1982
Neves, Paul (51)—October 2, 1981
Nuzzi, Nicolas (91)—December 22, 1981
Petrillo, Clement C. (67)—March 15, 1982
Pettiford, Ira (66)—June 13, 1981
Pineapple, Johnny K. (74)—June 13, 1981
Piper, Eddie (60)—October 12, 1981
Poulain, Dean (27)—January 3, 1982
Primrose, William (77)—May 2, 1982
Ptashne, Theodore (72)—May 19, 1982
Resener, Edward C. (85)—July 2, 1981
Rhoads, Randall (35)—March 19, 1982
Rothschild, Dorothy (44)—December 18, 1981
Rowe, Vern (59)—September 4, 1981
Rucci, Dominic M. (70)—January 17, 1982
Rudman, Albert (71)—April 28, 1982
Shaw, Elijah (83)—December 11, 1981
Stein, Emmanuel (68)—August 11, 1981
Stoiowski, Luisa M. (92)—March 4, 1982
Smith, Floyd G. (65)—March 29, 1982
Spivak, Charlie (77)—March 1, 1982
Thomas, Walter (74)—August 26, 1981
Thompson, Wilber H. (75)—October 21, 1981
Tjader, Cal (56)—May 5, 1982
Turk, Tommy (54)—August 4, 1981
Vogel, Adolph (88)—July 29, 1981
Weinberg, Herman (87)—February 1, 1982
Weintraub, Stefan (84)—September 1, 1981
William Anna K. (90)—August 25, 1981
Williams, Mary Lou (71)—May 28, 1981

PRODUCERS, DIRECTORS CHOREOGRAPHERS

Abramson, Charles—May 15, 1982
Barton, Charles T. (79)—December 5, 1981
Burke, Melville (97)—March 22, 1982

Callow, Reggie (80)—August 5, 1981
Camus, Marcel (69)—January 13, 1982
Carter, David (54)—November 16, 1981
Caton, Edward (96)—December 21, 1981
Dwan, Allan (96)—December 21, 1981
Factor, Alan Jay (56)—February 4, 1982
Feldkamp, Fred (67)—December 7, 1981
Greenwald, Phil (63)—January 18, 1982
Hanna, Arthur (75)—November 17, 1981
Harrison, Raymond (64)—July 27, 1981
Hatfield, Jack (80)—March 6, 1982
Hennessy, John J. (67)—January 24, 1982
Herget, Robert (56)—June 3, 1981
Ireland, Oscar Dale (53)—July 30, 1981
Liebman, Max (78)—July 21, 1981
Knight, Albert J. (72)—May 25, 1981
Lynn, Robert (64)—Winter 1982
May, Anita (71)—Summer 1981
Meister, Philip (56)—April 3, 1982
Michaelis, Diana Tead (56)—December 16, 1981
Michaels, Louis I. (79)—November 28, 1981
Patrick, Leonard (66)—October 1, 1981
Petrie, Robert E. (58)—January 1, 1982
Present, Jack (84)—August 1, 1981
Riskin, Everett (86)—March 27, 1982
Rollins, Leighton (80)—June 28, 1981
Rollo, Joe (73)—March 10, 1982
Rubber, Violla (70)—June 10, 1981
Santell, Alfred Allen (86)—June 19, 1981
Shelley, David (65)—April 8, 1982
Iff, Iris (58)—January 13, 1982
Sillman, Leonard (72)—January 23, 1982
Sloan, Mike (60)—October 19, 1981
Smith, Milton (91)—November 4, 1981
Stanley, Leonard (60)—December 9, 1981
Stark, Art (65)—April 23, 1982
Starr, Irving (76)—January 17, 1982
Strasberg, Lee (80)—February 17, 1982
Todisco, George (30)—February 2, 1982
Townsend, Irving J. (61)—December 17, 1981
Woods, Gene W. (54)—February 13, 1982

OTHERS

Anderson, Robert H. (62)—March 10, 1982
  Theater manager, Philadelphia
Andrews, Emmett (47)—November 26, 1981
  Photographer
Barr, Alfred Hamilton Jr. (79)—August 16, 1981
  Modern Art Museum
Barskin, Revin (71)—February 10, 1982
  Agent
Baxter, Frank C. (85)—January 18, 1982
  Professor of Shakespeare

Beard, Harry (73)—September 5, 1981
  Agent
Becker, Murray (58)—March 10, 1982
  Personal manager
Berger, Ruth (65)—October 16, 1981
  Booking agent
Blackstone, Dorothy (79)—February 20, 1982
  Personal manager
Bloch, Susan (42)—May 10, 1982
  Press agent
Boni, Albert (88)—July 31, 1981
  Publisher
Brewington, Walter Lewis (76)—January 25, 1982
  Attorney
Burke, George (50)—June 15, 1981
  Personal manager
Carlin, Alexis (87)—July 3, 1981
  Member, ATPAM
Carver, Lorena (95)—August 20, 1981
  Animal trainer
Clark, Mrs. Roscoe (89)—June 16, 1981
  Memphis Opera Theater
Comora, Sanford (60)—September 5, 1981
  Agent
Corley, Edwin R. (57)—November 7, 1981
  Advertising executive
Cort, Alaine Joseph (53)—February 24, 1982
  Editor
Cozzens, Dorothy Pitt (71)—June 1, 1981
  Educator
Cuneo, Fred (81)—May 25, 1981
  Company manager
Dempsey, Jack (86)—March 1, 1982
  Vaudeville agent
Dodge, Marshall (45)—January 28, 1982
  Maine humorist
Dunaway, John—November 30, 1981
  Otto Preminger's secretary
Edwards, Elenore (89)—June 22, 1981
  Hairdresser
Ellis, Martin B. (74)—August 28, 1981
  Allied Jewish Appeal
Fairburn, Evonne (57)—April 16, 1982
  Theater Authority West
Faris, Marvin L. (67)—September 9, 1981
  Association of Talent Agents
Ferrara, Anthony G. (63)—June 4, 1981
  Starlight Theater, Kansas City
Fishbein, Frieda (95)—September 6, 1981
  Agent
Foley, Thomas John (33)—November 18, 1981
  Agent
Forbes, Hazel (67)—November 29, 1981
  Press agent
Fox, Carol (55)—July 21, 1981
  Lyric Opera of Chicago

Frazer, Bernard J. (86)—June 25, 1981
Drama coach
Goldman, Joseph (73)—August 9, 1981
Theater manager
Goodkind, Karen Rose (74)—July 27, 1981
Agent
Gordon, Ann (65)—November 17, 1981
Press agent
Gore, Sonia (93)—September 23, 1981
Patron of opera
Graziadei, Ercole (81)—December 28, 1981
Attorney
Greenway, G. Lauder (77)—June 22, 1981
Metropolitan Opera Ass'n
Grossman, Joseph (78)—June 18, 1981
Company manager
Hamilton, Sara (89)—December 18, 1981
Editor
Hamlet (14)—January 20, 1982
Resident cat, Algonquin Hotel
Handlesman, Samuel (80)—September 3, 1981
Company manager
Hanshue, Jean Meredith (62)—November 14,
1981
Press agent
Harwan, Eva Walgus (84)—June 4, 1981
Theater owner
Hennessy, Rev. David (69)—March 25, 1982
Circus chaplain
Herford, Julius (80)—September 27, 1981
Music educator
Hessel, Paul R. (34)—March 22, 1982
Attorney
Hinson, Marie Rahner (94)—March 24, 1982
Costumer
Hirschhorn, Joseph (82)—August 31, 1981
Arts patron
Hollerith, Helen McVey (52)—October 9, 1981
Shubert Foundation
Johnson, Albert H. (76)—August 29, 1981
Carpenter
Joseph, Bertram Leon (66)—September 3, 1981
Authority on Shakespeare
Kalcheim, Jack (70s)—October 3, 1981
Agent
Katz, Henry (70s)—October 29, 1981
Attorney
Kaye, Frances (62)—November 3, 1981
Press agent
Kelem, Leslie K. (27)—April 6, 1982
Music copyist
Kieran, John (89)—December 9, 1981
Information Please panelist
Kingham, Warren (58)—January 26, 1982
William Morris Agency
Krause, Alvina (88)—December 13, 1981
Acting teacher

Krintzman, Donald J. (34)—November 10,
1981
Joffrey Ballet
Krugman, Saul John (63)—October 21, 1981
Agent
Landry, Paul B. (64)—August 1, 1981
Actors Equity benefits
Lane, Charlotte Lewis (69)—March 2, 1982
Monomoy Theater
Lane, Christopher (73)—March 3, 1982
Monomoy Theater
Lawrence, Stanley H. (59)—January 12,
1982
Nixon make-up expert
LeMunyon, Kenneth (69)—August 14, 1981
Theater party booker
Leone, Mary Sullivan (76)—March 20, 1982
Mama Leone's restaurant
Leppien, William (59)—July 7, 1981
Portrayed Uncle Sam
Levee, Sidney M. (78)—December 2, 1981
Agent
Lindsay, Harold W. (72)—April 1, 1982
Audio technology
Lyons, Mae (65)—August 2, 1981
Press agent
Marks, Paul (52)—September 15, 1981
Managing Director, ASCAP
Marsh, Ngaio (82)—February 18, 1982
Mystery writer
Martin, Victor (61)—September 6, 1981
Doorman
Mayers, Bertram A. (76)—August 24, 1981
Attorney
McNab, Horace Greeley (68)—November 23,
1981
Press agent
Mersand, Dr. Joseph (74)—October 19, 1981
Educator
Messenger, Lillie (81)—October 27, 1981
Agent
Michaels, Dewey (83)—February 21, 1982
Burlesque house owner
Mnich, William R. (55)—December 18, 1981
Southern Theater
O'Conner, Walter G. (82)—March 11, 1982
Ticket sellers union
Okun, Henry (79)—May 23, 1982
Press agent
Olesen, Oscar E. (65)—December 6, 1981
General manager
O'Rourke, James (76)—July 19, 1981
Press agent
Osterman, Judith (50s)—March 8, 1982
Agent
Paul, Art (66)—May 4, 1981
Source for gags, jokes

Peltz, Mary Ellen (85)—October 24, 1981
  Editor
Perry, Lou (74?)—August 12, 1981
  Personal manager
Petting, Arden A. (55)—March 30, 1982
  Stage manager
Pincus, George (78)—December 27, 1981
  Music publisher
Powers, Dorothy May (68)—March 10, 1982
  Civic Symphony of Boston
Rhodes, Julian (77)—October 18, 1981
  Boston night clubs
Robertson, Alec (89)—January 18, 1982
  Editor
Rogers, Louis E. (52)—June 3, 1981
  Fontainbleau Hotel
Schaded, Maurice (51)—September 24, 1981
  Company manager
Schoenfeld, Edward (79)—December 31, 1981
  Rabbi, Actor's Temple
Selznick, Joyce (53)—September 17, 1981
  Personal manager
Serreau, Genevieve (66)—October 1, 1981
  Theater historian
Shapiro, Simon (71)—Summer 1981
  Treasurer
Shiffrin, Bill (71)—March 12, 1982
  Agent
Siegel, Al (82)—July 25, 1981
  Voice coach
Silverman, Rose Linchuk (67)—July 23, 1981
  Dave Shore's restaurant
Skinner, Edith Warman—July 25, 1981
  Speech coach
Sobol, Harry (76)—June 13, 1981
  Press agent

Stark, Herman (86)—July 7, 1981
  Cotton Clubs
Stauffer, Oscar S. (96)—February 23, 1982
  Editor
Steinberg, Jeffrey (34)—June 1, 1981
  Editor
Stern, Francis E. (88)—August 14, 1981
  Columbia Records distributor
Sumner, Marnel (53)—February 7, 1982
  Stage manager
Turchen, Abe (66)—January 7, 1982
  Promoter
Underhill, Charles (46)—October 24, 1981
  Talent agent
Wald, Harry (72)—November 25, 1981
  Burlesque operator
Waterbury, Ruth (89)—March 23, 1982
  Editor
Weatherly, Tom (83)—May 12, 1982
  Press agent
Weaver, Frederick S. (69)—April 1, 1982
  Press agent
Whitney, John Hay (77)—February 8, 1982
  Publisher, *Herald Tribune*
Williams, Ned E. (84)—August 6, 1981
  Press agent
Witken, Benjamin—March 25, 1982
  Theater manager
Wood, Lee B. (88)—February 7, 1982
  Editor
Woodward, Margie C. (53)—November 25,
  1981
  Press agent
Zito, James M. (56)—September 1981
  Shakespearean scholar

THE BEST PLAYS, 1894–1981

Listed in alphabetical order below are all those works selected as Best Plays in previous volumes in the *Best Plays* series. Opposite each title is given the volume in which the play appears, its opening date and its total number of performances. Those plays marked with an asterisk (*) were still playing on June 1, 1982 and their number of performances was figured through May 31, 1982. Adaptors and translators are indicated by (ad) and (tr), the symbols (b), (m) and (l) stand for the author of the book, music and lyrics in the cast of musicals and (c) signifies the credit for the show's conception.

NOTE: A season-by-season listing, rather than an alphabetical one, of the 500 Best Plays in the first 50 volumes, starting with the yearbook for the season of 1919–1920, appears in *The Best Plays of 1968–69*.

PLAY	VOLUME	OPENED	PERFS
ABE LINCOLN IN ILLINOIS—Robert E. Sherwood	38–39.	.Oct. 15, 1938. .	472
ABRAHAM LINCOLN—John Drinkwater	19–20.	.Dec. 15, 1919. .	193
ACCENT ON YOUTH—Samson Raphaelson	34–35.	.Dec. 25, 1934. .	229
ADAM AND EVA—Guy Bolton, George Middleton	19–20.	.Sept. 13, 1919. .	312
ADAPTATION—Elaine May; and NEXT—Terrence McNally	68–69.	.Feb. 10, 1969. .	707
AFFAIRS OF STATE—Louis Verneuil	50–51.	.Sept. 25, 1950. .	610
AFTER THE FALL—Arthur Miller	63–64.	.Jan. 23, 1964. .	208
AFTER THE RAIN—John Bowen	67–68.	.Oct. 9, 1967. .	64
AH, WILDERNESS!—Eugene O'Neill	33–34.	.Oct. 2, 1933. .	289
AIN'T SUPPOSED TO DIE A NATURAL DEATH—(b, m, l) Melvin Van Peebles	71–72.	.Oct. 7, 1971. .	325
ALIEN CORN—Sidney Howard	32–33.	.Feb. 20, 1933. .	98
ALISON'S HOUSE—Susan Glaspell	30–31.	.Dec. 1, 1930. .	41
ALL MY SONS—Arthur Miller	46–47.	.Jan. 29, 1947. .	328
ALL OVER TOWN—Murray Schisgal	74–75.	.Dec. 12, 1974. .	233
ALL THE WAY HOME—Tad Mosel, based on James Agee's novel *A Death in the Family*	60–61.	.Nov. 30, 1960. .	333
ALLEGRO—(b,l) Oscar Hammerstein II, (m) Richard Rodgers	47–48.	.Oct. 10, 1947. .	315
*AMADEUS—Peter Shaffer	80–81.	.Dec. 17, 1981. .	605
AMBUSH—Arthur Richman	21–22.	.Oct. 10, 1921. .	98
AMERICA HURRAH—Jean-Claude van Itallie	66–67.	.Nov. 6, 1966. .	634
AMERICAN BUFFALO—David Mamet	76–77.	.Feb. 16, 1977. .	135
AMERICAN WAY, THE—George S. Kaufman, Moss Hart	38–39.	.Jan. 21, 1939. .	164
AMPHITRYON 38—Jean Giraudoux, (ad) S. N. Behrman	37–38.	.Nov. 1, 1937. .	153
ANDERSONVILLE TRIAL, THE—Saul Levitt	59–60.	.Dec. 29, 1959. .	179
ANDORRA—Max Frisch, (ad) George Tabori	62–63.	.Feb. 9, 1963. .	9
ANGEL STREET—Patrick Hamilton	41–42.	.Dec. 5, 1941. .	1,295
ANIMAL KINGDOM, THE—Philip Barry	31–32.	.Jan. 12, 1932. .	183
ANNA CHRISTIE—Eugene O'Neill	21–22.	.Nov. 2, 1921. .	177
ANNA LUCASTA—Philip Yordan	44–45.	.Aug. 30, 1944. .	957
ANNE OF THE THOUSAND DAYS—Maxwell Anderson	48–49.	.Dec. 8, 1948. .	286
*ANNIE—(b) Thomas Meehan, (m) Charles Strouse, (l) Martin Charnin, based on Harold Gray's comic strip "Little Orphan Annie"	76–77.	.Apr. 21, 1977. .	2,129
ANOTHER LANGUAGE—Rose Franken	31–32.	.Apr. 25, 1932. .	344
ANOTHER PART OF THE FOREST—Lillian Hellman	46–47.	.Nov. 20, 1946. .	182
ANTIGONE—Jean Anouilh, (ad) Lewis Galantiere	45–46.	.Feb. 18, 1946. .	64

458

PLAY

FIVE-STAR FINAL—Louis Weitzenkorn	30–31.	.Dec. 30, 1930. .	175
FLIGHT TO THE WEST—Elmer Rice	40–41.	.Dec. 30, 1940. .	136
FLOATING LIGHT BULB, THE—Woody Allen	80–81.	.Apr. 27, 1981. .	65
FLOWERING PEACH, THE—Clifford Odets	54–55.	.Dec. 28, 1954. .	135
FOLLIES—(b) James Goldman, (m, l) Stephen Sondheim	70–71.	.Apr. 4, 1971. .	521
FOOL, THE—Channing Pollock	22–23.	.Oct. 23, 1922. .	373
FOOLISH NOTION—Philip Barry	44–45.	.Mar. 3, 1945. .	104
FORTY CARATS—Pierre Barillet and Jean-Pierre Gredy, (ad) Jay Allen	68–69.	.Dec. 26, 1968. .	780
*42ND STREET—(b) Michael Stewart, Mark Bramble, (m,l) Harry Warren, Al Dubin, (add'l l) Johnny Mercer, Mort Dixon, based on the novel by Bradford Ropes	80–81.	.Aug. 25, 1980. .	729
FOURPOSTER, THE—Jan de Hartog	51–52.	.Oct. 24, 1951. .	632
FRONT PAGE, THE—Ben Hecht, Charles MacArthur	28–29.	.Aug. 14, 1928. .	276
GENERATION—William Goodhart	65–66.	.Oct. 6, 1965. .	299
GEORGE WASHINGTON SLEPT HERE—George S. Kaufman, Moss Hart	40–41.	.Oct. 18, 1940. .	173
GETTING OUT—Marsha W. Norman	78–79.	.Oct. 19, 1978. .	259
GIDEON—Paddy Chayefsky	61–62.	.Nov. 9, 1961. .	236
GIGI—Anita Loos, based on Colette's novel	51–52.	.Nov. 24, 1951. .	219
GIMME SHELTER—Barrie Keefe (Gem, Gotcha and Getaway)	78–79.	.Dec. 10, 1978. .	17
GIN GAME, THE—D. L. Coburn	77–78.	.Oct. 6, 1977. .	517
GINGERBREAD LADY, THE—Neil Simon	70–71.	.Dec. 13, 1970. .	193
GIRL ON THE VIA FLAMINIA, THE—Alfred Hayes, based on his novel	53–54.	.Feb. 9, 1954. .	111
GLASS MENAGERIE, THE—Tennessee Williams	44–45.	.Mar. 31, 1945. .	561
GOLDEN APPLE, THE—(b, l), John Latouche, (m) Jerome Moross	53–54.	.Apr. 20, 1954. .	125
GOLDEN BOY—Clifford Odets	37–38.	.Nov. 4, 1937. .	250
GOOD DOCTOR, THE—Neil Simon; adapted from and suggested by stories by Anton Chekhov	73–74.	.Nov. 27, 1973. .	208
GOOD GRACIOUS ANNABELLE—Clare Kummer	09–19.	.Oct. 31, 1916. .	111
GOODBYE, MY FANCY—Fay Kanin	48–49.	.Nov. 17, 1948. .	446
GOOSE HANGS HIGH, THE—Lewis Beach	23–24.	.Jan. 29, 1924. .	183
GRAND HOTEL—Vicki Baum, (ad) W. A. Drake	30–31.	.Nov. 13, 1930. .	459
GREAT DIVIDE, THE—William Vaughn Moody	99–09.	.Oct. 3, 1906. .	238
GREAT GOD BROWN, THE—Eugene O'Neill	25–26.	.Jan. 23, 1926. .	271
GREAT WHITE HOPE, THE—Howard Sackler	68–69.	.Oct. 3, 1968. .	556
GREEN BAY TREE, THE—Mordaunt Shairp	33–34.	.Oct. 20, 1933. .	166
GREEN GODDESS, THE—William Archer	20–21.	.Jan. 18, 1921. .	440
GREEN GROW THE LILACS—Lynn Riggs	30–31.	.Jan. 26, 1931. .	64
GREEN HAT, THE—Michael Arlen	25–26.	.Sept. 15, 1925. .	231
GREEN JULIA—Paul Ableman	72–73.	.Nov. 16, 1972. .	147
GREEN PASTURES, THE—Marc Connelly, based on Roark Bradford's Ol Man Adam and His Chillun	29–30.	.Feb. 26, 1930. .	640
GUYS AND DOLLS—(b) Jo Swerling, Abe Burrows, based on a story and characters by Damon Runyon, (l, m) Frank Loesser	50–51.	.Nov. 24, 1950. .	1,200
GYPSY—Maxwell Anderson	28–29.	.Jan. 14, 1929. .	64
HADRIAN VII—Peter Luke, based on works by Fr. Rolfe	68–69.	.Jan. 8, 1969. .	359
HAMP—John Wilson; based on an episode from a novel by J. L. Hodson	66–67.	.Mar. 9, 1967. .	101
HAPPY TIME, THE—Samuel Taylor, based on Robert Fontaine's book	49–50.	.Jan. 24, 1950. .	614

INDEX

Play titles appear in **bold face**. *Bold face italic* page numbers refer to those pages where complete cast and credit listings for New York productions may be found.

Dungeons and Gryphons, 65
Dunham, Ronald, 326
Dunleavy, Timothy, 400
Dunlop, Frank, 321
Dunn, Glenn, 95
Dunne, Griffin, 397
Dunnigan, Ann, 358
Durand, H.S., 388
Durang, Christopher, 4, 9, 16, 26, 339, 370, 397
Durante, Vito, 311
Dutchman's Breeze, 75
Dutton, Charles S., 88
Duvall, Robert, 34
Dwyer, Frank, 405
Dwyer, James E., 411
Dynamite Limited Partnership, The, 390
Dysart, Richard, 79

Easley, Holmes, 99
Easley, Richert, 104
East, Ian, 314
Eastman, Donald, 407
Ebb, Fred, 62, 64, 309, 335
Eberhard, Leslie, 395
Ebersole, Christine, 418
Ebert, Joyce, 87
Eckhart, Gary, 71
Eckhouse, James, 339
Economy Tires Theater, 40, 411
Eda-Young, Barbara, 39, 324, 386, 397, 407
Eddon, Richard, 350, 423
Ede, George, 100, 365, 368
Edeiken, Louise, 338
Edelstein, Gordon, 89, 400
Edenfield, Dennis, 420
Edgar, Bob, 360
Edgar, David, 3, 19, 313, 438, 442
Edgerson, Ventura, 76
Edgerton, Earl, 103
Edmead, Wendy, 335
Edmonds, Robert, 348, 401
Edmondson, James, 63, 98
Edmunds, Kate, 67, 68, 78, 399, 400
Edson, Jerome, 330
Edwards, Anne, 75, 76
Edwards, Ben, 324, 336, 442
Edwards, Daryl, 406
Edwards, Gus, 400, 444
Edwards, Jack, 87
Edwards, Jango, 43, 411
Edwards, Nazig, 384

Edwards, Richard, 99
Edwards, Ronnie Claire, 97
Edwards, Susan, 62
Edward-Stevens, Michael, 323
Een, Robert, 402
Effron, Howard P., 315
Egan, Clem, 377
Egan, Michael, 319
Egan, Patricia, 89
Egan, Patrick, 377, 378
Egan, Robert, 99, 100
Eggerth, Marta, 342
Ehman, Don, 91
Eichaker, Ron, 359
Eichler, Alan, 315
Eichler, Lawrence, 406
Eichorn, Lisa, 80
Eickhoff, Philip, 69
Eiding, Paul, 96
8½, 16, 339
'81 Theater, Inc, 354
'81 Varieties, *402*
Eigsti, Karl, 87, 103, 330, 332, 372, 380, 445
Eilber, Janet, 341
Einhorn, Marvin, 402
Einhorn, Susan, 403
Einstein and the Polar Bear, 7, 9, 16, 59, *317*
Eisen, Max, 309, 315, 372, 390
Eisenberg, Deborah, 406
Eisler, 92
Eisman, Mark, 65
Ekstrom, Peter, 82
El Bravo!, 23, 31, *350*
Elcar, Dana, 81
Elder, Adrian, 64
Elder, Eldon, 89
Elder, Suzanne, 445
Electra-Cution, or You're Under Orestes, *398*
Elephant Man, The, 91, 308
Elephants, *411*
Eley, Stephanie, 326
Elg, Taina, 338
Eli, 85
Eliasberg, Jan, 95
Elice, Eric, 354, 387
Elice, Rick, 356
Elio, Donna Marie, 321
Eliot, T.S., 366
Elizabeth Hull-Kate Warriner Award, 446
El-Kadi, Naseer, 397
Elkin, Paul M., 99

Elkow, Richard, 319, 347, 387
Ellenstein, Robert, 102
Ellerbe, Harry, 62, 94
Ellington, Alan, 400
Ellington, Duke, 308
Ellington, John, 72
Elliott, Alice, 395
Elliott, Harvey, 337
Elliott, Jean, 394
Elliott, Michael, 9, 12, 319
Elliott, Patricia, 353
Elliott, Robert, 71, 79
Elliott, Shawn, 403
Ellis, Helen Pearl, 397
Ellis, Joshua, 315, 319, 320
Ellis, Saun, 406, 412
Ellis, Scott, 410
Ellis, Sheila, 325, 326
Ellis, Terrance Terry, 352, 409
Ellison, Bill, 382
Ellyn, Maura, 408
Elmer, Todd, 362, 395
Elmore, Richard, 63
Elmslie, Kenward, 410
Elverman, Bill, 363
Embs, Lisa, 400
Emigrés, *396*
Eminent Domain, 5, 10, 14, 59, *316-317*, 439
Emmes, David, 72
Emmons, Beverly, 315, 319, 328, 338, 358, 388, 402, 407, 445
Emonts, Ann, 320, 371, 382
Emperor and the Nightingale, The, 411
Emperor of Self, The, *378*
Enchanted, The, *410*
Encompass Theater, 394
Encore, 18, 59, *335*
End of Ramadan, 94
End of the Teflon-Coated Life, The, 103
Enderle, Douglas E., 79
Endrizzi, Bettie, 409
Enea, John, 392
Enemy of the People, An, 62
Engbrecht, Susan, 74
Engel, Bernerd, 98
Engelbach, Jerry, 406
Engler, Michael, 65
English, Ellia, 99
English, Gary, 404
Englund, Lois, 396, 419
Engman, John, 84